DIGEST.

A NEW

DIGEST

OF THE ACTS AND DELIVERANCES

OF THE

General Assembly

OF THE

PRESBYTERIAN CHURCH

IN THE UNITED STATES OF AMERICA.

COMPILED

By the Order and Authority of the General Assembly.

BY

REV. WM. E. MOORE.

PHILADELPHIA:
PRESBYTERIAN PUBLICATION COMMITTEE.
1334 CHESTNUT STREET.
NEW YORK: A. D. F. RANDOLPH, 683 BROADWAY.

C. SHERMAN & SON, PRINTERS,
S. W. Cor. Seventh and Cherry Sts., Philadelphia.

EDITOR'S PREFACE.

It is with much satisfaction that this volume is presented to the churches by the Presbyterian Publication Committee. The need of a new, reliable, and complete Digest of the Acts and Deliverances of the General Assembly has been long and deeply felt. To the great body, whether of our laymen or of our ministers, it has been practically an impossibility to have the decisions of the highest judicatory of the Church upon topics of the greatest interest and importance. Full files of the Minutes of the Assemblies of even a single generation are rare. The records of earlier Assemblies are far more rare. And even were they in the hands of our church officers, they would be useful for reference only at an expenditure of time that would seldom be justifiable. Hence, the want of a well-arranged and fully-indexed Digest of these Acts and Deliverances. Such a Digest the committee have now the satisfaction of publishing. For its preparation, they and the churches are indebted to the patient, laborious, and skilful services of the Rev. William E. Moore, of West Chester, Pennsylvania. The time and toil which has thus been expended by one will be saved to many. Without the obtrusion of his personal opinions, or of unauthentic documents, the compiler has, with modesty and impartiality, allowed the successive General Assemblies to declare their own views and to expound their own positions. He has rigidly adhered to the preparation of *a Digest.*

By the aid of its full table of contents and alphabetical index, any topic discussed in the Digest will be readily found.

The typography and materials of the volume, it is hoped, will not disparage the excellence of its contents.

INTRODUCTION.

THE want of a Digest of the Acts of the Supreme Judicatory of the Presbyterian Church was early felt. In 1818 the following overture was adopted by the Assembly, viz.:

"*Resolved*, That Drs. Janeway, Neill, and Ely, be appointed a committee, and they are hereby appointed, to extract from the records of the General Assembly and of the late Synods of New York and Philadelphia all such matters as may appear to be of permanent authority and interest (including a short account of the manner in which Missions have been conducted, and their success), that the same may be published for the information of ministers and their people in our churches; and that they report the same to the next Assembly."—*Minutes*, 1818, p. 673.

The committee reported to the next Assembly, and were authorized to complete the work on the plan reported, and to publish it at the expense of the Trustees of the Assembly.—*Minutes*, 1819, p. 713.

The Digest thus authorized was published in 1820.—*Minutes*, p. 727.

In 1836, upon an overture on the subject of a new Digest, the Assembly—

"1. *Resolved*, That in the judgment of this Assembly, it is expedient that a new Digest of the acts and proceedings of the highest judicatory of our Church be prepared and placed within the reach of all our ministers and elders.

"2. *Resolved*, That Dr. John McDowell, Mr. Winchester, and Mr. Duffield, be a committee to prepare such a Digest, and report the same to the Assembly as soon as practicable, provided the expense of its publication be not defrayed out of the funds of the Assembly."—*Minutes*, 1836, p. 262.

This committee made no report. In 1838, the Assembly—

"*Resolved,* That the Stated Clerk (Erskine Mason, D.D.) and Dr. Patton be a committee to prepare and print a *complete Digest* of all the important acts of past General Assemblies."—*Minutes,* 1838, p. 661.

This committee "reported progress, and were continued."—*Minutes,* 1839, p. 11.

In 1841, they reported "that they were engaged in the duty assigned them, but were not at present prepared to make a final report." The committee was continued.—*Minutes,* 1841, p. 24.

In 1849, the committee to whom was referred the subject of the preparation of a new Digest, reported that they could not learn that any progress had been made in this matter by the committee who were appointed for this purpose by a former Assembly:

That it is desirable that a new and more complete Digest should be prepared; and that a committee be appointed to accomplish this object.

The plan which has seemed to them most likely to be useful, is to publish a volume containing the text of our standards, with marginal notes, exhibiting, in the proper place, the history of the changes in the Constitution, and the various acts of General Assemblies explanatory of our standards; the whole forming a complete commentary on the Constitution of the Presbyterian Church in the United States.

The report was adopted; and the Rev. Messrs. E. F. Hatfield, S. T. Spear, and A. E. Campbell, were appointed to prepare such a volume.—*Minutes,* 1849, p. 189.

In 1850, the committee "reported progress, and was continued."—*Minutes,* 1850, p. 308.

Also in 1851.—*Minutes,* p. 10.

In 1852, the committee appointed to prepare a Digest, reported that a Digest sufficient for the present had been prepared by other hands, and requested therefore to be discharged. Their report was accepted, and the committee discharged.—*Minutes,* 1852, p. 254.

The Digest referred to was that prepared by the Rev. Richard Webster, of Mauch Chunk, Pa., and published by the Presbyterian Board of Publication. It did not, however, prove satisfactory. In 1854, the Committee on Bills and Overtures reported "an overture respecting a new Digest; and recommended that a committee of three be appointed to prepare and publish such a Digest, if it can be done without expense to the Assembly. The report was adopted."—*Minutes,* 1854, p. 504.

The following committee were appointed, viz.: Rev. Messrs. George

Duffield, Jr., Henry Darling, and Wm. E. Moore. The Stated Clerk (Rev. Edwin F. Hatfield, D.D.) was added to this committee.—*Ibid.*, p. 505.

The committee reported from year to year till 1857, when

"The Committee on the Polity of the Church, to whom was referred the report of the Committee on the Digest, recommended that the course pursued by the Special Committee, in the preparation of the Digest thus far, be approved by the Assembly.

"That they be instructed to complete the work according to the plan heretofore followed, and to use their discretion in relation to the questions proposed in their report.

"That when completed, it be submitted to the Permanent Publication Committee, and, if approved by them, be published under their direction. The report was adopted."—*Minutes*, 1857, p. 400.

The committee thus appointed and authorized have been delayed in the performance of the duty assigned them by the want of funds to publish the Digest "without expense to the Assembly,"—a delay the less to be regretted, however, inasmuch as it has enabled them to add to the volume the acts of the last five years,—perhaps the most important years of the Assembly's history.

The difficulty of digesting the acts and deliverances of a series of Assemblies, *running through a century and a half*, each independent of the other, will readily be appreciated, and may, to some extent, excuse the imperfections of the work. That difficulty has been greatly enhanced, by the failure of the Minutes, in most cases, to present any clear and intelligible view of the questions which have come before the Assembly for its adjudication.

The plan adopted will, it is hoped, meet the approval of those who have occasion to use the work. The effort has been made to digest, under thirteen general heads or chapters, everything of importance in the Acts of the Assembly. The task assigned the committee *was not to prepare a history*, but a DIGEST of such Acts of the Assembly as interpret the Constitution of the Church, or express her views upon questions of morals and doctrines, or aim to increase and direct her power for good to the world. Much has been omitted that is now obsolete, or that was temporary, or that pertains to institutions not now under our control. For the most part, reports, protests, proposals, and other papers not the Acts of the Assembly, have been omitted. Where the very words of the records are not used, the fact is signified by brackets.

The labors of the committee extend over the whole period of the organized existence of the Presbyterian Church, from 1706 to 1860. The references in the Digest, from 1706 to 1835, are to the three volumes of Minutes published by the Presbyterian Board of Publication, viz.: "*Records of the Presbyterian Church, from* 1706 *to* 1788," "*Minutes of the General Assembly, from* 1789 *to* 1820," and "*Minutes of the General Assembly, from* 1821 *to* 1835." From 1836 to 1860, the references are to the annual Minutes.

The committee have freely availed themselves of the labors of their predecessors, so far as they have trodden common ground. They would cheerfully acknowledge their obligations to the Rev. S. J. Baird, the compiler of the Digest recently published by the Board of Publication.

It is proper to say that the chief responsibility of preparing the Digest has devolved upon one member of the committee.

The aim has been to furnish the office-bearers and intelligent laymen of our beloved Church a volume which will be of practical use to them in their endeavors to serve the cause of the Master through her organizations.

We rejoice in the confidence that no lover of Christ, of orthodoxy, of good morals, of large-hearted catholic liberality, of beneficence, of education, and of liberty, can ponder these acts and deliverances of the Supreme Judicature of our Church without wisdom and profit and grateful admiration. No Presbyterian can read this record without thanking God for his heritage. May the Head of the Church so use our labors as to advance His kingdom and glory, through the enlargement of our branch of His universal Church!

W. E. M.

WEST CHESTER, PA., December 31st, 1860.

CONTENTS.

CHAPTER I.

OF THE CHURCH.

CHAPTER III.

ON CANDIDATES.

CHAPTER IV.

ON THE SACRAMENTS.

CHAPTER V.

OF THE COURTS OF THE CHURCH.

CHAPTER VI.

OF DISCIPLINE.

CHAPTER IX.

ON MODES OF EVANGELIZATION.

CHAPTER XI.

CHAPTER XII.

PLAN OF UNION AND THE DIVISION.

APPENDIX.

DIGEST.

CHAPTER I.

OF THE CHURCH.

SECTION 1.—STANDARDS OF THE CHURCH.

1. Overture in reference to subscribing the Confession of Faith.—2. Confession of Faith. Larger and Shorter Catechisms of the Westminster Assembly adopted.—3. The "Directory" recommended.—4. Intrants or Candidates must adopt the standards.—5. The "Adopting Act" to be copied in the Presbytery books.—6. An act explanatory of the Adopting Act.—7. Plan of Union of 1758.—8. The Constitution of the Presbyterian Church in the United States of America, amended and adopted.—9. Proof texts added by order of the Assembly.—10. The marginal notes have no constitutional authority.—11. Use and obligation of the standards.—12. Subscription to them in every case required.—13. The Catechisms are an integral part of the Constitution.—14. The term "Standing Rule" in the Constitution defined. The Assembly may enact standing rules.

ADOPTION OF THE WESTMINSTER STANDARDS.

1.—*Overture laid over a year.*

"There being an overture presented to the Synod in writing having reference to the subscribing of the Confession of Faith, &c., the Synod, judging this to be a very important affair, unanimously concluded to defer the consideration of it till the next Synod, withal recommending it to the members of each Presbytery present to give timeous notice thereof to the absent members."—*Minutes,* 1728, p. 91.

2. *The Confession of Faith, Larger and Shorter Catechisms of the Westminster Assembly adopted.*

"The committee brought in an overture upon the affair of the Confession, which, after long debating upon it, was agreed upon, *in hæc verba:*

"Although the Synod do not claim or pretend to any authority of imposing our faith upon other men's consciences, but do profess our just dissatisfaction with, and abhorrence of such impositions, and do utterly disclaim all legislative power and authority in the Church, being willing to receive one another as Christ has received us to the glory of God, and admit to fellowship in sacred ordinances, all such as we have grounds to believe Christ will at last admit to the kingdom of heaven, yet we are undoubtedly obliged to take care that the faith once delivered to the saints be kept pure and uncorrupt among us, and so handed down to our posterity. And do therefore agree that all the ministers of this Synod, or that shall hereafter be admitted into this Synod, shall declare their agreement in, and approbation of, the Confession of Faith, with the Larger and Shorter Catechisms of the Assembly of Divines at Westminster, as being in all the essential and necessary articles, good forms of sound words and systems of Christian doctrine, and do also adopt the said Confession and Catechisms as the confession of our faith. And we do also agree, that all the Presbyteries within our bounds shall always take care not to admit any candidate of the ministry into the exercise of the sacred function, but what declares his agreement in opinion with all the essential and necessary articles of said Confession, either by subscribing the said Confession of Faith and Catechisms, or by a verbal declaration of their assent thereto, as such minister or candidate shall think best. And in case any minister of this Synod, or any candidate for the ministry, shall have any scruple with respect to any article or articles of said Confession or Catechisms, he shall at the time of his making said declaration declare his sentiments to the Presbytery or Synod, who shall, notwithstanding, admit him to the exercise of the ministry within our bounds, and to ministerial communion, if the Synod or Presbytery shall judge his scruple or mistake to be only about articles not essential and necessary in doctrine, worship, or government. But if the Synod or Presbytery shall judge such ministers or candidates erroneous in essential and necessary articles of faith, the Synod or Presbytery shall declare them uncapable of communion with them. And the

Synod do solemnly agree, that none of us will traduce or use any opprobrious terms of those that differ from us in these extra-essential and not necessary points of doctrine, but treat them with the same friendship, kindness, and brotherly love, as if they had not differed from us in such sentiments."

[In the afternoon.]

All the ministers of this Synod now present, except one, that declared himself not prepared, viz.: Masters Jedediah Andrews, Thomas Craighead, John Thomson, James Anderson, John Pierson, Samuel Gelston, Joseph Houston, Gilbert Tennent, Adam Boyd, Jonathan Dickinson, John Bradner, Alexander Hutchinson, Thomas Evans, Hugh Stevenson, William Tennent, Hugh Conn, George Gillespie, and John Willson, after proposing all the scruples that any of them had to make against any articles and expressions in the Confession of Faith and Larger and Shorter Catechisms of the Assembly of Divines at Westminster, have unanimously agreed in the solution of those scruples, and in declaring the said Confession and Catechisms to be the confession of their faith, excepting only some clauses in the twentieth and twenty-third chapters, concerning which clauses the Synod do unanimously declare, that they do not receive those articles in any such sense as to suppose the civil magistrate hath a controlling power over Synods with respect to the exercise of their ministerial authority; or power to persecute any for their religion, or in any sense contrary to the Protestant succession to the throne of Great Britain.

The Synod observing that unanimity, peace, and unity, which appeared in all their consultations and determinations relating to the affair of the Confession, did unanimously agree in giving thanks to God in solemn prayer and praises.—*Minutes*, 1729, p. 94.

3. *The "Directory" recommended.*

"A motion being made to know the Synod's judgment about the Directory, they gave their sense of that matter in the following words, viz.: The Synod do unanimously acknowledge and declare, that they judge the Directory for worship, discipline, and government of the Church, commonly annexed to the Westminster Confession, to be agreeable in substance to the word of God, and founded thereupon; and therefore do earnestly recommend the same to all their members, to be by them observed as near as circumstances will allow, and Christian prudence direct."—*Minutes*, 1729, p. 95.

4. *Intrants or Candidates to adopt the Confession and Catechisms in the same manner and as fully as those then present.*

a. "*Whereas,* some persons have been dissatisfied at the manner of wording our last year's agreement about the Confession, &c., supposing some expressions not sufficiently obligatory upon intrants:

"*Overtured,* That the Synod do now declare, that they understand these clauses, that respect the admission of intrants or candidates, in such a sense as to oblige them to receive and adopt the Confession and Catechisms at their admission, in the same manner and as fully as the members of the Synod did that were then present, which overture was unanimously agreed to by the Synod."—*Minutes,* 1730, p. 98.

b. "*Ordered,* That the Synod make a particular inquiry during the time of their meeting every year, whether such ministers as have been received as members since the foregoing meeting of the Synod have adopted, or have been required by the Synod, or by the respective Presbyteries, to adopt the Westminster Confession and Catechisms with the Directory, according to the acts of the Synod made some years since for that purpose, and that also the report made to the Synod, in answer to said inquiry, be recorded in our minutes."—*Minutes,* 1734, p. 109.

5. *To be inscribed on the Book of each Presbytery.*

"*Ordered,* That each Presbytery have the whole Adopting Act inserted in their Presbytery book."—*Minutes,* 1735, p. 115.

6. *An Act explanatory of the Adopting Act.*

"An overture of the committee upon the supplication of the people of Paxton and Derry was brought in, and is as followeth: That the Synod do declare, that inasmuch as we understand that many persons of our persuasion, both more lately and formerly, have been offended with some expressions or distinctions in the first or preliminary act of our Synod, contained in the printed paper, relating to our receiving or adopting the Westminster Confession and Catechisms, &c.; that, in order to remove said offence, and all jealousies that have arisen or may arise in any of our people's minds on occasion of said distinctions and expressions, the Synod doth declare, that the Synod have adopted and still do adhere to the Westminster Confession, Catechisms, and Directory, without the least variation or alteration, and without any regard to said distinctions.

And we do further declare, that this was our meaning and true intent in our first adopting of said Confession, as may particularly appear by our Adopting Act, which is as followeth: 'All the ministers of the Synod now present (which were eighteen in number, except one that declared himself not prepared), after proposing all the scruples any of them had to make against any articles and expressions in the Confession of Faith and Larger and Shorter Catechisms of the Assembly of Divines at Westminster, have unanimously agreed in the solution of these scruples, and in declaring the said Confession and Catechisms to be the confession of their faith, except only some clauses in the twentieth and twenty-third chapters; concerning which clauses the Synod do unanimously declare, that they do not receive these articles in any such sense as to suppose the civil magistrate hath a controlling power over Synods with respect to the exercise of their ministerial authority, or power to persecute any for their religion, or in any sense contrary to the Protestant succession to the throne of Great Britain.'

"And we hope and desire, that this, our Synodical declaration and explication, may satisfy all our people as to our firm attachment to our good old received doctrines contained in said Confession, without the least variation or alteration, and that they will lay aside their jealousies that have been entertained through occasion of the above hinted expressions and declarations as groundless. This overture approved *nemine contradicente.*"—*Minutes,* 1736, p. 126.

7. *Upon the reunion of the Synods of New York and Philadelphia, May* 29, 1758, *the following Plan of Union was agreed upon, viz.:*

"The Synods of New York and Philadelphia, taking into serious consideration the present divided state of the Presbyterian Church in this land, and being deeply sensible that the division of the Church tends to weaken its interests, to dishonor religion, and consequently its glorious Author; to render government and discipline ineffectual, and finally to dissolve its very frame; and being desirous to pursue such measures as may most tend to the glory of God, and the establishment and edification of his people, do judge it to be our indispensable duty to study the things that make for peace, and to endeavor the healing of that breach which has for some time subsisted amongst us, that so its hurtful consequences may not extend to posterity; that all occasion of reproach upon our society may be removed, and that we may carry on the great designs of religion to better advantage than we can do in a divided state; and since both Synods continue to profess the same principles of faith, and adhere to the same form of worship, government, and discipline, there is the greater reason to endeavor the compromising those differences which were agitated many years ago with too great warmth and animosity, and unite in one body.

"For which end, and that no jealousies or grounds of alienation may remain, and also to prevent future breaches of like nature, we agree to unite and do unite in one body, under the name of the Synod of New York and Philadelphia, on the following plan:

"I. Both Synods having always approved and received the Westminster Confession of Faith and Larger and Shorter Catechisms as an orthodox and excellent system of Christian doctrine, founded on the word of God, we do still receive the same as the confession of our faith, and also adhere to the plan of worship, government, and discipline, contained in the Westminster Directory, strictly enjoining it on all our members and probationers for the ministry that they preach and teach according to the form of sound words in said Confession and Catechisms, and avoid and oppose all errors contrary thereto.

"II. That when any matter is determined by a major vote, every member shall either actively concur with or passively submit to such determination; or, if his conscience permit him to do neither, he shall, after sufficient liberty modestly to reason and remonstrate, peaceably withdraw from our communion, without attempting to make any schism: Provided always, that this shall be understood to extend only to such determinations as the body shall judge indispensable in doctrine or Presbyterian government.

"III. That any member or members, for the exoneration of his or their conscience before God, have a right to protest against any act or procedure of our highest judicature, because there is no further appeal to another for redress, and to require that such protestation be recorded in their minutes. And as such a protest is a solemn appeal from the bar of said judicature, no member is liable to prosecution on the account of his protesting: Provided always, that it shall be deemed irregular and unlawful to enter a protestation against any member or members, or to protest facts or accusations instead of proving them, unless a fair trial be refused, even by the highest judicature. And it is agreed, that protestations are only to be entered against the public acts, judgments, or determinations of the judicature with which the protestor's conscience is offended.

"IV. As the protestation entered in the Synod of Philadelphia, Ann. Dom. 1741, has been apprehended to have been approved and received by an act of said Synod, and on that account was judged a sufficient obstacle to an union, the said Synod declare, that they never judicially adopted the said protestation, nor do account it a Synodical act, but that it is to be considered as the act of those only who subscribed it; and therefore cannot in its nature be a valid objection to the union of the two Synods, especially considering that a very great majority of both Synods have become members since the said protestation was entered.

"V. That it shall be esteemed and treated as a censurable evil, to accuse any member of heterodoxy, insufficiency, or immorality, in a calumniating manner, or otherwise than by private brotherly admonition, or by a regular process according to our known rules of judicial trial in cases of scandal; and it shall be considered in the same view, if any Presbytery appoint supplies within the bounds of another Presbytery without their concurrence; or if any member officiate in another's congregation, without asking and obtaining his consent, or the Session's in case the minister be absent; yet it shall be esteemed unbrotherly for any one, in ordinary circumstances, to refuse his consent to a regular member when it is requested.

"VI. That no Presbytery shall license or ordain to the work of the ministry any candidate, until he give them competent satisfaction as to his learning, and experimental acquaintance with religion, and skill in divinity and cases of conscience, and declare his acceptance of the Westminster Confession and Catechisms as the confession of his faith, and promise subjection to the Presbyterian plan of government in the Westminster Directory.

"VII. The Synods declare it is their earnest desire that a complete union may be obtained as soon as possible, and agree that the united Synod shall model the several Presbyteries in such manner as shall appear to them most expedient. Provided nevertheless, that Presbyteries where an alteration does not appear to be for edification, continue in their present form. As to divided congregations, it is agreed that such as have settled ministers on both sides be allowed to continue as they are; that where those of one side have a settled minister, the other being vacant, may join with the settled minister, if a majority choose so to do; that when both sides are vacant, they shall be at liberty to unite together.

"VIII. As the late religious appearances occasioned much speculation and debate, the members of the New York Synod, in order to prevent any misapprehensions, declare their adherence to their former sentiments in favor of them, that a blessed work of God's Holy Spirit in the conversion of numbers was then carried on; and for the satisfaction of all concerned, this united Synod agree in declaring, that, as all mankind are naturally dead in trespasses and sins, an entire change of heart and life is necessary to make them meet for the service and enjoyment of God; that such a change can be only effected by the powerful operations of the divine Spirit; that when sinners are made sensible of their lost condition and absolute inability to recover themselves, are enlightened in the knowledge of Christ, and convinced of his ability and willingness to save, and upon Gospel encouragements do choose him for their Saviour, and, renouncing their own righteousness in point of merit, depend upon his imputed righteousness for their justification before God, and on his wisdom and strength for guidance and support; when, upon these apprehensions and exercises, their souls are comforted, notwithstanding all their past guilt, and rejoice in God through Jesus Christ; when they hate and bewail their sins of heart and life, delight in the laws of God without exception, reverently and diligently attend his ordinances, become humble and self-denied, and make it the business of their lives to please and glorify God, and to do good to their fellow men: this is to be acknowledged as a gracious work of God, even though it should be attended with unusual bodily commotions, or some more exceptionable circumstances, by means of infirmity, temptations, or remaining corruptions; and wherever religious appearances are attended with the good effects above mentioned, we desire to rejoice in and thank God for them.

"But, on the other hand, when persons seeming to be under a religious concern, imagine that they have visions of the human nature of Jesus Christ, or hear voices, or see external lights, or have fainting and convulsion-like fits, and on the account of these judge themselves to be truly converted, though they have not the Scriptural characters of a work of God above described, we believe such persons are under a dangerous delusion; and we testify our utter disapprobation of such a delusion, wherever it attends any religious appearances, in any Church or time.

"Now as both Synods are agreed in their sentiments concerning the nature of a work of grace, and declare their desire and purpose to promote it, different judgments respecting particular matters of fact ought not to prevent their union; especially as many of the present members have entered into the ministry since the time of the aforesaid religious appearances.

"Upon the whole, as the design of our union is the advancement of the Mediator's kingdom, and as the wise and faithful discharge of the ministerial function is the principal appointed mean for that glorious end, we judge that this is a proper occasion to manifest our sincere intention unitedly to exert ourselves to fulfil the ministry we have received of the Lord Jesus. Accordingly, we unanimously declare our serious and fixed resolution, by divine aid, to take heed to ourselves that our hearts be upright, our discourse edifying, and our lives exemplary for purity and godliness; to take heed to our doctrine, that it be not only orthodox, but evangelical and spiritual, tending to awaken the secure to a suitable concern for their salvation, and to instruct and encourage sincere Christians, thus commending ourselves to every man's conscience in the sight of God; to cultivate peace and harmony among ourselves, and strengthen each other's hands in promoting the knowledge of divine truth, and diffusing the savor of piety among our people.

"Finally, we earnestly recommend it to all under our care, that instead of indulging a contentious disposition, they would love each other with a pure heart fervently, as brethren who profess subjection to the same Lord, adhere to the same faith, worship, and government, and entertain the same hope of glory. And we desire that they would improve the present union for their mutual edification, combine to strengthen the common interests of religion, and go hand in hand in the path of life; which we pray the God of all grace would please to effect, for Christ's sake. Amen.

"The Synod agree, that all former differences and disputes are laid aside and buried; and that no future inquiry or vote shall be proposed in this Synod concerning these things; but if any member seek a Synodical inquiry or declaration about any of the matters of our past differences, it shall be deemed a censurable breach of this agreement, and be refused, and he be rebuked accordingly."—*Minutes*, 1758, p. 285, 288.

8. *Constitution Amended and Adopted.*

[In 1787, preparatory to forming the General Assembly, the Synod ordered a thorough revision of the standards, altering the articles excepted to in the Adopting Acts, and making such amendments as were found necessary. The Constitution as thus amended was adopted.]

Form of Government and Discipline, as Amended, Adopted.

"The Synod having fully considered the draught of the Form of Government and Discipline, did, on review of the whole, and hereby do, ratify and adopt the same, as now altered and amended, as the Constitution of the Presbyterian Church in America, and order the same to be considered and strictly observed as the rule of their proceedings, by all the inferior judicatories belonging to the body. And they order that a correct copy be printed, and that the Westminster Confession of Faith, as now altered, be printed in full along with it, as making a part of the Constitution.

"*Resolved*, That the true intent and meaning of the above ratification by the Synod is, that the Form of Government and Discipline, and the Confession of Faith, as now ratified, is to continue to be our Constitution, and the Confession of our Faith and practice unalterable; unless two-thirds of the Presbyteries, under the care of the General Assembly, shall propose alterations or amendments, and such alterations or amendments shall be agreed to and enacted by the General Assembly."—*Minutes*, 1788, p. 546.

Directory as Amended Adopted. Larger and Shorter Catechisms Ratified as the Catechisms of the Church.

"The Synod having now revised and corrected the draught of a Directory for Worship, did approve and ratify the same, and do hereby appoint the said Directory, as now amended, to be the Directory for the worship of God in the Presbyterian Church in the United States of America. They also took into consideration the Westminster Larger and Shorter Catechisms, and having made a small amendment of the Larger, did approve, and do hereby approve and ratify the said Catechisms, as now agreed on, as the Catechisms of the Presbyterian Church in the said United States. And the Synod order, that the said Directory and Catechisms be printed and bound up in the same volume with the Confession of Faith and the Form of Government and Discipline; and that the whole be considered as the standard of our doctrine, government, discipline, and worship, agreeably to the resolutions of the Synod at their present session."—*Minutes*, 1788, p. 547.

9. *Proof Texts added by Order of the Assembly.*

The committee appointed to consider the expediency of a new impression of the Confession of Faith, Form of Government and Discipline of this Church, reported . . . . that another impression appeared expedient, in which, if the Scripture proofs were inserted at length, it would become more acceptable, and might be of greater utility to the churches; and proposed that a committee be appointed properly to select and arrange the Scripture texts to be adduced in support of the articles in the Confession of Faith, Form of Government and Discipline, and prepare the same to be laid before the next General Assembly.

"*Resolved*, That Dr. Robert Smith, and Messrs. Mitchell and Grier, be a committee to carry the above into execution."—*Minutes*, 1792, p. 59.

"A letter was received and read from Mr. Mitchell, one of the members of a committee appointed by the Assembly of 1792, to revise and prepare for publication an edition of the Confession of Faith, Catechisms, and Form of Government and Discipline of this Church, informing this Assembly that considerable progress had been made in the business, but that it was still incomplete. Whereupon the business was recommitted, and the Moderator [the Rev. James Latta], added to the committee in the place of the Rev. Dr. Robert Smith, deceased, and they were directed to report to the Assembly in 1794."—*Minutes*, 1793, p. 66.

[The letter was as follows:]

"UPPER OCTORARA, May 14th, 1793.

"THE REVEREND THE GENERAL ASSEMBLY.

"REVEREND FATHERS AND BRETHREN: The task assigned the Rev. Dr. Robert Smith, Mr. Grier, and myself, by the last General Assembly of our Church, was divided by your committee in the following manner: Doctor Smith undertook to adduce Scripture testimony in proof of the Larger Catechism, Mr. Grier the Shorter, and Mr. Mitchell the Confession of Faith and Church Government. Doctor Smith's remove from serving any longer in the Church militant, has left his part unfinished, and uncorrected (if correction it requires). I send his manuscript, and the printed book, which was the Doctor's property. Mr. Grier will inform the Reverend the General Assembly what progress he has made on his part. Your correspondent has completed the proofs for the Confession of Faith, and made some progress on Church Government, the first twelve chapters; but a severe pain in my right arm, attended with a paralysis in my hand, prevented me from finishing what I had inconsiderately undertaken. I hope I shall not tire nor repent of any poor service I may be called to perform to the Church of Christ; but this was a herculean labor for the time assigned to do it in.

"The General Assembly will perceive my method, which was to mention the chapter in the Confession, with its title and the several sections it contains; then insert the small letters of the Roman alphabet in the printed copy, and these serve to direct to those texts of Scripture adduced to prove the subject, or any part of it, where they are placed. Those texts that appear to me to be the most adequate and suitable to the design, I have wrote out in full. Where I have viewed them as serving either as parallel, or corroborating, I have only set down book, chapter, and verse in figures. There may be *lapsus pennæ*, which can be corrected when reviewed and examined. But these, with many other things, I submit to the Assembly's correction and inspection. Had it been pardonable, I should have taken the liberty to have altered some of the terms and phraseology in our translation, as more correspondent to the original; but to depart from established customs in religious matters is dangerous. I would also have abridged the proofs; but this would have raised a clamor among the people at large, that we had departed from the ancient faith. The printed copy belongs to the General Assembly, and accompanies my manuscript papers, together with the Scripture proofs on Church Government. May the great Head of the Church, the Lord Jesus Christ, be in the midst of you, to direct and assist you in all your consultations and deliberations for his glory and the prosperity of Zion. So prays your brother in the Gospel of Christ.

"A. MITCHELL."

Minutes, 1793, p. 66.

"The committee appointed to prepare the Scripture proofs in support of the doctrines of the Confession of Faith, the Catechisms, &c., of the Presbyterian Church, submitted their report, which was read, examined, and approved as a specimen of the work. Whereupon Dr. Green, Messrs. John B. Smith, James Boyd, William M. Tennent, Nathaniel Irwin, and Andrew Hunter, were appointed a committee to compare the proofs prepared by said committee, and now reported to the General Assembly, with the proofs annexed to the Westminster Confession of Faith, Catechisms, and Directory; to revise the whole, prepare it for the press, to agree with the printer for its publication, and to superintend the printing and vending of the same."—*Minutes*, 1794, p. 88.

10. *Authority of the Notes. The Text alone contains the Constitution.*

The committee to which was referred an inquiry, proposed to the Assembly by the Presbytery of Philadelphia, relative to the notes found in the book containing the Constitution, reported. Their report was adopted, viz.:

"That the book referred to was first published with nothing but the simple text, without any Scripture proofs, or any notes of any description whatsoever. This is evident not only from the minutes of the General Assembly, but from the numerous copies of this first edition of the standards of our Church which are now in existence. It is also equally evident, from examining the records of the General Assembly, that not a single note in the book has been added to or made a part of the Constitution of the Church, since it was first formed and published, in the manner above recited. Several alterations and additions have been made by referring them, when contemplated, to the Presbyteries for their decision thereon, in the manner pointed out in the Constitution itself. But among all the points thus referred, there is not found a single note which now appears in the book containing the Constitution of our Church. Hence it follows, beyond a doubt, that these notes are no part of that Constitution. If, then, it be inquired how these notes obtained the place which they now occupy, and what is the character, as to authority, which they possess, the answer is this: When a second edition of the standards of our Church was needed, it was thought by the General Assembly, that it would be of great use in itself, highly agreeable to the members of our Church generally, as well as conformable to the example of the Church of Scotland, from which we derive our origin, if the Scripture proofs were added in support of the several parts and clauses of the Confession of Faith, Catechisms, and Form of Government. A committee was accordingly appointed by the Assembly to select the Scripture proofs, and to prepare them for being printed in the second edition of the book. The work of this committee was, the following year, referred to another, and ultimately the committee charged with preparing the Scripture proofs reported, along with these proofs, the notes which now appear in the book, and which were approved by the General Assembly, and directed to be printed with the proofs, in the form in which they now appear. These notes, then, are explanations of some of the principles of the Presbyterian Church, given by the General Assembly, and which, of course, the General Assembly may modify or altogether exclude, at their pleasure, whereas the articles of the Constitution must govern the Assembly themselves, and cannot be altered or abrogated, but in the manner pointed out in the Constitution itself.

"On the whole, in the book containing the standards of our Church, the text alone contains the Constitution of our Church; the notes are an exposition of principles given by the highest judicature of that Church, of the same force, while they continue, with the other acts of that judicature, but subject to alterations, amendments, or a total erasure, as they shall judge proper.

"*Resolved,* That as it belongs to the General Assembly to give direction in regard to the notes which accompany the Constitution, of which they are the supreme judicatory, this Assembly express it as their opinion, that in printing future editions of the Constitution of this Church, the parenthesis on the note, on this part of the Form of Government, which defines a Synod, and which is expressed in these words, 'since a Synod is only a larger Presbytery,' be omitted, as well as the note connected with the Scripture proofs in answer to the question in the Larger Catechism, 'What is forbidden in the eighth commandment?' in which the nature of the crime of man-stealing and slavery is dilated upon. In regard to this last omission, the Assembly think proper to declare, that in directing it, they are influenced by far other motives than any desire to favor slavery, or to retard the extinction of that mournful evil as speedily as may consist with the happiness of all concerned."—*Minutes,* 1816, p. 630.

[NOTE.—These notes are not found in the Constitution as revised in 1820.]

"*Resolved,* That as the notes which have been expunged from our public formularies, and which some of the memorials referred to the committee request to have restored, were introduced irregularly, and never had the sanction of the Church, and therefore never possessed any real authority, the General Assembly has no power to assign them a place in the authorized standards of the Church, and does not deem it proper to take the constitutional measures for effecting their restoration."—*Minutes,* 1836, p. 248.

11. *Use and Obligation of the Confession.*

1. That, in the opinion of this Assembly, Confessions of Faith, containing formulas of doctrine, and rules for conducting the discipline and

worship proper to be maintained in the house of God, are not only recognized as necessary and expedient, but as the character of human nature is continually aiming at innovation, absolutely requisite to the settled peace of the Church, and to the happy and orderly existence of Christian communion. Within the limits of Christendom, few are to be found in the attitude of avowed hostility to Christianity. The name of Christian is claimed by all, and all are ready to profess their belief in the Holy Scriptures, too many reserving to themselves the right of putting upon them what construction they please. In such a state of things, without the aid of Confessions, Christian fellowship can exist only in a very limited degree, and the disorder of the Corinthian Church, condemned by the Apostle, would be realized: *"I am of Paul and I of Apollos."*

2. That, though the Confession of Faith and standards of our Church are of no original authority, independent of the Scriptures, yet we regard them as a summary of those divine truths which are diffused throughout the sacred volume.

They, as a system of doctrines, therefore, cannot be abandoned, in our opinion, without an abandonment of the word of God. They form a bond of fellowship in the faith of the Gospel, and the General Assembly cannot but believe the precious immortals under their care to be more safe in receiving the truth of God's holy word, as exhibited in the standards of our Church, than in being subject to the guidance of any instructor, whoever he may be, who may have confidence enough to set up his own opinions in opposition to the system of doctrines which men of sound learning, full of the Holy Ghost, and mighty in the Scriptures, have devised from the oracles of the living God. It should never be forgotten, that the Church is solemnly cautioned against the danger of being carried about by every wind of doctrine.

3. This Confession of Faith, adopted by our Church, contains a system of doctrines professedly believed by the people and the pastors under the care of the General Assembly, nor can it be traduced by any in the communion of our Church, without subjecting the erring parties to that salutary discipline which hath for its object the maintenance of the peace and purity of the Church, under the government of her great Master.—*Minutes,* 1824, p. 114.

12. *Subscription to the Standards in every case required.*

The committee appointed on an overture respecting the consistency of admitting into this Church ministers who manifest a decided hostility to ecclesiastical creeds, confessions, and formularies, make the following report, which was adopted, viz.:

1. That the Constitution, as is well known, expressly requires of all candidates for admission, a solemn declaration that they sincerely receive and adopt the Confession of Faith of this Church, as containing the system of doctrine taught in the Holy Scriptures.

2. That the last Assembly, in a report of their committee, to be seen on the minutes, have so explicitly and fully declared the sentiments of this Church in regard to her ecclesiastical standards, and all within her communion who may traduce them, that no further expression of our views on this subject is deemed necessary.—*Minutes*, 1825, p. 155.

13. *The Catechisms an Integral part of the Standards of the Church.*

The committee to whom was referred Overture No. 5, viz.: "On subscribing the Confession of Faith," made the following report, which was unanimously adopted, viz.:

That, in their judgment, any further legislation on the subject by the Assembly would be unnecessary and inexpedient. They consider the formula contained in our book, and the rule adopted by the Assembly in 1830, viz.: "That, in their judgment, every licentiate coming by certificate to any Presbytery, in connection with the General Assembly, from any portion of a corresponding ecclesiastical body, should be required to answer in the affirmative, the constitutional questions directed by chapter fourteenth of our Form of Government, to be put to our candidates before they are licensed; and that in like manner every ordained minister of the Gospel coming from any church in correspondence with the General Assembly by certificate of dismission and recommendation, should be required to answer affirmatively the first seven questions directed by chapter fifteenth of our Form of Government, to be put to one of our own licentiates when about to be ordained to the sacred office,' (p. 12, 1830), sufficiently explicit; and would earnestly recommend these to the attention of the Presbyteries under the care of the Assembly.

As to the question submitted to them, "Whether the Catechisms, Larger and Shorter, are to be considered as a part of the *Standards* of our Church, and are comprehended in the words, Confession of Faith of this Church?" the committee feel no hesitation in answering that question in the affirmative. It does not appear that any doubts on that subject have ever been entertained until very recently. The committee find in the minutes of the old Synod, at the union of the Synod of Philadelphia with the Synod of New York, in 1758, that the first article of the Plan of Union contains the following words (Digest, p. 118), viz.: "Both Synods, having always approved and received the Westminster Confession of Faith and Larger and Shorter Catechisms as an orthodox and excellent system of Christian doctrine founded on the word of God, we do still receive the same as the Confession of our Faith; and also the plan of worship, government, and discipline, contained in the Westminster Directory, strictly enjoining it on all our members and probationers for the ministry that they preach and teach according to the form of sound words in said Confession and Catechisms, and avoid and oppose all error contrary thereto." In the recital of the manner in which a Presbytery was received by the Synod of New York, 1763, we have the following record which is contained in the Assembly's Digest, p. 50: "It was agreed to grant their request, provided that they agree to adopt our Westminster Confession of Faith and Catechisms, and engage to observe the Directory as a plan of worship, discipline, and government, according to the agreement of this Synod."

In 1788, in the Adopting Act of the Confession, as entered in the Digest, p. 124, the Catechisms are distinctly mentioned as a part of our standards. "They also took into consideration the Westminster Larger and Shorter Catechisms, and having made a small amendment of the Larger, did approve, and do hereby approve and ratify the said Catechisms as now agreed on, as the Catechisms of the Presbyterian Church in the said United States. And the Synod order that the said Directory and Catechisms be printed and bound up in the same volume with the Confession of Faith and the Form of Government and Discipline; and that the whole be considered as the standard of our doctrine, government, discipline, and worship, agreeably to the resolutions of the Synod at their present sessions"—one of which resolutions was (p. 123), "that the Form of Government and Discipline, and the Confession of Faith, as now ratified, is to continue to be our constitution and the confession of our faith and practice unalterably, unless two-thirds of the Presbyteries under the care of the General Assembly shall propose alterations or amendments, and such alterations or amendments shall be agreed to and enacted by the General Assembly." Accordingly, in the Directory for the administration of baptism, the Larger and Shorter Catechisms of the Westminster Assembly are mentioned in connection with the Confession of Faith, as adopted by this Church, and are to be recommended as containing a summary of the principles of our holy religion, taught in the Scriptures of the Old and New Testament.

The committee therefore recommend to the Assembly the adoption of the following resolutions, viz.:

1. *Resolved* by the Assembly, that in receiving and adopting the Confession of Faith, as containing the system of doctrine taught in the Holy Scriptures, the Larger and Shorter Catechisms of the Westminster Assembly of Divines are included, and do constitute an integral part of the standards of this Church.

2. *Resolved*, That the use of the Catechisms in the religious instruction of the young and of the children under the care of the Church, be affectionately and earnestly recommended to the Sessions in connection with the General Assembly, as the most effectual means, under God, of preserving the purity, peace, and unity of our Church.—*Minutes*, 1832, p. 371.

14. *Power of the Assembly to make "Standing Rules."*

[The Presbytery of New York laid before the Assembly the following paper, viz.:]

"The Presbytery took into consideration the regulations adopted by the General Assembly at their last meeting, intended to embrace and extend the existing rules respecting the reception of foreign Ministers and Licentiates; whereupon the Presbytery were of opinion that if the General Assembly designed these regulations as a standing rule, supposing that having passed through their body, they became obligatory upon the subordinate judicatories, and ought to be carried into immediate effect, they therein violated the sixth section of the eleventh chapter of our Constitution, which says, 'Before any overtures or regulations, proposed by the Assembly to be established as standing rules, shall be obligatory upon the churches, it shall be necessary to transmit them to all the Presbyteries, and to receive the return of at least a majority of the Presbyteries, in writing, approving thereof.'"—*Minutes*, 1799, p. 172.

[To this the Assembly reply:]

"1. That the first reason assigned by the Presbytery of New York for their request is founded on a misinterpretation of an ambiguous expression in the Constitution. The sixth section of the eleventh chapter is thus expressed: 'Before any overtures or regulations proposed by the

Assembly to be established as *standing rules* shall be obligatory on the churches, it shall be necessary to transmit them to all the Presbyteries, and to receive the returns of at least a majority of the Presbyteries, in writing, approving thereof.' *Standing rules* in this section can refer only to one of the following objects: 1st. To articles of the Constitution which, when once established, are unalterable by the General Assembly; or 2d. To every rule or law enacted without any term of limitation expressed in the act. The latter meaning would draw after it consequences so extensive and injurious as forbid the Assembly to give the section that interpretation. It would reduce this Assembly to a mere committee to prepare business upon which the Presbyteries might act. It would undo, with few exceptions, all the rules that have been established by this Assembly since its first institution, and would prevent it forever from establishing any rule not limited by *the terms of the act* itself. Besides, *standing rules*, in the evident sense of the Constitution, cannot be predicated of any acts made by the Assembly and repealable by it, because they are limited, in their very nature, to the duration of a year, if it please the Assembly to exert the power inherent in it at all times to alter or annul them, and they continue to be rules only by the Assembly's not using its power of repeal. The law in question is no otherwise a *standing rule* than all other laws repealable by this Assembly."—*Minutes*, 1799, p. 179.

Section 2.—Of the particular Church.

1. A "Particular Church" defined.—2. How new Congregations are to be organized.—*a.* Application must be made to the Presbytery.—*b.* Order of proceeding in constituting a Church.—*c.* Covenant to be entered into.—*d.* Ruling Elders and Deacons to be elected and ordained.—*e.* The newly formed Church to be reported to Presbytery.—*f.* In exceptional cases congregations may be formed without Ruling Elders.—3. Churches not to be organized without an order of Presbytery.

1. *What is a particular Church?*

a. "A particular Church consists of a number of professing Christians, with their offspring, voluntarily associated together for divine worship and godly living, agreeably to the Holy Scriptures, and submitting to a certain form of government."—*Form of Gov.*, ch. ii, sec. 4.

b. The committee to whom was recommitted the report to the last Assembly on the organization of new churches, reported again, and their report was read and adopted, and is as follows, viz.:

That a particular Presbyterian Church, so far as adults are concerned, is constituted and organized, as such, by a number of individuals professing to walk together as the disciples of Jesus Christ, on the principles of the Confession of Faith and Form of Government of the Presbyterian Church, and the election and ordination of one or more ruling elders, who, by the ordination service, become the spiritual rulers of the persons voluntarily submitting themselves to their authority in the Lord. —*Minutes*, 1831, p. 325.

2. *How new Congregations are to be organized.*

a. This organization ought always to be made by application to the Presbytery within the bounds of which the church to be organized is found, unless this be exceedingly inconvenient, in which case it may be done by a duly authorized missionary, or a neighboring minister of the Gospel.

b. At the time appointed for the purpose, after prayer for divine direction and blessing, the presiding minister, or committee appointed by the Presbytery, should first receive from those persons to be organized into the new church, if they have been communicants in other churches, letters of dismission and recommendation; and in the next place, examine and admit to a profession of faith, such persons as may offer themselves, and may be judged suitable to be received on examination. If any of these persons, admitted to a profession on examination, have not been baptized, they should, in this stage of the business, be made the subject of Christian baptism.

c. The individuals ascertained in the foregoing manner to be desirous and prepared to associate as a church of Christ, should now, by some public formal act, such as rising, joining hands, or subscribing a written statement, agree and covenant to walk together in a church relation, according to the acknowledged doctrines and order of the Presbyterian Church.

d. The next step is to proceed to the election and ordination of ruling elders, in conformity with the directions given on this subject in the Form of Government of the Presbyterian Church.

Deacons are to be elected and ordained in like manner as in the case of ruling elders.—*Minutes*, 1831, p. 326.

e. When a church has been organized in the manner already described, report of the same should be made as soon as practicable to the Presbytery within whose bounds it is located. And when a missionary, or other minister of the Gospel, not specially appointed to the work by a Presbytery, has, in the manner above specified, organized a church, not within the known bounds of any Presbytery, the church thus organized should as soon as practicable make known to some Presbytery, with which it may be most naturally and conveniently connected, the time and manner of its organization, and desire to be received under the care of said Presbytery.

In cases in which churches are to be formed within the known boundaries of any Presbytery, it is most desirable that persons wishing to be organized as a Presbyterian Church should petition that Presbytery to receive them under its care for the purpose of organizing them in due form.

There may be people in destitute portions of our land who may be disposed to associate for the purpose of forming a Presbyterian congregation, when no minister of the Gospel can be obtained to aid them. The forming of associations for such a purpose, in the circumstances contemplated, should be considered not only as lawful, but highly commendable. And such associations when formed, should, as speedily as possible, take measures for obtaining the preaching of the Gospel, and for becoming organized as regular churches.—*Minutes*, 1831, p. 326.

f. "Cases may also occur in various places, in which a collection or association of people may desire the preaching of the Gospel, and be willing in whole or in part to support it, and yet may not have suitable men among them to sustain the office of ruling elders. Such people may and ought to obtain a preacher of the Gospel to labor among them, and occasionally to administer ordinances, under the direction of some Presbytery, till they shall find themselves in circumstances to make proper choice of ruling elders, and to have them regularly set apart to their office."—*Minutes*, 1831, p. 326–7.

3. *To organize Churches belongs to the Presbytery.*

The committee to whom was referred Overture No. 14, viz., "Is a minister of the Gospel in our connection ex-officio authorized to organize churches in the bounds of Presbyteries, without any previous order of Presbytery, directing such organization," made a report recommending the following resolution, which was adopted accordingly, viz.:

Resolved, That, except in frontier and destitute settlements, where, by Form of Government, chap. xv, sect. 15, it is made a part of the business of Evangelists to organize churches; and, except in cases where it is exceedingly inconvenient to make application to a Presbytery, for which provision is made in the act of Assembly of 1831, it is not the prerogative of a minister of the Gospel to organize churches without the previous action of some Presbytery directing or permitting it; since in Form of Government, chap. x, sect. 8, to form new congregations is enumerated among the powers of the Presbytery; and since in chap. iv, of Bishops or Pastors, no mention is made of any such power being lodged in the hands of an individual minister.—*Minutes*, 1833, p. 410.

SECTION 3.—MEMBERS OF THE CHURCH.

1. Universalists not to be admitted. Decision reaffirmed.—2. Persons refusing to present their children for baptism not to be refused communion; but the expediency of receiving them to membership left to the Session.—3. Postmasters officiating on the Sabbath to be excluded from communion. Decision reaffirmed.—4. Owners of stage coaches which run on the Sabbath ought not to be received to the communion of the Church.—5. Members to be admitted to the communion of the Church.—*a.* Only by an individual Session regularly constituted.—*b.* By the Session of that Church to which he will belong.—*c.* Undue haste is to be avoided.—6. Members by letter should produce a regular certificate of dismission.—7. Absent members whose residence is unknown.—*a.* Every member amenable to some tribunal.—*b.* Cannot avoid membership but by death or process.—*c.* Withdrawal irregularly from Church privileges censurable.—*d.* Absent members not to be stricken from the roll.—*e.* But those who wilfully withdraw are to be suspended.—8. Members wishing to be released from their obligations. The provisions of the book sufficient.

1. *Who may be received.*

a. A question from the Synod of the Carolinas was introduced as follows, viz.:

"Are they who publicly profess a belief in the doctrine of the universal and actual salvation of the whole human race, or of the fallen angels, or both, through the mediation of Christ, to be admitted to the sealing ordinances of the Gospel?"

The Assembly determined that such persons should not be admitted. —*Minutes*, 1792, p. 60.

b. The consideration of Dr. McCorkle's letter was resumed. On the proposition in the letter, requesting a reconsideration of the sentence of the General Assembly, respecting the doctrine of universal salvation, passed at Carlisle in 1792, the Assembly unanimously agreed to adhere to the aforesaid decision.—*Minutes*, 1794, p. 86.

2. *Persons refusing to present their Children in Baptism not to be refused Communion; but the expediency of receiving them to be judged of by the Session.*

The committee appointed on Overture No. 7, from the session of Union Grove church, Illinois, made the following report, which was adopted, viz.:

That two questions are submitted in this overture to the judgment of the Assembly, viz.:

1st. Is it the duty of Church Sessions to admit to membership persons who refuse to present their children to God in the ordinance of baptism?

2d. What is the duty of the Session in case of parents, members of the Church, who refuse from conscientious scruples to present their children for baptism?

For a reply to these questions, the Session are referred to the Digest, part iv, chap ii, sec. 7, p. 98, where the decision of the Assembly on the principle involved in both is recorded as follows:

"A letter also came, through the Committee of Overtures, from Bethuel Church, Esq., inquiring whether he may be admitted to occasional communion, whilst he has scruples concerning infant baptism.

"The letter from Bethuel Church, Esq., as overtured, was read, and the motion formerly made thus amended, 'That the Session of the church of Cambridge be permitted to receive Mr. Church upon satisfactory evidence of his good character, his scruples notwithstanding,' was taken up and agreed to."

But while it is clear, that persons otherwise of good Christian character, are not to be excluded from the communion of the Church, because they have scruples concerning infant baptism, there is in every case, where such persons apply for admission, a question as to the expediency of receiving them, upon which the Session of the Church must decide.—*Minutes*, 1834, p. 449.

3. *Postmasters officiating on the Sabbath.*

An appeal by Mr. Wiley, postmaster in Washington, Pennsylvania, from a decision of the Synod of Pittsburg, by which it is determined that Mr. Wiley's officiating as postmaster on the Sabbath day, under existing circumstances, is a sufficient reason to exclude him from the special privileges of the Church, was overtured and read. On motion,

Resolved, That the above decision of the Synod of Pittsburg be affirmed. And it is hereby affirmed.—*Minutes,* 1810, p. 456.

A petition signed by a number of persons in Washington, Pennsylvania, and its vicinity, praying the revision, with a view to its being rescinded, of the decision of the Assembly of 1810, respecting the case of Mr. Wiley, postmaster, was overtured.

Resolved, That the prayer of the petitioners be not granted.—*Minutes,* 1812, p. 508.

4. *May the Proprietor of a Stage running on the Sabbath be received in the Church?*

In answer to an "Overture relative to receiving a person as a member of the Church, who is a proprietor in a line of stages which carries the mail, and runs on the Sabbath;" the following was adopted.

Resolved, That it is the decided opinion of this Assembly, that all attention to worldly concerns on the Lord's day, farther than the works of necessity and mercy demand, is inconsistent both with the letter and spirit of the fourth commandment; and consequently, all engagements in regard to secular occupations on the Lord's day, with a view to secure worldly advantages, are to be considered inconsistent with Christian character; and that those who are concerned in such engagements ought not to be admitted to the communion of the Church, while they continue in the same.—*Minutes,* 1819, p. 713.

5. *By whom to be admitted, &c.*

The committee to whom was referred the subject involved in so much of the records of the Synod of Cincinnati as relates to the admission of persons to church privileges at the great meetings common in that region, made the following report, which was adopted, viz.:

That they have given this subject a careful consideration, and recommend the adoption of the following resolutions, viz.:

Resolved, 1. That the order of the churches requires that all persons making a public profession of religion be introduced to the communion of the Church only by an individual Session regularly constituted

Resolved, 2. That it is the right and duty of Sessions to take the exclusive oversight of their respective congregations, and that the practice of one Session admitting to a Christian profession persons belonging or intending to belong to a congregation under the care of another Session, is irregular, and ought not to be countenanced.

Resolved, 3. That the purity and prosperity of the Church, as well as the best interests of those immediately concerned, demand great circumspection in the admission of persons to church privileges; and that ordinarily it is deemed improper to receive persons immediately upon their indulging a hope of reconciliation with God, and especially in the case of the young, and of persons of previously immoral lives or lax principles, and of those concerning whom little is known.—*Minutes*, 1832, p. 373.

6. *Members received by Certificate.*

Nor can the Assembly forbear to regret that the Session of Chilicothe had not acted in a more formal manner, in receiving Mr. McCalla, and had not required a regular certificate of dismission from the church to which Mr. McCalla belonged before they received him.—*Minutes*, 1821, p. 21.

7. *Absent Members, whose Residence is unknown.*

a. The committee appointed on the overture from the Synod of New Jersey, inquiring what a church Session ought to do with members in communion, who have been absent for years without having taken a certificate of dismission, and whose place of residence is unknown, made a report, which, being read and amended, was adopted, and is as follows, viz.:

That although this particular case is not provided for by a specific regulation in our Book of Discipline, yet it is embraced by certain general principles, which are recognized in that book, and interwoven with many of its provisions. These principles, together with the result, bearing on the case in question, the committee beg leave most respectfully to state:

1. Every church member is amenable to some appropriate tribunal,

by the wisdom and fidelity of which, in case of his falling into any error, immorality, or negligence, he may be dealt with according to the word of God.

2. No member of a church can properly ever cease to be such but by death, exclusion, a regular dismission, or an orderly withdrawing to join some other Christian denomination; and must of necessity continue to be amenable to that church until he becomes regularly connected with another.

3. For a church member to withdraw from a use of his privileges as a member, either by irregularly connecting himself with another denomination, or by going to a distant part of the world, to reside for a number of years, without making known his removal to the church Session, and asking a certificate either of good standing, for the purpose of enjoying occasional communion elsewhere, or of dismission, to join some other church, is itself a censurable violation of the principles of church fellowship, and may infer suspension from its privileges.

4. Church members, therefore, who have been absent for a number of years in unknown places, are by no means to have their names erased from the churches to which they respectively belong, but are to be held responsible to their respective churches; and if they should ever return, or be heard from, are to be regularly dealt with according to the word of God, and the principles of our Church; and, although great caution and tenderness ought to be exercised toward those whose withdrawing from Christian privileges may be occasioned by the unavoidable dispensations of Providence, without any material fault of their own, yet in all cases in which a church Session has good reason to believe that any of the church under their care have absented themselves with design, either from a disregard of Christian privilege, or from a wish to escape from the inspection and discipline of the Church, they ought without unnecessary delay to declare such persons suspended from the privileges of the Church, until they give evidence of repentance and reformation; and, of course, in making their statistical reports, ought to enumerate such among the members under suspension.—*Minutes*, 1825, p. 138–9.

b. The Records of the Synod of New York and New Jersey were approved, with the exception of the action of the Synod (p. 381) in relation to the course of the Presbytery of North River, in the case of delinquent church members.—*Minutes*, 1853, p. 323.

[The record referred to is as follows, viz.: "The Committee on the Records of the Presbytery of North River, reported recommending that they be approved as far as written, with the following exception, viz.: On page 18, the Presbytery refused to sustain the following exception to the Records of the Session of Freedom Plains, viz.:

"That several members of the church have been suspended by the Session simply for having absented themselves for years, and having gone beyond the knowledge of the Session without applying for certificates. The Report was adopted."—*Minutes of the Synod of New York and New Jersey.*]

The Rev. William Homes, in behalf of himself and forty-three other commissioners, in accordance with notice given yesterday, submitted the following dissent from the action of the Assembly on the report of the Committee on the Records of the Synod of New York and New Jersey:

"The undersigned, acting in the fear of God, and unfeignedly regardful of the interests of the Presbyterian Church and the just rights of its individual members, in the full belief that the action of the Assembly, in excepting to the Records of the Synod of New York and New Jersey, was erroneous in judgment, and may prove the sanction of future action mischievous to the honor of the Church of Christ, involving principles injurious to the interests of religion and subversive of the constitutional rights of the members of the Presbyterian Church, ask leave respectfully to dissent from the action above mentioned for the following reasons:

"1. It concedes to the judicatories of the Church the right to inflict a judicial sentence upon members of churches, without a trial, contrary to the Form of Government, in which there is no authority whatever for sentence of any kind against such without a fair and impartial trial, a citation and a hearing.

"2. It violates the constitutional rights of individuals, not less sacred in the Church than out of it, to such trial for any alleged offence before sentence of condemnation can be pronounced upon them; reversing also the principle of common law, that innocence is to be presumed of every individual till proved guilty by due process of trial, he having fair opportunity to explain or defend.

"3. It is mischievous to the interests of justice and the credit of religion, in that it establishes the principle, that not only in the offence in question, but in any and every alleged offence, a judicatory may sit in judgment upon members of churches, and, without legitimate trial, record sentence of suspension or excommunication.

"4. Affording license as it does for such indiscriminate and unlimited illegal action, even if the course of the lower judicatory should be defined and limited to cases where Sessions could know that members had unworthily separated themselves from church association, yet sentence of suspension is utterly unwarranted in such cases without a citation and a hearing; and, moreover, the difficulty in ascertaining the real facts, and the possibility of committing a mistake, are so manifest, that such a proceeding is to be discountenanced in all cases.

"5. By assuming that members of churches have absented themselves without good and sufficient reasons, when, in many cases, it is impossible that the judicatory should know anything about it, it allows that a stigma may be inflicted upon members of the Church, worthy, and in other places fulfilling conspicuously their obligations as true and honorable members of Christ's Church universal, and upon others who are kings and priests unto God in the New Jerusalem.

"6. Even if it be affirmed that such sentence of suspension, as is sanctioned by the action from which we regret to be compelled to dissent, entails no obloquy; yet the Form of Government knows nothing of a sentence of suspension from the honorable and precious privileges of church membership that does not imply guilt and reproach, and furnishes no authority for a sentence of condemnation without dishonor.

"For these reasons, which seem to us to take deep hold of the foundations of justice and true religion in the Presbyterian Church, and believing that the offence for which it is implied that sentence of suspension may be pronounced without a trial, however, as we freely allow, it is one requiring the notice of Church Sessions, is not one so offensive to the honor of Christ, or destructive of the purity and edification of the Church, as to justify the alarming proceeding of a departure from the express enactment of our Form of Government, and an ignoring of those rights guaranteed by civil and ecclesiastical law, we beg leave to dissent from the action of the General Assembly, and to have these reasons spread upon the minutes."—*Minutes*, 1853, pp. 325, 326.

The Rev. Marcus Smith, Rev. E. J. Richards, Rev. J. C. Smith, and Hon. William Strong, were appointed a committee to answer the foregoing dissent, who subsequently presented a report, which was adopted, and is as follows:

"It is fully conceded and firmly maintained by the General Assembly that, in all cases where an offender can be reached by citation and brought to trial, it is the duty of the judicatory to which he is directly amenable, to proceed against him according to the process prescribed by the Book of Discipline.

"But the action complained of by the dissentients relates to a very different class of cases. The individuals in question have absented themselves from the church with which they are connected, and after diligent inquiry cannot be found. They are, therefore, beyond the reach of citation. They cannot possibly be brought to trial. Shall the Church, in such cases, be responsible for them? As they have placed themselves beyond the oversight of the Church, it is but reasonable that the Church should be permitted to secure itself against any reproach which might come upon it from the conduct of such absentees.

"In accordance with these principles, the Constitution of our Church makes provision (Book of Discipline, chapter xi), for the case of absent church members. It relieves the Church from the responsibility of sustaining a certificate of good standing when it has run on for more than one year. It implies that a church member may not absent himself a longer time from the ordinances, without a forfeiture of his good standing. In those cases, therefore, where individuals have absented themselves for years together, and after the most diligent inquiry cannot be found, it is but right that the Session of the church to which they are amenable should make entry of the fact on their records, and declare such persons to have forfeited their good standing, until they return and account for their absence. Such was the judgment of the Assembly of 1825, with which this Assembly perfectly accords."

The Rev. S. Holmes moved a reconsideration of the action of the Assembly in reference to the Records of the Synod of New York and New Jersey.

The motion was lost.—*Minutes*, 1853, p. 327.

8. *Members who wish to be released from their Obligations.*

The Committee on the Polity of the Church reported a paper, "asking what shall be done with certain Church members, against whose moral character no charges can be made, but who wish to be released from their Church obligations. The committee recommend that such cases be referred to the sound discretion of the Sessions to which such persons may be answerable; reminding the Sessions, that it is a fundamental law of the Church that no person can be suspended from the communion of the Church, or have any other penalty inflicted, without regular citation and trial, according to the form prescribed in our Book of Discipline."

The report was recommitted, "with instructions to report, that no new order be taken in the case."—*Minutes*, 1859, pp. 17, 18.

Subsequently, "The report of the Committee on the Case of Delinquent Church Members was taken up, and it was resolved, in accordance with their recommendation, that the provisions of the Book of Discipline are all that is needed."—*Minutes*, 1859, p. 48.

CHAPTER II.

OFFICERS OF THE CHURCH.

SECTION 1.—DEACONS.

1. Have no juridical power.—2. Their duty consists in distributing the charities of the Church to the poor.—3. To be ordained in the same manner as Ruling Elders.—4. The duties of Trustees and Deacons not identical, and Ministers not ex-officio members or Presidents of the Board of Trustees.

1. *Deacons have no Juridical Powers.*

"We need only represent unto you the ends and institution of Scripture Deacons, and that there is no juridical power allowed them in the Scriptures."—*Minutes*, 1716, p. 42.

2. *Their Duty consists in distributing the Charities of the Church to the Poor.*

The committee on Overture No. 4, viz., a reference from the Presbytery of West Tennessee, requesting an answer to the two following questions, viz., 1. What are the nature and duties of the office of deacon? 2. What is the Scriptural and appropriate mode of ordination?—made the following report, which was adopted, viz.:

In answer to the first inquiry, "What are the nature and duties of the office of deacon?" we reply: The answer we conceive to be explicitly given in our Form of Government, chapter vi. Their duties there are plainly made to consist in distributing the charities of the church to which they belong, to the poor of that church. Over charities collected for any other purpose than those specified, their office gives them no control. In addition to this the temporalities of the church generally may be committed to their care.—*Minutes*, 1833, p. 405.

3. *To be ordained in the same manner as Ruling Elders.*

In answer to the second inquiry, "What is the Scriptural and appropriate mode of ordaining them?" we reply: Our Form of Government, chap. xiii, sec. 4, declares that such, whether Elder or Deacon, shall be set apart to their respective offices by prayer. The imposition of hands, however, we are aware, in many of our churches, is practised, and, as it is plainly in accordance with apostolic example, it is the opinion of the committee that it is proper and lawful. We conceive that every church in this respect may with propriety be left to adopt either of these two modes, as they think suitable and best.—*Minutes*, 1833, p. 405.

4. *The appointment of Trustees, not inconsistent with Presbyterianism; their Duties distinct from those of Deacons. Ministers are not ex-officiò Members or President of the Board of Trustees.*

"It is not inconsistent with the Presbyterian plan of government, nor the institution of our Lord Jesus Christ, that Trustees, or a committee chosen by the Congregation, should have the disposal and application of the public money raised by said Congregation, to the uses for which it was designed; provided that they leave in the hands and to the management of the Deacons, what is collected for the Lord's table, and the poor. And that Ministers of the Gospel, by virtue of their office, have no right to sit with or preside over such Trustees or committees."—*Minutes*, 1752, p. 249.

Section 2.—Ruling Elders.

1. The Eldership is essential to the existence of a Presbyterian Church.—2. Elders must be duly elected.—3. Mode of Election.—4. Who are electors of Ruling Elders and Deacons?—*a.* Baptized persons only, legal voters.—*b.* No distinction is to be made as to the ages of the voters.—5. The office of a Ruling Elder is perpetual. Form of Government, chap. xiii, sec. 6. Election for a term of years is *irregular*, but not *invalid*.—6. An Elder may resign his office. Form of Government, chap. xiii, sec. 6.—7. In which case he has no seat in any Church court.—8. An Elder cannot hold office in two churches at the same time, nor adjudicate in a church in which he is not an Elder.—9. Elders censured for leaving, and also for non-attendance upon Church courts.—10. An

Elder who may sit in Presbytery, may sit in Synod by the same right.—11. Every church having a stated supply, entitled to be represented by an Elder.—12. A Minister with one Elder, may form a Session, if there be but one Elder.—13. Restoration to Church privileges, does not restore to office.—14. Elders are not to participate in the ordination of Ministers, by the laying on of hands.

1. *The Eldership essential to the Existence of a Presbyterian Church.*

"The report of the Committee to Examine the Records of the Synod of the Western Reserve was taken up and adopted; and is as follows, viz.: That the records be approved, with the exception of the sentiment on page 154, viz., that the Eldership is not essential to the existence of the Presbyterian Church. In the opinion of the committee, the Synod advance a sentiment that contravenes the principles recognized in our Form of Government, chap. ii, sec. 4; chap. iii, sec. 5; chap. v; chap. ix, sects. 1, 2."—*Minutes*, 1833, p. 404.

[This does not prevent the forming of congregations for religious worship, where they "may not have suitable persons among them to sustain the office of Ruling Elder." See *ante*, p. 37.]

2. *Elders must be duly elected.*

"The following inquiry was referred to the decision of the Assembly, by the Synod of the Carolinas, viz.:

"In what point of light are the Elders, nominated and ordained by Mr. Balch, to be viewed hereafter in Mount Bethel Congregation?

"It was determined by the Assembly that the 'Elders' mentioned in the inquiry, are to be henceforth viewed as private Church members only, unless they be duly elected and set apart as Church officers hereafter."—*Minutes*, 1798, p. 158.

3. *Mode of Election.*

"Every congregation shall elect persons to the office of ruling elder, and to the office of deacon, or either of them, in the mode most approved and in use in that congregation."—*Form of Government*, chap. xiii, sec. 2.

a. "And while the Assembly would recognize the undoubted right of each congregation to elect their elders in the mode most approved and in use among them, they would recommend that in all cases where any dissatisfaction appears to exist, the congregation be promptly convened to decide on their future mode of election. And they are inclined to believe that the spirit of our Constitution would be most fully sustained by having, in all cases, a direct vote of the congregation in the appointment of elders."—*Minutes*, 1827, p. 215.

b. The committee on Overture No. 9, relating to an amendment in the Form of Government, chap. xiii, sec. 20, reported, and their report was adopted, and is as follows, viz.:

"The committee to whom was referred the consideration of the Overture (No. 9) relating to an alteration of that part of the Constitution of our Church which gives the right of choosing ruling elders and deacons to the congregation, in the way most approved and in use in the congregation, reported, that after deliberating on the subject, they find themselves unable to devise any method by which a uniformity of practice can be established in this interesting concern throughout the different sections of our Church, and believe that any alteration effected in the Constitution, with a view to relieve the difficulties in one section, would produce difficulties in another section of the Church. The committee therefore judge it inexpedient to propose any alteration, and recommend that the Assembly dismiss this subject from any further consideration."—*Minutes*, 1826, p. 187.

c. "The Assembly gave their opinion, that the Session of a church has the authority to convene the congregation for all such purposes; but should the Session neglect or refuse to convene the congregation, the party feeling aggrieved has its remedy by application to Presbytery in the form of a complaint."—*Minutes*, 1822, p. 49.

4. *Who are the Electors of Ruling Elders and Deacons?*

a. The consideration of the report of the committee to which was referred the appeal of Messrs. Lowerie and Kelso from the decision of the Synod of Ohio, affirming the decision of the Presbytery of Miami, by which decision the Presbytery had pronounced the election of Messrs. Dillingham and Rice to the office of ruling elders in the Second Presbyterian Church of Cincinnati a valid election, was resumed and finished; and the report being amended and fully discussed, was adopted, and is as follows, viz.:

The General Assembly, having gone fully into the consideration of the appeal from the decision of the Synod of Ohio by Messrs. Lowerie and Kelso, and having seen, with deep regret, the appearance of much disorder in the whole business, which they disapprove; believing, as the Assembly do, that the election of elders should be conducted with all due deliberation, according to the letter of the Constitution of the Presbyterian Church, and in the spirit and temper of the Gospel, and that, although the Assembly are of the opinion that it would be most desirable to have the communicants only as the electors of ruling elders, yet, as it appears to be the custom in some of the churches in the Presbyterian connection to allow this privilege to others, they see no reason why the election should be considered void, nor any reason why the decision of the Synod of Ohio should not be affirmed.

Therefore *Resolved*, that the sentence of the Synod of Ohio be, and it hereby is affirmed.—*Minutes*, 1822, p. 49.

b. The committee on Overture No. 1, viz., the following reference from the Presbytery of Steubenville: Ought an unbaptized person, who yet pays his proportion for the support of a congregation, to be permitted to vote for ruling elders? made the following report, which was adopted, viz.:

That, in the opinion of your committee, the office of ruling elder is an office in the Church of Christ; that ruling elders, as such, according to our Confession of Faith, book i, on Government, chap. v, are "the representatives of the people by whom they are chosen, for the purpose of exercising government and discipline," in the kingdom of our Lord Jesus Christ; that the discipline lawfully exercised by them is the discipline exercised through them by their constituents, in whose name and by whose authority they act in all that they do. To suppose, therefore, that an unbaptized person, not belonging to the visible kingdom of the Redeemer, might vote at the election of ruling elders, would be to establish the principle, that the children of this world might, through their representatives, exercise discipline in the Church of God; which is manifestly unscriptural, and contrary to the standards of our Church; your committee would therefore recommend, that the question in the said overture be answered in the negative.—*Minutes*, 1830, p. 284.

c. The Committee on Polity reported paper No. 4, inquiring as to the right of minors to vote in the election of elders and deacons. The committee recommend to return for answer—

That it is not in accordance with the principles and usages of the Presbyterian Church to distinguish between members of the Church as to their ages in voting for officers of the Church.

The recommendation was adopted.—*Minutes,* 1859, p. 18.

5. *The office of Ruling Elder is perpetual. Election for a term of years is irregular, but not invalid.*

a. "The report of the committee on Overture No. 1 was amended and adopted, and is as follows, viz.:

The committee to whom was referred Overture No. 1, a communication from the Session of Wheatland congregation in reference to the appointment of Freeman Edson as a commissioner to this Assembly, beg leave to present the following report, viz.:

"Agreeably to the Constitution of our Church, the office of Ruling Elder is perpetual (see Form of Government, chap. xiii, sec. 6), and cannot be laid aside by the will of the individual called to that office, nor can any congregation form rules which would make it lawful for any one to lay it aside. Your committee are of opinion that the mode of electing Elders in the congregation of Wheatland for a term of years was irregular, and ought in future to be abandoned, but cannot invalidate the ordination of persons thus elected and ordained to the office of Ruling Elder. And whereas, it appears that Mr. Freeman Edson was once elected to the office of Ruling Elder in the church of Wheatland, and was regularly set apart to that office; whereas, there seems to be some material diversity of views between the Presbytery of Rochester and the church Session to which Mr. Edson once belonged, as to the manner in which, and the principle on which, he ceased to be an acting Elder in the said church, into which the Assembly have no opportunity at present of regularly examining; and whereas, the Presbytery, with a distinct knowledge, as is alleged, of all the circumstances attending this case, gave Mr. Edson a regular commission as a Ruling Elder to this General Assembly; therefore

"*Resolved,* That he retain his seat as a member of the Assembly."—*Minutes,* 1835, p. 471.

b. "The overture on limiting the term of service of Ruling Elders was, on motion, taken up for consideration. The report of the committee was adopted, and is as follows: Whereas, sundry memorials have been presented to the Assembly, asking for a change of the Constitution, respecting the term of service in the office of Ruling Elder.

"*Resolved,* That while the Assembly sympathize with those churches, which are more especially tried by the present rule, yet, believing that the evils of a change would far outweigh those of the present system, they are not prepared to recommend any overture on the subject."—*Minutes*, 1849, p. 182.

c. "An overture from the Presbytery of Pennsylvania, asking 'whether the Constitution of our Church shall be so altered as to make the term of office of Ruling Elder temporary in such churches as prefer it,' was taken up and answered as follows:

"The Assembly do not deem it expedient, or for the edification of the Church, to send down to the Presbyteries such an overture; the most obvious and natural construction of our Form of Government does not contemplate a rotatory Eldership; and while such an organization of a Session is not *Anti-presbyterial*, yet the Assembly would discourage the adoption of the principle in our Church, from respect to the plain meaning of our rule; but nothing in this resolution is intended to disturb the relations of those churches which have adopted the principle of a limited period in the service of Elders."—*Minutes*, 1852, p. 177.

6. *A Ruling Elder may cease to act as such.*

[See Form of Government, chap. xiii, secs. 6, 7.]

a. "A petition from the members of the Session of the Third Presbyterian Church in this city, asking advice of this Synod with respect to the execution of their office in consequence of the judgment of the Synod respecting that church. After it was duly considered, they returned the following answer, viz.: The Synod advise them to continue to act as elders, but in case they cannot, consistently with what they apprehend to be their duty, continue as such, and act upon the decisions of Synod, that they may resign their office, and the congregation proceed to choose other elders, who may have freedom to act according to the determinations of the Synod."—*Minutes*, 1772, p. 435.

b. "The Assembly earnestly recommend to the whole Session, including the majority and the minority, in view of the state of the Fifth Church, to take the constitutional steps, and cease from acting as Ruling Elders in that congregation, and that the entire church take immediate measures to elect a new bench of Elders, with a view to promote the peace of the church, and to secure the permanent settlement of the Gospel ministry among them. And further, that it be recommended to the persons so elected not to accept the office unless they shall obtain the suffrages of at least two-thirds of the electors participating in the election."—*Minutes,* 1834, p. 453.

7. *A Ruling Elder without Office has no Seat in a Church Court.*

"*Resolved,* That no Ruling Elder who has retired from the active exercise of his office in the church to which he belongs, can be admitted as a member of a Presbytery, Synod, or General Assembly."—*Minutes,* 1835, p. 489.

8. *An Elder cannot hold Office in two Churches at the same time.*

a. "The Judicial Committee reported that, by permission of the Assembly, a complaint was presented to them by the Rev. Dr. Ashbel Green, in behalf of a minority, against a decision of the Synod of Philadelphia,* recorded on the Synod book, page 168, by which complaint the following question is presented for the decision of the Assembly, viz.:

"Is it consistent with the Constitution of this Church for the same individual to hold the office of Ruling Elder in two different churches at the same time?

"The complainants were heard in support of their complaint; the Synod was heard in defence of their decision, and the complainants concluded with a reply:

"When it was resolved by the Assembly, that the decision of the Synod be affirmed, and the complaint dismissed."—*Minutes,* 1827, p. 204.

Nor Adjudicate in a Church of which he is not an Elder.

b. "Overture No. 14, viz., the following question from the Presbytery of Salem: 'Has a Ruling Elder in any case a legal right to adjudicate in another church than that of which he is an Elder?' was taken up and decided in the negative."—*Minutes,* 1831, p. 324.

9. *Elders Censured for leaving without Permission, and Sessions directed to defray Expenses.*

a. "Upon calling the roll, it being found that many of the Elders have gone home without leaving any reason for their doing so, the Synod

* The Synod having rejected a resolution declaring it lawful for an elder to exercise the office in two different congregations.

do order that such Elders as do withdraw from the Synod without leave, shall be left to the censure of their Sessions, and report made thereof to the next Synod. And the Synod do recommend it to the several congregations to defray the necessary charges that their Elders be at during their attendance upon the Synod."—*Minutes*, 1735, p. 117.

b. Whereas, the Synod is deeply affected that the judicatures of the Church are so exceedingly neglected, both by ministers and elders, especially the latter, and taking this matter into serious consideration, and apprehending that one reason of this non-attendance, particularly on the sessions of Synod, arises from the congregations making no provision for defraying the expenses of ministers and elders, do therefore request the Presbyteries to direct their members to recommend it to their respective congregations to make contributions for this purpose; and the Synod do further request that the Presbyteries take every proper measure to excite their members to attend upon this judicature.—*Minutes*, 1781, p. 491.

10. *Elders have the same Right to sit in Synod as in Presbytery.*

The committee also overtured this question: Has an elder, whom the discipline of our Church authorizes to sit as a member in Presbytery from a vacant congregation, or united congregations, a right by that discipline to sit in Synod as a representative of such congregation or congregations?

The vote being taken, the question was determined in the affirmative. —*Minutes*, 1808, p. 403.

11. *Every Church, having a Stated Supply, is entitled to be represented in Presbytery or Synod by a Ruling Elder.*

The Committee on Bills and Overtures reported Overture No. 2, from the Synod of West Pennsylvania, "*On Stated Supplies and Vacant Congregations*," in the form following:

"When a minister is at the same time *pastor* of one church, and acts as the *stated supply* of another church, has each of said churches a right to be represented by its own elder at the same meeting of Presbytery or Synod? Or does this case come under the rule, chap. x, sec. 4, p. 368, of Form of Government?" They recommend that the following answer be returned, viz.: "That churches, having stated supplies only, are not such churches as are contemplated in the article referred to, and have a right of representation according to the principles of the Form of Government, chap. x, sec. 5."

The report was adopted.—*Minutes,* 1851, p. 15.

12. *A Minister, with one Elder, may form a Session, if there be but one Elder.*

The question, "Can a minister, with one elder, form a Session capable of transacting judicial business?" is sufficiently answered in the Constitution, Form of Government, chap. ix, sec. 2, where it seems to be implied that cases may occur with infant or feeble churches in which it would be impracticable, for a time, to have more than one elder, and yet be necessary to perform acts of a judicial character. For such the Constitution provides; but if there be more than one elder, then two at least, with a minister, are necessary to form a Session.—*Minutes,* 1836, p. 263.

13. *When an Elder has been suspended from Church privileges and restored, he is not thereby restored to Office.*

"When an elder has been suspended from Church privileges, for an offence, and again restored to the privileges of the Church, is he also restored to his office as a ruling elder?" should be answered in the negative. The two things are distinct; and since an elder, as well as a minister, may be suspended from his office, and not from the communion of the Church, so there may be reasons for continuing his suspension from his office after he is restored to the privileges of the Church. He cannot be restored to the functions of his office without a special and express act of the Session for that purpose, with the acquiescence of the church.—*Minutes,* 1836, p. 263.

14. *Elders not to Participate in the Ordination of Ministers by the laying on of Hands.*

The Committee on the Polity of the Church reported an answer to the inquiry, "Ought the eldership to participate in the ordination of ministers by laying on of hands?" as follows:

It is a recognized principle of our Church polity, in accordance as we believe, with Apostolic teaching, that bishops, ministers, and elders, constitute but one grade or rank of officers in the Christian Church;

and hence that in all our Church judicatories they have equal rights and powers. In all the judicial business of the Church, all are Presbyters alike. (See Form of Gov., chap. ix, secs. 1, 2, 4; chap. x, secs. 2 to 7; chap. xi, secs. 1, 2; and chap. xii, sec. 2.) Still it cannot be denied that in the Bible a distinction is recognized between those Presbyters who rule only, and those who both rule and preach. In the practice of the Presbyterian Church in all its branches, this distinction has become very marked. Some are set apart expressly to preach the Gospel, and to administer the ordinances of God's house. They are Presbyters in common with others; but as ministers of Christ, they have functions and rights peculiar to themselves, and are required to possess peculiar qualifications. In the ordination of ministers, your committee believe there are two distinct things to be done: 1st. The examination and approval of the candidate. In this all the members of the Presbytery participate alike; and 2d. The formal act of induction into office, in which, by almost universal consent, as we suppose, only ministers officiate. It is true our Form of Government, chap. xv, sec. 14, speaks of the whole Presbytery as laying on hands, and giving the right hand of fellowship. But every statute should be construed consistently with itself, and with general usage under the statute. Your committee would suggest, that the act of induction is ministerial, not judicial. And, as in respect to baptism, the elders, jointly with the pastor, determine who shall be admitted to this ordinance; yet the pastor only administers it; so in ordination—the whole Presbytery determine the fitness of the candidate, but only the ministers present induct into office. This, we believe, has been the universal practice under this rule; and that this usage was intended by the framers of the book seems probable from the fact that, in the form of induction, those aiding in the service are directed to extend to the new minister their right hands, saying, "*We give you the right hand of fellowship to take part of this ministry with us.*" This language manifestly implies, that those thus welcoming him do themselves occupy places in that ministry to which they welcome him. The committee therefore recommend, that the question be answered in the negative. The report was adopted.—*Minutes*, 1860, p. 243.

SECTION 3.—PASTORS.

1. Mode of proceeding to elect a Pastor.—The Session to judge of the readiness of the Congregation to elect.—To procure a settlement as speedily as possible.

If remiss after being requested, a complaint to Presbytery will lie.—The Presbytery has full cognizance of the proceedings to avoid undue delay or haste. —2. Electors. None may vote for a Pastor but those who contribute to his support; and a major vote determines.—3. Case of a Pastorate by prescription.—4. Dissolution of the Pastoral relation; mode of proceeding.—5. To remove without consent of Presbytery, censurable.—6. Pastoral faithfulness enjoined, in visiting and in lecturing.—7. Catechetical instruction enjoined.—8. Stated supplies have no Pastoral relation.

1. *Order of Proceeding in the Election of a Pastor.*

"The business left unfinished in the morning was resumed, and, after a full discussion of the subject, the motion to sustain the appeal of the Session of the Third Presbyterian Church in this city from the decision of the Synod of Philadelphia, affirming a decision of the Presbytery of Philadelphia, by which the Presbytery directed the said Session, within twenty days from the date of their decision, or after the final determination of the case, to convene the congregation for the purpose of electing a Pastor, was determined in the affirmative; and Dr. Green, Dr. Neill, and Mr. Richards were appointed a committee to prepare a minute, stating the principles on which the Assembly sustained the appeal.

"The committee appointed to prepare a statement of the principles and grounds upon which the Assembly sustained the appeal of the Session of the Third Presbyterian Church in this city reported, and their report being read and amended, was adopted in the words following, viz.:

"That both to prevent misapprehension and to aid the congregations and judicatures of this Church in deciding on any similar cases that may arise, the Assembly therefore declare,—

"I. That in vacant congregations which are fully organized, the Session of each Congregation are to determine, under their responsibility to the higher judicatures, when the Congregation are prepared to elect a Pastor, as directed in the Form of Government of this Church, chap. xiv, sec. 1.

"II. That it is the duty of the Session when a Congregation is vacant, to use their best endeavors to promote the settlement of a Pastor in the same, in the speediest manner possible, consistently with the peace, order, and edification of the Congregation; and it is the privilege of the people, or of any portion of them, to complain to the Presbytery when they think that the Session, after being suitably requested, neglect, or refuse to convene the Congregation to elect a Pastor.

"III. That it belongs to the Presbyteries to take cognizance of the proceedings of Sessions and Congregations in the important concern of settling Pastors, and to adopt the most effectual measures on the one hand to prevent all undue delay by the Session, or the people, and on the other, to prevent all precipitancy in the settlement of any Minister, or the adoption of any system of proceedings in the Congregation inconsistent with the real and permanent edification of the people.

"IV. That by the due and discreet observance of these principles by all concerned, it will be found, that so far from the Session of a Congregation having it in their power to deprive a majority of a Congregation of their right to make an election of a Pastor, when sought in an orderly and Christian manner, or to keep a Congregation unsettled for an indefinite length of time, the rights of the people will be most effectually secured, and their precious and inalienable privilege of choosing their own Pastor will be exercised by them in the shortest period which their own real benefit will permit.

"V. That the conviction of this Assembly, that the foregoing obvious and constitutional principles had not been duly adhered to in the case before them; that the Congregation had not proceeded with a suitable respect to the Session, and that the Presbytery did not adopt the most suitable measure when they advised and directed the Session to convene the Congregation in twenty days, has led the Assembly to sustain this appeal as the measure most constitutional, best calculated on the whole to do justice to all the parties concerned, and to point the way to the most speedy settlement of the unhappy differences and disorders which have so long existed in the particular Congregation immediately concerned."—*Minutes*, 1814, p. 559–560.

2. *Who may Vote in the Election of a Pastor.*

"Agreed, that none shall be allowed to vote for the calling of a Minister, but those that shall contribute for the maintenance of him, and that the major vote of these shall be determinative."—*Minutes*, 1711, p. 24.

"In this election no person shall be entitled to vote, who refuses to submit to the censures of the Church regularly administered; or who does not contribute his just proportion, according to his own engagements, or the rules of that Congregation, to its necessary expenses."—*Form of Government*, chap. xv, sec. 4.

3. *A Pastoral Relation allowed where no Instalment had occurred.*

"It appears evident to this Synod, that Mr. Tennent having in all respects acted, and been esteemed and looked upon, not only by this Synod, but also by the Congregation of Neshaminy, and particularly by the appellants themselves, as the Minister and Pastor of the people of Neshaminy, that he is still to be esteemed as the Pastor of that people, notwithstanding the want of a formal instalment among them; which omission, though the Synod doth not justify, yet it is far from nullifying the pastoral relation between Mr. Tennent and said people."—*Minutes*, 1736, p. 127.

4. *The Translation of a Pastor.*

a. Amendment to chap. xvi, sec. 2, of Form of Government. Strike out *together with a written citation to him*, and insert *if the parties be not prepared to have the matter issued at that Presbytery, a written citation shall be given to the Minister.*—*Minutes*, 1804, p. 305.

Note by the Assembly. "This amendment [adopted 1805, p. 333], is intended to provide that consent of parties shall shorten the constitutional process for translating a Minister."—*Minutes*, 1804, foot of p. 305.

b. The committee on overture, viz.: "Is it contrary to chap. xvii of the Form of Government for a Presbytery to dissolve the connection between a Minister and his congregation at the time when he presents his request for its dissolution, and the congregation joins issue by commissioners duly appointed for that purpose?" made the following report, which was adopted, viz.:

"*Resolved*, That it is not expedient for this Assembly to give a decided answer to the question, but to leave every Presbytery to act according to their own discretion in the premises."—*Minutes*, 1832, p. 373.

5. *Removal without Consent of Presbytery censurable.*

a. "The Presbytery of East Jersey having reported that Mr. John Cross has, without the concurrence of Presbytery, removed from one congregation to another, the Synod do declare that the conduct of such Ministers that do neglect attendance upon the meetings of the Presbytery without necessity, or that take charge of any congregation without the Presbytery's concurrence, to be disorderly, and justly worthy of Presbyterial censure, and do admonish said Mr. Cross to be no further chargeable with such irregularities for the future."—*Minutes*, 1735, p. 115.

b. "The Synod having deliberately considered the affair of Mr. Alison's removal to Philadelphia, judge that the method he used is contrary to the Presbyterian plan. Yet considering that the circumstances which urged him to take the method he used were very pressing, and that it was indeed almost impracticable to him to apply for the consent of Presbytery or Synod, in the orderly way, and further, being persuaded that Mr. Alison's being employed in such a station in the Academy, has a favorable aspect in several respects, and a very probable tendency not only to promote the good of the public, but also of the Church; as he may be serviceable to the interests thereof in teaching philosophy and divinity, as far as his obligations to the Academy will permit, we judge that his proceedings in said affair are in a great measure excusable. Withal the Synod advises, that for the future its members be very cautious, and guard against such proceedings as are contrary to our known approved methods in such cases."—*Minutes*, 1752, p. 206.

6. *Pastoral Faithfulness enjoined in Visiting and Lecturing.*

a. Upon an overture to Synod, in pursuance of an order of the committee to that purpose, viz., to use some proper means to revive the declining power of godliness, the Synod do earnestly recommend it to all our ministers and members, to take particular care about ministerial visiting of families, and press family and secret worship, according to the Westminster Directory, and that they also recommend it to every Presbytery at proper seasons to inquire concerning the diligence of each of their members in such particulars.—*Minutes*, 1733, p. 105.

b. "That in the discharge of pastoral duties they take the utmost care that the word of God be known and understood by the people, and that for this purpose, in their public instructions, the practice of lecturing on certain portions of Holy Scripture be not laid aside, but rather revived and increased; that they endeavor, where it is prudent and practicable, to institute private societies for reading, prayer, and pious conversation; above all, that they be faithful in the duties of family visitation and catechetical instruction of children and youth."—*Minutes*, 1799, p. 182.

7. *Catechetical Instruction enjoined.*

The following resolutions on the subject of catechetical instruction were unanimously adopted, viz.:

"1. *Resolved*, That this General Assembly consider the practice of catechetical instruction as well adapted to the prosperity and purity of our Zion.

"2. *Resolved*, That this Assembly view also with deep regret the neglect, on the part of many of our churches, of this good old practice of our fathers; a practice which has been attended with such blessed results to the cause of pure and undefiled religion.

"3. *Resolved*, That the institution of Sabbath Schools does not exonerate ministers and parents from the duty of teaching the Shorter Catechism to the children of the Church.

"4. *Resolved*, That this Assembly earnestly and affectionately recommend to all the Ministers and Ruling Elders in its connection to teach diligently the young of their respective congregations the Assembly's Shorter Catechism."—*Minutes*, 1849, p. 181.

8. *Stated Supplies have no Pastoral Relation.*

a. The committee on Overture No. 9, viz., a memorial from East Hanover Presbytery on inefficiency in the ministry, made the following report, which was adopted, viz.: . . . . 3. That it be enjoined on all the Presbyteries to take such measures as they may deem expedient for forming the pastoral relation, in a regular manner, in all cases where churches are now served by stated supplies, unless there be special reasons to the contrary, of which reasons the Presbytery is required to judge, and to make their judgment matter of record on their minutes.—*Minutes*, 1834, p. 450.

b. The committee to whom was referred the complaint of the minority of the Session of the First Presbyterian Church in New Orleans, reported the following minute, which was adopted, viz.:

Resolved, That as Mr. Clapp was merely a stated supply of the church in New Orleans, the Presbytery of Mississippi had a right, and it was their duty, under existing circumstances, to adopt measures to detach him from said congregation.—*Minutes*, 1831, p. 340.

c. Churches having stated supplies only are not such churches as are contemplated in chap. x, sec. 4, Form of Government, and have a right of representation according to the principles of the Form of Government, chap. x, sec. 5.—*Minutes*, 1851, p. 15.

d. "The pastoral office should be more and more highly appreciated, practically honored, and mainly promoted, in all our judicatories and churches, as the ordinary, the permanent, and the incomparable way of the Lord, in promoting his own cause, and in educating his people for Heaven."—*Minutes*, 1840, p. 17.

SECTION 4.—MINISTERS WITHOUT CHARGE.

1. Ministers without charge have a right to sit in Church Courts.—2. A minister cannot cease to be such but by deposition; but if providentially incapacitated, he is still held to possess the ministerial character and privileges, and is under the inspection of his Presbytery. If, through a worldly spirit, or any other criminal motive, he lay aside his office, Presbytery is to endeavor to bring him to duty; and failing of this, at length to exclude him from office. When ministers have withdrawn wholly or in part from the work of the ministry, Presbytery is to require and record the reasons, with its approbation or disapprobation.—3. Demission of the ministry allowed in the case of Robert Laing; also of Wm. Woodhull. Case of Joseph Montgomery, leave refused by the Assembly.—4. On holding civil office; deliverance upon the subject.—5. Office of chaplain in the army allowed.—6. An ordination to a chaplaincy is not *sine titulo*.—7. A chaplain may not at the same time be pastor of a church.—8. Office of chaplain in the navy approved of.

1. *Have a Seat in Church Courts.*

a. The committee to which was referred the overture from the Presbytery of Baltimore, in the following words, viz., "Are ministers without charges constituent members of our Church judicatures, and have they an equal voice with settled pastors and ruling elders of congregations in ecclesiastical governments?" reported, and their report being read and amended, was adopted, and is as follows, viz.:

"In the judgment of this Assembly, this question is answered affirmatively, chap. ix, sec. 2, of the Form of Government of the Presbyterian

Church, in these words: 'A Presbytery consists of all the ministers and one ruling elder from each congregation within a certain district.'"—*Minutes*, 1816, p. 615.

The committee to whom was referred Overture No. 9, relative to the right of ministers without charge to a seat in our judicatories, made their report, which, after some discussion, was referred to a committee consisting of Dr. Blythe, Dr. Hoge, Mr. Montfort, Mr. Elliot, and Mr. A. O. Patterson, to take the subject into consideration, and report to the next General Assembly.—*Minutes*, 1835, p. 492.

The report of the committee on the rights of ministers without charges to a seat in the judicatories of the Church, was taken up, and indefinitely postponed.—*Minutes*, 1836, p. 294.

2. *Who Withdraw from the Discharge of the Duties of the Ministry, how regarded and dealt with.*

By a report of the Presbytery of Lewes, it appeared that a minister, heretofore a member of that Presbytery, had been declared to be no longer a member thereof, and, as the Assembly were informed, is considered by them as divested of the ministerial office, and this without deposition, suspension, or censure; wherefore—

Resolved, That it is a principle of this Church, that no minister of the Gospel can be regularly divested of his office, except by a course of discipline, terminating in his deposition.

That if any minister, by providential circumstances, become incapable of exercising his ministerial functions, or is called to suspend them, or to exercise them only occasionally, he is still to be considered as possessing the ministerial character and privileges; and his brethren of the Presbytery are to inspect his conduct; and while they treat him with due tenderness and sympathy, they are to be careful that he do not neglect his ministerial duty beyond what his circumstances render unavoidable.

That if any minister of the Gospel, through a worldly spirit, a disrelish for the duties of his office, or any other criminal motive, become negligent or careless, he is by no means to be suffered to pursue this course, so as at length to be permitted to lay aside the ministry, without censure; because this would be to encourage a disregard of the most solemn obligations, by opening a way to escape from them with impunity.

But in all such cases, Presbyteries are seasonably to use the means and pursue the methods pointed out in the word of God and the rules of this Church, to recall their offending brother to a sense of duty; and if all their endeavors be ineffectual, they are at length regularly to exclude or depose him from his office.

If any cases or questions, relative to this subject, arise in Presbyteries, which are not contemplated by the provisions of this rule, such cases or questions should be referred to the General Assembly for a special decision.—*Minutes*, 1802, pp. 258, 259.

Resolved, That when ministers have withdrawn, or may hereafter withdraw, wholly or in part, from the work of the ministry, it be enjoined upon the Presbyteries to which they belong to require of such ministers their reasons for so doing; which reasons are to be put upon record by the Presbytery, with an expression of their approbation or disapprobation of the same.—*Minutes*, 1834, p. 450.

Resolved, That the constitutional remedy of these evils is in the hands of the Presbyteries, to whom it belongs to ordain, instal, remove, and *judge* ministers (see Form of Government, chap. x, sec. 8), and whose duty it is to inspect the fidelity of those whom they have solemnly set apart to the work of the ministry by the imposition of hands.—*Minutes*, 1834, p. 450.

3. *Allowed to demit the exercise of the Ministry, for cause assigned.*

a. There being from time to time complaints of the weakness and deficiency of Mr. Robert Laing, rendering his exercise of the ministerial function a detriment to the interest of religion, and rather a scandal than a help to the Gospel; the Synod advised him to demit the whole exercise of the ministry, and not to take it up again, but by the approbation of at least three ministers of the Presbytery wherein he may reside. The said Mr. Laing did quietly and humbly acquiesce in the aforesaid advice.—*Minutes*, 1726, p. 84.

b. "The Presbytery of New York report, that the Rev. Mr. William Woodhull, one of their members, appeared before them at their last meeting, and stated to them his situation, as being still incapable of exercising his ministry by his continued indisposition, and the little or rather no probability of his ever being able to attempt the exercise of it in future; and that he was at the same time engaged in certain secular employments that would seem to render it improper to have his name in their records as a member, while he is incapable of attending their meetings or discharging any of the great duties of his ministry; and therefore submits to them the propriety of their continuing and considering him as a member from time to time; and that the Presbytery, on considering his situation, thought it best to leave his name out of their records in future, till he shall be able to return to the exercise of his ministry; an event that would give them great pleasure.

"The Synod considered the above report, and are of opinion that Mr. Woodhull ought to be continued a member of the Presbytery of New York, and therefore direct that Presbytery to insert his name in their roll."—*Minutes*, 1783, p. 497, 498.

c. [The Presbytery of New Castle reported], "that in consequence of Mr. Joseph Montgomery's having informed them that, through bodily indisposition, he was incapable of officiating in the ministry, and having also accepted an office under the civil authority, they have left his name out of their records."

"The Synod disapprove of the conduct of the Presbytery of New Castle, in striking the name of Mr. Montgomery off their roll, for the reasons given in their report, neither of which, nor both together, seem to be sufficient; and in future recommend to all Presbyteries, when any ministers under their inspection resign their charge, or discontinue the exercise of their office while they remain in the same bounds, to pass a regular judgment on the reasons given for such conduct; and continue their inspection of those who shall not have deserved to be deprived of the ministerial character, though they may be laid aside from immediate usefulness."—*Minutes*, 1785, pp. 507, 510.

d. [The Committee on Church Polity reported Overture No. 4, from the Presbytery of Portage, asking advice as to the case of a minister, "who, though charged with no disciplinable offence, had forsaken the ministry for ten or more years, had regularly and permanently engaged in secular employment, had become a private member of the Church, and had no design of again acting as a minister of the Gospel, and who on this ground had requested his Presbytery to strike his name from the roll of members."

The committee recommended, "that the Presbytery be directed to strike his name from the roll, without implying any censure or any imputation on his Christian character."]

"The action recommended by the Committee on the Polity of the Church was not adopted."—*Minutes*, 1852, p. 177.

e. "The Assembly resumed the consideration of the report of the special committee [Edwin F. Hatfield, D.D., Henry B. Smith, D.D., and Walter S. Griffith, Esq.] on the Demission of the Ministry. After considerable discussion, the report was adopted, and is as follows, viz.:

"The committee to whom was referred, by the last General Assembly, an Overture from the Presbytery of Philadelphia, Third, on the 'Voluntary Demission of the Ministry,' respectfully submit the following report:

"The Constitution of our Church, it is well known, provides for the deposition of the unworthy, by due process of discipline; but seems not to have anticipated that any other class would require to be separated from the responsibilities of an office so high and so sacred. It nowhere contemplates the dismission of the members of the Church to the world, nor the return of the ministry, at their own instance, to the mere secularities of every-day life.

"Such is the view that has been taken of our standards from the beginning. Neither the old Synod of New York and Philadelphia, nor any of our General Assemblies, has ventured to give any different interpretation. The Assembly of 1802, on the occasion of the exercise, by the Presbytery of Lewes, of the prerogative of divesting one of their ministers of his office, without deposition, suspension, or censure, passed the following resolution:

"'*Resolved*, That it is a principle of this Church, that no minister of the Gospel can be regularly divested of his office except by a course of discipline terminating in his deposition. That, if any minister, by providential circumstances, become incapable of exercising his ministerial functions, or is called to suspend them, or to exercise them only occasionally, he is still to be considered as possessing the ministerial character and privileges; and his brethren of the Presbytery are to inspect his conduct; and, while they treat him with due tenderness and sympathy, they are to be careful that he do not neglect his ministerial duties beyond what his circumstances render unavoidable.'

"The *office* is to be retained; but, for sufficient reason, the *exercise* of the office may be discontinued in whole or in part. Such was the judgment of the Synod of 1726, in the case of Mr. Robert Laing, who, by reason of the complaints of his 'weakness and deficiency,' brought against him, 'rendering his exercise of the ministerial function a detriment to the interests of religion, and rather a scandal than a help to the Gospel,' 'advised him to demit the whole exercise of the ministry, and not to take it up again, but by the approbation of at least three ministers of the Presbytery wherein he may reside.'

"Similar was the judgment of the Synod of 1783, in the case of Mr. William Woodhull, who had represented to the Presbytery of New York, of which he was a member, 'his situation as being still incapable of exercising his ministry by his continued indisposition; and the little, or rather no, probability of his ever being able to attempt the exercise of it in future; and that he was at the same time engaged in certain secular employments that would seem to render it improper to have his name in their records as a member.' The Synod judged, 'that Mr. Woodhull ought to be continued a member of the Presbytery of New York.'"

Two years afterwards, in the case of Mr. Joseph Montgomery of the Presbytery of New Castle, whose name had been dropped from the roll of the Presbytery, at his own instance, on account of indisposition of body, and the acceptance of "an office under the civil authority," the Synod expressed their disapprobation of the measure, and recommended "to all Presbyteries, when any ministers under their inspection resign their charge, or discontinue the exercise of their office while they remain in the same bounds, to pass a regular judgment on the reasons given for such conduct, and continue their inspection of those who shall not have deserved to be deprived of the ministerial character, though they may be laid aside from immediate usefulness."

Thus uniformly has the doctrine been maintained by the ecclesiastical authorities of our Church, "that no minister of the Gospel can be regularly divested of his office except by a course of discipline terminating in his deposition." The Assembly of 1852 took the same ground, or at least refused to take ground to the contrary. In the case of a member of the Presbytery of Portage, "who, though chargeable with no disciplinable offence, had forsaken the ministry for ten or more years, had regularly and permanently engaged in secular employments, had become a private member of the Church, and had no design of again acting as a minister of the Gospel, and who, on this ground, had requested his Presbytery to strike his name from the roll of members," the Presbytery took the position, "that presbyterial law contemplates the ministerial office as permanent, ceasing not but by death or deposition;" yet they referred the case to the wisdom of the General Assembly. And the Assembly of 1852, although the Committee on the Polity of the Church recommended "that the Presbytery be directed to strike his name from the roll, without implying any censure or any imputation upon his Christian character," refused to adopt the recommendation; thereby confirming the position taken by the Presbytery, and conforming their action to the uniform decisions of the highest ecclesiastical authorities of our Church from the beginning.

It is true that, in common with most of the evangelical denominations, we maintain that *ordination* is but a ceremony—an outward sign—a public recognition on the part of the ordainers of the fitness of him who is ordained for the office to which he is set apart, it does not impress a character or impart a fitness not previously possessed. But, in the case of a minister of the Gospel, it recognizes the fact that the man has consecrated himself to this high and holy calling; has, by irrevocable vows, set himself apart from merely secular pursuits to the service of the Lord Jesus Christ in the ministry. From these vows the Church has received no dispensation to release him; and, therefore, has ever disclaimed the power and right, even in the exercise of discipline.

So long, therefore, as it is in the power of the minister, he is to exercise his gifts and graces in this particular calling. He is under covenant, both to Christ and to the Church, thus to serve God. He may not, without breach of covenant, abandon, merely at his own instance, the ministerial for a secular calling. If the providence of God puts it out of his power, evidently and unmistakably, to pursue his ministerial work, it becomes his duty *to bring his case before his brethren of the Presbytery*, and submit it to their decision. If any minister neglects this obvious duty, and of his own accord devotes himself to secular pursuits, his Presbytery are to investigate the case, and pass judgment upon it. Such was the judgment of the General Assembly of 1834.

"When ministers have withdrawn," they say, "or may hereafter withdraw, wholly or in part, from the work of the ministry, it is enjoined upon the Presbyteries to which they belong to require of such ministers their reasons for so doing; which reasons are to be put upon record by the Presbytery, with an expression of their approbation or disapprobation of the same."

In like manner, also, the Assembly of 1802, in order, very properly, to guard against the practical demission of the office, determined and directed, "that if any minister of the Gospel, through a worldly spirit, a disrelish for the duties of his office, or any other criminal motive, becomes negligent or careless, he is by no means to be suffered to pursue this course, so as at length to be permitted to lay aside the ministry, without censure; because this would be to encourage a disregard of the most solemn obligations, by opening a way to escape from them with impunity. But, in all such cases, Presbyteries are seasonably to use the means and pursue the methods pointed out in the word of God and the rules of this Church, to recall their offending brother to a sense of duty; and, if all their endeavors be ineffectual, they are at length regularly to exclude or depose him from his office."

This rehearsal of the action of previous Assemblies, it is thought is a sufficient answer to the overture, without entering upon a discussion of the abstract question: "May an ecclesiastical body, in any case, demit from the office of the ministry without discipline or censure?" We simply refer to the usages of our own Church, and urge them upon the attention of our Presbyteries. They are not to allow any of their ministers to retire from the ministerial work of their own accord; but to require, of such as are desirous to enter into a secular calling, their reasons for such a course, which they are to put upon record, approvingly or otherwise. The circumstances of the age call loudly upon this Assembly to reaffirm these long-established principles, and to enjoin upon the Presbyteries the utmost carefulness in preventing the secularization of our ministry.—*Minutes*, 1860, pp. 234, 236.

4. *May they hold Civil Office?*

a. "The committee to whom were referred the communication from the Presbytery of Ohio, respecting the Rev. Boyd Mercer, and his letter to the Moderator of the Assembly, exhibited their report.

"The report having been read and amended, was adopted, and is as follows:

"With respect to the abstract question, whether the tenure of a civil office be or be not incompatible with that of the holy ministry; your Committee are of opinion that there is nothing in the Holy Scriptures, or in the Constitution, acts, or proceedings of the Presbyterian Church in these United States, expressly prohibitory of such union of offices.

"With respect to the particular case referred to their consideration, as Mr. Mercer in his letter expressly asserts, that it is not his intention to decline the office of the holy ministry, and that he was led to devote himself, for the present, to the functions of an Associate Judge, by a state of health so infirm as to interrupt the regular discharge of his public duties as a minister of religion; your committee are of opinion that the Presbytery of Ohio ought not to censure him, unless there be some circumstances in the case unknown to the Assembly.

"That none, however, may so far misconstrue these sentiments as to persuade themselves that they countenance a covetous, ambitious spirit; your committee farther beg leave to suggest the propriety of cautioning your clergy against worldly-mindedness; of exhorting them not to aspire after places of emolument or civil distinction; of reminding them that the cure of souls is their peculiar business, and that they who serve at the altar, ought, as far as possible, to avoid temporal avocations."—*Minutes*, 1806, pp. 363, 364.

b. "The Committee (of Overtures) also overtured the following question, preferred by the First Presbytery of South Carolina, viz.: 'Is it admissible for a Gospel minister to hold office?'

"*Resolved*, That the Presbytery be referred to the decision of the Assembly of 1806, on the same question."—*Minutes*, 1808, p. 399.

5. *May hold the Office of Chaplain in the Army or Navy.*

a. "Application was made to Synod by Mr. Beatty, desiring to know their mind with respect to his going chaplain to the forces that may be raised in the Province of Pennsylvania, if he shall by the Government be called to that service. The Synod do judge it to be his duty."—*Minutes*, 1756, p. 275.

b. "Application having been made to Mr. Beatty by Colonel Armstrong, to serve as chaplain to the first battalion of the Pennsylvania Provincials for the ensuing campaign, he requested the advice and judgment of this Synod with respect to his duty therein. The Synod do unanimously agree that it is his duty to go."—*Minutes*, 1758, p. 282.

c. "'Tis allowed that Messrs. Alexander McDowel, and Hector Allison, go as chaplains to the Pennsylvania forces, and that Mr. Kirkpatrick go with the New Jersey forces the ensuing campaign."—*Minutes*, 1760, p. 302.

d. "The First Philadelphia Presbytery report, that they have ordained Mr. Israel Evans, and Mr. William Lynn, to qualify them to act as chaplains in the Army, to which they had been appointed."—*Minutes*, 1776, p. 472.

e. "Also ordained Mr. Robert Keith, to qualify him to act as a chaplain in the Army."—*Minutes*, 1777, p. 477.

6. *An Ordination to a Chaplaincy, not sine titulo.*

"By the report now made by the New Castle Presbytery, it appears that there was a mistake in the report of last year, respecting Mr. Armstrong's ordination; that he was not ordained *sine titulo*, but in consequence of his having accepted a chaplaincy in the army."—*Minutes*, 1779, p. 484.

7. *May a Chaplain be at the same time Pastor of a Church.*

"The affair respecting the First Presbyterian Congregation in this city was resumed.

"In the course of reasonings upon it, a case of conscience was put, viz., Whether a minister, having connection with any part of His Majesty's regular forces as their chaplain, and receiving the salary, or any part thereof as such, may, or ought to accept of a stated pastoral relation to any congregation? Which question was answered in the negative."—*Minutes*, 1759, p. 294.

8. *Chaplains in the Navy.*

"A reference from the Presbytery of Philadelphia on the propriety of their ordaining to the work of the Gospel ministry, a licentiate under their care, who now holds the office of a chaplain in the Navy of the United States, was considered; whereupon the Assembly

"*Resolved*, That this judicature of the Presbyterian Church feels a deep and lively interest in the spiritual welfare of the mariners of this country; and especially of those who are engaged in the naval service of our Union; and that the Assembly therefore will rejoice, if any Presbytery under its care has the opportunity of ordaining any well-qualified persons, men of piety and learning, with a view to their rendering permanent ministerial services to large congregations of our fellow-citizens who dwell in ships of war."—*Minutes*, 1826, p. 171.

CHAPTER III.

CANDIDATES.

SECTION 1.—BEFORE LICENSURE AND AS LICENTIATES.

1. A liberal education required.—2. Waived in certain cases.—3. Time of study.—*a.* Three years proposed, but not adopted.—*b.* Rule of a Synod enjoining three years' study, unconstitutional.—*c.* A new proposal to extend to three years, negatived.—4. Candidates are under the care of Session till ordained.—*a.* They belong to the order of the laity; and, *b.* Discipline over them is to be exercised by the Session.—*c.* In case of discipline, the Session must notify the Presbytery under whose care he is.—*d.* When Presbytery drops a candidate, or deprives a licentiate, it must notify the Session to which he is amenable.—5. Candidates under the care of that Presbytery to which they most naturally belong; *i. e.*, in the bounds of which they have lived for the most part, and are best known.—6. For candidates to go to foreign bodies to be licensed, is irregular.—7. Candidates aided by the churches, to be placed under the care of Presbytery as soon as possible, and licensed by the Presbyteries to which they most naturally belong.—8. Candidates of one Presbytery not to be licensed by another.—9. Neglect to record the adoption of the standards; trying and licensing at the same meeting; ordaining without trial or licensure; and licensing for a certain time, condemned as irregular.—10. Irregularity does not invalidate licensure.—11. Lay-preaching and preaching before licensure, condemned.—12. Case of licensure by a self-constituted committee.—13. How soon students are to be reported as candidates.

1. *A Liberal Education required.*

a. It was requested by the First Presbytery of Philadelphia, that Synod declare to them their sense on this point, viz., Whether a person without a liberal education may be taken on trial or licensed to preach the Gospel? The question being put, it was carried in the negative.—*Minutes*, 1783, p. 499.

b. "An overture was brought in in the following terms, viz.: Whether in the present state of the Church in America, and the scarcity of ministers to fill our numerous congregations, the Synod, or Presbyteries, ought therefore to relax in any degree in the literary qualifications required of intrants into the ministry? And it was carried in the negative by a great majority."—*Minutes*, 1785, p. 511.

c. "Your committee recommend to the General Assembly to enjoin it upon all their Presbyteries to take the most effectual order in their power to increase, if possible, the qualifications of candidates for the Gospel ministry, with regard both to sincere piety and solid and extensive learning, that the improvements of the pulpit may keep full pace with the progress of society and letters."—*Minutes*, 1799, p. 181.

(See also letter to Dr. Rice, Minutes, 1804, p. 299).

2. *Liberal Education waived in certain cases.*

a. "Several very earnest applications were made to the Synod by Welsh people in different parts, representing that many among them understand not the English tongue, and unless they have a pastor capable of speaking in their own language, they must live entirely destitute of ordinances; that a certain Mr. John Griffith came some years ago from Wales, with good certificates of his Christian knowledge and piety, though he has not had a liberal education, and of being there licensed to preach the Gospel; that he has preached among them to their great satisfaction; and therefore pray the Synod to ordain him to the ministry, that he may both preach and also administer the sacraments among them.

"Upon considering the case, the Synod find that several members have seen his certificates from Wales, that some have conversed with him, and were much satisfied with his Christian knowledge and acquaintance with experimental religion; that those of the Welsh here who testify to the Synod concerning his useful preaching and pious conduct, are known to be men of judgment and integrity; and as the circumstances of that people are singular, and no other way appears in which they can enjoy ordinances, the Synod agree that the said Mr. John Griffith, though he has not the measure of school learning usually required, and which they judge to be ordinarily requisite, be ordained to the work of the ministry, and appoint Messrs. Samuel Daviės, Dr. Allison, Treat, Hunter, and Kettletas, to be a Presbytery '*pro re nata*' to ordain him tomorrow at 11 o'clock."—*Minutes*, 1758, p. 289.

[Mr. Griffith was accordingly ordained.]

Case of John Gloucester.

b. Whereas, from the communications from the Presbytery of Union, it appears that the said John Gloucester has been for some time under the care of the Presbytery of Union; that, in the opinion of that Presbytery, he possesses promising talents and eminent piety; that he has been for several years engaged in the study of literature and theology, but has not yet obtained all the literary qualifications usually required in candidates for licensure; and that if he were licensed, there is much reason to believe he might be highly useful in preaching the Gospel among those of his own color; and whereas, said Presbytery requests the advice of the General Assembly; therefore,

Resolved, 1. That the General Assembly highly approve the caution and prudence of the Presbytery of Union in this case. 2. That considering the circumstances of this particular case, viz., the evidence of unusual talents, discretion, and piety possessed by John Gloucester, the good reason there is to believe that he may be highly useful in preaching the Gospel among those of his own color, and the various difficulties likely to attend a farther delay in proceeding in this case, the General Assembly did, and hereby do, authorize the Presbytery of Philadelphia to consider the case of John Gloucester, and, if they think proper, to license him to preach the Gospel.—*Minutes,* 1807, p. 387.

3. *Time of Study.*

a. On motion *Resolved,* That it be recommended to the several Presbyteries of this Church to consider whether it would be proper to extend the time necessary for young men to apply to the study of Divinity before they be taken on trials, to three years at least, and to send up a report of their opinion to the next General Assembly.—*Minutes,* 1792, p. 60.

[No action of the Presbyteries is reported.]

Rule of a Lower Judicature Unconstitutional.

b. The records (of the Synod of New York and New Jersey) were approved, except a vote of that Synod by which they determine it to be constitutional for that Synod to enact, "That, in future, candidates who have the Gospel ministry in view, be required to attend to the study of Divinity at least three years before licensure;" which vote was determined by the Assembly to be unconstitutional.—*Minutes,* 1792, p. 59.

"A remonstrance was presented by the Synod of New York and New Jersey, against the decision of last year, by which they determine, that 'it is unconstitutional for the Synod of New York and New Jersey to enact that, in future, candidates who have the Gospel ministry in view, shall be required to attend to the study of Divinity at least three years before licensure.'

"It was moved to reconsider the above decision; which was agreed to.

"When it was unanimously *Resolved*, as the sense of this house, that the decision of the last General Assembly, which is the subject of complaint, ought not to be altered."—*Minutes*, 1793, p. 73.

Proposal to Extend the Time to Three Years.

c. "Overture No. 6 was taken up, viz.: Requests from several Presbyteries that the 6th section of chapter xiv, of our Form of Government, might be sent down to the Presbyteries, to be so altered as to read, 'to study theology at least *three* years, &c.' The overtures were read. And it was resolved that the proposed alteration be sent down as an overture to the Presbyteries; and that the Presbyteries be required to send up their answer to this overture, in writing, to the next General Assembly." —*Minutes*, 1835, p. 475.

"The committee to whom was referred the reports of Presbyteries, on the overture from the last General Assembly, proposing a change in the term of study of Theological Students, from *two* to *three* years, made a report, which being amended, was adopted, and is as follows, viz.:

"That they have had under their consideration, reports from *fifty-five* Presbyteries. Of these, *thirty-five* are in favor of the proposed change, and *twenty* are opposed to it. By the Constitution of our Church, the consent of a majority of the Presbyteries is necessary to authorize the alteration contemplated. And as a majority of the Presbyteries have sent up no report to this Assembly, that such Presbyteries be careful to send up their opinion in relation to the proposed alteration in the Constitution, to the next General Assembly."—*Minutes*, 1836, p. 276.

"The committee to whom was referred the reports of the Presbyteries in relation to certain changes of the Constitution, reported that *fifty-two* Presbyteries have reported in favor of, and *thirty-eight* against, the extension of the term of study to be required from Theological Students." —*Minutes*, 1837, p. 438.

[Since an affirmative vote of a majority of all the Presbyteries is needed for any change in the Constitution, the change proposed was not made.]

4. *Candidates under the Care of the Session until Ordained.*

The committee to whom was recommitted Overture No. 1, viz., The question at what period of their preparatory course are candidates for the Christian ministry to be considered as dismissed from the jurisdiction of the Session and transferred to that of the Presbytery, made a report, which, being read and amended, was adopted, and is as follows, viz.:

Whereas it appears necessary, in order to preserve the purity of the Church, and uniformity of procedure in the judicatories under the care of the General Assembly, that the manner of administering discipline to candidates and licentiates for the Gospel ministry should be distinctly specified; therefore,

Resolved, 1. That as the word of God, and the Constitution of the Presbyterian Church, recognize the distinction of laity and clergy, and a system of procedure in discipline in some respects diverse, as the one or the other of these orders of men is concerned, it becomes the judicatories of the Church to guard against the violation of this principle in the administration of discipline.

2. That, although candidates and licentiates are in training for the Gospel ministry, and in consequence of this are placed under the care of Presbyteries, and in certain respects become immediately responsible to them, yet they are to be regarded as belonging to the order of the laity till they receive ordination to the whole work of the Gospel ministry.

3. That it follows from the last resolution, that when candidates for the Gospel ministry are discovered to be unfit to be proceeded with in trials for the sacred office, it shall be the duty of the Presbytery to arrest their progress; and, if further discipline be necessary, to remit them for that purpose to the Sessions of the churches to which they properly belong; and that, when licentiates are found unworthy to be permitted further to preach the Gospel, it shall be the duty of the Presbytery to deprive them of their license; and if further discipline be necessary, to remit them for that purpose to the Sessions of the churches to which they properly belong.

4. That, in order to insure the proper effect of discipline in the per-

formance of the duties which severally belong to Sessions and Presbyteries, it will be incumbent on church Sessions, when they shall see cause to commence process against candidates or licentiates, before Presbytery has arrested the trials of the one, or taken away the licensure of the other, to give immediate notice to the moderator of the Presbytery to which the candidates or licentiates are amenable, that such process has been commenced, to the intent that the impropriety may be prevented of an individual proceeding on trials, or continuing to preach after committing an offence that ought to arrest him in his progress to an investiture with the sacred office; and when Presbyteries shall enter upon an investigation with the view of stopping the trials of a candidate, or taking away the license of a licentiate, the Session to which such candidates or licentiates are amenable shall be immediately informed of what the Presbytery is doing, that the Session may, if requisite, commence process and inflict the discipline which it is their province to administer.—*Minutes*, 1829, pp. 263, 264.

5. *Candidates under the care of the Presbytery to which they most naturally belong.*

"Query. Whether our students, bred in our colleges, have not a right to apply to any of our Presbyteries for improvement for the sacred work of the ministry, and whether they ought not to be received on sufficient recommendations?"—*Minutes*, 1760, p. 305.

The Synod judge that any student in divinity who professes a design to enter into the ministry has a right, in our present situation, to study for his improvement under the direction of any divine of reputation in the Synod, according to a former act; but that, when he proposes to enter upon trials, with a view to the ministry, he shall come under the care of that Presbytery to which he most naturally belongs; and he shall be deemed most naturally to belong to that Presbytery in whose bounds he has been brought up and lived for the most part, and where he is best known. But if another Presbytery desire that any student or students should come into their bounds, or if any such student or students, for greater conveniency, or from any circumstances that make it necessary, desire to enter on trials in a different Presbytery, upon his offering satisfactory reasons, he may be dismissed; but in either case, the Presbytery to which he removes shall not receive nor admit him to come under trials upon his having a certificate as a regular church member only; but he shall bring a testimonial from the Presbytery, or several neighboring ministers where he lived, recommending him as a candidate for the ministry, of exemplary piety and holiness of conversation; nor shall anything less be esteemed a sufficient recommendation.—*Minutes*, 1764, p. 337.

6. Query. Whether it is regular for our students of divinity, who intend to return and officiate in the bounds of the Synod, to go into New England, or elsewhere, in order to be licensed.—*Minutes*, 1760, p. 305.

Answer. "Though the Synod entertains a high regard for the associated Churches of New England, yet we cannot but judge that students who go to them, or to any other than our own Presbyteries to obtain license, in order to return and officiate among us, act very irregularly, and are not to be approved or employed by our Presbyteries, as hereby we are deprived of the right of trying and approving the qualifications of our own candidates; yet, if any case may happen, wherein such a conduct may, in some circumstances, be thought necessary for the greater good of any congregation, it shall be laid before the Presbytery to which the congregation belongs, and approved of by them."—*Minutes*, 1764, p. 338.

7. *Candidates should be placed under the care of Presbytery.*

a. "It is recommended to the agencies and committees to endeavor to have the young men aided by the Church, especially in their theological studies, placed under the care of Presbyteries, and that, in all ordinary cases, they be licensed by those Presbyteries where they naturally belong." (See Form of Government, chap. xiv, sec. 2.)—*Minutes*, 1854, p. 507.

b. "It is recommended that the young men aided by the Assembly's committee be ordinarily placed, as soon as possible, under the care of Presbyteries; and that, in all ordinary cases, they be licensed, if convenient, by the Presbyteries to which they naturally belong."—*Minutes*, 1856, p. 224.

8. *Candidates of one Presbytery may not be Licensed by Another.*

a. "The Presbytery of New Castle expressing some uneasiness at the conduct of the Second Philadelphia Presbytery, for having received and licensed a certain Mr. John McClean, who, they apprehend, most properly belonged to the Presbytery of New Castle, and had applied to them to be licensed; and while they were taking the proper steps for obtaining more full satisfaction concerning his church membership and Christian character, he, in the mean time, removed from them, and applied to the Second Philadelphia Presbytery, and was licensed by them: both the Presbyteries were fully heard in a free conference on this subject, and withdrew. The Synod, after mature deliberation, order Mr. McClean to be cited before the Presbytery of New Castle, with power to them to hear the charges against him, and issue the affair in a regular manner, and report to the next meeting of Synod. And the Synod do prohibit the Second Philadelphia Presbytery from employing him to preach till the affair shall be concluded."—*Minutes,* 1772, p. 435.

b. The consideration of the report of the Committee to Examine the Minutes of the Synod of Philadelphia was resumed. The report is as follows, viz.:

"Your committee observe in page 24th, that although the Synod were informed by the Presbytery of New Castle, that a certain Mr. Hindman had put himself under the care of the Presbytery of Donegal for trials, and afterwards, without certificate or dismission, offered himself to, and was received upon trials by the Presbytery of Lewes; and though in page 34th the Presbytery of New Castle represent that the said gentleman had been laid under censure by the Presbytery of Donegal, that they had no authentic proof that it was taken off, and that this gentleman had obtained license in opposition to a rule of the Synod of New York and Philadelphia, in their minutes of 1764, pages 79 and 80; yet the Synod recommended it to the Presbytery of New Castle to receive and treat this gentleman as a regular candidate, without any decision upon the matters referred to them."

[Whereupon the Assembly]

"*Resolved,* That the Synod be informed that the Assembly disapprove of the proceedings as represented in their records, in recommending a candidate to be received as in full standing, before they had given a decision upon the allegations against him."—*Minutes,* 1791, p. 37.

c. "At a meeting of the Presbytery of New Castle, in Wilmington, upon the first Tuesday of January, 1791, and continued by adjournments, the Rev. James McCoy, of Morris County Presbytery, with a commissioner from Queen Ann's Congregation, applied to be received as a member of this Presbytery. As Mr. McCoy had been under trials for licensure in the Presbytery of New York, and was licensed and ordained by the Presbytery of Morris, this Presbytery agreed not to receive him as a member, until his case be laid before the General Assembly, at their next stated meeting.

"The General Assembly, upon considering this case, determined that neither the Presbytery of New Castle, nor any other Presbytery, ought to receive Mr. McCoy into their connection, until he shall have produced a certificate from the Presbytery of New York, of his having given them the satisfaction which his case requires."—*Minutes*, 1791, p. 38.

9. *Certain Irregularities in Licensing condemned.*

"The Presbytery book of Suffolk approved, except that they have neglected to record their candidates' adopting our public standards at licensure, though they inform us it is a matter of constant practice; that they try and license at the same Presbytery; and in one instance, ordained without previous trial or licensure; and that they license for a certain time. All which we highly disapprove."—*Minutes*, 1764, p. 339.

10. *Irregularity does not invalidate the Licensure.*

a. "The committee appointed to draught a minute respecting the appeal from the decision of the Synod of Philadelphia, whereby they refused to revise a minute of their preceding sessions, in the case of Mr. Hindman, and refused to take into consideration the conduct of the Presbytery of Lewes in the affair of his licensure, produced a draught to that purpose, which, after some amendment, was approved, and is as follows, viz.:

"The Assembly having had the whole affair laid before them, and fully heard the parties, after mature deliberation, judged that in the case of Mr. Hindman there appeared to have been such a want of attention to the rules of this body, and neglect of order, as to afford just ground of uneasiness to the appellants, and to deserve the disapprobation of the Assembly. But inasmuch as acts which have been performed in an informal manner must often when done be sustained, the Assembly do hereby sustain the licensure and ordination of Mr. Hindman, while at the same time they enjoin it in the most pointed manner on the Synod of Philadelphia, to give particular attention that no Presbytery under their care depart in any respect from that rule of the former Synod of New York and Philadelphia, which is as follows:

"Any student in divinity, who professes a design to enter into the ministry, has a right, in our present situation, to study for his improvement under the direction of any divine of reputation in the Synod, according to a former act; but that when he proposes to enter upon trials, with a view to the ministry, he shall come under the care of that Presbytery to which he most naturally belongs; and he shall be deemed most naturally to belong to that Presbytery in whose bounds he has been brought up and lived for the most part, and where he is best known. But if another Presbytery desire that any student or students should come into their bounds, or if any such student or students, for greater convenience, or from any circumstances that make it necessary, desire to enter on trials in a different Presbytery, upon his offering satisfactory reasons, he may be dismissed; but in either case, the Presbytery to which he removes shall not receive nor admit him to come under trials, upon his having a certificate as a regular Church member only, but he shall bring a testimonial from the Presbytery, or several neighboring ministers where he lived, recommending him as a candidate for the ministry, of exemplary piety and holiness of conversation, nor shall anything less be deemed a sufficient recommendation."—*Minutes,* 1792, p. 56.

11. *Preaching before Licensure and Lay Preaching irregular.*

a. "Upon information that David Evan, a lay person, had taken upon him publicly to teach or preach among the Welsh in the Great Valley, Chester County, it was unanimously agreed that the said Evan had done very ill, and acted irregularly in thus invading the work of the ministry, and was, thereupon, censured."—*Minutes,* 1710, p. 17.

b. "The consideration of the business left unfinished yesterday afternoon, was resumed, viz., the complaint of the Presbytery of Washington, Ohio, against the Presbytery of West Lexington, for licensing and ordaining the Rev. William L. McCalla contrary, in the opinion of the complainants, to Presbyterial order, Mr. McCalla having been suspended from Church privileges by the Presbytery of Washington, in consequence of a reference on the subject from the Session of the Church of Chillicothe."

"After a long discussion of the subject, the Assembly adopted the following resolution and decision in the case, viz.:

"*Resolved,* That while the Assembly disapprove the conduct of Mr. McCalla in preaching the Gospel before he was regularly licensed;

and while they regret that the Presbytery of West Lexington, in the final trials of Mr. McCalla for licensure, did not pay sufficient attention either to his irregularity in preaching as just mentioned, or to the proceedings in the Session of the Church of Chilicothe, and of the Presbytery of Washington in his case, they nevertheless judge that the proceedings of the Presbytery of West Lexington, in licensing and ordaining Mr. McCalla, be sustained, and that Mr. McCalla be considered as a Minister in good and regular standing in the Presbyterian Church."—*Minutes*, 1821, p. 21.

Lay-Agency—no Organization needed. Rights and Duties of Lay-Members defined.

c. "The committee to which was referred the paper on the subject of lay-agency, presented a report, which was adopted, and is as follows:

"The committee appointed to consider the overture of the Presbytery of Philadelphia, Fourth, inquiring as to the expediency of organizing a lay-agency in the work of evangelization, beg leave respectfully to report:

"They have taken the inquiry presented in the overture under careful consideration, and are of the unanimous opinion, that no such organization is needed by the Church as is therein suggested. In declaring this opinion, they would not be understood as disparaging in any way the importance of lay efforts in advancing the Gospel. It is one of the cardinal doctrines of Protestants, that the proper sanctification and efficiency of the Church depends, in a large degree, on the constant exercise of all the natural talents and spiritual gifts of its members in the service of the Lord. Believing, though we do, in the divine appointment of a specially trained and ordained ministry, we do by no means confine to it the blessed work of bearing witness for Christ, by words and example. The divine word makes it the duty of every believer to let his light shine, and the savor of his salt be diffused; and so to contribute, according to his ability, unto the edification of the Church, and the saving of souls. This duty can never be too earnestly enforced and carried out. Its faithful observance is the very life of the Church, and the administrative skill of a minister and session is nowhere more signally shown, than in the means which they employ to bring every Church member under their care to realize and carry out the obligation. But, in order to this, your committee believe that no new ecclesiastical provision is required. Indeed, it is to be feared that such provision would hinder rather than promote the good sought. The excellence of lay-agency consists very largely in its voluntary character. It tells upon the people, because it is the free out-going of earnest and irrepressible sentiments and convictions, and because it is neither commissioned nor rewarded by man. We rob it of its peculiar power and efficiency, when we render it perfunctory. Very undesirable is it, therefore, to change its character, and convert it into a second-rate ministry, liable to assert pretensions for which it is not qualified. The history of the Church, in times past, too clearly sets forth the evils arising from the creation of such an order, for us to venture on the renewal of the measure.

"Accordingly, your committee recommend that no action be taken by the Assembly in the matter proposed, excepting,

"1. To declare it as our unanimous judgment, that the liberty conceded by our excellent polity, for the free exercise of all spiritual gifts in an orderly manner, renders the organization of any lay-agencies superfluous.

"2. To urge on all pastors and sessions, that they exert themselves, in all suitable ways, for the development, the employment, and direction of all the lay-talent existing in their churches, unto the upbuilding of the Redeemer's kingdom, and the glory of his name."—*Minutes*, 1859, p. 45.

12. *Case of licensure by a self-constituted Committee upon sufficient reasons approved.*

"It is reported that Mr. Samuel Davis, Mr. Hampton, and Mr. Henry, having, upon good and sufficient reasons, taken Mr. John Bradner under trials, in order to his being licensed to preach the Gospel, and having gone through the ordinary pieces of trial, and being satisfied with him therein, as also with respect to the orthodoxy of his faith, did license him accordingly in March last; which was approven."—*Minutes*, 1714, p. 36.

13. *When Students are to be Reported as "Candidates."*

The following overture from the Presbytery of New York, Third, was then adopted:

"*Resolved*, That it be recommended to the General Assembly, in order to ascertain the full number of individuals in the Church who are preparing for the ministry, to require of every Session to state in their annual report to their Presbytery how many of the communicants under their care are pursuing a course of study for the Gospel ministry; and that every Presbytery be required to report the whole number of these students, thus ascertained, among their churches, in their annual statement to the General Assembly, instead of reporting, as heretofore, only those who have formally been received under the care of the Presbytery."—*Minutes*, 1852, p. 176.

SECTION 2.—ORDINATION.

1. Ordination by a committee, frequent and approved.—2. Ordination of our candidates by foreign bodies, disapproved.—3. Ordination *sine titulo*, generally disapproved of. In cases where it seems desirable, the Presbytery to consult Synod. Leave granted in certain cases.—4. Ordination *sine titulo*. Overture upon, rejected.—5. A Presbytery censured by Synod for an ordination *sine titulo*. The censure disapproved of by the Assembly.—6. Ordination on the Sabbath disapproved of generally.—7. Reordination of Foreign Ministers.—8. Decisions reversed.—9. Rule as to receiving a Minister from any other Church. Not to be reordained, but all the qualifications demanded of our own candidates to be insisted on.—10. Lay-ordination invalid.

1. *By a Committee.*

a. "The Presbytery having seen Mr. George Gillespie's certificate from the Presbytery of Glasgow, concerning his being licensed to preach, and his conversation, did approve of them; and in case Providence make way for his ordination by a call from any congregation before next Presbytery, Mr. Andrews, McNish, Anderson, and Morgan, are ordered to ordain him; and that one of the said members, or two, as they shall see fit, preach at the solemnity."—*Minutes*, 1712, p. 26.

b. "It was reported by the ministers appointed to transact the affair relating to Mr. Wotherspoon's ordination, that they, in compliance with the last year's minutes, did solemnly, by prayer, fasting, and imposition of hands, ordain the said Mr. Robert Wotherspoon unto the sacred function and office of the ministry to the Presbyterian congregation at Apoquinomy, upon the 13th day of May, 1714."—*Minutes*, 1714, p. 35.

c. "An unanimous call from the people of Welsh tract to Mr. David

Evans, being presented to us and approven, we offered it to him, which he accepted; whereupon it was appointed as follows, viz.:

"That Messrs. Jedediah Andrews, Jones, Anderson, Gillespie, and Wotherspoon, solemnly ordain him to the work and office of the ministry, after having been satisfied with his ministerial abilities, in any pieces of trial they shall think fit to appoint him."—*Minutes*; 1714, p. 36.

[See Minutes of General Presbytery *passim.*]

d. "The appointment of the Synod with respect to the ordination of Masters John Clement and William Stewart, was complied with. They being solemnly set apart to the work of the ministry by the Rev. Masters Samuel Davis, John Hampton, and John Thompson, at Rehoboth, in Somerset County, in Maryland, upon the — day of June, 1719."—*Minutes*, 1719, p. 55.

[See, also, case of John Griffith, ordained by a Presbytery *pro re nata*, appointed by Synod, p. 74.

This mode of ordination by a committee was common with the Synod.]

2. *Ordination by Foreign Bodies not approved.*

The Assembly took up the report of the committee on Overture No. 3, which was laid on the table; which, being read and amended, was adopted, and is as follows, viz.:

Whereas many of the ministers, who are to supply the vacant churches and destitute places in the more new and growing parts of our Church, must, for some time to come, continue to be educated in the older sections of our country, and at a great distance from the field where they are to be employed; and whereas, it is important to the happy and useful settlement of these ministers, in their several fields of labor, that they should enjoy the full confidence of the ministers and churches among whom they are to dwell; and whereas, the ordination of ministers in the presence of the people among whom they are to labor, is calculated to endear them very much to their flocks, while it gives their fathers and brethren in the ministry an opportunity of knowing their opinions and sentiments on subjects of doctrine and discipline; and whereas, our Form of Government seems to recognize the right and privilege of each Presbytery to examine and ordain those who come to the pastoral office within their bounds, and who have never before exercised that office; therefore, *Resolved*,

1. That it be earnestly recommended to all our Presbyteries not to ordain, *sine titulo,* any men who propose to pursue the work of their ministry in any sections of the country where a Presbytery is already organized, to which they may go as licentiates and receive ordination.

2. That the several bodies with which we are in friendly correspondence in the New England States, be respectfully requested to use their counsel and influence to prevent the ordination, by any of their Councils or Consociations, of men who propose to pursue the work of the ministry within the bounds of any Presbytery belonging to the General Assembly of the Presbyterian Church; and that the Delegates from this Assembly to those bodies respectively be charged with communicating this resolution.—*Minutes,* 1834, p. 428.

3. *Ordination, sine titulo.*

a. "The Synod would bear testimony against the late too common, and now altogether unnecessary, practice of some Presbyteries in the north of Ireland, viz., their ordaining men to the ministry, *sine titulo,* immediately before they come over hither, thereby depriving us of our just rights, viz., that we, unto whom they are designed to be co-presbyters, and among whom they design to bestow their labors, should have just and fair inspecting into their qualifications; we say, it seems necessary that the Synod bear testimony against such practice by writing home to the General Synod, thereby signifying our dissatisfaction with the same. . . . . The Synod do agree that no minister ordained in Ireland, *sine titulo,* be for the future received to the exercise of his ministry among us, until he submit to such trials as the Presbytery among whom he resides shall think proper to order and appoint. And that the Synod do also advertise the General Synod in Ireland, that the ordaining any such to the ministry, *sine titulo,* before their sending them hither, for the future, will be very disagreeable and disobliging to us."—*Minutes,* 1735, p. 119.

b. "A question was proposed: Whether it be proper to ordain to the ministry *sine titulo,* except for some particular mission? The consideration of which is deferred till our next *sederunt.*"—*Minutes,* 1762, p. 314.

The question, Ought ministers to be ordained *sine titulo,* i. e., without relation or probable view had to a particular charge, resumed; and, after further deliberation, we judge as follows:

That in ordinary cases, where churches are properly regulated and organized, it is a practice highly inexpedient and of dangerous consequences, not to be allowed in our body except in some special cases, as missions to the Indians, and some distant places, that regularly apply for ministers. But as the honor and reputation of the Synod is much interested in the conduct of Presbyteries in such special cases, it is judged that they should previously apply to the Synod and take their advice therein, unless the cases require such haste as would necessarily prevent the benefit of such a mission if delayed to the next session of Synod; in which cases the Presbyteries shall report to the next Synod the state of the cases and the reasons for their conduct.—*Minutes*, 1764, p. 337.

c. Application was made to the Synod by the Presbytery of New Castle for advice respecting the propriety of Mr. Samuel Smith's being ordained by said Presbytery of New Castle, under whose care he is, in consequence of his having accepted a call from a congregation within the bounds of the Presbytery of Hanover.

The Synod having heard all the circumstances relative to this case, and deliberated thereon, agree that it is not expedient for the Presbytery of New Castle to ordain Mr. Smith, as the matter now stands.—*Minutes*, 1775, p. 465.

d. The Presbytery of Lewes, by their commissioner, Mr. Slemons, requested leave to ordain a certain Mr. James Lang, a licentiate under their care, *sine titulo.*

"*Resolved*, That the reasons offered for this measure are not sufficient, and therefore that the request be not granted."—*Minutes*, 1800, p. 199.

e. The following request was overtured by the Committee of Bills and Overtures:

"That the Synods of Virginia and the Carolinas have liberty to direct their Presbyteries to ordain such candidates as they may judge necessary to appoint on missions to preach the Gospel; whereupon—

"*Resolved*, That the above request be granted, the Synods being careful to restrict the permission to the ordination of such candidates only as are engaged to be sent on missions to preach the Gospel."—*Minutes*, 1795, p. 98.

f. "The Presbytery of Baltimore directed their commissioners to solicit the permission of the General Assembly to ordain Mr. William Maffit, a licentiate under their care, to the office of the Gospel ministry, if upon examination he should appear qualified. The request was made at the particular instance of the church of Bladensburg, where Mr. Maffit officiates as a stated supply.

"*Resolved,* That said request be granted."—*Minutes,* 1798, p. 146.

g. The Presbytery of Philadelphia submitted to the Assembly for their decision the case of Mr. John Jones, a licentiate under their care, who at their last session had requested that Presbytery would take measures to ordain him, *sine titulo.* The Presbytery stated that Mr. Jones had been a licensed candidate for a number of years; that he had always sustained a good and consistent character; that he was engaged in teaching an academy, and was so circumstanced, that his being ordained might render him more extensively useful. The Assembly, having considered the case—

"*Resolved,* That the Presbytery of Philadelphia be permitted and authorized to ordain Mr. Jones to the work of the Gospel ministry, *sine titulo:* provided, the Presbytery, from a full view of his qualifications and other attending circumstances, shall think it expedient so to ordain him."—*Minutes,* 1807, p. 386.

h. "Mr. Robert Smith was appointed a missionary to the western and northern frontiers of the State of New York, provided he shall be ordained by the Presbytery of New Castle for that purpose."—*Minutes,* 1794, p. 86.

[See also Minutes, 1799, p. 172; 1809, p. 415; 1810, p. 459.]

i. A reference from the Synod of Philadelphia, was laid before the Assembly. By an extract from the minutes of that Synod, it appeared that Mr. John Waugh, a licentiate under the care of the Presbytery of New Castle, had, for special reasons, requested the Presbytery to take measures for his ordination, *sine titulo.* The Presbytery accordingly presented the request to Synod, and the Synod finding that the authority in this case is by the Constitution expressly vested in the General Assembly, agree to refer the matter to them for their decision. The Assembly, having taken the subject into consideration—

Resolved, That the Presbytery of New Castle be, and they hereby are permitted and authorized to ordain the said Mr. Waugh to the work of the Gospel ministry, *sine titulo:* provided, that the Presbytery, from a full view of his qualifications and other attending circumstances, shall think it expedient.—*Minutes,* 1805, p. 337.

4. *Ordination sine titulo. Overture on rejected.*

a. "The following overture was brought in and read, viz.:

"In what cases, except the one provided for in the seventeenth chapter of the Constitution of our Church, may a Presbytery ordain a man to the work of the Gospel ministry without a call to particular charge?" —*Minutes*, 1810, p. 456.

This overture was referred to Drs. Miller and Green, Messrs. Nathan Grier, Anderson, and Campbell, as a committee.—*Minutes*, 1811, p. 464.

This committee reported as follows, viz.:

"*Whereas*, there may exist cases in which it may be needful for Presbyteries to ordain without a regular call; but as the frequent exercise of this power may be dangerous to the Church, and as this case does not appear to be fully provided for in our Constitution and Book of Discipline—

Resolved, That the following rule be submitted to the Presbyteries for their opinion and approbation, which, when sanctioned by a majority of the Presbyteries belonging to the Church, shall become a constitutional rule, viz.:

"That it shall be the duty of Presbyteries, when they think it necessary to ordain a candidate without a call to a particular congregation or congregations, to take the advice of their respective Synods, or of the General Assembly, before they proceed to this ordination."—*Minutes*, 1811, p. 474.

[Answered in the negative—11 to 7—and the subject dismissed.]—*Minutes*, 1812, p. 494.

b. [In 1813 another rule was proposed], viz.: The rule proposed, and on which an affirmative or negative vote of the Presbyteries is required, is in the following words, viz.:

"It shall be the duty of Presbyteries, when they think it necessary to ordain a candidate without a call to a particular pastoral charge, to take the advice of a Synod, or of the General Assembly, before they proceed to such ordination."—*Minutes*, 1813, p. 524.

[Of the Presbyteries answering this overture, twenty-six replied in the negative and four in the affirmative.]—*Minutes*, 1814, p. 558.

5. *Censure of Synod for Ordination, sine titulo, not sustained.*

The records of the Synod of Illinois were, on the recommendation of the committee, approved, with the exception of a censure, on p. 209, of the action of Knox Presbytery, for ordaining a man when there was no call from any part of the Church.—*Minutes*, 1843, p. 17.

6. *Ordination on the Sabbath.*

An overture was received from the Presbytery of Orange, requesting the opinion of the General Assembly on the question, whether it be proper to ordain licentiates to the office of the Gospel ministry on the Sabbath day. The General Assembly think it would not be for edification to adopt a uniform rule on the subject. In general they think it is not expedient that ordinations should take place on the Sabbath; yet that there may be cases in which urgent or peculiar circumstances may demand them. The Assembly, therefore, judged it best to leave it to the Presbyteries to act, in this concern, as they may judge that their duty requires.—*Minutes*, 1821, p. 10.

7. *Reordination of Methodist Ministers.*

a. A petition was laid before the General Assembly from the Presbyterian Church in the Island of Bermuda, requesting the settlement of a Mr. Enoch Matson, an elder formerly connected with the Methodist Church, who was represented as willing to subscribe the doctrine, discipline, and government of the Presbyterian Church, accompanied with a request from the Presbytery of Baltimore, for direction in what manner to proceed in receiving him into this Church.

"The Assembly recommend to the Presbytery of Baltimore to proceed in receiving Mr. Matson to trials for the ministry, in the same manner as if no licensure or ordination by the Methodist Church had taken place."—*Minutes*, 1792, p. 56.

b. "The following question from the Commissioners of Hudson Presbytery was brought in through the Committee of Overtures, viz.:

"Ought a Methodist minister, applying to one of our Presbyteries, and proposing to put himself under their care and to adopt their standards, to be again ordained?

"On motion, it was agreed that a sufficient answer is already given to this question by the Assembly in their sessions of 1792, where they direct a Presbytery in a similar situation to proceed as though no ordination had taken place."—*Minutes*, 1800, p. 199.

8. *These decisions reversed.*

"The Committee of Overtures brought in the following resolution, which, having been read and amended, was adopted, and is as follows, viz.:

"*Resolved*, That, in the opinion of this Assembly, the decisions of the General Assembly of 1792, and referred to by the Assembly of 1800, respecting the reordination of ministers regularly ordained in the Methodist Episcopal Church, and desiring to connect themselves with the Presbyterian Church in the United States of America, however expedient at the time of its formation, ought not to be considered as a precedent to guide the future decisions of the judicatories of this Church; and that the Presbyteries under the care of this Assembly, when they receive into their connection an ordained minister from any other denomination, be careful to record the circumstances of the case and the reasons which induced them to receive such ordained minister."—*Minutes*, 1810, p. 441.

9. *Rule in respect to receiving a Minister from another Church.*

The consideration of the report of the committee to which had been referred the question of validity of ordination in the case of a Baptist elder, was resumed, and the report being read was adopted, and is as follows, viz.:

It is not among the principles or usages of the Presbyterian Church to consider the ordination of ministers by other Protestant churches as invalid; on the contrary, the Presbyterian Church has always considered the ordinations of most other Protestant churches as valid in themselves, and not to be repeated, when those who have received them become members of the Presbyterian Church. Nor is it perceived that there is any sufficient reason why the ordinations in the Baptist Church should not be considered as valid, and be sustained as such.

But while the Presbyterian Church can act as has now been stated in regard to ordinations, it is among those principles and usages which she regards as most sacred and important, to secure for her churches both a pious and a learned ministry, and she cannot admit of any usage, or exercise any apparent liberality, inconsistent with security in this essential particular. On the whole, therefore, the committee recommend the following resolution:

Resolved, That when applications are made by ministers of the Baptist or any other Protestant denomination, to be connected with the Presbyterian Church, the Presbytery to which the applications are made shall require all the qualifications, both in regard to piety and learning, which are required of candidates for licensure or ordination of those who have originally belonged to the Presbyterian Church; and shall require the applicants from other denominations to continue their study and preparation till they are found on trial and examination to be qualified in learning and ability to teach in the manner required by our standards; but that when found to be thus qualified, it shall not be necessary to re-ordain the said applicants, but only to instal them when they are called to settle in Presbyterian congregations.—*Minutes*, 1821, p. 23.

10. *Lay Ordination invalid.*

a. The committee to whom was referred Overture No. 15, viz., on ordination by a deposed minister or by laymen, made the following report, which was adopted, viz.:

That this paper contains a letter from a minister in South Carolina to the stated clerk, requesting him to obtain a decision of the General Assembly on the question, "whether the ordination of a minister of the Gospel by the interposition of the hands of the laity is valid?" That the answer to this question should be in the negative is so obvious and evident, on all correct principles of ecclesiastical order, that your committee are of opinion that it is unnecessary for the General Assembly to give any further consideration to the subject.—*Minutes*, 1832, p. 366.

b. The committee on Overture No. 3, viz., a question from the Presbytery of Bethel, respecting holding communion with the followers of Wm. C. Davis, a deposed minister, and calling themselves Independent Presbyterians, reported that, in their judgment, the questions proposed in said overture ought to be answered in the negative. They, therefore, would recommend the adoption of the following resolution, viz.:

Resolved, That while this Assembly readily acknowledges the right of the Session to determine according to the Scriptures and the Constitution of our Church the qualifications for admission to sealing ordinances, yet they feel it to be their duty to declare that, in their judgment, the services of those who have received only lay-ordination, and of those who have been deposed from the Gospel ministry, are unscriptural and unwarrantable; and, therefore, an attendance on their ministrations cannot be in the order of the Gospel, and ought to be discouraged and discountenanced by every friend of the Redeemer's kingdom.—*Minutes*, 1833, p. 407.

CHAPTER IV.

THE SACRAMENTS.

Section 1.—Baptism.

1. By whom administered.—*a.* Baptism by an impostor invalid.—*b.* As also by a Unitarian.—*c.* And by a suspended Minister during his suspension.—Also, *d.* When administered by a deposed Minister.—*e.* Unworthiness of the Minister does not invalidate the ordinances dispensed by him; but the effect of irregularities to be judged of in each case by the Session.—2. Is Romish baptism Christian baptism? indefinitely postponed.—3. The parents or others presenting children for baptism.—*a.* To be examined as to character and knowledge.—*b.* And instructed in their duties.—*c.* Meaning of "a visible and credible profession" to be decided in each case by the proper judicatory.—*d.* Parents required to enter into an express engagement to perform their duties to the baptized.—4. The subjects of baptism.—*a.* Slaves of Christian masters and mistresses may be baptized.—*b.* Christian slaves of unbelieving masters should have their children baptized.—*c.* It is the duty of Christian masters to present the children of their servants, and of Ministers to baptize them.—*d.* The period of infancy is not defined, but must be decided in each case by the proper authorities.—5. Pastoral care to be exercised over baptized children.—And catechetical instruction imparted.—6. Discipline of baptized persons, not communicants.—7. Mode of baptism.—8. Baptism not ordinarily to be administered to adult converts previous to their reception to a particular church.

1. *By whom administered.*

a. Whereas a certain person pretending, at Egg Harbor, to be a minister regularly ordained among the Presbyterians, under that character baptized some adults and infants, and it appearing to the Synod that his pretences were false, having at that time no license or ordination, it is our opinion that all the Gospel ordinances he administered under that false and pretended character are null and void.—*Minutes,* 1752, p. 249.

b. The Committee to which was referred the question submitted by the member from the Presbytery of Harmony, and with the advice of that Presbytery in the following words, viz.:

"A person who had been baptized in infancy by Dr. Priestley applied for admission to the Lord's table; should the baptism administered by Dr. Priestley, then a Unitarian, be considered valid? reported, and their report being read was adopted, and is as follows, viz.:

"*Resolved*, That this question be answered in the negative. And it accordingly was determined in the negative.

"In the present state of our country, whilst Unitarian errors in various forms are making their insidious approaches, whilst the advocates of this heresy in many cases are practising a system of concealment and insinuating themselves into the confidence of multitudes who have no suspicion of their defection from the faith, the Assembly feel it their duty to speak without reserve.

"It is the deliberate and unanimous opinion of this Assembly, that those who renounce the fundamental doctrine of the Trinity, and deny that Jesus Christ is the same in substance, equal in power and glory with the Father, cannot be recognized as ministers of the Gospel; and that their administrations are wholly invalid."—*Minutes*, 1814, p. 549.

Baptism by a Suspended Minister.

c. "The following overture was presented by the Committee on Overtures, viz.:

"Can a Presbytery consistently acknowledge as valid the ordinance of Baptism, as administered by those who are regularly suspended by a higher judicatory of the Church? If not, how are we to regard the baptism of the Cumberland Presbyterians?

"The Assembly resumed the consideration of the report of the committee on the overture respecting the Cumberland Presbyterians. After considerable discussion, the report of the committee was adopted, and is as follows, viz.:

"1. That, in the opinion of this Assembly, Ministers of the Presbyterian Church, when regularly suspended by the competent judicatories, have no right to exercise the functions of a Minister during that suspension.

"2. That while those persons styling themselves the Cumberland Presbytery were under suspension, their administrations are to be considered as invalid; but after the General Assembly have declared them as no longer connected with our Church, their administrations are to be viewed in the same light with those of other denominations not connected with our body. This decision is grounded on the opinion, that the act of the Assembly of 1814 precluded the propriety of deposition, or any other process in the case.—*Minutes*, 1825, p. 156.

d. "A reference from the Presbytery of Hudson, requesting of the Assembly an answer to the following question, was received and read, viz.:

"Is baptism administered by a minister after he is deposed from office valid?

"*Resolved*, That in answer to this question, the Presbytery be referred to chap. vii, sec. 1, of the Directory for Public Worship."—*Minutes*, 1819, p. 701.

[The section thus referred to is as follows, viz.: "Baptism is not to be unnecessarily delayed; nor to be administered, in any case, by any private person; but by a minister of Christ, called to be the steward of the mysteries of God."]

e. "The following question was proposed by the Committee of Overtures, viz.:

"Ought such persons to be rebaptized as have been offered in baptism by notoriously profligate parents, and baptized by ministers of the same description?

"The question proposed by the Committee of Overtures respecting baptism was resumed; and after a full investigation of the subject, the following determination was adopted, viz.:

"*Resolved*, That it is a principle of this Church that the unworthiness of the ministers of the Gospel does not invalidate the ordinances of religion dispensed by them. It is also a principle, that as long as any denomination of Christians is acknowledged by us as a Church of Christ, we ought to hold the ordinances dispensed by it as valid, notwithstanding the unworthiness of particular ministers. Yet, inasmuch as no general rule can be made to embrace all circumstances, there may be irregularities in particular administrations by men not yet divested of their office, either in this or in other churches, which may render them null and void. But as these irregularities must often result from circumstances and situations that cannot be anticipated and pointed out in the rule, they must be left to be judged of by the prudence and wisdom of church Sessions, and the higher judicatories to which they may be referred. In such cases, it may be advisable to administer the ordinance of baptism in a regular manner, where a profane exhibition of the ceremony may have been attempted. These cases and circumstances, however, are to be inquired into by the church Sessions, and referred to a Presbytery before a final decision."—*Minutes*, 1790, p. 26.

2. *Romish Baptism.*

"The Committee on the Polity of the Church reported an overture from the Third Presbytery of New York, which is as follows: 'Is baptism, as administered by the Roman Catholic Church, to be regarded as Christian baptism?'" [Referred to a committee to consider the subject, and report an answer to the next General Assembly.]—*Minutes*, 1853, p. 342.

[The majority and minority of the committee made each a report, which were discussed at great length,] "and the whole subject indefinitely postponed."—*Minutes*, 1854, p. 512.

3. *Obligations and Qualifications of Parents.*

a. [The Synod] "do also exhort all the ministers within our bounds to take due care in the examination of all candidates for baptism, or that offer to dedicate their children to God in that sacred ordinance, that they are persons of a regular life, and have suitable acquaintance with the principles of the Christian religion; that that seal be not set to a blank, and that such be not admitted to visible Church relation that are manifestly unfit for it."—*Minutes*, 1735, p. 115.

b. "That previously to the administration of baptism, the minister shall inquire into the parent's knowledge of the great and fundamental doctrines of the Gospel, and the regularity of their lives; and being satisfied so as to admit them, shall, in public, point out the special duties of the parents, and particularly that they teach their children the doctrines and precepts of Christianity, contained in the Scriptures of the Old and New Testaments, and comprised in the Westminster Confession of Faith and Catechisms, which therefore he shall recommend unto them."—*Minutes*, 1755, p. 267.

c. "The following reference from the Synod of Philadelphia was laid before the Assembly: 'As baptism is to be administered to the infants of those who are members of the visible Church (but our Directory leaves the description of the visible and credible profession of Christian-

7

ity vague and indefinite), it is humbly proposed to the Assembly to give some precise direction and definition of such a profession for the information of its ministers.' In answer to the above reference, the Assembly judged it unnecessary, and perhaps impracticable, to deliver rules more explicit than those contained in the standards of our Church; but should cases of difficulty arise, they must be decided respectively, according to their own merits, before the proper judicatories."—*Minutes*, 1794, p. 91.

Parents required to enter into Engagements.

d. "The following question, through the Committee of Overtures, was read, viz.:

"Whether, besides requiring of parents dedicating their children to God in baptism, an express acknowledgment of the duties of parents, and recommending to them the observance thereof, it should be considered as essential to require that they come under an explicit vow or solemn engagement also to perform those duties? whereupon the Assembly—

"*Resolved*, That an answer to this question is contained in the Directory for Public Worship of this Church, under the head of the administration of baptism, which requires an express engagement on the part of the parents."—*Minutes*, 1794, p. 89.

4. *The Subjects of Baptism.*

a. "The following case of conscience from Donegal Presbytery was overtured, viz.: Whether Christian masters or mistresses ought in duty to have such children baptized as are under their care, though born of parents not in the communion of any Christian Church? Upon this overture, Synod are of opinion that Christian masters and mistresses, whose religious professions and conduct are such as to give them a right to the ordinance of baptism for their own children, may and ought to dedicate the children of their household to God in that ordinance when they have no scruples of conscience to the contrary."—*Records*, 1786, p. 527.

b. "It was overtured, whether Christian slaves, having children at the entire direction of unchristian masters, and not having it in their power to instruct them in religion, are bound to have them baptized; and whether a Gospel minister in this predicament ought to baptize them? And Synod determined the question in the affirmative."—*Records*, 1786, p. 527.

c. "The committee to which was referred the following question, viz.: 'Ought baptism on the profession and promise of the master to be administered to the children of slaves?' reported, and their report, being amended, was adopted, and is as follows, viz.:

"1. That it is the duty of masters, who are members of the Church, to present the children of parents in servitude to the ordinance of baptism, provided they are in a situation to train them up in the nurture and admonition of the Lord, thus securing to them the rich advantages which the Gospel provides.

"2. That it is the duty of Christ's ministers to inculcate this doctrine, and to baptize all children of this description when presented by their masters."—*Minutes*, 1816, p. 617.

Age of Infancy undetermined.

d. The committee to which was referred the question, "At what age ought children to be considered too old to be baptized on the faith of their parents?" reported the following answer, which, being read, was adopted, viz.:

The precise time of life when the state of infancy ceases is not determined in the Word of God, nor by the standards of our Church, and, from the nature of the case, is incapable of being regulated by any uniform rule, but should be left to the judgment of ministers and Sessions, to be determined according to the particular circumstances of each case. The Assembly therefore deem it inexpedient to attempt to fix the precise time at which children ought to be considered too old to be baptized on the faith of their parents.—*Minutes*, 1822, p. 53.

5. *Pastoral Care to be exercised over the Baptized.*

"*Whereas,* The Book of Discipline states that children born within the pale of the visible Church, and dedicated to God in baptism, are under the inspection and government of the Church, and specifies various important particulars in which that inspection and government should be exercised, as also directs the mode in which they shall be treated if they do not perform the duties of church members; *and whereas,* there is reason to apprehend that many of our congregations neglect to catechize the children that have been admitted to the sealing ordinance of baptism, and do not exercise suitable discipline over them, therefore—

"*Resolved,* That the different Presbyteries within our bounds are hereby directed to inquire of the different Sessions, whether a proper pastoral care be exercised over baptized children in their congregations; that they learn the principles of religion, and walk in newness of life before God; and that said Presbyteries do direct all Sessions that are delinquent in this respect, to attend to it carefully and without delay."—*Minutes*, 1809, p. 431.

To be Instructed as to their Duties.

b. "*Resolved*, That the General Assembly recommend, and they do hereby recommend to the pastors and Sessions of the different churches under their care, to assemble, as often as they may deem necessary during the year, the baptized children, with their parents, to recommend said children to God in prayer, explain to them the nature and obligations of their baptism, and the relation they sustain to the Church."—*Minutes*, 1818, p. 691.

Catechetical Instruction.

c. "The following resolutions on the subject of catechetical instruction were unanimously adopted, viz.:

"1. *Resolved*, That this General Assembly considers the practice of catechetical instruction as well adapted to the prosperity and purity of our Zion.

"2. *Resolved*, That this Assembly view also with deep regret the neglect, on the part of many of our churches, of this good old practice of our fathers,—a practice which has been attended with such blessed results to the cause of pure and undefiled religion.

"3. *Resolved*, That the institution of Sabbath-schools does not exonerate ministers and parents from the duty of teaching the Shorter Catechism to the children of the Church.

"4. *Resolved*, That this Assembly earnestly and affectionately recommend to all the ministers and ruling elders in its connection to teach diligently the young of their respective congregations the Assembly's Shorter Catechism."—*Minutes*, 1849, p. 181.

6. *Discipline of Baptized Children.*

a. "How far, and in what sense, are persons who have been regularly baptized in infancy, and have not partaken of the sacrament of the Lord's Supper, subject to the discipline of the Church?

"*Resolved*, That the public standards of this Church contain a sufficient answer to the question stated in the above reference."—*Minutes*, 1799, p. 171.

b. [The Book of the Synod of Kentucky] "contains a reference from said Synod to this Assembly of a case relative to the disciplining of baptized persons arrived at maturity, not in communion.

"This reference was committed to Dr. Clark, Messrs. Nathan Grier and Picton, who were directed to report to the Assembly on the subject."—*Minutes*, 1811, p. 468.

"The committee . . . brought in their report; which was read, and the subject indefinitely postponed."—*Minutes*, 1811, p. 475.

"*Resolved*, That Drs. Miller and Romeyn, and Rev. James Richards, be a committee to prepare and report to the next Assembly a full and complete answer to the following overture from the Synod of Kentucky, viz.:

"What steps should the Church take with a baptized youth, not in communion, but arrived at the age of maturity, should such youth prove disorderly and contumacious."—*Minutes*, 1811, p. 480.

"The committee appointed by the last Assembly to report to this Assembly on the subject of disciplining baptized children, reported, and the report was recommitted to the same committee for revision and publication; and it was

"*Resolved*, That the Assembly, without expressing any opinion on the principles it contains, recommend it to the serious consideration of all the Presbyteries and ministers, that in due time a decision may be had on the important subjects discussed in the report."—*Minutes*, 1812, p. 509.

c. [In 1814, the matter came up again, and it was]

"*Resolved*, That the whole subject be referred to a committee, to consider and report to the Assembly, what shall appear to them to be the correct method of procedure to be adopted relative thereto, in the circumstances in which it is now before the Assembly; and that Drs. Green, Woodhull, and Wilson, and Messrs. Caldwell and Connelly, be the committee."—*Minutes*, 1814, p. 543.

"The report on the subject of disciplining baptized children, which had at a former session of this Assembly been laid on the table, was again read, and recommitted to the same committee, with the addition of Drs. Griffin and Blatchford, and Messrs. Blackburn, Fisher, and Haslett."—*Ib.* p. 551.

"On motion,

"*Resolved*, That the committee appointed to report to the Assembly a correct method of procedure to be adopted relative to a report made by a former committee, on the subject of disciplining baptized children, be discharged.

"And they were accordingly discharged, and the subject was indefinitely postponed."—*Ib.* p. 567.

d. "A reference from the Presbytery of Fayetteville, on the subject of excommunicating a person who had been baptized, but had not been received into full communion with the Church, was overtured, and was committed to Dr. Miller, Messrs. Finley, Freeman, Cook, and Haslett."—*Minutes*, 1815, p. 578.

"The consideration of the report of the committee to which had been committed the reference of the Presbytery of Fayetteville, concerning the proper construction of the first article of the first chapter of the forms of process, relative to persons who have been baptized, but have not been admitted to the Lord's table, was resumed. After a long discussion of the subject, a motion was made and seconded for an indefinite postponement. The question being taken, was determined in the affirmative; and therefore the farther consideration of the subject was indefinitely postponed."—*Ib.* p. 589.

7. *Mode of Baptism.*

The committee to whom were referred Overtures 4 and 5, from the Synod of West Tennessee, made the following report, which was adopted, viz.: That two distinct questions are presented by the Synod:

1. "Is it expedient in the present state of the Church for a Presbyterian minister to baptize by immersion in any case?

2. "Is the baptism of the children of non-professing parents to be regarded as valid baptism?"

In relation to the first inquiry, the Confession of Faith, chap. xxviii, sec. 3, page 121, teaches as follows, viz.: "Dipping of the person into water is not necessary; but baptism is rightly administered by pouring or sprinkling of water upon the person." Your committee see no cause for adding anything to the doctrine of the Confession on this subject.

For a reply to the second inquiry, your committee refer to the Digest, part iv, chap. ii, sec. 1, on page 94, where the judgment of the Assembly in relation to it is fully recorded.—*Minutes*, 1834, p. 433.

[See ante, chap. iv, sec. 1, 3.]

8. *On Baptism on a General Profession of Faith in Christ.*

"The Committee on the Polity of the Church reported an answer to the following inquiry :

"'Is it forbidden by our standards to baptize adult converts upon a general confession of faith in Christ, previous to their being received into a particular church, and assenting to its articles of faith?' as follows, viz.:

"A profession of faith in Christ and obedience to Him is all that is required in our standards of those who are out of the visible church, in order to their being baptized. (See Con. of Faith, chap. xxviii, sec. 4; Larger Cat., quest. 166; Shorter Cat., quest. 95.) Hence, cases may occur in which, as in the case of Philip and the Ethiopian eunuch, it may be proper to baptize a person who does not expect immediately to connect himself with any particular church. But inasmuch as it was the obvious intent of the Saviour that all His disciples should be associated in local churches, and inasmuch as we cannot obey one of His commandments, that requiring us to remember Him at his table, without such connection; therefore, your committee believe that in no ordinary circumstances can a person give good evidence of a readiness to obey Christ in all things, who, having the opportunity, does not connect himself with some particular branch of the visible body of Christ. In the practice of our Church, and according to her standards, baptism is manifestly regarded as a part of the general profession of faith in, and obedience to, Christ, which constitute his initiation into the visible Church, and into some particular branch of it; and in no ordinary case ought the several parts of this solemn profession to be separated."—*Minutes*, 1860, p. 244.

SECTION 2.—THE LORD'S SUPPER.

1. Administration permitted where there is no organized church.—2. Not ordinarily to be administered within the bounds of a congregation without the consent of the minister and Session.

1. *Permitted where there is no organized Church.*

"It was moved that the restriction laid by the last General Assembly on our missionaries, which confines them to administer the ordinance of the Lord's Supper in such places only where there are church officers regularly appointed, be repealed, and it was repealed accordingly."—*Minutes,* 1798, p. 146.

2. *Not ordinarily to be administered within the bounds of a Congregation without consent of the Minister and Session.*

"The committee to which was referred the appeal of the Rev. R. B. Dobbins, from the decision of the Synod of Kentucky, affirming a decision of the Presbytery of Ebenezer, in the cases of the Rev. William L. McCalla, and the Session of the Church of Augusta, reported, and the report being read, was adopted, and is as follows, viz.:

"While the Assembly, as a general principle, disapprove of the administration of the sacraments by one of their ministers within the bounds of a congregation with which he is not connected, without the consent of the minister and Session of said congregation; yet under the peculiar local circumstances of the people, among which Mr. McCalla occasionally administered ordinances, the Assembly cannot decide that he deserves censure; therefore,

"*Resolved,* That the decision of the Synod of Kentucky, affirming a decision of the Presbytery of Ebenezer in regard to the complaint of the Rev. Mr. Dobbins, against the Rev. Mr. McCalla, be, and it hereby is, affirmed."—*Minutes,* 1824, p. 124.

CHAPTER V.

OF THE COURTS OF THE CHURCH.

Section 1.—Of Church Sessions.

1. Quorum of the Session. One elder, if there be but one, with a minister, may form a quorum.—2. The appointment of a special Session is unconstitutional.—3. The Session should be represented in Presbytery and Synod.—4. A Session may not invite a minister to sit as a corresponding member, nor assign him as counsel for the accused.—5. No one, not a member of the court, may act as counsel.—6. An elder has in no case a legal right to adjudicate in any other church than that in which he is an elder.—7. Records of the Session to be annually sent up for review.—8. The Session may not introduce a new Psalmody without the consent of the majority of the congregation.—9. Where a minister is the accuser, a minister should preside.—10. The Session cannot be set aside by an act of the church; nor would such attempted act deprive the church of its right to be represented by its elders in the courts of the Church.

1. *Quorum of Sessions.*

a. "I. The Church Session consists of the pastor or pastors and ruling elders of a particular congregation.

"II. Of this judicatory, two elders, if there be as many in the congregation, with the pastor, shall be necessary to constitute a quorum."—*Form of Government,* chap. ix.

b. The inquiry, which is in these words, "Can a minister with one elder form a Session capable of transacting judicial business?" is sufficiently answered in the Constitution, Form of Government, chap. ix, sec. 2, where it seems to be implied that cases may occur with infant or feeble churches, in which it would be impracticable for a time to have more than one elder, and yet be necessary to perform acts of a judicial character. For such the Constitution provides; but if there be more than one elder, then two at least, with a minister, are necessary to form a Session.—*Minutes,* 1836, p. 263.

2. *A Special Session unconstitutional.*

a. The Presbytery of Miami did appoint a special Session composed of elders belonging to different congregations, for the purpose of trying Mr. Lowrey, and the decision of such a special Session was affirmed by the Synod of Ohio; therefore—

Resolved, That the appeal of Mr. Lowrey be sustained, and it hereby is sustained; and that all the proceedings in the case be, and they hereby are reversed, on the ground that the appointment of such a special Session is entirely unconstitutional; and if Mr. Lowrey has done anything offensive, he ought to be tried by the courts that have been instituted by the Constitution of our Church.—*Minutes,* 1823, p. 92.

b. "This Assembly concur in opinion with the last General Assembly, that the special Session appointed by the Presbytery of Miami for the trial of S. Lowrey, was an unconstitutional court, and that all the proceedings of that body in this case, and of the Presbytery of Miami and of the Synod of Ohio, sanctioning the acts of that body, are irregular. And the allegation of the Synod, in their memorial, that this body, though called a Session, was, in reality, no more than a committee of Presbytery, is incorrect; for they are not only denominated a Session, but they performed the acts which belong peculiarly to a Church Session: they sat in judgment upon a member of the Church and an elder, and condemned and suspended him; but no Presbytery has authority, according to the Constitution of our Church, to delegate to a committee a power to perform such acts as those."—*Minutes,* 1824, p. 115.

3. *Of the Session: Duty to be represented in Presbytery and Synod.*

"The Synod do recommend it to the several Presbyteries belonging to their body to call those Sessions to account that do not send elders to attend upon the Synod and Presbyteries, and to enjoin these Sessions to call those elders to an account that do not attend upon judicatories when sent by them."—*Minutes,* 1753, p. 256.

4. *A Session may not invite a Minister to sit as Correspondent; nor assign him as Counsel for the Accused.*

The Committee on Bills and Overtures reported Overture No. 4 in these words, viz.:

"May a Session of a church invite a minister of the Gospel, belonging to the same Presbytery or Synod to which the church belongs, to sit as a corresponding member of said Session; and when so invited, may such minister, at the request of an accused brother, be assigned as counsel for the accused?

"The committee recommended that both questions be answered in the negative, and the report was adopted."—*Minutes*, 1851, p. 20.

5. *No one not a Member of the Judicatory may act as Counsel.*

The Committee on Bills and Overtures reported Overture No. 5, as follows:

"May the Session of a church, at the request of an accused brother, assign as his counsel a minister of the Gospel belonging to the same Presbytery to which the Session belongs?"

The committee answered: "There is no provision for such a case in our Constitution, and though it does not appear to contravene its spirit and design, and might, in special cases, be allowable with advantage, yet a strict interpretation of chap. iv, sec. 21, of the Book of Discipline seems to preclude the employment of any one as counsel who is not a member of the judicatory."

The report was adopted.—*Minutes*, 1851, p. 29.

6. *A Ruling Elder has no right to Adjudicate in another Church.*

"Overture No. 14, viz., the following question from the Presbytery of Salem, 'Has a ruling elder, in any case, a legal right to adjudicate in another church than that of which he is an elder?' was taken up, and decided in the negative."—*Minutes*, 1831, p. 324.

7. *Session Records to be annually sent up for Review.*

a. The following resolution was submitted to the Assembly, and after a long discussion, was adopted.

"*Whereas*, It appeared, in the course of the free conversation on the state of religion, that in one of the Presbyteries under the care of the General Assembly, the sessional records of the several church Sessions were not regularly called up and examined every year by the said Presbytery, and there is reason to believe that other Presbyteries had conducted in the same manner, therefore—

"*Resolved*, That it be and it hereby is required of all the Presbyteries within the bounds of the General Assembly annually to call up and examine the sessional records of the several churches under their care, as directed in the Book of Discipline."—*Minutes*, 1809, p. 429.

b. The committee appointed to consider the order of the last General Assembly, respecting the examination of Session books, and also the remonstrance of the Presbytery of Philadelphia, requesting this Assembly to review said order, brought in their report, which was read and adopted, and is as follows:

"The Assembly, after seriously reviewing the order of the last Assembly, and maturely deliberating on the remonstrance of the Presbytery of Philadelphia against it, can by no means rescind the said order, inasmuch as they consider it as founded on the Constitution of our Church, and as properly resulting from the obligation on the highest judicatory of the Church to see that the Constitution be duly regarded; yet, as it is alleged, that insisting on the rigid execution of this order, with respect to some of the church Sessions, would not be for edification, the Assembly are by no means disposed to urge any Presbytery to proceed, under this order, beyond what they may consider prudent and useful."—*Minutes*, 1810, p. 453.

[For duties of Session when a church is vacant, see under Election of Pastors, p. 58.]

8. *Session may not introduce a new Psalmody, without the Consent of the Congregation.*

"It being moved to the Synod, whether a church Session hath power to introduce a new version of Psalms into the congregation to which they belong, without the consent of the majority of said congregation; it was voted in the negative, *nemine contradicente*."—*Minutes*, 1753, p. 255.

9. *Where a Minister is the Accuser, a Minister must Preside.*

"*Ordered*, To hear the reference by the Second Philadelphia Presbytery of Mr. Alexander Alexander's appeal from the judgment of the Session of the Third Presbyterian Church in this city.

"After stating the cause and reading the judgment of the Session and the appeal, both parties were fully heard; and the Synod finding, that as the Session had not a minister of the word to preside through the course of the trial, and that a minister was the accuser of the appellant, it was judged it was at least inexpedient to proceed to trial; and upon the whole we think it best, and do remit the matter back to the Presbytery, to be heard and judged of by them *de novo*.—*Minutes*, 1773, p. 447.

10. *Deliverance in a Special Case.*

"The Committee on the Polity of the Church, to whom was referred the overture, 'When a church shall dismiss its ruling elders, and deny to its members the right of appeal and complaint, and deny the authority of Presbytery over it, has it a right to be represented in the judicatories of our Church?' reported as follows:

"Our Church is organized on constitutional principles, with powers and duties appropriate to each branch or part thereof; and, with a gradation of subordinate and superior judicatories, designed to preserve unity of doctrine, and orderly discipline, according to the Scriptures.

"This Constitution does not recognize a right of revolution, and makes no provision therefor, but treats all such cases simply as breaches of order, and visits them with appropriate constitutional remedies. Any individual church is represented in the Church judicatories constitutionally, only by the pastor or an elder, one or both; and it can find admission into such judicatories only through such a mode of representation.

"The overture supposes three cases: 1st, a dismissal of elders; 2d, a denial of the right of appeal and complaint; and 3d, a denial of the authority of the Presbytery.

"Each of these is an unconstitutional act, is utterly null and void, and subjects the offending church to visitation and discipline at the hands of the Presbytery. The Form of Government, chap. x, sec. 8, empowers the Presbytery 'to visit particular churches, for the purpose of inquiring into their state, and redressing the evils that may have arisen in them; to unite or divide congregations, at the request of the people; or to form or receive new congregations; and, in general, to order whatever pertains to the spiritual welfare of the churches under their care.'

"The above-named acts of insubordination, being void, work no effect; the Session have still the right, and it is their duty, to send one of the elders to the Presbytery and the Synod; and his votes and acts in these bodies are the votes and the acts of the church. So, too, the Presbytery may send any one of such elders to the General Assembly; and should such church refuse obedience to the acts of the judicatories so constituted, it would be subject to the discipline, in due form, of our ecclesiastical law. Such church has a right to be represented by *elders*, and it cannot pass by them and substitute a *private member* as its representative. A void act of deposition, or dismission of its elders, does not incapacitate the church. In sending one of its dismissed elders to the Presbytery or the Synod, it disaffirms its illegal act, and that is an end of it; and if it should send a delegate not an elder, he could not be received; and the church would simply be unrepresented (except by the pastor), *pro hâc vice;* but the church is still under the care of the Presbytery, and subject to its government. The bond of union, which was formed by mutual and concurrent consent and act, cannot be dissolved by an *ex parte* act of insubordination or revolution, until the other party has acted thereon. The committee, therefore, recommend the following answer to the overture:

"*Resolved*, That the acts of insubordination specified in the overture do not, of themselves, infer a forfeiture of the church's right to be represented in the Church judicatories; but such representation must be in the mode, and by the persons, specified in the Constitution of the Church.

"The report was adopted."—*Minutes*, 1860, pp. 260, 261.

SECTION 2.—THE PRESBYTERY.

I. ITS MEMBERS.—1. Ruling elders, in the absence of their pastors, entitled to a seat.—2. Ministers without charge are members of the Church courts.—3. But a ruling elder without charge has no seat in any judicatory of the Church.—4. The Presbytery alone is the judge of the fitness of its members.—5. It may reject an applicant at its discretion; but, 6, not without good reasons.—7. A new rule refused.—8. Rule as to a member of an extinct Presbytery, charged with an offence. The Presbytery to which he applies should receive him, and if charged with an offence, try him. But the Presbytery may refuse to receive him; in which case he is under the special jurisdiction of the Synod.—9. Ministers and licentiates, received from other bodies, are required to answer the questions, Form Gov. chaps. xiv, xv.—10. Members dismissed in good standing by sister Presbyteries ought to be received; but, 11, it is the right of every Presbytery to satisfy itself of the soundness of the applicant.—12. Examination made imperative, in every case; but, 13, the rule declared unconstitutional and void.—14. Rule for the reception of foreign ministers. The rule enforced. 15. Modification of the rules refused.

II. ITS JURISDICTION.—1. *a.* Over members non-resident, to try them. *b.* Difficulty of process does not relieve the Presbytery of responsibility. Discipline by a "mission," not recognized.—*c.* A case transferred to the Presbytery within whose bounds the accused resides.—*d.* Construction of chap. v, secs. 3 and 4, Book of Discipline.—2. Where a Session cannot act, the Presbytery is the proper court to try ruling elders.—3. When ministers withdraw irregularly, their name is to be stricken from the roll. Also churches, and church members.—4. When ministers withdraw partially or entirely from the work of the ministry, their reasons for so doing are to be recorded, with the approval or disapproval of the Presbytery.—5. A minister having left the Presbyterian Church, and wishing to return, must apply to the Presbytery from which he withdrew.—6. The Assembly refuses leave to prosecute ministers of other Presbyteries, who preach heresy within their bounds.—7. Jurisdiction over a deposed minister, is in the Presbytery that deposed him.—8. A minister holding a letter of dismission, is a member of the Presbytery, until received by another body.

III. DISMISSION OF MEMBERS.—1. The body to which he is dismissed must be specified.—2. May not dismiss by a "standing committee."—3. Where a sentence is reversed, and process not renewed within a certain time, a member may claim a dismissal in good standing.

IV. BOUNDARIES OF PRESBYTERIES.—1. Should have geographical limits.—2. "Elective affinity" condemned.—3. Exceptions permitted.—4. Ministers living out of the bounds of their Presbyteries, to show cause for non-residence; or to be transferred to the Presbytery within whose bounds they reside.—5. A Presbytery may not dismiss, nor receive, a church without the approval of Synod.

V. MISCELLANEOUS.—1. The Presbytery to inspect its members.—2. A Presbytery, organized without the act of Synod, recognized.—3. Duty of minorities, where the majority has withdrawn.—4. Resolutions excluding slaveholders from the pulpit and from communion unconstitutional, and Presbyteries requested to rescind such resolutions.—5. Church covenants belong to Presbyteries and Synods.—6. Two clerical members not a quorum.

I. ITS MEMBERS.

1. *Ruling Elder entitled to a Seat in the absence of the Pastor.*

"Mr. Edmundson being present as a representative of the congregation of Patuxent, and their minister absent, it was put to the vote whether the said Mr. Edmundson should act here as a representative, notwithstanding the minister's absence, and carried in the affirmative, *nem. con.*"—*Minutes,* 1716, p. 42.

2. *Ministers without Charge entitled to a Seat.*

"Are ministers without charges constituent members of our church judicatures, and have they an equal voice with settled pastors and ruling elders of congregations in ecclesiastical governments?"

"In the judgment of this Assembly, this question is answered affirmatively, chap. ix, sec. 2, of the Form of Government of the Presbyterian Church, in these words: 'A Presbytery consists of all the ministers and one ruling elder from each congregation within a certain district.'"—*Minutes,* 1816, p. 615.

3. *An Elder without Charge is not entitled to a Seat.*

Resolved, That no ruling elder who has retired from the active exercise of his office in the church to which he belongs, can be admitted as a member of a Presbytery, Synod, or General Assembly.

This resolution, after some discussion, was adopted by yeas and nays: yeas 76, nays 15.—*Minutes,* 1835, p. 489.

4. *The Presbytery alone must judge of the fitness of its Members.*

"Your committee doubted the correctness of the order given by the Synod to the Presbytery of Geneva, to reconsider their proceedings on the subject of the admission of the Rev. Shipley Wells, a constituent member of that Presbytery, which order, though it be not appealed from, appears to have given rise to the protest in question.

"The Synod of Geneva were beyond doubt, in the opinion of your committee, competent to censure the Presbytery of Geneva for admitting hastily, and on slight evidence, into their body, an unworthy or even a suspicious character. But it is, in the opinion of your committee, equally clear, that the right of deciding on the fitness of admitting Mr. Wells, a constituent member of the Presbytery of Geneva, belonged to the Presbytery itself; and that having admitted him, no matter how improvidently, that their decision was valid and final. The individual admitted became a member in full standing; nor could the Presbytery, though it should reconsider, reverse its own decision, or in any way sever the member so admitted from their body, except by a regular process. Adopted."—*Minutes,* 1816, p. 612.

5. *A Presbytery may reject an Applicant for cause.*

A complaint and appeal of the Rev. Thomas Ledlie Birch against certain proceedings of the Presbytery of Ohio in the case of Mr. Birch, particularly for refusing to receive him as a member of their body, on the ground of a supposed want of acquaintance with experimental religion, together with a representation of the congregation of Washington, in the bounds of said Presbytery, on the same subject, was brought in by the Committee on Bills and Overtures.

Subsequently, "*Resolved*, That no evidence of censurable procedure in the Presbytery of Ohio, in the case of Mr. Birch, has appeared to this house, inasmuch as there is a discretionary power necessarily lodged in every Presbytery to judge of the qualifications of those whom they receive, especially with respect to experimental religion."—*Minutes*, 1801, pp. 213, 218.

6. *But not without sufficient reasons.*

a. A complaint was brought in by the Rev. Mr. George Duffield against the Second Philadelphia Presbytery, that they had, by one of their members, obstructed his entrance into a church in this city under their care, to which he had accepted a call, and had also refused to receive him as a member, although he was dismissed from, and recommended by, the Presbytery of Donegal, which was read.

After having maturely considered this matter, the Synod judge that Mr. Duffield had just cause of complaint against the conduct and judgment of the Second Philadelphia Presbytery, who ought to have admitted him to membership with them, and allowed him a fair trial; wherefore we now declare him to be minister of the Pine Street or Third Presbyterian congregation in this city, and order that he be put upon the list of the aforesaid Presbytery.—*Minutes*, 1773, p. 446.

b. Resolved, That the appeal of the Presbytery of Abingdon from the decision of the Synod of Virginia, in the case of the Rev. Robert Glenn, be dismissed, on the ground that the substantial cause of appeal has been removed by the act of that Presbytery, in their receiving Mr. Glenn, in conformity with the decision of the Synod. The appeal was accordingly dismissed.—*Minutes*, 1822, p. 55.

7. *Assembly refuses to make an alteration in the Book.*

The following overture from the Presbytery of Baltimore was received and read, viz., "That after the 12th article of the 10th chapter of the revised Form of Government, the following be added: XIII. Every

Presbytery shall judge of the qualifications of its own members." On motion,

Resolved, That it is inexpedient to grant the request contained in this overture, or to make any new alterations at present in the Book of Discipline.—*Minutes,* 1821, p. 10.

8. *Rule as to a Member of an extinct Presbytery.*

The committee appointed to consider the overture sent up by the Presbytery of Baltimore, respecting the course proper to be pursued by a Presbytery, when a minister, with a certificate of good standing from a Presbytery which has no longer any existence, applies for admission, but is supposed to be chargeable with some offence subsequently to the date of that certificate, made the following report, which was adopted, viz.:

That after the most attentive consideration of the question presented in said overture, it appears to them that the proper answer is embraced in the following particulars, viz.:

1. It is well known that the Book of Discipline of our Church expressly provides, that when a minister shall be dismissed by one Presbytery with a view to his joining another, he shall always be considered as remaining under the jurisdiction of the Presbytery which dismissed him, until he actually becomes a member of another. In the case stated in the overture, however, as the dismissing Presbytery had become extinct, it was physically impossible to act according to the letter of this rule. In these circumstances, every principle of sound interpretation seems to direct that, in ordinary cases, the Presbytery into which admission is sought should receive the applicant; and, if he be charged with any offence, conduct the process against him.

2. Nevertheless it is the privilege of every Presbytery to judge of the character and situation of those who apply to be admitted into their own body, and unless they are satisfied, to decline receiving the same. A Presbytery, it is true, may make an improper use of this privilege; in which case the rejected applicant may appeal to the Synod or the General Assembly.

3. When any minister dismissed in good standing by an extinct Presbytery is charged with an offence subsequently to the date of his dismission, the Presbytery to which he applies for admission not only may, if they see cause, decline receiving him; but if their own situation be

such that there is no prospect of their being able to conduct process against him in an impartial and efficient manner, ought to decline admitting him into their body.

4. In this case, ministers dismissed by an extinct Presbytery, and not received into any other, are to be considered as under the direction of their proper Synod, and ought to be disposed of as the Synod may order. —*Minutes*, 1825, pp. 146, 147.

9. *How Ministers and Licentiates from corresponding Bodies are to be received.*

The committee appointed by the General Assembly of 1829, to consider and report to the Assembly of 1830 on the manner in which ministers and licentiates are to be received into any of our Presbyteries from ecclesiastical bodies in the United States which correspond with this General Assembly, made the following report, which was adopted, viz.:

That, in their judgment, every licentiate coming by certificate to any Presbytery in connection with the General Assembly from any portion of a corresponding ecclesiastical body, should be required to answer in the affirmative the constitutional questions, directed by chap. xiv of our Form of Government to be put to our own candidates before they are licensed; and that, in like manner, every ordained minister of the Gospel, coming from any church in correspondence with the General Assembly by certificate of dismission and recommendation, should be required to answer affirmatively the first seven questions directed by chap. xv of our Form of Government, to be put to one of our own licentiates when about to be ordained to the sacred office.

The course which is thus recommended by the committee, they believe, has been generally practised by our Presbyteries; and the impropriety of admitting strangers into our connection on other terms than our own licentiates and ministers is too obvious to require remark. It is the assent of licentiates and ministers to these questions which brings them under the watch and care of the Presbyteries which receive them, and without which they ought not to enjoy the privileges of preachers of the Gospel in our ecclesiastical connection.—*Minutes*, 1830, p. 287.

10. *Ministers dismissed in good standing should be received on their Testimonials.*

"*Resolved*, That a due regard to the order of the Church and the bonds of brotherhood require, in the opinion of this Assembly, that ministers dismissed in good standing by sister Presbyteries should be received by the Presbyteries which they are dismissed to join upon the credit of their constitutional testimonials, unless they shall have forfeited their good standing subsequently to their dismissal."—*Minutes*, 1834, p. 440.

11. *The right of Presbytery to satisfy itself of the soundness of the Applicant.*

"*Resolved*, That, in the judgment of this General Assembly, it is the right of every Presbytery to be entirely satisfied of the soundness in the faith and the good character in every respect of those ministers who apply to be admitted into the Presbytery as members, and who bring testimonials of good standing from sister Presbyteries, or from foreign bodies with whom the Presbyterian Church is in correspondence. And if there be any reasonable doubt respecting the proper qualifications of such candidates, notwithstanding their testimonials, it is the right, and may be the duty of such a Presbytery to examine them, or to take such other methods of being satisfied in regard to their suitable character as may be judged proper; and if such satisfaction be not obtained, to decline receiving them. In such case, it shall be the duty of the Presbytery rejecting the applicant to make known what it has done to the Presbytery from which he came, with its reasons. It being always understood, that each Presbytery is, in this concern, as in all others, responsible for its acts to the higher judicatories."—*Minutes*, 1835, p. 485.

12. *Examination made imperative in all Cases.*

"The report of the Committee on the right of Presbyteries to examine ministers applying for admission, which was adopted this morning, was reconsidered, amended, and adopted, as follows, viz.:

"That the constitutional right of every Presbytery to examine all seeking connection with them was settled by the Assembly of 1835. (See Minutes of 1835, p. 27.) And this Assembly now render it imperative on Presbyteries to examine all who make application for admission into their bodies, at least on experimental religion, didactic and polemic theology, and church government."—*Minutes*, 1837, p. 429.

13. *The above Rule unconstitutional.*

The committee to whom was referred Overture No. 14, reported the following resolution, which was adopted:

"*Whereas*, It is the inherent right of Presbyteries to expound and apply constitutional rules touching the qualification of their own members, therefore—

"*Resolved*, That the action of the last General Assembly (p. 429, printed Minutes), making it imperative on the Presbyteries to examine all who make application for admission to their bodies, not excepting ministers coming from other Presbyteries, is null and void."—*Minutes*, 1838, p. 660.

14. *Reception of Foreign Ministers the Rule.*

[The original rule on this subject may be found in the Minutes for 1735, p. 118. Action was also taken in 1773, p. 448, and 1774, p. 455. In 1784, the same matter forced itself upon the notice of Synod.]

"The Synod having reason, by information given since their present meeting, to apprehend the churches under their care in imminent danger from ministers and licensed candidates of unsound principles coming among us, do hereby renew their former injunction to the respective Presbyteries within their bounds, relative to this matter, and do also strictly enjoin on every member of this body, under pain of censure, to be particularly careful in this respect. And the stated clerk of the Synod is hereby directed to furnish each of our Presbyteries with an attested copy of the said injunctions, together with a copy of this minute."—*Minutes*, 1784, p. 504.

[In 1798 (*Minutes*, p. 148), the Assembly adopted "regulations intended to embrace and extend the existing rules." In 1800, it was modified and amended, and is now the rule, viz.:]

"The draught of certain regulations respecting the admission of foreign ministers and licentiates, reported by the committee appointed for that purpose, was again read, and having been fully considered and amended, was adopted by a large majority, and is as follows, viz.:

"When any minister or licentiate from Europe shall come into this country, and desire to become connected with the Presbyterian Church in the United States, he may apply to any committee appointed to direct the services of travelling ministers and candidates; which committee shall inspect his credentials, and, by examination or otherwise, endeavor to ascertain his soundness in the faith and experimental acquaintance with religion; his attainments in divinity and literature; his moral and religious character, and approbation of our public standards of doctrine and discipline. If the result shall be such as to encourage further trial, said committee may give him appointments to supply and recommend him to the churches till the next meeting of the Presbytery to which such committee belongs. It shall then become the duty of such minister or licentiate to apply to that Presbytery, or to any other, in whose bounds he may incline to labor; provided always, that he make his application to the Presbytery at their first meeting after his coming within their bounds; and also, that immediately on coming within the bounds of any Presbytery, he apply to their committee to judge of his certificate of approbation, and, if they think it expedient, to make him appointments; or, if it shall be more convenient, the application may be made to the Presbytery in the first instance; but it shall be deemed irregular for any foreign minister or licentiate to preach in any vacant church till he have obtained the approbation of some Presbytery or committee of Presbytery, in manner aforesaid.

"The Presbytery to which such minister or licentiate may apply, shall carefully examine his credentials, and not sustain a mere certificate of good standing, unless corroborated by such private letters, or other collateral testimony, as shall fully satisfy them as to the authenticity and sufficiency of his testimonials. After inspecting any evidences of his literary acquirements which may be laid before them, the Presbytery shall enter into a free conversation with him, in order to discover his soundness in the faith and experimental acquaintance with religion. If they shall obtain satisfaction on these several articles, they shall proceed to examine him on the learned languages, the arts, sciences, theology, Church history and government; nor shall they receive him, unless he shall appear to have made such attainments in these several branches as are required of those who receive their education or pass their trials among ourselves. But if, upon the whole, he appears to be a person worthy of encouragement, and who promises usefulness in the Church, they shall receive him as a minister or candidate on probation, he first adopting our standards of doctrine and discipline, and promising subjection to the Presbytery in the Lord. During this state of probation he may preach the Gospel where regularly called, either as a stated or occasional supply; and if an ordained minister, perform every part of the ministerial functions, except that he may not vote in any judicatory, or accept a call for settlement.

"If the foreigner who shall apply to any Presbytery or committee, as aforesaid, be an ordained minister, such committee and Presbytery may, at their discretion, dispense with the special examination on literature in this Act prescribed, provided he shall exhibit satisfactory evidence that he has received such education, and made such progress in languages, arts, and sciences, as are required by the Constitution of our Church as qualifications for the Gospel ministry. But in all other respects, the examination shall be the same as in the case of a licentiate.

"If from prospects of settlement, or greater usefulness, a minister or licentiate under probation in any Presbytery, shall wish to move into the bounds of another, he shall receive a dismission, containing a certificate of his standing and character, from the Presbytery under whose care he shall have been; which certificate shall entitle him to the same standing in the Presbytery into whose bounds he shall come, except that from the time of his coming under the care of this latter Presbytery, a whole year shall elapse before they come to a final judgment respecting his reception.

"When any foreign minister or licentiate, received on certificate, or pursuant to trials in any Presbytery, shall have resided generally and preached within their bounds and under their direction, for at least one year, they shall cause him to preach before them (if they judge it expedient), and taking into consideration, as well the evidence derived from their former trials as that which may arise from his acceptance in the churches, his prudence, gravity, and godly conversation, and from the combined evidence of the whole, determine either to receive him, to reject him, or to hold him under further probation. In case of receiving him at that, or any subsequent period, the Presbytery shall report the same to their Synod at its next meeting, together with all the certificates and other testimony on which they received them; or, if it shall be more convenient, this report may be made to the General Assembly. The said Assembly or Synod, as the case may be, shall then inquire into the proceedings of the Presbytery in the affair, and if they find them to have been irregular or deficient, they shall recommit them to the Presbytery, in order to a more regular and perfect process. But if the proceedings had in the Presbytery appear to have been conformable to this regulation, they shall carefully examine all the papers laid before them by the Presbytery, or which shall be exhibited by the party concerned, and considering their credibility and sufficiency, come to a final judgment, either to receive him into the Presbyterian body, agreeably to his standing, or to reject him.

"In order, however, to facilitate the settlement of foreign ministers as soon as may consist with the purity and order of the Church, it is further ordained, that if the proper Synod or the General Assembly are not to meet within three months after that meeting of a Presbytery at which a foreign minister on probation is expected to be received, the Presbytery may, if they see cause, lay his testimonials before that meeting of the Assembly or Synod which shall be held next before said meeting of the Presbytery. If this Assembly or Synod shall approve the testimonials, they shall give the Presbytery such information and direction as the case may require, and remit the same to them for final issue. In all other cases, it shall be deemed irregular for any Synod or General Assembly to receive a foreign minister or licentiate, until he shall have passed his period of probation, and been received and reported by some Presbytery, in manner aforesaid.

"No minister or licentiate, after being rejected by one Presbytery, shall be received by another, or if received through mistake or otherwise, he shall be no longer countenanced or employed, after the imposition is discovered. If, however, any minister or licentiate shall think himself aggrieved by the sentence of any Presbytery, he shall have a right to carry the matter by complaint to the proper Synod, or to the next General Assembly, giving notice thereof to the Presbytery during the meeting at which the sentence was pronounced, or at the meeting next following.

"These regulations and provisions relative to the reception of foreign ministers and licentiates, are to be considered as coming in place of all that have heretofore been established on this subject; and all judicatures and individuals under the care of the Assembly are to regard them accordingly."—*Minutes*, 1800, pp. 200–202.

The Rule enforced.

a. "The committee appointed to examine the records of the Synod of Albany, reported, and the book was approved to page 177, excepting the case of receiving a foreign licentiate by the Presbytery of St. Lawrence, without laying their proceedings in the case before the Synod or General Assembly."—*Minutes*, 1822, p. 38.

b. Overture No. 4 was taken up, viz., an application from the Presbytery of Watertown, for leave to receive Mr. William Lockhead, a foreign licentiate, who, after being under the care of the Presbytery of Champlain for five months, had been dismissed to the Presbytery of Watertown, and had been under the care of the latter Presbytery since the 9th of February last. The Presbytery of Watertown requests, that the Assembly will allow them to take into the account, for the term of trial, the time which Mr. Lockhead spent on trials in the Presbytery of Champlain. On this request the Assembly resolved, that the standing rule, which requires that the foreign licentiate must spend a year in the Presbytery to which he is dismissed, be not dispensed with."—*Minutes*, 1830, p. 299.

Leave granted to count the Year from the time of his first Reception.

c. "The committee appointed on Overture No. 14, from the Presbytery of Elizabethtown, respecting the case of Mr. John Anderson, a foreign licentiate, who, in October, 1834, was received under the care of the Presbytery of New York, and in April last transferred to the Presbytery of Elizabethtown,—requesting that Mr. Anderson's year of probation may be considered as commencing at the time when he was received by the Presbytery of New York, reported as follows:

"After examining all the documents put into their hands respecting the subject, they unanimously recommend that the request of the Presbytery of Elizabethtown be granted. This report was accepted and adopted."—*Minutes*, 1835, p. 470.

15. *Modification of the Rules Refused.*

"The Committee (on Polity) further report, an application from the Fourth Presbytery of New York, for such a modification of the rules in the Digest as will facilitate the reception of ministers from foreign bodies, with whom we are on terms of fraternal correspondence. The committee can see and appreciate the fact, that, in the great changes which have occurred, bringing the ends of the earth near together, instances of seeming hardship may occur; still, in their judgment, the time has not yet come, when it is wise for this Assembly to introduce the change in our arrangements referred to; and they therefore recommend that no action be taken by the Assembly in the premises."—*Minutes,* 1855, p. 26.

II. Of its Jurisdiction.

1. *Jurisdiction over Members non-resident.*

a. The Presbytery of New York represented to Synod that one of their members now resided in the bounds of New Brunswick Presbytery, whose moral character labored under some imputations, and requested the advice of the Synod as to which of the Presbyteries should make inquiry into the matter; whereupon the Synod judged it to be the duty of the Presbytery of New York.—*Minutes,* 1786, p. 495.

Difficulty of process does not relieve the Presbytery of responsibility. Discipline by persons not organized under any distinctive form of Church Government not recognized.

b. The Third Presbytery of New York, by overture, inquire what order it would be proper for them to take with reference to a member who has been excluded from Christian fellowship by a ministerial Association under the patronage of the American Board of Commissioners for Foreign Missions, and dismissed from the service of that Board for immorality, and with whom a regular process of discipline by the Presbytery is difficult, on account of his distance from them and from any ecclesiastical body of our connection. The General Assembly reply, that the ecclesiastical relations of the individual in question evidently remain unchanged by the action of persons not organized under any distinct form of government, and especially not guided by the principles of discipline to which he was subject; and the only correct course for the Presbytery to take, if they regard him as a proper subject of discipline, is to pursue precisely the forms of process given in our Book of Discipline, however difficult or protracted the actual process may be.—*Minutes,* 1856, p. 194.

A case transferred to the Presbytery in which the party resides.

c. Petitions from the churches at Mount Pleasant and Greensburg, in

New York, and from five ministers of the Gospel residing in the vicinity of Mr. George Bourne, requesting that Mr. Bourne might be restored to the office of the Gospel ministry, were overtured; and application on behalf of Mr. Bourne was made by Dr. Ely, that, on the profession of his penitence, he may be restored; whereupon, it was

"*Resolved*, That the case of Mr. George Bourne be referred to the Presbytery of New York, in whose bounds he now resides; and it is hereby ordered that the Presbytery of New York be furnished, by the Presbytery of Lexington, with all the documents relative to the deposition of Mr. Bourne, that they receive testimony as to the character and deportment of Mr. Bourne since his deposition, and also the evidences of repentance which Mr. Bourne may furnish; and it is ordered moreover, that the said Presbytery of New York do proceed to issue the case, and either continue the sentence of deposition or restore him, the said Bourne, to the Gospel ministry, as they may judge proper."—*Minutes*, 1824, p. 124.

The Presbytery within which a Minister resides may examine witnesses, and transmit the record, but may not try him.

d. The Judicial Committee also made a statement in the case of the Rev. Horace Belknap, and recommended the adoption of the following resolutions, which were adopted accordingly, viz.:

Resolved, 1. That, in the opinion of this Assembly, the resolution of the last General Assembly,* in answer to Overture No. 2, does not apply to the case of the Rev. Horace Belknap, as referred by the Presbytery of Harmony.

Resolved, 2. That, in the opinion of this Assembly, the Presbyteries both of Harmony and Steubenville appear to have misconceived the directions as laid down in chapter v, sections 3d and 4th of the Book of Discipline; inasmuch as those rules do not transfer jurisdiction from a Presbytery to which a minister belongs to the one within whose bounds he resides, so as to authorize the latter Presbytery to try such minister; but only to examine witnesses in the case, and transmit an authentic record of the testimony to the Presbytery which made the application; therefore,

Resolved, 3. That the Presbytery of Harmony is at liberty to pursue such a course in the case of Mr. Belknap as the circumstances of the case and the good of religion shall, in their opinion, require.—*Minutes*, 1831, p. 339.

* See 3, *b*, page 124; Reference for Advice from the Presbytery of St. Lawrence.

2. *The proper Court to try Ruling Elders in a given case.*

The following question from the Presbytery of Genesee was presented by the Committee of Overtures, viz.:

"Common fame accuses two ruling elders of a church [they being the only acting elders] of unchristian conduct, which took place several years ago, but which has lately been made known to the Presbytery with which said church is connected. What is the duty of the Presbytery in the case?"

Resolved, That the Presbytery is the competent court to try these two elders, and that it is their duty to cite the offending persons before them, and proceed to issue the case.—*Minutes,* 1825, pp. 142, 144.

3. *Ministers withdrawing from Presbytery irregularly, to be stricken from the roll.*

a. Overture No. 5, viz.: A reference from the Presbytery of Chenango, asking advice in the case of the Rev. Edward Andrews, a member of their body, who has recently withdrawn and received Episcopal ordination, was taken up and committed to Mr. Crothers, Mr. Weed, and Mr. Farrand.—*Minutes,* 1828, p. 239.

The committee on the reference from the Chenango Presbytery, in the case of the Rev. Edward Andrews, made the following report, which was adopted, viz.:

Resolved, as the sense of this Assembly, that though the conduct of Mr. Andrews was disorderly, it be recommended to the Presbytery to do nothing further in the case than simply to strike his name from the list of their members.—*Minutes,* 1828, p. 240.

b. "The Committee on Overture No. 2, viz., a reference for advice from the Presbytery of St. Lawrence, reported the following resolution as a suitable answer to be given in the case, which was adopted, viz.:

"*Resolved,* That when a minister otherwise in good standing gives notice in form to the Presbytery to which he belongs, that he renounces the fellowship of the Presbyterian Church, or by neglecting to attend the meetings of its judicatories after being dealt with for such neglect, gives evidence that he has done so in fact, his name ought to be struck from the roll of membership, a notice of this procedure communicated to the disowned member, and, if necessary, published to the Church. The congregation under the care of such minister ought to be held as still under the care of Presbytery, unless they give evidence that they also have withdrawn, in which case their name ought also to be struck from the list of congregations belonging to the Presbytery."—*Minutes*, 1830, p. 305.

c. *Resolved*, That it be recommended to majorities of church Sessions and Presbyteries to take no other action in relation to members who have left them to join other ecclesiastical bodies not in connection with us, than to strike their names from the roll.—*Minutes*, 1839, p. 24.

4. *Ministers withdrawing from the work of the Ministry to be questioned as to their reasons.*

"When ministers have withdrawn, or may hereafter withdraw, wholly or in part, from the work of the ministry, it is enjoined upon the Presbyteries to which they belong to require of such ministers their reasons for so doing, which reasons are to be put upon record by the Presbytery, with an expression of their approbation or disapprobation of the same." —*Minutes*, 1834, p. 450.

5. *A Minister who has withdrawn must return to his own Presbytery.*

"Mr. David Austin, who had been formerly a member of the Presbytery of New York, and had withdrawn from the Presbytery and the Presbyterian Church, appeared before the Assembly, and renewed his request of last year, to be again received into ministerial communion and regular standing in the Presbyterian Church.

"Mr. Austin, having been fully heard in support of his petition, withdrew; when the Assembly, after maturely considering the case,—

"*Resolved*, That, as it would be disorderly for this Assembly to restore Mr. Austin to his standing in the Presbyterian Church in the form in which it is sought by him, inasmuch as he withdrew from the Presbytery of New York, against whom he makes no complaint, and to whom of course he ought to apply; so this Assembly, in the course of the discussion had on the subject of Mr. Austin's application, have had before them sufficient evidence that it is inexpedient at present to recommend his reception by any judicature of this Church."—*Minutes*, 1802, p. 238.

6. *Leave to prosecute Heretics within their Bounds refused.*

Overture No. 13, being a proposition from the Presbytery of West

Lexington and Louisville, to the Assembly, to authorize them to prosecute ministers of other Presbyteries who may preach heresy within their bounds, was taken up and read: Whereupon, it was resolved, that the Constitution in sections 2, 3, or 4, of chap. v, of the Book of Discipline, contains sufficient provision on the subject overtured.—*Minutes*, 1834, p. 476.

7. *Jurisdiction over a deposed Minister is in the Presbytery which deposed him.*

[The Presbytery of Des Moines deposed Rev. James H. Shields from the ministry. Subsequently, Mr. Shields applied for restoration to the Presbytery of Keokuk, within whose bounds he resided at the time of his application.]

The Committee on Polity also reported Paper No. 2. An Overture from the Presbytery of Keokuk, asking if they have jurisdiction over the case of James H. Shields, deposed by the Presbytery of Des Moines.

The committee recommended to the Assembly, that the question submitted by the Presbytery of Keokuk be answered in the negative; and the recommendation was adopted.—*Minutes*, 1859, p. 18.

8. *A Minister, holding a Letter of Dismission, is a Member of the Presbytery dismissing him until received by another Body.*

[Overture to the Synod of Ohio. When a member of Presbytery has taken a letter to join another Presbytery or association, what relation does he sustain to, and what rights and privileges has he in the Presbytery from which he received the letter, during the time that intervenes between receiving the letter and uniting with that other Presbytery or consociation?

Answer by the Synod of Ohio. It is often a fact that dismissions are granted during the sessions of a Presbytery, to take effect at its close. This fact decides that in all ordinary cases all the rights and privileges of an individual in a Presbytery cease the moment his request for a dismission is granted. He may, however, at any time before he has used it, return his letter, and then claim all his former rights and privileges; but until he has used his letter, he is amenable to the Presbytery. See Form of Government, chap. x, sec. 1, 2.—*Minutes, Synod of Ohio*, p. 225.]

The Committee on the Records of the Synod of Ohio reported, and their report was adopted, recommending the approval of the Records as far as written, with the following exception:

That the answer to the question contained in Paper No. 2, p. 225, should be: "He is a member of the Presbytery until he is received by another body." See I. 8.—*Minutes*, 1860, p. 239.

III.—Dismission of Members.

1. *Presbytery must specify the Body to which a Member is dismissed.*

Resolved, That, whereas it is a fundamental principle of the government and discipline of the Presbyterian Church, that every minister of the Gospel belonging to it be subject, at all times, to his brethren in the Lord, and accountable to them for the orthodoxy of his principles, and for his moral, religious, and orderly deportment; it is therefore—

"*Ordered*, That every Presbytery under the care of this Assembly, whenever they dismiss a member, be careful particularly to specify with what Presbytery, association, or classis, or other religious body, he is to be associated after his dismission (to which some of the Presbyteries do not appear to have been sufficiently attentive); and that every member so dismissed be, in all cases, considered as amenable to the Presbytery which has dismissed him till he shall become connected with the ecclesiastical body which he shall have been directed to join."—*Minutes*, 1806, p. 351.

2. *May not dismiss by a Standing Committee.*

"The report of the committee on the reference from the Presbytery of Cayuga, relative to the constitutionality of a rule of that body, which had been laid on the table, was taken up. The rule of the Presbytery of Cayuga, referred to the Assembly, is as follows, viz.: The moderator for the time being, and the stated clerk *ex officio*, were appointed a committee to grant letters of dismission to ministers without charge, and to licentiates and candidates under the care of this Presbytery, to unite with other Presbyteries; and were directed to report at each stated meeting."

In relation to this rule, the following resolution reported by the committee was adopted, viz.:

"*Resolved*, That the rule hitherto acted upon by the Presbytery of Cayuga is inexpedient and unconstitutional."—*Minutes*, 1830, p. 302.

3. *Where Sentence has been reversed, and Process is not commenced anew within a certain time, a Member may claim a Dismission in good standing.*

The committee appointed to prepare a minute expressive of the sense of the Assembly, concerning the appeal of Mr. Joseph E. Bell, reported the following resolutions, which were adopted, viz.:

"1. *Resolved*, That, in the judgment of the Assembly, Mr. Bell was, and still continues to be, fully amenable to the Presbytery of Concord.

"2. That, while the Assembly do not wish to protect the guilty, they do judge that great caution, deliberation, and, as far as may be, the rules of discipline, where ministerial character is impeached, ought to be strictly observed, and that in this case the informality was exceptionable.

"3. That if it be deemed necessary for the good of religion, and the honor of the ministerial character, the Presbytery of Concord are entirely competent to commence a new trial. Or if Mr. Bell shall desire, for his own sake, a new trial, the door is still open.

"4. That in the mean time Mr. Bell's ministerial standing shall be considered regular; and if no process shall be commenced by either party within the space of six months, from the 1st of June next, then Mr. Bell may claim from the Presbytery of Concord a dismission declaring him to be in regular standing."—*Minutes*, 1828, pp. 240, 241.

IV.—Boundaries of Presbyteries.

1. *Presbyteries should have Geographical Boundaries.*

a. "A Presbytery consists of all the ministers and one ruling elder from each congregation, within a certain district." Form of Government, chap. ix, sec. 2.—*Minutes*, 1816, p. 615.

b. "*Resolved*, That, except in very extraordinary cases, this Assembly are of the opinion that Presbyteries ought to be formed with geographical limits."—*Minutes*, 1834, p. 441.

2. *Elective Affinity condemned.*

"*Resolved*, That the erection of Church courts, and especially of

Presbyteries and Synods, on the principle of 'elective affinity,' that is, judicatories not bounded by geographical limits, but having a chief regard in their erection to diversities of doctrinal belief, and of ecclesiastical policy, is contrary both to the letter and the spirit of our Constitution, and opens a wide door for mischiefs and abuses of the most serious kind. One such Presbytery, if so disposed, might, in process of time, fill the whole Church with unsound and schismatic ministers, especially if the principle were adopted that regular testimonials must of course secure the admission of those who bore them into any other Presbytery. Such a Presbytery, moreover, being without geographical bounds, might enter the limits and disturb the repose of any church into which it might think proper to intrude; and thus divide churches, stir up strife, and promote party spirit and schism, with all their deplorable consequences. Surely a plan of procedure in the Church of God which naturally and almost unavoidably tends to produce such effects as these, ought to be frowned upon, and as soon as possible terminated by the supreme judicatory of the Church."—*Minutes*, 1835, p. 486.

3. *Exceptions permitted.*

a. "The committee appointed to consider the petition of Union Presbytery (Overture No. 3) made the following report, which was adopted, viz.:

"The petition of the Presbytery states, that the missionaries of the American Board of Commissioners for Foreign Missions, laboring among the Cherokee Indians, have organized a number of churches according to the order of the Presbyterian Church in the United States; that these churches have been for the most part taken under care of the Union Presbytery, although some of the churches are within the territorial limits of other Presbyteries; that this measure was adopted on the presumption that no other judicatory of the Church would object to it; especially as the missionaries and their churches united with the Presbyterian body, on condition that they should be permitted to connect themselves with the Presbyteries that might be most agreeable to the natives, and most convenient to the missionaries. On this statement the Union Presbytery founds a petition that the General Assembly 'would give liberty to the missionaries and churches in the Cherokee nation, to unite to such adjacent Presbyteries as may be most agreeable to themselves.' Whereupon,

"*Resolved*, That the request herein made be granted; and the several Presbyteries to which the missionaries and churches aforesaid may unite themselves, are directed to report the names of ministers and number of communicants thus received to each future General Assembly; it being understood that in all other respects the said ministers and churches shall submit to the government and order of the Presbyterian Church."—*Minutes*, 1826, p. 181.

b. "The committee to whom was referred the memorial from the Synod of West Tennessee, complaining of the Assembly of 1826, because they admitted the verbal testimony of a delegate to set aside a written document from the Synod of Tennessee, and on that account, in dividing the Synod, granted them only a part of their request; complaining also of the privilege granted by the Assembly to the missionaries among the Cherokees, as found in the printed Minutes of 1826, pages 21, 24, and 27, and requesting that the privilege there referred to may be rescinded; made the following report, which was adopted, viz.:

"1. That it does not appear, either from the Minutes of the Assembly, or from the memorial, what part, if any, of the request of the Synod of Tennessee was refused to be granted. The Assembly, therefore, can grant no relief till the grievance be specified and understood.

"2. That in regard to the privilege granted to the Cherokee missionaries to join such Presbyteries as should be most convenient and agreeable to themselves, the Assembly do not perceive any particular grievance, either to the missionaries, or to the Synod of West Tennessee; yet, as it seems to have given some dissatisfaction, and is out of the usual course, therefore,

"*Resolved*, That the aforesaid Act, contained on page 27 of the printed Minutes of 1826, be rescinded, and that the missionaries be, and they hereby are directed, to connect themselves with those Presbyteries within whose territorial bounds they may reside."—*Minutes*, 1828, pp. 246, 247.

c. "The committee to whom was referred the representation of the Presbytery of Union, touching the ecclesiastical connection of the Rev. Messrs. Daniel S. Buttrick and Samuel A. Worcester, missionaries among the Cherokee Indians, with said Presbytery, and stating the grounds on which they request the continuance of said connection, having taken the said document into serious consideration, beg leave respectfully to recommend to this General Assembly the adoption of the following resolution, viz.:

"*Resolved*, That, in the opinion of this General Assembly, the peculiar circumstances in which the said missionaries are placed, renders the request now under consideration reasonable and proper; and to the end that the object thereof may with all practicable expedition be effectually secured, this General Assembly do hereby ratify and confirm such friendly and amicable arrangement as may hereafter be made between the Presbyteries of Hopewell and Union for this purpose."—*Minutes*, 1829, p. 259.

d. "Overture No. 2, from the Presbytery of Cincinnati, touching the condition of certain churches in Kentucky, seeking connection with us. The committee recommend that, for the present, such churches be allowed to connect themselves with the Presbyteries contiguous, most to their convenience. The report was adopted."—*Minutes*, 1859, p. 17.

e. "No. 3. A memorial from Rev. Benjamin Mills and others, of the Synod of Kentucky, with respect to himself and others, formerly members of the Synod of Kentucky, expressive of their attachment to us, and their desire to return to our connection, if, with their views on the subject of slavery, the way may be open to receive them. The committee recommend, that these ministers and churches, and others similarly situated, be referred to the Presbytery of Cincinnati or any other border Presbytery; and that such Presbyteries be authorized so to extend their jurisdiction as to receive any such ministers and churches, situated near their borders, whose principles and practice are found to harmonize with the position of the Church, as expressed and published to the world by former Assemblies."—*Minutes*, 1859, p. 18.

Adopted.

4. *Ministers Living out of the Bounds of their Presbyteries.*

"The committee to whom was referred an overture from the Synod of Albany, in regard to non-resident members of Presbyteries, made the following report, which was adopted, viz.:

"In conformity with the overture from the Synod of Albany, the committee would recommend to the Assembly the adoption of the following resolution, viz.:

"*Resolved*, That it be enjoined on the Presbyteries to inquire carefully in regard to any of their members, who may be residing without the bounds of their respective Presbyteries, whether there be sufficient cause for such non-residence; and if not, that measures be taken to transfer the relation of such ministers to the Presbyteries in the bounds of which they reside."—*Minutes,* 1836, p. 272.

5. *One Presbytery may not Dismiss a Church to another, without the Approbation of Synod.*

"*Resolved,* That it is unconstitutional for a Presbytery to dismiss a congregation under their care, and for any other Presbytery to receive the congregation so dismissed, without the approbation of the Synod to which such Presbyteries respectively belong."—*Minutes,* 1823, p. 91.

V.—Miscellaneous Decisions.

1. *Presbytery to inquire into the Fidelity of its Members.*

The Synod does recommend unanimously to all our Presbyteries to take effectual care that each of their ministers are faithful in the discharge of their awful trust; and in particular, that they frequently examine, with respect to each of their members, into their life and conversation, their diligence in their work, and their methods of discharging their ministerial calling; particularly, that each Presbytery do, at least once a year, examine into the manner of each minister's preaching; whether he insists in his ministry upon the great articles of Christianity, and, in the course of his preaching, recommends a crucified Saviour to his hearers as the only foundation of hope, and the absolute necessity of the Omnipotent influences of Divine grace to enable them to accept of this Saviour; whether he do, in the most solemn and affecting manner he can, endeavor to convince his hearers of their lost and miserable state whilst unconverted, and put them upon the diligent use of those means necessary in order to obtaining the sanctifying influences of the Spirit of God; whether he do, and how he doth, discharge his duties towards the young people and children of his congregation, in a way of catechising and familiar instruction; whether he do, and in what manner he doth, visit his flock, and instruct them from house to house.

And the Synod hereby orders, that a copy of this minute be inserted into the books of each of our Presbyteries, and be read at every of their Presbyterial meetings, and a record of its being read minuted in said books at the beginning of every session; and that there be also an annual record in each Presbytery book of a correspondence with this minute.

And in case any minister within our bounds shall be found defective in any of the above-mentioned cases, he shall be subject to the censure of the Presbytery; and if he refuse subjection to such censure, the Presbytery are hereby directed to represent his case to the next Synod.

And the Synod recommends to each of the ministers within our bounds to be as much in catechetical doctrines as they in prudence may think proper.—*Minutes*, 1734, p. 111.

2. *A Presbytery, organized without the Act of Synod, recognized.*

Mr. Judd, from the Committee of Elections, made a report in relation to the commissioners from the Presbytery of Hanover, which was considered and adopted, and is as follows:

After a full investigation of the facts in reference to the case of the Rev. A. D. Pollock, and Mr. James Caskie, elder, commissioners to this Assembly from the Presbytery of Hanover, the committee have come to the following results, viz.:

1. That, as a majority of the Presbytery of East Hanover had declared their adherence to a body claiming to be the General Assembly of the Presbyterian Church, which, by its palpable violations of the Constitution of said Church, had forfeited all claim to the appellation, the minority might have retained the name of the Presbytery of East Hanover.

2. Since they forbore to do this from courtesy to their brethren of the majority, and peaceably retired and assumed the name of the Presbytery of Hanover, without the agency of Synod, this deviation from the ordinary usages of our Church ought not, in their peculiar circumstances, to invalidate their organization.

3. The committee therefore recommend the recognition by this Assembly of the Presbytery of Hanover as a constituent part of the Presbyterian Church in these United States; the enrolment of the names of said commissioners on the list of its members; and that this Assembly determine the Synodical relations of said Presbytery.—*Minutes*, 1839, p. 9.

3. *Where Majorities have withdrawn, duty of the Minority.*

a. Resolved, That it be recommended to ministers, where majorities have left, to continue their ecclesiastical organizations as before, if in sufficient numbers; and if not, to connect themselves with the ecclesiastical bodies most convenient to their locality and circumstances which adhere to this General Assembly.—*Minutes*, 1839, p. 24.

b. Also, No. 8, "An inquiry by a commissioner of the Presbytery of Ottawa, whether, if a majority of a Presbytery withdraw from the General Assembly, the remaining members, if sufficient in point of numbers, are to be regarded as the Constitutional Presbytery?"

Answered in the affirmative.—*Minutes*, 1850, p. 320.

4. *Resolutions excluding Slaveholders unconstitutional.*

"*Whereas*, It appears from memorials sent up to this Assembly, that several of our Presbyteries have adopted resolutions excluding slaveholders from their pulpits, and from their communion: *And whereas*, Our Constitution requires that no member of the Presbyterian Church shall be thus disfranchised without a regular trial and conviction: *And whereas*, This proceeding is a repetition of the exscinding acts of the New Basis Assembly, against which we have taken our stand as friends of the Constitution; therefore—

"*Resolved*, That the said Presbyteries be requested to rescind such resolutions.

"The foregoing resolution was, with one dissenting voice, adopted." —*Minutes*, 1840, p. 24.

5. *Church Covenants belong to Presbyteries and Synods.*

Overture from the Synod of New York and New Jersey, and from the Presbytery of Pittsburg, "On Church Covenants," requesting the Assembly to take order in reference to some uniform mode and formula of receiving members into our churches, [the committee] recommend the following answer:

"That it is inexpedient for the Assembly to attempt such a measure, however desirable it is to have uniformity; but that it more properly belongs to the Presbyteries and Synods. Adopted."—*Minutes*, 1851, p. 15.

6. *Two Clerical Members not a Quorum.*

The Records of the Synod of Genesee were approved, with the following exception, viz.:

"The Synod made two clerical members of Presbytery a quorum for transacting business."—*Minutes*, 1857, p. 387.

SECTION 3.—OF THE SYNOD.

1. The Synod is a convention of Bishops and Elders.—2. Where a Synod has failed to meet on its adjournment, the Moderator may fix the time and place. —3. Special or called meetings of Synod are constitutional.—4. The Moderator has no power to change the place of meeting.—5. A Synod may not refuse the members of its Presbyteries.—Nor, 6. Order the erasure of their names from the roll of Presbytery.—7. The Synod may not act judicially when there is no reference or appeal to it.—8. The Records are to be sent up annually for review.—9. The members of an inferior Judicatory may not vote on the approval of their own Minutes.—10. When exceptions are taken to the records of inferior Judicatories, the exceptions should be stated and the reasons assigned.—11. Sessions on the Sabbath censured.—12. The Records should state the body to which a corresponding member belongs.—13. The Records should state that the meetings were opened and closed with prayer.—14. The Minutes should be read and approved.—15. They should be attested by the stated clerk.—16. A narrative of the State of Religion should be prepared and recorded.—17. Names of absentees should be recorded.—18. Reasons called for; and absentees not to be suspended without trial.—19. Formation of the Synods, 1–38.

1. *The Synod is a Convention of Bishops and Elders.*

"As a Presbytery is a convention of the Bishops and Elders within a certain district, so a Synod is the convention of several Presbyteries within a larger district, including at least three Presbyteries."—Form of Government, chap. xi, sec. 1, 1789. Amended, 1804–5, so as to read as at present: "So a Synod is a convention of the Bishops and Elders within a larger district including several Presbyteries."—*Minutes*, 1804, p. 304.

Approved by the Presbyteries.—*Minutes*, 1805, p. 333.

"This amendment goes to make a Synod consist not of *Presbyteries*, but, as it ought, of Bishops and Elders."—*Note, Minutes*, 1804, p. 304.

2. *Where a Synod has failed to meet on its Adjournment. The Remedy.*

"As it appeared from the representations of ministers and elders assembled at Yorktown, the 20th of October, 1795, and signed Robert

Davidson, that the Synod of Philadelphia did not meet according to its last adjournment, nor since the time to which it was adjourned. On motion,

"*Resolved*, That the Moderator of the Synod of Philadelphia, the Rev. Dr. Robert Davidson, ought to be considered as competent to call a meeting of the same, and that he do accordingly call a meeting, to be held in the Third Presbyterian Church in the city of Philadelphia, on the fourth Wednesday of October next; and that he give due notice thereof by a circular letter to the Moderators of the several Presbyteries composing the said Synod, whose duty it shall be to acquaint the other members.

"*Resolved*, as the opinion of the Assembly, That from the nature of the thing, two or more members of any judicatory, meeting according to adjournment, may adjourn from day to day until a sufficient number attend for the transacting of business; and in case a quorum should not attend within a reasonable time, that the Moderator shall be considered as competent to fix any time and place he may judge proper for convening the body; and if he be absent, that the members assembled shall represent the matter speedily to him that he may act accordingly."—*Minutes*, 1796, p. 113.

3. *Meetings pro re nata constitutional.*

a. The Committee of Overtures also reported Overture No. 13. This overture was taken up, and is as follows, viz.: "An answer is requested to the following question, viz., Has the Moderator of a Synod a right to call a meeting of the Synod during the interval of its stated sessions?"

Resolved, by the Assembly, That this question be answered in the affirmative.—*Minutes*, 1829, p. 268.

b. The Assembly took up the protest and complaint of a minority of the Synod of Virginia, against a decision of said Synod in favor of calling meetings of Synod. The complainants and Synod were heard, after which it was resolved that the complaint be not sustained.—*Minutes*, 1832, p. 368.

c. The Committee on the Records of the Synod of Tennessee reported, that after a careful examination of said Records, they find them correct; and the attention of the committee having been called to the report of a committee of the Synod of Tennessee, relating to the constitutionality of a called meeting of said Synod, convened in accordance with a declaratory resolution of the General Assembly of the Presbyterian Church, in 1796, and found on page 321 of the Digest published in 1820, after a careful examination of the whole subject, they recommend the following action in the case: That, in the judgment of this General Assembly, the meeting of the Synod of Tennessee at Knoxville, in said State, on the 9th day of November, was in accordance with the Constitution of the Presbyterian Church, and the Assembly do so declare. The report was adopted.—*Minutes*, 1855, p. 16.

4. *Moderator may not change the Time of Meeting.*

Records of the Synod of Illinois, approved: "Except in the case of the action of that body, as recorded on p. 415, sustaining the act of the Moderator of the Synod, in changing the time of its annual meeting." —*Minutes*, 1854, p. 500.

5. *Synod may not refuse to receive the Members of its Presbyteries.*

"The Records of the Synod of Michigan were, on the recommendation of the committee, approved, with the following exception, That on pages 137, 138, 139, 140, the Synod declined to receive two members, whose names appear on the minutes of two of the Presbyteries; and that the Synod also directed said Presbyteries to strike the names of said members of Presbytery from their roll: one of the members belonging to the Presbytery of Monroe, the other to the Presbytery of St. Joseph."—*Minutes*, 1849, p. 176.

6. *Nor enjoin the Erasure of their Names.*

"Overture No. 28. On the doings of the Synod of Michigan, the matter of enjoining the Presbyteries of St. Joseph and Monroe to erase the names of Rev. Marcus Harrison and Rev. A. L. Payson from their rolls, was taken up. It was *Resolved*, That the action of the Synod in the premises is unconstitutional."—*Minutes*, 1849, p. 177.

7. *The Synod may not act judicially upon Review, when there is no appeal or reference to it.*

"The Assembly, having maturely considered the appeal of Mr. Davis, from the proceeding of the Synod of the Carolinas in his case—

"*Resolved*, That although they highly approve of the zeal of the Synod to preserve the purity and peace of the Church within their bounds, yet they cannot but decide that, in their proceedings in the above case, in deciding that they had a right to try Mr. Davis, when there was no reference or appeal in his case before them, they have not strictly adhered to the Constitution of the Presbyterian Church."—*Minutes*, 1810, p. 448.

8. *The Synods to send up their Records annually.*

a. "*Ordered*, That the Minutes of the respective Synods be laid yearly before the General Assembly, to be by them revised."—*Minutes*, 1789, p. 7.

To report all Changes within their bounds.

b. "*Resolved*, That the respective Synods make yearly reports to the General Assembly of all the licensures, ordinations, instalments, translations, resignations, deaths, and whatever changes may take place among the members within their bounds."—*Minutes*, 1789, p. 7.

9. *The Members of an inferior Judicatory may not vote on the approval of their own Minutes.*

a. "A protest, signed by a number of members of the Synod of Geneva, against a decision of that Synod, excluding the Presbytery of Geneva from voting on the question, Whether their own records should be attested by the Moderator of the Synod, as approved. Your committee were, however, of opinion that the decision of the Synod was consonant to the prevalent usage of the judicatures of the Presbyterian Church, as well as to the usage of other analogous bodies in similar cases; and that it ought therefore to be approved." Adopted.—*Minutes*, 1816, p. 611.

b. The records of the Synod of Kentucky approved, except, "That the members of the West Lexington Presbytery voted in approbation of their own proceedings, which is deemed to be irregular."—*Minutes*, 1821, p. 23.

10. *When Exceptions are taken to the Records of the inferior Court, the Exceptions should be stated, and reasons assigned.*

a. "The committee appointed to examine the records of the Synod of Pittsburg, reported, and the book was approved, excepting the resolution on page 74, disapproving of the proceedings of a Presbytery without assigning the reason."—*Minutes,* 1820, p. 728.

b. "The records of the Synod of Ohio were approved, with the exception of a minute on page 243, disapproving of a decision of a Presbytery, and ordering said Presbytery to reconsider that decision, without any reasons being assigned."—*Minutes,* 1827, p. 202.

c. "The Synod of Pennsylvania, in approving the action of a Presbytery in a judicial case, assigned an entirely unsatisfactory reason, p. 259."—*Minutes,* 1850, p. 314.

d. "The records of the Synod of Indiana were approved, excepting that on page 342, the records of Greencastle Presbytery are reported as approved, with exceptions, while these exceptions are not spread upon the Minutes of the Synod, as required by the Form of Government, chap. vii, sec. 1, art. 3."—*Minutes,* 1857, p. 387.

11. *Session on the Sabbath censured.*

a. The committee appointed to examine the records of the Synod of North Carolina, reported, when the records were approved, with the exception that on page 48 it is recorded that Synod held a session on Sabbath evening. This was the closing meeting, and though it does not seem to have been one of much business, still, in the opinion of the Assembly, it was not proper.—*Minutes,* 1834, p. 445.

b. The records of the Synod of Peoria were approved, with the exception that "on p. 33, there is a record of a business meeting held on Sabbath evening."—*Minutes,* 1846, p. 18.

12. *The Record should state the Body to which a Corresponding Member belongs.*

a. "The proceedings of the Synod of Albany approved, with the exception of having invited several ministers to take their seats as corresponding members, without describing the ecclesiastical body to which such ministers belong."—*Minutes,* 1815, p. 578.

b. "The records of the Synod of Peoria were approved, with the exception that on page 28, mention is made of a minister being invited to sit as a corresponding member without designating the ecclesiastical body to which he belonged."—*Minutes,* 1846, p. 18.

c. The records of the Synod of Illinois, p. 440, "do not state the ecclesiastical connection of the Rev. Amasa Lord, who was invited to sit as a corresponding member."—*Minutes,* 1857, p. 387.

13. *The Records should state that the Meetings were opened and closed with Prayer.*

a. The records of the Synod of Pennsylvania approved, except that "there is no evidence from the records that the last meeting of the Synod was opened with prayer."—*Minutes,* 1850, p. 314.

b. "The records of the Synod of Tennessee were approved, with the following exceptions:

"1. On p. 34, it appears from the record that the Synod adjourned at the close of the day without prayer.

"2. On p. 36, it is recorded that the Synod was *constituted* with prayer, it being the second day of the sessions of the Synod."—*Minutes,* 1854, p. 500.

c. The records of the Synod of Kentucky approved, except that "there is no record of prayer in p. 176."—*Minutes,* 1854, p. 501.

d. Records of Synod of Minnesota approved, except "that on p. 54, in the record of the session of Friday, Sept. 30th, 1859, no mention is made of the opening services."—*Minutes,* 1860, p. 239.

e. "The opening minute of each session of the Synod of Cincinnati is defective, in not recording the meeting of the Synod before its being opened with prayer."—*Minutes,* 1849, p. 177.

14. *The Minutes should be read and approved.*

a. The records of the Synod of Cincinnati approved, except "the omission at the opening of each session to read the Minutes of the previous session, with no evidence in the records that the Minutes were approved by Synod."—*Minutes,* 1849, p. 177.

b. "The records of the Synod of Wabash were approved, with the following exceptions:

"1. On pages 51 and 52, the Synod met and proceeded to business without reading the Minutes of the previous day's session.

"2. On page 59, the Synod closed its annual sessions and adjourned without reading or approving the Minutes of the clerk."—*Minutes*, 1854, p. 500.

c. "The records of the Synod of Pennsylvania were approved, excepting, 'that it does not appear from the book that the records have ever been approved by the Synod.'"—*Minutes*, 1857, p. 387.

15. *The Minutes should be attested by the Stated Clerk.*

a. "The records of the Synod of Tennessee are not attested by the stated clerk."—*Minutes*, 1854, p. 500.

b. "The records of the Synod of Kentucky not approved by the Synod, and some not attested by the stated clerk."—*Minutes*, 1854, p. 501.

16. *A Narrative of the State of Religion should be prepared and recorded.*

a. The records of the Synod of Illinois were, on the recommendation of the committee, approved, with the following exception, viz.:

"At the sessions of Synod in October, 1846, it does not appear from the records, that a narrative of the State of Religion was prepared. Such an omission is considered contrary to the general usage of Synods, and not for the edification of the Church."—*Minutes*, 1849, p. 176.

b. "The records of the Synod of Illinois were approved, except, 'that they do not contain the narrative on the State of Religion, which was presented by the committee on that subject at the sessions of the Synod in 1854, p. 434.'"—*Minutes*, 1857, p. 387.

17. *Names of Absentees should be recorded.*

The Records of the Synod of Peoria were approved, except "that, in the roll of the Synod, record is made that no members of the Presbytery of Belvidere were present; but no record of the names of absentees."—*Minutes*, 1850, p. 314.

18. *Absentees must be called to answer.*

"The committee appointed to examine the Records of the Synod of Virginia reported, and the book was approved to page 83, with the exception of a resolution found in page 82, in which the Synod determined to discontinue the practice of calling upon their members for the reasons of their absence from its meetings."—*Minutes*, 1825, p. 140.

Absentees not to be disciplined without trial.

"The Records of the Synod of the Carolinas were approved to page 28 of the twenty-third sessions of said Synod, with the exception of the resolution to make a minister liable to suspension without trial for three years' absence from Synod, without sending forward his reason for absence."—*Minutes*, 1811, p. 468.

19. *Erection of the Synods.*

1–4. Synods of New York and New Jersey, Philadelphia, Virginia, and the Carolinas, 1788.—"Your committee beg leave to report that they conceive it will be most conducive to the interests of religion that this Synod be divided into four Synods; and therefore submit to the Synod the following plan for dividing the Synod of New York and Philadelphia into four distinct Synods, subordinate to a General Assembly, to be constituted out of the whole.

"1st. That one of the said Synods shall consist of the Presbyteries of Dutchess county, Suffolk, New York, and New Brunswick, to be known by the name of *The Synod of New York and New Jersey*.

"2d. That another Synod shall consist of the Presbyteries of Philadelphia, Lewistown, New Castle, Baltimore, and Carlisle, to be known by the name of *The Synod of Philadelphia*.

"3d. That another Synod shall consist of the Presbyteries of Redstone, Hanover, Lexington, and Transylvania, to be known by the name of *The Synod of Virginia*.

"4th. That another Synod shall consist of the Presbyteries of Abingdon, Orange, and South Carolina, to be known by the name of *The Synod of the Carolinas*."—*Minutes*, 1786, p. 523.

"1. *Resolved unanimously*, That this Synod be divided, and it is hereby divided, into four Synods, agreeably to an act made and provided for that purpose in the Sessions of Synod in the year one thousand seven hundred and eighty-six; and that this division shall commence on the dissolution of the present Synod.—*Minutes*, 1788, p. 547.

5, 6. THE SYNODS OF PITTSBURG AND KENTUCKY IN 1802.—"The committee appointed on the petition of the Synod of Virginia, praying to be divided into three Synods, reported. The report being read and amended, was adopted, and is as follows:

"It is the opinion of the committee that the said division ought to be made. They, therefore, submit the following resolutions, viz.:

"1. That the Presbyteries of Hanover, Lexington, and Winchester, constitute a Synod, to be known by the name of *The Synod of Virginia;* that they hold their first meeting at the Presbyterian church at Lexington, in Virginia, on the last Wednesday of September next, and be opened with a sermon by the Rev. Dr. James Waddel, or, in case of his absence, by the next senior minister who may be present, and that they afterwards meet on their own adjournments.

"2. That the Presbyteries of Redstone, Ohio, and Erie be constituted a Synod, to be known by the name of *The Synod of Pittsburg;* that they hold their first meeting in the Presbyterian church at Pittsburg, on the last Wednesday of September next, and be opened with a sermon by the Rev. James Power; and, in case of his absence, by the next senior minister who may be present, and that they afterwards meet on their own adjournments.

"3. That the Presbyteries of Transylvania, West Lexington, and Washington, be constituted a Synod, to be known by the name of *The Synod of Kentucky;* that their first meeting be held in the Presbyterian church, in the town of Lexington, in Kentucky, on the second Thursday in October next, and be opened with a sermon by the Rev. James Welch, and, in case of his absence, by the next senior minister who may be present, and that they afterwards meet on their own adjournments.

"4. That the southern boundary of the Synod of Pittsburg be, from the mouth of the Scioto, up the Ohio River to the mouth of the Great Kanawha, thence a line due east unto the top of the Alleghany mountains; and that the western boundary of the said Synod begin at the mouth of the Scioto, and thence up the said river to its source, &c.; and that the line between the States of Virginia and Kentucky be the boundary between those Synods."—*Minutes*, 1802, p. 250.

7. THE SYNOD OF ALBANY IN 1803.—"A communication was received from the Presbyteries of Albany, Oneida, and Columbia, requesting, among other things, that the said Presbyteries may be constituted a Synod, by the name of the Synod of Albany. Satisfactory evidence

was laid before the Assembly that the Synod of New York and New Jersey, to which said Presbyteries belong, has been consulted, and given their consent to the measures proposed; therefore,

"*Resolved*, That the Presbyteries of Albany, Oneida, and Columbia be, and they hereby are, constituted and formed into a Synod, to be known by the name of *The Synod of Albany;* that they hold their first meeting in the Presbyterian church of Albany the first Wednesday of October next, at two o'clock, P. M., and be opened with a sermon by the Rev. Jedediah Chapman, or, in case of his absence, by the next senior minister present, and that they afterwards meet on their own adjournments."—*Minutes*, 1803, p. 278.

8. THE SYNOD OF GENEVA IN 1812.—"The following application from the Synod of Albany was overtured by the Committee of Overtures, that said Synod be divided in the manner following, viz.:

"That the Presbyteries of Londonderry, Columbia, Albany, and Oneida, form the eastern division, and be constituted a Synod, to be called and known by the name of *The Synod of Albany.*

"That the Presbyteries of Onondaga, Cayuga, and Geneva, form the western division, and be constituted a Synod, to be called and known by the name of *The Synod of Geneva.* Adopted."—*Minutes*, 1812, p. 502.

9, 10. THE SYNODS OF NORTH CAROLINA AND SOUTH CAROLINA AND GEORGIA, IN 1813.—"*Resolved*, That the said Synod (of the Carolinas) be divided as follows, viz.:

"That the Presbyteries of Orange, Concord, and Fayetteville be constituted a Synod, to be known by the name of *The Synod of North Carolina.*

"That the Presbyteries of South Carolina, Hopewell, and Harmony be constituted a Synod, to be known by the name of *The Synod of South Carolina and Georgia.*"—*Minutes*, 1813, pp. 526, 527.

11. THE SYNOD OF OHIO, in 1814.—"The committee to which were referred the petition of the Presbytery of Lancaster, for the division of the Synod of Kentucky, and a resolution of the Synod on the same subject, reported in favor of the petition; and it was

"*Resolved by the Assembly*, That the Presbytery of Lancaster be separated from the Synod of Pittsburg, and the Presbyteries of Washington and Miami be separated from the Synod of Kentucky, and be erected into a new Synod, and called by the name of *The Synod of Ohio*, to meet at Chillicothe, on the last Thursday of October next; that the Rev. Robert G. Wilson, or, in case of his absence, the senior minister present, open the Synod with a sermon, and preside till a new moderator be chosen."—*Minutes*, 1814, p. 547.

12. THE SYNOD OF TENNESSEE, IN 1817.—"The committee to whom was referred the petition of the Synod of Kentucky, praying a division of said Synod, reported, and their report being read, was adopted, and is as follows, viz.:

"That, agreeably to the request of the Synod of Kentucky, the Presbyteries of Union, Shiloh, West Tennessee, and Mississippi, be constituted a Synod, to be known and called by the name of the *Synod of Tennessee;* that they hold their first session at Nashville, on the first Wednesday of October next; and that the Rev. James W. Stephenson, or, in case of his absence, the senior minister who may be present, open the Synod with a sermon, and preside until a new moderator be chosen." —*Minutes*, 1817, p. 643.

13. THE SYNOD OF GENESEE, IN 1821.—"The Synod of Geneva requested that said Synod be divided in the following manner, and their request was granted, viz.:

"That the Presbyteries of Niagara, Genesee, Rochester, and Ontario be erected into a Synod, to be known by the name of *The Synod of Genesee;* and that they hold their first meeting at Rochester, on the third Tuesday of September next, at 2 o'clock, P.M., and be opened with a sermon by the Rev. Ebenezer Fitch, D.D., or, in case of his absence, by the senior minister present; and afterwards meet on their own adjournments."—*Minutes*, 1821, p. 16.

14, 15. THE SYNOD OF NEW YORK AND NEW JERSEY DIVIDED, IN 1823.—"*Resolved*, That, agreeably to the petition of said Synod [of New York and New Jersey], the Presbyteries of New York, Long Island, Hudson, North River, and Second Presbytery of New York, be constituted, and they are hereby constituted a Synod, to be called *The Synod of New York;* that they hold their first meeting on the third Tuesday of October next, at 10 o'clock, A.M., in the First Presbyterian Church in the city of New York, and afterwards upon their own adjournments; that Dr. Rowan, or, in case of his absence, the senior

10

minister present, open the meeting with a sermon, and preside till a new moderator is chosen.

"That the Presbyteries of Jersey, New Brunswick, Newton, and Susquehanna be constituted, and they hereby are constituted a Synod, to be called *The Synod of New Jersey;* that they hold their first meeting on the third Tuesday of October next, at 10 o'clock, A.M., in the First Presbyterian Church in Newark, and afterwards on their own adjournments; that Dr. Woodhull, or, in case of his absence, the senior minister present, open the meeting with a sermon, and preside till a new moderator is chosen."—*Minutes*, 1823, p. 71.

16. SYNOD OF WESTERN RESERVE, IN 1825.—"*Resolved,* That the Presbyteries of Grand River, Portage, and Huron be, and they hereby are, detached from the Synod of Pittsburg, and constituted a new Synod, to be designated by the name of *The Synod of the Western Reserve;* that they hold their first meeting at Hudson, on the fourth Tuesday of September next, at 11 o'clock, A.M., and that the Rev. Joseph Badger preach the Synodical sermon, and act as moderator till another shall be chosen, or, in case of his failure, then the oldest minister present shall officiate in his place."—*Minutes*, 1825, p. 145.

17, 18. SYNODS OF WEST TENNESSEE AND INDIANA, IN 1826.—"The committee to whom was referred the petition from the Synod of Tennessee, requesting a division of said Synod, made the following report, which was adopted, viz.:

"*Resolved,* That the prayer of the Synod be granted, so far as to constitute the Presbyteries of West Tennessee, Shiloh, Mississippi, and North Alabama, into a Synod, to be denominated *The Synod of West Tennessee;* to meet in Huntsville, on the second Wednesday of October next, at 11 o'clock, A.M.; and that the Rev. Robert Hardin, or, in case of his absence, the senior minister present, open the Synod with a sermon, and preside till a moderator be chosen and the Synod regularly organized.

"The committee to whom was referred the petition from the Presbytery of Salem, requesting that the Presbyteries of Salem, Madison, Wabash, and Missouri be constituted a Synod, to be known by the name of *The Synod of Indiana,* made the following report, which was adopted, viz.:

"*Resolved,* That the prayer of the petition be granted, and that the said Synod meet in Vincennes, on the third Wednesday of October next; and that the Rev. William Martin, or, in case of his absence, the senior minister present, open the Synod with a sermon, and preside till a moderator be chosen and the Synod regularly organized."—*Minutes*, 1826, p. 179.

19. THE SYNOD OF UTICA, IN 1829.—"Overture No. 3, viz., an application from the Synod of Albany, for the erection of a new Synod, was taken up; when it was

"*Resolved*, That the request be granted; and, agreeably to the request of the Synod, the Presbyteries of Ogdensburg, Watertown, Oswego, Oneida, and Otsego are hereby constituted a new Synod, to be called *The Synod of Utica*."—*Minutes*, 1829, p. 260.

20. SYNOD OF MISSISSIPPI AND SOUTH ALABAMA, IN 1829.—"The committee on Overture No. 2, from the Judicial Committee, viz., the complaint and request of the Presbytery of Missisippi, reported, that in consequence of the insufficiency of testimony, they express no opinion respecting the correctness of the complaint; but they recommend that the request be granted,—which is, that the Presbyteries of Mississippi, South Alabama, and Bigby be formed into a new Synod. The report of the committee was adopted; and the Presbyteries of Mississippi, South Alabama, and Bigby are hereby formed into a new Synod, to be known by the name of *The Synod of Mississippi and South Alabama*."—*Minutes*, 1829, p. 263.

21. SYNOD OF CINCINNATI, IN 1829.—"*Resolved*, That a new Synod be constituted, by the name of *The Synod of Cincinnati*, to consist of the Presbyteries of Chillicothe, Cincinnati, and Miami; and that the line which divides the Presbyteries of Athens, Lancaster, and Columbus, on the east, from the Presbyteries of Chillicothe and Miami, on the west, shall be the dividing line between the Synods of Ohio and Cincinnati; excepting that the portion of the Presbytery of Columbus which lies in the counties of Clarke, Champaign, and Logan, and west of a line running due north from the northeast corner of the county of Logan, to the boundary of the Synod of the Western Reserve, shall be attached to the Presbytery of Miami; and the Synod of Cincinnati shall hold their first meeting in Lebanon, on the fourth Thursday of October next, at 11 o'clock, A.M., and shall be opened with a sermon by the

Rev. James Kemper, or, in case of his absence, by the senior minister present, who shall preside until a moderator shall be chosen."—*Minutes*, 1829, p. 271.

22. SYNOD OF ILLINOIS, IN 1831.—"The committee to whom was referred Overture No. 10, viz., an application for the division of the Synod of Indiana, reported in favor of the application; when it was resolved, agreeably to the request of the Synod, that the Presbyteries of Illinois, Kaskaskia, Sangamon, and Missouri, be, and they hereby are, erected into a new Synod, to be known by the name of *The Synod of Illinois.*" —*Minutes*, 1831, p. 324.

23. SYNOD OF MISSOURI, IN 1832.—"The Presbytery of Missouri requested the Synod of Illinois to take measures for the erection of a new Synod; whereupon the Synod divided the ministers and churches in the State of Missouri into three Presbyteries, viz., the Presbytery of St. Louis, the Presbytery of St. Charles, and the Presbytery of Missouri. The Synod of Illinois pray the General Assembly to erect a new Synod, to be composed of the above-named Presbyteries, and to be called *The Synod of Missouri.* Granted."—*Minutes*, 1832, p. 366.

24. SYNOD OF CHESAPEAKE, IN 1833.—[The Synod of Chesapeake, consisting of the Presbyteries of the District of Columbia, Baltimore, and East Hanover, was erected in 1833, see Minutes, p. 395, and dissolved in 1834. See Minutes, 1834, p. 451.]

25. SYNOD OF MICHIGAN, IN 1834.—"The Assembly took up Overture No. 11, viz.: A petition from the Synod of the Western Reserve to erect the Presbyteries of Detroit, Monroe, and St. Joseph, in said Synod, into a new Synod, to be called *The Synod of Michigan.*

"*Resolved,* That the petition be granted; and the said Presbyteries of Detroit, Monroe, and St. Joseph, are hereby erected into a Synod, to be known by the name of *The Synod of Michigan.*"—*Minutes*, 1834, p. 436.

26. SYNOD OF DELAWARE, IN 1834.—"*Resolved,* That the Second Presbytery of Philadelphia, and the Presbyteries of Wilmington and Lewes, be, and the same hereby are, erected into a new Synod, to be called *The Synod of Delaware;* that they hold their first meeting in the Second Church, Wilmington, the 4th Thursday in October next, at

11 o'clock, A. M., and that the opening sermon be preached by the Rev. James Patterson, or, in case of his absence, by the oldest minister present."—*Minutes*, 1834, p. 451.

DISSOLVED.—"*Resolved*, That at and after the meeting of the Synod of Philadelphia, in October next, the Synod of Delaware shall be dissolved, and the Presbyteries constituting the same shall be then and thereafter annexed to the Synod of Philadelphia."—*Minutes*, 1835, p. 486.

27. SYNOD OF ALABAMA, IN 1835.—"The committee to whom was referred Overture No. 26, being a petition from the Synod of Mississippi and South Alabama, for the erection of a new Synod, made their report, which was accepted and adopted, and is as follows, viz.:

"*Resolved*, 1. That the request of the Synod be granted.

"2. That the Presbyteries of South Alabama, Tuscaloosa, and Tombigbee, be erected into a new Synod, to be called *The Synod of Alabama*." —*Minutes*, 1835, p. 489.

28. SYNOD OF PENNSYLVANIA, IN 1838.—"A petition of certain members of the Presbyteries of Wilmington, Lewes, Philadelphia 2d, and Philadelphia 3d, praying for the erection of a new Synod, from the parts of the Synod of Philadelphia, was reported, and the following resolution was adopted:

"*Resolved*, That the ministers and congregations belonging to the Presbyteries of Wilmington, Lewes, Philadelphia 2d, Philadelphia 3d, Carlisle, Huntingdon, and Northumberland, be, and they hereby are, set off from the Synod of Philadelphia and erected into a new Synod, to be called *The Synod of Pennsylvania;* that they hold their first meeting in the Eleventh Presbyterian Church, in the city of Philadelphia, on the 2d Wednesday of July next, at 11 o'clock, A.M., and be opened with a sermon by the Rev. E. W. Gilbert, or, in case of his absence, by the oldest minister present."—*Minutes*, 1838, p. 657.

29. SYNOD OF NEWARK, IN 1839.—"Overtures No. 1 and 2, two memorials from the Presbyteries of Newark and Montrose, requesting the erection of a new Presbytery, by the name of *The Presbytery of Rockaway*, and also the erection of a new Synod, by the name of *The*

Synod of Newark, were taken up for consideration, and the following resolutions were adopted:

"1. *Resolved*, That the Presbytery of Newark be divided into two Presbyteries, and that the ministers and churches within the city of Newark and the townships of Paterson, Bloomfield, and Orange, together with the Rev. Samuel Fisher, D.D., Rev. Gideon N. Judd, and Rev. Henry A. Axtell, be and remain the Presbytery of Newark; and that the remaining ministers and churches belonging to the Presbytery of Newark be, and they hereby are, erected into a new Presbytery, to be called 'The Presbytery of Rockaway.'

"2. *Resolved*, That the Presbytery of Newark meet in the Third Presbyterian Church in Newark, on the second Tuesday in June next, at 4 o'clock, P.M., to transact any business which may become necessary in consequence of the division of said Presbytery, and that the last moderator preside until a new moderator be chosen.

"3. *Resolved*, That the Presbytery of Rockaway meet in the church in Parsippany, on the third Tuesday in June next, at 3 o'clock, P.M., to be opened with a sermon by the Rev. Barnabas King, or, in case of his absence, by the oldest minister present, who shall preside until a new moderator be chosen.

"4. *Resolved*, That the ministers and congregations belonging to the Presbyteries of Newark, Rockaway, and Montrose be, and they hereby are, set off from the Synod of New Jersey, and erected into a new Synod, to be called *The Synod of Newark;* that they hold their first meeting in the First Presbyterian Church in Newark, on the third Tuesday in October next, at 3 o'clock, P.M, and be opened with a sermon by the Rev. Asa Hillyer, D.D., or, in case of his absence, by the oldest minister present, who shall preside till a new moderator be chosen; and that they meet afterward on their own adjournment.

"And whereas it is understood that the Synod of New Jersey, at their last meeting, renounced the authority of this General Assembly, and declared their adherence to a different body; therefore,

"*Resolved*, That the territory heretofore comprehended within the bounds of the Synod of New Jersey, be attached to the Synod of Newark; and that if any of the Presbyteries heretofore belonging to the Synod of New Jersey, shall choose to be connected with the Synod of Newark, the said Synod is hereby authorized to receive them."—*Minutes*, 1839, pp. 10, 11.

30. Synod of New York and New Jersey, formed by union of Synods of Newark and New York, in 1840.—"The committee further report and recommend, that it be ordained by the General Assembly, in reference to the Synods of New York and of Newark, that they be united into one Synod, to be called *The Synod of New York and New Jersey;* and that said Synod meet in the city of New York, in the Pearl Street Presbyterian Church, on the evening of the third Tuesday of October next, at 7 o'clock, and be opened with a sermon by the Rev. Samuel Fisher, D.D., or, in case of his absence or inability to act, by the Rev. Erskine Mason, D.D.

"It was further ordered by the Assembly, that the Presbytery of Montrose may have their election, whether they shall belong to the Synod of New York and New Jersey, or to the Synod of Geneva, or to the Synod of Pennsylvania; provided they decide and signify their decision to the stated clerk of the Assembly before the first of October next; and in case of their failure to take the requisite order in the premises, that then they remain in their present connection with the Synod of New York and New Jersey."—*Minutes*, 1840, p. 18.

31. Synod of Peoria, in 1843.—"*Resolved*, That a new Synod be erected within the bounds of the Synod of Illinois, embracing the ministers and churches connected with the Presbyteries of Ottawa, Peoria, Knox, and Galena, to be known by the name of *The Synod of Peoria;* that the first meeting of the new Synod be held at Galena, on the second Thursday of October, 1843, at 6 o'clock, P.M., to be opened with a sermon by the Rev. George W. Gale, or, in his absence, by the oldest minister present, who shall preside till another moderator shall be chosen."—*Minutes*, 1843, p. 11.

32. Synod of West Pennsylvania, in 1843.—"*Resolved also*, That a new Synod be erected within the bounds of the Synod of Pennsylvania, embracing the ministers and churches connected with the Presbyteries of Erie, Meadville, and Pittsburg, to be known by the name of *The Synod of West Pennsylvania;* that the first meeting of the new Synod be held at Meadville, Crawford County, on the third Tuesday of October, 1843, at 6 o'clock, P.M., to be opened with a sermon by the Rev. D. H. Riddle, D.D., or, in his absence, by the oldest minister present, who shall preside till another moderator shall be chosen."—*Minutes*, 1843, p. 11.

33. SYNOD OF WABASH, IN 1851.—"The Committee on the Polity of the Church presented a report, which was adopted, recommending that the Synod of Indiana, at their own request, be divided in the following manner:

"*Resolved*, That the Presbyteries of Crawfordsville, Logansport, and Fort Wayne be detached from the Synod of Indiana, and constituted a Synod, to be called *The Synod of Wabash;* that they hold their first meeting at Fort Wayne, on the second Thursday of September next, at 11 o'clock, A.M.; and that the Rev. Charles White, D.D., or, in case of his absence, the senior minister present, preach the opening sermon, and preside until a new moderator be chosen; and that the Synod meet afterwards on their own adjournment."—*Minutes*, 1851, p. 13.

34. SYNOD OF IOWA, IN 1853.—"The Committee on the Polity of the Church presented a report, recommending the formation of a new Synod, to be called *The Synod of Iowa*, as follows:

"At the request of the Presbyteries of Des Moines, Iowa City, and Keokuk, and the concurring request of the Synod of Illinois, that the said Presbyteries be formed into a new Synod, it is hereby

"*Resolved*, That the Presbyteries of Des Moines, Iowa City, and Keokuk be, and they are hereby set off from the Synod of Illinois, and erected into a new Synod, to be styled *The Synod of Iowa*, to meet at Yellow Springs, Iowa, on the first Thursday of September next, at 2 o'clock, P.M.; that the Rev. W. W. Woods be appointed to preach the opening sermon, and preside till a moderator be elected, and, in case of his absence, the oldest minister present."—*Minutes*, 1853, p. 314.

35. SYNOD OF SUSQUEHANNA IN 1853.—"The same Committee (on Polity) also reported that they had received a request from the Presbyteries of Otsego, Delaware, and Chenango, to be erected into a new Synod, and recommended that it be granted, provided the commissioners from the Synods to which these Presbyteries are attached do not object,—the new Synod to take the name of *The Synod of Susquehanna*. Their report was put upon the docket.

"The committee, to whom was referred the subject of the erection of a new Synod, to be called *The Synod of Susquehanna*, made a report, which was adopted, and is as follows:

"1. The Presbyteries requesting the action of the Assembly occupy a large and important territory, sufficiently large and important for a separate Synod.

"2. There is a sufficient number of ministers and churches connected with those Presbyteries to warrant the formation of the proposed Synod; and—

"3. The geographical position of the members of those Presbyteries is such as to render it almost impossible for them to attend the meetings of their respective Synods.

"The committee would further report, that two of the three Synods more particularly interested on this subject, viz., the Synods of Geneva and Albany, make no objections to the erection of the proposed Synod; and the objection made by the Synod of Utica is, mainly, that it will reduce their number.

"While the committee think that the Presbyteries of Otsego and Delaware should have consulted their respective Synods in reference to the matter, yet, in view of the importance of the proposed change, they would recommend the adoption of the following resolution:

"*Resolved*, That the Presbyteries of Otsego, Chenango, and Delaware, belonging respectively to the Synods of Utica, Geneva, and Albany, be, and they hereby are, constituted into a new Synod, to be called *The Synod of Susquehanna*, to hold their first meeting at Franklin, Delaware Co., N. Y., on the third Thursday of October next, at 2 o'clock P. M.; opening with a sermon from the oldest minister present, who shall preside until a moderator shall be elected."—*Minutes*, 1853, pp. 314, 330, 331.

36. SYNOD OF ONONDAGA, IN 1855.—"The Committee on the Polity of the Church report, that an application has been made by the Synod of Geneva for the erection of a new Synod, to be composed of four Presbyteries of the Synod of Geneva; and, as the matter has been amicably arranged by those concerned, and no objection appears to such a course, they recommend that the Presbyteries of Onondaga, Cayuga, Cortland, and Tioga be erected into a new Synod, to be called *The Synod of Onondaga*.

"They also recommend that the first meeting of the Synod of Onondaga be appointed at Cortlandville, on the second Tuesday of October, 1855, at 7 o'clock, P. M.; that Rev. Levi Parsons preach the opening sermon, and preside until a moderator is chosen; or, in case of his absence, that the oldest member present preach and preside." Adopted.—*Minutes,* 1855, p. 26.

37. SYNOD OF WISCONSIN, IN 1857.—"The Committee on the Polity of the Church reported Overture No. 1, being a request from the Synod of Peoria for the erection of a new Synod.

"The committee recommend that the request be granted, and that the Presbyteries of Milwaukie, Fox River, and Columbus, now attached to the Synod of Peoria, be erected into a new Synod, to be called *The Synod of Wisconsin;* and that they hold their first meeting in Columbus, Wisconsin, on the third Thursday of October, 1857, at 7 o'clock, P. M., the oldest minister present to preach the sermon, and to preside until a moderator be chosen.

"The report was adopted."—*Minutes,* 1857, p. 383.

38. SYNOD OF ALTA CALIFORNIA, IN 1857.—"Also Overture No. 2, being a request from the Presbytery of San Francisco for the division of that Presbytery, and the erection of a new Synod.

"The committee recommend that the request be granted; that the Rev. Messrs. Silas S. Harmon, Laurentine Hamilton, Walter Frear, and Edward B. Walsworth, together with the churches of Columbia, Sonora, Placerville, and Marysville, be constituted into a new Presbytery, to be called *The Presbytery of Sierra Nevada,* to hold their first meeting at Sacramento, California, on Tuesday, October 6th, 1857, at 3 o'clock, P. M., and to be opened with a sermon by the oldest minister present, who is to preside until a moderator be chosen.

"That the Rev. Messrs. Samuel B. Bell, James Pierpont, William W. Brier, Eli Corwin, and Albert F. White, together with the churches of Oakland, Alemada, and Eden, be constituted into a new Presbytery, to be called *The Presbytery of San José;* to hold their first meeting at Sacramento, California, on Tuesday, October 6th, 1857, at 3 o'clock, P. M.; and to be opened with a sermon by the oldest minister present, who is to preside until a moderator be chosen.

"That the Presbyteries of San Francisco, Sierra Nevada, and San José, be erected into a new Synod, to be called *The Synod of Alta California;* to hold their first meeting at Sacramento, California, on Tuesday, October 6th, 1857, at 7½ o'clock, P.M.; and to be opened with a sermon by the oldest minister present, who is to preside until a moderator be chosen.

"The report was adopted."—*Minutes,* 1857, p. 383.

SECTION 4.—OF THE GENERAL ASSEMBLY.

1. *Formation of the General Assembly.*

a. "The Synod, considering the number and extent of the churches under their care, and the inconvenience of the present mode of government by one Synod,

"*Resolved*, That this Synod will establish out of its own body three or more subordinate Synods, out of which shall be composed a General Assembly, Synod, or Council, agreeably to a system hereafter to be adopted."—*Minutes*, 1786, p. 517.

b. "*Resolved unanimously,* That this Synod be divided, and it is hereby divided into four Synods, agreeably to an Act made and provided for that purpose in the sessions of Synod in the year one thousand seven hundred and eighty-six; and that this division shall commence on the dissolution of the present Synod.

"*Resolved,* That the first meeting of the General Assembly, to be constituted out of the above said four Synods, be held, and it is hereby appointed to be held, on the third Thursday of May, one thousand seven hundred and eighty-nine, in the Second Presbyterian Church in the city of Philadelphia, at eleven o'clock, A.M.; and that Dr. Witherspoon, or, in his absence, Dr. Rogers, open the General Assembly with a sermon, and preside till a moderator be chosen."—*Minutes,* 1788, p. 548.

2. *Organization of the Assembly.*

[Usage has fixed the third Thursday of May, at 11 A.M., as the time for the annual meeting of the Assembly. The last moderator present preaches the sermon, and then opens the session with prayer, and presides during the organization of the Assembly. The Committee on Commissions report; irregular commissions are referred to a special committee, who report, and the roll is completed. A moderator and temporary clerks are chosen, and the Assembly is ready for business.]

Rules of Organization—Committee of Commissions.

a. "I. Immediately after each Assembly is constituted with prayer, the moderator shall appoint a Committee of Commissions.

"II. The commissions shall then be called for, and delivered to the Committee of Commissions; and the person delivering each commission shall state whether the principal or the alternate is present.

"III. After the delivery of the commissions, the Assembly shall have a recess, until such an hour in the afternoon as will afford sufficient time to the committee to examine the commissions.

"IV. That the Committee of Commissions shall, in the afternoon, report the names of all whose commissions shall appear to be regular and constitutional; and the persons whose names shall be thus reported, shall immediately take their seats and proceed to business.

"V. The first act of the Assembly, when thus ready for business, shall be the appointment of a *Committee of Elections,* whose duty it shall be to examine all informal and unconstitutional commissions, and report on the same as soon as practicable."—*Minutes*, 1826, p. 191.

Standing Committee of Commissions.

b. "*Resolved*, That the permanent and stated clerks be, and they hereby are appointed a standing Committee of Commissions; and that the commissioners to future Assemblies hand their commissions to said committee, in the room in which the Assembly shall hold its sessions, on the morning of the day on which the Assembly opens, previous to 11 o'clock; and further, that all commissions which may be presented during the sessions of the Assembly, instead of being read in the house, shall be examined by said committee, and reported to the Assembly."—*Minutes*, 1829, p. 269.

3. *Commissioners from New Presbyteries.*

a. "The committee to which was referred an overture on the subject of admitting commissioners from newly-formed Presbyteries to seats in this house, reported the following resolutions, which were adopted, viz.:

"1. *Resolved*, That it be adopted as a standing rule of this house, that commissioners from newly-formed Presbyteries shall, before taking their seats as members of this body, produce satisfactory evidence that the Presbyteries to which they belong have been regularly organized according to the Constitution of the Church, and are in connection with the General Assembly.

"2. *Resolved also*, That such commissioners shall be entitled to furnish the evidence required in the foregoing resolution, before the house shall proceed to the choice of a moderator."—*Minutes*, 1822, p. 48.

b. "*Resolved* 1, That no commissioner from a newly-formed Presbytery shall be permitted to take his seat, nor shall such commissioner be reported by the Committee on Commissions, until the Presbytery shall have been duly reported by the Synod, and recognized as such by the Assembly; and that the same rule apply when the name of any Presbytery has been changed.

"2. When it shall appear to the satisfaction of the General Assembly, that any new Presbytery has been formed for the purpose of unduly increasing the representation, the General Assembly will by a vote of the majority refuse to receive the delegates of Presbyteries so formed, and may direct the Synod to which such Presbytery belongs to reunite it to the Presbytery or Presbyteries to which the members were before attached."—*Minutes*, 1837, p. 446.

4. *Ratio of Representation and Quorum.*

a. "Every Presbytery shall, at their last stated meeting preceding the meeting of the General Assembly, depute to the General Assembly commissioners, in the following proportion: Each Presbytery consisting of not more than six ministers, shall send one minister and one elder; each Presbytery consisting of more than six ministers, and not more than twelve, shall send two ministers and two elders; and so in the same proportion for every six ministers. And these commissioners, or any fourteen of them, whereof seven to be ministers, being met on the day and at the place appointed, shall be competent to enter upon business. And the judicatory thus constituted shall bear the style and title of *The General Assembly of the Presbyterian Church in the United States of America.*"—*Minutes*, 1786, p. 524.

In 1819, the ratio was altered by "substituting the word nine for the word six, and the word eighteen in place of the word twelve."—*Minutes*, 1819, p. 700.

In 1826 the ratio was increased from nine to twelve, and from eighteen to twenty-four.—*Minutes*, 1826, p. 168.

The Present Ratio.

b. "*Resolved*, That the 2d section of the 12th chapter of the Form of Government be, and the same is, hereby so amended as to read thus: The General Assembly shall consist of an equal delegation of bishops and elders from each Presbytery, in the following proportion, viz.: Each Presbytery consisting of not more than twenty-four ministers, shall send one minister and one elder; and each Presbytery consisting of more than twenty-four ministers, shall send two ministers and two elders; and in like proportion for every twenty-four ministers in every Presbytery; and these delegates so appointed shall be styled *Commissioners to the General Assembly.*"—*Minutes*, 1833, p. 401.

"The Assembly rule and ordain that the ratio of Presbyterial representation be reduced to its minimum, altering our Form of Government (chap. xii, sec. 2), so that said section shall be hereafter alone, and in all, and read as follows, viz.: The General Assembly shall consist of an equal delegation of bishops and ruling elders from the Presbyteries, in the simple proportion of one minister and one elder from each Presbytery. And these commissioners so appointed shall be styled *Commissioners to the General Assembly*."—*Minutes*, 1840, p. 17.

[This, though acted on from 1841 to 1850, was "never submitted to the Presbyteries and constitutionally adopted" (Minutes, 1849, p. 183). It was sent down as an overture in 1849, and rejected, 28 to 56 (Minutes, 1850, p. 318). The ratio remains, therefore, as fixed in 1833, above.]

5. *Where a Presbytery sends more than its proportion of Commissioners, the last elected are refused.*

"The right of two persons to a seat in the Assembly from the Presbytery of Portage was questioned; whereupon their case was referred to the Committee of Elections. After considering the subject, the committee reported that the names of the minister and elder last appointed should be erased; because the Presbytery is entitled to no more than two commissioners. This report was adopted."—*Minutes*, 1835, p. 466.

6. *Such Commissioners only should be appointed as will remain throughout the Sessions.*

"It is, in the opinion of this General Assembly, highly important that commissioners should not be appointed, unless it shall satisfactorily appear to the several Presbyteries that they design to remain throughout the sessions."—*Minutes*, 1827, p. 207.

7. *In case of the Defect of a Commission, or its Absence.*

[The case of the claimant is referred to a special committee, who, on satisfactory evidence to them that he has been elected, recommend that his name be enrolled.]

a. The committee further reported, that the commission of David M. Wilson, a ruling elder from the Presbytery of the District of Columbia, wants the signature of the clerk; and that the Rev. F. W. Graves, of the Presbytery of Alton, is without a regular commission, but has presented a certificate of his election from the stated clerk of that Presbytery.

"These cases were referred to Messrs. Judd, Lathrop, and Rood, as a Committee of Elections. The committee reported favorably, and, at their recommendation, the names of Messrs. Wilson and Graves were inserted on the roll."—*Minutes*, 1839, p. 8.

Where the Form is substantially observed, and the Commission authenticated by either Moderator or Clerk, the name is to be enrolled.

b. "The Committee on Commissions further reported, that the commissions from the Presbyteries of Buffalo, Otsego, Bath, Elyria, and Logansport, want the signature of the moderator, that the commission from the Presbytery of Hudson wants the signature of the stated clerk, and that the commissions from the Presbytery of Tioga, though regularly signed, are not after the form prescribed by the Constitution.

"It was ordered that, where the form is substantially observed, and the commission authenticated by either moderator or clerk, the name be enrolled; and the commissioners from these Presbyteries were enrolled accordingly."—*Minutes*, 1849, p. 166.

c. "The committee further reported the case of the Rev. A. Cogswell Frissell, from the Presbytery of North River, as appearing without a commission.

"The Assembly having received other and satisfactory evidence of his appointment as a commissioner, it was resolved that Mr. Frissell be received as a member, and his name was put upon the roll of the Assembly."—*Minutes*, 1852, p. 151.

d. "The Committee on Elections reported, and, on their recommendation, the Rev. Eleazar T. Ball, of the Presbytery of Ithaca, Elder Wm. Hubbard, of the Presbytery of Grand River, and Elder John D. Armstrong, of the Presbytery of Providence, who had appeared without commissions, were admitted to seats in the Assembly."—*Minutes*, 1853, p. 305.

Change of Usage.

e. "The stated clerk also reported the following persons as appearing without commissions, and that their appointment is sustained by the testimony of commissioners present:

"Rev. George Painter, of the Presbytery of New River; Elder Milton J. Snow, of the Presbytery of Portage; Rev. Reed Wilkinson, of the

Presbytery of Athens; Elder John C. Bestow, of the Presbytery of Athens; Rev. James B. Shaw, D.D., of the Presbytery of Rochester; Elder Orlando Hastings, of the Presbytery of Rochester; Elder Marvin Freeman, of the Presbytery of Troy; Elder Peter B. Ackart, of the Presbytery of Troy; Rev. George A. Howard, of the Presbytery of Catskill; Rev. Thomas Brainerd, D.D., of the Presbytery of Philadelphia 4th.

"Whereupon it was

"*Resolved*, That the above names be inserted in the roll as commissioners.—*Minutes*, 1854, p. 480.

f. "The permanent clerk also reported the following persons as appearing without commissions, and that their appointment is sustained by testimony satisfactory to the committee:

"Rev. Seth G. Clark, of the Presbytery of Cleveland; Rev. John G. Atterbury, of the Presbytery of Salem; Elder Solomon Beckley, of the Presbytery of Keokuk; Elder William Porter, of the Presbytery of Franklin.

"Whereupon it was

"*Resolved*, That the names of the above persons be inserted in the roll as commissioners.—*Minutes*, 1855, p. 8. 1856, p. 182.

"The stated clerk also reported that Elder John Dunning had presented an irregular commission from the Presbytery of Rockaway; which was referred to a committee, consisting of Rev. Horace P. Bogue and Rev. Henry Kendall.

"The Committee reported that the name of Mr. Dunning be added to the roll."—*Minutes*, 1857, p. 374.

8. *Principals and Alternates.*

[From the origin of the General Assembly, it was frequent usage for the principal to resign his seat to the alternate, and *vice versa*. But in 1827, the following act was adopted.]

"The Committee to whom were referred Overtures No. 4 and 5, containing resolutions of the Presbyteries of Richland and Charleston Union, disapproving the practice of permitting members of the General Assembly 'at various stages of the sessions to resign their seats to others, called alternates,' made the following report, viz.:

"These overtures present two points of inquiry.

"1. Whether the Constitution of the Church, according to a fair interpretation, permits the practice complained of by these Presbyteries.

"2. If this practice is allowed by the Constitution, whether it is expedient that it should be continued.

"As to the first question, the only authority on this subject, as far as appears to your committee, is found in Form of Government, chap. xxii, sec. 1, in these words: 'And as much as possible to prevent all failure in the representation of the Presbyteries, arising from unforeseen accidents to those first appointed, it may be expedient for each Presbytery, in the room of each commissioner, to appoint also an alternate commissioner to supply his place in case of necessary absence.'

"The first remark obviously presenting itself here is, that the language quoted, so far from making the appointment of alternates necessary, contains nothing more than a recommendation of the measure, expressed in very gentle terms.

"In the next place, although the terms of the article may be so interpreted as to make it provide for the necessary absence of a commissioner at any time during the sessions of the Assembly, yet it appears most reasonable to suppose that the intention of the framers of the Constitution was to provide for those unforeseen events which might altogether prevent the attendance of the primary commissioners. For it is not at all probable that wise men, in drawing up a Constitution for a Church judicature of the highest dignity, whose business is often both very important and extremely difficult, would provide for a change in the members of the court, after it should be constituted, and become deeply engaged in the transaction of weighty affairs, and the investigation of perplexing questions. A measure of this kind is, the committee believe, without example, and therefore the construction, which would support it, is thought to be erroneous.

"If, in this case, the committee have judged correctly, they are much more confident in the remarks that the Constitution does not justify the practice, now very common, of the arrangements, for convenience, made by the primary commissioner and his alternate, according to which the one or the other, as the case may be, takes his seat for a few days in the Assembly, resigns it, and goes to his secular business.

"But, secondly, if it should be determined that the Constitution permits these changes, in some instances, the committee are constrained to believe that the practice is, on the whole, entirely inexpedient.

"1. Because it creates dissatisfaction among many brethren, as well those who have complained of it, as others who have held their peace.

"2. It gives an invidious advantage to the neighboring Presbyteries over those which are remote.

"3. It may be the occasion of a number of abuses, against which the Assembly ought to guard, but which the committee do not think it needful to specify.

"4. But chiefly, it often embarrasses and retards the proceedings of the Assembly, because members of committees resign to alternates before the committees to which they belong have finished their business, or received a discharge from the house; because new members, coming into the Assembly in the midst of business, often cannot possibly understand it sufficiently to decide on it wisely, and because speeches made in relation to matters imperfectly understood often shed darkness, and throw perplexity on them, and thus very much time is wasted in discussions which profit nothing.

"Finally, the practice is thought to be derogatory to the dignity and usefulness of the General Assembly. For these reasons, the committee recommend the adoption of the following resolution:

"*Resolved*, That, in the judgment of this General Assembly, the construction of the Constitution, Form of Government, chapter xxii, section 1, which allows commissioners, after holding their seats for a time, to resign them to their alternates, or which allows alternates to sit for a while, and then resign their places to their principals, is erroneous; that the practice growing out of this construction is inexpedient, and that it ought to be discontinued.

"The above report was accepted, and the resolution with which it closes was adopted."—*Minutes*, 1827, pp. 209, 210.

Rule dispensed with under peculiar Circumstances.

b. "Rev. Jacob D. Mitchell informed the Assembly that, as the alternate named in the commission from West Hanover, his principal, Rev. James Wharey, not being present, he had, at the commencement of the Assembly, taken his seat as a member, and that Mr. Wharey had now arrived, having been detained in the Providence of God. Mr. Mitchell moved that he have leave to resign his seat in favor of Mr. Wharey. It was then moved and carried, that under the peculiar circumstances of the case, the standing rule be dispensed with, and that Mr. Wharey be admitted a member in the place of Mr. Mitchell."—*Minutes*, 1836, p. 245.

9. *Commissioners under the Plan of Union.*

a. "A commission, signed by the moderator and clerk of the Presbytery of Hartford, appointing Mr. Daniel W. Lathrop, one of the standing committee of the church in Ellsworth a commissioner to this Assembly, was read.

[The subject was referred to a committee, who reported as follows. The report was adopted unanimously.]

"Whereas, a conventional agreement was entered into with the General Association of Connecticut by the General Assembly of the Presbyterian Church, in the year one thousand eight hundred and one, for the purpose of preventing alienation, and promoting harmony in those new settlements which are composed of persons adhering to both those bodies:

"And whereas, in the said agreement it is provided, that in a church composed in part of Congregationalists and in part of Presbyterians, the church may choose a standing committee for the exercise of discipline; and moreover, that the standing committee of any church may depute one of their body to attend the Presbytery, and that the person so deputed may have the same right to sit and act in Presbytery as a ruling elder of the Presbyterian Church:

"And, moreover, as in the mixed state of Christian society contemplated in the agreement aforesaid, Presbyteries have sometimes appointed members of standing committees so admitted into their body as commissioners to represent them in General Assembly. Therefore,

"*Resolved*, In order to carry into effect the friendly object of the above agreement, that Daniel W. Lathrop be admitted as a member of this Assembly.

"*Resolved*, That it be affectionately recommended to the brethren who compose mixed societies of this kind, so far as expediency will allow, to conform to the letter of the Constitution of the Presbyterian Church in making their appointments and organizing their congregations."—*Minutes*, 1820, pp. 721, 722, 724.

b. "Mr. Josiah Bissell, from the Presbytery of Rochester, appeared in the Assembly, and produced a commission as an elder from that Presbytery. A member of that Presbytery informed the Assembly that Mr. Bissell had not been set apart as an elder; but that he was appointed, as was supposed by the Presbytery, in conformity with the conventional agreement between the General Assembly and the General Association of Connecticut. After considerable discussion, it was

"*Resolved*, That Mr. Bissell be admitted as a member of the Assembly."

"The following protest was offered, and ordered to be entered on the Minutes, viz.:

"The subscribers enter their dissent and protest against the resolution by which Mr. Josiah Bissell was admitted as a member of this General Assembly, for the following reasons:

"1. Because he was neither an ordained minister, nor a ruling elder; and consequently he was destitute of the qualifications which the Constitution of our Church requires in commissioners appointed by Presbyteries as their representatives in this body.

"2. Because he was not even a 'committee-man,' on which ground some might, in existing circumstances, have been disposed to advocate his admission as a member.

"3. Because he had not, either from the Constitution, or from the conventional agreement [the Plan of Union], the shadow of a claim to a seat in this house."

[In reply, it is said that] "Mr. Bissell was admitted by the Assembly for the following reasons:

"1. The commission which Mr. Bissell produced was in due form, and signed by the proper officers of the Presbytery.

"2. Every Presbytery has a right to judge of the qualifications of its own members; and it is amenable to Synod, and not to the General Assembly, except by way of appeal, or reference, or complaint, regularly brought up from the inferior judicatories, which has not been done in the present case.

"3. It would be a dangerous precedent, and would lead to the destruction of all order in the Church of Christ, to permit unauthorized verbal testimony to set aside an authenticated written document."—*Minutes*, 1826, pp. 164, 178, 181.

c. [The Committee of Elections reported]: "With respect to the case of the standing committee-man from Grand River Presbytery, they decline expressing any opinion as to the constitutional question of the right of such to a seat in the Assembly.

"The Assembly proceeded to consider the case of the person denominated 'standing committee' in the commission; and after considerable discussion, it was

"*Resolved*, That the member be received and enrolled among the list of members."—*Minutes*, 1831, p. 318.

d. "The consideration of the overture on the right of members of standing committees to be members of the General Assembly was resumed. After considerable discussion, the overture was adopted, and is as follows, viz.:

"*Resolved*, That in the opinion of the General Assembly the appointment by some Presbyteries, as has occurred in a few cases, of members of standing committees to be members of the General Assembly, is inexpedient and of questionable constitutionality, and therefore ought not in future to be made."—*Minutes*, 1831, p. 338.

e. "The Committee [of Commissions] also reported two commissions for members of standing committees, instead of ruling elders, from the Presbytery of Grand River. These commissions were referred to the Committee of Elections.

"The Committee of Elections reported that the commissions referred to them from the Presbytery of Grand River had been withdrawn by the persons presenting them."—*Minutes*, 1832, pp. 354, 356.

f. "The Committee [of Commissions] reported that Mr. Erastus Upson, a standing committee-man from the Presbytery of Oswego, had been appointed a member of this body. A motion was made to refer this case to the Committee of Elections, which was negatived. It was then

"*Resolved*, That Mr. Upson have leave to withdraw his application."—*Minutes*, 1833, p. 392.

g. "The committee appointed to examine the records of the Synod of South Carolina and Georgia made a report; when the records were approved, with the exception of a resolution recorded on pages 218 and 219, on the subject of admitting the representatives of Congregational and Independent churches to be members of their Presbyteries and Synod, in the same manner as ruling elders."—*Minutes*, 1832, p. 370.

10. *Corresponding Members. Ministers casually present, not invited.*

a. "Upon motion, it was agreed, That, whereas this Assembly, copying the example of their predecessors, have admitted several ministers, who are not commissioners, to join in their deliberations and conclusions, but not to vote on any question; and although this Assembly has been much indebted to the wise counsels and friendly assistance of these corresponding ministers, nevertheless, on mature deliberation, it was

"*Resolved*, As the opinion of this house,

"1. That no delegated body has a right to transfer its powers, or any part thereof, unless express provision is in its Constitution.

"2. That this Assembly is a delegated body, and no such provision is in its Constitution.

"3. Although such admission has hitherto produced no bad consequences, it may, nevertheless, at some future day, be applied to party purposes, and cause embarrassment and delay: wherefore,

"*Resolved*, 4. Lastly, that the practice of this Assembly, in this case, ought not to be used as a precedent in future."—*Minutes*, 1791, p. 42.

Delegates from other Bodies.

b. [At first these were not allowed to vote; but in 1794, the Assembly asked, and the General Association of Connecticut acceded to the request, "That the delegates from these bodies, respectively, shall have a right, not only to sit and deliberate, but also to vote on all questions which may be determined by either of them."—*Minutes*, 1794, p. 80; 1795, p. 96.

[The Assembly afterwards, 1827, asked that the right of voting be given up; and, since 1830, corresponding members have the right only to sit and deliberate, but not to vote.] See chap. xi, sec. 2.

The Secretary of any of the permanent Committees, the stated and temporary Clerks, have the privileges of corresponding Members.

c. "*Resolved*, That it be a standing rule of the Assembly, that the secretary of any of the permanent committees shall be entitled to the same privilege as the delegates from corresponding bodies, while the business intrusted to that committee is under consideration in the house.

"The Assembly voted that the same privilege be extended to the stated and permanent clerks, in reference to matters pertaining to their official duties."—*Minutes*, 1858, p. 581.

11. *Of the mode of Choosing the Moderator of the Assembly.*

"On motion agreed, that it be the standing rule of the General Assembly, in choosing a moderator, that any commissioner may nominate a candidate for the chair. The candidates so pointed out shall then severally give their votes for some one of their number, and withdraw; when the remaining commissioners shall proceed *viva voce*, to choose by a plurality of voices one of the said candidates for moderator."—*Minutes,* 1791, p. 39.

12. *Rules of the General Assembly of the Presbyterian Church.*

The Moderator's address to his successor in office, introductory to the Rules of Order.

"SIR: It is my duty to inform you, and announce to this house, that you are duly elected to the office of moderator in this General Assembly. For your direction in office, and for the direction of this Assembly in all their deliberations, before I leave this seat, I am to read to you and this house, the rules contained in the records of this Assembly; which, I doubt not, will be carefully observed by both in conducting the business that may come before you.

"1. The moderator shall take the chair precisely at the hour to which the Assembly stands adjourned; shall immediately call the members to order; and, on the appearance of a quorum, shall open the session with prayer.

"2. If a quorum be not assembled at the hour appointed, any two members shall be competent to adjourn from time to time, that an opportunity may be given for a quorum to assemble.

"3. After calling the roll, the minutes of the last sitting shall be read, and if requisite, corrected.

"4. The General Assembly, at every meeting, shall appoint a Committee of Bills and Overtures, to prepare and digest business for the Assembly. Any person thinking himself aggrieved by this committee, may complain to the Assembly.

"5. Petitions, questions relating either to doctrine or order, and, usually, all new propositions tending to general laws, shall be laid before the Committee of Bills and Overtures, before they be offered to the Assembly.

"6. The Assembly shall also, at every meeting, appoint a committee, to be styled the Judicial Committee, whose duty it shall be to take into consideration all appeals and references brought to the Assembly; to ascertain whether they are in order, to digest and arrange all the documents relating to the same, and to propose to the Assembly the best method of proceeding in each case.

"7. It shall be the duty of the moderator, at all times, to preserve order; and to endeavor to conduct all business before the Assembly to a speedy and proper result.

"8. It shall be the duty of the clerk, as soon as possible after the commencement of the sessions of the Assembly, to form a complete roll of the members present, and put the same into the hands of the moderator; and it shall also be the duty of the clerk, whenever any additional members take their seats, to add their names, in their proper places, to the said roll.

"9. It shall be the duty of the clerk, immediately to file all papers, in the order in which they have been read, with proper endorsements, and to keep them in perfect order.

"10. The moderator may speak to points of order in preference to other members, rising from his seat for that purpose; and shall decide questions of order, subject to an appeal to the Assembly by any two members.

"11. Business left unfinished at the last sitting, is, ordinarily, to be taken up first.

"12. A motion made must be seconded, and afterwards repeated by the moderator, or read aloud, before it is debated; and every motion shall be reduced to writing, if the moderator, or any member require it.

"13. Any member who shall have made a motion, shall have liberty to withdraw it, with the consent of his second, before any debate has taken place thereon; but not afterwards, without the consent of the Assembly.

* "14. On questions of order, adjournment, postponement, commitment, or the previous question, no member shall speak more than once; on all other questions, each member may speak twice, but not oftener, without the express permission of the Assembly.

"15. When a question is under debate, no motion shall be received, except to amend it, to commit it, to postpone it, for the previous question, or to adjourn.

"16. An amendment may be moved on any motion, and shall be decided before the original motion.

"17. If a motion under debate contains several parts, any two members may have it divided, and a question taken on each part.

* "18. The previous question shall be in this form: 'Shall the main question be now put?' and, until it is decided, shall preclude all amendment, and further debate on the main question.

† "19. If the previous question be decided in the affirmative, the debate

* Modified by act of Assembly of 1851. See p. 172. The 14th and 18th, here, correspond with the 13th and 17th of the "Rules for Judicatories."

† Modified by act of Assembly of 1835. See p. 172.

on the main question may proceed; if in the negative, the effect shall be to arrest the discussion, and to produce an indefinite postponement.

"20. A question shall not be again called up, or reconsidered at the same sessions of the Assembly at which it has been decided, except by the consent of two-thirds of the members who were present at the decision; and unless the motion to reconsider be made and seconded by persons who voted with the majority.

"21. A subject which has been indefinitely postponed, either by the operation of the previous question, or by a direct motion for indefinite postponement, shall not be again called up, during the same sessions of the Assembly, except by the consent of three-fourths of the members who were present at the decision.

"22. Every member, when speaking, shall address himself to the moderator; and shall treat his fellow-members, and especially the moderator, with decorum and respect.

"23. Without express permission, no member, while business is going on, shall engage in private conversation; nor shall members address one another, nor any person present, but through the moderator.

"24. No speaker shall be interrupted, unless he be out of order, or for the purpose of correcting mistakes or misrepresentations.

"25. It is indispensable, that members maintain great gravity and dignity while judicially convened; that they attend closely, in their speeches, to the subject under consideration, and avoid prolix and desultory harangues; and when they deviate from the subject, it is the privilege of any member, and the duty of the moderator, to call them to order.

"26. No member, in the course of debate, shall be allowed to indulge in personal reflections.

"27. If more than one member rise to speak at the same time, the member who is most distant from the moderator's chair shall speak first.

"28. When more than three members shall be standing at the same time, the moderator shall require all to take their seats, the person only excepted who may be speaking.

"29. If any member act, in any respect, in a disorderly manner, it shall be the privilege of any member, and the duty of the moderator, to call him to order.

"30. If any member consider himself aggrieved by a decision of the moderator, it shall be his privilege to appeal to the Assembly; and the question on such appeal, shall be taken without debate.

"31. Any member who may think himself aggrieved by a decision of the General Assembly, shall have his dissent, or protest, with his reasons, entered on the records of the Assembly, or filed among their papers, if given in before the rising of the Assembly.*

"32. It is the duty of the moderator to appoint all committees, except in those cases in which the Assembly shall decide otherwise.

"33. The person first named on any committee, shall be considered as the chairman thereof, whose duty it shall be to convene the committee; and in case of his absence, or inability to act, the second-named member shall take his place, and perform his duties.

"34. When various motions are made with respect to the filling of blanks with particular numbers or times, the question shall always be first taken on the highest number, and the longest time.

"35. When the moderator has commenced taking the vote, no further debate or remark shall be admitted, unless there has evidently been a mistake; in which case, the mistake shall be rectified, and the moderator shall recommence taking the vote.

"36. When a vote is taken by ballot, the moderator shall vote with the other members; but he shall not vote in any other case, unless the Assembly be equally divided, when, if he do not choose to vote, the question shall be lost.

"37. The yeas and nays on any question, shall not be recorded, unless it be required by one-third of the members present.

"38. Whenever the Assembly is about to sit in a judicial capacity, it shall be the duty of the moderator, solemnly to announce from the chair, that the Assembly is about to pass to the consideration of the business assigned for trial, and to enjoin on the members to recollect and regard the high character, as judges of a court of Jesus Christ, and the solemn duty, in which they are about to act.

"39. No member shall retire from the Assembly, without the leave of the moderator; or withdraw from it, to return home, without the consent of the Assembly.

"40. The moderator, in finally closing the sessions of the Assembly, in addition to prayer, may cause an appropriate psalm or hymn to be sung; and shall pronounce the Apostolical Benediction."

Conclusion of the Moderator's address to his successor in office.

"Having now read these rules, according to order, for your instruction, as moderator, and for the direction of all the members, in the

* See Form of Government, Book II, Chap. 8.

management of business, praying that Almighty God may direct, and bless all the deliberations of this General Assembly, for the glory of his name, and for the edification and comfort of the Presbyterian Church in the United States, I resign my place and office as moderator."—*Minutes*, 1822, p. 42–45.

Modifications of Rules.

[The 13th, 17th, and 18th of the "Rules for Judicatories" correspond with the 14th, 18th, and 19th of the Rules for the Assembly given above. The "Rules for Judicatories as they now stand will be found in full in the last chapter of this Digest.]

The Assembly resumed the consideration of the Report of the Committee on the 17th and 18th Rules for Judicatories. The Report was amended and adopted, and is as follows, viz.: That the 17th Rule remain as it now stands, and that the 18th be so altered as to read thus: "If the previous question be decided in the affirmative the main question shall be immediately put without debate; if in the negative, the debate may proceed."—*Minutes*, 1835, p. 473.

The Committee (Hon. William Strong, Mr. Abraham B. Conger, and Mr. William H. Brown), to whom was referred the interpretation of the 17th rule, presented a report, and, on their recommendation, the 13th and 17th rules were amended, so as to read as follows:

"The previous question shall be put in this form: *Shall the main question be now put?* It shall only be admitted when demanded by a majority of the members present; and its effect shall be to put an end to all debate, and bring the body to a direct vote,—first, upon a motion to commit the motion under consideration (if such motion shall have been made); secondly (if the motion to commit does not prevail), upon pending amendments; and, lastly, upon the main question. To call for the previous question shall not be debatable.

"The 13th rule shall be amended by striking out the words, '*or the previous question.*' "—*Minutes*, 1851, p. 27.

13. *The Moderator has no other than the casting vote.*

"On the question being taken, the moderator [Dr. John Blair Smith] claimed a right to a vote as a commissioner from the Presbytery of Albany, distinct from the casting vote. He left it to the house to decide on the claim. The house, having taken a vote on the subject, decided by a great majority against the moderator's claim."—*Minutes*, 1798, p. 140.

[See *ante* 36, p. 171.]

14. *Communications to the Assembly through the Moderator.*

"On motion,

"*Resolved,* That every letter or communication addressed to the moderator, be opened and read by him, and at his discretion be either communicated immediately to the Assembly for their decision, or to the Committee of Overtures, to be by them brought before the house in the ordinary channel."—*Minutes,* 1794, p. 79.

15. *The "last Moderator present," not necessarily a Member of the Assembly.*

"PITTSBURG, May 21st, 1835.

"The General Assembly of the Presbyterian Church met in the First Presbyterian Church in this city, and the Rev. Dr. Lindsley, the moderator of the last Assembly, being absent, was opened with a sermon by the Rev. Samuel Miller, D.D., at the request of the Rev. Dr. William A. McDowell, the last moderator present, with a sermon on 2 Corinthians 4 : 7 : 'But we have this treasure in earthen vessels, that the excellency of the power may be of God and not of us.'

"After sermon the stated clerk called the house to order, and informed them, that the Rev. Dr. Lindsley, the moderator of the last Assembly, being absent, the duties of the chair devolved upon the last moderator, who is present, and has a commission to sit in this Assembly, and therefore he moved that the Rev. Nathan S. S. Beman, D.D., be called to the chair. This motion prevailed, and Dr. Beman took the chair, and constituted the Assembly with prayer.

"Thursday afternoon, 3 o'clock.

"The Assembly met.

"A motion was made to reconsider the vote by which Dr. Beman was called to the chair, on the ground that many persons voted in the apprehension that Dr. Wm. A. McDowell, the moderator immediately preceding Dr. Lindsley, was not in the house; and that many others believed the rule of the house required the constituting moderator to be in commission, which Dr. McDowell was not. This motion, after considerable discussion, was adopted unanimously.

"After some further remarks, it was agreed that the original motion of the stated clerk should be again submitted to the house, and the vote be taken by him. Whereupon Dr. Ely put the question: 'All who are in favor of sustaining the resolution passed in the morning, by which

Dr. Beman was called to the chair, will signify it by saying aye.' This motion was lost.

"It was then moved that the Rev. Wm. A. McDowell, D.D., being the last moderator present, be requested to take the chair. This motion prevailed, and Dr. McDowell took the chair accordingly."—*Minutes*, 1835, pp. 461, 466.

16. The Stated Clerk.

Appointment.

a. "Ordered, that Dr. Duffield be appointed stated clerk of the Assembly, procure a proper book into which to transcribe their minutes, and lay the expense of the book and of transcribing the minutes, before the General Assembly at their next meeting."—*Minutes*, 1789, p. 13.

Duties of the Stated Clerk.

b. "The stated clerk shall transcribe for the press such parts as may be necessary of the minutes ordered to be published from year to year. He shall correct the press, and superintend the printing of all the minutes and papers which shall be ordered to be printed by the General Assembly. As soon as the extracts are printed from year to year, he shall send one copy by mail to each Presbytery, and apportion and send the rest by private conveyance to the Presbyteries and other bodies, as shall be prescribed by the Assembly, only reserving a sufficient number of copies for binding. He shall have the charge of all the books and papers of the General Assembly, shall cause their minutes to be fairly transcribed into the book or books provided for the purpose, and give attested copies of all minutes and other documents, when properly required so to do."—*Minutes*, 1807, p. 377.

To Notify Presbyteries whose Commissioners have left without Leave.

c. "Whereas, it has frequently happened that members of this Assembly, neglecting their duty and inattentive to the rules of decorum, have abruptly left the Assembly, and returned home without leave of absence,

"*Resolved*, That in all similar cases which shall occur in future, it shall be the duty of the clerk of this House to give notice thereof to the Presbyteries to which such delinquent members may belong; and that it be recommended to the said Presbyteries, in their settlements with such delinquents, not to allow them any compensation for services as members of the Assembly."—*Minutes*, 1801, p. 233.

"*Resolved*, That it be the duty of the stated clerk hereafter, to report to the several Presbyteries the names of the commissioners who, at the calling of the roll at the close of the Assembly, may appear to have left the Assembly without permission."—*Minutes*, 1820, p. 723.

"*Resolved*, That as the names of persons who have left the Assembly without leave are to be published in the printed journals, therefore the stated clerk is liberated from the duty enjoined by a standing rule, of writing to the Presbyteries on the subject."—*Minutes*, 1824, p. 125.

Salary of the Stated Clerk.

d. "*Resolved*, That the salary of the stated clerk be hereafter one hundred dollars per annum, exclusive of the expense of having the minutes transcribed."—*Minutes*, 1837, p. 467.

17. Permanent Clerk.

Appointment and Duties.

"*Resolved*, That a permanent recording clerk be chosen, whose duty it shall be, from year to year, to draught the minutes of the Assembly during their sessions, and afterwards to perform such services respecting the transcribing, printing, and distributing the extracts as shall be assigned to him, from time to time; and that he be paid out of the funds of the Assembly three dollars per day, for the time he shall be employed, as well during the sessions of the Assembly as after their dissolution."—*Minutes*, 1802, p. 235.

"*Resolved*, That hereafter the permanent clerk shall receive for his services two dollars per day, during the sessions of the Assembly, and one dollar and fifty cents per day, while necessarily attending upon the business of the Assembly after their adjournment."—*Minutes*, 1806, p. 372.

"The permanent clerk shall furnish all the stationery for the use of the Assembly and the several clerks. He shall make the original draught of all the minutes, and give certified copies, as occasion may require, of all such as may be proper to be transmitted to the trustees of the General Assembly, or any of their officers. After the Assembly rises, from year to year, he shall carefully revise the manuscript, render it correct and legible, and deliver it over to the stated clerk. He shall receive a reasonable compensation for the stationery supplied by him, and the pay (per diem) fixed by the last Assembly" (*i. e.*, two dollars per day during the sessions of the Assembly, and one dollar and fifty cents per day, while necessarily attending on the business of the Assembly after their adjournment).—*Minutes*, 1807, p. 377.

[Restored to three dollars per diem.—*Minutes*, 1826, p. 188.]

18. Temporary Clerks.

a. "*Resolved*, That a temporary clerk be chosen by each Assembly as heretofore, to read the minutes and communications to the Assembly, and otherwise aid the permanent clerk as occasion may require, and that he be paid one dollar per day for his services."—*Minutes*, 1802, p. 235.

b. "The temporary clerk shall hereafter receive no pecuniary compensation for his services."—*Minutes*, 1806, p. 372.

Choice of Clerks not confined to Members of Assembly.

c. "On motion,

"*Resolved*, That it be considered as the right of every member of the Assembly to vote for a clerk who is not a member of the body."—*Minutes*, 1793, p. 64.

19. *The Standing Committees.*

"*Resolved*, That the committees appointed at the opening of each Assembly be called *Standing Committees*, and those outside of the Assembly, *Permanent Committees*."—*Minutes*, 1856, p. 192.

I. Committee of Bills and Overtures.

a. "The General Assembly at every meeting shall appoint a Committee of Bills and Overtures, to prepare and digest business for the Assembly. Any person thinking himself aggrieved by this committee may complain to the Assembly."—*Minutes*, 1789, p. 8.

b. "Petitions, questions relating either to doctrine or order, intended to be brought before the Assembly for decision, and in general, all new propositions tending to general laws, shall usually be laid before the Committee of Bills and Overtures before they be offered to the Assembly." —*Minutes*, 1819, p. 718. [See Rules 4 and 5, p. 168.]

II. Judicial Committee.

"The Assembly shall also at every meeting appoint a committee, to be styled the Judicial Committee, whose duty it shall be to take into consideration all appeals and references brought to the Assembly; to ascertain whether they are in order; to digest and arrange all the documents relating to the same; and to propose to the Assembly the best method of proceeding in each case."—*Minutes*, 1819, p. 718. [See Rule 6, p. 168.]

III. Committee on Polity of the Church.

"*Resolved*, That a Committee of seven members be appointed on the Polity of the Church; and that it be referred to this committee to examine and settle the true roll of the Presbyteries and Synods connected with the Assembly; and that they receive the reports of the several Presbyteries on amending the Constitution of the Church."—*Minutes*, 1840, p. 7.

IV. Committee on Church Extension.

"There shall hereafter be appointed, with the other standing committees of the General Assembly, one on Church Extension, to whom shall be committed, at an early period of their sessions, the Synodical and Presbyterial reports on the subject, whose duty it shall be to present a condensed view of them to the Assembly, with such further propositions to promote this work as they may deem desirable. This standing committee shall be required to report as soon as a faithful discharge of its duties will permit."—*Minutes*, 1852, p. 172.

V. Committee on Education.

VI. Committee on Publication.

"*Resolved*, That hereafter there be appointed, at the opening of each Assembly, Standing Committees on Education and Publication, to whom may be referred appropriate reports and communications."—*Minutes*, 1856, p. 192.

VII. Committee on Devotional Exercises.

"*Resolved*, That it be hereafter a standing rule of the General Assembly to spend the first Wednesday of their sessions in religious exercises, as follows, viz.:

"It is recommended that each member should spend from eight till nine o'clock, A. M. of that day in secret devotion. At ten, the Assembly shall meet together, and spend a season in prayer, praise, reading the Scriptures, and exhortation. In the afternoon, there shall be a public meeting of the Assembly, with all who may choose to convene with them, to engage again in religious exercises.

"Each Assembly shall, at an early period of its sessions, appoint a committee to make arrangements for the observance of this day, in conformity with the above general plan."—*Minutes*, 1828, p. 239.

VIII. Committee on the Narrative.

The following proposition was introduced through the Committee of Bills and Overtures, viz.:

"That the General Assembly take measures to bring into distinct view, at its different sessions, the situation of the Presbyterian Church under its jurisdiction in the United States of America, with respect to the state of religion in the different Presbyteries, the state of religious denominations amongst them, and the most probable expedients for reviving and promoting the essential interests of Christ's kingdom in the world; whereupon—

"*Resolved*, That it be recommended to each Synod to enjoin it upon the respective Presbyteries within their bounds, to specify the above particulars in the annual reports which they make of the state of their respective churches, to be laid before the General Assembly at its stated meetings."—*Minutes*, 1792, p. 59.

Narrative to notice the Decease of Ministers.

"*Resolved*, That the narrative on the state of religion annually contain a notice of the decease of all the ministers of our Church, who may have been removed by death during the preceding year; and the several Presbyteries are ordered to incorporate with their reports on the state of religion, made to the Assembly, the case of every such removal within their bounds."—*Minutes*, 1822, p. 38.

IX. Committee on Leave of Absence.

"*Resolved*, That, as a standing rule of the Assembly, a committee of five be appointed, whose duty it shall be to consider all applications for leave of absence, with power to decide on the same, in place of the house, and with instructions to require in every case satisfactory reasons for the necessity of such absence, and report to the house, at the commencement of every session, the members so dismissed; and that an appeal to the Assembly may be made in any instance of refusal on the part of the committee to grant the application."—*Minutes*, 1833, p. 390.

X. Committee on Mileage.

"*Resolved*, That the members entitled to mileage shall give to the Committee on the Commissioners' Fund, within three days after the appointment of said committee, in writing, their names, the names of their Presbyteries, and their distance from home to the Assembly; and if any member neglects to comply with this resolution, he shall forfeit his portion of said fund. And that no member may be ignorant of this resolution, the moderator shall read it as soon as the committee on said fund is appointed each year."—*Minutes*, 1818, p. 687.

"The Committee on Mileage reported in part, when it was

"*Resolved*, That the commissioners from Newburyport, Clinton, and Madison be struck off from the list of applicants for a portion of the commissioners' fund, on the ground that their respective Presbyteries have paid nothing into this fund.

"*Resolved further*, That the commissioners from the following Presbyteries, viz., Cortland, Genesee, Onondaga, Oswego, Rochester, and Ontario be allowed to draw from the commissioners' fund only the amount that their Presbyteries have respectively paid in."—*Minutes*, 1833, p. 404.

"It is hereby ordered, that no commissioner who shall obtain leave of absence within the first six days of the sessions shall be entitled to receive anything from the commissioners' fund, unless the General Assembly shall order otherwise, when the reasons of the application are given."—*Minutes*, 1827, p. 207.

XI. Committee on Foreign Missions.

"*Resolved*, That a *standing* Committee on Foreign Missions be annually appointed, who shall have charge of this general subject in the sessions of the Assembly."—*Minutes*, 1858, p. 596.

20. *Commissioners' Fund.*

a. "1. *Resolved*, That it be, and hereby is earnestly recommended to the several Presbyteries, and all the ministers under the care of the General Assembly, to urge upon the people under their care the equity, the importance, and the absolute necessity of contributing to the commissioners' fund, in order to secure the attendance of commissioners at the sessions of the General Assembly, from those sections of the Church which are at the greatest distance from the place of the Assembly's meetings, and which in the Divine Providence are least able to sustain the burden of expense, both of time and money, in giving such attendance.

"2. *Resolved*, That in the judgment of this General Assembly, those Presbyteries that are wealthy, and that have judged it proper to pay the expenses of their own commissioners, are bound in a peculiar manner to contribute liberally to the general fund, in order that they may bear their due proportion of the expenses of commissioners who attend from distant Presbyteries; which Presbyteries and their commissioners, in the Providence of God, are not able to pay their own expenses; and this General Assembly would fain hope that the wealthy Presbyteries will esteem it both their privilege and their duty to make such contributions."—*Minutes*, 1833, p. 410.

b. "The committee to whom was referred the subject of mileage, presented a report, which was adopted, and is as follows:

"The commissioners' fund is distributed at the present time in the following manner: The money contributed for the general fund is paid into the hands of the Committee on Mileage, and distributed to such commissioners as claim it (whose Presbyteries have contributed anything to the fund, and who have not otherwise been paid), according to the number of miles each has travelled to the place of meeting.

"This mode of distribution appears to be as simple and equitable as any that can be adopted; and the committee recommend that it remain unchanged.

"Our Form of Government, chap. xxii, sec. 3, makes it proper for each Presbytery to pay its own commissioners; consequently, if any Presbytery shall choose to do so, the Assembly cannot *require* them to contribute to the general fund; but it is most earnestly *recommended* to the older and abler Presbyteries, in view of the wide extent of our Church, and the great importance of our rising Presbyteries being represented in the meetings of the Assembly, if they shall still choose to exercise their right to pay their own commissioners in full, that they be particular in making additional collections for the general fund, so that the younger and feebler Presbyteries may be fully represented. And it is hereby made the duty of the stated clerk to give due notice of this recommendation previous to the meeting of the General Assembly."—*Minutes*, 1851, p. 24.

c. "The Committee on the Polity of the Church made the following report, which was adopted:

"Whereas, a full representation, both of ministers and of elders, from all the Presbyteries, is essential to the efficiency and welfare of the Church; and whereas this can be secured only by the co-operation of all the Presbyteries in raising an adequate fund to defray the necessary expenses of all the commissioners to the Assembly. Therefore,

"*Resolved*, 1. That there be a Permanent Committee on Mileage, of which the stated clerk shall be *ex officio* a member, who shall estimate the probable amount that will be required to defray the travelling expenses of commissioners and the contingent expenses of the Assembly, shall apportion the same to the several Presbyteries, and recommend to them prompt measures to secure the amount,—the apportionment for each successive Assembly to be reported to the preceding Assembly. And if any Presbytery supposes its apportionment unjust, it may make representation to the Permanent Committee on Mileage, who shall reconsider their case, and make such changes as they shall deem proper.

"*Resolved*, 2. That on the fourth day after the opening of the Assembly, the Presbyteries be called upon to report, whether the amount assigned them has been paid into the treasury of the Assembly.

"*Resolved*, 3. That the commissioners to the Assembly, whose Presbyteries have paid the amounts assigned them, are expected, within four days after the opening of the Assembly, to present a bill of their necessary travelling expenses to the Permanent Committee on Mileage, to be audited by them, and paid in equal proportions according to the funds furnished by those Presbyteries.

"*Resolved*, 4. That since the question has arisen, whether this plan is constitutional, it be referred to the Presbyteries for their approval; and, if approved, it shall become part of the Constitution, and all prior regulations of the Assembly on the subject of mileage, inconsistent with these regulations, shall be rescinded."—*Minutes*, 1856, pp. 216, 217.

d. "The Committee on the Polity of the Church reported that fifty Presbyteries had taken action upon the overture on the subject of mileage, thirty-one answering in the affirmative, and nineteen in the negative; and, as a majority of all the Presbyteries had taken no action upon the subject, that the overture was not adopted. The whole subject was again referred to the Committee on the Polity of the Church."—*Minutes*, 1857, p. 380.

"The Committee on the Polity of the Church, to whom was referred the consideration of a permanent system of mileage, present the following report:

"The Constitution affirms that, 'in order, as far as possible, to procure a respectable and full delegation to all our judicatories, it is proper that the expenses of ministers and elders, in their attendance on these judicatories, be defrayed by the bodies which they respectively represent.'

"The following recommendations are therefore submitted:

"That each Presbytery be earnestly requested to contribute annually their full proportion towards the expenses of our General Assemblies.

"That this proportion be determined by the number of communicants connected with the Presbytery.

"That the rate, *per capita*, for the next Assembly be five (5) cents for each communicant.

"That each Presbytery be at liberty to apportion their quota among their churches as they shall deem best.

"That the Standing Committee on Mileage, annually appointed, estimate and report the probable amount that will be needed to defray the necessary travelling expenses of the commissioners, and the contingent expenses of the next succeeding Assembly, together with the rate that will be adequate.

"That, on or before the fourth day of the sessions of each Assembly, the amount thus contributed be paid to the Committee on Mileage, and a bill be presented by each commissioner of his necessary travelling expenses and mileage.

"That these bills, having been duly audited by the Mileage Committee, be paid as fully as the funds will permit, after appropriating an amount sufficient to defray the contingent expenses of the Assembly.

"That each minister and vacant church connected with those Presbyteries who have contributed their full quota to this fund be entitled to a copy of the annual Minutes.

"That, in order to avail themselves of the privileges of this plan, the Presbyteries must contribute and forward to the Assembly, their full proportion of this fund as thus determined. The report was adopted." —*Minutes*, 1857, pp. 399, 400.

21. *Contingent Fund.*

"*Resolved*, That it be recommended to the congregations under the care of this Assembly to make annually a collection for a contingent fund to defray the incidental expenses of the Assembly, such as recording and printing the Minutes, clerks' salaries, janitor's bill, stationery, and expenses of delegates to corresponding bodies.

"*Resolved*, That this collection be reported annually by the congregations to their respective Presbyteries; and by the Presbyteries be paid over to the treasurer of the Trustees of the General Assembly, and be reported in the annual report to the Assembly."—*Minutes*, 1830, p. 305. [See above, p. 182.]

22. *The Publication and Distribution of the Minutes.*

"The committee would submit to the Assembly the following plan for the publication of the Minutes in future, viz.: That each Presbytery shall forward to the treasurer, for the contingent fund of the Assembly, at or before the meeting of the Assembly in each year, a sum equal to 31¼ cents for each member of the Presbytery, and for any licentiate or other person who shall desire the Minutes, and whose post-office address shall be given. And the stated clerk shall not forward the Minutes to the members of any Presbytery from which no such remittance shall be made; but only to the stated clerk of such Presbytery, and to such members as shall forward the sum above stated. Adopted."—*Minutes*, 1836, p. 277.

"The price, either with or without postage, of a copy of the Annual Minutes, with the usual appendix, is forty cents. Every Presbytery that contributes to the contingent fund an amount equal to forty cents for each minister, will have one copy of the Minutes forwarded by mail, as soon as published, to each of its ministers whose post-office address is given in the Statistical Report. The Minutes will also be sent, free of postage, when ordered, to any address at the same rate. The postage on all orders must be prepaid.

"Agreeably to a resolution of the Assembly, a copy of the Minutes will be sent, post-paid, to each of the stated clerks of the Presbyteries and Synods, for the use of those bodies respectively."—*Minutes*, 1854, p. 540 (Appendix).

23. *The Charter of the Trustees of the Assembly.*

An Act for incorporating the Trustees of the Ministers and Elders constituting the General Assembly of the Presbyterian Church in the United States of America.

"*Whereas*, The ministers and elders forming the General Assembly of the Presbyterian Church of the United States of America, consisting of citizens of the State of Pennsylvania, and of others of the United States aforesaid, have by their petition represented, that by donations, bequests, or otherwise, of charitably disposed persons, they are possessed of moneys for benevolent and pious purposes; and the said ministers and elders have reason to expect farther contributions for similar uses; but from the scattered situation of the said ministers and elders, and other causes, the said ministers and elders find it extremely difficult to manage the said funds in the way best calculated to answer the intention of the donors; therefore—

"SEC. 1. Be it enacted by the Senate and House of Representatives of the Commonwealth of Pennsylvania in General Assembly met, and it is hereby enacted by the authority of the same, That John Rodgers, Alexander McWhorter, Samuel Stanhope Smith, Ashbel Green, William M. Tennent, Patrick Allison, Nathan Irvin, Joseph Clark, Andrew Hunter, Jared Ingersoll, Robert Ralston, Jonathan B. Smith, Andrew Bayard, Elias Boudinot, John Nelson, Ebenezer Hazard, David Jackson, and Robert Smith, merchant, and their successors duly elected and appointed in manner as is hereinafter directed, be, and they are hereby made, declared, and constituted a corporation and body politic and corporate, in law and in fact, to have continuance forever, by the name, style, and title of 'Trustees of the General Assembly of the Presbyterian Church in the United States of America;' and by the name, style, and title aforesaid, shall, forever hereafter, be persons able and capable in law as well to take, receive, and hold, all and all manner of lands, tenements, rents, annuities, franchises, and other hereditaments, which at any time or times heretofore have been granted, bargained, sold, enfeoffed, released, devised, or otherwise conveyed, to the said ministers and elders of the General Assembly of the Presbyterian Church of the

United States, or any other person or persons, to their use, or in trust for them; and the same lands, tenements, rents, annuities, liberties, franchises, and other hereditaments, are hereby vested and established in the said corporation, and their successors forever, according to the original use and intent for which such devises, gifts, and grants, were respectively made; and the said corporation and their successors are hereby declared to be seized and possessed of such estate and estates therein as by and in the respective grants, bargains, sales, enfeoffments, releases, devises, and other conveyances thereof, is or are declared limited and expressed; also, that the said corporation and their successors, at all times hereafter, shall be capable and able to purchase, have, receive, take, hold, and enjoy, in fee simple, or of lesser estate or estates, any lands, tenements, rents, annuities, franchises, and other hereditaments, by the gift, grant, bargain, sale, alienation, enfeoffment, release, confirmation, or devise, of any person or persons, bodies politic and corporate, capable and able to make the same: And farther, that the said ministers and elders, under the corporate name aforesaid, and their successors, may take and receive any sum or sums of money, and any portion of goods and chattels, that have been given to the said ministers and elders, or that hereafter shall be given, sold, leased, or bequeathed to the said corporation by any person or persons, bodies politic or corporate, that is able or capable to make a gift, sale, bequest, or other disposal of the same; such money, goods, or chattels, to be laid out and disposed of for the use and benefit of the aforesaid corporation, agreeably to the intention of the donors, and according to the objects, articles, and conditions of this act.

"Sec. 2. And be it further enacted by the authority aforesaid, That no misnomer of the said corporation and their successors shall defeat or annul any gift, grant, devise, or bequest, to or from the said corporation, provided the intent of the party or parties shall sufficiently appear upon the face of the gift, will, grant, or other writing, whereby any estate or interest was intended to pass to or from the said corporation.

"Sec. 3. And be it further enacted by the authority aforesaid, That the said corporation and their successors shall have full power and authority to make, have, and use one common seal, with such device and inscription as they shall think fit and proper; and the same to break, alter, and renew, at their pleasure.

"Sec. 4. And be it further enacted by the authority aforesaid, That the said corporation and their successors, by the name, style, and title aforesaid, shall be able and capable in law to sue and be sued, plead and be impleaded, in any court, or before any judge or justice, in all and all manner of suits, complaints, pleas, matters, and demands, of whatsoever nature, kind, and form they may be; and all and every matter and thing to do, in as full and effectual a manner as any other person, bodies politic or corporate, within this Commonwealth, may or can do.

"SEC. 5. And be it further enacted by the authority aforesaid, That the said corporation and their successors shall be, and hereby are authorized and empowered to make, ordain, and establish by-laws and ordinances, and do everything incident and needful for the support and due government of the said corporation, and managing the funds and revenues thereof: provided, the said by-laws be not repugnant to the Constitution and laws of the United States, to the Constitution and laws of this Commonwealth, or to this act.

"SEC. 6. And be it further enacted by the authority aforesaid, That the said corporation shall not at any time consist of more than eighteen persons; whereof the said General Assembly may, at their discretion, as often as they shall hold their sessions in the State of Pennsylvania, change one-third in such manner as to the said General Assembly shall seem proper; and the corporation aforesaid shall have power and authority to manage and dispose of all moneys, goods, chattels, lands, tenements, and hereditaments, and other estate whatsoever, committed to their care and trust by the said General Assembly; but in cases where special instructions for the management and disposal thereof shall be given by the said General Assembly in writing, under the hand of their clerk, it shall be the duty of the said corporation to act according to such instructions: provided, the said instructions shall not be repugnant to the Constitution and laws of the United States, or to the Constitution and laws of this Commonwealth, or to the provisions and restrictions in this act contained.

"SEC. 7. And be it further enacted by the authority aforesaid, That six members of this corporation, whereof the president, or in his absence the vice-president, to be one, shall be a sufficient number to transact the business thereof, and to make by-laws, rules, and regulations: provided, that previous to any meeting of the board or corporation, for such purposes, not appointed by adjournment, ten days' notice shall be previously given thereof, in at least one of the newspapers printed in the city of Philadelphia. And the said corporation shall and may, as often as they shall see proper, and according to the rules by them to be prescribed, choose out of their number, a president and vice-president, and shall have authority to appoint a treasurer, and such other officers and servants as shall by them, the said corporation, be deemed necessary; to which officers the said corporation may assign such a compensation for their services, and such duties to be performed by them, to continue in office for such time, and to be succeeded by others, in such way and manner as the said corporation shall direct.

"SEC. 8. And be it further enacted by the authority aforesaid, That all questions before the said corporation, shall be decided by a plurality of votes, whereof each member present shall have one, except the president, or vice-president when acting as president, who shall have only the casting voice and vote, in case of an equality in the votes of the other members.

"SEC. 9. And be it further enacted by the authority aforesaid, That the said corporation shall keep regular and fair entries of their proceedings, and a just account of their receipts and disbursements, in a book or books to be provided for that purpose; and their treasurer shall, once in a year, exhibit to the General Assembly of the Presbyterian Church in the United States of America, an exact state of the accounts of the corporation.

"SEC. 10. And be it further enacted by the authority aforesaid, That the said corporation may take, receive, purchase, possess and enjoy, messuages, houses, lands, tenements, rents, annuities, and other hereditaments, real and personal estate of any amount not exceeding ten thousand dollars a year value, but the said limitations not to be considered as including the annual collections and voluntary contributions made in the churches under the care of the said General Assembly.

"CADWALADER EVANS, JR.,
"*Speaker of the House of Representatives.*
"ROBERT HARE,
"*Speaker of the Senate.*

"Approved March 28, 1799.

"THOMAS MIFFLIN,
"*Governor of the Commonwealth of Pennsylvania.*"
—*Minutes*, 1799, pp. 173, 175.

24. *Mode of Electing the Trustees.*

"*Resolved*, That it is expedient to adopt and recommend the following system:

"1. That when this subject is called up annually, a vote shall first be taken whether for the current year the Assembly will or will not make any election of members in the Board of Trustees.

"2. If an election be determined on, the day on which it shall take place shall be specified, and shall not be within less than two days of the time at which such election shall be decided on.

"3. When the day of election arrives, the Assembly shall ascertain what vacancies in the number of the eighteen trustees incorporated, have taken place, by death or otherwise, and shall first proceed to choose other members in their places. When this is accomplished, they shall proceed to the trial whether they will elect any, and if any, how many of that third of the number of the trustees which by law they are permitted to change, in the following manner, viz.: The list of the trustees shall be taken, and a vote be had for a person to fill the place of him who is first on the list. In voting for a person to fill said place, the vote may be given either for the person who has before filled it, or for any other person. If the majority of votes shall be given for the person who has before filled it, he shall continue in office. If the majority of votes shall be given for another person, this person is a trustee duly chosen in place of the former. In the same form the Assembly shall proceed with the list, till they have either changed one-third of the trustees (always including in the third those who have been elected by the sitting Assembly, to supply the places become vacant by death or otherwise), or by going through the list, shall determine that no farther alteration shall be made."—*Minutes*, 1801, p. 217.

Rules for Intercourse between the Trustees and the Assembly.

"The committee appointed to meet a committee of the Board of Trustees of the Assembly, to digest and prepare a regular and stated mode of intercourse between the Assembly and the trustees, made a report, which was read and approved, as follows, viz.:

"That the management and disposal of all moneys, goods, chattels, lands, tenements, hereditaments, and all other estate whatever, committed to their care and trust by the General Assembly, is invested in the said trustees; unless where special instructions for the management and disposal thereof shall be given by the General Assembly in writing under the hand of their clerk; in which case, the corporation is to act according to said instructions. That an exact state of the accounts of the trustees is to be exhibited by their treasurer to the General Assembly, once in every year; whereupon it is recommended,

"1. That this state of the accounts be laid before the General Assembly as early in their sessions as possible, in order that the General Assembly may know what appropriations it may be in their power to make, or what instructions to give to their trustees, respecting the moneys in hand.

"2. That when any appropriations are made by the General Assembly, a copy of their minute for that purpose, signed by the clerk, shall be transmitted to the trustees, and shall be their warrant for the payment of all moneys thus appropriated.

"3. That when any measures are taken, or any resolutions adopted by the General Assembly, or the Board of Trustees, which it concerns the other to be acquainted with, due information of the same shall be given, as soon as possible, to the other."—*Minutes*, 1801, p. 232.

25. *Powers of the General Assembly.*

[The Assembly has exercised the power *Of transferring churches from one Synod and Presbytery to another.*—*Minutes*, 1824, p. 105; 1827, p. 201, 202, 205; 1829, p. 260; 1831, p. 324.

Usually the record states the consent of the parties interested.

Of forming new Presbyteries. Huntingdon, Minutes, 1794, p. 89; Columbia and Oneida, 1802, p. 252. In this case: "Whereas, doubts arose, whether it is proper for the Assembly to interfere for the purpose of making such division (of the Presbytery of Albany),—the proposal not having first been laid before the Synod,—as it would establish a precedent which might tend to confusion, and in the end to schism. The Assembly think it expedient to declare, that their decision in this case has been particularly influenced by the pressure of circumstances, and is not to be considered a precedent for future conduct." Oneida, 1805, p. 324; Chenango, 1826, p. 176; Detroit, 1827, p. 206; Philadelphia 2d, 1832, p. 361; Philadelphia 3d, 1836, p. 278; San Francisco, 1849, p. 176; Milwaukie, 1851, p. 15; Sierra Nevada and San José, 1857, p. 383.

Of dividing Presbyteries. Either to alter their bounds or to form new Presbyteries.—Minutes, *passim*.

Of dissolving Presbyteries. Philadelphia 3d. Minutes, 1837, p. 472.

Of erecting Synods. Chap. v, sec. 2.

Of dividing Synods and changing their boundaries.

Of managing the whole business of Missions. Minutes, 1791, p. 38; 1802, p. 226; 1809, p. 427. See chap. ix.

Powers with reference to slavery. See chap. vii, sec. 9.]

26. *The Assembly will not ordinarily decide questions in thesi.*

a. "But while the General Assembly is invested with the power of deciding in all controversies, respecting doctrine and discipline; of reproving, warning, or bearing testimony against error in doctrine in any church, Presbytery, or Synod; or of suppressing schismatical contentions and disputations, all such matters ought to be brought before the Assembly in a regular and constitutional way. And it does not appear that the Constitution ever designed that the General Assembly should take up abstract cases, and decide on them, especially when the object appears to be to bring those decisions to bear on particular individuals, not judicially before the Assembly. Neither does it appear, that the Constitution of the Church intended that any person or persons should have the privilege of presenting for decision, remonstrances, respecting points of doctrine, on the conduct of individuals, not brought up from the inferior judicatories, by appeal, reference, or complaint; and this especially, when such remonstrances contain no evidence whatsoever, of the facts alleged, but mere statements, of the truth or justness of which the Assembly have no means of judging, inasmuch as a contrary course would allow of counter and contradictory remonstrances, without end."—*Minutes,* 1822, p. 50.

b. "It is ordinarily undesirable for the General Assembly to decide questions *in thesi,* which are liable to be brought before it in its judicial capacity, as it may thus virtually prejudge cases of discipline; it appears better that it should ordinarily follow, in this respect, the uniform practice of civil courts, to decide legal principles only upon actual cases presented."—*Minutes,* 1856, p. 213.

CHAPTER VI.

OF DISCIPLINE.

SECTION 1.—GENERAL PRINCIPLES.

1. Censure, without trial, is informal; and connecting names with charges of a serious nature, without evidence, disapproved of.—Circulating evil reports, not in the performance of indispensable duty, is slander.—Ministers are not to be excluded from the pulpits of the churches, nor members from communion, without trial.—2. The charges must be specific.—*a.* What must be specified in a charge of heresy.—3. The rules must be observed. An appeal is sustained, because the judicature did not observe the constitutional rules. The defendant is entitled to a copy of the proceedings.—*a.* A judgment of Synod reversed; four reasons assigned.—*b.* An appeal may not be entertained when due notice has not been given; nor may the fact of an appeal be established otherwise than as ordered by the book.—*c.* A superior judicature may not try a man when there is no reference or appeal before it.—*d.* An unconstitutional act ordered to be reversed; but the order for a new trial does not restore the defendant.—4. The authority for judicial oaths.—5. Testimony in a judicial case should be under oath.—6. A husband and wife may be joint witnesses, but great care should be taken to guard against collusion.—7. The accused should be present at his trial. Having excused himself by letter for non-attendance, he is not guilty of contumacy.—8. A disproportionate censure will not be sustained; either in case the charges are not fully substantiated, or the sentence too severe. On an appeal, the judicatory may not pass a new sentence.—9. Suspension from the ministry, during process. For a specified time.—10. When an elder has been suspended from church privileges, removal of suspension does not restore him to office. He can be restored to office only by express act of the Session, and acquiescence of the church.—11. A suspended minister is not to be regarded as possessing the rights of a common Christian in good standing.—12. Deposition and excommunication are distinct acts.—13. When deposed ministers continue to perform ministerial functions, their names are to be published.—14. Refusal to submit to the decision debars the right of petition.—15. Refusal to submit does not invalidate the sentence.—16. A Presbytery is censured for restoring a man without due evidence of penitence; but—17. When a minister has been restored he can be deprived of his office only by a new process and

conviction.—18. New trial may be had on new testimony. If it seem desirable for a court to review its decisions without new testimony, it should refer the case to the next higher judicatory.—19. A Synod corrects its own hasty action, and is sustained; but a judicatory may not call back a case after an appeal has been taken.—20. The accused, on trial, has no right to introduce testimony which would inculpate others not on trial.—21. The Assembly cannot reverse the judicial acts of a former Assembly, unless in case of error.—22. The decisions of the superior courts are binding on the inferior.—23. The judicial sentences of sister churches are to be respected.

1. *Censure without trial informal.*

a. "Messrs. Ker and Rankin, the commissioners to this Assembly from the Presbytery of Lewes, in behalf and by the order of the said Presbytery, applied to the Assembly, and remonstrated against a decision of the last Assembly, in the case of Mr. Hindman, in which they conceive the Presbytery of Lewes is virtually condemned, without their having had an opportunity of defending themselves, which they conceive they could readily have done.

"After considerable discussion, it was

"*Resolved*, As the sense of this house, that no man, or body of men, agreeably to the Constitution of this Church, ought to be condemned, or censured, without having notice of the accusation against him or them, and notice given for trial. And therefore, that if the General Assembly of last year meant, by the minute in question, to pass a censure on the Presbytery of Lewes, it was informal."—*Minutes*, 1793, p. 71.

b. "The committee appointed to examine the records of the Synod of the Carolinas reported, and the book was approved to page 28 of the twenty-third sessions of said Synod, with the exception of the resolution to make a minister liable to suspension without trial, for three years' absence from Synod, without sending forward his reasons for absence."—*Minutes*, 1811, p. 468.

Censure upon an Absent Person, without Citation, disapproved of.

c. "The Assembly moreover cannot forbear expressing their regret that the Presbytery of Washington should have passed a vote of censure upon Mr. McCalla, without citing him to appear before them, or giving him any opportunity of making a defence; since this mode of proceeding seems to have occasioned a portion of the irregularity in the Presbytery of West Lexington, of which the Presbytery of Washington have complained."—*Minutes*, 1821, p. 21.

Names should not be connected with serious Charges, unless in connection with a Prosecution.

d. "That while it is unquestionably the privilege of individuals and members of the Presbyterian Church, when they think they see the peace, purity, or prosperity of the Church in danger, either from an individual, or from an inferior court, to apply to the General Assembly, in an orderly manner, for redress or direction; yet, in such cases, unless they mean to come forward as prosecutors, with the necessary testimony, they should most carefully avoid mentioning names connected with charges of the most serious kind, in support of which no evidence has been orderly adduced; nor have the individuals thus accused had an opportunity of replying to those charges, or of making any defence of themselves. The Assembly, therefore, cannot witness a procedure of this kind, without expressing their disapprobation of it."—*Minutes*, 1824, p. 113.

To circulate Evil Reports, not in the way of Duty, is Slander.

e. "*Resolved*, That the Assembly sustain the appeals of the Session of the church of Bloomington, and of Dr. Wylie, against a decision of the Synod of Indiana; and the judgment of the Presbytery and Session is hereby confirmed, on the ground that Mr. Harney circulated evil reports against Dr. Wylie, without showing that he did it in the due performance of some indispensable duty; but it is the judgment of this Assembly, that Mr. Harney shall still have the privilege, if he desire it, of commencing a prosecution against Dr. Wylie, before the Presbytery of Vincennes; and in such case, said Presbytery are hereby authorized and directed to hear the whole cause, and issue the same in a constitutional way."—*Minutes*, 1834, p. 443.

Ministers may not be Excluded from the Pulpits of the Churches, nor Members from Communion, without Trial.

f. "Whereas, it appears from memorials sent up to this Assembly, that several of our Presbyteries have adopted resolutions excluding slaveholders from their pulpits, and from their communion; and whereas, our

Constitution requires that no member of the Presbyterian Church shall be thus disfranchised, without a regular trial and conviction; and whereas, this proceeding is a repetition of the exscinding acts of the New Basis Assembly, against which we have taken our stand as friends of the Constitution. Therefore,

"*Resolved,* That the said Presbyteries be requested to rescind such resolutions."—*Minutes,* 1840, p. 24.

2. *Charges must be Specific.*

a. "The Synod orders that all their judicatures shall, for the future, be particularly careful not to receive or judge of any charges, but such as shall be seasonably reduced to a specialty in the complaint laid before them."—*Minutes,* 1770, p. 406.

b. "There was a great deficiency in the charges preferred against Mr. Craighead, as it relates to precision. All charges for heresy should be as definite as possible. The article or articles of faith impugned should be specified, and the words supposed to be heretical shown to be in repugnance to these articles, whether the reference is made directly to the Scripture as a standard of orthodoxy, or to the Confession of Faith, which our Church holds to be a summary of the doctrines of Scripture."—*Minutes,* 1824, p. 121.

3. *The Rules must be Observed.*

a. "The Assembly sustained the appeal of Mr. Arthur from the sentence of the Presbytery, by which he was suspended from the Gospel ministry, on the ground of contumacy, because the Presbytery appeared to have been precipitate, and not to have observed the constitutional rules. See Discipline, chap. iv, secs. 6, 10, and 11. They deem, too, the request of Mr. Arthur, for a copy of the first sentence, to have been reasonable, and that it ought to have been complied with. But the appeal from the first sentence, by which the charge of slander, preferred against him by the Rev. Joshua L. Wilson, was declared to be substantiated, and Mr. Arthur required to submit to a rebuke, the Assembly could not sustain. For, although the Assembly noticed the omission of Presbytery to assign Mr. Arthur counsel to manage his defence (see Discipline, chap. iv, sec. 13), yet they did judge the pamphlet, of which Mr. Arthur admitted himself to be the author, to contain slander against

Mr. Wilson, and could not but disapprove of the spirit, under the influence of which it appeared to have been written."—*Minutes*, 1822, p. 53.

Judgment of the Synod of Genesee Reversed.

b. On the complaint of William H. Beecher and others against the Synod of Genesee, in the case of the appeal of Dr. Frank from the decision of the Presbytery of Genesee, the General Assembly *sustain the complaint*, and reverse the judgment of the Synod on the following grounds, viz.:

"1. That the merits of the case seem to be expressly declined by the Synod, as the subject-matter of adjudication.

"2. That the Synod appear not to have adhered to the alternatives prescribed by the Constitution. See Book of Discipline, chap. vii, sec. 3, sub-section 10.

"3. That the Synod seem to have forgotten the nature and the limits of their appellate, as distinguished from the original jurisdiction in the case,—in that they censure at their bar the appellant, in a way competent, in any circumstances, only to the Session of the church to which the appellant was primarily amenable.

"4. That they seem to have forgotten also, in restoring the appellant, that some expression of repentance ought to have been exacted, especially if their reprimand could, from any tribunal, have been deserved.

"The Assembly therefore rule that the Synod of Genesee should review their proceedings in this case, and regarding alike the rules of the Constitution and the merits of the case, that they proceed to issue the same with equity and wisdom."—*Minutes*, 1840, p. 11.

Due Notice of an Appeal must be given.

c. "The records of the Synod of Utica were approved, with the following exceptions:

"1. That the Synod issued an appeal from the inferior judicatory, when it appeared before them that an appellant had not given notice in writing that he should appeal, with his reasons assigned for appealing, as required by the Book of Discipline, before the rising of the judicatory appealed from, or within ten days thereafter.

"2. That the Synod violated the principles of the Constitution in qualifying the members of the inferior judicatory to ascertain whether an appeal had been given, when the Book of Discipline requires that the appeal shall be lodged in the hands of the moderator; and further, that the inferior judicatory shall send authentic copies of all the records, and of all the testimony relating to the matter of appeal, up to the Synod, whose duty it is to issue the appeal, when found to be in order, and in accordance with the Book of Discipline."—*Minutes*, 1840, p. 12.

A Superior Judicatory may not try a Man on review of Records.

d. "In the case of the appeal of W. C. Davis, the Assembly—

"*Resolved*, That although they highly approve of the zeal of the Synod to preserve the purity and peace of the Church within their bounds, yet they cannot but decide that in their proceedings in the above case, in deciding that they had a right to try Mr. Davis, when there was no reference nor appeal in his case before them, they have not strictly adhered to the Constitution of the Presbyterian Church."—*Minutes*, 1810, p. 448.

Unconstitutional Action ordered to be reversed.

e. "The proceedings of the Synod of Cincinnati, in the institution and prosecution of judicial process against William Graham, subjecting him first to censure, and afterwards to suspension, under which he now labors, are unconstitutional and irregular, and therefore null and void; and the Synod is hereby enjoined to take constitutional action in the case, and to revise and correct its proceedings accordingly.

"While the Assembly thus speaks on the constitutionality of the matter, they do it without reference to the error or truth of the sentiments he advanced."—*Minutes*, 1846, pp. 31, 32.

An Order for a New Trial does not restore the Defendant.

"It was—

"*Resolved*, That the General Assembly do not intend by the above decision to restore Mr. Graham to his ministerial standing; that action being left entirely to the Synod."—*Ibid.* p. 33.

4. *The Authority for Judicial Oaths.*

"The committee appointed to draft an answer to the following question, overtured from the Presbytery of Georgia, viz., 'Whence do the General Assembly derive authority to empower the moderator of a church session to administer an oath?' reported the following, which was adopted, viz.: 'An oath for confirmation (saith the Apostle), is to men an end of all strife.' Heb. 6 : 16. It is a solemn affirmation, wherein we appeal to God as the witness of the truth of what we say, and with an imprecation of his vengeance if what we affirm is false, or what we promise be not performed. Its force results from a belief that God will punish false swearing with more severity than a simple lie, or breach of promise; because perjury is a sin of greater deliberation, and violates superior confidence.

That oaths are lawful is evident from the fact that our Lord, when interrogated on certain occasions, answered upon oath. See Matt. 26 : 63, 64. Paul also uses several expressions which contain the nature of an oath. See Rom. 1 : 9; 9 : 1; 1 Cor. 15 : 31; 2 Cor. 1 : 18; Gal. 1 : 20. They are solemn appeals to God. It is manifest that oaths are not to be used on light or trivial occasions. We are expressly commanded not to take God's name in vain. But as the Bible does not point out the particular occasions when oaths are to be used, nor the persons who are to administer them, these circumstances are left to the discretion of individuals and communities. The necessity of oaths is founded in expediency; and all associations, whether civil or ecclesiastical, have a right to use them for confirmation, when, in the exercise of a sound discretion, they are deemed important. It is lawful for every community, in the compact on which their union is founded, to point out the cases in which oaths shall be used, and who shall administer them. The authority of moderators in the Presbyterian Church to administer oaths is not derived from the General Assembly, but from the Constitution, or articles of compact, which our churches have adopted, and by which they have agreed to be governed as a Christian community. It may be proper also to add, that the oaths prescribed by ecclesiastical authority, and administered by civil authority, in no respect interfere with our relations to civil society. Nor can the administering of them, if rightly viewed, be considered as a violation of those laws of the State which prescribe the manner in which civil oaths shall be administered."—*Minutes*, 1823, pp. 87, 88.

5. *Testimony in a Judicial Case should be under Oath.*

"There is only one other thing in the proceedings on which the General Assembly will remark; which is, that statements were given as evidence by the members of Presbytery which are not recorded, and which do not appear to have been given under the usual solemnity of an oath." [Craighead's case.]—*Minutes*, 1824, p. 122.

6. *A Husband and Wife may be Joint Witnesses.*

"The Assembly went into the consideration of the case reported by the Presbytery of Ohio, which was in the following terms, viz.: 'A certain married woman charges an unmarried man with immodest conversation and conduct in attempts upon her chastity, of which her husband and another, or indifferent person, were at a certain time witnesses. Whereas our Constitution declares that a person accused shall not be convicted by a single witness, can the said woman and her husband be admitted witnesses in the above case?'

"To the above question the Assembly answered, that in all such cases as that submitted by the Presbytery of Ohio, it is a principle that both the husband and wife are to be admitted to give testimony. But in every particular case as it occurs, the judicature before whom it is tried ought, in order to guard against collusion, to pay a very scrupulous regard to all the circumstances attending it, and especially to the characters of those who are admitted as evidences, so that on the one hand the necessity of the case may be consulted, and, on the other, that no injury may result to an innocent person."—*Minutes*, 1797, p. 128.

7. *The Accused must be Present at the Trial.*

"In the progress of this case, the Presbytery proceeded regularly to cite the accused, once and again; and upon his not appearing, they proceeded to the trial, and having gone through the evidence, they referred the whole to the Synod to adjudicate upon it, with the expression of their own opinion, that Mr. Craighead ought to be suspended. The Synod met immediately after Presbytery, and took up the case, and, in concurrence with the opinion of the Presbytery, suspended Mr. Craighead from the Gospel ministry.

"In this proceeding, the General Assembly are of opinion that there was too much haste. Mr. Craighead was not guilty of contumacy, for he wrote two letters to the Presbytery, excusing himself for non-attendance; and if he had been guilty of contumacy, he ought to have been suspended on that ground. Perhaps no man ought to be tried on charges preferred, and to be supported by evidence, who is not present, without his own consent. A trial, in the nature of things, cannot be impartial, when there is but one party heard."—*Minutes*, 1824, p. 121.

8. *A Disproportionate Censure not sustained.*

a. "It being the order of the day, the Assembly proceeded to consider the appeal of Mr. Jabez Spicer from the decision of the Synod of Geneva, by which Mr. Spicer had been deposed from the Gospel ministry. The documents on the subject were read, and the parties were heard. After a considerable discussion, the following resolution was adopted, viz.:

"*Resolved*, That the appeal of Mr. Spicer be sustained, on the ground that the sentence pronounced on him was disproportioned to his crime, it not appearing substantiated that he was guilty of more than a single act of prevarication. While, therefore, the Assembly express their entire disapprobation of the conduct of Mr. Spicer, as unbecoming a Christian and Christian minister, they reverse the sentence of deposition passed upon him by the Presbytery, and direct that, after suitable admonitions and acknowledgments, he be restored to the ministerial office."—*Minutes*, 1821, p. 24.

b. "The discussion left unfinished yesterday afternoon was resumed, viz., of the motion to reverse a decision of the Presbytery of Lexington, by which decision Mr. George Bourne was deposed from the Gospel ministry. This motion, after it had been amended and fully discussed, was determined in the affirmative, and is as follows, viz.:

"The Assembly judge that the charges in the case of Mr. Bourne were not fully substantiated, and that if they had been, the sentence was too severe. Therefore,

"*Resolved*, That the sentence of the Presbytery of Lexington, deposing Mr. Bourne, be reversed, and it is hereby reversed; and that the Presbytery commence the trial anew."—*Minutes*, 1817, p. 646.

c. "The Assembly sustain the appeal of David Price from the decision of the Synod of Geneva, on the ground that the charge of intoxication was not sufficiently supported by the testimony; although it does appear, principally from his own confession, that he had made an unbecoming use of ardent spirits; and that an admonition was, in the view of the Assembly, deserved, and would have been sufficient."—*Minutes*, 1825, p. 155.

The Superior Judicature may not Pass a New Censure without a New Trial.

d. "*Resolved*, That the General Assembly, having heard and considered in detail the circumstances and merits of the appeal of Newton Hawes, are of the opinion that in the proceedings of the Synod of Genesee in the case, there appears to be nothing irregular or censurable, until they come to their last decision, in which they pass a new and severe censure on the appellant. In this particular, the Assembly judge that the proceedings of the Synod were not regular, inasmuch as they inflicted a new censure, without a new and regular trial. Had the Synod contented themselves with approving the doings of the church of Warsaw, in declining to restore the appellant to their communion, and left him in the condition of a suspended member, they would have acted with entire regularity. But not pausing at this point, the Assembly consider them as acting on matters not regularly brought before them; and, therefore,

"*Resolved*, That the sentence of the Synod, requiring the appellant to make a new and second confession, be reversed, and it is hereby reversed; and that the other part of their proceedings and decision be affirmed, and they are hereby affirmed."—*Minutes*, 1823, p. 79.

9. *Suspension from the Ministry during Process.*

a. "*Overtured*, that a committee be sent to Rehoboth, with full power from the Synod to act in their names and by their authority, in the affair between Mr. Clement and that people; and that Mr. Clement be suspended from the exercise of his ministry, until the determination of that committee. This overture was carried by a vote in the affirmative, *nemine contradicente*."—*Minutes*, 1720, p. 62.

b. "The consideration of Mr. Alexander Miller's complaint resumed, and upon full inquiry the Synod conclude that, as the Presbytery of Hanover are not present, and it has not been made appear before us that they were cited to be present, or informed that Mr. Alexander Miller intended to lodge a complaint against them before the Synod at this time, we cannot now enter upon the consideration of the merits of the complaint, but order both the Presbytery and Mr. Alexander Miller to attend our next Synod, prepared for a full hearing, and, in the meantime, on account of Mr. Miller's unjustifiable delay for some years to enter his complaint before us, the irregularity of his proceedings during that time, and the atrocious nature of the crimes laid to his charge, we do hereby declare him suspended from the exercise of the ministerial office till his complaint can be fully heard."—*Minutes*, 1769, p. 396.

Suspension from the Ministry for a Specified Time.

c. "The affair of Mr. Robert Cross, transmitted from the interloquitur of the Synod, came into consideration before the Synod, wherein the charges of fornication laid against him, with its aggravations, were fully heard and considered with great deliberation, and also charged upon him by the moderator, in the face of the Synod, and before several other discreet persons who were desired to be present. And the said Mr. Robert Cross did, with great seriousness, humility, and signs of true repentance, confess the charge laid against him, and in all respects did so behave himself as was universally satisfactory to the Synod and the other persons present.

"*Overtured*, That Mr. Cross be suspended by act of the Synod four Sabbaths, and at the expiration of said time he have liberty again to preach the Gospel. And that, at the desire of the congregation of New Castle, or their representatives in their name, he may be again restored to the exercise of his ministry in that place by a committee of the Synod; and that the said committee meet at said place at least three days before the expiration of the said time."

"This overture was agreed to by Synod."—*Minutes*, 1720, p. 63.

10. *Restoration to Communion does not restore to Office.*

"When an elder has been suspended from Church privileges for an offence, and again restored to the privileges of the Church, is he also restored to his office as a ruling elder?"

"Answer. The two things are distinct; and since an elder, as well as a minister, may be suspended from his office, and not from the communion of the Church, so there may be reasons for continuing his suspension from his office after he is restored to the privileges of the Church. He cannot be restored to the functions of his office without a special and express act of the Session for that purpose, with the acquiescence of the church."—*Minutes*, 1836, p. 263.

11. *A Suspended Minister is not a Christian in good standing.*

"The committee appointed to examine the records of the Synod of Geneva reported, and their report being read, was adopted, and is as follows, viz.:

"That the book be approved to page 235, with the exception of pages 215, 224, 229, relative to certain appeals, in which the nature of the offence on which the appeals are founded is not specified; and of pages 227 and 228, in which the conduct of the Presbytery of Cayuga is censured without prosecuting the subject to a proper issue; and in pages 270 and 271, where the conduct of the Presbytery of Ontario is censured for condemning the conduct of Mr. Foreman, a suspended minister, for exercising the rights of a common Christian, in illustrating Scripture and delivering exhortations; because, without deciding on the rights of common Christians in this matter, Mr. Foreman being suspended from the ministry, ought by no means to be considered as occupying the ground of a common Christian in good standing."—*Minutes*, 1821, p. 15.

12. *Deposition and Excommunication distinct Acts.*

"The records of the Synod of Geneva are approved, with the exception of a resolution on page 28, which declares that a deposed minister ought to be treated as an excommunicated person.

"In the judgment of this Assembly, the deposition and excommunication of a minister are distinct things, not necessarily connected with each other; but when connected, ought to be inflicted by the Presbytery, to whom the power of judging and censuring ministers properly belongs."—*Minutes*, 1814, p. 549.

13. *If the Deposed do not submit, his Name to be published.*

"*Resolved*, That it be recommended to the Presbyteries under the care of the General Assembly, when they shall depose any of their members from the exercise of the ministerial office; and when any person so deposed shall, without having been regularly restored, assume the ministerial character, or attempt to exercise any of the ministerial functions, that in such case, with a view to prevent such deposed person from imposing himself on the churches, Presbyteries be careful to have his name published in the Assembly's Magazine as deposed from the ministry, that all the churches may be enabled to guard themselves against such dangerous impositions."—*Minutes,* 1806, p. 360.

14. *Refusal to Submit debars the Right of Petition.*

"The committee to which was referred the petition of Mr. Bourne reported, and their report being read, was accepted; whereupon it was—

"*Resolved,* That, as it appears to be a fact that Mr. Bourne has not submitted to the judgment of the Assembly in affirming a decision by which he was deposed from the Gospel ministry, he be permitted to withdraw his petition."—*Minutes,* 1823, p. 93.

15. *Does not Invalidate the Sentence.*

a. "The Assembly proceeded to the consideration of the appeal of Mr. Josiah B. Andrews. The roll was called, to give each member an opportunity to express his opinion; after which the final vote was taken, when it was—

"*Resolved,* That the decision of the Synod of New Jersey, affirming the decision of the Presbytery of Elizabethtown, whereby Mr. Josiah B. Andrews was suspended from the office of the Gospel ministry, be and it hereby is affirmed."—*Minutes,* 1826, p. 187.

"The following communication, dated June 2d, 1826, the day after the rising of the last Assembly, and addressed to the moderator of that Assembly, from Mr. Josiah B. Andrews, was laid before the Assembly, viz.:

"Notice is hereby most respectfully given to the General Assembly of Presbyterians in the United States, that the undersigned conscientiously believes it to be his duty to continue to preach the Gospel, and to perform all other ministerial services, according to the rule of God's word, wherever he may be providentially called, any resolutions or decisions of the Assembly, or of any other ecclesiastical body under their jurisdiction, made to the contrary notwithstanding. God alone is my judge.

"JOSIAH B. ANDREWS.

"Philadelphia, June 2d, 1826." —*Minutes,* 1827, p. 198.

"*Resolved,* That, in the opinion of this Assembly, the said letter is highly contumacious; and the sentiments avowed in it, a gross infraction of Mr. Andrews's ordination vows."—*Minutes,* 1827, p. 201.

b. "Mr. Alexander Miller was called in, and the above determination of the Synod [see p. 200] read in his hearing. Whereupon he gave in a paper, renouncing the authority of the Synod. Upon which the Synod find, that as Mr. Miller was deposed by the Presbytery of Hanover, he declined the judgment of that Presbytery, and appealed to this Synod; and while we were taking measures to try and issue his complaint, he, in the paper aforesaid, hath renounced our authority. The Synod, therefore, declare he is not a member of this body, and forbid all their Presbyteries and congregations to employ him."—*Minutes*, 1769, p. 396.

c. "*Resolved*, That the Church of Geneva be referred to the minute of the Assembly formed in the case of David Price, in the year 1825, from which it will appear that, in the judgment of the Assembly, an admonition was deserved by the said Price, in consequence of his unchristian conduct. And it is the judgment of this Assembly, that the Session ought immediately to have administered such admonition; that they ought still to administer it; and that if the said Price refuse to submit to such admonition, or do not thereupon manifest repentance and Christian temper to the satisfaction of the Church, he ought not to be received into the communion of that or any other Presbyterian church." [See 8, *c*, p. 199.]—*Minutes*, 1827, p. 203.

16. *A Presbytery is Censured for restoring a Man without due Evidence of Penitence.*

"The business left unfinished on Saturday was resumed, viz., the appeal of the Presbytery of Onondaga, from a decision of the Synod of Geneva, relative to the restoration of the Rev. John Shepherd to the Gospel ministry, who had been deposed by the Association of Fairfield, Connecticut. After considerable discussion of the subject, the following resolutions were adopted, viz.:

"*Resolved*, That the decision of the Synod of Geneva, relative to the restoration of the Rev. John Shepherd to the office of the Gospel ministry, so far as it censures the restoration of said Shepherd, who was deposed by a judicatory of the Church of Christ in fellowship with us, be and hereby is confirmed; because it did not appear from the records of the Presbytery of Onondaga, that said restoration took place in consequence of any confession of the alleged crime for which the said Shepherd was deposed, or of any profession of penitence for it, or of any conference with the judicatory which deposed him."—*Minutes*, 1818, p. 687.

17. *But the action of Presbytery in such case is final.*

"That the appeal of the Presbytery of Onondaga, so far as it relates to the rescinding of their vote to restore the Rev. John Shepherd, be and hereby is sustained, on the second reason of appeal, and upon that alone; because the Assembly judges that a minister of the Gospel, when once restored by Presbyterial authority, cannot be deprived of his office, except it be by a new process and conviction."—*Minutes,* 1818, p. 687.

18. *New Trial on new Testimony being produced.*

a. "The Assembly took into consideration the report of the committee on an appeal from a decision of the Synod of New York and New Jersey, in the case of Mr. Aaron C. Collins; and, after mature deliberation thereon, resolved as follows:

"1. That the decision of the Synod, as founded on the evidence and the circumstances which were presented to them at the time, was proper, and is therefore confirmed.

"2. That as new evidence, apparently of an important kind, has been alleged on this case since the decision of the Synod, it is proper that a new trial be instituted thereon."—*Minutes,* 1793, p. 68.

b. "*Resolved,* That it is the well-known privilege of Mr. Hindman, if he consider himself as having new evidence to offer in this case, to apply to the Presbytery for a new trial upon that new evidence."—*Minutes,* 1811, p. 479.

c. "The Judicial Committee reported on the appeal of John Ward, from a decision of the Synod of Genesee; that having duly considered the case, they recommend, that on the ground of new testimony, the appellant be directed to apply to the Church of Bergen for a new trial. The above report was adopted."—*Minutes,* 1829, p. 266.

New Trial may be granted on the discovery of new Testimony; but if a court thinks proper to review a case, without new testimony, it should refer it to the next higher judicatory.

d. "The committee appointed to consider and report on Overture No. 2, which is in the following words: 'Is it lawful and consistent with the order of our Church, for a church court to reconsider and set aside its own decision in a case of discipline, after a lapse of five or six years from the time the decision was made, after the court has so changed, that many of its members were not members at the time of the decision, and when no new testimony is proposed?' beg leave to report, that, in their opinion, the proper answer to this overture, will be found included in the following principles, viz.:

"1. Our Book of Discipline, chap. ix, sec. 1, provides, that if after a trial before any judicatory, new testimony be discovered, which is supposed to be highly important to the exculpation of the accused, it is proper for him to ask, and for the judicatory to grant, a new trial.

"2. It is very conceivable that, after the lapse of five or six years, the sentence of an ecclesiastical court, which was originally considered as just and wise, although no new testimony, strictly speaking, has appeared, may in the view of the Church, appear under an aspect, equivalent to new testimony, and calling for reconsideration; yet,

"3. Inasmuch as the frequent reconsideration of cases adjudged by the inferior judicatories, without the appearance of new testimony, admits of great and mischievous abuse, and might lead to an endless recurrence of reviews and reversals of former decisions, in the absence of a majority of the court pronouncing the same; it is evidently more regular, safe, and for edification, when a review of a decision, without the disclosure of new testimony, is thought desirable, to refer the case to the next higher judicatory."—*Minutes*, 1833, p. 405, 406.

19. *A Synod corrects its own hasty action, and is sustained.*

a. "The committee to whom the records of the Synod of the Carolinas were recommitted, beg leave to report: That your committee find that a judgment of the Session of Salem was confirmed by the Presbytery of Abingdon, and brought by appeal before the Synod of the Carolinas, who remitted the cause to a select Session. The sentence of this Session, which appears to your committee to have been irregular, was affirmed by the Synod of the Carolinas, at their sessions in October, 1790. At the same sessions, however, they resumed the cause, and rescinded the decision made by the Synod two days before. Here your committee conceive, that the Synod did right as to matter, but were wrong in point of form; for it does not appear from the minutes that there was more than merely a majority of the members of the Synod for resuming the cause."—*Minutes*, 1791, pp. 41, 42.

But a Judicatory may not call back a case after an Appeal has been taken.

b. "The Synod next proceeded to consider the appeal; but, before they came to a decision, a meeting was held by the members of Abingdon Presbytery, then attending on Synod, at which meeting they professed to reverse the former sentence of that Presbytery, and reported the same to Synod, in order to preclude the farther proceedings. Here your committee observe that, in their opinion, the Presbytery had no right to call back the cause, after sentence by them passed, and an appeal from it carried up to the superior court. The Synod having agreed that they had a right to proceed, notwithstanding this information, did accordingly proceed, and, in a regular way, as your committee conceive, reversed the sentence of the Session of Salem, and declared the appellant restored to the privileges of the Church.

"Upon the whole, your committee conceive that the proceedings of that Synod should be sustained in point of order by the General Assembly, and their decision confirmed. In that instance in which their proceedings seem to be most contrary to regular discipline, and which is particularly pointed at in the reasons of protest by the members of Abingdon Presbytery,—we mean, resuming a case during the same session after a decision first had upon it,—your committee judge that the first decision was made in a way that was entirely informal, and therefore they had a right to resume the cause, and issue it in an orderly and constitutional way; which they have accordingly done, though your committee conceive that this reason should have been assigned upon their minutes."—*Minutes*, 1791, p. 42.

20. *The Accused has no right to introduce Testimony which would inculpate those not on Trial.*

"No. 3, an overture on a case of discipline, was taken up, and is as follows:

"'Suppose a member of the Church is on trial, and his accuser is "common fame." One specification against him is, "Speaking evil of his brethren, A. and B., while he neglects to take any Gospel steps to bring them to repentance or to trial."

"'The specification is abundantly sustained by testimony; but the person on trial proposes to introduce testimony to prove that the reports which he circulated, and the opinions which he pronounced derogatory to the brethren named, were true. Has the accused a right to introduce such testimony, tending to injure the character of parties not on trial, nor connected at all with the prosecution, and having no opportunity for defence?

"'Would the Session be authorized to reject such testimony, on the ground that, if introduced, it would not exculpate the accused, inasmuch as he had no right to circulate evil reports against his brethren, whether true or false, while neglecting to bring them to trial?'

"To this the following answer was given:

"'The person on trial, under charges tabled on the ground of "common fame," has no right to introduce testimony which inculpates his brethren who are not on trial, and who have no opportunity to defend themselves, because it was his previous duty to take proper steps, if the persons were guilty of the evils which he had alleged against them, to bring them to repentance, or free the Church from the scandal.'"—*Minutes*, 1852, p. 177.

21. *The Assembly cannot reverse the Judicial Acts of a former Assembly, unless Error be shown.*

"This Assembly has no authority to reverse the judicial acts of a former General Assembly, except in cases of such palpable error as would manifestly tend to interfere with the substantial administration of justice." [Case of Samuel Lowry.]—*Minutes*, 1824, p. 115.

22. *The Decisions of the Superior Courts binding on the Inferior.*

"The Assembly cannot but express their disapprobation of the concluding paragraph of the memorial of the Synod of Ohio, in which they say, 'The Synod consider the judgments entered upon their records against Samuel Lowry, in October, 1822, as remaining in full force,' &c.

"This declaration, notwithstanding the respectful expressions of the Synod, is apparently wanting in the respect due from an inferior to a superior judicatory; and is repugnant to the radical principles of the government of the Presbyterian Church. If an inferior court has authority to declare that its own decisions are in force, after they have been reversed by a superior court, then all appeals are nugatory, and our system, as it relates to judicial proceedings, is utterly subverted. The

Assembly are willing to believe, however, that the Synod of Ohio did not mean to set themselves in opposition to the highest judicatory of the Church, and that when they have reconsidered the matter, they will rescind what is so manifestly inconsistent with the principles of the Constitution, which they have bound themselves to support."—*Minutes*, 1824, p. 116.

"On the sixth exception to the minutes of the Synod of Cincinnati, viz., '6th. The vote of the Synod not to comply with the injunction of the last Assembly in the case of Mr. Graham;* in respect to which vote the Synod is directed to reconsider their action, and proceed in conformity with the instructions of the last Assembly,'—a long discussion ensued. Mr. Spear moved to amend, by inserting 'ought' in the place of 'is directed.' Before the question was taken, at 6¼ o'clock, on motion of the Rev. W. H. Beecher, the whole subject was indefinitely postponed."—*Minutes*, 1849, p. 177.

23. *Judicial Sentences of Sister Churches to be respected.*

[See *ante*, sec. 16, p. 204.]

[For other cases of Discipline, see chap. vii, secs. 1 and 2; also chap. vi and viii, secs. 2 and 3.]

SECTION 2.—OF APPEALS.

1. An appeal defined. How it differs from a "complaint."—2. The right to appeal is limited to the original parties.—3. Limitation of time. It must be prosecuted at the first ensuing meeting of the judicature appealed to, or the sentence will be made final. Personal attendance is not essential.—4. The appeal must be lodged with the clerk on the first or second day of the sessions of the court appealed to.—5. Due notice must be given of the intention to appeal. See Book of Discipline, chap. vii, sec. 3, 5.—6. On the failure of the inferior judicatory to send up their records and copies of the testimony, the appeal was sustained.—7. An appeal postponed, where the appellant failed to give notice.—8. The case may be postponed at the instance of the appellant.—9. May an appeal be carried over the next higher court? Various decisions; general principle.—10. The best evidence which the case admits of required, and in all trials this is the record of the judicatory.—11. A copy made by the appellant is not sufficient.—12. Neglect of the inferior judicatory shall not harm the appellant.—13. Testimony not on record may be received by agreement.—14. Leave refused to introduce testimony going to show that the appellant has not submitted to the sentence of the court.—15. An appeal arrests all further process

* See p. 196, *e*.

until it is issued; 16. But does not arrest the sentence, where the delay is asked for by the appellant.—17. Who may sit in the trial of an appeal? No one who was a member of the judicature when the vote appealed from took place; nor one who is interested in the case.—18. The death of the respondent bars the prosecution of an appeal by the prosecutor.—19. An express vote must be taken in an appeal, and the sentence must be definite, precise, and just.—20. Irregularities of the inferior judicatures censured.—21. Appeal of George Sheldon.—22. Appeal of Lewis Tappan. Appeal sustained, and both parties censured.—23. Order for issuing an appeal.

1. "*An appeal is the removal of a cause already decided, from an inferior to a superior judicatory, by a party aggrieved.*"—Form of Gov., chap. vii, sec. 3.

[Prior to the revision of the Constitution (1820), no distinction was made between appeals and complaints. The usual formula was, "We appeal and complain." Appeals are now limited to the "parties aggrieved." "All persons who have submitted to a regular trial in an inferior, may appeal to a higher judicatory." Form of Gov., chap. vii, sec. 3. "A complaint is a representation made to a superior by any member or members of an inferior judicatory, or by any other person or persons, respecting a decision by an inferior judicatory, which, in the opinion of the complainants, has been irregularly or unjustly made." Form of Gov., chap. vii, sec. 4.]

2. *The Right to Appeal is limited to the Original Parties.*

a. "The Judicial Committee reported a paper, signed by Dr. Cathcart and others, members of the Presbytery of Carlisle, purporting to be an appeal or complaint relative to a decision of the Synod of Philadelphia. The committee gave it as their opinion, that the subject could not be taken up on the ground of an appeal, because these persons were not one of the original parties; but that it might be taken up in the character of a complaint.

"*Resolved*, That the consideration of this complaint be the order of the day for next Tuesday morning."—*Minutes*, 1823, p. 69.

b. "The Judicial Committee also reported on judicial business No. 8, viz., the appeal of Dr. Joshua L. Wilson and others, against a decision of the Synod of Cincinnati, in the case of Dr. Beecher, that they have examined the same, and are of opinion that Dr. Wilson and others were not a party in the case, and consequently cannot constitutionally appeal;

and recommend that they have leave to withdraw their appeal. This report was adopted."—*Minutes*, 1834, p. 432.

3. *Limitation of Time. The Appeal must be Prosecuted at the First Meeting of the Superior Judicatory.*

"*Resolved*, That in case of an appeal or complaint, entered in an inferior judicatory to a superior, if the appellant or appellants do not appear at the first meeting of the superior judicatory, protest may be admitted, at the instance of the respondents, at the last session of such meeting, that the appeal is fallen from; and the sentence so appealed from shall be considered as final."—*Minutes*, 1791, p. 39.

a. "A protest was admitted in behalf of the Synod of the Carolinas, that an appeal of the Presbytery of Abingdon, from a judgment of the said Synod, October 7, 1790, was not prosecuted, and was therefore fallen from, and the judgment became final."—*Minutes*, 1791, p. 45.

b. "Rev. Thomas B. Craighead having appealed to the General Assembly, from a decision of the Synod of Kentucky, made in the month of October last, by which decision the said Synod directed the Presbytery of Transylvania to depose the said Thomas B. Craighead from the Gospel ministry, which was done accordingly; and whereas the said Mr. Craighead has not prosecuted his appeal to the General Assembly, and the subscribers, members of the Synod of Kentucky, have waited till the last day of the session of the Assembly, to afford opportunity for the prosecution of said appeal, we do therefore now protest, in our own name and on behalf of the Synod of Kentucky, against the future prosecution of said appeal, and declare the sentence of the Synod to be final, agreeably to a standing order of the General Assembly."

"The protest was accepted."—*Minutes*, 1811, pp. 481, 482.

c. [In 1822 the case came up again, when the following report was adopted:]

"In the year 1811, an appeal from a decision of the Synod of Kentucky, by T. B. Craighead, accompanied by a letter from the same, was laid before the General Assembly; but Mr. Craighead not appearing in person to prosecute his appeal, permission was given by the Assembly, on the last day of their sessions, to the members of the Synod of Kentucky who were present, to enter a protest against the prosecution of the aforesaid appeal at any future time. This was supposed to be required by a standing rule of the Assembly. The appeal of Mr. Craighead was therefore not heard, and the sentence of the Synod of Kentucky was rendered final.

"It moreover appears, that the General Assembly of the year aforesaid, having adopted the protest of the members of the Synod of Kentucky as their own act, did declare that Mr. Craighead had been deposed, whereas the decision of the Synod was suspension; and although the Synod did direct the Presbytery to which Mr. Craighead belonged to depose him, if he did not, at their next stated meeting, retract his errors, yet this sentence could not have been constitutionally inflicted, because Mr. Craighead appealed from the decision of Synod, the effect of which was to arrest all further proceedings in the case until the appeal should be tried; therefore the sentence of the Assembly, declaring Mr. Craighead deposed, does not accord with the sentence of the Synod, which was suspension.

"From the above history of facts, your committee are of opinion that Mr. Craighead has just grounds of complaint, in regard to the proceedings of the General Assembly of 1811, in his case, and that the construction put on the standing rule of the Assembly was not correct; for personal attendance on the superior judicatory is not essential to the regular prosecution of an appeal. Moreover, the sentence of the Assembly being founded in error, ought to be considered null and void, and Mr. Craighead ought to be considered as placed in the same situation as before the decision took place, and as possessing the right to prosecute his appeal before this judicatory."—*Minutes*, 1822, pp. 52, 53.

d. "From the records of the Synod of Kentucky it appeared that Guernsey G. Brown had appealed from a decision of that body in his case to the General Assembly. As Mr. Brown has not appeared to prosecute his appeal, and the commissioners from the Synod of Kentucky require that his absence may, according to a rule of the Assembly on the subject, preclude him from a future hearing: therefore—

"*Resolved*, That Guernsey G. Brown be considered as precluded from prosecuting his appeal."—*Minutes*, 1821, p. 30.

In the absence of the Appellant, the Appeal dismissed, but leave granted to renew the Appeal.

e. "The appeal of Dr. James Snodgrass against a decision of the Synod of Pittsburg was called up, and the appeal was dismissed, on the ground that the appellant has not appeared, either in person or by proxy, to prosecute said appeal.

"The Assembly, however, give to Dr. Snodgrass the privilege of prosecuting his appeal before the next General Assembly, if he can then show sufficient cause for its further prosecution."—*Minutes*, 1832, p. 376.

In the absence of the Appellant, the Appeal dismissed, and Sentence affirmed.

f. "Judicial business No. 2, viz., the appeal of Benedict Hobbs from a decision of the Synod of Kentucky, was taken up, and the appellant not being present to prosecute his appeal, it was dismissed, and the sentence of the inferior court affirmed.

"Judicial business No. 5, viz., the appeal of Chloe G. Giles from a decision of the Synod of Utica, was taken up, and the appellant not being present to prosecute her appeal, it was dismissed, and the sentence of the inferior court affirmed."—*Minutes*, 1834, p. 452.

Personal attendance is not necessary.

g. "The construction put, by the Assembly of 1811, on the standing rule of the Assembly (in Craighead's case), was not correct; for personal attendance on the superior judicatory is not essential to the regular prosecution of an appeal."—*Minutes*, 1822, p. 52.

4. *The Appeal must be lodged with the clerk in due time*, i. e., "*On the first or second day of the meeting of the judicatory appealed to next ensuing the date of his Appeal.*"—Form of Government, Discipline, chap. vii, secs. 3, 11.

a. "The Judicial Committee reported the appeal of R. Taylor against the Synod of Michigan, which was not put into the hands of the clerk within the constitutional time. The appeal was therefore dismissed."—*Minutes*, 1837, p. 480.

Ignorance of the Rule plead.

b. "The chairman of the Judicial Committee stated to the Assembly, that an appeal had been put into his hands, from Duncan Hamilton and his wife, from a decision of the Synod of Pittsburg, which appeal had not been reported to the clerk of the house, and asked the direction of the Assembly in the case. On inquiry, it appeared this appeal was in the house in season; and the persons to whom it was intrusted were not aware of the constitutional rule requiring that it be lodged with the clerk.

"On motion, it was—

"*Resolved*, That, in the opinion of the Assembly, the rule has virtually been complied with."—*Minutes*, 1830, p. 302.

5. *Due Notice must be given of the intention to Appeal.*

a. "The records of the Synod of Utica were approved, with the following exceptions:

"1. That the Synod issued an appeal from the inferior judicatory, when it appeared before them that an appellant had not given notice in writing that he should appeal, with his reasons assigned for appealing, as required by the Book of Discipline, before the rising of the judicatory appealed from, or within ten days thereafter.

"2. That the Synod violated the principles of the Constitution in qualifying the members of the inferior judicatory to ascertain whether an appeal had been given, when the Book of Discipline requires that the appeal shall be lodged in the hands of the moderator; and further, that the inferior judicatory shall send authentic copies of all the records, and of all the testimony relating to the matter of appeal, up to the Synod, whose duty it is to issue the appeal, when found to be in order, and in accordance with the Book of Discipline."—*Minutes*, 1840, p. 12.

b. "An appeal of Mr. Benjamin Bell from a decision of the Presbytery of Geneva, and also an appeal of Mr. Bell from the decision of the Synod of Geneva, were laid before the Assembly by the Judicial Committee. These appeals were both dismissed on account of the judicatories, from whose decisions they had been taken, not having received due notice from Mr. Bell that he designed to prosecute them before this Assembly."—*Minutes*, 1821, p. 25.

c. "The appeal of Mr. Charles Yale from a sentence of the Presbytery of Bath, deposing him from the Gospel ministry, was taken up and dismissed, because it appeared that Mr. Yale gave notice to said Presbytery that he should appeal to the Synod of Geneva several days before he signified his desire to the moderator of Presbytery to appeal to the General Assembly."—*Minutes*, 1826, p. 187.

d. "The Judicial Committee, to whom was recommitted the appeal of the Church of Bergen, made the following report, which was adopted, viz.:

"They recommend that said appeal be dismissed, on the ground that the only paper which appears to be intended as an appeal, is without date or signature, or evidence that it was ever before the Synod of Genesee, or lodged with the moderator of said Synod."—*Minutes*, 1830, p. 292.

e. "*Resolved*, That the appeal [of certain pew-owners of the First Presbyterian Church, in Troy] be dismissed, on the ground that the Synod has not had the constitutional notice of the reasons of the appeal." —*Minutes*, 1828, p. 242.

6. *On the failure of the Inferior Judicatory to send up copies of Testimony, the Appeal was sustained.*

"The committee appointed to prepare a minute on the decision of the Assembly sustaining the appeal of Mr. Pope Bushnell, from a decision of the Synod of New York, affirming the decree of the Presbytery of Hudson, by which the said Mr. Bushnell had been suspended from the privileges of the Church, made the following report, which was adopted, viz.:

"That the appellant having given due notice that he did appeal, appeared regularly before the Assembly; and that while the Presbytery and Synod have sent up their records in the case, neither has forwarded to this Assembly an authentic copy of the testimony taken on the trial. The Assembly did therefore decide, that Mr. Bushnell's appeal be, and it hereby is sustained, so that he is restored to all his rights and privileges as a member of the Church of Christ."—*Minutes*, 1826, p. 187.

7. *Postponed because of failure of Appellant to file Notice.*

"The appeal of Mr. Craighead from a decision of the Synod of Kentucky was taken up, and being read, it appeared on inquiry that the Synod of Kentucky was not ready for trial, because Mr. Craighead had failed to give them notice that he intended to avail himself of the privilege granted by the last Assembly, by prosecuting his appeal; therefore,

"*Resolved*, That the further consideration of this appeal be postponed, and that Mr. Craighead be informed, that if he wishes to prosecute his appeal before the next General Assembly, he must give notice of his intention to the Synod of Kentucky.

"*Resolved*, That the Synod of Kentucky and the Presbytery of Transylvania, be directed, and they hereby are directed, to send up to the next Assembly a copy of their minutes in Mr. Craighead's case."—*Minutes*, 1823, p. 92.

8. *The Case may be Postponed at the instance of the Appellant.*

a. "The Judicial Committee reported an appeal by Mr. James Taylor, from a decision of the Synod of Pittsburg; and that the communication of Mr. Taylor gave information that, by reason of ill health, he was unable to attend, to prosecute his appeal before the present Assembly.

"*Resolved*, That Mr. Taylor have leave to prosecute his appeal before the next General Assembly."—*Minutes*, 1827, p. 211.

b. "The Judicial Committee reported that a paper had been put into their hands, purporting to be a request from Mr. C. H. Baldwin, to the moderator of the Assembly, that his appeal from a decision of the Synod of Genesee be continued to the next General Assembly, and offering reasons for his failure to appear and prosecute it. It appears, from the Form of Discipline, chap. vii, sec. 3, art. 2, that his case is regularly before us, for reference to the next General Assembly, if his excuse for now failing to appear shall be deemed sufficient." [The request was granted.]—*Minutes*, 1858, p. 580.

9. *May an Appeal be carried over to the next higher Court?*

a. "Inasmuch as the request of Mr. Bourne, to be tried on an appeal before the General Assembly, rather than the Synod, may be reasonable; and, inasmuch as the words of our Constitution, viz., 'The Assembly shall receive and issue all appeals and references which may be regularly brought before them from the inferior judicatures,' &c., have been interpreted favorably to such a request, the General Assembly do order that a certified copy of the records of the Lexington Presbytery, in this case, be duly made and transmitted to the next Assembly, unless the Synod of Virginia, to which the Assembly can have no objection, shall have previously received the appeal (but that this constitutional question, as well as the merits of the case, shall remain open for discussion at that time)."—*Minutes*, 1816, pp. 626, 627.

b. "*Resolved*, That the records of the Synod of Virginia be approved, except their censure of the Presbytery of Lexington, for allowing an appeal from their decision directly to the Assembly, without noticing the supposed irregularity of such appeal."—*Minutes*, 1818, p. 688.

c. [The "appeal and complaint of Lewis Tappan from a decision of the Third Presbytery of New York," was received and issued by the Assembly.]—*Minutes*, 1839, p. 11.

d. "The Committee on Overture No. 7, viz., An overture from the Presbytery of Baltimore, in relation to the practice of inferior judicatories in carrying appeals and complaints directly to the General Assembly, without first bringing them to their respective Synods, made the following report, which was adopted, viz.: That the Constitution of our Church is so explicit that it requires no order of the Assembly in relation to the case brought to view in this overture."—*Minutes*, 1833, p. 396.

[The principle which has guided the Assembly seems to be, that where there is no sufficient reason for passing by the next superior court, the case should go there. But where good reasons are assigned for carrying it directly to the Assembly, it will be entertained.]

e. "The Judicial Committee reported two appeals of Samuel Lowery, the first, from a special decision of the Session of the Second Presbyterian Church of Cincinnati; the second from a decision of the Presbytery of Miami. These appeals were dismissed, because the appellant had not prosecuted his appeals before the inferior judicatories."—*Minutes*, 1822, p. 36.

f. "The Judicial Committee made the following report on the complaint of the Presbytery of Philadelphia against the Presbytery of Columbia, relative to the licensure of Mr. Samuel Shaffer, which was adopted, viz.: That it is a desirable thing to prevent the unnecessary accumulation of business before the General Assembly; that no good reason appears why the Synod of Albany, who must be entirely competent to issue the complaint, should be passed by, and that, therefore, in their judgment, the matter ought to go before that body."—*Minutes*, 1828, p. 237.

g. "The Judicial Committee made a report in relation to the appeal of Mr. Matthew H. Rice, from a decision of the Presbytery of East Hanover, which was adopted, and is as follows, viz.:

"That the appellant had leave to withdraw his appeal on the following ground, viz.: No reasons are assigned by the appellant for making this appeal to the General Assembly instead of the Synod."—*Minutes*, 1830, p. 298.

h. "The Judicial Committee reported on judicial business No. 7, viz.: The appeal from the decision of the Presbytery of Otsego, by the Church at Cooperstown, that it appears from the documents that the appeal is made by said church immediately from Presbytery to the Assembly; and they recommend that the appellants have leave to withdraw their appeal, and prosecute it before the Synod of Utica. This report was adopted."—*Minutes,* 1834, p. 432.

i. "A letter from several members of the First Presbyterian Church of the town of Ovid, in the State of New York, complaining of the conduct of the Presbytery of Oneida, in erecting another congregation in their neighborhood; also of Mr. Chapman for preaching in said congregation, &c., was received and read.

"The Assembly having considered the same—

"*Resolved,* That as the complainants have not stated their grievances to the Presbytery, nor applied to it for redress, the petition be returned to them, and that they be directed to proceed in this case as the Constitution prescribes."—*Minutes,* 1804, p. 309.

10. *The best Evidence which the Case admits of required.*

"This Assembly are of opinion that the correct mode of proceeding for the last General Assembly would have been to have suspended a decision on the appeal, until the records of the inferior judicatories should have been present; because the rules in our Form of Government prescribe, that before a judgment is given, all the proceedings of the inferior judicatories in the case should be read, and it is a sound maxim, generally admitted in courts of justice, that the best evidence which the case admits of should be required, which in all trials is undoubtedly the record of the judicatory."—*Minutes,* 1824, p. 115.

[Case of Samuel Lowery.]

11. *A Copy made by the Appellant not sufficient.*

"By 'the forms of process,' Mr. Bourne ought to be allowed copies of the whole proceedings in his case, yet the judicatory appealed from is, by the same rules, 'to send authentic copies of the whole process.' His copy, therefore, which he says was taken by himself, but is not shown to the Assembly, is not sufficient. His affidavit is not required by the course of proceeding in this body, and the three papers presented by him are not to be considered as the commencement of a cause, or the entry of an appeal in this judicatory."—*Minutes,* 1816, p. 627.

12. *Neglect of the Inferior Court shall not work harm to the Appellant.*

a. [Mr. Bourne having brought in an appeal from the Presbytery of Lexington, and the record not sent up, the Assembly say that] "Mr. Bourne shall not suffer any inconvenience which the Assembly can prevent, on account of any failures of the inferior judicatures; if a default should in future appear on their part, the evidence of such circumstance being not as yet made clear to this Assembly."—*Minutes,* 1816, p. 627.

b. "The appellant having given due notice that he did appeal, appeared regularly before the Assembly; and that while the Presbytery and Synod have sent up their records in the case, neither has forwarded to this Assembly an authentic copy of the testimony taken on the trial. The Assembly did, therefore, decide that Mr. Bushnell's appeal be, and it hereby is sustained, so that he is restored to all his rights and privileges as a member of the Church of Christ."—*Minutes,* 1826, p. 187.

13. *Testimony not on Record may be received by Consent of Parties.*

"The following papers were offered and ordered to be entered on the Minutes, viz.:

"I offer to the Assembly the paper called 'An Appendix,' as the records furnished by the Presbytery in my case, and request that it may be read, as containing evidence which I deem important, which was before the Presbytery, and which was not before the Synod.

"ALBERT BARNES.

"The prosecutor in the case of Mr. Barnes, and the committee appointed by the Synod of Philadelphia, to defend their decision in the same case, hereby agree to the introduction of the document entitled 'An Appendix,' &c.; not, however, as a part of the records of the inferior judicatory, but as testimony adduced by the appellant to substantiate any statements which he has made, or may yet make.

"GEORGE JUNKIN,
"S. G. WINCHESTER,
"G. W. MUSGRAVE,
"DAVID MCKINNEY,
"Committee of Synod of Philadelphia.

"The document called the Appendix, numbered from pp. 1 to 58 inclusive, containing the trial, testimony of the parties, Junkin and Barnes, and final decision of the Second Presbytery of Philadelphia, in the said case of Junkin and Barnes, was read."—*Minutes,* 1836, p. 256.

14. *Leave refused the Respondents to introduce Testimony going to show that the Appellant has not submitted to the Sentence of the Court.*

"During their defence the question arose, Shall the respondents have leave, the parties consenting, to introduce evidence to show that the appellant has not submitted to the decision of the Presbytery? Leave was refused." [Appeal of Lewis Tappan from Third Presbytery of New York.]—*Minutes,* 1839, p. 23.

15. *An Appeal arrests all further Process until it is issued.*

"It moreover appears, that the General Assembly of the year aforesaid, having adopted the protest of the members of the Synod of Kentucky as their own act, did declare that Mr. Craighead had been deposed, whereas the decision of the Synod was suspension; and although the Synod did direct the Presbytery to which Mr. Craighead belonged to depose him, if he did not, at their next stated meeting, retract his errors; yet this sentence could not have been constitutionally inflicted, because Mr. Craighead appealed from the decision of Synod, the effect of which was to arrest all further proceedings in the case until the appeal should be tried. Therefore, the sentence of the Assembly declaring Mr. Craighead deposed, does not accord with the sentence of the Synod, which was suspension."—*Minutes,* 1822, p. 52.

16. *But does not Arrest the Sentence, where Delay is asked by the Appellant.*

"The Judicial Committee reported that a paper had been put into their hands, purporting to be a request from Mr. C. H. Baldwin, to the moderator of the Assembly, that his appeal from a decision of the Synod of Genesee be continued to the next General Assembly, and offering reasons for his failure to appear and prosecute it. It appears from the Form of Discipline, chap. vii, sec. 3, art. 2, that his case is regularly before us for reference to the next General Assembly, if his excuse for now failing to appear shall be deemed sufficient.

"The committee recommend that the Assembly, in view of the reasons offered, and out of a desire to grant the appellant every reasonable indulgence, continue his case agreeably to his request; it being understood, that the sentence of the Presbytery remain in full force against him till the case be finally issued, in accordance with the provisions of our Form of Discipline, chap. vii, sec. 3, art. 15."—*Minutes*, 1858, p. 580.

17. *Who may Sit in an Appeal.*

a. "*Resolved*, That no minister belonging to the Synod of Philadelphia, nor elder who was a member of the judicature when the vote appealed from took place, shall vote in the decision thereof by this Assembly.

"The moderator, being a member of the Synod of Philadelphia, withdrew, and Dr. McKnight took the chair."—*Minutes*, 1792, p. 56.

b. "A question was raised by Mr. Cunningham, an elder from the Synod of Philadelphia, who was not a member of Synod at the meeting at which the case of Mr. Barnes was tried and issued, whether he has a right to vote in this case in the Assembly. After some discussion, the moderator decided that Mr. Cunningham, and any other members of the Assembly from that Synod similarly situated, have a right to vote in the Assembly. From this decision of the moderator an appeal was taken, when, by a vote of the Assembly, the decision of the moderator was not sustained, and it was decided that Mr. Cunningham, and others similarly situated, have no right to vote on the case in the Assembly."—*Minutes*, 1836, p. 265.

"A motion was made that Dr. Skinner and Mr. Dashiell, who, at the time the trial was commenced in the Second Presbytery of Philadelphia, were either not dismissed from that body, or had not yet connected themselves with any other, though they did not meet with the Presbytery, and before the meeting of the Synod were members of other Presbyteries, should not sit in judgment in the case of Mr. Barnes. This motion was decided in the negative."—*Ibid.* 266.

c. "The appeal of Mr. Pope Bushnell was resumed. The moderator being a member of the Synod appealed from, Mr. Jennings, the last moderator present, took the chair."—*Minutes*, 1826, p. 184.

An Interested Party should not Sit on a Trial.

d. "The Records of the Synod of Genesee were, on recommendation of the committee, approved, with the following exception : Of a decision of the moderator, recorded on page 151, that a member of a Synod, who might be interested in a case under trial, cannot be challenged; which decision is unconstitutional, and ought to be reversed by that Synod."—*Minutes*, 1846, p. 20.

18. *The Death of the Respondent bars the Prosecution of an Appeal by his Prosecutor.*

"The records of the Synod of New York were approved, except that, on p. 277, it appears that the Synod decided that the death of the Rev. Mr. Griffith should be no bar in the way of the prosecution of an appeal by his prosecutor from the decision of the Presbytery of Bedford, acquitting Mr. Griffith."—*Minutes*, 1833, p. 400.

19. *An express Vote must be taken in an Appeal, and the Sentence must be definite, precise, and just.*

"*Resolved*, That inasmuch as the Synod of Indiana did not take an express vote on sustaining the appeal of Mr. Harney, and the sentence on record is vague and inconsistent with itself, the whole case be remitted to the said Synod, with an injunction to them to reconsider the same, and pass a definite, precise, and just sentence."—*Minutes*, 1837, p. 480.

20. *Irregularities of the Inferior Judicatory censured.*

a. "The Minutes of the Synod of Genesee were approved, with the exception of an irregularity, recorded on p. 170, in allowing the original parties in a trial to speak after a lower judicatory had given the reasons for their decision, which was contrary to our Book of Discipline."—*Minutes*, 1846, p. 20.

b. "There is no record of calling the roll for remarks of the members, before taking the vote, in the case of an appeal by A. King." [Exceptions to records of the Synod of Cincinnati.]—*Minutes*, 1849, p. 177.

c. "On pp. 215, 224, 229 (Records of the Synod of Geneva), relating to certain appeals, 'the nature of the offence on which the appeals are founded is not specified.'"—*Minutes*, 1821, p. 15.

21. *Appeal of George Sheldon. Protest. Answer of the Assembly.*

[Mr. Sheldon was deposed by the Presbytery of Portage, on the ground of adultery, in having married a second wife during the life of his first wife, from whom he had obtained a divorce in the civil courts, in the judgment of the Presbytery on other than scriptural grounds. From the decision of the Presbytery he took an appeal to the Synod of the Western Reserve. The Synod decided as follows, viz.: "After a full and patient hearing of the whole case of appeal by George Sheldon from the Presbytery of Portage, the Synod are constrained to believe that the decision of the Presbytery was just; and that the Presbytery conducted the case with as much order and tenderness as the inherent difficulties of the case would admit.

"In view of the whole case: '*Resolved*, That the decision of the Presbytery of Portage be sustained.']

"The Assembly resumed the consideration of the appeal of the Rev. George Sheldon.

"The original parties having been fully heard, the roll was called, and opportunity was given to the members of the Assembly to express their opinions on the case. After which the final vote was taken, and the appeal was not sustained, nineteen voting in the affirmative, and fifty-four in the negative.

"The following protest was ordered to be entered on the Minutes: We, the undersigned, members of the General Assembly, feel constrained to protest against the decision of the General Assembly, in not sustaining the appeal of Mr. George Sheldon, for the following reasons, viz.:

"1. It is shown by the records in the case that Mr. Sheldon failed to appear on the second citation, and that the Presbytery, instead of immediately suspending him for contumacy, according to the rule of our Discipline, chap. v, sec. 11, merely passed a vote of censure, and proceeded not only to take testimony, but to issue the whole case upon its merits, in the absence of the accused. In allowing a judicatory to take testimony in the absence of the accused, our Book of Discipline does not authorize them to try and issue a case, but only to take the testimony, in order to preserve it on record, in case the man should repent of his contumacy on a third citation, and submit himself to trial.

"The course of the Presbytery should have been to suspend Mr. Sheldon for contumacy on the second citation, and then, when he appeared on a third citation, the Presbytery could have removed the sentence of suspension for contumacy, and given him a fair trial.

"But, instead of this course, the Presbytery tried the case during Mr. Sheldon's absence, and found him guilty of the charge on merely *ex parte* testimony. And then, when Mr. Sheldon appeared, prepared with testimony in his defence, it was not admitted, nor put on record. He was not, therefore, tried according to our Form of Government; and any evidence adduced by him, touching his guilt or innocence, was entirely excluded from the record.

"All of which is contrary to the principles of our Form of Government, and to the past decisions of the General Assembly, especially in the case of the Rev. Dr. Craighead, of Kentucky, A. D. 1806.

"2. In the evidence on record before the Presbytery, when parts of several letters of Mr. Sheldon were given and allowed in evidence, the Presbytery should have required the whole documents in the case; and also when part of the record of the court was admitted, the testimony, on the ground of which the divorce was sought to be obtained, was ruled out. And the Presbytery proceeded upon these partial extracts to form a decision, when the whole document, if allowed in court, or produced there, might have given an entirely different construction to the parts read.

"All of which is contrary to the established legal principle, that the best evidence to be had should be demanded in every case; and that, when parts of a document touching any subject are introduced in evidence, the whole document must be admitted.

"3. So many and great were the irregularities in this assumed trial as to enable the General Assembly to form no proper judgment of the real merits of the case. And, on account of these irregularities, the case should have been remanded for a new trial.

"On these grounds, we protest against the action of the General Assembly, virtually confirming the act of deposition pronounced against Mr. Sheldon, as being contrary to the former decisions of the General Assembly, contrary to the established practice of our judicatory, contrary to the personal rights of Mr. Sheldon, and derogatory to the honor of Jesus Christ, as represented by his Church in the highest judicatory. And, because we are unwilling to be thought consenting to such action, we here respectfully enter our solemn protest, and pray that it may be admitted upon the Minutes of the Assembly."—*Minutes*, 1858, pp. 607, 608.

Answer of the Assembly.

"The committee appointed to answer the protest of Rev. H. A. Rowland, D.D., and others, presented a report, which was adopted, and is as follows:

"In answer to the protest against the decision of the Assembly in the case of George Sheldon, the Assembly make the following statement:

"1. The action of the Presbytery in the case was irregular, only technically, and not in such a sense as to vitiate the substantial justice of the result. The case had been on trial during a period of some three years, and ample opportunity had been given in this period for the accused to defend himself.

"2. Although it is asserted, that only extracts from Mr. Sheldon's letters were admitted in evidence, yet it appears that one letter, and the most important one, is given in full; that the extracts from the other letters are undisputed, and that these fairly and clearly present the truth in the case.

"3. As to the alleged new evidence, it appears that it was before the Judicial Committee of the Presbytery, and read in full before the Synod, and was unanimously decided by these judicatories to be no ground for reopening the case; and it also appears, that this testimony is wholly irreconcilable with statements made by Mr. Sheldon in the letters above referred to.

"4.. Inasmuch as the Assembly, after a full hearing of the case, by a vote of more than two-thirds, decided that there have been no material deviations from the rules of the Book of Discipline for conducting judicial cases, it is deemed unnecessary, at this late hour of their sessions, to reply further to the allegations of the protestants."—*Minutes*, 1858, p. 609.

22. *An Appeal directly to the Assembly allowed.*

"Dr. Fisher, from the Judicial Committee, reported the appeal and complaint of Lewis Tappan against the decision of the Third Presbytery of New York, as in order. The report was accepted, and the subject was taken up for consideration. A motion was made to send it down to the Synod, for adjudication.—*Minutes*, 1839, p. 13.

"The consideration of Mr. Rowland's motion to refer to the Synod of New York, the adjudication of the appeal of Lewis Tappan, was taken up. The motion to refer the case to Synod was lost. The Assembly then decided to hear the case."—*Minutes*, 1839, p. 13.

The Decision Sustaining the Appeal, and Censuring both the Appellant and the Courts below; Case of Lewis Tappan.

"*Resolved*, That, in view of the whole case, the Assembly, while they sustain the appeal, and cannot pass without censure some of the acts of the courts below, are constrained to rule as follows, viz.:

"1. That the act of the Session, excluding the stenographer, even if it were within the ultimate prerogatives of the court, was of very questionable wisdom, as well as of dangerous precedent, in reference to the rights of respondents at their bar.

"2. That there seems to have been, in the proceedings of the Session, too much precipitation and absoluteness, and too little of that calm and practical vindication of their own dignity, which mildness and forbearance, in the spirit of our Master, are largely necessary to inspire; and this especially in reference to the sentence they pronounced.

"3. That the appellant seems in several respects to have manifested a resolute opposition to the court of the first resort, which certainly, as a whole, amounts to contumacy; though we are not disposed to graduate it as flagrant or unmingled, or in circumstances of no severe probation.

"4. The Assembly therefore decide in the premises, that the sentence of the Session, suspending the appellant, be, and it hereby is reversed, as also the decision of the Presbytery confirming that of the Session.

"5. That the appellant be advised to review his conduct, in the spirit of solemn and faithful self-examination; and henceforth to order his way with more meekness and reverence of the authority of the great Head of the Church, as the Supreme President of all our judicatories.

"6. That all the parties, the Session and the appellant in the first instance, and after that, if necessary, the Presbytery with them, be required solemnly and prayerfully to confer together in the whole case, with the sincere purpose of preventing further proceedings and pacificating all concerned, according to the order and honor of the kingdom of Christ; and that they resume not their formal proceedings of trial before the Session, unless or until it is demonstrated that no other measures can preventively avail; and the Assembly do solemnly and affectionately exhort all persons at all connected with the case, and especially the parties themselves, to seek the things that make for peace, and the things whereby one may edify another."—*Minutes*, 1839, pp. 13–25.

23. *An Appeal arrests all further proceedings in the case until the Appeal shall be tried.*

[The Synod of Kentucky directed] "the Presbytery to which Mr. Craighead belonged to depose him, if he did not at their next meeting retract his errors; yet this sentence could not have been constitutionally inflicted, because Mr. Craighead appealed from the decision of the Synod, the effect of which was to arrest all further proceedings in the case until the appeal should be tried."—*Minutes*, 1822, p. 52.

24. *Order for Issuing an Appeal.*

a. "The order of the day, viz., an appeal by William H. Shumway from a decision of the Synod of Utica, confirming a decision by which he was suspended from the church of Watertown, was taken up.

"The sentence appealed from, the reasons assigned by the appellant for his appeal, the whole record of the proceedings of the inferior judicatories in the case, including all the testimony, and the reasons of their decision, were read. The parties were then heard, and the roll called, to give every member an opportunity to express his opinion; after which the final vote was taken, by which the appeal of Mr. Shumway was dismissed, and the sentence of the Session affirmed."—*Minutes*, 1835, p. 488.

b. "The moderator read the rule, enjoining on the members to recollect and regard their high character, as judges of a court of Jesus Christ, and the solemn duty in which they were about to act.

"The sentence appealed from, the reasons assigned by the appellant for his appeal, and which were on record, and the proceedings of the inferior judicatories in the case, including the testimony, and the reasons of the Presbytery for their decision, were read. The original parties were then heard; first Mr. Tappan, the appellant, and then the Presbytery in defence. The Presbytery having finished their defence, Mr. Tappan replied, and the Presbytery made some explanations. The parties having been fully heard, were considered as withdrawn. The roll was called, and the following adopted as the decision in the case." [See *ante*, p. 226.]—*Minutes*, 1839, pp. 17–25.

SECTION 3.—OF COMPLAINTS.

1. Distinction between a complaint and an appeal must be observed.—2. The complaint should be carried to the next superior court, unless valid reason be shown for a different course.—3. Complaint dismissed, for want of evidence of the complaint itself; also for want of evidence that notice was given of the intent to complain.—4. Through failure of the prosecutor to appear in person, or by proxy.—5. On account of informality.—6. After conference with the parties.—7. In the absence of the records.—Postponed for the same cause.—8. Complaint sustained for reasons assigned.—9. Referred back by consent of parties.—10. Referred to the court below, with instructions.—11. Judgment of a Synod reversed, because they decline the merits of the case; because they do not adhere to the rules; because they do not distinguish their appellate and original jurisdiction; and because they restore the appellant, without any evidence of repentance.—12. The superior court may reverse, either in whole or in part, but must observe the rules of Discipline.—13. The nature of the complaint, and the grounds on which it is issued, should be stated in the record.—14. A complaint against a Synod for dissolving a Presbytery sustained, and the Presbytery restored.—15. A complaint may be issued in the absence of the complainant.—16. A complaint must be specific.—17. The record must state that the minutes in the case have been read.—18. Advice given by a judicatory is not a ground of complaint.—19. The discussions must not involve the character of a party in his absence; regularity of proceedings only to be inquired into.—20. Order of issuing a complaint.

[For the distinction between an appeal and a complaint, see under "Appeal," p. 210, as also for the limitation of time within which a complaint may be laid.]

1. *The Distinction between an Appeal and a Complaint should be observed.*

"The records of the Synod of Utica were, on the recommendation of the committee, approved, with the exception that, on page 275, the Synod recognizes a reference to them *as an appeal,* which should have been considered and acted on merely as a *complaint against,* and not *as an appeal from* the decision of Presbytery concerning the settlement of a pastor."—*Minutes,* 1843, p. 22.

2. *A Complaint should be carried to the next Superior Court.*

a. "The complaint of John Cochran against a decision of the Session of the Eighth Presbyterian Church, Philadelphia, which was dismissed by the Presbytery of Philadelphia, as irrelevant and unfounded, appears to have been regularly conducted, except that it is brought directly to the Assembly from the Presbytery, instead of being carried first to the Synod; and no reasons are assigned for this course. Your committee would therefore recommend that this case be sent to the Synod for adjudication, should Mr. Cochran choose to prosecute his complaint." Adopted.—*Minutes*, 1833, p. 409.

b. [Members of a church complain of the conduct of a Presbytery. Complaint dismissed] because "complainants have not stated their grievances to the Presbytery, nor applied to it for redress."—*Minutes*, 1804, p. 309.

c. [The Session of a church present a paper, in a case acted upon and decided by a Synod. Complaint dismissed] because—

"1. This memorial is, in fact, a complaint against the decision of the Synod of Iowa; and it does not appear that any notice of intention to complain to the Assembly was given to the Synod by the complainants.

"2. No evidence has been presented by the complainants of the injustice of the decision of the Synod.

"The committee therefore recommend that the paper be returned to the complainants.

"The report was adopted."—*Minutes*, 1855, p. 16.

3. *Complaint Dismissed, for want of Evidence of the Complaint itself.*

a. "The Judicial Committee reported on the paper purporting to be a complaint of a minority of the Synod of Kentucky, against the proceedings of said Synod in the case of Dr. A. Smith, and recommended that the paper be returned for want of evidence of the complaint itself. This report was adopted."—*Minutes*, 1831, p. 339.

b. [Complainant had leave to withdraw] "because there is no evidence that notice of said complaint was given to Synod."—*Minutes*, 1834, p. 434.

c. "The Judicial Committee reported, that the complaint of E. W. Gilbert and others, in relation to the Synod of Philadelphia, for dissolving the church at Newark; also, the complaint of E. W. Gilbert and others, against the decision of the Synod of Philadelphia, dissolving the Presbytery of Wilmington; and also, the complaint of St. George's Church against the same Synod, for dissolving the Presbytery of Wilmington, are informal, there being no evidence before the committee that due notice of said complaints was given to the Synod of Philadelphia. This report was laid on the table."—*Minutes*, 1836, p. 252.

"The Judicial Committee reported in relation to the complaint of E. W. Gilbert and J. W. Pickands, on behalf of the Presbytery of Wilmington, against the Synod of Philadelphia, for dissolving said Presbytery, accompanied with a petition for their restoration, that since their last report, which was laid on the table, they had received satisfactory evidence that due notice of said complaint was given to the moderator of the Synod of Philadelphia, and that therefore the complaint is in order."—*Minutes*, 1836, p. 274.

4. *Dismissed through Failure of the Prosecutor.*

a. "The complaint of Rev. Dr. Henry Davis, against a decision of the Synod of Utica, was taken up, and dismissed on the ground that the complainant has not appeared to prosecute his complaint, nor any other person in his behalf."—*Minutes*, 1834, p. 454.

b. "The complaints of Rev. G. Duffield and W. R. Dewitt were dismissed on the ground that neither the complainants themselves, nor any person in their behalf, are present to prosecute those complaints."—*Minutes*, 1835, p. 490.

5. *Dismissed on account of Informality.*

"The subject of the complaint of the Session of Indianapolis was taken up, and after considerable discussion and mature deliberation, it was—

"*Resolved*, That this business be dismissed on account of informality, and that the papers be returned to the respective parties."—*Minutes*, 1829, p. 269.

6. *After Conference with Complainants, leave given to withdraw.*

"The committee to whom was referred the complaint of the Second Presbytery of Philadelphia against the Synod of Philadelphia, and also the complaint of Robert Cathcart, George Duffield, and E. W. Gilbert, against the Synod of Philadelphia; also the complaint of E. W. Gilbert, in behalf of himself and the Hanover Street Church of Wilmington, Delaware, against the Synod of Philadelphia; and also the remonstrance and petition of the Synod of Philadelphia; and also the remonstrance of the Presbytery of Philadelphia, both against proceedings of the last General Assembly in relation to the Second Presbytery of Philadelphia; together with the complaint of the Synod of Cincinnati on the same subject, reported that they have had an interview with several members of the Second Presbytery of Philadelphia, and subsequently with the Presbytery itself, on the subject of their complaint against the Synod of Philadelphia; and that they have also had an interview with thirty-one members of the Synod of Philadelphia, assembled at the request of the committee; that after a free conference with both these parties, during which the subject of their conference was treated with much tenderness and Christian affection, the committee are enabled to recommend to the Assembly the following resolution, viz.:

"*Resolved*, That the complainants in these cases have leave to withdraw their complaints, and that the consideration of all the other papers relating to the Second Presbytery of Philadelphia be indefinitely postponed."—*Minutes*, 1833, p. 399.

7. *Complaint dismissed in the absence of Records.*

"The Assembly took up the complaint of the Presbytery of Missouri against the Presbytery of St. Charles, laid over by the last Assembly, and the records of the Presbytery of St. Charles not being present—

"*Resolved*, That the complaint be dismissed."—*Minutes*, 1837, p. 429.

Postponed for the same Cause.

"The Assembly took up the appeal and complaint of the church of St. Charles against the Synod of Missouri, laid over by the last Assembly. The church appeared, and was ready for trial, but the records of the Synod not being present, the appeal was postponed, and it was ordered that the Synod of Missouri send up their records to the next General Assembly."—*Minutes*, 1837, p. 429.

8. *Complaint sustained for Reasons assigned.*

"Judicial business No. 12, viz., A complaint of Daniel Hayden and others against a decision of the Synod of Cincinnati, in the case of the Rev. George Beecher, was taken up.

"*Resolved*, That the complaint of the minority against the majority of the Synod of Cincinnati be, and the same is hereby sustained, on the ground that the Synod was, and is, competent to receive and examine witnesses called before them to support or to rebut the charges preferred by the minority of the Presbytery of Cincinnati against the majority of said Presbytery."—*Minutes*, 1834, p. 453.

9. *Referred back by consent of Parties.*

"Judicial business No. 9, reported by the Judicial Committee, viz., the complaint of Alexander M. Cowan against the Synod of Utica, was taken up and the complaint read, when, with the consent of Mr. Cowan and the members of the Synod present, it was—

"*Resolved*, That the subject be referred back to the Synod of Utica; and they are hereby directed to issue the case as referred to them by the Presbytery of Otsego."—*Minutes*, 1834, p. 434.

10. *Referred back to the Court below with Instructions.*

"Whereas, It appears that the decision of the Synod of Missouri, in the case of the complaint of Franklin Knox, has been recorded in resolutions, which set forth, not the reasons for the decision in the case, but which are, in fact, a compromise; which also admit that, at most, there is a strong presumption of guilt, but not evidence, agreeably to the Constitution, sufficient to convict; therefore—

"*Resolved*, That the complaint of Franklin Knox against the Synod of Missouri be referred back to the lower judicatory, and that the Synod be and hereby is instructed to reconsider said resolutions, and record their decision agreeably to the evidence and the principles of justice recognized in our Constitution."—*Minutes*, 1852, p. 173.

11. *Judgment of Synod reversed.*

"On the complaint of Mr. William H. Beecher and others against the Synod of Genesee, in the case of the appeal of Dr. Frank from the decision of the Presbytery of Genesee, the General Assembly sustain the complaint and reverse the judgment of the Synod on the following grounds, viz.:

"1. That the merits of the case seem to be expressly declined by the Synod as the subject-matter of adjudication.

"2. That the Synod appear not to have adhered to the alternatives prescribed by the Constitution. (See Book of Discipline, chap. vii, sec. 3, subsection 10.)

"3. That the Synod seem to have forgotten the nature and the limits of their appellate, as distinguished from the original jurisdiction in the case; in that they censure at their bar the appellant in a way competent, in any circumstances, only to the Session of the church to which the appellant was primarily amenable.

"4. That they seem to have forgotten also, in restoring the appellant, that some expression of repentance ought to have been exacted, especially if their reprimand could, from any tribunal, have been deserved.

"The Assembly therefore rule, that the Synod of Genesee should review their proceedings in this case; and, regarding alike the rules of the Constitution and the merits of the case, that they proceed to issue the same with equity and wisdom.

"In the matter of defining in what calumny consists, as connected with the case, the Assembly feel it not necessary to express any opinion farther than to recommend the principles of our constitutional discipline." —*Minutes*, 1840, p. 11.

12. *The Superior Court has a Right to Reverse either in whole or in part, but must observe the Principles of Discipline.*

"The Assembly having heard the complaint of the Presbytery of Carlisle against the Synod of Philadelphia, in the case of William S. McDowell, with the facts and arguments offered both by the Presbytery and the Synod, judged that the Synod had a constitutional right to reverse the decision of the Presbytery in the case, either in whole or in part, as to them might seem proper; but that in the exercise of this right, the Synod have not duly regarded the principles of discipline prescribed in the Constitution; inasmuch as it appears by their records that they have removed all censure from a man whom they declare to be deserving of rebuke, without directing that rebuke to be administered, and without receiving any evidence of his penitence."—*Minutes*, 1823, p. 81.

13. *The Nature of the Complaint, and the Grounds on which it is sustained, when it reverses the Action of the Court below, should be stated.*

On p. 571 (Minutes of the Synod of Geneva), "a complaint against a decision of a Presbytery, which is not named, is there represented as having been sustained, and the decision of the Presbytery reversed, without stating the nature of the complaint, or the grounds of the Synod's reversal. This your committee regard as a defective minute."—*Minutes*, 1835, p. 475.

14. *A Complaint against a Synod for Dissolving a Presbytery sustained, and the Act of the Synod reversed.*

"The Assembly took up the complaint of Mr. Gilbert and Mr. Pickands, in behalf of themselves and other members of the late Presbytery of Wilmington, against the Synod of Philadelphia, for dissolving them, and a petition to be restored to their former state, as a Presbytery.

"The sentence complained of, the reasons assigned by the complainants for their complaint, and the whole record of the proceedings of the Synod in the case, were read. The complainants were then heard by Mr. Duffield, who, by their request, appeared in their behalf, and the Synod, in explanation of their decision. After which, it was

"*Resolved*, That the complaint be sustained, and the petition granted; and the Presbytery are hereby restored to the state in which they were at the time of their organization by the Synod,—except that the church of New Castle, if they desire it, shall have the privilege of uniting with the Presbytery of New Castle."—*Minutes*, 1836, p. 279.

15. *A Complaint Issued in the Absence of the Complainants.*

"The Assembly took up the complaint against the Synod of Virginia, by the Rev. Samuel Houston and the Rev. Samuel B. Wilson, reported by the Judicial Committee. The complainants did not appear, but a written communication, containing the reasons of their complaint, was laid before the Assembly. At the request of the complainants, Mr. Weed was appointed to manage their cause in their absence."—*Minutes*, 1827, p. 210.

16. *A Complaint must be Specific.*

"The committee to whom was referred the memorial from the Synod of West Tennessee complaining of the Assembly of 1826, because they admitted the verbal testimony of a delegate to set aside a written document from the Synod of Tennessee, and on that account, in dividing the Synod, granted them only a part of their request; complaining also of the privilege granted by the Assembly to the missionaries among the Cherokees, as found in the printed Minutes of 1826, pages 21, 24, and 27, and requesting that the privilege there referred to may be rescinded, made the following report, which was adopted, viz.:

"That it does not appear, either from the Minutes of the Assembly, or from the memorial, what part, if any, of the request of the Synod of Tennessee was refused to be granted. The Assembly, therefore, can grant no relief till the grievance be specified and understood."—*Minutes*, 1828, p. 246.

17. *The Records must state that the Minutes in the Case have been read.*

"In the case of a complaint against the decision of a Presbytery, no evidence appears that the records of the Presbytery were read."

[Exceptions to Records, Synod of Indiana.]—*Minutes*, 1837, p. 480.

18. *Advice not a Ground of Complaint.*

The "complaint of members of the Park Church, Newark, New Jersey, against the Synod of New York and New Jersey," was dismissed, "on the ground that the action of the Presbytery was not a subject-matter of complaint, or removal of the case to a higher judicatory, their proceedings having been merely advisory, upon the memorial of the complainants."—*Minutes*, 1852, p. 166.

19. *The Character of the Absent not to be involved.*

"The following report of the Judicial Committee, in the case of the complaint of members of the Carlisle Presbytery against the decision of the Synod of Philadelphia, was received, which, being read, was adopted.

"*Resolved*, 1. That no discussion ought to be allowed which may involve the character of Mr. McDowell, in his absence.

"2. That the complaint ought to be considered by the Assembly, only so far as it regards the *regularity* of the proceedings of the Synod in reversing the judgment of Presbytery in the case."—*Minutes*, 1823, p. 74.

20. *Mode of Issuing a Complaint.*

"The Judicial Committee reported as being in order, a complaint of the Rev. Thompson Bird, in behalf of the Presbytery of Des Moines, against a decision of the Synod of Iowa, in the case of Rev. James H. Shields, who had been deposed by the Presbytery, for marriage with a woman divorced, as alleged, for insufficient grounds, and whom the Synod had restored. They recommend that it be taken up, and issued; and that in doing this the following order be observed:

"1. That the action of the Synod complained of be read.

"2. The reasons of the complaint.

"3. The action of the Synod in the case.

"4. The doings of the Presbytery, including all the testimony on which the action of the Synod was based.

"5. That the original parties then be heard; first, the complainant, and then the Synod.

"6. That any of the members of the inferior judicatory be heard in explanation of the grounds of their decision, or dissent from it."—*Minutes*, 1858, p. 580.

CHAPTER VII.

MORAL QUESTIONS.

SECTION 1.—ON MARRIAGE.

1. Marriage with a brother's widow declared incestuous, and the parties debarred communion while living together. A similar case referred to the discretion of the Session.—2. With a wife's sister. The offender restored, but such marriages condemned. Proposal for a change of the Confession negatived.—3. Marriage of the relicts of a brother and sister not incestuous.—4. With a wife's brother's daughter to be censured, but the parties not to be excluded from the Church.—5. With a niece, referred to the lower judicatories. Declared incestuous, and to demand judicial action.—6. Marriage engagements may be dissolved by consent of parties, but hasty engagements are to be censured.—7. Clandestine marriages discountenanced.—8. Publication of purpose of marriage. The Presbyteries to judge.—9. A bigamist not to be received to the Church. Wilful and obstinate desertion a lawful cause of divorce. If just cause of divorce exist, and divorce be refused him, he may be received to the Church, but only with great caution.—10. Marriage with a woman divorced on grounds not recognized by the Book, declared to be adultery, and the offender deposed from the ministry and excommunicated.—11. A deposition for having obtained a divorce on other than scriptural grounds, and marrying again, sustained.

1. *Marriage with a Brother's Widow declared incestuous.*

a. "The affair of Andrew Van Dyke, that was referred from the Presbytery of New Castle to the Synod, came under consideration, and a considerable time being spent in discoursing upon it, it was determined, *nemine contradicente,* that his marriage with his brother's wife or widow was incestuous and unlawful, and their living together as the consequence of that marriage is incestuous and unlawful; and that so long as they live together, they be debarred from all sealing ordinances."—*Minutes,* 1717, p. 50.

A similar Case referred to the Session.

b. "The appeal of Mr. William Adams from a decision of the Synod of Pittsburg was laid before the Assembly. The minutes of the Synod respecting the case being read, it appeared that the said William Adams had married his brother's widow; that his case having been brought before the Presbytery of Erie, the said Presbytery had pronounced his marriage unconstitutional, and that the Synod, upon an appeal, had confirmed the judgment of the Presbytery. From this judgment of the Synod, Mr. Adams appealed to the General Assembly.

"The Assembly, having taken the subject into consideration, were informed by some of their members, who are also members of the Synod of Pittsburg, that Mr. Adams's moral and religious character is perfectly fair and exemplary, except in what respects his marriage, which was contracted above fifteen years ago."—*Minutes,* 1805, p. 338.

[The report of the committee to whom the appeal was referred] "having been read and amended, was adopted, and is as follows, viz.:

"Whereas, Frequent decisions on marriages of a similar nature have been given by the late Synod of New York and Philadelphia, and by the General Assembly; and whereas, it appeared on these occasions that while such marriages are offensive to some, to others they appear lawful, therefore this Assembly consider the subject doubtful and delicate, and do not think it expedient to express any opinion on the decision of the Synod of Pittsburg in the present case. But in conformity to a decision made by last Assembly on a marriage somewhat similar, this General Assembly refers the case of Mr. Adams to the Session of the church of Rocky Spring, or that of any other in which he may be, and leave it to their discretion to act according to their own best light, and the circumstances in which they find themselves placed."—*Minutes,* 1805, p. 340.—See p. 243, *c.*

2. *Marriage with a deceased Wife's Sister.*

a. "In the case of a man's marrying two sisters, one after the other's death, the Synod judge, "That, as the Levitical law, enforced also by the civil laws of the land, is the only rule by which we are to judge of marriages, whoever marry within the degrees of consanguinity and affinity forbidden therein act unlawfully, and have no right to the distinguishing privileges of the Church; and as the marriages in question appear to be within the prohibited degrees, they are to be accounted unlawful, and the persons suspended from special communion while they continue in this relation."—*Minutes*, 1761, p. 312.

b. "Anthony Dushane, who has married the sister of his former wife, and whose case has been before the Synod for two years past, preferred a petition that he might no longer be debarred the privileges of the Church on the account of said marriage.

"After full and deliberate discussion, the question was put, 'Shall Anthony Dushane and his wife be capable of Christian privileges, their marriage notwithstanding?' which was carried in the affirmative by a considerable majority."—*Minutes*, 1782, p. 495.

"Remonstrances from sundry congregations were brought in by the Committee of Overtures, requesting a reversing of the decision of the last Synod, respecting the marriage of a man with his former wife's sister.

"The Synod having again resumed the consideration of the judgment which they passed last year concerning Anthony Dushane, declare their dissatisfaction with all such marriages as are inconsistent with the Levitical law, and that persons marrying within the degrees of consanguinity prohibited in that law, ought to suffer the censures of the Church; and they further judge, that, although the marriage of a man to two sisters successively, viz., to the one after the death of the other, may not be a direct violation of the express words of that law, yet, as it is contrary to the custom of the Protestant Churches in general, and an evidence of great untenderness toward many serious and well-disposed Christians, and may, through the prejudices or generally received opinions of the members of our Church, be productive of very disagreeable consequences; the persons contracting such marriages are highly censurable, and the practice ought to be disallowed in express terms by the Synod, and we do therefore condemn such marriages as imprudent and unseasonable. Yet as some things may be done very imprudently and unseasonably, which when done ought not to be annulled, we are of opinion that it is not necessary for the persons whom this judgment respects, to separate from one another, yet they should not be received into the communion of the Church without a solemn admonition, at the discretion of the Session of the congregation to which they belong; and the Synod publicly recommend it to all their members to abstain from celebrating such marriages, and to discountenance them by all the proper means in their power."—*Minutes*, 1783, p. 500.

c. "A reference from Bethel Church, South Carolina, was overtured, requesting the decision of the Assembly in relation to a case in which a person had married the sister of his deceased wife.

"*Resolved*, That this reference be answered by the following decision of the Assembly of 1804."—*Minutes*, 1810, p. 456.

[See case of James Gaston, p. 243, *c.*]

Marriage with a Deceased Wife's Sister inexpedient, unfriendly to Domestic Purity, and offensive to the Church, but not undoubtedly incestuous.

d. "The following appeal was then taken up, viz., the appeal of William Vance from the decision of the Presbytery of Washington, affirming the judgment of the Session of Cross Creek, which pronounces his marriage with his deceased wife's sister to be incestuous.

"The committee to which had been referred the appeal of Mr. William Vance from the judgment of the church Session of Cross Creek, and the judgment of the Presbytery of Washington, Pennsylvania, by which judgment Mr. Vance had been excluded from Church privileges on account of his being married to the sister of his deceased wife, reported, and their report was read, and the consideration and discussion of it was postponed, to take into consideration the following resolutions, which, after a full discussion, were adopted by the Assembly as their decision in the case, viz.:

"*Resolved*, That, in the opinion of this General Assembly, the marriage of a man to the sister of his deceased wife, and all similar connections, are highly inexpedient, unfriendly to domestic purity, and exceedingly offensive to a large portion of our churches.

"*Resolved*, That it be, and it hereby is earnestly enjoined upon the ministers, elders, and churches of our communion, to take every proper occasion to impress the sentiments contained in the foregoing resolution on the public mind, and by all suitable means to discourage connections so unfavorable in their influence on the peace and edification of the Church.

"*Resolved*, That while the Assembly adopt the opinion, and would enforce the injunction above expressed, they are by no means prepared to decide that such marriages as that in question are so plainly prohibited in Scripture, and so undoubtedly incestuous, as necessarily to infer the exclusion of those who contract them from Church privileges. They therefore refer the case of Mr. Vance back again to the Session of the church of Cross Creek, agreeably to former decisions of the General Assembly in similar cases, to be disposed of in such manner as the said Session may think most conducive to the interests of religion."—*Minutes*, 1821, pp. 21, 22.

Proposal for a Change in the Confession negatived.

e. "The committee on Mr. McCrimmon's appeal from a decision of the Presbytery of Fayetteville, confirming his suspension from the communion of the Church for having married his deceased wife's sister, reported, that, in their opinion, no relief can be given to the said McCrimmon, without an alteration of the Confession of Faith, chap. xxiv, sec. 4, the last clause of which declares, that "the man may not marry any of his wife's kindred nearer in blood than he may of his own, nor the woman of her husband's kindred nearer in blood than of her own;" but inasmuch as a diversity of opinion and practice obtains on this very important subject, your committee beg leave to submit the following resolution, viz.:

"*Resolved*, That the Presbyteries be, and they are hereby directed to take this matter into serious consideration, and send up in writing to the next General Assembly an answer to the question, whether the above-quoted clause of our confession shall be erased.

"The above report was adopted."—*Minutes*, 1826, p. 177.

"In regard to the proposed erasure of the 4th section of the 24th chapter of the Confession of Faith, sixty-eight Presbyteries have reported; fifty of them against the erasure, and eighteen in favor of it. The section, therefore, is not to be erased."—*Minutes*, 1827, p. 218.

3. *Where the Relicts of a Brother and Sister had Married.*

"That such a marriage, however inexpedient it be, yet, as we cannot find it prohibited by the Levitical law, is not to be condemned as incestuous."—*Minutes*, 1760, p. 303.

4. *With a Wife's Brother's Daughter.*

a. "After mature deliberation, the Synod declare their great dissatisfaction with all such marriages as are inconsistent with the Levitical law, which in cases matrimonial we understand is the law of our nation, and that persons intermarrying in these prohibited degrees, are not only punishable by the laws of the country, but ought to suffer the censures of the Church; and further judge, though the present case is not a direct violation of the express words of the Levitical law, yet as it is contrary to the custom of Protestant nations in general, and an evidence of great untenderness, and so opposite to such precepts of the Gospel as require Christians to avoid things of ill report, and all appearance of evil, and what is offensive to the Church; that the person referred to in this instance, ought to be rebuked by the Church Session, and others warned against such offensive conduct; and in case these persons submit to such rebuke, and are in other respects regular professors, that they be not debarred of Christian privilege."—*Minutes*, 1772, p. 427.

With a Wife's Half-Brother's Daughter.

b. "A reference from the Synod of Virginia was received through the Committee of Overtures, respecting a certain Charles Mitchel, who had married his former wife's half-brother's daughter, requesting the opinion of the Assembly whether such persons may be admitted to Church privileges. Whereupon,

"*Resolved*, That though the Assembly would wish to discountenance imprudent marriages, or such as tend in any way to give uneasiness to serious persons, yet it is their opinion, that the marriage referred to is not of such a nature as to render it necessary to exclude the parties from the privileges of the Church."—*Minutes*, 1797, p. 127.

5. *With a Deceased Wife's Sister's Daughter.*

a. "Reference on the petition of John Latham, who has married his deceased wife's sister's daughter, praying a reconsideration of his case, which was tried and issued against him, nine years ago, in the Synod of the Carolinas.

"After mature deliberation, it was

"*Resolved*, That the case of John Latham, referred for the decision of the General Assembly, by the Synod of the Carolinas, be remitted to the said Synod, and that they be directed to review the case, and if they shall judge it to be consistent with the existing laws of the State and the peace of the Church, they may admit the persons alluded to, to its privileges."—*Minutes*, 1799, p. 176.

b. "The Session of the Church of Westminster, in Jefferson County, State of Tennessee, having requested the direction of this Assembly in a case of discipline, viz.: Whether a man and his wife were admissible to Church privileges who had been related to each other as uncle and niece; that is to say, the woman being sister's daughter to the man's former wife, whereupon the Assembly

"*Resolved*, That such marriages as that in question have been determined both by the late Synod of New York and Philadelphia, and by the General Assembly, to be on the one hand not forbidden by the laws of God, and on the other hand to be contrary to the general practice of Protestant churches, and the feelings and opinions of many serious Christians among ourselves, and on that account to be discountenanced, therefore,

"*Resolved*, That when such marriages take place, the Session of the church where they happen, are carefully to consider the case, and if they think it expedient, to administer such discipline, as they may judge to be deserved, for that want of Christian tenderness and forbearance that are incumbent on all the professors of our holy religion, or for violating any municipal law, if this has been done; and then to admit or restore them to good standing in the Church. And if the Session judge that the state of society is such where these marriages take place, as that neither the duty of Christian tenderness and forbearance, nor the laws of the State have been violated, they may admit the persons concerned to Christian privileges without censure."—*Minutes*, 1802, p. 248.

c. "It appeared that a Mr. James Gaston had been censured as being guilty of incest for having married a woman who was sister's daughter to his former wife; and had brought the cause by appeal to the Synod of Pittsburg. The Synod, conceiving that the cause involved a high question of discipline, chose to refer it to the General Assembly for their decision.

"The Assembly having given repeated decisions on similar cases, cannot advise to annul such marriages, or to pronounce them to such a degree unlawful, as that the parties, if otherwise worthy, should be debarred from the privileges of the Church. But as great diversity of opinion seems to exist on such questions in different parts of the Church, so that no absolute rule can be enjoined with regard to them that shall be universally binding, and consistent with the peace of the Church, and as the cases in question are esteemed to be doubtful, the Assembly is constrained to leave it to the discretion of the inferior judicatories under their care, to act according to their own best lights, and the circumstances in which they find themselves placed."—*Minutes,* 1804, p. 306.

d. With a Sister's Daughter.

"The report of the Committee on Bills and Overtures in answer to the two questions, 'May a man, in accordance with the teachings of the Scriptures, marry a daughter of his own sister?' and 'When members of the Church have contracted such a marriage, may they still retain their standing in the Church?' was taken up for consideration.

"A motion was made for indefinite postponement, which was lost.

"The report of the committee was postponed; and the following substitute, proposed by Rev. S. P. M. Hastings, was adopted:

"'*Resolved,* 1. That the first question be answered in the negative, such marriages being evidently contrary to the teachings of the Scriptures, and incestuous. See Lev. 18 : 6, 12, 13.

"'*Resolved,* 2. That the second question in the overture be answered as follows, viz.: In the judgment of this Assembly, such a connection as is contemplated by the overture demands the judicial action of the Church, and, if not repented of, should incur Church censure.'"—*Minutes,* 1853, p. 339.

6. *Marriage Engagements may be dissolved, but hasty Engagements are to be censured.*

"An affair concerning promises of marriage between —— and a young woman, being laid before the Synod by the Presbytery of New Castle, the Synod on the consideration thereof, and because —— desired on some accounts to be loosed from said obligation, and it was found the young woman scrupled the lawfulness of their being loosed from said obligation, the first question put in the affair was, Whether a single man and woman having promised marriage to each other, may lawfully agree again to release each other from the promise; and after mature deliberation, the Synod resolved the case, that it was lawful, *nemine contradicente.*

"—— being called before the Synod and asked, whether he had promised to this young woman marriage, he acknowledged he had, and that he was culpable in entering into such rash and unwarrantable methods of engaging.

"The question was put, censure or not, and it was carried censure.

"Another question was put, what censure is to be inflicted upon him for his misconduct in the above mentioned affair?

"And after serious consideration and much reasoning on this head, the Synod came to a resolution, that a rebuke before the Synod was necessary to show our detestation of such rash proceedings in young people. And that Mr. John Thompson admonish him.

"—— being called, the minute in respect to his affair was read and he censured accordingly, to which he submitted."—*Minutes,* 1750, p. 198.

7. *Clandestine Marriage discouraged.*

"The Synod do recommend it to all their members to use the greatest caution that they do not countenance any clandestine marriages, and especially that they do not marry any that they have reason to suspect to go contrary to the minds of their parents and guardians in seeking it."—*Minutes,* 1735, p. 115.

8. *Publication of Purpose of Marriage.*

"What is a sufficient publication of the purpose of marriage according to the second sentence of the sixth section of the eleventh chapter of the Book of Discipline?

"*Resolved,* That the following be given as an answer to this question, viz.: That the Presbyteries are the best judges in the case."—*Minutes,* 1820, p. 740.

9. *Bigamy and Divorce.*

A Bigamist to be excluded from the Communion. Wilful Desertion a just cause of Divorce. If just cause exist, and Divorce be refused, he may be admitted to Church privileges, but only with the greatest caution.

"A married man left Ireland a number of years ago, leaving his family behind him, with hopes of providing better for them in this country. He afterwards returned to Ireland three sundry times, with an intention of bringing in his family. But by no arguments could his wife be persuaded to come with him; and the last time peremptorily refused all further cohabitation. He afterwards returned, and remained in single life ten years in this country. He is since married, and has children in second marriage: his wife and he are desiring communion.

"This man ought not to be admitted to the privileges of the Church; because, although wilful and obstinate desertion is a legal cause of divorce, yet it does not appear that this man has actually been divorced from his wife; and it is improper and dangerous to receive to Church communion such persons as, in the eye of the civil law, are living in vice. And although a good man may sometimes be oppressed by power, and prevented from obtaining a divorce where sufficient causes exist, yet it does not appear from your representation that he has used the proper means to obtain a legal divorce, nor even to authenticate the facts upon which he founds his application for the privileges of the Church by sufficient evidence from Ireland,—the place in which they happened, and where alone they can be substantiated; and it is contrary to all just rules of proceeding to take any evidence or representation *ex parte*. But, the decision of the Assembly notwithstanding, if it shall appear that this man has separated from his wife by her wilful and obstinate desertion, and that he has taken all just means to obtain a divorce, to which he was lawfully entitled, but was prevented and oppressed by the power of antagonists or of unjust courts; and if he shall moreover produce such evidence of these facts from the place in which they happened, as would entitle him to a divorce by the laws of this land and of this Church, then, in that case, it is the opinion of the General Assembly that such man behaving himself otherwise as a good Christian, may be admitted to Church privileges. But in such case, it is necessary that the most authentic evidence be required and great caution used, both that the proceedings of the Church may not be inconsistent with the civil law, and that a door be not opened to laxness on this important subject of morals."—*Minutes*, 1790, p. 28.

10. *Marriage with a Divorced Woman.*

"The Assembly resumed the consideration of the unfinished business of the morning, viz., the complaint against the Synod of Iowa. Every member having had an opportunity to express his opinion in the case, the roll was called, and the complaint of the Presbytery of Des Moines against the Synod of Iowa, in the case of Rev. James H. Shields, was sustained by a vote of 106 to 52. Excused from voting, 1.

"The Rev. Messrs. Theodore Spencer, James Eells, and John W. Dulles, with Hon. Arnold Naudain, M.D., and Thomas W. Fry, M.D., were appointed a committee to prepare a minute on this case.

"The committee appointed to prepare a minute on the complaint against the Synod of Iowa in the case of the Rev. James H. Shields, report as follows:

"In the year 1853, Maria C. Cowles presented a petition under oath to the District Court of Wayne County, Iowa, praying for a divorce from her husband, William A. Cowles, in which it was stated substantially, that she had been lawfully married to said Cowles in January, 1839, in the State of Massachusetts; that they had lived together there until August, 1851, when she separated herself from him, and proceeded to Iowa, where she has since resided. That, previous to her departing from him in 1851, her husband was in the habit of becoming intoxicated, and when so intoxicated, was ill-natured and abusive,—so much so, that her situation as his wife became intolerable; and she had been under the necessity of leaving his house and of making her own living since that time, the defendant having neglected to make provision for her support since the period of her separation from him. No pertinent proof of the truth of these allegations was made; but the court, notwithstanding, granted her a divorce *a vinculo matrimonii;* when James H. Shields, then a member of the Presbytery of Des Moines, being cognizant of all the facts in the case, was married to the said Maria C. Cowles, and has continued to cohabit with her as his wife. In April, 1856, the Presbytery instituted proceedings against him for adultery, and finally convicted him of that offence, and deposed him from the ministry and excommunicated him from the Church. Thereupon the said Shields appealed to the Synod of Iowa, who reversed the decision of Presbytery. The case is before this General Assembly, on a complaint of the Rev. Thompson Bird, on behalf of the Presbytery, against the action of Synod.

"In view of all the testimony brought before the Assembly, the complaint is sustained.

"It has not been made to appear, that the said Maria C. Cowles attempted to establish the fact of adultery against her husband, William A. Cowles. Neither has there been proved 'such wilful desertion' on his part, 'as can no way be remedied by the Church or civil magistrate,' as is recognized in the Confession of Faith (chap. xxiv, sec. 6) as 'cause sufficient of dissolving the bond of marriage.'

"The General Assembly do, therefore, consider that the said James H. Shields was properly convicted of adultery; and the decision of the Synod of Iowa in this case is hereby reversed, and the judgment of the Presbytery of Des Moines therein confirmed.

"The Assembly, whilst rendering this decision, takes occasion to call the attention of the churches under its care to a tendency, manifest in some portions of our country, to relax the sacredness of the marriage tie. Lying, as the institution of marriage does, at the very foundation of order, purity, and prosperity in the State and in the Church, the Assembly cannot view without abhorrence any attempt to diminish its sanctity or to extend beyond the warrant of the Holy Scriptures the grounds of divorce."—*Minutes*, 1858, pp. 599, 600.

11. [A sentence of the Presbytery of Portage, suspending, and ultimately deposing, the Rev. Geo. Sheldon, on the charge of adultery, in having married a second wife in the lifetime of his first, from whom he had obtained a divorce in the civil courts, on other than scriptural grounds, was sustained.—*Minutes*, 1858, p. 607, 609. See chap. vi, sec. 2, 21, p. 223.]

Section 2.—On the Sabbath.

1. A postmaster officiating on the Sabbath is rightly excluded from the Church. —2. Ownership in stages running upon the Sabbath, inconsistent with Christian character.—3. Petitions in reference to Sunday mails.—4. A deliverance on the profanation of the Sabbath. Ministers enjoined to preach upon it, and Sessions to enforce discipline.—5. Deliverance of the Assembly of 1836 upon the same subject.—6. On Sabbath desecration. Travelling on the Sabbath specially condemned.—7. Church Sessions urged to greater fidelity.

1. *Officiating as Postmaster on the Sabbath excludes from Communion of the Church.*

a. "An appeal by Mr. Wiley, postmaster in Washington, Pennsylvania, from a decision of the Synod of Pittsburg, by which it is determined that Mr. Wiley's officiating as postmaster on the Sabbath day, in existing circumstances, is a sufficient reason to exclude him from the special privileges of the Church, was overtured and read. On motion,

"*Resolved*, That the above decision of the Synod of Pittsburg be affirmed, and it hereby is affirmed."—*Minutes*, 1810, p. 456.

b. "A petition, signed by a number of persons in Washington, Pennsylvania, and its vicinity, praying the revision, with a view to its being rescinded, of the decision of the General Assembly of 1810, respecting the case of Mr. Wiley, postmaster, was overtured.

"*Resolved*, That the prayer of the petitioners be not granted."—*Minutes*, 1812, p. 508.

2. *Ownership in Stages running on the Sabbath inconsistent with Christian Profession.*

"In an overture relative to receiving a person as a member of the Church, who is a proprietor in a line of stages which carries the mail and runs on the Sabbath—

"*Resolved*, That it is the decided opinion of this Assembly that all attention to worldly concerns on the Lord's day, farther than the works of necessity and mercy demand, is inconsistent both with the letter and spirit of the fourth commandment; and consequently all engagements in regard to secular occupations on the Lord's day, with a view to secure worldly advantages, are to be considered inconsistent with Christian character, and that those who are concerned in such engagements ought not to be admitted into the communion of the Church while they continue in the same."—*Minutes*, 1819, p. 713.

[See also 5, resolution 5, p. 253, on owning stock in steamboats, canals, railroads, &c., which run on the Sabbath.]

3. *Petitions to Congress on Carrying the Mails on the Sabbath.*

[In 1812, the Assembly addressed a petition to Congress, setting forth the evils of Sabbath profanation, and praying] "for such an alteration in the law relative to the mails as will prevent the profanation of the Sabbath which now takes place in conveying and opening the mail."—*Minutes*, 1812, pp. 513, 514.

Again, in 1814, a petition on the same subject was prepared, and "each Presbytery directed to take order that the same be circulated for subscription in all the congregations under their care," and "forwarded to Congress by the first day of January next."—*Minutes*, 1814, p. 566.

[In 1815, the Assembly again considered the subject, and after adopting the report of a committee (Minutes, p. 597), sent out another petition to be signed and forwarded to Congress, viz.:]

"The undersigned, inhabitants of ———, and State of ———, beg leave to represent to the honorable the Senate and House of Representatives of the United States, in Congress assembled, that in the opinion of your petitioners, the transportation and opening of the mail on the Sabbath day is inconsistent with the proper observance of that sacred day, injurious to the morals of the nation, and provokes the judgments of the Ruler of nations. We perceive from the report of the Postmaster-General, at your last session on this subject, that it is his opinion that when peace shall arrive, the necessity of carrying and opening the mail on the Sabbath day will greatly diminish. While, therefore, we congratulate you on the return of peace, we approach you with confidence, and beseech you to take this subject into your serious consideration, and enact such laws as you in your wisdom may deem necessary for the removal of this evil. And we, your petitioners, as in duty bound, will ever pray."—*Minutes*, 1815, p. 601.

4. *Deliverance on the Profanation of the Sabbath.*

a. "The committee to whom was referred the overture respecting the profanation of the Lord's day, presented the following resolutions, which were adopted, viz.:

"1st. *Resolved*, That this Assembly regard with pain and deep regret the profanation of the Lord's day, which exists in our country in various forms, and which is calculated in an alarming degree to create a neglect of public worship, a contempt of the authority of Almighty God, a corruption of morals, and eventually to bring down the judgment of God on our land.

"2d. *Resolved*, That the Assembly repeat the warnings which have heretofore been frequently given on this subject, and do solemnly and earnestly exhort the churches and individuals in their connection, to avoid a participation in the guilt of profaning this holy day.

"3d. *Resolved*, That it be earnestly recommended to the ministers of the Presbyterian churches who have pastoral charges, frequently and solemnly to address their people on the subject of the sanctification of the Lord's day, and to urge its vital importance to our moral, social, and civil, as well as religious welfare.

"4th. *Resolved,* That it be solemnly enjoined on all the Presbyteries and church Sessions in our connection, to exercise discipline on their respective members whenever guilty of violating the sanctity of the Sabbath; and that an inquiry should be annually instituted in each Presbytery relative to this subject; and that each pastor should, at the earliest opportunity practicable, present this subject, in all its solemn importance, to the Session of the church under his pastoral charge, and invite the co-operation of its members in all proper and prudent measures for the suppression of Sabbath-breaking; and further, that it be recommended to all our ministers and church members, when travelling, to give preference to such livery establishments, steamboats, canal-boats, and other public vehicles, as do not violate the law of God and of the land, in relation to the Sabbath."—*Minutes*, 1826, pp. 182, 183.

b. "*Resolved,* That this Assembly renewedly enjoin upon their Presbyteries and churches the duty of enforcing the discipline of the Church in every case of a violation of the Sabbath."—*Minutes,* 1828, p. 242.

5. *Another Deliverance upon the same Subject.*

"The committee to whom was referred Overture No. 5, relating to the Christian Sabbath, respectfully report:

"That they have given to the consideration of it all that attention which circumstances would permit; and are prepared to submit to the Assembly the results of their deliberations.

"One important fact cannot be denied. The desecration of the Sabbath is certainly increasing with fearful rapidity in almost every part of our beloved country. A solemn and alarming crisis has already come. Unless the slumbering energies of the Church are speedily aroused to arrest the progress of this growing evil, the entire obliteration of the Sabbath will, at no distant period, be the result. It is necessary only to look into our large cities and villages on the Sabbath, or to glance the eye along our navigable rivers and over our beautiful lakes, or to trace the extended lines of our canals and railroads, or listen to the perpetual rumbling of loaded vehicles on all our travelled routes, in order to be convinced that Sabbath-breaking has already become a sin of giant growth in our land. It is, indeed, a wide-spread, deep-seated, unblushing evil. It enters boldly into almost every commercial interest in the country, and embraces, directly or indirectly, in its broad sweep of mischief, a vast multitude of individuals; and, what is still worse, an alarming proportion of these offenders belong to the Church of the living God. Here is the root of the evil. The Church has become a deliberate partaker in this great sin. In this way has her warning voice been well-nigh silenced, her redeeming power over the community paralyzed, and the salutary restraints of a consistent example effectually vacated. Reformation, then, must begin at the house of God. If the Church alone can save the Sabbath from being abolished, she must first reform her own conduct. In entering upon the work, it must not be forgotten that, in its failure or success are involved the best interests of the Church, of our country, and the world. The rest of the Sabbath is the only wise and adequate provision for the wants of the animal system. The influence of the Sabbath can alone be relied on to sustain our free institutions, to extend the empire of law, to preserve domestic order and happiness, and to continue the bare existence of morality and religion in the world. The abandonment of the Sabbath is, therefore, nothing less than resigning all that is sacred and dear to a Christian people, for time and for eternity. It is certain that whatever is done to rebuke and arrest the profanation of the Sabbath, must be done immediately. The work of reform cannot be delayed, without hazarding the irretrievable loss of all the blessings which flow from the observance of that day. The task has already become formidable and difficult. It is not, however, altogether hopeless. The Sabbath may yet be restored, and its blessings perpetuated. The Church and the ministry can, under God, do all that the exigency demands. Let this Assembly do their whole duty; let them lift up a voice of strength; let them send out a loud note of alarm; let them determine, in the strength of the Lord, to carry out, in their practical relation to the Sabbath, the true principles of Christian discipline, and the whole Church may be cleansed, the Sabbath reinstated, and this great and guilty nation saved. Till this is done, the power of every other Christian enterprise will be circumscribed and fluctuating. Nothing that is pure and holy can flourish without the Sabbath. The Sabbath reform is the fundamental enterprise. It is utterly vain to think of substituting any other conservative power. The question of rescuing the Sabbath from general profanation is, absolutely, a question of life and death to every Christian denomination in the world. Such is the momentous nature of the subject under consideration. Your committee rejoice that in this work all hearts may unite, and every minor difference be forgotten. Here is common ground. The Sabbath of the Lord is the inheritance of all true Christians; and there is work enough for all. The Church must revive her wholesome discipline. The ministry must cry aloud and spare not. The press must be enlisted; the whole community aroused. The entire instrumentality which God has prepared for preserving his own institutions must be called forth, and kept in untiring requisition. For the purpose of enabling the General Assembly more effectually to speak their sentiments to the churches and the nation, your committee recommend the adoption of the following resolutions:

"1. *Resolved,* That the observance of the Sabbath is indispensable to the preservation of civil and religious liberty, and furnishes the only security for eminent and abiding prosperity, either to the Church or the world.

"2. *Resolved,* That the growing desecration of the Sabbath in our country must be speedily arrested, and the habits of the community essentially reformed, or the blessings of the Sabbath, civil, social, and religious, will soon be irrecoverably lost.

"3. *Resolved,* That inasmuch as the work of a general reformation belongs, under God, to the Christian Church, it is the duty of the Church to apply the corrections of a firm and efficient discipline to all known violations of the Sabbath, on the part of her members.

"4. *Resolved,* That inasmuch as ministers of the Gospel must act a conspicuous part in every successful effort to do away the sin of Sabbath-breaking, it is their duty to observe, both in their preaching and their practice, the rule of entire abstinence from all profanation of the Lord's day, studiously avoiding even the appearance of evil.

"5. *Resolved,* That, in the judgment of this General Assembly, the owners of stock in steamboats, canals, railroads, &c., which are in the habit of violating the Sabbath, are lending their property and their influence to one of the most wide-spread, alarming, and deplorable systems of Sabbath desecration which now grieves the hearts of the pious, and disgraces the Church of God.

"That it be respectfully recommended to the friends of the Lord's day, as soon as possible, to establish such means of public conveyance as shall relieve the friends of the Sabbath from the necessity under which they now labor of travelling at any time in vehicles which habitually violate that holy day, and thus prevent them from being in any way partakers in other men's sins in this respect.

"6. *Resolved,* That the power of the pulpit and the press must be immediately put in requisition on behalf of a dishonored Sabbath, that the magnitude and remedy of the evils, which its violation involves, may be fully understood by the whole community.

"7. *Resolved,* That this Assembly solemnly enjoin it upon the churches under their care to adopt, without delay, all proper measures for accomplishing a general and permanent reformation from the sin of Sabbath-breaking, and all its attendant evils.

"8. *Resolved,* That a committee of one from each Synod under the care of this Assembly be now appointed, to hold correspondence with ministers and churches, for the purpose of carrying out and applying the leading principles of the foregoing report and resolutions.

"9. *Resolved,* That the foregoing report and resolutions be published in such newspapers, secular and religious, as are friendly to the observance of the Sabbath."—*Minutes,* 1836, pp. 281–283.

6. *For the better Observance of the Sabbath.*

"The committee to whom was referred Overture No. 5, to wit, 'A memorial from the Presbytery of Cleveland on the subject of Sabbath mails,' having been instructed to report on the general subject of 'Sabbath desecration,' submit the following:

"In the deliberate judgment of your committee, it is an unquestionable fact that, in despite of all which has been said and done to check it, the profanation of the Lord's day is, on the whole increasing. There are, indeed, some local and cheering exceptions to this remark, which we are happy to acknowledge. As a national sin, however, it steadily gathers strength, and puts on a more unblushing face every year. We hear much of the moral machinery which has been set in motion for the salvation of our country and of the world—of the blessed light of the nineteenth century, and the glory of our free institutions. Too often do we seem to forget that the very institution which is the chief support of liberty, learning, and religion, is itself standing in fearful jeopardy. All those whose lot is cast in any of the great centres of business, or on any of the principal avenues of intercommunication, know that what your committee assert is true. Their own eyes have seen it, their own ears have heard it, and their hearts have bled over it a thousand times. It is, in fact, universally conceded, that the desecration of the Sabbath has become a giant evil, calling loudly for the most efficient measures of reform. Your committee desire not unnecessarily to publish the faults of the Christian Church. But they are compelled to confess, that in many parts of the country the frequent violations of the Sabbath by ministers of the Gospel, and by other professors of religion, is a serious obstacle in the way of all attempts at radical and permanent reformation. Till the ministry and the Church have purified themselves, all else will be, as it has been, 'beating the air.' Travelling on the Sabbath, a practice to which the convocation of the highest judicatory of our Church lends its guilty sanction; voluntary participation in enterprises and improvements which are prosecuted at the expense of the Sabbath; the legalized profanation of this holy day by the transmission of the mail on all the principal routes; and the frequent neglect of Church discipline, are among the many causes of the rapid spread of this enormous evil. The bare enumeration of these causes suggests the proper remedy. Resolutions, addresses, conventions, and all the stirring appeals which the subject has called forth, are, by themselves, utterly ineffectual. The leviathan with which we are now contending is not to be so tamed. A more potent corrective must be applied, or we shall become more and more a nation of Sabbath-breakers. The Church undoubtedly possesses the power to cleanse her own garments, and till she has done this, she has no strength to put on for the reformation of others. Having done this, the next step will be to lift up a united voice against all that immoral legislation behind which the sin of Sabbath-breaking now stands intrenched. What has been found true in the 'Temperance Reform,' will be found true in the 'Sabbath Reform.' The sanction of law must be removed from every evil which you would frown upon and exterminate. To do this, the public mind must be waked up, and held awake till the combined energy of patriotism and piety is enlisted and pledged for the protection of the Sabbath against every tangible form of profanation and abuse. Your committee accordingly recommend for your adoption the following resolutions, viz.:

"*Resolved*, That this Assembly regard the prosecution of a journey on any part of the Sabbath, whether by ministers, elders, or church members, for the sake of convenience or of avoiding expense, as deserving of special notice and unqualified disapprobation.

"*Resolved*, That this Assembly affectionately urge upon all the judicatories of the Church to take suitable measures for enforcing the wise discipline of the Church against all violations of the Sabbath within their own cognizance and jurisdiction.

"*Resolved*, That it is the duty of the Christian ministry to unite in more concentrated and persevering efforts to assert the claims of the Christian Sabbath upon the habitual regard of the whole community.

"*Resolved*, That the Assembly will give its most cordial approbation to any and every wise plan for uniting the sympathies and strength of all evangelical denominations in defence of the Christian Sabbath.

"*Resolved*, that a committee of nine be appointed to correspond with other evangelical denominations on the subject of measures for promoting a better observance of the Lord's day.

"*Resolved*, That the clerks of this Assembly be requested to cause these resolutions to be officially published and circulated as widely as possible, through the religious press, and that all ministers within our bounds be requested to present them before their respective congregations."—*Minutes*, 1838, pp. 658, 659.

[See also Minutes, 1840, p. 14; 1843, p. 13; 1846, p. 15, for substantially the same action.]

7. *Church Sessions enjoined to greater fidelity.*

"The Committee on Bills and Overtures made a report on the subject of the Sabbath, which was adopted, and is as follows:

"The Assembly are at a loss what to say more than what they have repeatedly said, by way of urging on all our churches and congregations, and the community generally, a better observance of the holy Sabbath. Of its Divine original and authority we have no doubt. Nor can we doubt its indisputable necessity in keeping up the institutions of religion, and promoting the cause of salvation and pure morality. What could we do without the Sabbath? And where, in half a century, will be our glorious civil and religious liberty, if the terrible process of Sabbath desecration be permitted to go on as it has done for the past ten years? Let the history of other nations answer. Let the fearful declarations of God's word admonish us to anticipate the result. 'For the nation and kingdom that will not serve thee shall perish.'

"While, therefore, we earnestly entreat our fellow-citizens of every class 'to remember the Sabbath day to keep it holy,' the Assembly do hereby, in a special manner, enjoin it upon the church Sessions to watch over their brethren with tenderness and great fidelity in respect to the observance of the Sabbath; and to exercise wholesome discipline on those who, by travelling or other ways, presume to trample upon this sacred institution. And we further enjoin it upon the Presbyteries annually to institute inquiries of the eldership, as to the manner in which this injunction has been attended to in their respective churches."—*Minutes*, 1853, p. 323.

Section 3.—Intemperance.

1. Action of the Assembly. Recommendation to preach upon the sin and mischiefs of intemperate drinking.—2. Temperance societies, on the basis of total abstinence from the use of ardent spirits, approved.—3. Manufacture and traffic in ardent spirits condemned.—4. Total abstinence from all that will intoxicate, the only true principle of temperance.—5. Prohibitory laws commended and urged.—6. An overture on temperance. Relation of the Church to voluntary associations.

[1. A committee was appointed "to endeavor to devise measures which, when sanctioned by the General Assembly, may have an influence in preventing some of the numerous and threatening mischiefs which are experienced throughout our country, by the excessive and intemperate use of spirituous liquors," to report to the next Assembly. On the report of the committee (Minutes, 1811, p. 474), it was]

"*Resolved*, That it be recommended to all the ministers of the Presbyterian Church in the United States to deliver public discourses, as often as circumstances may render it expedient, on the sin and mischiefs of intemperate drinking; in which, as well as on other suitable occasions, both public and private, it will be proper pointedly and solemnly to warn their hearers, and especially members of the Church, not only against actual intemperance, but against all those habits and indulgences which may have a tendency to produce it.

"2. That it be enjoined on all church Sessions within the bounds of the General Assembly, that they exercise a special vigilance and care over the conduct of all persons in the communion of their respective churches, with regard to this sin, and that they sedulously endeavor, by private warning and remonstrance, and by such public censures as different cases may require, to purge the Church of a sin so enormous in its mischiefs, and so disgraceful to the Christian name.

"3. That it be recommended to the ministers and other officers and members of our Church, that they exert themselves to diffuse as extensively as possible, among their congregations, and the community at large, such addresses, sermons, tracts, or other printed compositions on this subject, as may have a tendency to produce a suitable impression against the use of ardent spirits, and to recommend sobriety and temperance.

"4. That it be recommended to the officers and members of our

Church to take such measures as may be judged proper and effectual for reducing the number of taverns and other places of vending liquors by small measure, in all those parts of our country in which either their excessive numbers, or the improper character of such places, renders them a public nuisance.

"It is believed that the evils arising from these sources are incalculably great, and that by prudent management they admit, under Providence, of very considerable diminution."—*Minutes*, 1812, p. 511.

[In 1818 the evils of intemperance are enlarged upon in the pastoral letter, and the officers and members of our Church are urged "to abstain even from the common use of ardent spirits." Minutes, p. 689. In 1828, the Assembly commends the "American Society for the Promotion of Temperance." Minutes, p. 214. The same year they "appoint the fourth Thursday of January, 1829, a day of fasting, humiliation, and prayer, with especial reference to this sin." Minutes, p. 244.]

2. *Entire Abstinence from the Use of Ardent Spirits.*

"The report of the Committee on Temperance was taken up, and after mature consideration, was unanimously adopted, and is as follows, viz.:

"*Resolved*, 1. That this Assembly regard with devout gratitude and praise the great success which has attended the efforts of the friends of the cause of temperance during the past year, as evinced in the increase of the number and zeal of temperance societies, in the diminution of the sale of ardent spirits, and in the existence of a strong and increasing public sentiment against the use of it.

"2. That they cordially approve and rejoice in the formation of temperance societies on the principle of entire abstinence from the use of ardent spirits, as expressing disapprobation of intemperance in the strongest and most efficient manner, and making the most available resistance to this destructive and wide-spreading evil.

"3. That they deeply deplore the apathy manifested by many professing Christians towards the cause of temperance, while many distinguished persons who make no religious profession, are prompt and powerful fellow-laborers with Christians in this worthy and divinely sanctioned cause. And especially do they grieve and wonder that members of our churches, in view of an evil so desolating and so awful in its prospective bearings on all the interests of our country, should not only take no part in the exertions of their brethren and fellow-citizens against intemperance, but by using and trafficking in ardent spirits, be actively engaged in promoting it.

"4. That they earnestly recommend, as far as is practicable, the forming of temperance societies in the congregations under their care; and that all members of the churches adopt the principle of entire abstinence from the use of ardent spirits.

"5. That as friends of the cause of temperance, this Assembly rejoice to lend the force of their example to that cause as an ecclesiastical body by an entire abstinence themselves from the use of ardent spirits."—*Minutes*, 1829, p. 262.

"The committee appointed to prepare a minute expressive of the views of the Assembly on the subject of temperance, reported the following resolutions, which were adopted, viz.:

"*Resolved*, 1. That this Assembly considers itself called upon to make a public acknowledgment of the goodness of God for the unparalleled success with which he has crowned the efforts of those who are actively concerned in the promotion of temperance.

"2. That the experience of the past year furnishes additional and most abundant evidence of the wisdom and importance of the plan adopted by the American Temperance Society.

"3. That this Assembly feels bound to repeat a former recommendation to the ministers, elders, and members of the churches under its care, to discountenance the use of distilled liquors, not only by abstaining themselves from the use of such liquors, but by actively promoting every prudent measure devised for the purpose of furthering the cause of temperance.

"4. That this Assembly earnestly recommends to all persons for whose spiritual interests it is bound to consult, that they favor the formation of temperance societies on the plan of entire abstinence."—*Minutes*, 1830, p. 298.

3. *Manufacture and Traffic in Ardent Spirits.*

a. "5. That while this Assembly would by no means encroach upon the rights of private judgment, it cannot but express its very deep regret that any members of the Church of Christ should, at the present day, and under existing circumstances, feel themselves at liberty to manufacture, vend, or use ardent spirits, and thus as far as their influence extends, counteract the efforts now making for the promotion of temperance."—*Minutes*, 1830, p. 298.

b. "*Resolved,* That the traffic in ardent spirits, to be used as a drink by any people, is, in our judgment, morally wrong, and ought to be viewed as such, by the churches of Jesus Christ universally."—*Minutes*, 1834, p. 445.

c. "It is with the utmost surprise and pain that we learn from the reports of two or three Presbyteries, that some of their members, and even ruling elders, still manufacture and sell ardent spirits. These things ought not so to be. They are a stumbling-block to many, and have a manifest tendency to bring overwhelming calamities, both temporal and spiritual, on society at large. No church can shine as a light in the world, while she openly sanctions and sustains any practices, which are so evidently destructive of the best interests of society."—*Minutes*, 1837, p. 510.

4. *Total Abstinence from all that will Intoxicate.*

"The Assembly would also recommend to all the members of the churches under its care, to be found the fast, unflinching, and active friends of temperance; abstaining from all forms and fashions which would countenance to any extent the sin of intemperance; avoiding even the appearance of evil; disentangling themselves from all implication with the traffic and manufacture, and especially presenting in their whole lives a standing and unvarying exemplification of the *only true principle of temperance,—total abstinence from everything that will intoxicate.*"—*Minutes*, 1840, p. 15.

5. *Prohibitory Laws.*

a. "The following resolution upon the subject of temperance was unanimously adopted:

"*Resolved,* That the General Assembly continue to view, with deep interest, the progress of the temperance reformation, most intimately connected with the vital interests of men for time and eternity; and they do especially hail its new phase through the action of several State legislatures, by which the traffic in intoxicating liquors as a beverage is entirely prohibited. They commend this new system of legislation to the attention and support of all ministers and churches connected with this body, for its blessed results, already experienced; and as able, if universally adopted, to do much to seal up the great fountains of drunkenness, pauperism, and crime, and relieve humanity of one of its most demoralizing and distressing evils."—*Minutes*, 1854, p. 503.

b. "The resolutions upon the subject of temperance were taken from the docket, adopted, and are as follows:

"Whereas, Intemperance is the great antagonist of domestic peace and social happiness, of sound morality and pure Christianity, and at war with all the dearest interests of man for this world and the future; and whereas, the experience of two hundred years proves, that this evil can never be removed or effectively resisted, while the traffic in intoxicating drinks is continued, it being necessary if we would stop the effect to remove the cause; therefore

"*Resolved*, 1. That this Assembly, as lovers of our holy religion, of our country, and our race, and as office-bearers in the church, can but feel a lively interest in the progress of the temperance reform.

"*Resolved*, 2. That we here record our devout thanksgiving to Almighty God, for the recent unparalleled progress of this reform, as evinced by the action of the legislatures of thirteen States and two Territories of our Union, in the passage of laws prohibiting entirely the traffic of all intoxicating beverages.

"*Resolved*, 3. That, in the opinion of this body, laws prohibiting the sale of intoxicating drinks, can interfere with the rights of no man; because no man has a right of any name or nature, inconsistent with the public good, or at war with the welfare of the community; it being a well-known and universally acknowledged maxim of law, that 'no man has a right to use his own to the injury of his neighbor.'

"*Resolved*, 4. That we earnestly recommend to the ministers and congregations in our connection, and to all others, to persevere in vigorous efforts until laws shall be enacted in every State and Territory of our beloved country, prohibiting entirely a traffic which is the principal cause of the drunkenness, and its consequent pauperism, crime, taxation, lamentation, war, and ruin to the bodies and souls of men, with which the country has so long been afflicted."—*Minutes*, 1855, pp. 30, 31.

6. *An Overture on Temperance. Relation of the Church to voluntary Associations.*

"The Committee on Bills and Overtures reported an overture from W. F. Stuart, Samuel Polkey, Robert Barry, Joseph H. Leonard, and

Parker Earle, representatives of different temperance organizations in Illinois, praying that this General Assembly would 'give the temperance cause a proper prominence among the means of reform sustained by the Church;' and especially suggesting, that it would 'arrange or recommend that some proper temperance movement should sustain the same relation to the churches, as the tract, the Bible, and the missionary causes do, both morally and financially, it would be of immense advantage to the cause.'

"The committee report, that this overture did not come into their possession until near the close of the sessions of the Assembly, affording but little time for such action as the importance of the subject demands. In compliance with the request of the petitioners, the Assembly are willing to assign to the cause of temperance a relation to our Church not dissimilar to that which has been given to the benevolent objects with which it is compared. But with none of these do we maintain any other connection, than that which their own moral power secures upon the free affection and esteem of our members. Very cheerfully and earnestly would this Assembly commend the cause of temperance to all the ministers and members of our Church, and urge them heartily to co-operate with every judicious effort in a Christian spirit to promote it; that pastors frequently preach upon the subject, and especially that no countenance be given to those social usages, by which great temptations to intemperance are thrown before their fellow-men."—*Minutes*, 1860, p. 262.

Section 4.—On the Theatre and Dancing.

1. Theatrical exhibitions and dancing condemned.—2. Dancing dangerous to morals, and to be condemned.—3. Promiscuous dancing calls for faithful and judicious discipline.

1. *Theatrical Exhibitions and Dancing condemned.*

"On the fashionable though, as we believe, dangerous amusements of theatrical exhibitions and dancing, we deem it necessary to make a few observations. The theatre we have always considered as a school of immorality. If any person wishes for honest conviction on this subject, let him attend to the character of that mass of matter which is generally exhibited on the stage. We believe all will agree that comedies at least, with a few exceptions, are of such a description, that a virtuous and modest person cannot attend the representation of them, without the most painful and embarrassing sensations. If indeed custom has familiarized the scene, and these painful sensations are no longer felt, it only proves that the person in question has lost some of the best sensibilities of our nature, that the strongest safeguard of virtue has been taken down, and that the moral character has undergone a serious depreciation."—*Minutes*, 1818, p. 690.

2. *Dancing a dangerous Amusement, and to be discouraged.*

"With respect to dancing, we think it necessary to observe, that however plausible it may appear to some, it is perhaps not the less dangerous on account of that plausibility. It is not from those things which the world acknowledges to be most wrong, that the greatest danger is to be apprehended to religion, especially as it relates to the young. When the practice is carried to its highest extremes, all admit the consequences to be fatal; and why not then apprehend danger, even from its incipient stages? It is certainly in all its stages a fascinating and an infatuating practice. Let it once be introduced, and it is difficult to give it limits. It steals away our precious time, dissipates religious impressions, and hardens the heart. To guard you, beloved brethren, against its wiles and its fascinations, we earnestly recommend that you will consult that sobriety which the sacred pages require. We also trust that you will attend, with the meekness and docility becoming the Christian character, to the admonitions on this subject of those whom you have chosen to watch for your souls. And now, beloved brethren, that you may be guarded from the dangers we have pointed out, and from all other dangers which beset the path of life, and obstruct our common salvation, and that the great Head of the Church may have you in his holy keeping, is our sincere and affectionate prayer. Amen."—*Minutes*, 1818, p. 690.

3. *Promiscuous Dancing calls for faithful and judicious Discipline.*

"*Resolved*, That the fashionable amusement of promiscuous dancing is so entirely unscriptural, and eminently and exclusively that of 'the world which lieth in wickedness,' and so wholly inconsistent with the spirit of Christ, and with that propriety of Christian deportment and that purity of heart which his followers are bound to maintain, as to render it not only improper and injurious for professing Christians either to partake in it, or to qualify their children for it, by teaching them the art; but also to call for the faithful and judicious exercise of discipline on the part of church Sessions, when any of the members of their churches have been guilty."—*Minutes,* 1843, p. 14.

Reaffirmed, Minutes, 1853, p. 340.

Section 5.—Gambling, Lotteries, and Betting.

1. These sins to be denounced and avoided.—2. Lotteries to be discountenanced, and, if possible, done away.

1. *These Sins to be denounced and avoided.*

"The vice of gambling has also been forced upon our attention. We indeed hope that few, or perhaps none of our actual professors, have indulged themselves in the practice of what they consider as coming under the denomination of gambling. But perhaps there are some addicted to this practice who have evinced a predilection for our Church and forms of worship, and who are not unwilling to receive the word of admonition from us. Such we would earnestly exhort to consider in the most serious manner the consequences of the course they are pursuing, and the awful lessons which the experience of the world is every day exhibiting on this subject. But it is our duty further to testify, that all encouragement of lotteries and purchasing of lottery-tickets, all attendance on horse-racing, and betting on such, or any other occasions, and all attempts, of whatever kind, to acquire gain without giving an equivalent, involve the gambling principle, and participate in the guilt which attaches to that vice."—*Minutes,* 1818, p. 690.

2. *Lotteries discountenanced.*

"The report of the Committee on the subject of Lotteries was taken up and adopted, and is as follows, viz.:

"That although so often sanctioned by legislative acts; although the proceeds of lotteries have not unfrequently been appropriated to benevolent and religious objects; although many wise and good men have in periods past, by their participation or agency, given countenance to lotteries, yet your committee cannot view them in any other light than that of legalized gambling.

"It would require volumes to record all the evils resulting from this system of predatory speculation. It adds nothing to the wealth of the community. It too often takes from the uninformed poor the property obtained by labor and skill, and transfers the same, without the least equivalent, into the hands of the idle and unworthy. It thus becomes the means of introducing and extending habits of gambling in all forms. Hundreds of families yearly are reduced to dependence and beggary, and not unfrequently its deluded victims terminate their miserable existence in this world by suicide. Contemplating this multitude of evils to individuals, to families, and to the community at large, your committee beg leave to submit the following resolutions:

"1. *Resolved*, That, in the opinion of this General Assembly, all lotteries should be discountenanced by every professed member of the Presbyterian Church, as immoral in their nature, and ruinous in their effects upon individual character and the public welfare.

"2. That the purchase and sale of lottery-tickets should be avoided by every member of our Church, even when the professed object of the lottery may be praiseworthy, inasmuch as it is not allowable to do evil that good may come.

"3. That all the Presbyteries under the care of this General Assembly be, and they hereby are recommended to take order on the subject of lottery gambling, to press the consideration of it and its attendant evils upon ministers and Sessions, and to adopt such plans of operation as may free the Church from all participation in this sin, enlighten, arouse, and direct public opinion, and save our country from this and every other species of gambling."—*Minutes*, 1830, p. 306.

SECTION 6.—ON DUELLING.

Duellists excluded from Church Privileges, and Ministers recommended to refuse attendance on the Funeral of a fallen Duellist.

"The General Assembly, having taken into serious consideration the unhappy prevalence of the practice of duelling in the United States, and being anxiously desirous to contribute what may be in their power, consistently with their character and situation, to discountenance and abolish this practice—

"*Resolved unanimously*, That they do, in the most unequivocal manner, declare their utter abhorrence of the practice of duelling and of all measures tending thereto, as originating from the malevolent dispositions of the human heart, and a false sense of honor; as a remnant of Gothic barbarism; as implying a presumptuous and highly criminal appeal to God as the Sovereign Judge; as utterly inconsistent with every just principle of moral conduct; as a direct violation of the sixth commandment, and destructive of the peace and happiness of families; and the Assembly do hereby recommend it to the ministers in their connection to discountenance, by all proper means in their power, this scandalous practice.

"*Resolved also*, That it be, and it is hereby recommended to all the ministers under the care of the Assembly, that they scrupulously refuse to attend the funeral of any person who shall have fallen in a duel; and that they admit no person, who shall have fought a duel, given or accepted a challenge, or been accessary thereto, unto the distinguishing privileges of the Church, until he manifest a just sense of his guilt, and give satisfactory evidence of repentance."—*Minutes*, 1805, p. 339.

SECTION 7.—ON SLAVERY.

1. First notice of the matter in Synod, 1774.—2. Action of the Synod, 1787.—3. Overture on communion with slaveholders, 1795, 1840.—4. Deliverance of the Assembly of 1815.—5. Overture on selling a slave, a member of the Church, and deliverance of the Assembly of 1818.—6. Indefinitely postponed, 1836.—7. Referred to the lower judicatories, 1839, 1843.—8. Declaration of the Assembly, 1846.—9. Action of 1849.—10. Slaveholding declared to be an offence, 1850.—11. Information asked for from the Southern churches, 1853.—12. Committee appointed to report on the constitutional powers of the Assembly on the subject of slaveholding, 1855.—13. Report of the committee, 1856.—14. Deliverance of the Assembly at Cleveland, 1857.—15. The Assembly refuses to instruct the Church Extension Committee not to assist a church having slaveholders in its communion, 1860.

1. FIRST NOTICE OF THE MATTER IN SYNOD, A.D. 1774.

"A representation from the Rev. Dr. Ezra Stiles and the Rev. Samuel Hopkins, respecting the sending two natives of Africa on a mission to propagate Christianity in their native country, and a request that the Synod would countenance this undertaking by their approbation of it, was brought in and read. The consideration of the above deferred."— —*Minutes*, 1774, p. 456.

"The representation and request relative to sending negro missionaries to Africa was taken into consideration, in consequence of which the subject of negro slavery came to be considered, and, after much reasoning on the matter, Dr. Rodgers, Messrs. John Miller, Caldwell, and Montgomery were appointed a committee to bring in an overture on Wednesday morning."—*Ib.* p. 456.

"The committee appointed to prepare an overture on the representation from Dr. Stiles and the Rev. Samuel Hopkins, and also on the subject of negro slavery, brought in a draught, the first part of which being read and amended, was approved, and is as follows:

"The Synod is very happy to have an opportunity to express their readiness to concur with and assist in a mission to the African tribes, and especially where so many circumstances concur, as in the present case, to intimate that it is the will of God, and to encourage us to hope for success. We assure the gentlemen aforesaid that we are ready to do all that is proper for us in our station for their encouragement and assistance.

"But some difficulties attending the discussion of the second part of that overture, the Synod agree to defer the affair to our next meeting." —*Minutes*, 1774, p. 458.

2. Action in Synod, A.D. 1787.

"The following was brought in by the Committee of Overtures:

"The Creator of the world having made of one flesh all the children of men, it becomes them, as members of the same family, to consult and promote each other's happiness. It is more especially the duty of those who maintain the rights of humanity, and who acknowledge and teach the obligations of Christianity, to use such means as are in their power to extend the blessings of equal freedom to every part of the human race.

"From a full conviction of these truths, and sensible that the rights of human nature are too well understood to admit of debate, overtured, that the Synod of New York and Philadelphia recommend, in the warmest terms, to every member of their body, and to all the churches and families under their care, to do everything in their power, consistent with the rights of civil society, to promote the abolition of slavery, and the instruction of negroes, whether bond or free.

"The Synod, taking into consideration the overture concerning slavery, transmitted by the Committee of Overtures last Saturday, came to the following judgment:

"The Synod of New York and Philadelphia do highly approve of the general principles in favor of universal liberty that prevail in America, and the interest which many of the States have taken in promoting the abolition of slavery; yet, inasmuch as men introduced from a servile state to a participation of all the privileges of civil society, without a proper education, and without previous habits of industry, may be, in many respects, dangerous to the community, therefore they earnestly recommend it to all the members belonging to their communion to give those persons, who are at present held in servitude, such good education as to prepare them for the better enjoyment of freedom; and they moreover recommend that masters, wherever they find servants disposed to make a just improvement of the privileges, would give them a *peculium*, or grant them sufficient time and sufficient means of procuring their own liberty at a moderate rate, that thereby they may be brought into society with those habits of industry that may render them useful citizens; and, finally, they recommend it to all their people to use the most prudent measures, consistent with the interest and state of civil society, in the counties where they live, to procure eventually the final abolition of slavery in America."—*Minutes*, 1787, pp. 539, 540.

"*Ordered*, That the records of the General Synod of the year 1787, on the subject of slavery, be published among the extracts to be printed of the proceedings of this Assembly."—*Minutes*, 1793, p. 76.

3. Sessions at Carlisle, A.D. 1795.

Communion with Slaveholders.

a. "The following overture was brought in by the Committee on Bills and Overtures, viz.:

"A serious and conscientious person, a member of a Presbyterian congregation, who views the slavery of the negroes as a moral evil, highly offensive to God and injurious to the interests of the Gospel, lives under the ministry of a person, or amongst a society of people, who concur with him in sentiment on the subject upon general principles, yet for particular reasons hold slaves and tolerate the practice in others. Overtured, Ought the former of these persons, under the impressions and circumstances above described, to hold communion with the latter?

"Whereupon, after due deliberation, it was

"*Resolved*, That, as the same difference of opinion with respect to slavery takes place in sundry other parts of the Presbyterian Church, notwithstanding which they live in charity and peace according to the doctrine and practice of the Apostles, it is hereby recommended to all conscientious persons, and especially to those whom it immediately respects, to do the same.

"At the same time, the General Assembly assure all the churches under their care that they view with the deepest concern any vestiges of slavery which may exist in our country, and refer the churches to the records of the General Assembly published at different times, but especially to an overture of the late Synod of New York and Philadelphia, published in 1787, and republished among the extracts from the Minutes of the General Assembly of 1793, on that head, with which we trust every conscientious person will be fully satisfied.

"*Resolved*, That Mr. Rice and Dr. Muir, ministers, and Mr. Robert Patterson, an elder, be a committee to draught a letter to the Presbytery of Transylvania on the subject of the above overture, and report in the afternoon.

"The committee appointed to prepare a draught of a letter to the Presbytery of Transylvania reported a draught, which being read and debated for some time, a motion was made, Shall this draught of a letter be read and debated by paragraphs, or not? The vote being taken, the question was carried in the affirmative. The consideration of the draught was resumed; and, after a very considerable time spent therein, it was amended and adopted, and ordered to be signed and sent to the Presbytery of Transylvania by their commissioners. As follows:

"To our brethren, members of the Presbyterian Church under the care of the Transylvania Presbytery:

"DEAR FRIENDS AND BRETHREN: The General Assembly of the Presbyterian Church hear with concern from your commissioners that differences of opinion with respect to holding Christian communion with those possessed of slaves agitate the minds of some among you, and threaten divisions, which may have a most ruinous tendency. The subject of slavery has repeatedly claimed the attention of the General Assembly, and the commissioners from the Presbytery of Transylvania are furnished with attested copies of these decisions, to be read by the Presbytery when it shall appear to them proper, together with a copy of this letter to the several churches under their care.

"The General Assembly have taken every step which they deemed expedient or wise to encourage emancipation, and to render the state of those who are in slavery as mild and tolerable as possible.

"Forbearance and peace are frequently inculcated in the New Testament. Blessed are the peacemakers. Let no one do anything through strife and vain-glory. Let each esteem others better than himself. The followers of Jesus ought conscientiously to walk worthy of their vocation, with all lowliness and meekness, with long-suffering forbearing one another, and endeavoring to keep the unity of the spirit in the bond of peace. If every difference of opinion were to keep men at a distance, they could subsist in no state of society, civil or religious. The General Assembly would impress this upon the minds of their brethren, and urge them to follow peace and the things which make for peace.

"The General Assembly commend our dear friends and brethren to the grace of God, praying that the peace of God, which passeth all understanding, may possess their hearts and minds.

"Signed by order of the Assembly."—*Minutes*, 1795, pp. 103, 104.

b. "Whereas, it appears from memorials sent up to this Assembly, that several of our Presbyteries have adopted resolutions excluding slaveholders from their pulpits and from their communion; and whereas our Constitution requires that no member of the Presbyterian Church shall be thus disfranchised without a regular trial and conviction; and whereas this proceeding is a repetition of the exscinding acts of the New Basis Assembly, against which we have taken our stand as the friends of the Constitution: therefore,

"*Resolved*, That the said Presbyteries be requested to rescind such resolutions.

"The foregoing resolution was, with one dissenting voice, adopted."—*Minutes*, 1840, p. 24.

4. Sessions at Philadelphia, A.D. 1815.

"The committee to which was committed the report of the committee to which the petition of some elders who entertain conscientious scruples on the subject of holding slaves, together with that of the Synod of Ohio concerning the buying and selling of slaves, had been referred, reported; and their report, being read and amended, is as follows, viz.:

"The General Assembly have repeatedly declared their cordial approbation of those principles of civil liberty which appear to be recognized by the Federal and State Governments in these United States. They have expressed their regret that the slavery of the Africans and of their descendants still continues in so many places, and even among those within the pale of the Church, and have urged the Presbyteries under their care to adopt such measures as will secure, at least to the rising generation of slaves within the bounds of the Church, a religious education, that they may be prepared for the exercise and enjoyment of liberty when God in his providence may open a door for their emancipation. The committee refer said petitioners to the printed extracts of the Synod of New York and Philadelphia, for the year 1787, on this subject, republished by the Assembly in 1793, and also to the Extracts of the Minutes of the Assembly for 1795, which last are in the following words, viz.:

"A serious and conscientious person, a member of a Presbyterian congregation, who views the slavery of the negroes as a moral evil, highly offensive to God and injurious to the interests of the Gospel, lives under the ministry of a person, or amongst a society of people, who concur with him in sentiment on the subject upon general principles, yet for particular reasons hold slaves and tolerate the practice in others. Overtured, Ought the former of these persons, under the impressions and circumstances above described, to hold communion with the latter?

"Whereupon, after due deliberation, it was

"*Resolved*, That, as the same difference of opinion with respect to slavery takes place in sundry other parts of the Presbyterian Church, notwithstanding which they live in charity and peace according to the doctrine and practice of the Apostles, it is hereby recommended to all conscientious persons, and especially to those whom it immediately respects, to do the same.

"This is deemed a sufficient answer to the first petition; and, with regard to the second, the Assembly observe that, although in some sections of our country, under certain circumstances, the transfer of slaves may be unavoidable, yet they consider the buying and selling of slaves by way of traffic, and all undue severity in the management of them, as inconsistent with the spirit of the Gospel. And they recommend it to the Presbyteries and Sessions under their care to make use of all prudent measures to prevent such shameful and unrighteous conduct."—*Minutes*, 1815, p. 586.

5. Sessions at Philadelphia, A.D. 1818.

Overture on Selling a Slave, a Member of the Church.

"The following resolution was submitted to the Assembly, viz.:

"*Resolved*, That a person who shall sell as a slave a member of the Church, who shall be at the time of sale in good standing and unwilling to be sold, acts inconsistently with the spirit of Christianity, and ought to be debarred from the communion of the Church.

"After considerable discussion, the subject was committed to Dr. Green, Dr. Baxter, and Mr. Burgess, to prepare a report to be adopted by the Assembly, embracing the object of the above resolution, and also expressing the opinion of the Assembly in general as to slavery.

[The report of the committee] "being read, was unanimously adopted, and referred to the same committee for publication. It is as follows, viz.:

"The General Assembly of the Presbyterian Church, having taken into consideration the subject of slavery, think proper to make known their sentiments upon it to the churches and people under their care.

"We consider the voluntary enslaving of one part of the human race by another as a gross violation of the most precious and sacred rights of human nature, as utterly inconsistent with the law of God, which requires us to love our neighbor as ourselves, and as totally irreconcilable with the spirit and principles of the Gospel of Christ, which enjoin that 'all things whatsoever ye would that men should do to you, do ye even so to them.' Slavery creates a paradox in the moral system: it exhibits rational, accountable, and immortal beings in such circumstances as scarcely to leave them the power of moral action. It exhibits them as dependent on the will of others whether they shall receive religious instruction; whether they shall know and worship the true God; whether they shall enjoy the ordinances of the Gospel; whether they shall perform the duties and cherish the endearments of husbands and wives, parents and children, neighbors and friends; whether they shall preserve their chastity and purity, or regard the dictates of justice and humanity. Such are some of the consequences of slavery,—consequences not imaginary, but which connect themselves with its very existence. The evils to which the slave is always exposed often take place in fact, and in their very worst degree and form: and where all of them do not take place—as, we rejoice to say, in many instances, through the influence of the principles of humanity and religion on the mind of masters, they do not—still, the slave is deprived of his natural right, degraded as a human being, and exposed to the danger of passing into the hands of a master who may inflict upon him all the hardships and injuries which inhumanity and avarice may suggest.

"From this view of the consequences resulting from the practice into which Christian people have most inconsistently fallen, of enslaving a portion of their brethren of mankind,—for 'God hath made of one blood all nations of men to dwell on the face of the earth,'—it is manifestly the duty of all Christians who enjoy the light of the present day, when the inconsistency of slavery both with the dictates of humanity and religion has been demonstrated, and is generally seen and acknowledged, to use their honest, earnest, and unwearied endeavors to correct the errors of former times, and as speedily as possible to efface this blot on our holy religion, and to obtain the complete abolition of slavery throughout Christendom, and, if possible, throughout the world.

"We rejoice that the Church to which we belong commenced as early as any other in this country the good work of endeavoring to put an end to slavery, and that in the same work many of its members have ever since been, and now are, among the most active, vigorous, and efficient laborers. We do, indeed, tenderly sympathize with those portions of our Church and our country where the evil of slavery has been entailed upon them,—where a great, and the most virtuous, part of the community abhor slavery, and wish its extermination as sincerely as any others,—but where the number of slaves, their ignorance, and their vicious habits generally, render an immediate and universal emancipation inconsistent alike with the safety and happiness of the master and the slave. With those who are thus circumstanced, we repeat that we tenderly sympathize. At the same time, we earnestly exhort them to continue, and, if possible, to increase, their exertions to effect a total abolition of slavery. We exhort them to suffer no greater delay of slavery. We hope that those portions of the American Union whose inhabitants are by a gracious Providence more favorably circumstanced, will cordially and liberally and earnestly co-operate with their brethren in bringing about the great end contemplated.

"We recommend to all the members of our religious denomination, not only to permit, but to facilitate and encourage, the instruction of their slaves in the principles and duties of the Christian religion, by granting them liberty to attend on the preaching of the Gospel when they have opportunity, by favoring the instruction of them in the Sabbath-school, wherever those schools can be formed, and by giving them all other proper advantages for acquiring the knowledge of their duty both to God and to man. We are perfectly satisfied that it is incumbent on all Christians to communicate religious instruction to those who are under their authority; so that the doing of this, in the case before us, so far from operating, as some have apprehended that it might, as an incitement to insubordination and insurrection, would, on the contrary, operate as the most powerful means for the prevention of those evils.

"We enjoin it on all church Sessions and Presbyteries under the care of this Assembly to discountenance and, as far as possible, to prevent all cruelty, of whatever kind, in the treatment of slaves, especially the cruelty of separating husband and wife, parents and children, and that which consists in selling slaves to those who will either themselves deprive these unhappy people of the blessings of the Gospel, or who will transport them to places where the Gospel is not proclaimed, or where it is forbidden to slaves to attend upon its institutions. And if it shall ever happen that a Christian professor in our communion shall sell a slave who is also in communion and good standing with our Church, contrary to his or her will and inclination, it ought immediately to claim the particular attention of the proper church judicature; and, unless there be such peculiar circumstances attending the case as can but seldom happen, it ought to be followed without delay by a suspension of the offender from all the privileges of the Church till he repent and make all the reparation in his power to the injured party.

"*Resolved*, That fifteen hundred copies of this report be printed or published in the newspapers."—*Minutes*, 1818, pp. 692–694.

Sessions at Pittsburg, A.D. 1836.

6. *Indefinitely Postponed.*

"The Assembly resumed the subject of slavery.

"The following motion was made by Dr. Hoge:

"Inasmuch as the Constitution of the Presbyterian Church, in its preliminary and fundamental principles, declares that no Church judicatory ought to pretend to make laws to bind the conscience, in virtue of their own authority; and as the urgency of the business of the Assembly, and the shortness of the time during which they can continue in session, render it impossible to deliberate and decide judiciously on the subject of slavery in its relations to the Church: therefore,

"*Resolved*, That this whole subject be indefinitely postponed.

"Adopted. Yeas, 154; Nays, 87."—*Minutes*, 1836, p. 272.

Sessions at Philadelphia, A.D. 1839.

7. *Referred to the Lower Judicatories.*

"Whereas, certain memorials have been sent up to this Assembly from several Presbyteries desiring some action on the subject of slavery; and whereas, these memorials have been read and freely discussed by this body; and whereas, this Assembly is made up of members from different portions of our extended country, who honestly differ in opinion, as well in regard to the propriety as the nature of the ecclesiastical action desired in the case: therefore,

"*Resolved*, That this Assembly does most solemnly refer to the lower judicatories the subject of slavery, leaving it to them to take such order thereon as in their judgment will be most judicious, and adapted to remove the evil."—*Minutes*, 1839, p. 22.

Sessions at Philadelphia, A.D. 1840.

In 1840, the whole subject was indefinitely postponed.—*Minutes*, pp. 18, 19.

Sessions at Philadelphia, A.D. 1843.

"Whereas, there is in this Assembly great diversity of opinion as to the proper and best mode of action on the subject of slavery; and whereas, in such circumstances, any expression of sentiment would carry with it but little weight, as it would be passed by a small majority, and must operate to produce alienation and division; and whereas, the Assembly of 1839, with great unanimity, referred this whole subject to the lower judicatories, to take such order as in their judgment might be adapted to remove the evil:

"*Resolved*, That the Assembly do not think it for the edification of the Church for this body to take any action on the subject.

"Passed. Yeas, 66; Nays, 33."—*Minutes*, 1843, p. 19.

Sessions at Philadelphia, A.D. 1846.

8. *Declaration of the General Assembly on the subject of Slavery.*

"1. The system of slavery, as it exists in the United States, viewed either in the laws of the several States which sanction it, or in the actual operation and results in society, is intrinsically an unrighteous and oppressive system, and is opposed to the prescription of the law of God, to the spirit and precepts of the Gospel, and to the best interests of humanity.

"2. The testimony of the General Assembly, from A.D. 1787 to 1818 inclusive, has condemned it; and it remains still the recorded testimony of the Presbyterian Church of these United States against it, from which we do not recede.

"3. We cannot, therefore, withhold the expression of our deep regret that slavery should be continued and countenanced by any of the members of our churches; and we do earnestly exhort both them and the churches among whom it exists to use all means in their power to put it away from them. Its perpetuation among them cannot fail to be regarded by multitudes, influenced by their example, as sanctioning the system portrayed in and maintained by the statutes of the several slaveholding States wherein they dwell. Nor can any mere mitigation of its severity, prompted by the humanity and Christian feeling of any individuals who continue to hold their fellow-men in such bondage, be regarded either as a testimony against the system, or as in the least degree changing its essential character.

"4. But while we believe that many evils incident to the system render it important and obligatory to bear testimony against it, yet would we not undertake to determine the degree of moral turpitude on the part of individuals involved by it. This will doubtless be found to vary in the sight of God, according to the degree of light and other circumstances pertaining to each. In view of all the embarrassments and obstacles in the way of emancipation interposed by the statutes of the slaveholding States and by the social influence affecting the views and conduct of those involved in it, we cannot pronounce a judgment of general and promiscuous condemnation, implying that destitution of Christian principle and feeling which should exclude from the table of the Lord all who stand in the legal relation of masters to slaves, or justify us in withholding our ecclesiastical and Christian fellowship from them. We rather sympathize with, and would seek to succor them in their embarrassments, believing that separation and secession among the churches and their members are not the methods that God approves and sanctions for the reformation of his Church.

"5. While, therefore, we feel bound to bear our testimony against slavery, and to exhort our beloved brethren to remove it from them as speedily as possible, by all appropriate and available means, we do at the same time condemn all divisive and schismatical measures, tending to destroy the unity and disturb the peace of our churches, and deprecate the spirit of denunciation, and that unfeeling severity, which would cast from the fold those whom we are rather bound by the spirit of the Gospel and the obligations of our covenant to instruct, to counsel, exhort, and try to lead in the ways of God, and towards whom, even though they may err, to exercise forbearance and brotherly love.

"6. As a court of our Lord Jesus Christ we possess no legislative authority, and as the General Assembly of the Presbyterian Church we possess no judiciary power. We have no right to institute and prescribe tests of Christian character and church membership not recognized and sanctioned in the Sacred Scriptures and in our standards by which we have agreed to walk. We must, therefore, leave this matter with the Sessions and Presbyteries and Synods—the judicatories to whom pertains the right of judgment—to act in the administration of discipline as they may judge it to be their duty, constitutionally subject to the General Assembly only in the way of general review and control.

"[Yeas, 92; Nays, 29; *non liquet*, 3.]"—*Minutes*, 1846, pp. 28–30.

9. Sessions at Philadelphia, A.D. 1849.

"The committee to whose consideration were submitted sundry papers on the subject of slavery now present to the Assembly the following report, consisting of preamble and resolutions:

"These documents are nineteen in number, embracing memorials from four Synods, thirteen Presbyteries, one church, and one from certain individuals. The object of these papers is one and the same, namely, to free the Presbyterian Church from all participation and connection with slaveholding. The measures proposed are various,—some more and some less stringent. Some ask for discipline, others for a pastoral letter, a third class for separation from the evil complained of, without defining the mode; one proposes the reorganization of the Church to which we belong into three General Assemblies; one threatens secession if something is not done; and others ask for nothing definite. While these voluminous papers furnish a considerable variety as to tone and manner and intimations as to the future, and likewise as to a knowledge of the intrinsic difficulties attending this complicated evil, they are sufficiently respectful in their language and grave and weighty in their opinions and arguments to demand the wise and prayerful consideration of this Assembly. This consideration we believe we may say, without boasting or arrogance, they have received from your committee; and we have a cheerful confidence they will now receive the same from this body.

"The subject is not a new one: it has occupied the attention of the Presbyterian Church from the commencement of its organization,—even before the General Assembly had an existence; and your committee are happy to avail themselves of the lights of former times in presenting this difficult matter to you, and through you to the judicatories and churches under our care. Your committee would deprecate two errors into which minds of different and opposite structures, on this and all similar subjects, are liable to fall. One class forget that we live in an age of progress, and the other forget that the first step in progress is not perfection. In relation to both of these great truths here alluded to, we should, as rational beings and as Christians, be ready to obey the intimations of Providence, and to follow the guidance of the torchlight of truth which the hand of God holds up before us,—to go forward as that goes onward, and to move no faster than its blessed radiance is shed upon our pathway. All theories, when they come to put on the forms of experiment, must yield to the authority of uniform and universal facts; and both progressives and conservatives might render themselves much more comfortable as well as useful in our world if they were more deeply imbued with this one practical truth. These remarks apply with great force to all evils which are interwoven with the very texture of social organization; and slavery is by no means an exception.

"Your committee propose to embody the sentiments of this Assembly, in relation to this evil, in the following resolutions:

"*Resolved*, That we reaffirm the sentiments expressed by the Assembly of 1815, and especially in the following quotations:

"'The General Assembly have repeatedly declared their cordial approbation of those principles of civil liberty which seem to be recognized by the Federal and State Governments of the United States. They have expressed their regret that the slavery of the Africans and of their descendants still continues in so many places, and even among those within the pale of the Church, and have urged the Presbyteries under their care to adopt such measures as will secure, at least to the rising generation of slaves within the bounds of the Church, a religious education, that they may be prepared for the exercise and enjoyment of liberty when God in his providence may open a door for their emancipation.'

"Again: 'The General Assembly assure all the churches under their care, that they view with the deepest concern any vestiges of slavery which may exist in our country.'

"And again: 'The Assembly observe that, although in some sections of our country, under certain circumstances, the transfer of slaves may be unavoidable, yet they consider the buying and selling of slaves by way of traffic, and all undue severity in the management of them, as inconsistent with the spirit of the Gospel. And they recommend it to Presbyteries and Sessions under their care to make use of all prudent measures to prevent such shameful and unrighteous conduct.' [See *ante*, pp. 270, 271.]

"2. *Resolved*, That this General Assembly reaffirms the opinions expressed by the General Assembly of 1818. The following extracts are commended to special notice, viz.:

"'We consider the voluntary enslaving of one part of the human race by another as a gross violation of the most precious and sacred rights of human nature, as utterly inconsistent with the law of God, which requires us to love our neighbors as ourselves, and as totally irreconcilable with the spirit and principles of the Gospel of Christ, which enjoins that "all things whatsoever ye would that men should do to you, do ye even so to them." Slavery creates a paradox in the moral system: it exhibits rational, accountable, and immortal beings in such circumstances as scarcely to leave them the power of moral action. It exhibits them as dependent on the will of others whether they shall receive religious instruction; whether they shall know and worship the true God; whether they shall enjoy the ordinances of the Gospel; whether they shall perform the duties and cherish the endearments of husbands and wives, parents and children, neighbors and friends; whether they shall preserve their chastity and purity, or regard the dictates of justice and humanity. Such are some of the consequences of slavery,—consequences not imaginary, but which connect themselves with its very existence.'

"Again: 'From this view of the consequences resulting from the practice into which Christian people have most inconsistently fallen of enslaving a portion of their *brethren* of mankind,—for "God hath made of one blood all nations of men to dwell on the face of the earth,"—it is manifestly the duty of all Christians who enjoy the light of the present day, when the inconsistency of slavery, both with the dictates of humanity and religion, has been demonstrated and is generally seen and acknowledged, to use their honest, earnest, and unwavering efforts to correct the errors of former times, and as speedily as possible to efface this blot on our holy religion, and to obtain the complete abolition of slavery throughout Christendom, and, if possible, throughout the world.' [See *ante*, pp. 272, 273.]

"3. *Resolved*, That we reaffirm the 'declaration of the General Assembly on the subject of slavery' made in the year 1846. The following sentiments are particularly commended to the serious and prayerful attention of our judicatories and churches, viz.:

"'The system of slavery as it exists in these United States, viewed either in the laws of the several States which sanction it or in its actual operation and results in society, is intrinsically an unrighteous and oppressive system, and is opposed to the prescriptions of the law of God, to the spirit and precepts of the Gospel, and to the best interests of humanity.'

"Again: 'But, while we believe that many evils incident to the system render it important and obligatory to bear testimony against it, yet would we not undertake to determine the degree of moral turpitude on the part of the individuals involved by it. This will doubtless be found to vary in the sight of God according to the degree of light and other circumstances pertaining to each. In view of all the embarrassments and obstacles in the way of emancipation interposed by the statutes of the slaveholding States, and by the social influence affecting the views and conduct of those involved in it, we cannot pronounce a judgment of general and promiscuous condemnation, implying that destitution of Christian principle and feeling which should exclude from the table of the Lord all who stand in the legal relation of master to slaves, or justify us in withholding our ecclesiastical and Christian fellowship from them. We rather sympathize with and would seek to succor them in their embarrassments, believing that separation and secession among the churches and their members are not the methods which God approves and sanctions for the reformation of his Church.' [See *ante*, pp. 276, 277.]

"4. *Resolved*, That, in the judgment of this Assembly, these declarations of former General Assemblies bear an explicit, frank, honest, and honorable testimony against the evils of slavery, and they ought to be 'known and read of all men.'

"The following principles are clearly stated in the documents above referred to and quoted:

"1. That civil liberty is the right of man as a rational and moral being.

"2. That the institution of slavery, in the language of a former Assembly, 'is intrinsically an unrighteous and oppressive system,' and injurious to the highest and best interests of all concerned in it.

"3. That it is 'the duty of all Christians who enjoy the light of the present day' 'to use their honest and unwearied endeavors' 'as speedily as possible to efface this blot on our holy religion, and to obtain the complete abolition of slavery throughout Christendom, and, if possible, throughout the world.' This General Assembly do most solemnly exhort all under our care to perform this duty, and to be ever ready to make all necessary sacrifices in order to effect a consummation so much to be desired.

"4. When circumstances over which good men have not the control inevitably prevent the attainment of this ulterior and desirable purpose at once, there are other and important duties which cannot be neglected without great guilt, such as a watchful care for the interests of the soul, direct religious instruction, and the communication of that practical knowledge of life and its objects which may prepare this portion of our fellow-men for 'the exercise and enjoyment of liberty when God in his providence may open a door for their emancipation.'

"5. There are incidental evils which belong to this system, which, when they occur in the Church, should be corrected by discipline, such as 'buying and selling of slaves by way of traffic, and all undue severity in the management of them.' To these may be added the breaking up of the family relationship, and separating husbands and wives, parents and children, 'thus rendering it impossible for rational, moral, and immortal beings to perform the duties and cherish the endearments of social life.'

"All these things are fairly and fully presented in the declaration of preceding Assemblies, and quite as explicitly before the division of the Presbyterian Church as since.

"5. *Resolved*, That while we bear this testimony against the system of slavery as it exists in this country and elsewhere, and which testimony coincides with the almost uniform testimony of all good men in every age, and especially with that borne by the fathers of the Presbyterian Church, to which we have herein referred, and while we commend these DECLARATIONS OF SENTIMENT to the attention of all the judicatories, and all the churches under our care, we feel ourselves bound to add that there has been no information before this Assembly to prove that members of our Church in the slave States are not doing all that they can (situated as they are in the providence of God) to bring about the possession and enjoyment of liberty by the enslaved; nor are there any facts before us to show that they are living in the violation of the duties growing out of their relations to slavery, as it is continued in existence by the laws of their respective States; nor do we know that they tolerate any of those evils which ought to call forth the discipline of the Church; but, if there are such cases, we would direct the attention of the proper judicatories to them in the exercise of a kind and salutary discipline.

"Commending these views to the consideration of all under our care, and especially of those whose lot is cast where the institution of slavery exists, and which the smallness of their numbers forbids us to suppose they have the power of controlling, we leave this whole matter with God and the consciences of all those who love his blessed cause."—*Minutes*, 1849, pp. 185–188.

10. SESSIONS AT DETROIT, A.D. 1850.

[The committee report] "That after a careful and thorough examination of the whole subject, they have been brought to the conclusion that, in consideration of the previous action of the Assembly had at different times for a series of years, and what they believe to be its present sentiments, and the expectations of the churches in its connection, the cause of truth and righteousness, of peace and unity, will be best subserved by the adoption of the following resolutions:

"*Resolved*, 1. That we exceedingly deplore the working of the whole system of slavery as it exists in our country, and is interwoven with the political institutions of the slaveholding States, as fraught with many and great evils to the civil, political, and moral interests of those regions where it exists.

"*Resolved*, 2. That the holding of our fellow-men in the condition of slavery, except in those cases where it is unavoidable by the laws of the State, the obligations of guardianship, or the demands of humanity, is an offence in the proper import of that term as used in the Book of Discipline, chap. i, sec. 3, and should be regarded and treated in the same manner as other offences.

"*Resolved*, 3. That the Sessions and Presbyteries are, by the Constitution of our Church, the courts of primary jurisdiction for the trial of offences.

"*Resolved*, 4. That after this declaration of sentiment, the whole subject of slavery, as it exists in the Church, be referred to the Sessions and Presbyteries, to take such action thereon as, in their judgment, the laws of Christianity require.

"Adopted. Yeas, 87; nays, 16."—*Minutes*, 1850, p. 325.

Sessions at Utica, A.D. 1851.

"The memorials are few in number (four in all), kind in spirit, decorous in matter, and no doubt conscientious in origin. The committee have carefully read and considered these documents, and unanimously and cordially agree to the following result:

"That the Assembly have reason to be thankful to Divine Providence for the wisdom and prudence vouchsafed to the last Assembly in coming to conclusions on this vexed question which have so generally met with the acquiescence of the Church at this crisis; and that it seems obviously our duty at the present session to leave the whole subject as it was placed by that action, and to devote our time to other subjects which demand attention, always praying that God will hasten on the day of universal freedom throughout our land and the world."—*Minutes*, 1851, p. 13.

Sessions at Washington, A.D. 1852.

"The Committee on Bills and Overtures reported four memorials on the subject of slavery. These memorials ask of the Assembly:

"1. A further expression of opinion on the subject of slavery.

"2. That it be enjoined on the lower judicatories to bring every case of slaveholding under examination for particular condemnation or vindication.

"3. That the several Synods be cited to appear before the next General Assembly, to answer charges which it is alleged common fame brings against them in connection with slavery.

"The committee are of opinion:

"1. That the General Assembly has already so clearly and explicitly defined its views on the subject that no further expression of opinion is demanded at the present time.

"2. That the demand for an injunction on the lower judicatories, to take action with respect to this subject, is not in accordance with the provisions of our Constitution. (Vide chapter on Review and Control.)

"3. That the several memorials which ask for the citation of the Synods should be referred to the Judicial Committee.

"In view of these reasons, the committee ask to be discharged from the further consideration of the subject.

"Adopted."—*Minutes*, 1852, pp. 160, 161.

11. Sessions at Buffalo, A.D. 1853.

"The report of the committee was adopted, and is as follows:

"The committee to whom was referred the subject of slavery respectfully report, that twelve memorials touching this grave matter, from various Synods and Presbyteries, have been put into their hands. Of these, eleven are from the North, praying the Assembly for further action, and asking for precise information in regard to the extent of the practice of slaveholding in our body, and in regard also to certain alleged aggravations of it in the unchristian and cruel treatment of slaves. One is from the South, complaining of unkindness and injustice on the part of many Northern brethren, in charging upon the memorialists practices of which they are not guilty, and in attributing to them motives which they utterly disclaim and abominate, protesting also against the continued agitation of this subject, as tending more to rivet than to loose the chains of the slave, and seriously to embarrass them in their Gospel work.

"Your committee, after much serious and prayerful consideration of this whole subject, in all its complicated and perplexing relations, and with a solemn sense of responsibility to God and to his Church, are of one mind in recommending to the Assembly the following action:

"1. That this body reaffirm the doctrines of the second resolution adopted by the Assembly in its action at Detroit in 1850.

"2. That we do earnestly exhort and beseech all those who are happily free from any personal connection with the institution of slavery to exercise patience and forbearance towards their brethren less favored in this respect than themselves, remembering the embarrassments of their position; and to cherish for them that fraternal confidence and love which they the more need in consequence of the peculiar trials by which they are surrounded.

"3. To correct misapprehensions which may exist in many Northern minds, and allay causeless irritation, by having the real facts in relation to this subject spread before the whole Church, it is recommended earnestly to request the Presbyteries in each of the slaveholding States to take such measures as may seem to them most expedient and proper for laying before the next Assembly, in its sessions at Philadelphia, distinct and full statements touching the following points:

"1. The number of slaveholders in connection with the churches under their jurisdiction, and the number of slaves held by them.

"2. The extent to which slaves are held by an unavoidable necessity 'imposed by the laws of the States, the obligations of guardianship, and the demands of humanity.'

"3. Whether a practical regard, such as the word of God requires, is evinced by the Southern churches for the sacredness of the conjugal and parental relations as they exist among slaves; whether baptism is duly administered to the children of slaves professing Christianity; whether slaves are admitted to equal privileges and powers in the church courts; and, in general, to what extent and in what manner provision is made for the religious well-being of the enslaved.

"Adopted. Yeas, 84; Nays, 39."—*Minutes*, 1853, p. 333.

12. Sessions at St. Louis, A.D. 1855.

"The committee recommend—

"1. That the General Assembly address a pastoral letter to all the churches under their care, reaffirming the testimony of past Assemblies in regard to the sinfulness of the system of slavery as it generally exists in these United States, and expressing their deep regret at the intemperateness of word and action that has too often characterized the spirit of those who have conscientiously aimed at its overthrow; and that they urge upon their churches earnest efforts, by all Christian and constitutional modes, to remove the evil from the midst of us.

"2. That a committee be appointed to report to the next Assembly on the constitutional power of the Assembly over the subject of slaveholding in our churches; and that we recommend that this evil be removed from our Church as soon as it can be done in a Christian and constitutional manner.

"Adopted."—*Minutes,* 1855, p. 30.

SESSIONS AT NEW YORK, A.D. 1856.

13. *Report of the Committee "On the Constitutional Power of the General Assembly over the Subject of Slaveholding in our Churches.*

"The report of the committee was adopted, and is as follows:

"The committee appointed by the last General Assembly 'to report to the next Assembly on the constitutional power of the Assembly over the subject of slaveholding in our churches,' respectfully submit the following report:

"It should be observed at the outset that the committee are instructed to report on but a single point,—that of 'power.' The question before them is not what it may be wise for the Assembly to do,—not what in a particular case, or in general (authority being presupposed), would be for edification, but what is the *power* of the Assembly in the matter of slaveholding? This is a question which can be determined only by reference to our Form of Government. The 'power' on which we are to report is fitly designated as 'constitutional.' We are a constitutional body. No judicatory of our Church has any legitimate functions save those which, either expressly or by clear implication, the Constitution confers. Emphatically should this be said of our highest judicatory, in view of the tendency of human nature, in ecclesiastical connections, to a grasping and tyrannous centralism. The one-man power at Rome is hardly more abhorrent to the genius of Presbyterianism than would be a many-headed Papacy, under the name and form of a General Assembly. It should be remembered, also, that as a visible Church or particular denomination, our Constitution is the sole bond of our union. We are united, externally and formally, only as that unites us. That, of course, must measure and limit the responsibility for each other which grows out of our union. No one part of our body can be held answerable for the evils in another, which, by the terms of our confederation, it has no power to reach.

"The committee would further remark, that they do not feel themselves called on to present their views of the moral character of slavery, or to reargue the question whether slaveholding is, in any case, a disciplinable offence. They do not suppose that they were appointed with reference to that question. It was thoroughly discussed in the Assembly of 1850, and the conclusion reached, 'that the holding of our fellowmen in the condition of slavery, except in those cases where it is unavoidable by the laws of the State, the obligations of guardianship, or the demands of humanity, is an offence in the proper import of that term, as used in the Book of Discipline, chapter i, section 3, and should be regarded and treated in the same manner as other offences.' This opinion has been reaffirmed, either expressly or virtually, by nearly every succeeding Assembly, including the last. Nor do the committee anticipate that any considerable portion of the present Assembly will either stand in doubt concerning it, or incline in the least to a retrograde course. The doctrine set forth at Detroit—set forth simply as a doctrine, and not as a law or judicial decision—is yet, they judge, the settled view of our Church. Taking this for granted, their sole concern is with the relations of the Assembly to the matter. To determine this point, we have only to ascertain what are the constitutional powers of that body in respect to disciplinable offences generally.

"Its functions in this regard, we judge, are of two kinds, *advisory* and *authoritative;* and between these there should be a careful discrimination. The *advisory* function of the Assembly is of very wide scope. According to the Form of Government, chapter xii, section 5, they have the power of 'reproving, warning, or bearing testimony against error in doctrine or immorality in practice in any church, Presbytery, or Synod,' and 'of recommending . . . reformation of manners . . . through all the churches under their care.' This function of reproof may be exercised in reference to any evil grave enough to call for it. Nor is it an unimportant function. The testimony of such a body as the General Assembly, especially if unanimously given, must have great weight. It has, indeed, only a moral influence. It is not authoritative. It binds no other body, not even a succeeding General Assembly. It binds no individual; yet cases are not unfrequent in which a moral influence of this sort, if not the only one that could be employed, is the most efficacious. It has greater power over the conscience, often, than the most stringent exercise of bare authority.

"As it respects the *authoritative* function of the Assembly, or its power of discipline, that, we judge, can only be exercised in the forms and methods marked out in the Constitution. It is by no means co-extensive with its testifying power. As counsel or testimony has only a moral force, the manner in which it shall be put forth is wisely left to the discretion of the Assembly. Not so with discipline. Concerning, as it does, the dearest rights and interests, it is of the highest importance that the mode of its exercise should be particularly prescribed. So we find it in our Form of Government. Every step is distinctly set forth, and the greatest care taken to guard all concerned against mistake and abuse. Nor is any exception made as to any particular class of offences. If slaveholding is in any case to be dealt with as a disciplinable matter, it must be in some one of the ways explicitly authorized in the Constitution.

"The methods in which the *authoritative* action of the Assembly may be invoked, as appears from the seventh chapter of the Book of Discipline, are four: by *reference*, by *appeal*, by *complaint*, and—to state that last which in the Book of Discipline comes first—by *general review and control.* The three processes first named do not, of course, originate in the Assembly. Their inception is in a lower judicatory. In one or another of them, it is presumed, most of the matters which call for disciplinary action on the part of the highest judicatory will, in due time, come before it. There is, however, a possibility of neglect in this regard; and for such a contingency our Constitution—framed with a wisdom best appreciated by those who have most thoroughly studied it—has made a specific provision. This provision is found in the section on 'General Review and Control.' See Book of Discipline, chap. viii, sec. 1.

"Under this section, there are two methods in which any disciplinable offence—and slaveholding, of course, when it assumes that character—may be reached authoritatively by the Assembly. (1.) It may appear from the records of a Synod, as submitted for inspection, that there has been some wrong-doing or culpable omission in the matter.

A case may have been incorrectly decided, or refused a hearing. Or it may be obvious that the records of some Presbytery have not, according to the 2d and 3d articles of this section, been properly disposed of. Or it may appear that the duty enjoined in the 6th article—that of citing a lower judicatory in a given contingency—has been entirely neglected. In cases of this sort there may be 'animadversion or censure,' or, according to article 3d, the Synod 'may be required to review and correct its proceedings.' (2.) 'Any important delinquency, or grossly unconstitutional proceedings,' not apparent from the records, may yet be charged against a Synod 'by common fame.' It may be reported, for example, that through some neglect of the Synod 'heretical opinions or corrupt practices' are 'allowed to gain ground,' or that 'offenders of a very gross character' are 'suffered to escape.' See Articles 5 and 6 of this same section. In such case, provided the rumor is of the character specified in the Book of Discipline, chap. 3, sec. 5,—for a process against a Synod should certainly not be commenced on slighter grounds than against an individual,—the Assembly 'is to cite the judicatory alleged' to have offended to appear at a specified time and place, and to show what it has done, or failed to do, in the case in question; after which the judicatory thus issuing the citation shall remit the whole matter to the delinquent judicatory, with a direction to 'take it up and dispose of it in a constitutional manner, or stay all further proceedings in the case, as circumstances may require.' See Book of Discipline, chap. vii, sec. 1, art. 6.

"In view of the aforenamed and other provisions of our Form of Government touching the authority of the Assembly, two things are to be carefully noted.

"1. It has no power to *commence* a process of discipline with an individual offender. That, by a just and wise arrangement, belongs to the Session in the case of a layman, to the Presbytery in the case of a minister. The disciplinary function of the Assembly as to individuals is simply appellate and revisionary. It is not the court of first, but of last resort.

"2. In the way of 'general review and control,' it can reach *directly* only the judicatory next below,—that is, the Synod. (See Book of Discipline, chap. vii, sec. 1, art. 6.) Indirectly, indeed, the doings of other bodies may be involved. A Session may grossly neglect discipline, for example, and the recorded indication or the common fame thereof may not be properly heeded by the Presbytery. The fruit of this heedlessness, or the evidence of it in the Presbyterial records, may call forth no appropriate action on the part of the Synod; and this may be brought, by the Synodical records, or by general rumor, to the knowledge of the Assembly. On the ground of either the record or the rumor, the Assembly may cite the Synod before them. Thus, *mediately*, may even a Session be reached, but not directly.

"Such are the metes and bounds which our Form of Government has prescribed, and which the Assembly may not overpass. It is quite possible that, in connection with them, offenders of various sorts may sometimes escape. To a human administration, of however Divine a system, imperfection always pertains. Our Book of Discipline, indeed (chap. iii, sec. 3), distinctly recognizes a class of cases in which, 'however grievous it may be to the pious to see an unworthy member in the Church, it is proper to wait until God in his righteous providence shall give further light.' Waiting may be rendered necessary by a lack of fidelity on the part of the lower judicatories, as well as by a lack of evidence. We speak of it, of course, not as an actual, but only as a supposable case. And it may seem to some a great evil that the General Assembly is not invested with larger powers. Yet it would be a greater evil to allow any departure from the carefully-devised processes of discipline set forth in the Constitution. To permit the Assembly to adopt at its pleasure new processes—to suit its own powers to real or fancied exigencies—would not only invest it with legislative functions, but would virtually annul the Constitution, and transform the highest judicatory of the Church into an overshadowing ecclesiastical despotism.

"It has, indeed, been urged—though we see not with what reason—that the advisory function of the Assembly, or its power of bearing testimony, implies the authority necessary to enforce that testimony. Is there then no just and salutary distinction between persuasion and compulsion? Must the two be ever conjoined? Are there no cases in which a simple moral power may, in the nature of things, be most potent? Must the Assembly utter no counsels which are not to be interpreted as mandatory and coercive? If they may enforce all their counsels, how are they to do it? By processes which they themselves devise,—extra-constitutional processes? Or are they to be held to the provisions of the Book of Discipline? They have, it is true, the right, according to the Form of Government, chap. xii, sec. 5, of 'attempting,' as well as 'recommending, reformation of manners.' But the attempt must be made, if discipline is to be involved, only in the method prescribed in the Constitution. To all desirable ends, the committee believe, that method will be found adequate; especially as connected with that testifying and reproving function so often exercised in time past, and which, by a body like the Assembly, can never be wisely exercised but with salutary results.

"ALBERT BARNES,
"ASA D. SMITH,
"WM. JESSUP,
"AUGUSTUS P. HASCALL."
—*Minutes*, 1856, pp. 197–201.

14. SESSIONS AT CLEVELAND, A.D. 1857.

"The General Assembly, in view of the memorials before them and of the present relations of the Church on the subject of slavery, feel called upon to make the following exposition of principle and duty:

"The Presbyterian Church in these United States has from the beginning maintained an attitude of decided opposition to the institution of slavery.

"The Synod of New York and Philadelphia, in 1787, two years before the organization of the General Assembly, declared that they did 'highly approve of the general principles in favor of universal liberty that prevail in America, and the interest which many of the States have taken in promoting the abolition of slavery, and did recommend it to all their people to use the most prudent measures, consistent with the interest and state of civil society in the parts where they live, to procure eventually the final abolition of slavery in America.'

"In 1793, while the Constitution of the Presbyterian Church was in process of formation and publication, the action of the Synod just referred to was approved by the General Assembly, and republished by its order.

"The Assembly of 1815 declared 'that, although in some sections of our country, under certain circumstances, the transfer of slaves may be unavoidable, yet they consider the buying and selling of slaves by way of traffic, and all undue severity in the management of them, as inconsistent with the spirit of the Gospel. And they recommend it to the Presbyteries and Sessions under their care to make use of all prudent measures to prevent such shameful and unrighteous conduct.'

"The Assembly of 1815 'expressed their regret that the slavery of the Africans and of their descendants still continues in so many places, and even among those within the pale of the Church,' and called particular attention to the action of 1795, with respect to the buying and selling of slaves.

"In 1818, the Assembly unanimously adopted a report on this subject, prepared by Dr. Green, of Philadelphia, Dr. Baxter, of Virginia, and Mr. Burgess, of Ohio, of which the following is a part:

"'We consider the voluntary enslaving of one part of the human race by another as a gross violation of the most precious and sacred rights of human nature, as utterly inconsistent with the law of God, which requires us to love our neighbor as ourselves, and as totally irreconcilable with the spirit and principles of the Gospel of Christ, which enjoins that "all things whatsoever ye would that men should do to you, do ye even so to them." Slavery creates a paradox in the moral system: it exhibits rational, accountable, and immortal beings in such circumstances as scarcely to leave them the power of moral action. It exhibits them as dependent on the will of others whether they shall receive religious instruction; whether they shall know and worship the true God; whether they shall enjoy the ordinances of the Gospel; whether they shall perform the duties and cherish the endearments of husbands and wives, parents and children, neighbors and friends; whether they shall preserve their chastity and purity, or regard the dictates of justice and humanity. Such are some of the consequences of slavery,—consequences not imaginary, but which connect themselves with its very existence. The evils to which the slave is *always* exposed often take place in fact, and in their very worst degree and form; and, where all of them do not take place,—as we rejoice to say that in many instances, through the influence of the principles of humanity and religion on the minds of masters, they do not,—still, the slave is deprived of his natural right, degraded as a human being, and exposed to the danger of passing into the hands of a master who may inflict upon him all the hardships and injuries which inhumanity and avarice may suggest.

"'From this view of the consequences resulting from the practice into which Christian people have most inconsistently fallen of enslaving a portion of their *brethren* of mankind,—for God hath made of one blood all nations of men to dwell on the face of the earth,—it is manifestly the duty of all Christians who enjoy the light of the present day, when the inconsistency of slavery both with the dictates of humanity and religion has been demonstrated and is generally seen and acknowledged, to use their honest, earnest, and unwearied endeavors to correct the errors of former times, and as speedily as possible to efface this blot on our holy religion, and to obtain the complete abolition of slavery throughout Christendom, and, if possible, throughout the world.'

"The Assembly also recommended 'to all the members of our religious denomination, not only to permit, but to facilitate and encourage the instruction of their slaves in the principles and duties of the Christian religion;' and added, 'We enjoin it on all church Sessions and Presbyteries under the care of this Assembly to discountenance, and, as far as possible, to prevent, all cruelty of whatever kind in the treatment of slaves, especially the cruelty of separating husband and wife, parents and children, and that which consists in selling slaves to those who will either themselves deprive these unhappy people of the blessings of the Gospel, or who will transport them to places where the Gospel is not proclaimed, or where it is forbidden to slaves to attend upon its institutions.'

"The foregoing testimonials on the subject of slavery were universally acquiesced in by the Presbyterian Church up to the time of the division in 1838.

"In the year 1846, the General Assembly made a declaration on this subject, of which the following is the introductory paragraph:

"'1. The system of slavery as it exists in these United States, viewed either in the laws of the several States which sanction it, or in its actual operation and results in society, is intrinsically an unrighteous and oppressive system, and is opposed to the prescriptions of the law of God, to the spirit and precepts of the Gospel, and to the best interests of humanity.'

"In 1849, the Assembly explicitly reaffirmed the sentiments expressed by the Assemblies of 1815, 1818, and 1846. In the year 1850, the General Assembly made the following declaration: 'We exceedingly deplore the working of the whole system of slavery as it exists in our country and is interwoven with the political institutions of the slaveholding States, as fraught with many and great evils to the civil, political, and moral interests of those regions where it exists.

"'The holding of our fellow-men in the condition of slavery, except in those cases where it is unavoidable by the laws of the State, the obligations of guardianship, or the demands of humanity, is an offence in the proper import of that term as used in the Book of Discipline, chap. i, sec. 3, and should be regarded and treated in the same manner as other offences.'

"Occupying the position in relation to this subject which the framers of our Constitution held at the first, and which our Church has always held, it is with deep grief that we now discover that a portion of the Church at the South has so far departed from the established doctrine of the Church in relation to slavery as to maintain that 'it is an ordinance of God,' and that the system of slavery existing in these United States is scriptural and right. Against this new doctrine we feel constrained to bear our solemn testimony. It is at war with the whole spirit and tenor of the Gospel of love and good-will, as well as abhorrent to the conscience of the Christian world. We can have no sympathy or fellowship with it; and we exhort all our people to eschew it as serious and pernicious error.

"We are especially pained by the fact that the Presbytery of Lexington, South, have given official notice to us that a number of ministers and ruling elders, as well as many church-members, in their connection, hold slaves 'from principle' and 'of choice,' 'believing it to be according to the Bible right,' and have, without any qualifying explanation, assumed the responsibility of sustaining such ministers, elders, and church-members in their position. We deem it our duty, in the exercise of our constitutional authority 'to bear testimony against error in doctrine or immorality in practice in any church, Presbytery, or Synod,' to disapprove and earnestly condemn the position which has been thus assumed by the Presbytery of Lexington, South, as one which is opposed to the established convictions of the Presbyterian Church, and must operate to mar its peace and seriously hinder its prosperity, as well as bring reproach on our holy religion; and we do hereby call on that Presbytery to review and rectify their position. Such doctrines and practice cannot be permanently tolerated in the Presbyterian Church. May they speedily melt away under the illuminating and mellowing influence of the Gospel and grace of God our Saviour!

"We do not, indeed, pronounce a sentence of indiscriminate condemnation upon all our brethren who are unfortunately connected with the system of slavery. We tenderly sympathize with all those who deplore the evil, and are honestly doing all in their power for the present well-being of their slaves and for their complete emancipation. We would aid and not embarrass such brethren. And yet, in the language of the General Assembly of 1818, we would 'earnestly warn them against unduly extending the plea of necessity,—against making it a cover for the love and practice of slavery, or a pretence for not using efforts that are lawful and practicable to extinguish this evil.'

"In conclusion, the Assembly call the attention of the Publication

Committee to this subject, and recommend the publication, in a convenient form, of the testimony of the Presbyterian Church touching this subject, at the earliest practicable period.

"The vote upon its adoption was by yeas and nays.

"Adopted: Yeas, 169; Nays, 26; *non liquet*, 2."—*Minutes*, 1857, pp. 401–404.

15. Sessions at Chicago, 1860.

"The Standing Committee on Church Extension, to whom was referred the resolution proposing that the General Assembly should instruct the Church Extension Committee to offer no assistance to any church that has in its communion one or more slaveholders, reported as follows:

"1. The Permanent Committee on Church Extension is appointed to act for the whole Church, being an organ of the General Assembly, which represents the whole Church, and we can see no defensible principle on which such a committee could make discriminations, on moral grounds, between churches that are recognized as having the same ecclesiastical standing under our common Constitution.

"2. The position of our Church is well understood to be one of opposition to the spirit and the system of slavery; and we have no reason to believe that any churches connected with us are using their influence to sustain and fortify that institution.

"3. If it be true, that any members of churches in our connection hold slaves, under mistaken views of their duty towards them, we do not see that this affords any sufficient reason for withholding from them the bread of life, and such enlightened teachings as we believe our ministry are qualified and disposed to impart, in relation to all the great principles of Christian duty. We sympathize with all Christian endeavors to remove imperfection and sin from the Church of Christ; but we think this end is to be accomplished, not by withdrawing the Gospel from those who need it, but by affectionate and prayerful efforts to apply the principles of our holy religion to the heart and conscience of every Christian who is willing to receive instruction.

"4. The Church Extension Committee are fully aware of the ground which our Church occupies with reference to this subject, and we have confidence that they will conscientiously discharge their duty, with an enlightened regard to the promotion of righteousness and holiness in the Church and in the world.

"The report was adopted."—*Minutes*, 1860, p. 258.

CHAPTER VIII.

DELIVERANCES ON DOCTRINE.

Case of Samuel Harker. Views condemned.—2. Testimony against the doctrine of universal salvation, and the finite duration of hell torments.—3. Testimony against Socinianism.—4. Case of Rev. Hezekiah Balch. Doctrines condemned; acknowledgment required, and made.—5. "Gospel Plan," by W. C. Davis, condemned.—6. Case of Thomas B. Craighead.—7. Case of Albert Barnes.—8. Testimony against certain disorders.—9. Against errors in doctrine.—10. An explication of doctrines.

1. *Case of Samuel Harker.*

"A reference was brought into the Synod from the New Brunswick Presbytery, respecting Mr. Samuel Harker, one of their members, as having imbibed and vented certain erroneous dectrines. The further consideration of this affair deferred till the next *sederunt.*"—*Minutes,* 1758, p. 283.

[The matter was continued from year to year, Synod endeavoring to remove the difficulty, and bring Mr. Harker to a sense of his error. In 1761, Mr. Harker printed and published his views, and the Synod (1762) appointed a committee to examine the book, who reported next year.]

"The Synod proceeded to consider Mr. Harker's principles, collected from his book by the committee, which are in substance as follows:

"1. That the covenant of grace is in such a sense conditional, that fallen mankind in their unregenerate state, by the general assistance given to all under the Gospel, have a sufficient ability to fulfil the conditions thereof, and so, by their own endeavors, to insure to themselves regenerating grace and all saving blessings.

"2. That God has bound himself by promise to give them regenerating grace, upon their fulfilling what he (Mr. Harker) calls the direct conditions of obtaining it; and, upon the whole, makes a certain and an infallible connection between their endeavors and the aforesaid blessings.

"3. That God's prescience of future events is previous to, and not dependent on his decrees; that his decrees have no influence on his own conduct, and that the foresight of faith was the ground of the decree of election.

"It is further observed, that he often uses inaccurate, unintelligible, and dangerous modes of expression, that tend to lead people into false notions in several important matters, as that Adam was the federal father of his posterity in the second covenant as well as in the first; that the regenerate are not in a state of probation for heaven, and several such like.

"The Synod judge that these principles are of a hurtful and dangerous tendency, giving a false view of the covenant of grace, perverting it into a new-modelled covenant of works, and misrepresent the doctrine of the Divine decrees, as held by the best Reformed Churches, and in fine, are contrary to the word of God and our approved standards of doctrine."—*Minutes*, 1763, p. 329.

2. *Testimony against Universalism.*

"Whereas, the doctrine of universal salvation, and of the finite duration of hell torments, has been propagated by sundry persons who live in the United States of America, and the people under our care may possibly, from their occasional conversation with the propagators of such a dangerous opinion, be infected by the doctrine, the Synod take this opportunity to declare their utter abhorrence of such doctrines as they apprehend to be subversive of the fundamental principles of religion and morality; and therefore earnestly recommend it to all their Presbyteries and members to be watchful upon this subject, and to guard against the introduction of such tenets among our people." [See chap. i, sec. 3 : 1, p. 38.]—*Minutes*, 1787, p. 540.

3. *Against Socinianism.*

a. "If there is a religion revealed by God, it is as important to have correct views of its principles, to perform the duties which it enjoins in the various relations of life, as it is to have correct views of morality, that our lives may be moral. Error in principle invariably produces error in practice. To be ever learning and never coming to the knowledge of the truth, is characteristic of none but those who assume for the human understanding the prerogative of sitting in judgment upon the inspired truth of God, either condemning the whole as an imposition, or undertaking to correct its alleged mistakes by abridging and falsifying its contents. Of the former class, we rejoice that their number and influence are diminished. Not many years past, they triumphed, to the regret and anguish of the followers of Christ. With brazen front, infidelity threatened the annihilation of the Church, and the ruin of her Lord's authority. But the Church not merely survives its attacks; she has increased in numbers and in grace, whilst her adversaries are compelled, though unwillingly, to pay homage to the paramount claims of her God and her Saviour, who is King of kings, and Lord of lords. Few are to be found, who respect themselves, openly opposing the truth of God as contained in the Scriptures. There are, however, some within our bounds who, whilst they profess to honor the authority of the Bible, with unhallowed hands would cut out of its pages those passages which command us to honor the Son as we honor the Father, and rob the trembling sinner of the only hope of acceptance with God which his soul can cherish. The well-beloved and only-begotten Son of God they reduce to the level of frail humanity, and his work of redemption to the mere fact of furnishing us a perfect example of conversation and conduct. By denying his character as a covenant-surety to bear our sins and carry our sorrows, they lower his example, as a righteous and holy man, below that which his Apostles and primitive followers afford us. And so far as we have had the opportunity of judging from facts which have fallen under our observation, their principles have introduced among all who have embraced them, so great a conformity in their practice to the world which lieth in wickedness, as to render it impossible to discriminate them from the children of that world.

"In connection with these anti-Trinitarians, for we reject the name which they have assumed, of Unitarians, holding the unity of God as strictly as they do, are the Universalists, or the supporters of the doctrine of universal salvation. It is a tribute, however, which we owe to truth, to say, that whilst the anti-Trinitarians, for the sake of consistency, are compelled to maintain the ultimate and eternal salvation of all, the Universalists believe in the doctrine of the Trinity, and the atonement of the Lord Jesus. They, however, by assuring all that they will be in the end forever happy, provide for the gratification of present desires and continuance in sin whilst they live.

"As these errors in principle do exist in some portion of our Church, though we have good reasons to believe that they are not increasing, the Assembly trust that they will be opposed, and their ruinous tendency unfolded with fidelity and success."—*Minutes*, 1818, p. 677.

b. "In some parts of our land, attempts are made to propagate the most pernicious errors. With a zeal worthy of a better cause, and under lofty pretensions to superior rationality and to deeper discoveries in religion, some are endeavoring to take away the crown from the Redeemer's head; to degrade Him who is the mighty God and the Prince of life to a level with mere men, and to rob us of all our hopes of redemption through his blood. Pretending, too, a more expanded benevolence to man, and more ennobled ideas of the goodness and mercy of God, they assiduously propagate the sentiment, that all men will ultimately obtain eternal happiness, however sinful their present temper and conduct may be, without any regard to the cleansing of the blood, of atonement, or the sanctifying influences of the Spirit of God. Believing that these sentiments are utterly subversive of Gospel truth and holiness; that they are alike dishonoring to God and destructive to the present and eternal welfare of men, we cannot but affectionately warn you against them. Beware, brethren, lest ye also, being led away with the error of the wicked, fall from your own steadfastness. Cherish an ardent attachment to the truth which is according to godliness, and seek to experience in your own souls its sanctifying influence."—*Minutes*, 1822, p. 58.

4. *Case of Rev. Hezekiah Balch.*

"The consideration of the references relative to Mr. Balch was resumed, and after some amendments made on the draught brought in by the committee, it was adopted, and is as follows, viz.:

"They remark upon the first article of the creed aforesaid, that Mr. Balch is erroneous in making disinterested benevolence the only definition of holiness or true religion; because this may perplex the minds of those not accustomed to abstract speculations, is questionable in itself, and may convey the idea that an absolute God, or a God out of Christ, is the object of the highest affection to the renewed mind.

"Upon the second article, they remark, that Mr. Balch has confounded self-love with selfishness in an abstract speculation, calculated to puzzle plain Christians and lead to unprofitable disputes.

"Upon the third article, they remark, that the transferring of personal sin, or righteousness, has never been held by Calvinistic divines, nor by any person in our Church, so far as is known to us, and therefore that Mr. Balch's observations on that subject appear to be either nugatory or calculated to mislead. But with regard to his doctrine of original sin, it is to be observed, that he is erroneous in representing personal corruption as not derived from Adam; making Adam's sin to be imputed to his posterity, in consequence of a corrupt nature already possessed, and derived from we know not what; thus, in effect, setting aside the idea of Adam's being the federal head or representative of his descendants, and the whole doctrine of the covenant of works.

"It is also manifest that Mr. Balch is greatly erroneous in asserting that the formal cause of a believer's justification is the imputation of the fruits and effects of Christ's righteousness, and not that righteousness itself; because righteousness, and that alone, is the formal demand of the law, and consequently the sinner's violation of the divine law can be pardoned only in virtue of the Redeemer's perfect righteousness being imputed to him, and reckoned as his. It is also not true, that the benefits of Christ's righteousness are, with strict propriety, said to be imputed at all; as these benefits flow to, and are possessed by, the believer as a consequence of his justification, and having an interest in the infinite merits of the Saviour.

"On article fourth, no remark is necessary.

"With regard to the fifth article, they remark, that Mr. Balch appears to confound sentiment with the mere perception of truth, whereas it always partakes of the disposition of the heart, and consequently involves in it either sin or holiness. The article, as stated by him, contradicts the principle laid down in the introduction to our Form of Government, and levels the important distinction between truth and falsehood, so as to be liable to the construction that it is no matter what a man believes. And though Mr. Balch may not, and probably did not, intend to insinuate anything disrespectful to the Holy Scriptures, where he asserts that 'there are wrong sentiments in the Bible,' yet, as his expression is liable to such a construction, we judge it highly censurable.

"With regard to the sixth and seventh articles, no remarks seem to be necessary, except that the offence given by the reflection cast on his brethren, the Presbyterians, in the seventh, has been sufficiently removed by his candid acknowledgment before the Synod and General Assembly.

"The eighth, ninth, and tenth articles require no remark, except that they appear to be unimportant.

"With regard to the twelfth article, it is remarked, that his observation upon love, as exercised by the human race, so far as it may be applicable to a state of infancy, is unintelligible; and that, though a distinction may be made between regeneration and conversion, yet the terms in which the article is expressed are exceptionable, as they seem to discourage the use of the means of grace.

"With regard to the thirteenth article, it is remarked, that in making repentance and faith to proceed wholly from love or charity, Mr. Balch has expressed an opinion unnecessary and improper.

"In regard to the subject of false doctrine, in discoursing from Psalm 51 : 5, and Isa. 48 : 8, nothing seems necessary to be added to the remarks made on the subject of original sin, as contained in Mr. Balch's creed, except that he charges Calvinistic divines with holding sentiments relative to infants which they do not hold; and that he makes positive declarations in regard to the state of infants, when it has pleased a wise and holy God to be silent on this subject in the revelation of his will. . . . . . .

"On the whole, your committee recommend that Mr. Balch be required to acknowledge before the Assembly that he was wrong in the publication of his creed; that in the particulars specified above, he renounce the errors pointed out; that he engage to teach nothing hereafter of a similar nature; that the moderator admonish him of the divisions, disorder, trouble, and inconvenience which he has occasioned to the Church and its judicatories by his imprudent and unwarrantable conduct, and warn him against doing anything in time to come that may tend to produce such serious and lamentable evils.

"That if Mr. Balch submit to this, he be considered as in good standing with the Church, and that the reference and queries of the Synod of the Carolinas be considered as fully answered by the adoption of these measures."—*Minutes*, 1798, pp. 155, 156.

[Mr. Balch appeared before the Assembly, and acknowledged that he was wrong in publishing his creed, and did "solemnly declare, as in the presence of his final Judge, that he never did entertain the ideas nor intend to teach the doctrines which are pointed out as errors by the Assembly." He was accordingly solemnly admonished and declared to be in good standing with the Church.]—*Minutes*, 1798, p. 158.

5. *Case of Rev. William C. Davis.*

"The overture from the Synod of the Carolinas, which had been laid on the table, referring to the Assembly an overture laid before that Synod, requesting their attention to a late publication of the Rev. W. C. Davis, denominated the 'Gospel Plan,' was read; Messrs. Robert G. Wilson, Calhoun, and Anderson were appointed a committee to examine said book and report to this Assembly the doctrines it contains, if any such they find, that are contrary to the standards of the Presbyterian Church.

"The report of the committee was adopted, viz.:

"The committee, presuming that a complete and perfect enumeration of all the objectionable parts of said book is not expected, called the attention of the Assembly only to the following doctrines, supposed to be contrary to the Confession of Faith of the Presbyterian Church:

"Doctrine I. That the active obedience of Christ constitutes no part of that righteousness by which a sinner is justified, pp. 257, 261, 264, 3d corollary.

"Doctrine II. That obedience to the moral law was not required as the condition of the covenant of works, pp. 178, 180.

"These pages being read, the Assembly resolved that they do consider these doctrines as contrary to the Confession of our Church.

"Doctrine III. God himself is as firmly bound in duty (not obedience) to his creatures, as his creatures are bound in obedience or duty to him, pp. 164, 166. Also, that God's will is not the standard of right and wrong. If God's will is the primary rule of his own actions, he would be: 1st. Entirely void of holiness; 2d. There could be no justice in God; 3d. It would be impossible for God to be unchangeable; 4th. If the will of God is the standard of right and wrong, then it would be no infringement on the divine character to be unfaithful to his word and promise, pp. 168–171.

"These pages were read,

"*Resolved*, That, without deciding on the question whether these sentiments are contrary to our Confession of Faith, the Assembly consider the mode in which they are expressed as unhappy, and calculated to mislead the reader.

"Doctrine IV. God could not make Adam, or any other creature, either holy or unholy. Compare page 194 with 166.

"Doctrine V. Regeneration must be a consequence of faith. Faith precedes regeneration, p. 352.

"Doctrine VI. Faith, in the first act of it, is not a holy act, p. 358, &c.

"These pages being read,

"*Resolved*, That the Assembly do consider the three last-mentioned doctrines contrary to the Confession of Faith of our Church.

"Doctrine VII. Christians may sin wilfully and habitually, pp. 532, 534.

"These pages being read,

"*Resolved*, That the Assembly consider the expressions in the pages referred to as very unguarded; and so far as they intimate it to be the author's opinion that a person may live in an habitual and allowed sin, and yet be a Christian, the Assembly considers them contrary to the letter and spirit of the Confession of Faith of our Church, and in their tendency highly dangerous.

"Doctrine VIII. If God has to plant all the principal parts of salvation in a sinner's heart to enable him to believe, the 'Gospel Plan' is quite out of his reach, and consequently does not suit his case; and it must be impossible for God to condemn a man for unbelief, for no just law condemns or criminates any person for not doing what he cannot do, p. 413.

"This page, and several others on the same subject, being read,

"*Resolved*, That the Assembly do consider this last-mentioned doctrine contrary to the Confession of Faith of our Church.

"On the whole,

"*Resolved*, That this Assembly cannot but view with disapprobation, various parts of the work entitled 'The Gospel Plan,' of which William C. Davis is stated in the title-page to be the author. In several instances in this work, modes of expression are adopted so different from those which are sanctioned by use and by the best orthodox writers, that the Assembly consider them as calculated to produce useless or mischievous speculations.

"In several other instances, there are doctrines asserted and advocated, as has been already decided, contrary to the Confession of Faith of our Church, and the word of God; which doctrines the Assembly feel constrained to pronounce to be of very dangerous tendency; and the Assembly do judge, and do hereby declare, that the preaching or publishing of them, ought to subject the person or persons so doing to be dealt with by their respective Presbyteries, according to the discipline of the Church, relative to the propagation of errors."—*Minutes*, 1810, pp. 448, 452, 453.

6. *Case of Rev. Thomas B. Craighead.*

[On an appeal from the Synod of Kentucky. After speaking of certain irregularities in the conduct both of the Synod and of the appellant, the committee say:]

"But from matters of form, the General Assembly will now pass to the merits of the case; and, for the sake of brevity, the first and second charges only shall be brought into view.

"Charge 1. We charge him with denying and vilifying the real agency of the Spirit in regeneration, and in the production of faith and sanctification in general.

"And first, they would observe, that there can be no doubt, that the denial of the *real agency of the Spirit* is a dangerous and fundamental error; and if Mr. Craighead taught such an error, he ought to have been suspended.

"The question then is: Do the passages of Mr. Craighead's sermon, referred to in the charge, prove that he did deny the *reality* of the operations of the Spirit?

"Here, it will be important to remark, that a man cannot fairly be convicted of heresy, for using expressions which may be so interpreted as to involve heretical doctrines, if they may also admit of a more favorable construction: because, no one can tell in what sense an ambiguous expression is used, but the speaker or writer, and he has a right to explain himself; and in such cases, candor requires that a court should favor the accused, by putting on his words the more favorable, rather than the less favorable construction.

"Another principle is, that no man can rightly be convicted of heresy by inference or implication; that is, we must not charge an accused person with holding those consequences which may legitimately flow from his assertions. Many men are grossly inconsistent with themselves; and while it is right, in argument, to overthrow false opinions, by tracing them in their connections and consequences, it is not right to charge any man with an opinion which he disavows.

"With these principles in view, the General Assembly proceed to observe, that there is abundant evidence, that Mr. Craighead did deny the *immediate agency* of the Spirit, but no clear evidence that he denied the *real agency* of the Spirit. These are very different things, and the proof of the one, does by no means establish the other. *Immediate* agency or operation, is opposed to *mediate.* This is a well-known distinction in theology; and a point which has been greatly controverted. The Reformed Church, of which ours is a part, in all their purest times, maintained the doctrine of the immediate operation of the Spirit, not without the word, but distinct from it, and in the order of nature preceding it. Other Protestant churches, never charged with fundamental error, have as uniformly maintained the doctrine of a *mediate* agency; and those commonly believe, that this operation is not occasional, but uniform, and diversified in its effects, by the difference of resistance with which it meets. Neither the Presbytery nor the Synod appear to have attended sufficiently to this distinction. They appear to have thought, that a denial of *immediate agency* was a denial of all *real* agency. It deserves special *regard* here, that our Confession takes no notice of these nice distinctions, about the mode in which the Holy Spirit operates. It usually mentions the word and the Spirit together, and the former as the instrument of the latter. And they who believe in the immediate agency of the Spirit do not exclude the instrumentality of the word; they however explain it in a different way from those who hold, that there is no agency of the Spirit, distinct from the word. But this is the more favorable construction; there is another, which if not more probable, is more obvious. Mr. Craighead may be understood as teaching, that the only real agency of the Spirit was in inspiring the Scriptures, and confirming them by signs and miracles. There is much in his discourse that has this bearing; and undoubtedly this is the common impression among the people where it is best known. This was the idea of the Synod of Kentucky, when they condemned him; and this is, in fact, denying the reality of the operation of the Spirit, in our days: and whether his expressions have been fairly interpreted or not, they are dangerous, and ought to be condemned. In justice to Mr. Craighead, however, it ought to be remembered, that he utterly disclaims this meaning, in his defence sent up to this Assembly. And would it be fair to continue to charge upon him opinions which he solemnly disavows? Of the sincerity of his disavowal, God is the judge. The conclusion is, that the first charge, though supported by strong probabilities, is not so conclusively established as to remove all doubt, because the words adduced in proof, will bear a different construction from that put on them by the Presbytery and Synod.

"The evidence in support of the second charge is still less clear and conclusive. The charge is—

"'We charge him with denying, vilifying, and misrepresenting the doctrine of divine foreordination, and sovereignty, and election.'

"It might, perhaps, be shown by argument, that Mr. Craighead uses many expressions not consistent with these doctrines; but agreeably to the principle laid down above, he must not be charged with holding these consequences, unless he has avowed them. These passages of his discourse, it is true, contain erroneous and offensive things, but they do not establish the charge of denying, vilifying, &c. In one single instance, he seems to deny that everything should be referred to the sovereignty of God's will; but the words, in their connection, may have an innocent meaning. Here again it must be observed, that Mr. Craighead solemnly declares his belief in the doctrine of decrees and election, as expressed in our standards.

"But whilst the General Assembly are of opinion that the charges against Mr. Craighead are not clearly and fully supported by the references, they feel it to be their duty to say, that the impression which they have received from hearing extracts from this discourse are very unfavorable; and they do believe that Mr. Craighead, by preaching and printing this sermon, did subject himself justly to censure.

"Moreover, the Assembly are of opinion, that the doctrines of this sermon, in the most favorable construction, are different from those of the Reformed Churches, and of our Church, and are erroneous; although the error is not of fundamental importance. They have observed, also, that this discourse contains many unjust and illiberal reflections on the doctrines which have been the common and uniform belief of the great majority of the preachers and writers of the Reformed Churches. He mentions the names of a few persons as favoring the doctrine which he opposes; but he might have put into the list almost every standard writer of our own and sister churches, since the Reformation.

"The sermon also contains much declamation which confounds fanaticism and piety; and representations of opinions which are true and important, so associated with error and absurdity, as to exhibit them in a ridiculous and odious light.

"Finally, the General Assembly are deeply impressed with the evidences of an improper spirit, and an evil tendency in this sermon, and are of opinion that Mr. Craighead ought so to retract or to explain his sentiments, as to afford reasonable satisfaction to his brethren."—*Minutes*, 1824, pp. 122–124.

[The case was transmitted to the Presbytery of West Tennessee, which was ordered, on satisfactory explanations and retractions, to restore him to the ministry, from which he had been suspended. Mr. Craighead was restored.]

7. *Case of Rev. Albert Barnes.*

[On an appeal from the action of the Synod of Philadelphia, suspending him from the Gospel ministry, the appeal was sustained, Yeas, 134; Nays, 96; and the decision of the Synod *reversed*, Yeas, 145; Nays, 78. The following resolution was then offered by Dr. Miller, viz.:]

"*Resolved*, That while this General Assembly has thought proper to remove the sentence of suspension under which the Rev. Mr. Barnes was placed by the Synod of Philadelphia; yet the judgment of the Assembly is, that Mr. Barnes, in his notes on the Epistle to the Romans, has published opinions materially at variance with the Confession of Faith of the Presbyterian Church, and with the word of God,—especially with regard to original sin, the relation of man to Adam, and justification by faith in the atoning sacrifice and righteousness of the Redeemer. The Assembly consider the manner in which Mr. Barnes has controverted the language and doctrine of our public standards, as highly reprehensible, and as adapted to pervert the minds of the rising generation from the simplicity and purity of the Gospel plan. And although some of the most objectionable statements and expressions which appeared in the earlier editions of the work in question have been either removed, or so far modified or explained as to render them more in accordance with our public formularies, still the Assembly considers the work, even in its present amended form, as containing representations which cannot be reconciled with the letter or spirit of our public standards, and would solemnly admonish Mr. Barnes again to review this work, to modify still further the statements which have grieved his brethren, and to be more careful in time to come to study the purity and peace of the Church.

"After considerable discussion, the previous question was moved and carried, to put the main question.

"The main question was then put, on the adoption of the above resolution, offered by Dr. Miller, and was decided in the negative, as follows, viz.: Yeas, 109; Nays, 122."—*Minutes*, 1836, p. 270.

[To this action two protests were offered and entered on the Minutes. The following reply of the Assembly to the protests gives the only view, found on the Minutes, of the merits of the case:]

"In reply to the two protests of the minority, against the decision of the Assembly in refusing to censure the first edition of Barnes's Notes on the Romans, the Assembly remark:

"1. That by their decision they do not intend to, and do not, in fact, make themselves responsible for all the phraseology of Mr. Barnes; some of which is not sufficiently guarded, and is liable to be misunderstood; and which we doubt not Mr. Barnes, with reference to his usefulness and the peace of the Church, will modify so as to prevent, as far as may be, the possibility of misconception.

"2. Much less do the Assembly adopt as doctrines, consistent with our standards, and to be tolerated in our Church, the errors alleged by the prosecutor, as contained in the book on the Romans. It was a question of fact, whether the errors alleged are contained in the book; and by the laws of exposition, in conscientious exercise of their own rights and duties, the Assembly have come to the conclusion that the book does not teach the errors charged. This judgment of the Assembly is based on this maxim of equity and charity, adopted by the Assembly of 1824, in the case of Craighead, which is as follows, namely: 'A man cannot be fairly convicted of heresy for using expressions which may be so interpreted as to involve heretical doctrines, if they also admit of a more favorable construction. It is not right to charge any man with an opinion which he disavows.' The import of this is, that when language claimed to be heretical admits, without violence, of an orthodox exposition, and the accused disclaims the alleged error, and claims as his meaning the orthodox interpretation, he is entitled to it, and it is to be regarded as the true intent and import of his words. But in the case of the first edition of the Notes on the Romans, the language is, without violence, reconcilable with an interpretation conformable to our standards; and, therefore, all the changes of phraseology which he has subsequently made, and all his disclaimers before the Assembly, and all his definite and unequivocal declarations of the true intent and meaning of his words in the first edition, are to be taken as ascertaining his true meaning, and forbid the Assembly to condemn the book as teaching great and dangerous errors.

"3. When the Assembly sustained the appeal of Mr. Barnes, by a majority of thirty-eight; and by a majority of sixty-seven removed the sentence of his suspension, and restored him in good standing to the ministry, it is not competent for the same judicature, by the condemnation of the book, to inflict on Mr. Barnes indirectly, but really, a sentence of condemnation, as direct in its effects, and as prostrating to his character and usefulness, as if it had been done directly, by refusing to sustain his appeal, and by confirming the sentence of the Synod of Philadelphia; and what this Assembly has declared that it cannot in equity do directly, it cannot, in equity or consistency, attempt to do indirectly.

"4. The proposed condemnation of Mr. Barnes's book, as containing errors materially at variance with the doctrines of our standards, after sustaining his appeal, and restoring him to good standing in the ministry, would be a direct avowal that great and dangerous errors may be published and maintained with impunity in the Church. For if the book does in fact inculcate such errors, it were wrong to attempt to destroy the book and spare the man. If the charges are real, they are not accidental. Therefore, should the Assembly decide the alleged errors of the book to be real, it would, by its past decision, declare that a man suspended for great and pernicious errors, may be released from censure, and restored to an unembarrassed standing in the ministry; a decision to which this Assembly can never give its sanction.

"5. The attempt to condemn Mr. Barnes, by a condemnation of his book, after he had been acquitted on a hearing on charges wholly founded on the book, is a violation of the fundamental maxim of law, that no man shall be twice put in jeopardy for the same offence; and if it were otherwise, and the man might be tried in his person, and tried on his book, the same process of specification and defence is due to personal and public justice.

"6. So far is the Assembly from countenancing the errors alleged in the charges of Dr. Junkin, that they do cordially and *ex animo* adopt the Confession of our Church, on the points of doctrine in question, according to the obvious and most prevalent interpretation, and do regard it, as a whole, as the best epitome of the doctrines of the Bible ever formed. And this Assembly disavows any desire, and would deprecate any attempt, to change the phraseology of our standards, and would disapprove of any language of light estimation applied to them; believing that no denomination can prosper whose members permit themselves to speak slightly of its formularies of doctrine; and are ready to unite with their brethren in contending earnestly for the faith of our standards.

"7. The correctness of the preceding positions is confirmed, in the opinion of the Assembly, by a careful analysis of the real meaning of Mr. Barnes under each charge, as ascertained by the language of his book, and the revisions, disclaimers, explanations, and declarations which he has made.

"In respect to the first charge, that Mr. Barnes teaches that all sin is voluntary, the context and his own declarations show that he refers to all actual sin merely, in which he affirms the sinner acts under no compulsion.

"The second charge implies neither heresy nor errors, but relates to the expression of an opinion on a matter, concerning which no definite instruction is contained, either in the Bible or in the Confession of Faith.

"In respect to the third charge, Mr. Barnes has not taught that unregenerate men are able, in the sense alleged, to keep the commandments, and convert themselves to God. It is an inference of the prosecutor from the doctrine of natural ability, as taught by Edwards, and of the natural liberty of the will, as taught in the Confession of Faith, chap. ix, sec. 1. On the contrary, he does teach in accordance with our standards, that man, by the fall, hath wholly lost all ability of will to any spiritual good accompanying salvation.

"In respect to the fourth charge, that faith is an act of the mind, Mr. Barnes does teach it in accordance with the Confession of Faith and the Bible; but he does not deny that faith is a fruit of the special influence of the Spirit, and a permanent holy habit of mind, in opposition to a created physical essence. That faith 'is counted for righteousness,' is the language of the Bible, and, as used by Mr. Barnes, means, not that faith is the meritorious ground of justification, but only the instrument by which the benefit of Christ's righteousness is appropriated.

"In respect to the fifth charge, Mr. Barnes nowhere denies, much less 'sneers' at the idea that Adam was the covenant and federal head of his posterity. On the contrary, though he employs not these terms, he does, in other language, teach the same truths which are taught by this phraseology.

"In respect to the sixth and seventh charges, that the sin of Adam is not imputed to his posterity, and that mankind are not guilty or liable to punishment on account of the first sin of Adam, it is to be observed, that it is not taught in the Confession of Faith that the *sin* of Adam is imputed to his posterity. The imputation of the guilt of Adam's sin, Mr. Barnes affirms, though not as including personal identity and the transfer of moral qualities, both of which are disclaimed by our standard writers, and by the General Assembly.

"In respect to the eighth charge, that Christ did not suffer the penalty of the law, as the vicarious substitute of his people, Mr. Barnes only denies the literal infliction of the whole curse, as including remorse of conscience and eternal death; but admits and teaches, that the sufferings of Christ, owing to the union of the divine and human natures in the person of the Mediator, were a full equivalent.

"In respect to the ninth charge, that the righteousness of Christ is not imputed to his people, Mr. Barnes teaches the imputation of the righteousness of Christ, but not as importing a transfer of Christ's personal righteousness to believers, which is not the doctrine of our Church. And when he says, that there is no sense in which the righteousness of Christ becomes ours, the context and his own declarations show that he simply means to deny a literal transfer of his obedience; which, on the contrary, he teaches is so imputed or set to our account as to become the only meritorious cause or ground of our justification.

"In respect to the tenth charge, Mr. Barnes has not taught that justification consists in pardon only; but has taught clearly that it includes the reception of believers into favor, and their treatment as if they had not sinned."—*Minutes*, 1836, pp. 287–289.

8. *Testimony against certain Disorders and Irregularities.*

"Whereas, It is represented to the Assembly, that the following disorders and irregularities are practised in some portions of the Presbyterian Church, the Assembly, without determining the extent of them, would solemnly warn all in our connection against them. They are as follows, viz.:

"1. The formation of Presbyteries without defined and reasonable limits, or Presbyteries covering the same territory, and especially such a formation founded on doctrinal repulsions or affinities, thus introducing schism into the very vitals of the body.

"2. The licensing of persons to preach the Gospel, and the ordaining to the office of the ministry such as not only accept of our standards merely for substance of doctrine, and others who are unfit and ought to be excluded for want of qualification, but of many even who openly deny fundamental principles of truth, and preach and publish radical errors, as already set forth.

"3. The formation of a great multitude and variety of creeds, which are often incomplete, false, and contradictory of each other, and of our Confession of Faith and the Bible; but which, even if true, are needless, seeing that the public and authorized standards of the Church are fully sufficient for the purposes for which such formularies were introduced, namely, as public testimonies of our faith and practice, as aids to the teaching of the people truth and righteousness, and as instruments for ascertaining and preserving the unity of the Spirit in the bonds of peace, it being understood that we do not object to the use of a brief abstract of the doctrines of our Confession of Faith in the public reception of private members of the Church.

"4. The needless ordination of a multitude of men to the office of Evangelist, and the consequent tendency to a general neglect of the pastoral office; frequent and hurtful changes of pastoral relations; to the multiplication of spurious excitements, and the consequent spread of heresy and fanaticism,—thus weakening and bringing into contempt the ordinary and stated agents and means for the conversion of sinners, and the edification of the body of Christ.

"5. The disuse of the office of Ruling Elder in portions of the Church, and the consequent growth of practices and principles entirely foreign to our system; thus depriving the pastors of needful assistants in discipline, the people of proper guides in Christ, and the churches of suitable representatives in the ecclesiastical tribunals.

"6. The unlimited and irresponsible power assumed by several associations of men under various names, to exercise authority and influence, direct and indirect, over Presbyteries, as to their field of labor, place of residence, and mode of action in the difficult circumstances of our Church; thus actually throwing the control of affairs, in large portions of the Church, and sometimes in the General Assembly itself, out of the hands of the Presbyteries into those of single individuals or small committees, located at a distance."—*Minutes*, 1837, p. 471.

9. *Testimony against Doctrinal Errors.*

"As one of the principal objects of the memorialists is to point out certain errors, more or less prevalent in our Church, and to bear testimony against them, your committee are of opinion, that as one great object of the institution of the Church was to be a depository and guardian of the truth; and as, by the Constitution of the Presbyterian Church in the United States, it is made the duty of the General Assembly to testify against error, therefore—

"*Resolved*, That the testimony of the memorialists concerning doctrine be adopted as the testimony of this General Assembly (with a few verbal alterations), which is as follows:

"1. That God would have prevented the existence of sin in our world, but was not able without destroying the moral agency of man; or that, for aught that appears in the Bible to the contrary, sin is incidental to any wise moral system.

"2. That election to eternal life is founded on a foresight of faith and obedience.

"3. That we have no more to do with the first sin of Adam than with the sins of any other parent.

"4. That infants come into the world as free from moral defilement as was Adam, when he was created.

"5. That infants sustain the same relation to the moral government of God in this world as brute animals, and that their sufferings and death are to be accounted for, on the same principles as those of brutes, and not by any means to be considered as penal.

"6. That there is no other original sin than the fact that all the posterity of Adam, though by nature innocent, or possessed of no moral character, will always begin to sin when they begin to exercise moral agency; that original sin does not include a sinful bias of the human mind, and a just exposure to penal suffering; and that there is no evidence in Scripture, that infants, in order to salvation, do need redemption by the blood of Christ, and regeneration by the Holy Ghost.

"7. That the doctrine of imputation, whether of the guilt of Adam's sin, or of the righteousness of Christ, has no foundation in the word of God, and is both unjust and absurd.

"8. That the sufferings and death of Christ were not truly vicarious and penal, but symbolical, governmental, and instructive only.

"9. That the impenitent sinner is, by nature, and independently of the renewing influence or almighty energy of the Holy Spirit, in full possession of all the ability necessary to a full compliance with all the commands of God.

"10. That Christ does not intercede for the elect until after their regeneration.

"11. That saving faith is not an effect of the special operation of the Holy Spirit, but a mere rational belief of the truth, or assent to the word of God.

"12. That regeneration is the act of the sinner himself, and that it consists in a change of his governing purpose, which he himself must produce, and which is the result, not of any direct influence of the Holy Spirit on the heart, but chiefly of a persuasive exhibition of the truth, analogous to the influence which one man exerts over the mind of another; or that regeneration is not an instantaneous act, but a progressive work.

"13. That God has done all that *he can do* for the salvation of all men, and that man himself must do the rest.

"14. That God cannot exert such influence on the minds of men, as shall make it certain that they will choose and act in a particular manner without impairing their moral agency.

"15. That the righteousness of Christ is not the sole ground of the sinner's acceptance with God; and that in no sense does the righteousness of Christ become ours.

"16. That the reason why some differ from others in regard to their reception of the Gospel is, that they make themselves to differ.

"Against all these errors, whenever and wherever, and by whomsoever taught, the Assembly would solemnly testify; and would warn all in connection with the Presbyterian Church against them. They would also enjoin it upon all the inferior judicatories to adopt all suitable measures to keep their members pure from opinions so dangerous. Especially does the Assembly earnestly enjoin on all the Presbyteries to guard with great care the door of entrance to the sacred office. Nor can the Assembly regard as consistent with ministerial ordination vows, an unwillingness to discipline according to the rules of the word of God and of our standards, any person already a teacher, who may give currency to the foregoing errors. Yeas, 109; Nays, 6; *non liquet*, 11."—*Minutes*, 1837, pp. 468, 470.

10. *An explication of Doctrines.*

[The following final article of a protest on the general action of the Assembly in reference to the "Memorial," was ordered to be placed upon the minutes, viz.:]

"We protest finally, because, in view of all the circumstances of the case, we feel that while we were prevented from uniting in the final vote with the majority in their testimony against error, for the reasons above stated, we owe it to ourselves, to our brethren, to the Church, and to the world, to declare and protest, that it is not because we do, directly or indirectly, hold or countenance the errors stated. We are willing to bear our testimony in full against them, and now do so, when, without misapprehension and liability to have our vote misconstrued, we avow our real sentiments, and contrast them with the errors condemned, styling them, as we believe, the true doctrine, in opposition to the erroneous doctrine condemned, as follows, viz.:

"*First Error.* 'That God would have prevented the existence of sin in our world, but was not able, without destroying the moral agency of man; or, that for aught that appears in the Bible to the contrary, sin is incidental to any wise moral system.'

"*True Doctrine.* God permitted the introduction of sin, not because he was unable to prevent it, consistently with the moral freedom of his creatures, but for wise and benevolent reasons which he has not revealed.

"*Second Error.* 'That election to eternal life is founded on a foresight of faith and obedience.'

"*True Doctrine.* Election to eternal life is not founded on a foresight of faith and obedience, but is a sovereign act of God's mercy, whereby, according to the council of his own will, he hath chosen some to salvation; 'yet so as thereby neither is violence offered to the will of the creatures, nor is the liberty or contingency of second causes taken away, but rather established;' nor does this gracious purpose ever take effect independently of faith and a holy life.

"*Third Error.* 'That we have no more to do with the first sin of Adam than with the sins of any other parent.'

"*True Doctrine.* By a divine constitution, Adam was so the head and representative of the race, that, as a consequence of his transgression, all mankind became morally corrupt, and liable to death, temporal and eternal.

"*Fourth Error.* 'That infants come into the world as free from moral defilement as was Adam when he was created.'

"*True Doctrine.* Adam was created in the image of God, endowed with knowledge, righteousness, and true holiness. Infants come into the world, not only destitute of these, but with a nature inclined to evil, and only evil.

"*Fifth Error.* 'That infants sustain the same relation to the moral government of God, in this world, as brute animals, and that their sufferings and death are to be accounted for on the same principles as those of brutes, and not by any means to be considered as penal.'

"*True Doctrine.* Brute animals sustain no such relation to the moral government of God as does the human family. Infants are a part of the human family; and their sufferings and death are to be accounted for, on the ground of their being involved in the general moral ruin of the race induced by the apostacy.

"*Sixth Error.* 'That there is no other original sin than the fact, that all the posterity of Adam, though by nature innocent, will always begin to sin when they begin to exercise moral agency; that original sin does not include a sinful bias of the human mind, and a just exposure to penal suffering; and that there is no evidence in Scripture, that infants, in order to salvation, do need redemption by the blood of Christ, and regeneration by the Holy Ghost.'

"*True Doctrine.* Original sin is a natural bias to evil, resulting from the first apostasy, leading invariably and certainly to actual transgression. And all infants, as well as adults, in order to be saved, need redemption by the blood of Christ, and regeneration by the Holy Ghost.

"*Seventh Error.* 'That the doctrine of imputation, whether of the guilt of Adam's sin, or of the righteousness of Christ, has no foundation in the word of God, and is both unjust and absurd.'

"*True Doctrine.* The sin of Adam is not imputed to his posterity in the sense of a literal transfer of personal qualities, acts, and demerit; but by reason of the sin of Adam, in his peculiar relation, the race are treated as if they had sinned. Nor is the righteousness of Christ imputed to his people in the sense of a literal transfer of personal qualities, acts, and merit; but by reason of his righteousness, in his peculiar relation, they are treated as if they were righteous.

"*Eighth Error.* 'That the sufferings and death of Christ were not truly vicarious and penal, but symbolical, governmental, and instructive only.'

"*True Doctrine.* The sufferings and death of Christ were not symbolical, governmental, and instructive only, but were truly vicarious, *i. e.*, a substitute for the punishment due to transgressors. And while Christ did not suffer the literal penalty of the law, involving remorse of conscience and the pains of hell, he did offer a sacrifice which infinite wisdom saw to be a full equivalent. And by virtue of this atonement, overtures of mercy are sincerely made to the race, and salvation secured to all who believe.

"*Ninth Error.* 'That the impenitent sinner is by nature, and independently of the renewing influence or almighty energy of the Holy Spirit, in full possession of all the ability necessary to a full compliance with all the commands of God.'

"*True Doctrine.* While sinners have all the faculties necessary to a perfect moral agency and a just accountability, such is their love of sin and opposition to God and his law, that, independently of the renewing influence or almighty energy of the Holy Spirit, they never will comply with the commands of God.

"*Tenth Error.* 'That Christ does not intercede for the elect until after their regeneration.'

"*True Doctrine.* The intercession of Christ for the elect is previous as well as subsequent to their regeneration, as appears from the following Scripture, viz.: 'I pray not for the world, but for them which thou hast given me, for they are thine. Neither pray I for these alone, but for them also which shall believe on me through their word.'

"*Eleventh Error.* 'That saving faith is not an effect of the operations of the Holy Spirit, but a mere rational belief of the truth or assent to the word of God.'

"*True Doctrine.* Saving faith is an intelligent and cordial assent to the testimony of God concerning his Son, implying reliance on Christ alone for pardon and eternal life; and in all cases it is an effect of the special operations of the Holy Spirit.

"*Twelfth Error.* 'That regeneration is the act of the sinner himself, and that it consists in change of his governing purpose, which he himself must produce, and which is the result, not of any direct influence of the Holy Spirit on the heart, but chiefly of a persuasive exhibition of the truth, analogous to the influence which one man exerts over the mind of another; or that regeneration is not an instantaneous act, but a progressive work.'

"*True Doctrine.* Regeneration is a radical change of heart, produced by the special operations of the Holy Spirit, 'determining the sinner to that which is good,' and is in all cases instantaneous.

"*Thirteenth Error.* 'That God has done all that *he can do* for the salvation of all men, and that man himself must do the rest.'

"*True Doctrine.* While repentance for sin and faith in Christ are indispensable to salvation, all who are saved are indebted from first to last to the grace and Spirit of God. And the reason that God does not save all, is not that he wants the *power* to do it, but that in his wisdom he does not see fit to exert that power further than he actually does.

"*Fourteenth Error.* 'That God cannot exert such influence on the minds of men, as shall make it certain that they will choose and act in a particular manner, without impairing their moral agency.'

"*True Doctrine.* While the liberty of the will is not impaired, nor the established connection betwixt means and end broken by any action of God on the mind, he can influence it according to his pleasure, and does effectually determine it to good in all cases of true conversion.

"*Fifteenth Error.* 'That the righteousness of Christ is not the sole ground of the sinner's acceptance with God; and that in no sense does the righteousness of Christ become ours.'

"*True Doctrine.* All believers are justified, not on the ground of personal merit, but solely on the ground of the obedience and death, or, in other words, the righteousness of Christ. And while that righteousness does not become theirs, in the sense of a literal transfer of personal qualities and merit; yet, from respect to it, God can and does treat them as if they were righteous.

"*Sixteenth Error.* 'That the reason why some differ from others in regard to their reception of the Gospel is, that they make themselves to differ.'

"*True Doctrine.* While all such as reject the Gospel of Christ do it, not by coercion, but freely—and all who embrace it do it, not by coercion, but freely—the reason why some differ from others is that *God* has made them to differ.

"George Duffield,
"E. W. Gilbert,
"Thomas Brown,
"Bliss Burnap,
"N. S. S. Beman,
"E. Cheever,
"E. Seymour,
"George Painter,
F. W. Graves,
Obadiah Woodruff,
N. C. Clark,
Robert Stuart,
Nahum Gould,
Absalom Peters,
Alexander Campbell."

—*Minutes*, 1837, pp. 484–486.

CHAPTER IX.

ON MODES OF EVANGELIZATION.

SECTION 1.—ON DOMESTIC MISSIONS.

1. The earliest missionary appointments temporary.—2. Missionaries appointed to itinerate for some months.—3. Ministers sent out to organize churches, ordain elders, administer the ordinances, and instruct the people.—4. Candidates sent out on missionary duty.—5. Plan of missions adopted by the Assembly.—6. Operation of the plan.—7. Leave granted in special cases to the Synods to prosecute their own missionary work.—8. The work resumed by the Assembly.—9. Collections ordered. They may not be prohibited by a church Session.—10. The Assembly refuse to exempt a Presbytery from contributing to its funds; as, also, to appropriate their own funds.—11. Instructions of the missionaries. Form of commission.—12. Kind of men required as missionaries, and their duties.—13. "Standing Committee on Missions;" its duties.—14. Its powers enlarged, and its name changed to "The Board of Missions."—15. Recommendations to raise funds, and to furnish men.—16. Powers of the Board enlarged and defined.—17. Proposal to unite with the American Home Missionary Society. Any change in the Assembly's mode of conducting missions inexpedient.—18. The Board is not the judge of the orthodoxy or morality of a minister.—19. Action of the Assemblies, 1837, 1838, 1849, with regard to the American Home Missionary Society.—20. A "Standing Committee on Home Missions" appointed.—21. History of the subsequent relation to and intercourse with the American Home Missionary Society. Committee of Conference.

1. *The earliest Missionary Appointments, temporary.*

"A representation being made by some of our members of the earnest desire of some Protestant dissenting families in Virginia, together with a comfortable prospect of the increase of our interest there, the Synod have appointed that Mr. Hugh Conn, Mr. John Orme, and Mr. William Stewart, do each of them severally visit said people, and preach four

Sabbaths to them, between this and the next Synod."—*Minutes,* 1722, p. 74.

"Mr. Hugh Conn, John Orme, and William Stewart, fulfilled their appointments with respect to Virginia."—*Minutes,* 1723, p. 76.

[The same year the same appointments were again made. *Vide* Minutes, *passim.*]

2. *Itinerant Missionaries appointed, temporary.*

"*Ordered,* That Messrs. McWhorter, Kirkpatrick, and Latta, take a journey to Virginia and Carolina, as soon as they can, this summer or ensuing fall, and spend some months in those parts.

"The Synod, further considering the destitute condition of Hanover, and the uncertainty of their being supplied, if supplies are left to their own discretion respecting the time of their going to Virginia, do order that Mr. Kirkpatrick prepare for his journey, so as to be at Hanover the third Sabbath of July, at the furthest, and supply there for some time, according to the order of that Presbytery; that Mr. McWhorter be at Hanover the first of September; that Mr. Latta be there the first of November, at the furthest; and that the Presbyteries of Philadelphia and New Brunswick take care that these gentlemen fulfil this appointment, and neither prescribe nor allow them employment in our bounds, so as to disappoint this our good intention."—*Minutes,* 1759, p. 293.

[Appointments of this kind are found on the Minutes of almost every year.]

3. *Ministers sent to organize Churches, ordain Elders, &c.*

"The Synod, more particularly considering the state of many congregations to the southward, and particularly North Carolina, and the great importance of having those congregations properly organized, appoint the Rev. Messrs. Elihu Spencer and Alexander McWhorter to go as our missionaries for that purpose; that they form societies, help them in adjusting their bounds, ordain elders, administer sealing ordinances, instruct the people in discipline, and finally direct them in their after-conduct; particularly in what manner they shall proceed to obtain the stated ministry, and whatever else may appear useful or necessary for those churches, and the future settlement of the Gospel among them. And also, that they assure those people wherever they go, that this

Synod has their interest much at heart, and will neglect no opportunities of affording them proper candidates and supplies to the utmost of our power.

"*Ordered*, That the clerk give said missionaries an attested copy of this minute, and proper testimonials, signed by the moderator and clerk.

"And that these brethren may not suffer by so long and expensive a journey, the Synod agree to defray their expenses, and make them a proper acknowledgment for the damages they may sustain in their domestic affairs; and for this purpose a collection is ordered through our bounds, and each Presbytery required to see it be duly observed."—*Minutes*, 1764, p. 340.

[These gentlemen being pastors, Synod made arrangements for the supply of their pulpits in their absence.]

4. *Candidates sent on Missionary Service.*

a. "The Synod appoint Messrs. Enoch Green and William Tennent, Jr., to go as soon as they conveniently can, so as they defer it no longer than next October, to supply six months under the direction of Hanover Presbytery."—*Minutes*, 1762, p. 320.

b. "The Synod find that many of their candidates do not attend their meetings, and for this reason many of their appointments are not fulfilled. They judge that candidates should constantly attend their respective Presbyteries, and, as often as they can conveniently, they should attend our Synods.

"They therefore recommend it to all our Presbyteries to propose one or more of their candidates, as persons that they think proper to be sent to preach to our frontier settlements; and that they let these candidates know that they intend to propose them as such to the Synod, that so our Synodical appointments may be more punctually fulfilled, and that no candidate, without very weighty reasons, presume to break our appointments."—*Minutes*, 1763, p. 325.

[Such appointments occur thenceforward with great frequency.]

[On the formation of the General Assembly, the subject of missions became one of the first subjects of action.]

5. *Plan of Missions adopted.*

"The Committee of Bills and Overtures overture, that the state of the frontier settlements should be taken into consideration, and missionaries sent to them, to form them into congregations, ordain elders, administer the sacraments, and direct them to the best measures for obtaining the Gospel ministry regularly among them."

"The committee [Drs. Allison and S. S. Smith] appointed to devise measures to carry the mission to the frontiers into execution, made the following report, which was adopted, viz.:

"*Resolved*, That each of the Synods be, and are hereby requested to recommend to the General Assembly, at their next meeting, two members, well qualified, to be employed in missions on our frontiers, for the purpose of organizing churches, administering ordinances, ordaining elders, collecting information concerning the religious state of those parts, and proposing the best means of establishing a Gospel ministry among the people.

"And in order to provide means for defraying the necessary expenses of the mission, it is strictly enjoined on the several Presbyteries, to have collections made during the present year, in the several congregations under our care, and forwarded to Isaac Snowden, Esq., the Treasurer of the General Assembly, with all convenient speed."—*Minutes*, 1789, p. 10.

6. *Operation of the Plan.*

a. "Dr. Rodgers, Dr. Allison, Mr. Ker, Mr. Hanna, and Mr. Chambers were appointed a committee to prepare certain directions necessary for the missionaries of the Assembly, in fulfilling the design of their mission, and to specify the compensation that it will be proper to make them for their services, and to make report to-morrow morning."—*Minutes*, 1790, p. 23.

b. "The Committee of Missions brought in their report, which was read and approved, and is as follows, viz.:

"The Rev. Messrs. Nathan Ker and Joshua Hart were appointed missionaries on the frontier settlements of New York and Pennsylvania, to the west branch of the Susquehanna, for at least three months, from an early day in June, to preach the Gospel, administer other ordinances, organize churches, ordain elders, collect every useful information they can about the religious state of those parts, and lay before the Assembly the result of their inquiries respecting the most effectual means of establishing the Gospel ministry among the people; together with the probable proportion of the different denominations, and the number of our vacancies,—carefully distinguishing those who are able and willing to support a minister from such as are of a different description. It was at the same time

"*Ordered*, That the Treasurer advance to the missionaries fifty dollars each; and agreed that they shall receive for their services one hundred dollars each, including what may be received by them on their tour, and the sum advanced before their departure, and of this they are to render an account at their return."—*Minutes*, 1790, p. 26.

7. *Leave granted the Synods in special Cases, to prosecute their own Missionary work.*

a. [Leave was granted the Synod of the Carolinas "to manage the matter of sending missionaries to places destitute of the Gospel" within their bounds,—they reporting annually to the Assembly, an account of their proceedings, moneys raised, &c.]—*Minutes*, 1791, p. 38; 1792, p. 59.]

"*Resolved*, That the Synod of the Carolinas be authorized and requested to continue and conduct, with their wonted zeal and diligence, the missionary business on their frontiers and elsewhere at discretion, and report to next Assembly."—*Minutes*, 1803, p. 265.

b. [The Synod of Virginia also had liberty to conduct their own missions. Minutes, 1791, p. 44, 45; 1793, p. 67, &c. This right they proposed to resign (Minutes, 1807, p. 377); but the Assembly declined. Minutes, 1807, p. 380.]

8. *The work resumed by the Assembly.*

"An overture was received from the Synod of the Carolinas, requesting the General Assembly to take upon them the direction of the missionary business within their bounds. This overture being read, it was

"*Resolved*, That the request of the Synod be granted."—*Minutes*, 1812, p. 508.

9. *Collections ordered. They may not be prohibited by a Church Session.*

a. "*Ordered*, That every minister, according to our former agreement, propose the collection for the fund to his congregation, and as it is a synodical appointment, it is inconsistent with our Church government to be under the check or prohibition of a church session; they indeed may give or withhold their charity, but may not prevent a minister to propose it publicly, according to our appointment. *Ordered*, likewise, That every Presbytery take care of the conduct of their members, how they observe this agreement previous to their coming to the Synod, and that they gather the collection from absent members."—*Minutes*, 1755, p. 215.

b. "Whereas, it appears that some of the congregations under the care of this Assembly, though duly informed of the injunction made at our last sessions respecting the raising of contributions for the support of missionaries to the frontiers of the country, have not complied with the same, the Assembly, therefore, thought proper to continue the above-mentioned order, and do hereby enjoin it on all the Presbyteries to give particular attention that every congregation raise the specified contribution; and that all the contributions be sent forward, as soon as possible, to the Treasurer of the General Assembly."—*Minutes*, 1790, p. 24.

10. *The Assembly refuse to exempt a Presbytery from Contributing to its Funds, as also leave to Appropriate their own Funds.*

a. "The Assembly took into consideration that part of the communication from the Presbytery of Oneida, wherein they pray that the churches under the care of that Presbytery may be exempted from pecuniary contributions to the funds of the Assembly. On motion, it was

"*Resolved*, That the request be not granted."—*Minutes*, 1803, p. 279.

b. "The committee to whom was referred the request of the Presbytery of Oneida, that they be permitted to appropriate their own funds collected for missionary purposes, submitted the following resolution, which was adopted:

"*Resolved*, That the Presbytery of Oneida be again referred to the plan proposed by the Board of Missions, and approved by this Assembly, with instructions to conform to the same on the subject of their request."—*Minutes*, 1820, p. 733.

11. *Instructions of the Missionaries; Form of Commission.*

"The General Assembly of the Presbyterian Church in the United States of America, now sitting at Carlisle, reposing confidence in your piety, prudence, and abilities for the important business, do hereby appoint you one of their missionaries.

"In discharge of the trust committed to you, much must be left to your discretion. But the General Assembly, viewing with concern the state of our frontiers and other settlements, destitute of the regular administration of the worship and ordinances of God, and desirous to do all in their power to extend the blessings to be derived from the means of grace, confidently expect that you will faithfully preach the Gospel, administer its ordinances, organize churches, and ordain elders; doing all these things according to the word of God, and the standards of our Church, contained in our Confession of Faith, Larger and Shorter Catechisms, the Government and Discipline, and Directory for the Worship of God: commending you to the grace and protection of our Lord Jesus Christ, we wish abundant success to your mission.

"Of your diligence wherein, of the state of religion, and of society, of the most probable means of establishing the Gospel in these parts, with every useful and necessary information, you will give an account to the next General Assembly.

Attested, { ——— ——— } *Clerks of Assembly.*

Signed, ——— *Moderator.*

—*Minutes,* 1795, p. 103.

12. *Kind of Men required as Missionaries, and their Duties.*

"The Committee on Missions beg leave to report, that they ought to be conducted by men of ability, piety, zeal, prudence, and popular talents. That missionaries should preach the most important doctrines of grace during the short period which they can afford to stay in a particular place. That they organize churches where opportunity offers, and administer ordinances. And that they catechize and instruct from house to house, as far as practicable, when they remain for any length of time in a settlement. That they refrain from all political and party discussions of any kind, and, with the self-denial of their Master, be wholly devoted to their ministry, and exemplary in their lives and conversation. That, in keeping their journals, they distinctly record the subjects on which they preach, and the apparent effect on their hearers."—*Minutes,* 1798, p. 150. [See also Minutes, 1799, pp. 183, 184.]

13. *Standing Committee of Missions appointed; its Duties.*

"1. *Resolved,* That a committee be chosen annually by the General Assembly, to be denominated *The Standing Committee of Missions.* That the committee shall consist of seven members, of whom four shall be clergymen and three laymen; that a majority of this committee shall be a quorum to do business; that it shall be the duty of this committee to collect, during the recess of the Assembly, all the information in their power relative to the concerns of missions and missionaries; to digest this information, and report thereon at each meeting of the Assembly; to designate the places where, and to specify the periods during which, the missionaries should be employed; to correspond with them if necessary, and with all other persons on missionary business; to nominate missionaries to the Assembly, and report the number which the funds will permit to be employed; to hear the reports of the missionaries, and make a statement thereon to the Assembly, relative to the diligence, fidelity, and success of the missionaries, the sums due to each, and such parts of their reports as it may be proper for the Assembly to hear in detail; to ascertain annually whether any money remains with the trustees of the College of New Jersey which ought to be used for missionary purposes, agreeably to the last will of James Leslie, deceased; that they also engage a suitable person annually to preach a missionary sermon, on the Monday evening next after the opening of the General Assembly, at which a collection shall be made for the support of missions; and superintend generally, under the direction of the Assembly, the missionary business.

"2. *Resolved,* That although this standing committee shall be elected annually, yet each committee shall continue in office till the end of the sessions of that Assembly which succeeds the one by which the said committee was chosen.

"3. *Resolved,* That this Standing Committee of Missions, in addition to the duties above specified, shall be, and they hereby are, empowered to direct the trustees of the General Assembly, during the recess of the Assembly, to issue warrants for any sums of money which may become due, in consequence of contracts, appropriations, or assignments of duty made by the Assembly, and for which orders may not have been issued by the Assembly; and on this subject the committee shall report annually to the Assembly."—*Minutes,* 1802, pp. 257, 258.

"4. *Resolved,* That it be again solemnly enjoined on all the Presbyteries and Synods within the bounds of the General Assembly on no account to interfere with the instructions given by the Committee of Missions to missionaries."—*Minutes*, 1809, p. 427.

14. *Standing Committee enlarged in its Powers, and its style changed to "The Board of Missions."*

"The committee appointed to consider whether the missionary business cannot be carried on with more efficacy, and to greater extent, reported; and their report, being amended, was adopted, and is as follows, viz.:

* * * * * * * *

"For the purpose of enlarging the sphere of our missionary operations, then, and infusing new vigor into the cause, your committee would respectfully recommend a change of the style, and enlargement of the powers, of the Standing Committee of Missions. If, instead of continuing to this body the character of a committee, bound, in all cases, to act according to the instructions of the General Assembly, and under the necessity of receiving its sanction to give validity to all the measures which it may propose, the Committee of Missions were erected into a board, with full powers to transact all the business of the missionary cause, only requiring the board to report annually to the General Assembly, it would then be able to carry on the missionary business with all the vigor and unity of design that would be found in a society originated for that purpose, and, at the same time, would enjoy all the benefit that the counsel and advice of the General Assembly could afford. With these views of the subject, it is respectfully recommended—

"1. That the style of the committee be changed for that of *The Board of Missions*, acting under the authority of the General Assembly of the Presbyterian Church in the United States.

"2. That the Board of Missions be enlarged by the addition of the Rev. John B. Romeyn, D.D., Samuel Miller, D.D., and Messrs. Samuel Bayard, Robert Ralston, Robert Lenox, John R. B. Rodgers, John E. Caldwell, Divie Bethune, and Zechariah Lewis.

"3. That in addition to the powers already granted to the Committee of Missions, the Board of Missions be authorized to appoint missionaries whenever they may deem it proper; to make such advances to missionaries as may be judged necessary; and to pay balances due to missionaries who have fulfilled their missions, whenever, in their judgment, the particular circumstances of the missionaries may require it.

"4. That the Board be authorized and directed to take measures for establishing throughout our churches auxiliary missionary societies; and that the General Assembly recommend to their people the establishment of such societies, to aid the funds and extend the operations of the Board.

"5. That the members of the Board of Missions be annually chosen by the Assembly, and that they continue in office until the rising of the next General Assembly, when they are to be succeeded by the persons chosen for the current year."—*Minutes*, 1816, p. 633.

15. *Recommendation to raise Funds, and to supply Waste Places in the New States in advance.*

a. "1. *Resolved*, That the report of the Board of Missions be accepted and approved.

"2. *Resolved*, That it be earnestly recommended to all the congregations under the care of the Assembly to send annual and liberal contributions to aid the Board in their future operations; but this recommendation shall not involve in censure any congregation belonging to the Synods to whom the General Assembly has given permission to manage their own missionary concerns, who shall think themselves unable to contribute to the funds of the Board of Missions.

"3. *Resolved*, That the Assembly highly approve the sentiments expressed by the Board, with respect to the new States in the western and southern parts of our country, and to the importance of supplying them with the preaching of the Gospel, that their character, which is now forming, may be formed under the influence of religion."—*Minutes*, 1823, p. 76.

b. "*Resolved*, That it be recommended, and it is hereby earnestly recommended to all the churches under our care, to take up and forward one annual missionary collection for this purpose, and that Presbyteries take order on the subject."—*Minutes*, 1827, p. 216.

16. *Enlargement of Powers.*

a. "*Resolved*, That the Board of Missions, in addition to the powers already granted to them, be authorized to manage, appoint, and direct the whole concerns and business of the Assembly's missions definitively, and report annually their doings to the Assembly.

"*Resolved*, That the Board be authorized to appoint, if they think proper, an executive committee of their own number, to carry into effect the details of their plan; and that they also be authorized to appoint and employ an agent or agents at their discretion."—*Minutes*, 1827, p. 217.

[In 1828, an overture was brought in for the reorganization of the Board.] "The committee reported as follows, viz.: The committee consider the matter contained in this overture of the first importance to the interests of the Church and the world, and they believe that they cannot better discharge the duties intrusted to them, than to lay the overture, as it now stands, before the General Assembly for their consideration."—*Minutes*, p. 234.

[While the subject was under discussion] "a communication was received from the Executive Committee of the American Home Missionary Society, announcing the appointment of Rev. James M. Matthews, D.D., Rev. Absalom Peters, and Knowles Taylor, Esq., a committee of that body to communicate to the Assembly the views of said Executive Committee in relation to the subject of the overture, now before the Assembly, for a reorganization of the Board of Missions of the General Assembly.

"Dr. Herron, Mr. Hardin, and Mr. Holmes were appointed a committee to confer with the committee from the American Home Missionary Society; and it was resolved to suspend the business of reorganizing the Board of Missions until said committee shall report."—*Minutes*, 1828, p. 236.

[The subject was discussed at great length, and then "indefinitely postponed." Against this result a protest was offered, and a committee of conference appointed.]

b. "The Committee of Conference reported, that, after mature deliberation, they recommend the following resolutions, which were adopted, viz.:

"*Resolved*, That the Board of Missions already have the power to establish missions, not only among the destitute in our own country, or any other country, but also among the heathen in any part of the world; to select, appoint, and commission missionaries, to determine their salaries, and to settle and pay their accounts; that they have full authority to correspond with any other body on the subject of missions; to appoint an executive committee, and an efficient agent or agents to manage their missionary concerns; to take measures to form auxiliary societies, on such terms as they may deem proper; to procure funds; and, in general, to manage the missionary operations of the General Assembly.

"It is therefore submitted to the discretion of the Board of Missions, to consider whether it is expedient for them to carry into effect the full powers which they possess.

"*Resolved*, That an addition of seven laymen be made to the present number of the Board of Missions."—*Minutes*, 1828, p. 244.

17. *Proposal to unite with the American Home Missionary Society.*

a. "Agreeably to the order of the day, the Assembly took up Overture No. 10, viz., a request of the Presbytery of Cincinnati, that the General Assembly would unite with the American Home Missionary Society in the appointment of one Board of Agency, to manage the missionary concerns of both Boards in the Western country. After some discussion, this subject was committed to Dr. Green, Dr. McAuley, Mr. Russell, Mr. Slack, and Mr. Beckwith, to confer with delegates, which the Assembly are informed have been appointed by the Home Missionary Society, on the request of the Presbytery of Cincinnati, and report to the Assembly as soon as practicable."—*Minutes*, 1830, pp. 298, 299.

"The committee to whom was committed Overture No. 10, reported the following resolution, viz.:

"*Resolved*, That it is expedient for the Board of Missions of the General Assembly and the Board of the Home Missionary Society to conduct their missionary operations in the West through a common Board of Agency in that part of the country.

"This report was accepted, and the committee discharged.

"A motion was then made to dismiss the whole subject; and, after considerable discussion, this motion was carried in the affirmative, and the subject was accordingly dismissed."—*Minutes*, 1830, p. 301.

b. [The same subject came up next year. The Assembly having refused by yeas and nays, 87 to 109, to reappoint the committee, a compromise committee was appointed, who reported as follows:]

"1. In view of existing evils, resulting from the separate action of the Board of Missions of the General Assembly, and the American Home Missionary Society, the General Assembly recommend to the Synods of Ohio, Cincinnati, Kentucky, Tennessee, West Tennessee, Indiana, and Illinois, and the Presbyteries connected with the same, to correspond with each other, and endeavor to agree upon some plan of conducting domestic missions in the Western States, and report the result of their correspondence to the next General Assembly: it being understood that the brethren of the West be left to their freedom to form any organization which in their judgment may best promote the cause of missions in these States, and also, that all the Synods and Presbyteries in the valley of the Mississippi may be embraced in this correspondence, provided they desire it.

"*Resolved by this Assembly*, That the present Board of Missions be reappointed."—*Minutes*, 1831, p. 337.

Change Inexpedient.

c. "The committee to whom was referred Overture No. 1, viz., sundry documents on the subject of missions, made the following report, which was unanimously adopted, viz.:

"*Resolved*, That, under existing circumstances, it is deemed inexpedient to propose any change in the Assembly's mode of conducting missions."—*Minutes*, 1832, p. 364.

18. *The Board has no Power to Judge of the Orthodoxy, or Morality of a Minister who is in Good Standing in his own Presbytery.*

"The committee to whom was recommitted the report on Overture No. 9, made the following report, which was adopted, viz.:

"In answer to the questions propounded by the Presbyteries of Union and French Broad, the Assembly would say, that though they do not recognize in the Board of Missions the authority to sit in judgment upon the orthodoxy or morality of any minister who is in good standing in his own Presbytery, yet, from the necessity of the case, they must exercise their own sound discretion upon the expediency or inexpediency of appointing or withholding an appointment from any applicant, holding themselves amenable to the General Assembly for all their official acts."—*Minutes*, 1830, p. 290.

19. *The American Home Missionary Society. Action of the Assemblies of* 1837, 1838–1849.

a. [In 1837, the Assembly adopted a resolution, 124 to 86, declaring the operations of the American Home Missionary Society to be "exceedingly injurious to the peace and purity of the Presbyterian Church," and "recommend accordingly that they should cease to operate within any of our churches."—*Minutes*, 1837, p. 442.

b. The Assembly of 1838 rescinded the above resolution, and adopted the following, viz.:]

"*Resolved*, That the General Assembly recognize, with devout gratitude to God, the eminent usefulness of those societies [the American Home Missionary and Education] to the Church and the world, and cordially commend them to the continued confidence and increasing patronage of our churches."—*Minutes*, 1838, p. 649.

c. [The "Board of Missions," remaining under the control of the "Old School" party, refused to report to the Assembly. Minutes, 1838, p. 655. Next year the following resolution was adopted, viz.:]

"*Resolved*, That we recommend to all our churches the American Board of Commissioners of Foreign Missions, the American Home Missionary Society, and the American Education Society, as the most suitable channels, under present circumstances, through which they can dispense their charities in aiding the propagation of the Gospel among the heathen, and in our own country, and for training up young men for the Gospel ministry; without, however, wishing to restrict the liberty of individuals to use their own discretion in this matter."—*Minutes*, 1839, p. 24.

d. [In 1840, the Assembly renewed their recommendations of these and several other voluntary societies] "as every way worthy of patronage and support; and as affording *safe, convenient*, and, perhaps, the best channels through which their contributions may reach the objects contemplated by those societies respectively."—*Minutes*, 1840, p. 21.

20. *A "Standing Committee on Home Missions" appointed.*

"*Resolved*, That a committee of *five*, from the Western Synods, be appointed to consult and correspond on this and the other subjects embraced in this paper; and to present a detailed report to the next General Assembly embodying the different plans tried by the Presbyteries which have proved most successful, and presenting such recommendations and suggestions as the whole subject may seem to require. [See Appendix, Minutes, 1847, p. 152.]

"The Rev. Messrs. Thornton A. Mills, A. T. Norton, John M.

Dickey, Henry Little, C. P. Wing, and T. Cleland, D.D., were appointed a '*Standing Committee on Home Missions*,' under the foregoing resolution."—*Minutes*, 1847, p. 143.

[This committee reported a series of resolutions, which, after much discussion, were adopted. See Minutes, 1849, p. 178.]

21. *History of, subsequent relation to, and Intercourse with the American Home Missionary Society.*

[See also chap. x, sec. 1, on Church Extension.]

a. "A committee, consisting of five, viz., Rev. George Duffield, D.D., N. S. S. Beman, D.D., Rev. Thornton A. Mills, Robert W. Patterson, and Hon. John L. Mason, is hereby appointed to confer with the Executive Committee of the American Home Missionary Society, expressing to it the kind feelings and confidence of the General Assembly and the churches it represents, and requesting its co-operation in this plan (church extension), as far as its principles will admit; and also requesting a statement of the principles on which its appropriations are made to the churches of the several denominations of Christians who support it: the results of which conference shall be reported to the next General Assembly."—*Minutes*, 1852, p. 173.

b. [The committee reported. See chap. x, sec. 1. Minutes, 1853, p. 340; also, Minutes, 1854, p. 514. In 1857, a committee of nine (Drs. George L. Prentiss, J. F. Stearns, Thos. Brainerd, Wm. C. Wisner, D. Howe Allen, Rev. H. Curtis, Timothy Hill, and Messrs. Samuel H. Perkins, and Cyrus P. Smith) were appointed "to confer with the Executive Committee of the American Home Missionary Society, in reference to our relations with that society." Minutes, p. 409. The next year, 1858, the committee reported; their report, with other documents, were referred to a special committee, who report as follows:]

"The special committee on the documents relating to the Committee of Conference with the American Home Missionary Society, recommend the adoption of the following resolutions:

"1. That the Committee of Conference with the American Home Missionary Society be continued, and consist of the following members: Rev. Jonathan F. Stearns, D.D., Rev. Thomas Brainerd, D.D., Rev. William C. Wisner, D.D., Rev. D. Howe Allen, D.D., Rev. Harvey Curtis, D.D., Rev. A. Augustus Wood, D.D. (in the place of Rev. George L. Prentiss, D.D., resigned), Rev. Thompson Bird, Mr. Cyrus

P. Smith, and Mr. Norman White, and that four of their number constitute a quorum.

"2. That this committee report to the next General Assembly upon our general relations with the American Home Missionary Society; upon its appointment of agents and missionaries; upon the number of our churches and ministers aided by it; upon the amount contributed by our churches to its funds; and upon any other points of interest connected with our home missionary work; that we may come to a more full comprehension of our duties, and be aroused to greater zeal and liberality.

"3. That this committee, as far as is practicable, procure from our Presbyteries information as to home evangelization; and that our Presbyteries give diligent heed to this work, as far as is practicable, raising money to be expended within their own bounds, and seeing to it that annual collections for home missions be made in all their churches."—*Minutes*, 1858, p. 604.

[The report of the committee of 1858, with other papers, were referred to the Standing Committee on Church Extension, who reported as follows:]

c. "The Committee on Church Extension beg leave to report on the papers referred to them relating to church extension.

"The annual report of the permanent committee impresses us, more deeply than ever, with the indispensableness and vast importance of the work with which they are charged; and contains gratifying evidence of its enlargement, and of the rapidly growing interest that is enlisted in it. The contributions to their treasury are seventy per cent in advance of those of the previous year, and two hundred and fifty per cent in advance of those of the year prior to that; and, while the missionaries and exploring agents employed have been considerably multiplied, the openings and calls for the service they perform, urgently demanding immediate attention, far exceed the means in the hands of the committee, and earnestly appeal to our churches, to place this cause on a par with the most prominent objects of their pecuniary benevolence. Our own country is the field for which American Christians are especially responsible, and for which they should feel especially concerned, in fulfilling the command to evangelize the world; and the teaching of the Gospel, by the living pastor and preacher, is the chief instrumentality by which the duty is to be discharged. The denomination of Christians, represented by this General Assembly, has hitherto principally employed the American Home Missionary Society, as its agency for the prosecution of domestic missions. The organization, from which that society proceeded, was formed in the bounds, and by the members of our Church; and its origin, and the capital of various kinds which it has accumulated, make it impossible, as a matter of feeling, of interest, and of justice, that we should abandon it to those whom we have received as partners in it. We can leave it, only on the dissolution of the firm, and the setting up of its members in new establishments. But, while this is true, the number and magnitude of the cases, for which the American Home Missionary Society cannot or does not provide, make it imperative upon us, largely to swell our contributions to the church extension scheme, so that its operations may correspond to the demands upon it, without the incurring of a farthing of debt. The purpose of the Permanent Committee, to equalize their appropriations and receipts, deserves cordial approbation; and the Standing Committee respectfully propose that the Assembly should be understood as recognizing this principle, for the guidance of the Permanent Committee, in complying with the recommendations made in a subsequent part of this report.

"So important are all the departments of labor assigned to the Permanent Committee, that it is almost impossible to give the precedence to either. The Standing Committee, however, have been particularly impressed with the necessity and value of the work of exploring new and destitute fields, and organizing churches on them. It cannot be dispensed with. To neglect or inefficiently conduct it, is unfaithfulness to our trust. Its results are immediate, as well as abundant and large. An exploring agent, for example, entered Kansas, about six months since, and during the sessions of this Assembly we have received the Presbytery of Kansas into our connection. The committee recommend that this branch of the Church extension work be prosecuted with quickened energy and zeal; and they would designate Nebraska, California, and Oregon, as fields for which exploring agents should be commissioned forthwith, if the requisite funds can be procured. The peculiar circumstances of Missouri commend it to us. The fast increasing portion of its people, in sympathy with the spirit of our Church, and accordant with its position on matters of controlling movement and interest, makes the summons irresistible to help her. The near approach of the settlement of titles to land in California, the dubiousness of which has thus far hindered Church extension there, by hindering church erection, opens the way for our building fund, and so gives a free course for the advancement of our Church; while the geographical position and natural resources of Nebraska and Oregon, render certain the gathering of a vast population, the laying of the foundations of society there is a work in which love to God and man requires us to take part. . . . .

"The Presbyteries of Alton, Bloomington, and Chicago complain of the action of the American Home Missionary Society, in withholding appropriations from churches connected with Presbyteries that employ exploring agents without the commission of the American Home Missionary Society; and from such as are connected with Presbyteries, the churches of which do not contribute, to the full measure of their ability, to the treasury of the American Home Missionary Society. The following resolutions of the Executive Committee of the American Home Missionary Society have been published in a letter from the pen of one of the Secretaries:

"'A communication having been received by the Presbytery of Alton, inclosing a minute adopted by that body at its late meeting, in reference to the terms of co-operation,—

"'*Resolved*, 1. That the Presbytery be informed that the following principles govern the Society in co-operating with auxiliaries and ecclesiastical bodies, and this Committee will be happy to co-operate with the Presbytery on the same terms, viz.:

"'1st. That the missionaries laboring within the bounds of an auxiliary or ecclesiastical body be commissioned by this Society, and be governed in their labors by its principles.

"'2d. That the funds raised on the field be applied to cancel the pledges contained in the commissions, and be acknowledged by the Society as contributed to its treasury.

"'3d. That the churches on the field co-operate cordially with the Society in the raising of funds, and contribute yearly to its treasury, according to the full measure of their ability.

"'*Resolved*, 2. That this committee continue to regard the work of exploring and occupying new fields of labor, as one of great importance; and, by sustaining general exploring agents and other itinerant laborers, having missionary circuits more or less extensive, as circumstances may require, they are enabled to reach every portion of the field, and carry forward with harmony and efficiency every department of the missionary work.'

"The General Assembly can never approve of these resolutions, if they are to be interpreted as,

"1. Denying the right of our Presbyteries, in our present relations to the American Home Missionary Society, to appoint, solely on their own authority, one or more exploring missionaries within their bounds; or as,

"2. Asserting it as a sufficient reason why the Society should withhold aid from the feeble churches of a Presbytery, that other churches of such Presbytery contribute the whole, or a portion, of their home missionary funds elsewhere than to the treasury of that Society.

"Churches in the condition of those just referred to, ought not to be left to suffer, and perhaps to perish; and, with a view to them, and also to churches situated like those in Missouri, the powers and duties of the Church Extension Committee ought to be expanded. It has hitherto devolved upon them, 1. To employ agents for purposes of exploration; 2. To aid churches in the chartered limits of cities and large towns; 3. To plant Presbyterian churches in places where sister denominations had not previously occupied the ground; and, 4. To answer applications that require prompt and immediate replies, and that will not admit of the delay incident to requests preferred in other directions.

"In view of the new classes of exceptional cases to which they have referred, the committee recommend that the province of the Permanent Committee be still further enlarged, so that they may be authorized to provide for churches that can receive adequate aid from no other source. And to meet the increased draft that must thus be made upon their treasury, it is desirable that additional force should be given to their agency for collecting funds.

"The report of the Committee of Conference with the American Home Missionary Society has been referred to this committee, and the following preamble and resolution are recommended for the adoption of the General Assembly.

"Whereas, the Presbyterian Church in the United States of America, represented in this General Assembly, has hitherto prosecuted the work of domestic missions, principally through the agency of the American Home Missionary Society; and whereas, complaints have been made to the General Assembly, from year to year, and with increasing earnestness, of the mode in which that agency has been conducted, particularly in the Western and Northwestern States and Territories; therefore,

"*Resolved*, That a commission of the General Assembly is hereby raised, consisting of Rev. Jonathan F. Stearns, D.D., Rev. A. Augustus Wood, D.D., Rev. Philemon H. Fowler, D.D., Rev. Thos. Brainerd, D.D.,

Rev. Robert W. Patterson, D.D., Rev. Harvey Curtis, D.D., Rev. D. Howe Allen, D.D., Jesse W. Benedict, Esq., Mr. Norman White, Mr. James B. Pinneo, and Hon. William Jessup (any four of them, at a meeting properly called, to constitute a quorum), to ascertain, by a thorough investigation, the facts in the case, and to procure such other information as may be in their power, relating to the history of our connection with the work of home missions, and our present relations to it; also, to learn the principles and modes of the administration of the American Home Missionary Society over the entire field of its operations; and to submit the whole, well authenticated, to the next General Assembly."—*Minutes*, 1859, pp. 40–43.

Report of the Committee, 1860.

d. "The report of the Special Committee on Home Missions, after further discussion, and prayer for Divine guidance, was adopted without dissent, and is as follows:

"The committee to whom was referred the general subject of home missions, together with the report of the Commission appointed by the General Assembly at Wilmington, to make investigation respecting the same, submit, and recommend for adoption, the following paper:

"1. We regard the statements and representations made in the report of the commission as essentially correct and just. And we believe that this lucid and faithful exposition of facts and principles, if brought before our churches and the public at large, would remove many misapprehensions, and do an important service to the cause of truth. It is therefore ordered, that at least 5000 copies of the report be printed, under the direction of the stated clerk of the Assembly, for general circulation.

"2. We deeply regret that our relations to the American Home Missionary Society seem to grow more and more complicated and embarrassing. We see no prospect of any such effectual removal of the difficulties which have sprung up between that society and our Church as will fully re-establish the harmonious and beneficent co-operation in the Home Missionary work, which was so happily maintained in former years. All endeavors to effect a satisfactory adjustment of the matters of difference between us and the Executive Committee of the American Home Missionary Society have proved fruitless. And the position which has been assumed in relation to our church extension operations, and the action of the General Assembly, by the leading Congregational associations with which we are in correspondence, indicates a deep and settled feeling on their part which appears to foretoken a speedy dissolution of the copartnership in home missions, unless we shall consent to abandon a great work, which we believe Divine Providence has set before us, and shall retrace steps which we have taken under a most solemn conviction of our duty to God and to his Church.

"3. It is with us no longer an open question, whether we should continue to prosecute our church extension work, so as to supply any lack of service that may exist on our field, according to our own judgment and ability. In maintaining this position, we are guilty of no breach of good faith towards the American Home Missionary Society. For we have never expressly, nor by remote implication, bound ourselves to make that society the exclusive agency of our Church in the home missionary work.

"In pursuing our church extension work, we feel that we are only discharging an imperative duty which the Great Head of the Church has laid upon us. The necessity for this work is becoming increasingly urgent, in consequence of new circumstances over which we have no control; and we must go forward, and not backward, in the prosecution of it.

"4. While we deem it incumbent on our Church to maintain firmly the principles and policy regarding this subject, which have been heretofore adopted and acted upon by the General Assembly, we earnestly desire to effect a good understanding with our Congregational brethren. We have no disposition to take any advantage of them in our co-operation with them; nor do we assert any right or liberty for ourselves which we do not freely accord to them.

"We have earnestly desired continued co-operation with our brethren in the work of home missions, provided it could be carried forward in consistency with the proper liberty of our churches, Presbyteries, and higher judicatories, and in fraternal confidence. But, if a separation must take place, we trust that it may be effected in Christian love, and solely with a view to the greater peace and efficiency of both denominations.

"And, that we may do all in our power to secure a wise and Christian adjustment of the difficulties by which we are encompassed, in relation to this subject, the General Assembly hereby appoint a committee of ten, to meet, in a fraternal conference, a committee of Congregational brethren (should such a committee be appointed), consisting of two members from each of the Congregational bodies with which this General Assembly is in correspondence, namely: The General Association of Connecticut, the General Association of Massachusetts, the General Convention of Vermont, the General Association of New Hampshire, and the General Conference of Maine. To carry into effect this arrangement, the Committee of Conference are hereby instructed to address a communication to each of the bodies already named, inviting them to appoint a like committee to meet with the committee of this General Assembly.*

"5. It shall be the duty of the committee of the Assembly, herein provided for, to use their utmost endeavors to secure such an understanding between us and our Congregational brethren, in regard to our co-operation with them in the work of home missions, as may conduct to an equitable and final settlement of this whole question.

"It shall also be the duty of this committee to make a full report to the next General Assembly, and to recommend to that body such plans and measures pertaining to the home missionary work as they may deem wise and necessary.

"6. We would lay no restrictions whatever on our Presbyteries or churches, as to the exercise of their liberty, in choosing for themselves, through what agency they shall bestow their contributions for the promotion of the domestic missionary work. But we would earnestly urge them to do all in their power for the furtherance of this great cause, either through the American Home Missionary Society or the Church Extension Committee, or both, or through some other agency; and to suffer no feeling of suspense, as to the channels through which they are to send forth the waters of life, to dry up the fountains of their Christian beneficence.

"*Resolved*, That four of the Committee of Conference appointed by the above report be a quorum; and that they be authorized to fill their own vacancies."—*Minutes*, 1860, pp. 252, 254.

"The committee, appointed to nominate the Committee of Conference with a similar committee to be appointed by the General Associations of New England, made the following nominations: Rev. Albert Barnes, Rev. Jonathan F. Stearns, D.D., Rev. Robert W. Patterson, D.D., Rev. Thornton A. Mills, Rev. Edwin Hall, D.D., Rev. Asa D. Smith, D.D., Rev. D. Howe Allen, D.D., Rev. Samuel T. Seelye, Hon. William Jessup, LL.D., and Walter S. Griffith.

* These bodies respectively refused to appoint committees.

"In regard to the distribution of the five thousand copies of the report of the commission, the committee recommend that the stated clerk be instructed to place one thousand copies at the disposal of the Committee of Conference, and to send the remainder to the stated clerks of the several Presbyteries, dividing them in proportion to the number of communicants in each Presbytery.

"The report was adopted."—*Minutes*, 1860, p. 260.

[On this subject, see also Church Extension.]

Section 2.—On Education for the Ministry.

1. Early efforts by the Synod and Assembly.—2. The Board of Education established. Passes into the hands of the "Old School" party at the division.—3. Other action. American Education Society commended. Action leading to the establishment of the Permanent Committee on Education.

1. *Early Efforts.*

[The subject of education for the ministry early attracted the attention of the General Presbytery and Synod (Minutes, 1733, p. 106; 1751, p. 246), and the churches were urged to aid pious youth in their course of study. Out of these efforts to supply the lack of candidates grew Princeton College. In 1806, the Assembly adopted a report, recommending to the Presbyteries to use their utmost endeavors to increase the number of candidates, and to give such assistance as they need. (Minutes, 1806, p. 366.) The Presbyteries were annually called on to report what they had done in the matter. In 1819, the Assembly resolved to establish a General Board of Education.]

2. *The Board of Education established; its Constitution.*

a. "The committee appointed to draught a Constitution for establishing a General Board of Education, agreeably to the resolutions adopted by the Assembly on the subject, reported one, which being read and amended, was adopted, and is as follows, viz.:

"I. There shall be a General Board of Education, known by the name of *The Board of Education*, under the care of the General Assembly of the Presbyterian Church in the United States of America.

"II. The board shall consist of thirty-six members; of whom there shall be twenty ministers and sixteen elders, one minister and one elder to be chosen from each Synod, and the remainder from Philadelphia, and from a distance convenient to it. Seven members, including the President or Vice-President, shall be a quorum to transact business.

"III. The whole number of members shall be divided into four classes, one-fourth to be annually elected.

"IV. The election of the members of the board shall be made by nomination and ballot by the General Assembly.

"V. The officers shall be a president, three vice-presidents, a recording and a corresponding secretary, and a treasurer, to be annually elected by the board.

"VI. The objects of this board shall be—

"1. To recognize such Presbyteries and other associations as may form themselves into education societies, as auxiliary to the general board.

"2. To assist such Presbyteries and associations in educating pious youth for the Gospel ministry, both in their academical and theological course.

"3. To assign according to their best discretion, to the several auxiliary societies, a just proportion of the whole disposable funds under their control.

"4. To concert and execute such measures as they shall judge to be proper for increasing their funds, and promoting the general object.

"VII. No young man shall be patronized or assisted by any auxiliary society, unless he shall produce a testimonial of his hopeful piety and talents from some Presbytery under whose care he shall have been taken.

"VIII. Auxiliary societies may make such arrangements and selection of a seminary for the young men under their patronage, as, in their opinion, shall be most eligible for the prosecuting of their education, whether classical or theological.

"IX. The auxiliary societies shall send to the board all the surplus funds in their hands which shall not be necessary for the accommodation of those immediately depending on them for support.

"X. Every auxiliary society shall annually forward a report of their proceedings to the board, sufficiently early to enable the board, whose duty it shall be, to report to the General Assembly.

"XI. The board shall have power to make such by-laws to regulate their own proceedings, and effectually to accomplish the great objects of their appointment, as shall not be inconsistent with this Constitution.

"XII. The board may propose to the General Assembly, from time to time, such plans as they may consider useful and necessary for the success of this institution, to be recommended to the several societies or churches, as the Assembly may think proper.

"XIII. No addition or amendment to the provisions of this Constitution shall be made, unless by the consent of two-thirds of the members of the General Assembly present at any of their sessions; of which notice shall be given at least one day previous."—*Minutes*, 1819, pp. 714, 715.

[This board, in 1838, passed into the hands of the "Old School" party.]

3. *Other Action of the Assembly. American Education Society commended.*

[The American Education Society was recommended by the Assembly. 1838, p. 649; 1839, p. 24; 1840, p. 21. In 1852, the subject came up in connection with the general matter of church extension. The Assembly adopted an extended report, which ultimately led to the formation of the Permanent Committee on Education for the Ministry. See Minutes, 1852, p. 170. In 1853, the subject came up again, and was referred to a committee of five, to digest a plan and report to the next Assembly.—*Minutes*, 1853, p. 320. See chap. x, sec. 5.]

SECTION 3.—ON FOREIGN MISSIONS.

1. Earliest effort to evangelize the heathen.—2. First missionary appointment of the Synod.—3. Minute on the Indian Mission.—4. The Assembly declines to form a board of missions co-operative with the American Board.—5. The United Missionary Society formed. Amalgamation with the American Board. The American Board commended.

1. *Earliest Efforts to Evangelize the Heathen.*

"The exigencies of the great affair of propagating the Gospel among the heathen being represented unto the Synod, the Synod, in order to promote so important and valuable a design, do enjoin all their members to appoint a collection, in their several congregations, once every year, to be applied for that purpose; and that the money raised by such collections, be yearly sent to the Synod."—*Minutes*, 1751, p. 246.

[In 1756 (Minutes, p. 266), "Mr. Gilbert Tennent reported that he had lately received a bill for two hundred pounds sterling, generously given for the propagation of the Gospel among the Indians, and to be under the direction of this Synod." A committee was appointed "to draw up a plan for the application of the money contributed in Great Britain for the use of the Indians."]

2. *First Missionary Appointed. John Brainerd.*

a. "Upon application made to this Synod, they agreed to allow the interest of the money under their direction for the propagation of the Gospel among the Indians, unto Mr. Brainerd, a missionary to the Indians, in order to assist him in laboring among them for this year."—*Minutes*, 1756, p. 273.

b. "Mr. Brainerd applied to the Synod for their advice whether it was his duty to leave his present charge at Newark, and resume his mission to the Indians.

"Arguments on both sides were fully heard.

"Though the Synod are tenderly affected with the case of Newark congregation, yet in consideration of the great importance of the Indian mission, they do unanimously advise Mr. Brainerd to resume it.

"The Synod do further agree to give him the interest of the Indian fund for this year, in order to his more comfortable subsistence." *Minutes*, 1759, p. 294.

3. *Minute on the Indian Mission.*

"Mr. Brainerd has received the greater part of the interest of the Indian fund, according to the vote of the Synod.

"It is known to many in the bounds of this Synod, that some ministers, moved with an holy zeal to promote the kingdom of Christ among the Indian tribes, applied to the society in Scotland for propagating Christian knowledge, and obtained a grant of a certain sum of money yearly, to support two missionaries to promote the conversion of the savage nations; they employed Mr. David Brainerd, whose praise is in the churches of Christ, and whose endeavors were blessed with remarkable success in this great work of bringing the Indians to the knowledge of Christ.

"It pleased God soon to remove him from his useful labor on earth to the joys of his heavenly kingdom. As the name of Brainerd was dear to these poor tribes, his brother was chosen to succeed him in the mission, in which station he continued for seven or eight years; but, as the prospect of a troublesome war made the mission dangerous and disagreeable, the commissioners who employed him dismissed him from his care of the Indians, and he was employed to preach the Gospel at Newark.

"At an Indian treaty, the province of New Jersey bought all the small tracts of land that the Indians claimed in different parts of the government; and, that they might still encourage the native inhabitants to reside among them in their own country, they bought and bestowed on the remnant of these people about four thousand acres of land, which they gladly accepted; and, as many of them were converted to Christianity, they earnestly requested that Mr. Brainerd might be granted to them again as a Gospel minister.

"The annuity which the society in Scotland had allowed to the missionary, was stopped upon Mr. Brainerd's dismission, though there was and is hope of procuring it again. Mr. Brainerd was requested by the governor and commissioners of Jersey to undertake the Indian mission. He applied to the Synod for advice, and though he had a very comfortable settlement at Newark, yet the Synod, through an earnest desire to promote the kingdom of Christ among these poor Indians, advised him to give up these temporal advantages, and settle as a missionary among those poor Indians, with which advice he readily and generously complied. But as there is no provision yet made to support him, and to answer many and various expenses in preaching to, and settling schools among these people, the Synod think themselves obliged to use all lawful endeavors to support said mission, and have now at their Synodical meeting agreed to contribute themselves, and to make application to the congregations in the bounds of this Synod, for a general collection to promote this pious and good design; and to order that a collection for this purpose be made in every congregation under the care of this Synod, and that the respective collections be sent by the moderators of the Presbyteries before the beginning of September, to Mr. Jonathan Sergeant, near Princeton, who is to receive it and pay it to the correspondents of the Indian mission, to be by them used for this purpose.

"*Ordered*, That a copy of this minute be taken by the moderators of such Presbyteries as are present, and sent to such as are absent."—*Minutes*, 1760, p. 299.

[For other efforts, see Minutes, 1763, p. 324; 1767, p. 375; 1768, p. 380; 1802, p. 238; 1806, p. 361, 365; 1805, p. 331, &c.]

4. *Answer of the Assembly to the American Board, declining to Form a Board of Foreign Missions.*

"The committee to which was referred a letter addressed to the moderator, by the secretary of the 'American Board of Commissioners for Foreign Missions,' reported, and the report being read, was adopted, and is as follows:

"That having had under consideration the important and interesting vote of the American Board of Commissioners, by which they submit to the Assembly 'the expediency of forming an institution similar to theirs, between which and them may be such a co-operation as shall promote the great object of missions amongst unevangelized nations,' it appears proper to state—

"1. That it is a matter of sincere joy in their apprehension, to all who love the Lord Jesus Christ and the souls of men, a joy in which the committee doubt not that the Assembly has a lively participation, that the brethren of the American Board of Commissioners for Foreign Missions have, by the exertions they have used, and the success of those exertions, demonstrated that the Churches of America are desirous to embark with their Protestant brethren in Europe in the holy enterprise of evangelizing the heathen.

"2. That as the churches under the care of the Assembly rejoice in the foreign missions organized and about to be organized by the American Board of Commissioners, so, as opportunity favors, they ought to aid them, as they have, in a measure, already aided them, by contributions to their funds, and by every other facility which they could offer to so commendable an undertaking.

"3. That as the business of foreign missions may probably be best managed under the direction of a single Board, so the numerous and extensive engagements of the Assembly, in regard to domestic missions, renders it extremely inconvenient, at this time, to take a part in foreign missions. And the Assembly, it is apprehended, may rather decline these missions, inasmuch as the committee are informed that missionary societies have lately been instituted in several places within the bounds of the Presbyterian Church, which make foreign missions a particular object of their attention."—*Minutes*, 1812, p. 515.

5. *The "United Foreign Missionary Society" formed, and amalgamated with the American Board of Commissioners for Foreign Missions.*

a. [In 1817, the "United Foreign Missionary Society" was formed and approved by the Assembly. It embraced "the Presbyterian, Dutch Reformed, Associate Reformed, and all other Churches which may choose to join them." *Minutes*, 1817, p. 657. This society reported to the Assembly, and was recommended by it from year to year, until 1826, when it was united with the American Board of Commissioners for Foreign Missions.]

b. "The report of the committee on a communication from a committee of the Managers of the United Foreign Missionary Society was taken up, and, after mature deliberation, it was

"*Resolved*, That the General Assembly do consent to the amalgamation of the American Board of Commissioners for Foreign Missions and the United Foreign Missionary Society.

"*Resolved further*, That this General Assembly recommend the American Board of Commissioners for Foreign Missions to the favorable notice and Christian support of the Church and people under our care." —*Minutes*, 1826, p. 175.

Committee of Conference.

a. "The committee on Overture No. 6, viz., 'A memorial on the subject of Foreign Missions,' made a report, which being read and amended, was adopted, and is as follows, viz.:

"*Resolved*, That a committee of three be elected to attend the next annual meeting of the American Board of Commissioners for Foreign Missions, and confer with that body in respect to measures to be adopted for enlisting the energies of the Presbyterian Church more extensively in the cause of missions to the heathen; and that said committee report the results of this conference, and their views on the whole subject, to the next General Assembly."—*Minutes*, 1831, p. 328.

b. "The report of the committee who were appointed by the last Assembly to attend the Board of Commissioners for Foreign Missions, and confer with that body, &c., was taken up, and after some discussion the following resolution was adopted, viz.:

"*Resolved*, That while the Assembly would express no opinion in relation to the principles contained in the report, they cordially recommend the American Board of Commissioners for Foreign Missions to the affection and patronage of their churches."—*Minutes*, 1832, p. 370.

c. [In 1831, the Western Foreign Missionary Society was formed by the Synod of Pittsburg, and offered to the Assembly. *Minutes*, 1835, p. 488. The transfer was refused by the Assembly. *Minutes*, 1836, p. 278. In 1837, "The Board of Foreign Missions" was organized by the Assembly, and is now in possession of the "Old School" Assembly. Since the division, the General Assembly has continued to approve and to co-operate with the American Board of Commissioners for Foreign Missions. Minutes, *passim*. See chap. x, sec. 6.]

Section 4.—On the Bible.

1. Gratuitous distribution. Aitkin's edition.—2. Collins's edition. Ostervald's Notes commended.—3. The American Bible Society. The Bible to be given to every family, and to the whole world.—4. The common version commended, and a "new version" deprecated.—5. Co-operation with the Society urged.

1. *Gratuitous Distribution. Aitkin's Edition.*

"The Synod, taking into consideration the situation of many people under their care, who, through the indigence of their circumstances, are not able to purchase Bibles, and are in danger of perishing for lack of knowledge—

"*Ordered*, That every member of this body shall use his utmost influence in the congregation under his inspection, and in the vacancies contiguous to them, to raise contributions for the purchasing of Bibles, to be distributed among such poor persons; and that Drs. Sproat and Ewing, and Mr. Duffield, be a committee to receive such contributions, to purchase Bibles therewith, and send them to the several members of this Synod, who, in conjunction with their respective Sessions, shall distribute them. And as Mr. Aitkin, from laudable motives, and with great expense, hath undertaken and executed an elegant impression of the Holy Scriptures, which, on account of the importation of Bibles from Europe, will be very injurious to his temporal circumstances, Synod further agree that the above committee shall purchase Bibles of the said impression and no other, and earnestly recommend it to all to purchase such in preference to any other."—*Minutes*, 1783, p. 500; also, 1784, p. 503; 1785, p. 506.

2. *Collins's Edition. Ostervald's Notes recommended.*

[" Mr. Collins, printer to the State of New Jersey," proposing to issue an edition, the Assembly appointed a committee to procure subscriptions.] "The General Assembly also confirm the appointment made by the Synod of New York and New Jersey, that Dr. John Witherspoon, Dr. Samuel S. Smith, and Mr. James F. Armstrong, be a committee to concur with any such committee as may be appointed, whether from any other denomination, or from any other Synod of our denomination, to revise and correct the proof-sheets, and, if necessary, to fix upon the most correct edition of the Scriptures to be recommended to the printer, from which to make his impression; and that the said committee be ordered to agree with the printer, that Ostervald's Notes, if not inconsistent with the views of other denominations of Christians engaged in this undertaking, be printed with it, in such manner as may best promote the publication.

"The General Assembly, desirous to spread the knowledge of eternal life contained in the Holy Scriptures, earnestly recommend to all the congregations under their care to encourage this undertaking."—*Minutes*, 1789, pp. 12, 13. [Also 1790, p. 25; 1791, p. 41.]

3. *American Bible Society.*

a. "The General Assembly record with gratification and heartfelt pleasure the information they have received of the formation of an American Bible Society, a few days since, in the city of New York; and from the unanimity manifested by all denominations of Christians on that occasion, the fervor of zeal displayed, and eagerness manifested by the numerous and highly respectable delegation which attended, to combine their exertions in promoting the best interests of their fellow-men, by furnishing them with the word of life, they cannot but believe that it is the work of God; that it will stand, and prove a rich blessing to those who may enjoy the fruits of its exertions."—*Minutes*, 1816, p. 620.

The Bible to be given to every Family in our Land.

b. "On motion, it was—

"*Resolved unanimously*, That the General Assembly view with peculiar satisfaction the measure recently proposed by the American Bible

Society, to supply every destitute family in the United States with a copy of the Bible in the course of two years; and that it be cordially recommended to the Presbyteries, individual ministers, and churches, connected with the Assembly, to use their endeavors to carry the above measure, in reliance on the blessing of the Almighty, into full and prosperous effect."—*Minutes*, 1829, p. 269.

The Bible to be given to the whole World.

c. "The committee recommend the following resolutions for the adoption of the Assembly, viz.:

"1. It is the duty of the people of God to give the Bible to every family and dweller upon earth, in the earliest period of time in which it is possible to do it.

"2. *Resolved*, That, in the judgment of the General Assembly, the Church of Christ is, under God, able to give the Word of God in a comparatively short time, and much shorter than is ordinarily supposed, to the whole world; and that, from the peculiar position and resources of the American, and especially of the Presbyterian Church in the United States, our responsibility in this momentous service is, beyond all other people, great and pressing.

"3. *Resolved*, That inasmuch as the fixing of a definite period has some important benefits connected with it, and as, in the judgment of the General Assembly, the period agreed upon is sufficiently long, it be recommended to all the churches under the care of this Assembly, and respectfully proposed to all the sister churches in correspondence with our own, to follow the noble example, and unite in the important resolution, of the Society of Virginia, viz.: To endeavor to give the Bible to the whole world, in a period of not more than twenty years.

"Adopted."—*Minutes*, 1835, p. 483.

Recommendation to fix a Month for Annual Collections.

d. "1. Believing, as this Assembly does, in the great Protestant doctrine that the Bible is indispensable to the well-being of the State and the Church, of families and individuals, therefore—

"*Resolved*, That it becomes one of the clearest of duties to promote the diffusion of this sacred volume as extensively as possible.

"2. As the history of Bible society organizations in the present century shows, that, through their instrumentality, an unparalleled increase of translations and distributions has been effected; that the best of all books has thus become the lowest of all in price, is kept clear from sectarian perversions, and is primarily and mainly furnished to the destitute, therefore—

"*Resolved,* That this mode of preparing and circulating the Word of God has the hearty approbation of this General Assembly.

"3. As the American Bible Society has co-operating branches and auxiliaries in most parts of the country, designed and calculated to facilitate the supply of our own population with the Scriptures, therefore—

"*Resolved,* That the churches and congregations be invited to co-operate with these local organizations, and render them efficient in furnishing destitute families, Sunday schools, and all who need, with Bibles and Testaments.

"4. As the parent society, by the growth of new States and Territories, by the revolutions of Europe, and by the progress of missions in Mahommedan and Pagan countries, is now called upon annually for a much larger amount of means than it can furnish towards preparing and circulating the Scriptures (having a deficiency of nearly $30,000 the past year), therefore—

"*Resolved,* That it be considered the duty of our respective charges, where circumstances will permit, to assign a month in each year when a collection shall be taken up, whether a Bible agent be present or not, in furtherance of this important object.

"Adopted."—*Minutes,* 1849, pp. 179, 180.

4. *Common Version commended, and a New Version deprecated.*

"Your committee report an overture from the Synod of Missouri, respecting the common version of the Bible. The said memorial sets forth the fact that strenuous efforts have been made for years, and are now made, especially in the West, to destroy confidence in, and set aside, our common and most excellent version of the Bible, as very defective and sectarian, and to introduce a new one.

"The memorial, moreover, sets forth, that we, as Presbyterians, have been misrepresented, and the idea conveyed that some of our ministers favor this scheme. Our silence on the subject has resulted in making the impression, among some of our people, that the common version of the Bible is not worthy of confidence; therefore—

"*Resolved*, 1. That we have unshaken confidence in our common version, and a firm belief that a better one, on the whole, for common use cannot be had.

"*Resolved*, 2. That we deprecate the incalculable evils that would inevitably result from such an attempt, by any denomination or denominations, to introduce a new version, destroying, as it would, confidence in our common version, ejecting it from our schools, opening the way for conflicting, sectarian versions, and sadly wounding and marring our beautiful Protestantism.

"*Resolved*, 3. That, in the judgment of this Assembly, not one of our judicatories, and not one minister, approves of, or sympathizes with, this injudicious sectarian movement.

"*Resolved*, 4. That all our ministers be careful, in expounding the word publicly, so to expound as to inspire and sustain confidence in our excellent version as truly the Word of God: believing, as we do, that the honest-hearted inquirer searching after the truth, with a teachable spirit, will find it.

"Adopted."—*Minutes*, 1855, p. 28.

5. *Co-operation urged.*

"The following preamble and resolution were unanimously adopted:

"As the American Bible Society resolved, at its late anniversary, that, with Divine aid and the co-operation of its friends, it would endeavor, as early as practicable, to supply every destitute family in our country with the Bible, therefore—

"*Resolved*, That this General Assembly, now convened, have great satisfaction in expressing their warm approval of the undertaking; and to secure its accomplishment, would not only pledge their own exertions, but invite the pastors and churches here represented to lend their assistance in carrying it forward, particularly in their connection, respectively with the local auxiliaries, the main channels through which the sacred Word is to reach those who are without it."—*Minutes*, 1856, p. 197.

SECTION 5.—ON RELIGIOUS BOOKS AND TRACTS.

1. Religious books and tracts distributed gratuitously.—2. Formation of tract societies commended.—3. American Sunday-School Union approved.—4. The "American" societies endorsed.

1. *Religious Books, Tracts, &c., distributed Gratuitously.*

a. "The Synod finding the money collected some years ago for defraying the expense attending the missions appointed on our frontiers is nearly expended, agree to have a collection this year through their bounds upon the same plan with the former. And, as it is judged it might be useful to extend this public charity to purchase such religious books as the Synod may approve of, to be given to poor congregations, the following members are appointed to consider this matter, and bring in an overture to be subjected to the Synod as soon as they conveniently can, viz.: Messrs. McWhorter, Montgomery, and Ogden."—*Minutes*, 1772, p. 428.

b. "The committee appointed last Friday to draw up an overture with respect to the general collection and the distribution of books, brought one in, which, after correction, is as follows:

"1. That the Synod recommend a general collection in all the churches under their care.

"2. That the Synod write a pastoral letter, in which they shall return thanks to their several congregations for their former generosity, and solicit their future favors.

"3. That the Synod particularly desire the charity of the public for those purposes, viz.: For defraying the expenses of sending missionaries to the frontiers, and such other places as are unable to support the Gospel; for purchasing useful books to distribute in said places under the direction of committees to be appointed for that purpose; for propagating Christian knowledge among the Indians; and for such other pious uses as may occur from time to time.

"The following books were proposed and agreed to be procured and distributed, viz.: Bibles, Westminster Confessions of Faith, small edition of Vincent's Catechism, Doddridge's Rise and Progress of Religion, A Compassionate Address to the Christian World, Allein's Alarm to the Unconverted, Dr. Watt's Divine Songs for Children, and the Assembly's Catechism.

"And for the purpose of procuring and distributing those books we appoint for a committee at Philadelphia, Dr. Alison, Mr. Sproat, Mr. Montgomery, Mr. Bayard, and Mr. Jonathan Smith; and at New York, Dr. Rodgers, Mr. Treat, Mr. McWhorter, Mr. Caldwell, Mr. V. B. Livingston, and Mr. Robert Ogden. And the committees are restricted not to lay out this year above ten pounds proclamation currency each for the purposes aforesaid. But if any well-disposed person will send the committees books or pamphlets which they judge will answer the intention of the Synod to promote Christian knowledge, they are desired to distribute these also."—*Minutes*, 1772, p. 429.

c. "For the purpose of procuring books to bestow on the poor: in Philadelphia, Dr. Francis Alison, Mr. Sproat, Mr. Montgomery, Mr. John Bayard, and Mr. Jonathan Smith; and in New York, Dr. Rodgers, Mr. Treat, Mr. McWhorter, Mr. Caldwell, and Mr. Noel are appointed as committees, and that they do not exceed the sum of twenty pounds proclamation currency, to be laid out by each committee, and that they draw on the treasurer for this sum."—*Minutes*, 1773, p. 441.

d. "The committees appointed last Synod to purchase books and distribute them among the poor on the frontiers, report, that they have complied with the order, and disposed of the whole of the sum allowed at New York, and the whole also of the sum allowed at Philadelphia, except one pound seven shillings and eight pence, but as the committee at Philadelphia have not yet received an account of any distribution made by the persons to whose care they have committed them on the frontiers, the Synod direct them to inquire as soon as possible into that matter, and use their best endeavors to have said distribution made (if not already done), and procure what information they can, of the success attending said distribution, and make report at next meeting of Synod."—*Minutes*, 1774, p. 452. See also, 1794, p. 93, &c.

e. "That there be made a purchase of as many cheap and pious books as a due regard to the other objects of the Assembly's funds will admit, with the view of distributing them, not only along the frontiers of these States, but also among the poorer classes of people, and the blacks, or wherever it is thought useful; which books shall be given away, or lent, at the discretion of the distributor. And that there be received from Mr. Robert Aitken, toward the discharge of his debt, books to such amount as shall appear proper to the Trustees of the Assembly, who are hereby requested to take proper measures for the distribution of the same."—*Minutes*, 1801, p. 229.

[See also, 1802, p. 259; 1803, p. 268; 1805, p. 346; 1806, p. 361, &c.]

2. *Formation of Tract Societies recommended.*

The committee appointed to report on the establishment of a society for procuring and distributing religious tracts, reported the following resolution, and it was adopted:

"*Resolved*, That whereas it appears to this Assembly, that great and increasing good has accrued to the Church of Christ, by the distribution of small, cheap religious tracts; it is hereby earnestly recommended that each Synod take measures for establishing as many religious tract societies within their bounds, by association of one or more Presbyteries, as may be most convenient for this purpose; and that such societies may adopt such plan for carrying into effect the object of this resolution, as may be most conducive in their judgment to this end."—*Minutes*, 1809, p. 429.

[See chap. x, sec. 3, on Publication.]

3. *American Sunday-School Union.*

a. "The committee to whom was referred the communication from the American Sunday-School Union, recommended the following resolution, which was adopted, viz.:

"*Resolved*, That the General Assembly do cordially approve of the design and operations of the American Sunday-School Union; and they do earnestly recommend to all the ministers and churches under their care, to employ their vigorous and continued exertions in the establishment and support of Sabbath-schools."—*Minutes*, 1826, p. 181.

b. [On memorial of the Sunday-School Union, stating their purpose, by Divine aid, to establish a Sunday-school, where practicable, in every destitute place in the valley of the Mississippi, the Assembly]

"*Resolved*, That it be earnestly recommended to the pastors and sessions of all our churches and congregations, to present this subject to their people, and solicit their prayers and labors, and contributions, to aid the society in the accomplishment of this important work."—*Minutes*, 1830, p. 297.

4. *The "American Societies" commended.*

"That the Assembly recommend to all the congregations connected with this body, the American Board of Commissioners for Foreign

Missions, the American Bible Society, the American Education Society, the American Home Missionary Society, the American Tract Society, and the American Sunday-School Union, as institutions every way worthy of patronage and support; and as affording *safe, convenient*, and perhaps the best channels through which their contributions may reach the objects contemplated respectively by these societies."—*Minutes*, 1840, p. 21.

Section 6.—On African Colonization.

1. First notice of the scheme; recommended.—2. Collections on the Fourth of July recommended.—3. Recognition of Liberian independence urged.

1. *First Notice.*

a. "The Assembly notice with pleasure the general attention and exertion to alleviate the condition of the people of color in almost all parts of the country. A society for the colonization of free people of this description is formed, and is patronized by the first characters of our nation."—*Minutes*, 1817, p. 651.

American Colonization Society recommended.

b. "We recommend to all our people to patronize and encourage the Society lately formed for colonizing in Africa, the land of their ancestors, the free people of color in our country. We hope that much good may result from the plans and efforts of this Society. And while we exceedingly rejoice to have witnessed its origin and organization among the holders of slaves, as giving an unequivocal pledge of their desires to deliver themselves and their country from the calamity of slavery, we hope that those portions of the American Union whose inhabitants are, by a gracious Providence, more favorably circumstanced, will cordially, and liberally, and earnestly co-operate with their brethren in bringing about the great end contemplated."—*Minutes*, 1818, p. 693.

c. "The following overture was submitted to the Assembly, which being read and amended, was adopted, viz.:

"The objects and plans of the American Society for colonizing the free people of color of the United States, having been stated to the General Assembly, and the same having been considered and discussed, the Assembly—

"*Resolved*, That, in their opinion, the plan of the society is benevolent in its design, and, if properly supported, and judiciously and vigorously prosecuted, calculated to be extensively useful to this country and to Africa.

"The situation of the people of color in this country has frequently attracted the attention of this Assembly. In the distinctive and indelible marks of their color, and the prejudices of the people, an insuperable obstacle has been placed to the execution of any plan for elevating their character, and placing them on a footing with their brethren of the same common family. In restoring them to the land of their fathers, the Assembly hope that the way may be opened, not only for the accomplishment of that object, but for introducing civilization and the Gospel to the benighted nations of Africa.

"From the information and statements received, the Assembly believe that the proposed colony in Africa may be made a powerful auxiliary in the efforts which are making to abolish the iniquitous traffic in slaves carried on in Africa, and happily calculated to lay the foundation of a gradual emancipation of slaves in our own country, in a legal and constitutional manner, and without violating the rights or injuring the feelings of our Southern brethren.

"With these views, the Assembly feel it a duty to recommend the American Society for colonizing the free people of color of the United States to the patronage and attention of the churches under their care, and to benevolent individuals throughout the Union."—*Minutes*, 1819, p. 710.

2. *Collections on Fourth of July recommended.*

"*Resolved*, That this Assembly recommend to the churches under their care to patronize the objects of the American Colonization Society, and particularly that they take up collections in aid of its funds on the Fourth of July next, or on the Sabbath immediately preceding or succeeding that day, and whenever such course may be thought expedient to give their assistance, in such manner as may be most conducive to the interests of the general cause."—*Minutes*, 1825, p. 154. [See also 1826, p. 180; 1831, p. 332; 1832, p. 365; 1833, p. 411.]

3. *Recognition of Liberian Independence urged.*

"The following resolutions were presented and unanimously adopted:

"The committee appointed to draft a minute and resolutions relative to colonization, and the desirableness of a recognition of the republic of Liberia by the Government of the United States, report as follows:

"The enterprise of colonization has been before the American people about forty years, and has been thoroughly discussed. Whatever diversity of views may prevail as to its capacity or incapacity, its effect or lack of effect upon the subject of a final abolition of slavery, your committee believe that very little diversity exists as to the fact that a great practical blessing to Africa, and a real social and civil benefit to the emigrant colonists, have resulted from the establishment of the republic of Liberia. By it, the colored man, removed from those impediments which, in this land, hindered the full and immediate development of his capabilities for self-government, has been enabled at once, on a theatre to which the eyes of the civilized world are turned, to demonstrate them beyond the power of disputation, and thus to exert a mighty moral influence for the benefit and elevation of his race. By it, schools, churches, the Christian Sabbath, regulated government, freedom, have been set up upon the shores of a barbarous, despotic, superstitious continent, and are sending abroad their benign influences from year to year in an ever-increasing measure.

"Thirty years after the organization of the first Colonization Society, the colony of Liberia, yet feeble, was compelled to set forth its Declaration of Rights, and to assume the constitutional organization of an independent republic. This event, which marks an era in the history of Africa and her children, occurred in 1846; since which period, with a rapidity which has exceeded the anticipation of the most sanguine minds, this new nation has been steadily acquiring strength and respectability.

"The nations of Europe answered the appeal of this rising State, and cordially encouraged it by liberal treaties and an open recognition. We regret to say that our own Government has not hitherto afforded to it the same moral support. A strange anomaly is seen in the fact, that the great republic of the North, looked to for sympathy and support by all people struggling for liberty, fails to afford sympathy or acknowledgment to a sister republic, whose origin, whose similarity of form, and whose successful attempt at self-government, it should seem, would make the claim almost imperative.

"In view of such facts and considerations, the committee recommend the following resolutions to be adopted as the sense of this Assembly:

"1. That the original project of colonization, so far as it proposed to introduce civilization, free government, and Christianity among the people of Africa, merits, as it has already received, the cordial approbation and friendly sympathy of the Presbyterian Church.

"2. That, as Christians and Americans, we look with delight upon the success already achieved in the rescue of more than five hundred miles of seacoast from the manifold crimes and miseries which the slave trade inflicted upon it, and in the successful organization and administration of republican government by the emigrants to Liberia, thus triumphantly vindicating their capacity for the highest duties of society.

"3. That, in view of the origin of the people of Liberia, of the entire correspondence of their laws and Constitution with our own, and of their rapidly growing commerce and greatness, their republic has peculiar claims, both of justice and policy, for an open recognition by the American Government; and that we sincerely regret that the empires of France and Brazil, and the monarchies of England, and Russia, and Belgium, have been permitted to anticipate the action of our country.

"4. That whenever colored emigrants, already free, or offered liberty by their masters at the South, on the condition of their emigrating, solicit aid to reach Liberia, we cordially recommend them to the sympathies and assistance of the churches under our care."—*Minutes*, 1853, pp. 329, 330.

SECTION 7.—ON SYSTEMATIC BENEFICENCE.

1. The plan endorsed, and urged upon the churches.—2. The American Systematic Beneficence Society recommended.

"The report of the Committee on Benevolent Societies was adopted, viz.:

"1. This Assembly would recognize, with devout gratitude to God, the success that has attended the labors of most of our great national societies during the last year; that notwithstanding the unprecedented commercial embarrassments by which the year has been distinguished, most of these societies have been enabled to prosecute their work, and, with few exceptions, to meet and sustain all their responsibilities.

"The Assembly have in these facts an additional proof that some at least of these contributions to this cause are made from principle, and that Christians are ready, to some extent, to make sacrifices in the cause of Christ.

"2. That the Assembly recognize with pain the fact, that while some have done so nobly and so well, yet the number of contributors to the cause, compared with the whole number in our communion, is lamentably small, the largest portion, by far, of our communicants withholding their contributious altogether.

"3. That it be recommended to our Synods, Presbyteries, and church Sessions to devise, if possible, some method by which a more general application shall be made to every member of the Church; so that our whole Church may be engaged to take a part in the glorious enterprise of reclaiming the world to Christ.

"4. That it be commended to the attention of pastors and stated preachers in our Church to consider well if more cannot be done by *them* in the advocacy of benevolent action, and in the *collection of funds*, than has hitherto been attempted; the Assembly being fully satisfied that no person can be so well qualified to judge what are the best means to be employed in any given case as the pastor of the congregation.

"5. * * * *

"6. That this Assembly are fully satisfied that neither of these enterprises is in a condition at present to dispense with the employment of agents, yet they are fully satisfied that a much smaller number would be demanded, and those employed enabled to extend their labors, each to a much larger field, if a portion of the labor in collecting funds could be performed by *collectors, male and female,* appointed in each congregation for the purpose. They therefore recommend to pastors, Sessions, and friends of the cause generally, such organizations in the respective congregations as shall bring the leading enterprises of benevolence before every member of the Church, without the personal application of an agent every year."—*Minutes,* 1840, pp. 21, 22.

"American Systematic Beneficence Society" commended.

"*Resolved,* 1. That the subject of systematic beneficence be earnestly commended to the attention and action of our churches.

"2. That 'The American Systematic Beneficence' Society, already organized in Philadelphia, be commended to the co-operation of all our Synods, Presbyteries, and Sessions."—*Minutes,* 1856, pp. 195, 196.

CHAPTER X.

THE PERMANENT COMMITTEES.

"*Resolved,* That the committees appointed at the opening of each Assembly be called *Standing Committees,* and those outside of the Assembly, *Permanent Committees.*"—*Minutes,* 1856, p. 192.

SECTION 1.—PRELIMINARY ACTION.

1. Reports of committees in 1849 and 1850, looking to raising up ministers, gathering and organizing churches, and building church edifices.—2. A full report on Church extension. The American Home Missionary Society recommended. Each Presbytery to appoint a standing committee on Church extension, and to take the oversight of the work within their own bounds. The Home Missionary Society requested not to require the *official sanction* of any of its agents to a Presbyterial application. Exploring missionaries encouraged. Committee of Conference with the American Home Missionary Society.—3. Report of the Committee of Conference.

1. *Preliminary Action.*

"The committee to whom was referred the report of the committee of the last Assembly on Home Missions, reported the following resolutions, which, after much discussion, were adopted:

"1. *Resolved,* That the Providence of God, as indicated in the wonderful improvements of the age, in the commotions of the Old World, the influx of foreigners, and the unparalleled increase of population in our extensive and extending country, calls for the entire consecration and most self-denying and efficient action of the Christian ministry.

"2. That the friends of Christ are called upon to use all wise and Christian means to raise up ministers, and meet the emergencies of coming years.

"3. That our Presbyteries are admonished to secure, so far as possible, a good supply for all the feeble churches under their care, and to gather congregations and organize churches in the towns and settlements in which it may be practicable; either by employing a permanent missionary agent, or by such other means as the circumstances and necessities of these destitute fields demand.

"4. That those ministers who preach to two or more congregations should use their best endeavors to induce the elders of the churches to hold Sabbath-schools, in connection with some form of religious worship, at a regular hour every Sabbath-day, when their ministers cannot be present.

"5. That we should make efforts to induce the children of immigrants to attend our Sabbath-schools, and the adults, our congregations; and when they are converted, to join our churches, or to organize churches of their own in connection with us; that, as soon as possible, they may be Americanized in their language and feelings, and become evangelical in their religion.

"6. That every congregation which has no church edifice should, without unnecessary delay, build themselves a suitable house of worship; that generally this should be done by their own exertions, or by such aid only as can be secured in their own vicinity.

"But if, in any case, a church or churches of a district of country really need assistance from abroad, then the strong ought to help bear the burdens of the weak; and, in all such cases, those asking aid should bear such testimonials from the Synods to which they belong that the benefactors may know that their charities will be well bestowed."—*Minutes*, 1849, p. 178.

Church Extension.

a. "The following resolutions were then adopted on the subject of home missions:

"1. "*Resolved*, That in the last command of Christ to his disciples we recognize a command obligatory on our branch of the Church, to preach the Gospel and establish religious institutions throughout the entire extent of our national domain, as far, and as fast, as that domain becomes inhabited.

"2. *Resolved*, That our Presbyteries be recommended to take such action within their respective bounds that, either by themselves, or by the aid of the Home Missionary Society, new churches may be organized wherever circumstances will permit, and the stated preaching of the Gospel be supplied in churches now destitute, as speedily as possible."—*Minutes*, 1850, p. 315.

Church Erection.

b. 3. "*Resolved*, That it be recommended to all our churches to strive earnestly to render our religious institutions permanent, by the erection of church edifices, and the settlement of pastors, whenever this can be done; and in this work the older and wealthier churches ought to co-operate with the younger and feebler."—*Ibid.*

Education.

c. "4. *Resolved*, That the searching out and bringing forward of young men, of hopeful piety and talent, as candidates for the Gospel ministry, is an integral and essential part of the missionary enterprise, and, as such, demands the constant vigilance and untiring efforts of the ministers and elders of our churches in all parts of the land."—*Ibid.*

2. *A full Report on the general subject of Church Extension.*

"The whole subject [of Church extension] was accordingly referred to a special committee, consisting of the Rev. Thornton A. Mills, Rev. Nathan S. S. Beman, D.D., Rev. Frederick A. Ross, Rev. Artemas Bullard, D.D., Rev. Asa D. Smith, D.D., Rev. D. Howe Allen, D.D., Rev. James B. Townsend, Rev. Samuel W. Fisher, and Rev. Robert W. Patterson; four of whom to form a quorum."—*Minutes*, 1851, p. 29.

[The report of the committee was the next year presented, amended, and adopted, viz.:]

"To promote more extensively the work of domestic missions, the General Assembly hereby adopts the following arrangement:

"1. The American Home Missionary Society is hereby recommended to the Presbyteries as the agency through which, as heretofore, the work of domestic missions shall be done; and the Presbyteries and Synods are requested to adopt, as far as they may deem proper in their circumstances, the following or similar arrangements:

"2. Each Presbytery shall elect a Standing Committee on Church

Extension to serve one year, and continue in office till successors are appointed, who shall, under its direction, attend to the general interests of this work within its bounds.

"3. Each Presbytery shall see that, by its own ministers or other suitable agency, the claims of home missions shall be presented annually to each of its churches, and that proper efforts are made to bring their liberality into free and becoming exercise towards this cause; these contributions to be paid into the treasury of the American Home Missionary Society, or any of its auxiliaries, and to be raised with as little expense to that Society as possible.

"4. Each Presbytery shall recommend all applications for aid from any of its churches; and shall be careful to see that the amount asked for is the lowest which will fairly answer the purpose. And it is recommended, that the appropriations sought be diminished from year to year, if it can be safely done, that the churches may be brought to a self-sustaining standard as soon as possible.

"5. The American Home Missionary Society is hereby requested to arrange its system of appropriations, so that applications made by any Presbytery for its churches shall not require the *official sanction* of any agent of that Society. It is not intended, however, by this recommendation, to abridge the right of the Society to obtain information as to such applications, or to use its full discretion as to granting them in whole or in part.

"6. Each Presbytery, whose circumstances as to territory, churches, and numbers demand it, is recommended to appoint an itinerant missionary within its bounds. Or each Synod, where it is best that two or more, or all, of its Presbyteries shall be united in this work, is recommended to appoint such a missionary, whose duty it shall be to act as a travelling evangelist, after the scriptural pattern, to explore destitute fields; to prepare the way for the formation of new churches by the Presbyteries; to seek for ministers to take charge of them; to assist and direct in building houses of worship in destitute places; and in all other suitable ways, under the direction of Presbyterial or Synodical committees, promote the work of Church extension.

"7. Each Synod shall appoint yearly a Church Extension Cemmittee, whose duty it shall be to take the supervision of any agencies which shall be established, to arrange and carry out some plan to aid in the erection of churches in destitute places, to conduct the home missionary business of the Synod generally, and make a full report at each meeting.

"8. Each Synod shall require a yearly collection from its churches, to assist, by loan or gift, feeble churches to erect houses of worship in destitute places; which funds shall be distributed by the Synod's committee among those churches which may apply for it, according to their necessities. And the older and abler Synods of the Church are earnestly recommended to contribute of their abundance to aid the feebler Synods in this work.

"9. Each Synod is hereby charged with the review of the course of its Presbyteries in the duties now assigned them; and is further required to report to the General Assembly, through its Standing Committee, its proceedings up to the first of April in each year.

"10. Each Presbytery is further required, in addition to its statistical report and narrative, to forward yearly to the General Assembly a full report of its various arrangements for Church extension, stating the number of its ministers, and the particular manner in which they are employed; the number of its churches, and how they are supplied; the gross amount of funds collected in its bounds for home missions and church erection; the amount received by its churches from the American Home Missionary Society, or any similar institution; the number of houses of worship, with their probable value, and whether they are free from debt; the number of new churches organized, and new houses of worship erected; what itinerant arrangements have been adopted for preaching the Gospel; what and how much agency has been employed; together with all such other facts and suggestions as will show from year to year what has been accomplished, and what may need to be undertaken to bring all the churches to a proper degree of effort to promote the kingdom of Christ.

"11. The stated clerk is required, in due time previous to the meeting of each General Assembly, to notify the stated clerks of the Synods and Presbyteries, by a circular letter, of the foregoing requirement as to reports.

"12. There shall hereafter be appointed, with the other standing committees of the General Assembly, one on Church extension, to whom shall be committed, at an early period of their sessions, the Synodical and Presbyterial reports on the subject, whose duty it shall be to present a condensed view of them to the Assembly, with such further propositions to promote this work as they may deem desirable. This standing committee shall be required to report as soon as a faithful discharge of its duties will permit.

"13. A committee, consisting of five, is hereby appointed to confer with the Executive Committee of the American Home Missionary Society, expressing to it the kind feelings and confidence of the General Assembly and the churches it represents, and requesting its co-operation in this plan, as far as its principles will admit; and also requesting a statement of the principles on which its appropriations are made to the churches of the several denominations of Christians who support it; the results of which conference shall be reported to the next General Assembly.

"The Rev. George Duffield, D.D., Rev. Philemon H. Fowler, and Hon. Daniel Haines were appointed a committee to nominate the committee of five contemplated in the 13th article; and on the nomination of the committee the following persons were appointed, viz., Rev. George Duffield,D.D., Rev. Nathan S. S. Beman, D.D., Rev. Thornton A. Mills, Rev. Robert W. Patterson, and Hon. John L. Mason."—*Minutes*, 1852, pp. 171–173.

3. *Report of the Committee of Conference with the American Home Missionary Society*, 1853.

"The Committee of Conference with the American Home Missionary Society report as follows:

"That they have been much gratified in receiving the assurance, from this correspondence, and from personal conference with the Rev. D. B. Coe, one of the Secretaries of the American Home Missionary Society, that said Society has no disposition to interfere in anywise with the ecclesiastical functions of the Synods and Presbyteries, but rather, in just so far as it can, consistent with its organization and principles as a voluntary association, to blend its agency with theirs in the promotion of the one great common object, the extension of the Redeemer's kingdom. The Missionary Committee of each Presbytery is recognized by the Society as the appropriate body to certify the wants of any particular church seeking aid, the standing of the minister and his prospects of usefulness, and to endorse and recommend the application.

"The Society utterly disclaims any purpose of permitting its agents to interfere with the ecclesiastical relations of the churches, or to overrule the recommendations of the Presbyterial Missionary Committees, or the intention to make any discrimination in the appropriations in favor of one denomination and against another.

"The long connection which has existed between our churches and the American Home Missionary Society, as the receiving and disbursing agent of the churches in carrying forward their domestic missionary work, the efficiency with which the Society has performed its duties, and the general impartiality and fidelity with which it has discharged its important and sometimes difficult trust, force upon us the conviction that our home missionary work can be more successfully prosecuted, in existing circumstances, under our present arrangements, than by any new organization.

"At the same time, we are fully satisfied that the rules of the Society, well designed, and undoubtedly wise and beneficial in their general working, do, nevertheless, sometimes prevent the extension of the Gospel under its auspices, in many of our new and rapidly-growing cities and towns of the West, in cases where the importance of the work, and the incalculable good which might result therefrom, demand some aid. We are aware, also, that the recent revival of denominational zeal which has occurred, will render the continued co-operation of different sister denominations in the missionary work much more delicate and difficult than heretofore, and may occasion injustice to be done through subordinate agents, without intention to do so on the part of the Executive Committee of the Society. Mutual forbearance, however, and that charity which the apostle commends to his Corinthian brethren, and that fear of God which will lead one to suffer rather than inflict a wrong, may, we believe, enable the co-operating parties to continue thus their joint labors happily and successfully, cultivating, also, thereby, the most difficult graces, by often exercising them."—*Minutes*, 1853, pp. 340, 341.

SECTION 2.—THE CHURCH EXTENSION COMMITTEE.

1. The powers and duties of the Assembly in regard to home missions. Committee on Church Extension established; located in Philadelphia. Powers only such as are conferred by the Assembly. The functions of the committee designated. Intention to interfere with the American Home Missionary Society disavowed. Number of the committee, classes, and term of office. Five a quorum. The committee has power to fill its vacancies in the recess of the Assembly.—2. Intent of the appointment of the committee, not to change the co-operative policy of the Church, but to supplement existing agencies.—3. The committee authorized to use their own discretion in cases where prompt action is required. —4. The powers and duties of the committee enumerated and enlarged. Au-

thorized to provide for churches which can receive aid from no other source.—5. The committee instructed to prosecute their work with all energy. Feeble churches to ask the least sum possible. General contributions urged in all the churches not aided by the American Home Missionary Society.—6. The Board of Missions has no authority to sit in judgment upon the orthodoxy or morality of a minister in good standing in his own Presbytery.—7. The committee can make no discrimination between churches having the same standing under the Constitution.—8. Rules of the committee.

1. *The Report of the Standing Committee. The Church Extension Committee established.*

"The Assembly resumed the consideration of the report of the Committee on Church Extension, relative to the overtures on the subject of home missions, when, after full discussion, it was adopted, and is as follows:

"The Committee on Church Extension, to whom was referred the overtures and memorials on the subject of home missions from the Third and Fourth Presbyteries of Philadelphia, the Synod of Iowa, and the Presbyteries of Chicago and Iowa City, respectfully report: That their attention has been especially directed to those cases of home missionary effort which are excluded by the rules of the American Home Missionary Society. Such are, for example, the employment of Synodical, Presbyterial, and generally of exploring or itinerant Presbyterian Missionaries, and the planting of Presbyterian churches in advance of all others in towns and neighborhoods, and the founding of churches within the chartered limits of cities and large villages.

"The Form of Government of our Church, chapter xviii, expressly authorizes the inferior judicatories to apply to the General Assembly for missionary assistance, and in express terms authorizes the Assembly to send missionaries to any part of the Church. The principles of our Presbyterianism, applicable to this subject, are, that the Church is one; that, in accordance with this idea, the stronger parts of the Church must assist the weaker, and that the reservoir into which the surplus shall flow to be equalized and distributed, is the General Assembly. It is obvious that the details of the reception and distribution of funds for this object cannot be arranged by the whole body of the Assembly, but that the Assembly must employ some agency for this purpose; and our opinion is, that it is entirely free to choose any agency whatever. Of course, it may operate through a voluntary association like the American

Home Missionary Society; but your committee do not conceive that its use of that society for specific purposes either gives that society a right to control the whole subject of Church extension for our denomination, or releases the General Assembly from its own obligation to do so. The older and richer Synods, indeed, do not feel so much the pressure of this necessity, as they are able to afford the needed supplementary aid from their own resources; but it is urged upon us from the more new and destitute portions of our Church, that our interests are grievously suffering, because neither the American Home Missionary Society nor any other agency meets their wants in certain respects, such as those which have been already mentioned; and their appeal in this behalf is made just where the Constitution of our Church directs that it should be made,—to the General Assembly itself.

"This being obviously, therefore, a case which cannot be reached so effectually by any action of the inferior judicatories, your committee connot see how the Assembly can refuse to exercise, in regard to it, that power of 'superintendence of the concerns of the whole Church,' expressly confided to it by the Constitution. They therefore recommend the following action:

Name, Powers, and Functions of the Committee.

a. "*Resolved,* 1. That the General Assembly hereby establishes a standing committee, to be called *The Church Extension Committee,* a majority of whom shall reside in or near the city of Philadelphia. This committee shall have no other powers than those conferred by the Assembly; and the functions now assigned to them are those of employing Presbyterial, Synodical, and other Presbyterian itinerant or exploring agents, and affording aid in such exceptional cases as those already mentioned, and also the receiving and disbursing of funds for these objects.

Intention to interfere with the American Home Missionary Society disavowed.

b. "2. That, in recommending this course of action, the General Assembly distinctly declare that it is not their intention thus to establish an ecclesiastical board, or to interfere with the proper functions of the American Home Missionary Society, but, as heretofore, they recommend that society to the confidence and co-operation of the churches under their care.

Number, Classes, and Term of Office, of the Committee.

c. "3. That the Standing Committee on Church Extension, now constituted, shall consist of fifteen members, to be chosen by the Assembly in such manner as the Assembly may direct, and the committee shall, at its first meeting, divide itself into three equal parts, to serve respectively one, two, and three years; but the same persons shall be re-eligible at the pleasure of the Assembly."

Quorum; Power to fill Vacancies in the Recess of the Assembly.

d. "4. Five members of the committee shall be a quorum; but in order to elect any salaried officer of the committee, or to increase or diminish the salary of the same, a majority of the committee shall be necessary to constitute a quorum. The committee shall have power to fill any vacancies occurring while the Assembly is not in session, and they shall make an annual report to the Assembly of all their proceedings."—*Minutes*, 1855, pp. 20–22.

2. *Intent of the Appointment of the Committee.*

"In establishing the Committee on Church Extension, the General Assembly distinctly declared, that it was not their intention to change the co-operative policy of our Church on the subject of home missions, but merely to provide a supplementary agency to attend to the cases needing assistance, which could not be met in consistency with the rules of the American Home Missionary Society. The committee clearly apprehend the object of their appointment, and correctly defined it in a document put forth in August last; and this Assembly commend the strict and prudent adherence of the committee to the principles therein contained. There is nothing in the original appointment of the committee, when properly understood, nor in its action, to excite the fears which have been expressed by corresponding bodies, that our Church has started on a crusade to propagate sectarianism."—*Minutes*, 1856, pp. 219, 220.

3. *The Committee to use its discretion in Cases requiring prompt Action.*

"*Resolved*, That while this Assembly would make no change in the general basis of our operations in the department of Church extension, yet, in view of the fact that, as experience shows, great and perplexing delays are found to result in many cases from a literal and rigid adherence to the restrictions under which the Committee on Church Extension have acted hitherto, they are hereby authorized to exercise their discretion in relation to such applications for aid as may seem to require prompt and immediate action."—*Minutes*, 1857, p. 409.

4. *Powers of the Committee enlarged.*

"Churches in the condition of those just referred to (from whom aid has been withheld by the Home Missionary Society), ought not to be left to suffer, and perhaps to perish; and with a view to them, and also to churches situated like those in Missouri, the powers and duties of the Church Extension Committee ought to be expanded. It has hitherto devolved upon them: 1. To employ agents for purposes of exploration; 2. To aid churches in the chartered limits of cities and large towns; 3. To plant Presbyterian churches in places where sister denominations had not previously occupied the ground; and 4. To answer applications that require prompt and immediate replies, and that will not admit of the delay incident to requests preferred in other directions.

"In view of the new classes of exceptional cases to which they have referred, the committee recommend that the province of the Permanent Committee be still further enlarged, so that they may be authorized to provide for churches that can receive adequate aid from no other source. And to meet the increased draught that must thus be made upon their treasury, it is desirable that additional force be given to their agency for collecting funds.

"Adopted."—*Minutes*, 1859, p. 43.

5. *Committee instructed to prosecute their Work with energy.*

"The report of the Permanent Committee affords encouraging proof of progress in the work of church extension. This work is steadily growing on the hands of the committee, and is carried forward by them with wisdom and efficiency. An increase of about fifty per cent. in the receipts of the committee within the past year shows that this cause is taking a deep hold on the hearts of our people. The importance of the exploring agencies that are employed by the committee can hardly be overestimated. New and wide fields are opening, that must not be neglected by our Church. The number of our feeble churches that can receive aid only from this Church Extension Committee is, from special causes, rapidly increasing. These churches must not be suffered to die, or be driven to other denominations for support, as the condition of their continued existence. The present condition of our home missionary affairs multiplies, and will multiply, the demands for the efficient prosecution of our Church extension enterprise. The coming year will be one of great importance in the history of this work. A large increase upon the present receipts of the committee will be urgently needed.

"In view of the whole case, we recommend the adoption of the following resolutions:

"*Resolved*, 1. That the report of the Church Extension Committee be approved, and that the committee are hereby instructed to prosecute their work with all the energy that they can command.

"2. That we urge our feeble churches that make application to the committee for aid to use their utmost endeavors to help themselves, and to ask the committee for the smallest amount with which they can adequately support their ministers.

"3. That we request all the churches in our connection, that are not aided by the American Home Missionary Society, to take up collections at an early day for the Church extension cause."—*Minutes*, 1860, p. 255.

6. *The Board of Missions has no authority to sit in Judgment upon the Orthodoxy or Morality of a Minister in good standing in his own Presbytery.*

"In answer to the questions propounded by the Presbyteries of Union and French Broad, the Assembly would say, that, though they do not recognize in the Board of Missions the authority to sit in judgment upon the orthodoxy or morality of any minister who is in good standing in his own Presbytery, yet, from the necessity of the case, they must exercise their own sound discretion upon the expediency or inexpediency of appointing or withholding an appointment from any applicant, holding themselves amenable to the General Assembly for all their official acts." —*Minutes*, 1830, p. 290.

7. *The Committee can make no discriminations between Churches having the same standing under the Constitution.*

"The Standing Committee on Church Extension, to whom was referred the resolution proposing that the General Assembly should instruct the Church Extension Committee to offer no assistance to any church that has in its communion one or more slaveholders, reported as follows:

"1. The Permanent Committee on Church Extension is appointed to act for the whole Church, being an organ of the General Assembly, which represents the whole Church, and we can see no defensible principle on which such a committee could make discriminations, on moral grounds, between churches that are recognized as having the same ecclesiastical standing under our common Constitution.

"2. The position of our Church is well understood to be one of opposition to the spirit and the system of slavery; and we have no reason to believe that any churches connected with us are using their influence to sustain and fortify that institution.

"3. If it be true that any members of churches in our connection hold slaves under mistaken views of their duty towards them, we do not see that this affords any sufficient reason for withholding from them the Bread of Life, and such enlightened teachings as we believe our ministry are qualified and disposed to impart, in relation to all the great principles of Christian duty. We sympathize with all Christian endeavors to remove imperfection and sin from the Church of Christ; but we think this end is to be accomplished not by withdrawing the Gospel from those who need it, but by affectionate and prayerful efforts to apply the principles of our holy religion to the heart and conscience of every Christian who is willing to receive instruction.

"4. The Church Extension Committee are fully aware of the ground which our Church occupies with reference to this subject, and we have confidence that they will conscientiously discharge their duty with an enlightened regard to the promotion of righteousness and holiness in the Church, and in the world.

"Adopted."—*Minutes*, 1860, p. 258.

8. *Rules of the Church Extension Committee.*

"1. Quarterly meetings of the committee shall be held alternately in the cities of Philadelphia and New York, on the third Tuesdays of April, July, October, and January, at one o'clock P. M., at which meetings alone the more important business not requiring haste shall be transacted; such as the appointing of officers, determining the policy of the committee, adopting rules or changing them, and agreeing upon the annual report to the General Assembly. Beside the quarterly meetings, there shall be held monthly meetings, excepting in those months in which the quarterly meetings occur, at the Presbyterian House in Philadelphia, at which meetings all ordinary executive business, not reserved as above, may be transacted. The chairman may convene the committee at any other time by causing suitable notice to be given. The necessary travelling expenses of the ministerial members of the committee shall be paid by the treasurer.

"2. A secretary and a treasurer shall be chosen annually, by nomination and ballot.

"3. While the secretary shall be careful not to interfere with the collections made for the American Home Missionary Society or its auxiliaries, yet it is understood that the claims of the committee are to be so presented to individuals and churches, as to secure adequate funds to carry out all the objects designed by the General Assembly in its appointment.

"4. The ordinary mode of operation of the committee will be through the Synods or Presbyteries of our Church, upon the following plan: Each Synod or Presbytery which thinks proper to do so, may appoint a Committee on Church Extension, where such a committee does not already exist, composed of members so situated that they can readily meet. When cases occur such as come within the range of our appointment, the Synodical or Presbyterial Committee will recommend the field, or church, or minister, as the case may be, and in general co-operate with this committee in regard to this class of domestic missionary operations. It will be understood, however, in cases where the Synod or Presbytery has not acted, that churches or ministers may address the committee directly.

"5. Synods or Presbyteries co-operating with the committee will either send to it all their funds collected for the class of cases appropriate to the committee, and the appointments be made by it; or they may raise their own funds and make appointments to be confirmed by this committee, and pay over to it their surplus.

"6. Applications should always be specific. They should state such particulars as the following: The circumstances which make the case one proper for the action of this committee, and not for that of the American Home Missionary Society; the extent and location of the field; the name of the agent or missionary; if a church or congregation, its name and location; the number of communicants; the average number of attendants on public worship; the state of the country and population, and prospects of the field; the denominations and size of congregations immediately contiguous; the total amount of salary which they can raise for the given time, or which can be raised in the Synod or Presbytery; and every other particular calculated to throw light upon the case.

"7. All co-operating committees will make an annual report to the committee, and all agents or missionaries receiving from it the whole or a part of their support, will make a quarterly report. The annual reports shall be forwarded in time to be received by the second Tuesday of April in each year, and the quarterly reports by the second Tuesdays of July, October, and January."

Section 3.—Committee on Church Erection.

1. Initiatory measures.—2. The committee appointed; its number, classification, and duties.—3. The church erection plan of the Assembly.—4. The charter accepted by the Assembly. The fund transferred to the trustees. The Synods enjoined to appoint committees of Church extension.—5. The fund completed. —6. The trustees authorized to require church edifices to be kept insured, at their discretion.—7. Rigid adherence to the plan required. Amendment of art. xiv, sec. 3.—8. Appropriations not to be made, when there is no organized congregation. The trustees are the sole custodians of the fund. The Assembly refuse to alter the plan.—9. Act of incorporation of the Trustees of the Church Erection Fund.—10. By-laws of the trustees.—11. Rules and regulations for the use of applicants for aid from the fund.

1. *Initiatory Measures.*

"*Resolved,* That it be recommended to our churches to strive earnestly to render our religious institutions permanent, by the erection of church edifices and the settlement of pastors, whenever this can be done; and in this work the older and wealthier churches ought to co-operate with the younger and feebler."—*Minutes,* 1850, p. 315.

2. *Committee appointed; its Duties, &c.*

[The Committee on "Church Extension" reported, reciting certain statistical facts, and recommending the following action. Adopted.]

"*Resolved*, 1. That the General Assembly, relying on the assisting grace of God and the hearty co-operation of his people, will undertake to raise, within the present year, the sum of $100,000, which shall constitute a permanent fund to aid feeble congregations in erecting houses of worship.

"*Resolved*, 2. That, in the furtherance of this object, the Assembly do now elect, by ballot, and annually hereafter, a Church Erection Committee, to be composed of ten members, one-half of whom shall be ministers, six to reside in or near the city of New York, and four in or near the city of Philadelphia,—including the stated and permanent clerks and the treasurer of the Assembly, with power to fill their own vacancies; said committee to employ, at their discretion, a corresponding secretary, who shall be paid a suitable salary, together with his travelling expenses.

"*Resolved*, 3. This Church Erection Committee shall meet in the city of New York, on the second Wednesday of June next, and thereafter, on their own adjournment, in the cities of Philadelphia and New York alternately, at least once in three months, their necessary taavelling expenses being defrayed.

"*Resolved*, 4. The General Assembly hereby authorize said committee to take such measures as to them may seem best to bring the claims of this great object before our churches, so as to secure as soon as possible the fund above named; said committee to be authorized, also, to renew the appeal annually to our churches, in order to make up any deficiency which may exist in the first simultaneous subscriptions to complete the fund, or which may arise thereafter; it being the purpose of the Assembly to raise and maintain a permanent fund of $100,000, for the purposes herein specified.

"*Resolved*, 5. The General Assembly recommend that a collection or subscription be taken in all our churches in behalf of this object, on the second Sabbath of November next; and that the money thus raised be forwarded to Anthony P. Halsey, Esq., the treasurer of the General Assembly, or to his successor duly appointed, to be held in trust for the use, and subject to the order, of the above-named committee.

"*Resolved*, 6. The stated clerks of the several Presbyteries shall constitute a committee of correspondence for their respective Presbyteries, with the Church Erection Committee; communicating all needed information in respect to the state and wants of their churches; and the Church Erection Committee, thus informed, shall report to the General Assembly, from year to year, the facts as they exist in respect to the relative wants of the different Synods, and also, the amount and condition of the fund under their direction, and their opinion of the proper apportionment of the same; whereupon the Assembly shall determine the amount to which each Synod shall be entitled for the year next ensuing. And thus, at each successive Assembly, the committee shall report as aforesaid; and, further, they shall report a full statement of all moneys loaned or donated from the fund, and the securities taken therefor. And the Assembly shall direct, as before, the distribution of said fund among the Synods in our connection.

"*Resolved*, 7. Each Synod, through its Committee on Church Extension, of which the stated clerk of the Synod shall be ex-officio secretary, shall draw on the Church Erection Committee for such portion of the fund as has been allotted to it, in such sums as it shall, from time to time, loan or donate to particular churches within its bounds. But no draft shall be made by any Synod for any portion of the fund allotted to it, until, where the money is loaned, each particular loan shall have been definitely agreed upon, and sufficient security in bond and mortgage or personal notes shall have been duly executed and placed in the hands of the stated clerk of said Synod, who shall with his draft transmit a statement of the loan thus made and the security taken; nor shall any draft be made until such accompanying statement, satisfactory to the committee, shall have been received.

"*Provided*, That the Church Extension Committee of each Synod, when, in their estimation, the circumstances of the case demand it, may also donate to feeble churches within their bounds, or remit on previous loans, such sums as they shall judge proper; not to exceed, however, in the aggregate, a sum equal to one-fourth part of the amount apportioned to said Synod for the current year. And the Church Erection Committee shall pay the drafts for such donations in the same manner as for the loans above authorized. All moneys thus donated or remitted to be secured on the house, in case of a change in the ecclesiastical relations of the church thus aided.

"*Provided further*, That all churches, to whom moneys are thus donated or remitted, shall take an annual collection in behalf of the Church Erection Fund, at least until they shall have thus repaid the amount which was granted them. No interest shall ever be demanded for any moneys loaned to congregations from this fund, until by the terms of the loan the principal has become due."—*Minutes*, 1853, pp. 317, 318.

3. *Church Erection Plan.*

"The Church Erection Committee, appointed by the General Assembly of 1853, after a full consideration of the trust committed to them, beg leave to report the following plan for the proper control and management of the Church Erection Fund:

"PREAMBLE. The General Assembly of the Presbyterian Church in the United States of America, now holding its sessions in the city of Philadelphia, in the State of Pennsylvania, having, through the liberality of the congregations connected with this body, established a fund for the purpose of aiding feeble congregations in erecting houses of worship, do hereby adopt the following plan, under which this fund shall be held, administered, and used:

"ART. 1. This fund having been committed to the General Assembly as a special trust, no part of it as now established, nor any additions which may hereafter be made to it, shall ever be used for any other purpose, than that of aiding feeble congregations in connection with the General Assembly in erecting houses of worship; except so much as may be absolutely necessary to defray the expenses incident to the administration of this plan.

"ART. 2. The custody, care, and management of this fund, and of all securities of every kind belonging to it, or growing out of it, together with all claims, dues, and property that may at any time pertain to it, and all additions that may hereafter be made to it by donations, bequests, or otherwise, shall be committed to a board of trustees, to be called 'The Trustees of the Church Erection Fund of the General Assembly of the Presbyterian Church in the United States of America.' The board shall consist of nine members, four of them being ministers and five of them elders, in connection with some Presbytery or church under the care of the General Assembly, who shall reside in the city of New York, or its immediate vicinity, and whom the General Assembly shall elect by ballot, on a nomination to be made at least one day before such election. The trustees shall continue in office until the election and induction of their successors. The certificate of the stated clerk of the General Assembly shall be necessary, to entitle a trustee to take his seat as a member of the board, which certificate it shall be his duty to furnish as soon as practicable after the election.

"The trustees first elected shall arrange themselves into three equal classes. The term of office of the first class shall expire in one year from their election; that of the second class in two years; and that of the third class in three years. After the first election, the General Assembly shall annually elect three trustees, to supply the place of the class whose term is about to expire, to hold their office for three years, the same persons always being re-eligible; and each General Assembly shall also by election supply any vacancy in the board, caused by death, resignation, or otherwise. If any trustee shall, during the term for which he is elected, cease to be connected with a Presbytery or church under the care of the General Assembly, he shall thereby cease to be a member of the board; and the vacancy shall be reported to the next General Assembly.

"ART. 3. The first meeting of the board shall be held on the second Tuesday of June next, in the city of New York, at such place and hour as the stated clerk of the General Assembly may appoint, who shall preside until the board is organized by the choice of its president.

"ART. 4. The board shall make their own by-laws. They shall annually, at their first meeting after the adjournment of the General Assembly, elect one of their number president of the board; and shall appoint a secretary, and a treasurer who shall give security to the board for the faithful performance of his duties. They shall keep complete books of record and account, in which shall be recorded all their proceedings, and the true state at all times of all matters relating to this fund; which records and accounts, or any part of them, shall at all times be open to the inspection of any committee appointed by the General Assembly for this purpose. They shall also keep full and correct copies and files of all the correspondence which may be conducted or received by them, or in their name; and shall annually present to the General Assembly, not later than the third day of its sessions, a full written report of their proceedings and of the state of the fund, together with any suggestions or recommendations which they may deem necessary or suitable. The General Assembly shall annually appoint a committee of three of its members, to audit the accounts and to examine the securities of the board, and report at the next General Assembly.

"ART. 5. The board are hereby directed, either by procuring a special act of the Legislature of the State of New York, or in accordance with the existing statutes of said State, to incorporate themselves, and their successors in office, always to be elected as aforesaid, into a body corporate and politic, invested with all such legal powers, as may be necessary to enable them to hold and administer this fund, in conformity with the provisions of this plan.

"ART. 6. The board are directed, as far as practicable, to keep at interest, on sufficient security, payable on call or short notice, any portion of the fund that may not be appropriated by the General Assembly; or, if appropriated, may not be in use in the Synods.

"ART. 7. The board shall prepare blank forms of all such legal and other papers as may be required in the proper distribution and management of the fund; and they shall furnish a sufficient quantity of such forms to the Committee on Church Extension of each Synod; the forms so prepared and furnished, and none others, shall be used in all matters and transactions relating to the fund, to which they may be applicable. They shall designate such legal advisers within the bounds of each Synod, as by a correspondence with the Church Extension Committees of the Synods may be found desirable, to examine all certificates of title, and all conveyances and other documents connected with the loan or donation of any part of this fund, including a careful investigation in regard to the legal incorporation of the boards of trustees of the congregations concerned; and they shall further have power to appoint an agent in each Synod, and to require that all payments of money that may become due to this fund shall be made to such agent.

"ART. 8. The fund thus established is, in the first instance, hereby appropriated to be used within the bounds of the respective Synods, in the following proportions:

" Synod of	Albany,	2.5	per ct.	" Synod of	Ohio,	3	per ct.
"	Cincinnati,	3	"	"	Pennsylvania,	3	"
"	Genesee,	3	"	"	Peoria,	7	"
"	Geneva,	3	"	"	Susquehanna,	3	"
"	Illinois,	6	"	"	Tennessee,	4	"
"	Indiana,	5	"	"	Utica,	2.5	"
"	Iowa,	5	"	"	Virginia,	3.5	"
"	Kentucky,	2.5	"	"	Wabash,	5	"
"	Michigan,	8	"	"	Western Reserve,	5	"
"	Mississippi,	2.5	"	"	West Pennsylvania,	3	"
"	Missouri,	2.5	"	"	West Tennessee,	3	"
"	New York and New Jersey,	15	"				

"ART. 9. Each General Assembly shall determine the proportion to be appropriated within the bounds of the respective Synods, of any part of the fund that the board may have received since the meeting of the preceding General Assembly, by the payment of loans, gifts, legacies, or otherwise; and every such appropriation, without reference to any previous one, shall be made by the General Assembly in view of the relative wants and necessities of the Synods at the time.

"ART. 10. If any Synod shall deem it inexpedient to aid their feeble churches in accordance with the provisions of this plan; or shall fail to elect a Committee on Church Extension, to act in conjunction with the board, as herein provided; or shall notify the board that any portion of the amount hereby appropriated to be used within their bounds, or of any amount that may be hereafter so appropriated, is not needed; then, in each of these cases, the General Assembly may, at their discretion, appropriate the portion of the fund, or any surplus amount, assigned to such Synod, to other Synods in the same manner as is provided for in the preceding article.

"ART. 11. In order to be entitled to the use of any portion of the fund, each Synod connected with the General Assembly shall annually elect a Committee on Church Extension, consisting of at least five members. The stated clerk of the Synod shall, immediately after the election of said committee, transmit to the president or secretary of the board his certificate of such election, giving the name and residence of each member.

"ART. 12. All applications for aid from the fund shall be made, in the first instance, to the Committee on Church Extension of the Synod to which the applicants belong, or within whose bounds they are situated. Every such application shall be in writing, and shall particularly state: the location of the house or site for its erection; the number of families or persons attached to the congregation, or that propose to unite in building a house of worship; the description of the house which they propose to build, with its estimated and probable cost, or the description and cost of the house and lot owned by the congregation; the amount of reliable subscriptions which have been obtained, and how much has been paid thereon; the amount of available means possessed by the congregation, if any; whether the congregation is in debt, and if so, to what amount, and when the same becomes due; and also any other facts which may aid the committee of the Synod in judging of the application. This application shall be accompanied by the certificate of one of the legal advisers of the board, that the title to the lot on which the house is built or to be built is vested in said congregation, and is free from all legal incumbrance and liability.

"ART. 13. If the committee of the Synod, to whom application for aid has been made as above provided, shall, after a careful examination into the condition and prospects of the congregation so applying, be satisfied that such congregation have done all that should reasonably be expected of them, and that, with the aid which can be afforded from this fund, they can build or possess a house of worship adapted to their wants, and be free from other indebtedness than that to this fund; then the committee shall sign a certificate addressed to the board, stating the application, and that they have examined and approve of it; and also stating the amount which it is proper to loan or donate to the congregation. This certificate, together with a copy of the application made to the committee of the Synod, shall be transmitted to the board. On the receipt of this certificate and application, the board shall, as soon as practicable, if the application is in due form, forward the necessary papers, to be executed by the trustees of the congregation, and to be approved by their legal adviser, or some other attorney proposed by the congregation and accepted by the board. When the papers, so executed, approved, and properly recorded, are returned to the board, they shall authorize the treasurer of the trustees of the congregation, or any other person duly appointed by them for this purpose, to draw on the treasurer of the board for the amount thus provided for and secured.

"ART. 14. The Board shall not in any case loan or donate any portion of the fund to any congregation, unless such congregation own, in fee simple and free from all legal incumbrance, the lot on which their house of worship is situated, or on which they propose to build; nor shall any loan or donation be made for the payment of any debt, except that which may have been contracted within one year previous, in erecting a house of worship.

"The amount loaned to any congregation shall never be more than one-third of the amount contributed for the house and lot, nor exceed the sum of five hundred dollars; nor shall the amount given to any congregation as a donation be in any case more than two hundred dollars, or exceed one-fourth of the amount contributed for their house and lot; nor shall a loan and a donation be made to the same congregation. The donations within the boundaries of any Synod shall never be more than one-fourth of the amount appropriated to that Synod.

"All loans shall be made on the following conditions:

"1. The principal shall be paid in four equal annual instalments, the first instalment becoming due in three years from the date of the loan.

"2. If all the instalments are punctually paid, no interest will be required on any part of the loan.

"3. In default of the payment of any instalment, interest shall be required on the whole loan unpaid, from the time of such default, until such instalment, with all the interest that may thus accrue, shall be paid.*

"The conditions of all donations from this fund shall be, that, in case the church or congregation shall cease to be connected with the General Assembly, or their corporate existence shall cease, or their house of worship be alienated, except for the building or purchase of a better house of worship, they shall refund to the Board the amount which they have so received, with interest from the time of receiving it; and further, that every congregation receiving a donation shall annually make a collection in aid of the fund, transmitting the same to the treasurer, until the amount so collected and paid over shall equal the sum received as a donation.

"The fulfilment of the above conditions, in respect to both loans and donations, shall in all cases be secured by the bond of the trustees of the congregation, and a mortgage on their house and lot, made in favor of the Board; which bond and mortgage, duly executed and recorded, shall always be placed in the possession of the Board, before any money is paid over to the congregation.

"ART. 15. The Board shall not make a loan or donation to any congregation, until the full sum of one hundred thousand dollars shall have been actually paid to the treasurer of the General Assembly. When this amount has been received, the treasurer of the General Assembly is hereby directed to pay over the whole amount to the treasurer of this fund, upon the written order of the Board, signed by its President and Secretary.

"ART. 16. In accepting this trust and adopting this plan, the General Assembly hereby declares, that the first article shall admit of no alteration or amendment; and that no change shall be made in any other part

* "And in case any church or congregation receiving a loan shall afterwards withdraw from the General Assembly, the whole amount unpaid shall at once become due."—*Amendment*, *Minutes*, 1858, p. 586.

of the plan by any future General Assembly, except by an affirmative vote of two-thirds of all the members whose names have been entered upon the roll.

"The following resolutions were also adopted:

"*Resolved*, 1. That this General Assembly express its full approbation of the action of the last Assembly, for raising the sum of one hundred thousand dollars, as a permanent fund for church erection.

"*Resolved*, 2. That efficient measures should now be taken to make up the deficiency of this fund, in the shortest time practicable,—say, by the first day of October next.

"*Resolved*, 3. That the trustees, who are to be appointed to take charge of this whole business, be instructed to make an early and earnest appeal to those churches—more than one-half of our whole number—who have contributed nothing to this fund, asking their co-operation in this labor of love; that they solicit additional assistance from those who have afforded but slender aid; and that they state our remaining wants to those whose liberality has already abounded."—*Minutes*, 1854, pp. 493–498.

4. *Approval of the Charter, &c.*

"The committee to whom was referred the report of the trustees of the Church Erection Fund, having had the matters therein contained under consideration, present the following report:

"1. The Charter.

"The trustees having, according to the direction of the last General Assembly, obtained from the Legislature of the State of New York an act of incorporation, and having accepted the same, which act they have reported to this General Assembly; therefore,

"*Resolved*, That this General Assembly approve said act of incorporation, and the acceptance thereof by the trustees.

"2. Election of Trustees.

"The term of service of the following trustees, Walter S. Griffith, William E. Dodge, and Oliver H. Lee, having expired, the committee nominate them as suitable persons for re-election for three years, according to the provisions of the plan for the management and distribution of the Fund; and recommend that the election be held on Friday morning, immediately after the opening of the Assembly.

"3. TRANSFER OF THE FUND, 1855.

"At the close of the last General Assembly, the Board not being incorporated, or even organized, the amount of the fund then collected was properly left in the custody of the treasurer of the Assembly; but the Board now being fully organized, and having a legal existence, it appears to the committee desirable and proper that the custody of the fund, as far as completed, should be committed to those who are responsible for its future management, and they therefore recommend the adoption of the following resolution:

"*Resolved,* That the closing sentence of the 15th article of the Plan for Distribution be altered to read as follows: 'The treasurer of the General Assembly is hereby directed to transfer the moneys and securities belonging to the Church Erection Fund, in his hands, to the treasurer of the Board of Trustees of the General Assembly's Church Erection Fund, upon the written order of the Board, signed by its president and secretary.'

"4. THANKS TO THE TREASURER.

"*Resolved,* That the thanks of the General Assembly are hereby tendered to Anthony P. Halsey, Esq., its treasurer, for the accommodating, patient, and faithful attention that he has bestowed on the reception and the management of the Church Erection Fund, while it has been in his hands; and that the stated clerk communicate this resolution to Mr. Halsey.

"5. AUDITING COMMITTEE.

"*Resolved,* That the Auditing Committee appointed by the last General Assembly be reappointed for the coming year.

"6. CHANGE OF THE PLAN.

"In reply to the memorial of the Presbytery of Kalamazoo, requesting a change in the conditions of the 12th and 14th sections of the Plan of Distribution, the committee recommend the adoption of the following resolution:

"*Resolved,* That, upon a careful examination, it will be found that the Plan contains no conditions or requirements not necessary to the permanence and perpetuity of the fund ; and that essentially to modify or change the conditions of distribution would jeopard its perpetuity.

"7. Premature Distribution of the Fund.

"In reply to the suggestion of the Presbytery of Ithaca, that the distribution of the fund should be commenced before the amount originally contemplated is paid in, the committee recommend the adoption of the following resolution :

"*Resolved,* That good faith towards many of the contributors to the fund, and a becoming regard to consistency on the part of the Assembly in its reiterated declaration of its purposes and pledges on this subject, alike forbid any distribution till the whole sum is completed.

"8. Injunction to the Synods.

"*Resolved,* That the Synods be enjoined to give particular attention to Article 11 of the Plan of Distribution, requiring the appointment of Committees of Church Extension, and the transmission of the names and residences of the members to the board of trustees."—*Minutes,* 1855, pp. 23, 24.

5. *The Fund completed.*

"The Trustees of the Church Erection Fund made their annual report, which was read and accepted.

"*Resolved,* That the General Assembly will now proceed to provide for the deficit reported in the Church Erection Fund, by the personal pledges of individuals present, to the amount of that deficit.

"In accordance with the above resolution, the Assembly received pledges from several individuals, members and others, to the full amount of $2900 ; and the fund of $100,000 for church erection was thus completed."—*Minutes,* 1856, p. 190.

6. *Trustees authorized to require the Churches mortgaged to be kept Insured.*

"To render the security for loans in all cases satisfactory, the trustees are hereby authorized to require that the churches on which they take mortgages shall be kept insured, whenever they may deem this precaution necessary."—*Minutes,* 1857, p. 386.

7. *Rigid Adherence to the Plan required. Section* 3, *Article* 14, *amended.*

"*Resolved*, 1. That while we regard the whole course of the trustees, during the past year, as worthy of our approval, we especially approve, in their disbursement of the Church Erection Fund, their rigid adherence to that portion of the Assembly's plan which restricts the board from loaning or donating any portion of the fund to any congregation, unless such congregation own in fee simple and free from incumbrance the lot on which their house of worship is already, or is to be, erected. And we would recommend a rigid adherence to this feature of the plan for the future, regarding such a course as especially adapted to secure an increasing confidence in the Assembly's plan, and increasing donations from its friends.

"*Resolved*, 2. That the following words be added to the first paragraph in section third of the fourteenth article of the Plan, namely: 'And in case any church or congregation receiving a loan shall afterwards withdraw from the General Assembly, the whole amount unpaid shall at once become due.' "—*Minutes*, 1858, p. 585.

8. *Appropriations cannot be made where there is no Church organization. The Trustees are the sole Custodians of the Fund.*

"The second special report of the trustees relates to a proposal, that the trustees should appoint agents for the collection of money to assist churches, in certain cases, beyond the amount allowed by the existing regulations of the Fund; and also to a proposal, that these regulations should be so altered as to permit appropriations to communities, in special circumstances, where no church had been organized. The terms of the charter forbid a compliance with the last; and the repeated and widely-published statements, while the Church Erection Fund was in the process of collection, that the scheme was to check, if not arrest, appeals for help in building houses of worship, dissuade us from acceding to the first.

"Various overtures have been referred to this committee. The Presbytery of Iowa City prays, that the trustees of the Church Erection Fund may appoint agents for the collection of funds in the cases described in the second special report; and the Presbyteries of Iowa City, Keokuk, and Knox, pray that a day may be appointed for a general collection, to assist churches beyond the amount allowed by the existing regulations of the Church Erection Fund. The committee recommend the answer given to these petitions, in form or substance, in the second special report of the trustees.

"The Presbytery of Iowa City renews the prayer, that grants may be allowed, in some extraordinary cases, where no church has been yet constituted; to which the committee recommend the reply in the second special report of the trustees.

"The Presbyteries of Winona, Iowa City, and Knox, pray that the portions of the Church Erection Fund allotted to the different Synods, may be paid over to the Synodical Committees for distribution at their discretion. And the Presbytery of Kansas prays that $3000 may be paid over to it, to be distributed at its discretion; or, if this be declined, that the money be remitted to the Synod to which that Presbytery may be attached, for distribution at the discretion of the Synodical Committee.

"The charter constitutes the trustees the sole custodians and managers of the Church Erection Fund; and the committee recommend this as the answer to these petitions of the Presbyteries.

"The Synod of Iowa pray that the trustees of the Church Erection Fund may be clothed with discretionary power to grant to congregations in cities and large towns loans as large, if necessary, as $1000; and donations as large, if necessary, as $400.

"While it has seemed, to a majority of the committee, desirable, in itself considered, that appropriations of the amount now named should be allowable in certain extraordinary cases, there are too many considerations presenting the proposed alteration as of questionable expediency, and too many brethren whose experience and observation of the workings of the scheme entitle their judgment to respect, clear and decided in their convictions against it, to justify our venturing upon it at the present time; and the committee cordially agree in recommending that the existing rates of grants be adhered to, until a further trial shall make it more obvious, whether they should be retained or changed, and secure greater unanimity in regard to them.

"The trustees of the Synod of Iowa pray that $100, with interest from 1855, transmitted, as they state, by mistake, to the Church Erection Fund of the General Assembly, should be returned to them. It appears, however, from the records of the Synod of Iowa, that that body sanctioned the act of the chairman of its Church Erection Committee in transmitting the said $100 to the trustees of the Assembly's fund, in payment of the assessment made upon its churches for the purposes of this fund; and the committee therefore recommend that the trustees of the Synod of Iowa be referred to the Synod of Iowa, and to the churches under its care for the sum they ask of the Assembly."—*Minutes*, 1859, pp. 26, 27.

9. *An Act to Incorporate the Trustees of the Church Erection Fund of the General Assembly of the Presbyterian Church in the United States of America, passed March* 31, 1855.

"The people of the State of New York, represented in Senate and Assembly, do enact as follows:

"1. Samuel T. Spear, Asa D. Smith, Edwin F. Hatfield, James W. McLane, Walter S. Griffith, Oliver H. Lee, Norman White, William E. Dodge, and Stephen H. Thayer (designated for the purpose by the General Assembly of the Presbyterian Church, which met in Philadelphia, in May, 1854), and their successors in office, are hereby constituted a body corporate and politic, by the name of 'The Trustees of the Church Erection Fund of the General Assembly of the Presbyterian Church in the United States of America,' for the purpose of aiding feeble congregations in connection with the said General Assembly in erecting houses of worship, and by that name, they and their successors shall and may have perpetual succession. Provided, that no money shall be furnished by said corporation for the erection of any house of worship in any State or Territory, in which there shall exist at the time a law for the incorporation of religious societies, the title to which is not held by a religious corporation under and according to the laws of the respective States or Territories in which such places of worship are located. Provided also, that the title shall in no instance be vested in any priest, bishop, or other ecclesiastic.

"2. The said corporation shall possess the general powers, and be subject to the provisions, contained in title 3 of chapter 18 of the first part of the Revised Statutes, so far as the same are applicable and have not been repealed or modified.

"3. The management and disposition of the affairs and funds of said corporation shall be vested in the individuals named in the first section of this act, and their successors in office, who shall remain in office for such period, and be displaced and succeeded by others, to be elected at such time and in such manner as the said General Assembly shall direct and appoint; and such election shall be made, and the said fund shall be held and administered, invested and disposed of, for the purposes aforesaid, in conformity with the provisions of the plan adopted by the said General Assembly.

"4. The said corporation shall in law be capable of taking, receiving and holding any real or personal estate, which has been or may hereafter be given, devised, or bequeathed to them for the purposes of their incorporation, or which shall accrue from the use of said fund; but the said corporation shall not take and hold real and personal estate above the sum of two hundred and fifty thousand dollars.

"5. This act shall take effect immediately.

STATE OF NEW YORK,
Secretary's Office.

I have compared the preceding with the original law on file in this office, and I do hereby certify that the same is a correct trans-
[L. S.] cript therefrom, and of the whole of such original.

Given under my hand and seal of office, at the city of Albany, this second day of April, 1855.

A. G. JOHNSON,
Deputy Secretary of State.

10. *By-Laws adopted by the Trustees of the Church Erection Fund of the General Assembly of the Presbyterian Church in the United States of America, May,* 1855.

"I. Five members of the Board shall constitute a quorum.

"II. The Board shall meet annually on the third Wednesday of June, when, if a quorum is present, they shall proceed to elect from their number a president and a vice-president. They shall also appoint a secretary and treasurer. The Board shall also meet on the third Wednesday of September, December, and March. Special meetings of the Board may be called by the president, or, in his absence or inability to act, by the vice-president, or by the secretary, at the written request of three members of the Board. If no quorum shall be present at the time fixed for the annual or other regular meeting of the Board, the members present shall adjourn from time to time until a quorum shall be present.

"III. The Board, at its annual meeting, shall appoint three standing committees, viz.:

"1st. A Committee of Finance, who shall take the oversight and direction of all the financial affairs of the Board, and direct the treasurer in the discharge of his duties. No money shall be paid out or invested by the treasurer without the written authority of the Finance Committee. The Finance Committee shall not authorize any loan or donation to be made to any congregation until they have before them the certificate of the Committee on Applications, as hereinafter provided for.

"2d. A Committee on Applications, to whom shall be referred all applications for loans or donations from the Fund, with the securities offered and the vouchers and correspondence accompanying the same. It shall be their duty to certify in writing to the Finance Committee, that they have carefully examined the same, and that the applications and securities are according to the provisions of the Plan of the Assembly. It shall also be the duty of the committee to recommend to the Board such persons as legal advisers within the bounds of the Synods as, after correspondence with the Church Extension Committees of the Synods, they shall approve, to make the examinations of title provided for in Art. 8 of the Plan; and generally to secure a strict compliance with the Plan of the Assembly and the Charter of the Board, with respect to loans and donations from the Fund. And

"3d. A Committee on Correspondence, whose duty it shall be to take the oversight and direction of all the correspondence of the Board, except that pertaining to the duties of the other standing committees, and to supervise the reports and all communications to the General Assembly or other religious or public bodies.

"IV. The standing committees shall be subject to the direction of the Board; they shall each keep a book of minutes, in which all their proceedings shall be recorded, which shall be laid before the Board at each meeting.

"V. The Board, at their regular meeting in March of each year, shall fix the amount of salaries to be paid the secretary and treasurer, and the sums so fixed shall not be changed during the year next ensuing.

"VI. It shall be the duty of the treasurer to take the custody of the funds and securities belonging to the Board, and to hold, invest, and pay over the same, as he shall be directed from time to time by the Board or by the Finance Committee. He shall keep complete books of account of all matters pertaining to the Fund, and shall furnish to the Board at each regular meeting, and at any other time when directed by the Board or by the Finance Committee to do so, a full and methodical statement in writing of the amount of the Fund; the amount not in use in the Synods, how invested, on what security, and at what rate of interest; the amount in use in each Synod, by what congregations and when due; the amount loaned or donated since the last previous meeting of the Board; in what Synods and to what congregations. He shall have the custody of the corporate seal, and shall keep all the books, securities, and valuable papers, belonging to the Board, in a fireproof safe, to be provided by them for the purpose. He shall be subject at all times in the discharge of his duties to the direction of the Board or of the Finance Committee, and shall hold his office during the pleasure of the Board.

"VII. No money belonging to this Fund shall be drawn, except upon the check of the treasurer, countersigned by the chairman of the Finance Committee.

"VIII. It shall be the duty of the secretary to keep the minutes of the Board and of all the standing committees, to correspond in the name of the Board as he shall be directed to do by the Board or by the standing or special committees, and to attend to such other duties as the Board shall prescribe. He shall hold his office during the pleasure of the Board.

"IX. All reports made to the Board by any of its committees or officers shall be in writing, and, unless otherwise ordered, shall be entered at length on the minutes.

"X. At all meetings of the Board, the following order shall be observed:

"1. Prayer.
"2. Reading the minutes of the last meeting.
"3. Report of the treasurer.
"4. Reports of the standing committees.
"5. Reports of special committees.
"6. Unfinished business.
"7. New business.
"8. Concluding prayer.

"XI. In case of the absence of the president and vice-president, the Board shall elect a president pro tem.

"XII. The Board at any meeting may fill any vacancy that shall occur in the officers or standing committees of the Board; provided, that notice of such vacancy shall be given when the meeting is called.

"XIII. All elections shall be by ballot.

"XIV. These by-laws shall not be changed, except by a vote of two-thirds of all the members of the Board. Previous notice of any proposed change shall be given in writing to each member of the Board."

11. *Rules and Regulations for the Use of Applicants for Aid from the Church Erection Fund, as required by the Assembly's Plan.*

"1. All applications for aid must first be made to the Synodical Committee on Church Extension.

"2. All such applications must be made in the forms prepared by the trustees of the Fund, and placed by them in the hands of the chairman of the Synodical Committee.

"3. The Synodical Committee will designate to applicants for aid what lawyer they shall employ to fill up and sign the certificate on the last page of the form used in making the application.

"4. The expense incurred in obtaining this certificate must be borne by the applicants.

"5. The congregation applying for aid must own in fee simple, and free from all legal incumbrance, the lot on which their house stands, or on which it is to be erected.

"6. Each congregation, in order to be aided from this Fund, must be free from all other indebtedness than that to this Fund.

"7. Each congregation must first do what they can to erect a house of worship, before applying for help.

"8. As the amount apportioned by the General Assembly to each Synod is not large, and as it is desirable to aid as many feeble congregations as possible, all applicants should keep this fact in view in fixing the amount asked for.

"9. No congregation can receive more than one-third of the amount actually paid by them for their house and lot.

"10. No loan or donation can be made for the payment of any debt, except that which may have been contracted in erecting their house, and within one year previous to the time of making their application.

"11. No donation can be made to any congregation of more than two hundred dollars; nor can it in any case exceed one-fourth of the amount actually paid by them for their house and lot.

"12. A loan and donation can not be made to the same congregation."

SECTION 4.—THE PUBLICATION COMMITTEE.

1. Preliminary history.—2. The "Doctrinal Tract" Committee appointed. Located at Philadelphia. Its duties and powers. Unanimous consent required before any book or tract is published. Empowered to fill its own vacancies.—3. The committee enlarged to eleven. Rule requiring unanimous consent changed to three-fourths.—4. The committee further enlarged to fifteen, nine of whom to reside at or near Philadelphia. Five a quorum. The consent of a majority required to the publication of anything issued by the committee. The committee divided into three classes of five each. Names.—5. Name changed to "Publication Committee."—6. Negotiations respecting the Church Psalmist. The committee are authorized to apply for, and accept, an act of incorporation.—7. The committee authorized to issue works of a general evangelical character, in addition to strictly doctrinal works. The trustees of the House authorized and directed to act as trustees of the Publication Committee. The Psalmist recommended. An appendix to be added.—8. Churches permitted to receive the publications of the committee to the amount of half their collections. 9. A working capital of twenty-five thousand dollars urged. The committee authorized to employ an agent.—10. Presbyterial depositories recommended.

1. *Preliminary Action.*

[In 1846, an overture on the subject of "*Doctrinal Tracts,*" was referred to a committee of two from each Synod, Rev. H. A. Rowland chairman. *Minutes*, 1846, p. 11. "The Rev. H. A. Rowland, from the Committee on 'Doctrinal Tracts,' presented a report, which was accepted and put on the docket." *Ib.* p. 19. Subsequently, "the whole subject was referred to a committee, consisting of Messrs. William Patton, D.D., T. H. Skinner, D.D., E. F. Hatfield, and H. A. Rowland, to act in the premises, and report at the meeting of the Assembly in Cincinnati." *Ib.* p. 38. The committee made a report, which was referred to a new committee, Messrs. Hatfield, Cox, Mason, Stowe, and Parker, with instructions to report to the next Assembly. *Minutes*, 1847, p. 145. This committee seem to have made no report. In 1850, on an overture, the subject was referred to a select committee, consisting of Rev. J. C. Stiles, D.D., J. B. Townsend, J. Holmes Agnew, and F. A. Ross, with Elders Abner Bryant and George Kellogg, to report to the next Assembly. *Minutes*, 1850, p. 309. No further action appears until 1852, when "the Assembly proceeded to consider the third section of the report on Church extension," viz., in relation to doctrinal tracts. The report was adopted, and is as follows, viz. :]—*Minutes*, 1852, p. 175.

2. *The Committee appointed; its Powers and Duties.*

a. "To promote the diffusion of those truths which distinguish us as a Church, the General Assembly adopts the following arrangement:

"1. There is hereby established at Philadelphia a standing committee of nine persons, whose duty it shall be to superintend the publication of a series of tracts explanatory of the doctrines, government, and missionary policy of the Presbyterian Church, as the General Assembly shall from time to time direct. One-third of this committee shall serve for one year, one-third for two years, and the remaining third for three years. The election, to fill the places of those whose terms expire, to be held at each meeting of the General Assembly.

"2. This committee shall elect a secretary and treasurer, the former of whom shall receive such a salary per annum, as shall be agreed upon by the committee; and shall be the editor of the tracts published; and also, as far as may be necessary, the soliciting agent for such an amount of funds as may be required to carry out the objects for which this committee is appointed.

"3. It shall be the duty of this committee to meet at Philadelphia, and, after due organization, to take measures to procure the preparation and publication, in cheap, neat, and substantial form, of a series of Tracts for the purposes above stated. No tract to be published, which does not receive the unanimous approbation of the committee.

"4. This committee shall, if consistent with the interests of the Assembly, enter into a contract with some publisher or publishers to assume, for a time, the publication of such tracts as may be furnished them, at certain rates, which shall be agreed upon in writing. And if no such arrangement can be profitably and satisfactorily made, then the said committee shall, by solicitation from the churches, proceed to provide a sufficient fund for their publication in behalf of the Assembly.

"5. This committee shall make a full report of its proceedings to the General Assembly, at each annual meeting.

"The following persons were appointed the committee to superintend the preparation and publication of doctrinal tracts, viz.: Rev. Thomas Brainerd, D.D., Rev. Albert Barnes, and Mr. S. T. Bodine, for one year; Rev. E. W. Gilbert, D.D., Rev. Thomas H. Skinner, D.D., and Rev. George Duffield, Jr., for two years; Rev. Asa D. Smith, D.D., Rev. Jonathan F. Stearns, D.D., and Hon. William Darling, for three years.

"*Resolved,* That the committee have power to fill their own vacancies."—*Minutes,* 1852, p. 176.

b. "In regard to the publication of the annual reports, we would state, that each permanent committee now publishes and circulates, to a considerable extent, its own report, and bears the expense; that our religious weeklies insert synopses of them free of charge; and that the only satisfactory change, at present practicable or desirable, seems to be, that the several committees, each bearing its own expense as now, intrust the printing of their reports to the Publication Committee; and that the latter print them in uniform style, with their own *imprimatur.* The reports will then be in shape, both for easy circulation, and also for binding and preservation. This change in the publication of the annual reports of our permanent committees we recommend."—*Minutes,* 1859, p. 37.

3. *Committee enlarged. Rule modified so as to require the assent of three-fourths to the Publication of any Book or Tract.*

"The committee to whom was referred the report of the Standing Committee for the preparation and publication of doctrinal tracts, reported the following resolutions, which were adopted:

"1. That the Rev. Thomas Brainerd, D.D., Rev. Albert Barnes, and Mr. Samuel T. Bodine, whose term of service on the committee has expired, be re-elected.

"2. That the Rev. George Chandler and Samuel H. Perkins, Esq., of Philadelphia, be added to the committee.

"3. That the rule requiring the unanimous consent of the committee for the publication of any book or tract, be so modified, that a majority of three-fourths only shall be required.

"4. That the committee be authorized to take such measures as they may deem advisable, to secure the necessary funds for the erection of a house of publication.

"5. That it be earnestly recommended to all our churches to take up collections, annually or otherwise, in aid of the publishing fund under the control of this committee.

"6. That we suggest to the Publication Committee the desirableness of issuing, as soon as practicable, a few tracts which shall clearly and distinctly exhibit our peculiar views of doctrine, government, and missionary policy, with a view to answer the calumnies against us, and show our true position in the Church and in the world."—*Minutes*, 1853, p. 330.

4. *Committee enlarged. Quorum. Nothing to be Published without the Assent of a Majority of the Committee.*

a. "The committee to whom was referred the report on doctrinal tracts, and also the overture from the Presbytery of Philadelphia 4th, on the subject of a Presbyterian publication house, report, that they concur cordially in the expressions of the report on the subject of the press, and its great importance as an organ of usefulness; also, on the desirableness of a religious literature suitable to the wants of our denomination; and congratulate the Assembly on the prospect that this want will be supplied by the future efficiency of this committee.

"Your committee, moreover, fully concur in the views of the report, as to the inexpediency of ourselves entering upon the business of printing, and the superior advantages of doing the work by the agency of existing printing establishments.

"Your committee further recommend, that the Publication Committee be enlarged to the number of fifteen, nine of whom shall reside in the city of Philadelphia, or vicinity; that of this number, five shall constitute a quorum for ordinary business, whose sittings shall be in the city of Philadelphia; but nothing shall be authorized for publication, issued, or endorsed by said committee, except by a majority of its members. All publications to issue simultaneously in the two cities of New York and Philadelphia, with the *imprimatur* of the committee. Adopted."—*Minutes*, 1854, p. 508.

Committee divided into Three Classes, one Class to go out of Office Yearly.

b. "The members of the Publication Committee, whose term of office expires at this time, are the Rev. Thomas H. Skinner and George Duffield, Jr. In addition to these, the committee recommend the appointment of thirteen others; and that this committee arrange themselves at their first meeting into three classes, five going out of office yearly. Adopted."—*Minutes*, 1854, p. 508.

c. "The committee to nominate members of the Doctrinal Tract Committee made the following report, which was adopted.

"*Publication Committee:* Rev. A. Barnes, Rev. N. S. S. Beman, D.D., LL.D., Rev. Wm. Eagleton, D.D., Rev. Thos. Brainerd, D.D., Rev. Asa D. Smith, D.D., Rev. S. H. Gridley, Rev. A. H. H. Boyd, D.D., Rev. S. T. Spear, D.D., Rev. Geo. Duffield, Jr., Rev. H. Darling, Rev. J. Jenkins, and Messrs. S. H. Perkins, S. T. Bodine, C. S. Wurts, and E. S. Whelen."—*Minutes*, 1854, p. 510.

5. *Name changed to "The Presbyterian Publication Committee."*

"*Resolved*, That the name of the Doctrinal Tract Committee of the General Assembly, be changed to 'The Presbyterian Publication Committee.'"—*Minutes*, 1855, p. 13.

6. *The Church Psalmist to be secured for the Assembly.*

a. "The Assembly took from the docket the report of the Committee on Church Psalmody, and the following substitute was adopted:

"*Resolved*, 1. That the Publication Committee confer with the proprietors of the Church Psalmist, and secure, if possible, the transfer, on reasonable terms, of the copyright of said book to the General Assembly, and that the committee have full powers to close arrangements binding on the Assembly.

"*Resolved*, 2. That, in case of failure, said committee report to the next General Assembly, and at the same time recommend to that body the course which they deem it most advisable to pursue in the premises."—*Minutes*, 1855, p. 32.

The Committee authorized to negotiate for the Church Psalmist; also, to apply for an Act of Incorporation.

b. "The committee to whom was referred the annual reports of the Publication Committee, and of 'the Trustees of the Presbyterian House,' respectfully report:

"That they recommend the approval of these reports and the course of action which has been pursued by these bodies the past year. Your committee believe that there is an important field to be occupied by the Publication Committee, without interference with the societies whose object is to supply a more general evangelical literature. It is necessary, also, that the committee should have a house in which their operations may be carried on, and which may be used for other purposes connected with our Church.

"It appears from the reports, that three objects are now particularly engaging the attention of the Publication Committee and the Board of Trustees, viz.: the necessary arrangements for a uniform psalm and hymn book for the whole Church; the endowment of the committee with a suitable capital for carrying on its operations; and the raising of funds to complete the payment for the Presbyterian House, agreeably to the plan adopted by the General Assembly in 1854. These objects strike your committee as reasonable and important, and, in view of the whole case, they recommend the following resolutions, viz.:

"*Resolved*, 1. That the reports of the Presbyterian Publication Committee, and of the Board of Trustees of the Presbyterian House, be approved, and that extracts from the same be published in the Appendix to the Minutes of the Assembly, at the discretion of the stated clerk.

"2. That in view of the wants of these institutions; for the purpose of securing uniformity in Church psalmody; of endowing the Publication Committee, and paying the balance of the sum required for the purchase of the Presbyterian House, agreeably to the plan agreed upon by the General Assembly of 1854; it be and hereby is recommended to all the churches under our care, to take up a simultaneous collection on the first Sabbath of December next; and that an effort be made at that time to raise the sum of thirty thousand dollars for these objects; one-half of which is to be appropriated to the Publication Committee, for the two objects first mentioned, and the other one-half to the trustees of the Presbyterian House, for the last object mentioned; and that, in case less than the sum mentioned be raised by said collection, it be equally divided between the two bodies for the respective purposes mentioned.

"3. In order to preserve uniformity in Church psalmody, that the Publication Committee be authorized to negotiate with the compilers and publishers of the *Church Psalmist*, and to purchase that book, if this can be done on reasonable terms; but, if such terms cannot be obtained, then that they be instructed to inquire whether a new book of psalms and hymns may not be compiled, which shall meet all our wants, and to report to the next General Assembly.

"4. That the Publication Committee is hereby authorized to apply to the Legislature of Pennsylvania to obtain a charter to enable them more perfectly to carry on their operations, and to accept the same when granted.

"5. That the following persons, whose term of office in the Publication Committee now expires, are hereby re-elected for three years, viz.: Rev. S. H. Gridley, D.D., Rev. A. H. H. Boyd, D.D., Rev. Samuel T. Spear, D.D., Rev. George Duffield, Jr., Rev. Henry Darling.

"Adopted."—*Minutes*, 1856, pp. 214, 215.

7. *The Press to be employed. Works of a general Evangelical Character to be published.*

a. "*Resolved*, That the power of the press, in promoting true piety and a wide-spread intelligence among our population, is an instrumentality appointed of God, and now put into our hands, to be employed for the advancement of the general interests of religion, and for the prosperity of our own denomination.

"*Resolved*, That the Publication Committee be encouraged to publish not only such works as may present the peculiarities of our branch of the Christian Church in doctrine and practice, but, from time to time, such works of an evangelical character as may be profitable to the Church at large."—*Minutes*, 1857, p. 410.

The Trustees of the Presbyterian House authorized and directed to act as Trustees of the Publication Committee.

b. "*Resolved*, by the General Assembly of the Presbyterian Church in the United States of America, that 'The Trustees of the Presbyterian House' be, and they hereby are, authorized and directed to act, in their corporate capacity as trustees of the Permanent Committee of this Assembly, called 'The Presbyterian Publication Committee,' as fully, and in the same manner, as if 'The Presbyterian Publication Committee' were themselves constituted a corporation by the same authority which incorporated 'The Trustees of the Presbyterian House.'—*Ibid.* p. 410.

Church Psalmist commended. An Appendix to be added. A Book of Tunes to be prepared.

"*Resolved*, That we recognize, with gratitude to God, the completion of the labors of the Publication Committee, by which the Assembly is furnished with a book of psalmody which they can call their own, the profits of which will materially aid the funds of the Church in the publication cause; and the Assembly hereby recommend to the pastors and the churches that they use all reasonable diligence in promoting uniformity, by the introduction of this book.

"*Resolved*, That a committee of three be appointed by the Publication Committee, to prepare a book of *tunes* adapted to the Church Psalmist, and that this committee be instructed to consult and correspond with pastors and leaders of choirs in the churches, as to the particular tunes most in use and most popular in the congregations; and that this committee report to the next General Assembly.

"*Resolved*, That the preparation of an appendix to the Church Psalmist, of such hymns as may be necessary to make the work complete, be committed to N. S. S. Beman, D.D., Rev. Albert Barnes, and S. W. Fisher, D.D., and that this committee report to the next General Assembly."—*Ibid.* 411.

"*Resolved*, That the committee appointed by the last General Assembly to prepare an arrangement of the Book of Psalms for chanting, a specimen of which is presented with their report, be directed, in the completion of their work, for the sake of bringing the book into as small compass as possible, to leave out the titles of the psalms, and all comments upon the text, and only arrange the words to the music; and in publishing the work, the copy of an English print, accompanying the report, is commended as a model."—*Ibid.*, pp. 410, 411.

Adjustment of Claims of the Publisher of the Parish Psalmody.

d. "*Resolved*, That, as the publisher of the 'Parish Psalmody,' in a memorial made to the Assembly, seems to suppose that he has some pecuniary claim upon the Assembly, though the Permanent Committee of Publication, to whom this subject has been referred, have decided that there is no just claim, yet, as a Christian method of answering the memorial and settling the question in dispute, the whole subject be referred to a committee, to report to the next General Assembly in respect to this claim; of which committee one shall be appointed by said publisher, one by the Permanent Committee of Publication, and the third by these two.

"*Resolved*, That the treasurer's accounts of the Publication Committee, and of the Board of Trustees of the Presbyterian House, which have been presented duly audited, be approved."—*Ibid.*, p. 411.

Collections enjoined. Sermon.

e. "*Resolved,* That it be enjoined upon all our churches to make an annual collection for the Publication cause, in the month of October.

"*Resolved,* That an annual sermon be preached before the General Assembly, on the subject of Publication, and that for the next year Rev. Albert Barnes be the preacher, and Rev. Henry B. Smith, D.D., be the alternate."—*Ibid.*, p. 411.

8. *Churches permitted to receive Publications to the amount of one-half their Collections.*

"*Resolved,* That all churches making this annual collection be permitted, if they so elect, to order for their own use any publications of the committee to the amount of one-half their respective collections."—*Minutes*, 1859, p. 39.

9. *Report of the Standing Committee; a Working Capital recommended; authorized to employ an Agent.*

"The Standing Committee of Publication respectfully report:

"It is a matter of satisfaction to notice, from year to year, the indication of advance, slow but sure, in this important department of the Church's activity.

"The Presbyterian Publication Committee, in their report (which, with the treasurer's account and vouchers, has been carefully considered by us), furnish evidence that they have been faithful stewards of the very limited resources placed at their control.

"They have added to their list of publications a number of tracts and volumes which promise to be useful; among which is the long-needed Tune Book, literally, as it is named, 'Eclectic' of the melodies widely familiar in our congregations. This, with the admirable Church Psalmist, will contribute to promote a uniformity in the service of song of our beloved Zion. These new publications, as their report remarks, must 'add moral, as well as material strength' to the Publication cause.

"The sales of the year furnish a grateful indication of the growth of this scheme. The amount, for a period of eleven months included in the report, exceeds $15,000, being an advance of 60 per cent. over that of last year, and of 200 per cent. over that of the year previous.

"The donations, likewise, are represented under the respectable figure of $8095 81; though an abatement from the satisfaction of this item must be had, in view of the fact that it is mainly the result of a special appeal to the churches of Philadelphia, which have before done so much for the caùse; and, consequently, it does not express the interest felt by the body at large.

"The present capital of the Publication Committee may, perhaps, be estimated as high as $15,000; which, considering the newness of the scheme, and the difficulties under which it has been prosecuted, is certainly honorable to the energy and management of the brethren who have had it in hand, if not particularly creditable to the liberality of the denomination at large.

"But, while we recognize this advance, we must not ignore the fact that the publication enterprise is yet in its infancy and weakness, and needs the fostering help of the churches.

"The Publication Committee, in discharging the trust laid upon them, painfully realize the need of resources greatly beyond what have yet been supplied them. Indeed, in order to sustain the scheme, to keep it alive by meeting the demands of its natural growth, the brethren who compose that committee are compelled to lie under a heavy personal pecuniary responsibility, to which they ought not for one day to be subjected.

"The only relief for this weakness and inconvenience is the formation of a working capital, in some measure proportioned to the aims of the General Assemblies which have established and continued the Publication Committee. And, until individuals of wealth may be inclined adequately to endow this enterprise, we must look to the annual and continued collections from our churches to raise it gradually to a position of ability, in which it may wield the power for good that was contemplated in its organization.

"This committee therefore recommend: 1. That the Publication Committee be endowed with a working capital of not less than twenty-five thousand dollars; 2. That the General Assembly earnestly request all their churches to make a special contribution for this object in the month of October next; and 3. That the Publication Committee be authorized, in their discretion, to employ an agent for the furtherance of this design.

"It appears from the report before us, that less than one-half the number of our churches have done anything for the publication cause; a fact which plainly and painfully suggests the want of instruction on the relations of this cause to our denominational interests, as well as the promotion of sound doctrine and godliness among the people. The committee would therefore recommend, 4. That the Assembly earnestly request the pastors to preach to their congregations on this subject, in connection with the call for a contribution in October. . . .

"The General Assembly last year ordered that churches making collections for the publication cause should be allowed to receive one-half the amount of their contributions in publications of the committee. This provision it is thought desirable should be renewed and brought to the attention of the churches." . . .

10. *Presbyterial Depositories recommended.*

"The suggestion is an important one, that in Synods or Presbyteries a small amount of capital might be invested in the committee's publications; and these put into the hands of some suitable person, in a central position, for sale. The receipts from sales, being reinvested from time to time, a perpetual stock would be maintained.

"The report was adopted."—*Minutes*, 1860, pp. 246–248.

SECTION 6.—TRUSTEES OF THE PRESBYTERIAN HOUSE.

1. Preliminary action and acceptance of the House conditionally authorized. Legal Position of the Assembly.—2. The trustees.—3. The charter. The Board of Trust enlarged to ten,—five ministers and five laymen. Duties and powers of the trustees.—4. The charter.—5. The trustees under the charter.—6. The legal title secured.

1. *Preliminary Action.*

[The first action of the General Assembly on the subject of a publication house, appears in the minutes for 1853, under date Monday, May 30. A committee having been appointed to consider the report of the Standing Committee for the Preparation and Publication of Doctrinal Tracts (now the Presbyterian Publication Committee), report, *inter alia*, as follows, and their report was adopted :]

"4. That the committee [the Doctrinal Tract Committee] be authorized to take such measures as they may deem advisable, to secure the necessary funds for the erection of a house of publication."—*Minutes*, 1853, p. 330.

[Under date Monday, May 22, 1854, the Committee of Bills and Overtures report:]

"Overture No. 2. On a Presbyterian Publication House. The committee recommend the acceptance of the overture, and its reference to a special committee, to report to this Assembly." Adopted.

[Same date:] "The Assembly voted to hear statements from John A. Brown, Esq., of this city [Philadelphia], in reference to the Presbyterian Publication House, when the thanks of the Assembly were tendered to Mr. Brown for the information imparted."

[Same date:] "The unfinished business of the morning,—the consideration of the report of the Standing Committee on the Publication of Doctrinal Tracts,—was resumed; when it was

"*Resolved*, That the report just read be referred to a select committee of nine, with directions to consider the whole subject of the publication of books and tracts by authority of the General Assembly, and also Overture No. 2, upon the Presbyterian Publication House."

[Under date Friday, May 26:] "The Committee on the Polity of the Church, to whom was referred the report on the subject of the legal powers, claims, and liabilities of the General Assembly, submitted the following report:

"1. Whereas, we regard the rights of this body as complete under the charter of 1799, therefore no action is required in respect to a new charter.

"2. [Relates to the Trustees of the Church Erection Fund.]

"3. It is recommended that, provided this General Assembly appoint a Board of Trustees of the Presbyterian Publication House, or for any other specific purpose, in the city of Philadelphia, that that board obtain a special act of incorporation under the laws of this State; and that a committee of three members of the legal profession be appointed, to whom the subject shall be committed, with instructions to examine and determine the question, whether a general provision in said charter or act of incorporation, like that provided for in the preceding article, will, in respect to all the interests of the Church, be safe and expedient; and if they so judge, to secure its insertion.

"The report was adopted, and Messrs. Samuel H. Perkins, Henry J. Williams, and Hon. William Darling were appointed the committee."

[The "provision" referred to in the "preceding article," is in the following words: "A general provision authorizing them to hold in trust for this Assembly any property committed to them by donations, bequests, or otherwise."]—*Minutes,* 1854, pp. 502, 503.

[The report of the committee of three legal gentlemen is contained in the First Annual Report of the Board of Trustees of the Presbyterian House to the General Assembly, May 21, 1855.]

"By the fourth section of the act of incorporation, the trustees and their successors have power to execute any trusts that may be confided to them. This section was submitted to the committee of three members of the legal profession, appointed by the last General Assembly. They thought it both safe and expedient, with respect to all the interests of the Church, and its insertion was accordingly secured as recommended." —*Minutes,* 1855, pp. 52, 53.

Acceptance of the House conditionally authorized.

"The committee finally recommend, that the Assembly take its possession of the house in Philadelphia, referred to in the overture from the Presbytery of Philadelphia 4th, as a House of Publication, on the terms and conditions, as to the price and payments, following, viz.:

"The General Assembly will authorize the conditional acceptance of the property, so soon as $12,500 shall have been pledged by responsible persons, connected with the churches of Philadelphia; and, when this pledge has thus been made, suitable measures shall be authorized to raise a like sum of $12,500; and the balance—say $20,000—shall be left on mortgage, to be liquidated by a sinking-fund arising from the annual proceeds of the House. When the measures to complete the purchase have been perfected, the Assembly will take the property unconditionally; and, to the end that the legal measures may be taken to perfect the title prior to the next meeting of the Assembly, five trustees of the House of Publication shall be elected, who shall be authorized to obtain an act of incorporation."—*Minutes,* 1854, p. 508.

2. *Trustees.*

"The committee to nominate members of the Doctrinal Tract Committee and Trustees for the Presbyterian Publication House, made the following report, which was adopted:

"Trustees of the Presbyterian Publication House: Messrs. J. A. Brown, S. H. Perkins, C. S. Wurts, M. W. Baldwin, and J. C. Farr."—*Minutes,* 1854, p. 510.

3. *The Charter accepted. Board of Trust enlarged; Duties and Powers.*

"The committee to whom was referred the report of the trustees of the Presbyterian House, and of the Publication Committee, have considered the same, and report the following preamble and resolutions, for the adoption of the Assembly, namely:

"Whereas, the Legislature of the State of Pennsylvania, by an act approved by the Governor, April 21, 1855, incorporated 'The Trustees of the Presbyterian House,' in Philadelphia, who are by said act to be elected by this body, therefore

"*Resolved*, by the General Assembly of the Presbyterian Church in the United States of America: 1. That the said charter be, and the same is hereby accepted; and that the trustees, created by said act of incorporation, be directed to perform all the duties required by their appointment.

"*Resolved*, 2. That the said trustees be directed to give such official notification to the proper authorities of the State of Pennsylvania, as may be necessary, of the acceptance of the charter by the General Assembly.

"*Resolved*, 3. That the Assembly do now elect ten trustees, under this charter, five of whom shall be ministers, and five laymen, all of whom shall be connected with some Presbytery or church under the care of the General Assembly.

"*Resolved*, 4. That the first meeting of the trustees shall be at such time and place as shall be fixed by the trustee first elected, or in case of his inability to act, the trustee next elected, who shall act as chairman, until the board is constituted by the election of a president and secretary.

"*Resolved*, 5. That the trustees, at their first meeting, be directed to divide themselves into two portions, and in such manner that there shall always be in the board five ministers and five laymen.

"*Resolved*, 6. That, in electing these trustees, a nomination shall be made in the Assembly, and that the election shall be by ballot on the day following that on which the nomination is made.

"*Resolved*, 7. That these trustees be directed to keep an accurate record of all their proceedings, and report the same annually to the Assembly.

"*Resolved*, 8. That these trustees be directed to take such measures for raising the amount pledged by the last Assembly, for the purchase of the 'Presbyterian House,' as they may deem expedient and proper.

"*Resolved*, 12. That the trustees of the Presbyterian House be directed to report to the next Assembly a plan of rules and regulations for the government of said trustees in the discharge of their duties.

"Nominations for trustees of the Presbyterian House were made; the election to take place to-morrow."—*Minutes*, 1855, pp. 26, 27.

4. *The Charter.*

"AN ACT TO INCORPORATE THE TRUSTEES OF THE PRESBYTERIAN HOUSE.

"*Whereas*, the General Assembly of the Presbyterian Church in the United States of America, which held its sessions in the first Presbyterian Church, on Washington Square, in the city of Philadelphia, in May, Anno Domini one thousand eight hundred and fifty-four, did appoint John A. Brown, Samuel H. Perkins, Charles S. Wurts, Matthew W. Baldwin, and John C. Farr, trustees of the Presbyterian Publication House, and recommended that the said Board obtain an act of incorporation under the laws of this State, and that the said act should contain a general provision, authorizing the said trustees to hold in trust for said Assembly any property committed to them by donations, bequests, or otherwise;

"*And whereas*, several gentlemen in the city of Philadelphia, feeling the necessity of some suitable place for the business of the societies and churches connected with the said Assembly, purchased a property for that purpose, which they are desirous of conveying to the said trustees;

"*And whereas*, the said trustees will labor under serious disadvantages, as to receiving and holding the title of said property, as well as any that may be committed to them by donations, bequests, or otherwise, in trust for said Assembly; therefore,

"SEC. 1. *Be it enacted by the Senate and House of Representatives of the Commonwealth of Pennsylvania, in General Assembly met, and it is hereby enacted by the authority of the same*, That John A. Brown, Samuel H. Perkins, Charles S. Wurts, Matthew W. Baldwin, and John C. Farr, citizens of the United States and of this Commonwealth, and their successors, are hereby constituted and declared to be a body politic and corporate, by the name of '*The Trustees of the Presbyterian House*;' and as such shall have perpetual succession, and be able to sue and be sued, and to purchase and receive, take and hold, to them and their successors forever, lands, tenements, and hereditaments, goods, money, and chattels, and all kinds of property and estate, which may be devised, or bequeathed, or given to them, or to the said Assembly for them, and the same to sell, alien, demise, and convey; also to make a common seal, and the same to alter and renew at their pleasure; and also to make such rules, by-laws, and ordinances, as may be needful for the government of said corporation, and not inconsistent with the Constitution and laws of the United States and of this State: *Provided always*, That the clear yearly income of the real estate held by the said corporation shall not at any time exceed the sum of five thousand dollars.

"SEC. 2. That the trustees above named shall hold their office till the first day of June, Anno Domini one thousand eight hundred and fifty-five, and until their successors are duly qualified to take their places, who shall be chosen by the said Assembly and their successors, who may, at any annual meeting, increase the number of said trustees to ten, if in their judgment the interest of the churches under their care require it.

"SEC. 3. That the said Assembly and their successors shall, at their annual meeting in each and every year, wherever held, elect at least five trustees, who shall hold their office for one year, and until their successors are elected and qualified: *Provided*, That the said corporators shall be citizens of Pennsylvania.

"SEC. 4. That the trustees hereby incorporated, and their successors, shall, subject to the direction of the said Assembly and their successors, have full power to manage all funds, property, and effects committed to their care by gift, purchase, bequest, or otherwise, and to execute any trusts confided to them by the said General Assembly or their successors, in such manner as shall be deemed most advantageous, and not contrary to law, or the intention of the donor or testator.

"SEC. 5. That the act, entitled 'An act to incorporate the trustees of the Constitutional Presbyterian Publication House,' approved the thirteenth day of April, Anno Domini one thousand eight hundred and fifty-five, be, and the same is, hereby repealed.

"HENRY K. STRONG,
"Speaker of the House of Representatives.

"WM. M. HIESTER,
"Speaker of the Senate.

"Approved the twenty-first day of April, Anno Domini one thousand eight hundred and fifty-five.

"JAMES POLLOCK."

—*Minutes*, 1855, pp. 53, 54.

5. *The Trustees.*

"As trustees of the Presbyterian House, the following individuals were elected: John A. Brown, M. W. Baldwin, Charles S. Wurts, Samuel H. Perkins, John C. Farr, Rev. Albert Barnes, Rev. Thomas Brainerd, D.D., Rev. Benjamin J. Wallace, Rev. Henry Darling, and Rev. David H. Riddle, D.D."—*Minutes*, 1855, p. 29.

6. *The Legal Title secured through the Liberality of John A. Brown, Esq.*

"*Resolved*, That the General Assembly notice with pleasure the manifestation of promptness and liberality in the president of the Board of Trustees of the Presbyterian House, John A. Brown, Esq., of Philadelphia, who, by a munificent donation, has secured to the trustees the legal title of the Presbyterian House."—*Minutes*, 1857, p. 410.

SECTION 6.—THE EDUCATION COMMITTEE.

1. Formation of the Permanent Committee. Located in New York. Consisting of fifteen, seven of whom must reside in or near New York. Five constitute a quorum. Classes and term of office. Duties of the committee. The Synods and Presbyteries urged to co-operate. Plans of co-operation.—2. Organization and report of the committee. Plan for aiding beneficiaries, adopted.—3. The plan of the committee endorsed and commended. The charter approved and accepted. Candidates to retain their Church and Presbyterial relations unchanged during their studies. The act of incorporation.—4. The plan again commended. No student ought to receive from educational funds a larger appropriation than is contemplated by the plan of the Assembly. The endowment of scholarships urged.—5. The committee instructed to continue their work, and to revise the plan and submit it to the Presbyteries.

1. *Formation of the Permanent Committee.*

[In 1854, the committee reported a plan, which was adopted, and which will be found substantially merged in the following action of 1856. See Minutes, 1854, pp. 506, 507.]

"The special committee, to whom was referred the report of the Permanent Committee on the education of young men for the Gospel ministry, presented a report, which was adopted, and is as follows:

"The committee to whom was referred the reports of the Committee on Education, and of the several education societies co-operating with this Assembly, respectfully report, that, having carefully considered the resolutions proposed by the Committee on Education, they would recommend their adoption by the Assembly, with divers alterations and additions, in the following form:

"*Resolved*, 1. That a committee of fifteen ministers and members of the Presbyterian Church, of whom five shall be laymen, shall be appointed by the General Assembly, to be called *The Permanent Committee on Education for the Ministry;* seven at least of whom shall reside in or near the city of New York, which shall be the seat of its operations. Five members of this committee shall constitute a quorum; but for the election of a secretary of education, or for action upon his salary, a majority shall be necessary to constitute a quorum.

"*Resolved*, 2. This committee, as thus constituted, shall divide itself into three equal classes,—the first, second, and third,—whose terms of office shall expire respectively in one, two, and three years. The General Assembly shall annually elect, after its first organization, five members of this committee for three years, to fill such vacancies. It shall also fill any vacancy which may have occurred in the other classes. The committee shall have power to fill any vacancies occurring in the interval between the sessions of two Assemblies, for such an interval.

"*Resolved*, 3. The duties of the Assembly's committee shall be, to superintend the whole cause of education in behalf of the Assembly; to appoint a general secretary; to determine his salary and direct his movements; and also a treasurer, to take charge of the funds which may be collected and paid into the treasury, for the purposes of education; to devise and adopt such principles, rules, and regulations, in reference to aiding candidates for the ministry, as they shall deem proper and feasible; to receive and disburse funds raised within the bounds of the Presbyterian Church or elsewhere, and, when so directed by the donors, to invest funds for the purposes of ministerial education; to take the general oversight of such beneficiaries as receive assistance directly from the treasury of the committee; to make a full annual report of all that has been done, so far as they can learn, throughout the Church in behalf of education for the ministry;—in a word, to do all that is proper and necessary to the development of an educational spirit and activity throughout the Church, and the successful prosecution of this great and important cause of Christian benevolence.

"*Resolved*, 4. It shall be the duty of the secretary of Education to visit, as far as may be, the Synods, Presbyteries, and churches throughout our bounds, for the purpose of awakening the interest and concentrating the energies of the whole Church; to visit the colleges and seminaries where young men, aided by the Permanent Committee, are pursuing their studies, for the purpose of counsel and encouragement, and for the purpose of presenting to young men the claims of the ministry upon them; to present the cause to the churches and collect funds as directed by the Assembly's committee; and to make a quarterly report, in writing, of his labors to the said committee.

"*Resolved*, 5. The treasurer of the committee shall render quarterly accounts of all moneys received and disbursed; and he shall pay out no moneys, unless thus directed by a written order of the committee, which order or orders shall constitute his vouchers.

"*Resolved*, 6. The Synods, Presbyteries, and churches are earnestly requested to co-operate with the Assembly's committee in a work of such urgent and inestimable importance; to correspond with them on all points, where mutual sympathy and action are necessary to bring up the cause to its legitimate position in the prayers and efforts of God's people; to search out candidates for the ministry within their respective bounds, and to raise funds necessary for their support while in a course of preparation for the sacred office. It is particularly urged upon them to take up an annual collection in behalf of the education cause, which, if not required within their own bounds, may be transmitted to the treasury of the Assembly's committee, to be used for the support of such beneficiaries as may be under their patronage.

"*Resolved*, 7. Synods, Presbyteries, and churches may, at their own election, carry forward educational operations within their bounds, through their own agencies and local organizations, and assist their young men directly from their own funds, and according to their own rules and regulations, or operate through the Assembly's committee, contributing their funds to the general treasury, and placing their candidates under the patronage and supervision of the said committee. Where the former of these methods is adopted, it is very desirable that a yearly report be made to the Permanent Committee, in order that the combined results of the whole cause may appear in the committee's annual report to the General Assembly.

"*Resolved*, 8. The Permanent Committee shall be empowered to make such arrangements with the Central American Education Society at New York, and the Philadelphia Education Society at Philadelphia, as shall insure, if possible, the harmonious co-operation of these societies in the work of educating men for the Gospel ministry.

"*Resolved*, 9. It is recommended that the young men aided by the Assembly's committee, be ordinarily placed as soon as possible under the care of Presbyteries; and that in all ordinary cases they be licensed, if convenient, by the Presbyteries to which they naturally belong. [See Form of Government, chap. xiv, sec. 2.]

"*Resolved*, 10. That it be recommended that the annual collection in aid of education for the ministry be taken up on the Sabbath succeeding the day of prayer for colleges; and it is also recommended that an appropriate sermon be preached on the occasion of that collection.

"*Resolved*, 11. That the Presbyteries be directed to report to the General Assembly the amounts contributed by the several churches under their care, in aid of the education of young men for the ministry, and that the said sums be placed in a separate column in the statistical minutes of the Assembly.

"The following were appointed the Education Committee, in accordance with the above resolutions: Rev. John J. Owen, D.D., Rev. George L. Prentiss, D.D., Rev. Asa D. Smith, D.D., Mr. Jesse W. Benedict, Mr. Anson G. Phelps, Mr. Joseph B. Sheffield, Mr. Walter S. Griffith, Mr. William A. Booth, Rev. John Jenkins, Rev. George Duffield, Jr., Hon. William Darling, Rev. Jonathan F. Stearns, D.D., Rev. Henry Smith, D.D., Rev. Harvey Curtis, and Hon. William Jessup, LL.D."—
—*Minutes*, 1856, pp. 222–224.

2. *Organization and Report of Committee. Plan for aiding Beneficiaries.*

"The Standing Committee, to whom was referred the report of the Permanent Committee on Education for the Ministry, respectfully report, recommending the adoption of the following resolutions:

"*Resolved*, 1. The General Assembly recognizes, with gratitude to God, the organization of the Permanent Committee on Education for the Ministry, and the appointment of a General Secretary, Rev. Thornton A.

Mills, D.D., who has entered on the duties of his office; also, the fact that the report of the committee presents and enforces the foundation principles of this work, especially in its relation to churches and Presbyteries.

"*Resolved*, 2. The Assembly, deeply impressed with the importance of a plan of action which shall develop the resources of the whole Church, and bring each section of the Church to the work of training its own ministry, adopts the arrangement recommended in the report of the Permanent Committee, with some additions and alterations, in the following form:

"1. It is the duty of the Church, in obedience to the Saviour's last command to preach the Gospel to every creature, to give constant and becoming attention to the increase of the ministry.

"2. The Presbyterian Church, in its congregations, Sessions, Presbyteries, Synods, and General Assembly, possesses a superior system of means for conducting this work in a most successful manner.

"3. It is particularly desirable that each Presbytery should make the subject of the ministry a topic of serious consideration in its stated meetings, at least once every year, and adopt arrangements to have presented to the churches, through their own ministers as far as possible, the wants of our Church, our country, and the world, in this respect; to press on young men their duty to give themselves to this work; on parents their obligation to dedicate their children to it, and train them for it; and on individual churches their privilege and duty to see that all their sons, who give promise of suitable qualifications for the ministry, are sought out and encouraged to enter it; to make adequate provision for the education of all such as are in circumstances to need their aid, and who show by their characters and improvement that they are worthy of it; and to see that in each church an annual collection is made in behalf of this cause.

"4. It is important that the claims of the Christian ministry on pious young men, in a course of education, should be publicly presented once every year in all the colleges within our bounds; and it is recommended that the general secretary, in connection with the officers in these institutions, secure the performance of this service.

"5. While the General Assembly does not design to interfere with the action of separate churches and Presbyteries, or the combined action of a number of them in their synodical capacity, it decidedly recommends its Permanent Committee as the bond of union and medium of co-operation in this work; and it is hereby urged upon each Presbytery and Synod, whether co-operating or not with that committee, to forward, through its stated clerk, to said Permanent Committee, at some time in the month of April in each year, a full report of its doings, in reply to such questions as may be proposed to it; and the information so given shall be embodied in the annual report of the committee to the General Assembly.

"6. Each Presbytery, designing to co-operate with the Permanent Committee, shall appoint annually a Standing Committee on Education for the Ministry, whose duty it shall be to examine and recommend, in the vacation of the Presbytery, such young men as require assistance from the funds at the disposal of the Permanent Committee; and to exercise over them such pastoral supervision as may be possible, while they are prosecuting their studies. And all such committees are hereby enjoined, to give strict attention to the rules prescribed by the Permanent Committee, in any recommendation which they may make, so as to avert dishonor from this enterprise of the Church, and avoid the waste and misapplication of its funds.

"7. Every Presbytery, co-operating with the Permanent Committee by presenting the subject to its churches annually, and taking collections to be paid to the general treasury, shall be entitled, as far as the means placed at the disposal of that committee will allow, to receive aid for all candidates for the ministry under its care, however much the appropriations to them may exceed the contributions of such Presbytery.

"8. It is recommended to all the churches so to arrange their contributions to benevolent operations, that the uniform time for that in behalf of education for the ministry shall be the Sabbath preceding, or succeeding the last Thursday in February of each year, the day of the Annual Concert of Prayer for Colleges.

"9. As it is desirable that this cause should assume a prominent and permanent place in the contributions of the churches, it is recommended, to those whom Providence has favored with means, to endow temporary scholarships, by the contribution of the requisite sum each year to assist a student through his theological course; or the contribution of such a sum each year to assist one through his literary and theological course; or by the establishment of permanent scholarships by donations or legacies, under the management of the Permanent Committee; and, to afford facility and security in doing this, the Permanent Committee are hereby directed to apply to the Legislature of the State of New York for a suitable act of incorporation. And, until such act is obtained, individuals designing permanent gifts or legacies, are requested to place them in the legal charge of the trustees of the Presbyterian House in Philadelphia, for the use of the Permanent Committee on Education for the Ministry.

"10. The General Assembly would not claim any authority over the institutions where our ministry are educated; but it is hereby requested of the Faculties of the Union and Auburn Theological Seminaries in New York, of Lane Seminary near Cincinnati, and Maryville Seminary in Tennessee, and of any other similar institutions hereafter established, to furnish the General Assembly each year, through its Permanent Committee on Education for the Ministry, with a written statement of their condition, advantages, and prospects, the names of their professors, the ordinary yearly expenses, and any other matters of general interest to the Church, to be read to the Assembly, and published as an appendix to the annual report of the said committee; and the general secretary is hereby charged with the duty of presenting this request annually to said Faculties, in time to receive their written reports before the meeting of the General Assembly.

"*Resolved*, 3. This General Assembly approves the rules adopted by the Permanent Committee, for aiding young men in their preparatory studies for the ministry, with some alterations, as fitted to prevent the introduction of incompetent and unworthy men to this office, and at the same time to afford suitable encouragement to those whose piety and talents give promise of usefulness. When any alterations are made in these rules, the Permanent Committee are requested to report the same to the General Assembly.

"PLAN FOR AIDING BENEFICIARIES.

"1. Each applicant for assistance shall present a certificate of recommendation from a Presbytery (or its Standing Committee on Education), stating that he has been in the communion of the Church at least one year, and that he has been carefully examined as to his experimental piety, his motives for desiring the sacred office, his attachment to the doctrines of the Presbyterian Church, his general habits, his prudence, his talents, his studies, his gifts for public speaking, his need of assistance, his disposition to do all in his power to sustain himself, and his willingness to observe the rules of the committee. Such certificate must also state, whether the candidate is in his academic, collegiate, or theological course, and the amount requisite to carry him through the first year.

"2. While it is highly desirable, that all who receive assistance should be under the supervision of the Presbyteries to which they would naturally belong, and should be recommended by them, yet if, owing to the present position of the education cause, or other important reasons, a Presbyterial certificate cannot be obtained, it may, at the option of the Permanent Committee, be substituted by a certificate of the same import, from any examining committee, appointed by them for such purposes, at any educational institution where the student is pursuing his course.

"3. The amount granted to any applicant shall not, unless in very peculiar circumstances, exceed one hundred dollars for the academic, one hundred and twenty dollars for the collegiate, and one hundred and forty for the theological course per annum, to be paid in quarterly instalments upon the return of schedules to be filled up by the student and his instructors, and the approbation of the same by the Permanent Committee.

"4. Each applicant shall give a receipt or acknowledgment to the treasurer, for the amount which from time to time he may receive, promising to repay the same with interest, if he fail to enter upon the work of the ministry within a reasonable time, or turn aside to any secular pursuit; unless the Presbytery to which he belongs shall certify, that there are good reasons for his relinquishing the active duties of the office, and recommend the cancelling of the obligation.

"5. Individuals receiving aid shall be under the pastoral supervision of the Presbyteries recommending them, and also of the general secretary of the Permanent Committee; and will be expected to undergo renewed examinations on passing from one grade of their general course to another.

"6. No payment shall be made in advance.

"7. As the appropriations of the committee are made on the principle of helping those who help themselves, and are insufficient for the entire support of a student, it is expected, that the student and his friends will make all proper exertions to assist in defraying the expenses of his education.

"8. Each student aided is required to pursue a thorough course of study preparatory to a three years' course of theological studies, unless the Permanent Committee, and the Presbytery under whose care he is, in the exercise of a wise discretion, shall decide that his circumstances require that his studies shall be abbreviated.

"9. When any student shall find it necessary to relinquish study for a time, to teach, or otherwise increase his means of support, he shall first obtain the consent of the Permanent Committee; and, if he shall not be absent from study more than three months, his appropriations will be continued; but if longer, they will be discontinued, or continued in part, according to circumstances.

"10. When a student has ceased, for a period longer than a year, to receive assistance from the committee, he shall be required to produce new testimonials before his name can be restored to the roll.

"11. When the official relation between a student and the committee ceases, or is about to cease, he is required to notify the general secretary of the fact, stating the reason.

"12. The reception of an appropriation, by a student, shall be considered as expressing a promise, to comply with all the rules and regulations of the committee.

"13. If at any time there be discovered in any student such defect in capacity, diligence, prudence, and especially in piety, as would render his introduction into the ministry a doubtful measure, it shall be considered the sacred duty of the committee to withdraw their appropriations. Students shall also cease to receive assistance, when their health shall become such as to unfit them for study, and for the work of the ministry; when they are manifestly improvident, and contract debts without reasonable prospects of payment; when they marry; when they receive the assistance of any other educational committee; when they fail to make the regular returns; or cease, by change of circumstances, to need aid.

"14. As all intellectual acquisitions are comparatively of little value without the cultivation of piety, it is expected and required of every candidate, to pay special attention to the practical duties of religion; such as reading the Scriptures, secret prayer and meditation; to attend upon religious meetings on the Sabbath, and during the week; to endeavor to promote the salvation of others; and to exhibit at all times a pious and consistent example.

"*Resolved*, 4. While the Assembly feels the importance of a thorough organization of the Church, for the accomplishment of the work of ministerial education, it is at the same time deeply convinced that success will not attend the enterprise, unless the earnest efforts of its friends are united with prayer to God, that, by the abundant outpouring of the

Spirit, the life of the Church may be made more vigorous, and large numbers of the youth of our land be converted to Christ.

"*Resolved*, 5. The General Assembly recommends the observance of the last Thursday in February as a day of prayer for the blessing of God on our various institutions of learning.

"*Resolved*, 6. That the election to fill the vacancies in the Permanent Committee be the first order of the day for Friday morning, and that the election be by ballot.

"*Resolved*, 7. That the report of the Permanent Committee be published under their direction, and circulated through all the churches.

"The same committee reported the following resolution, which was adopted :

"*Resolved*, That the memorial of the Presbytery of Iowa City, on the subject of Christian education, asking the General Assembly, through its Permanent Committee on Education for the Ministry, to aid in erecting academies and collegiate institutions, be referred to that committee, with instructions to consider and extend aid at their discretion during the year; and to report to the next General Assembly."—*Minutes*, 1857, pp. 388–392.

3. *Injunctions of the Assembly of* 1858. *The Charter approved and accepted.*

"*Resolved*, That this Assembly find, in the practical workings of the plan for ministerial education inaugurated by the last General Assembly, reason to regard it with increasing confidence, and consider it eminently wise, and admirably adapted to develop the zeal and activity of the whole Church in this department of her duty.

"*Resolved*, That in laying the foundation for this work in a living Christianity of the body, and devolving the execution of it on individual churches and Presbyteries, the Assembly has proposed the most evangelical and effective method of accomplishing the enterprise.

"*Resolved*, That while the responsibility of performing this part of her mission rests on Christian parents, and the individual members and elders of the Church, it also presses with peculiar weight on ministers; and from a becoming spirit and example in their daily labor, and a faithful and frequent presentation to Christian parents and youth of their obligations of covenanted consecration, the happiest results may be reasonably expected.

"*Resolved*, That it is deeply to be lamented that the Saviour's command, 'Pray ye the Lord of the harvest that he would send forth laborers into his harvest,' has so extensively passed from the minds and hearts of his people, and that this Assembly admonish all its ministers and churches of this neglect, and earnestly exhort them to give attention to it in their private, domestic, social, and public devotions, and that they especially remember it at the monthly concert, as well as at the annual concert of prayer for educational institutions, on the last Thursday of February.

"*Resolved*, That inasmuch as a large number of Presbyteries have disregarded the urgent recommendation of the last Assembly to forward full reports of their action in reference to ministerial education, this Assembly readopts that recommendation, considering a faithful compliance with it essential to a successful enlistment of the whole Church in this important enterprise.

"*Resolved*, That it is highly desirable that the subject of the increase of the ministry should be annually presented to the churches on the Sabbath preceding or succeeding the annual concert of prayer for colleges, and that contributions be made on one of the Sabbaths above named, when it will not interfere with or disturb systematic arrangements already adopted.

"*Resolved*, That it is the conviction of this Assembly that a large and useful increase of the ministry cannot be secured without constant vigilance on the part of the Presbyteries in the introduction of men into the sacred office, in arrangements to direct their efforts and facilitate their settlement, and in holding them to a just responsibility in the discharge of their work, and also without a disposition on the part of the churches to furnish it with an adequate and equitable support.

"*Resolved*, That the Assembly recommend, as a general principle, that candidates for the ministry, especially those who are connected with churches under the care of our newer and smaller Presbyteries, retain their church and Presbyterial relations unchanged during the progress of their studies.

"*Resolved*, That the Permanent Committee be directed to publish this annual report, or such portions of it as they may deem advisable."

"ACT OF INCORPORATION.

"An Act to incorporate the Permanent Committee on Education for the Ministry, of the General Assembly of the Presbyterian Church in the United States of America.

"The people of the State of New York, as represented in Senate and Assembly, do enact as follows:

"SEC. 1. John J. Owen, Asa D. Smith, George L. Prentiss, William A. Booth, Joseph B. Sheffield, Jesse W. Benedict, Walter S. Griffith, Anson G. Phelps, William Hogarth, Jonathan F. Stearns, Henry Smith, Harvey Curtis, John Jenkins, William Darling, and William Jessup (designated for the purpose by the General Assembly of the Presbyterian Church, which met in Cleveland, Ohio, in May, eighteen hundred and fifty-seven), and their successors in office, are hereby constituted a body corporate and politic, by the name of 'The Permanent Committee on Education for the Ministry of the General Assembly of the Presbyterian Church in the United States of America;' whose duty it shall be to superintend the whole cause of education in behalf of the said General Assembly, as said General Assembly may from time to time direct; also to receive, take charge of, and disburse any property or funds which at any time, and from time to time, may be intrusted to said General Assembly, or said Permanent Committee, for educational purposes.

"SEC. 2. The said corporation shall possess the general powers, and be subject to the provisions contained in title three, of chapter eighteen of the first part of the Revised Statutes, so far as the same are applicable, and have not been repealed or modified.

"SEC. 3. The management and disposition of the affairs and funds of said corporation shall be vested in the individuals named in the first section of this act, and their successors in office, who shall remain in office for such period, and be displaced and succeeded by others, to be elected at such time and in such manner as the said General Assembly shall direct and appoint.

"SEC. 4. The said corporation shall in law be capable of taking, receiving, and holding any real or personal estate which has been or may hereafter be given, devised, or bequeathed to it, or to said General Assembly, for the purposes aforesaid, or which may accrue from the use of the same; but the said corporation shall not take and hold real and personal estate above the sum of two hundred thousand dollars.

"SEC. 5. This act shall take effect immediately.

"Passed April 17, 1858."

"APPROVAL BY THE GENERAL ASSEMBLY.

"*Resolved*, That the Assembly approve of the act of incorporation obtained by the Permanent Committee of Education, from the Legislature of New York, and of its acceptance by that committee; and that said committee thus incorporated, is hereby cordially and confidently recommended to such persons as may be disposed to devote property to ministerial education, as a safe and responsible agency for its investment and disbursement."—*Minutes,* 1858, pp. 597, 598.

4. *Report and Resolutions of* 1859. *Endowment of Scholarships urged.*

"The committee, therefore, recommend to the General Assembly the adoption of the following resolutions:

"1. That the Assembly has undiminished confidence in the plan for promoting the increase of the ministry, adopted by the Assembly of 1857; the more it is examined, and the better it is understood, the more worthy of confidence does it appear.

"2. That, though the Permanent Committee and their secretary have encountered many embarrassments, in the incipiency of their enterprise, yet, in the judgment of the Assembly, they are doing a great work; and we heartily concur with the two Assemblies last past, in commending them to the favor of the churches.

"3. That the ultimate result towards which we should aim, is the universal adoption of this plan, as soon as practicable, and that it be commended to the favorable notice of all our Presbyteries; and further, that all local societies within our bounds, whose existence seems necessary for the time being, be requested, as far as possible, to adjust themselves to it.

"4. That, in the judgment of this Assembly, no student ought to receive from educational funds a larger appropriation than is contemplated in the plan of the General Assembly; and that ministers, and professors in colleges and seminaries, be requested to discountenance all partiality, and scrupulously adhere to the Assembly's plan in this regard.

"5. That, for this purpose, *all* Presbyteries and colleges and theological seminaries be requested to send to the Permanent Committee the names of all students under their care who receive aid, with the amount apportioned by them.

"6. That, in order to facilitate the connection of the Permanent Committee with every part of the Church, every Synod be requested to appoint a corresponding member, as a medium of communication between the Committee and the Presbyteries, pastors, and churches.

"7. That the common mode of raising funds for this cause is, at present, a necessity; but that the perfection of the work, in the judgment of the Assembly, is the endowment of scholarships, held in trust by the Assembly's Committee under its charter; and that anything short of this is liable to affect injuriously the churches and the young men who receive their benefactions.

"8. That we cannot disguise the fact, that no plans or rules can compensate for the want of a livelier interest on this subject in all our churches; which interest would obviate all our difficulties, and silence all complaints in all parts of the Church.

"9. That the Permanent Committee be requested to appeal to the churches to make immediate and special efforts to replenish the general treasury for education; and that they be urged to contribute both for present exigencies and wants, and also for a permanent endowment, that the support of applicants may not depend upon the scanty and uncertain contributions of the Church.

"10. That it is the opinion of this Assembly, that $35,000, which is but little more than twenty-five cents for each member in our churches, is the very least amount that our Church, or its members, ought to be content to raise for this cause during the coming year." . . .—*Minutes*, 1859, p. 34–36.

5. *Committee to revise the Plan, and submit it to the Presbyteries.*

"*Resolved*, 1. That the Permanent Committee continue their work as heretofore; and that they be instructed, at an early day, to revise the present plan of the Assembly, and submit the revised plan to the Presbyteries, with the earnest request that they express their views and wishes concerning it to the Permanent Committee previous to the meeting of the next Assembly; and that Rev. Albert Barnes, D. Howe Allen, D.D., Ezra A. Huntington, D.D., and Henry B. Smith, D.D., be appointed to confer with said committee concerning the revision of the plan.

"*Resolved*, 2. That this Assembly are gratified to learn that the Permanent Committee have begun to aid students from their own treasury; and that the churches be earnestly requested to replenish that treasury, that the work may go on in a manner worthy of the cause and of the Church at large."—*Minutes*, 1860, p. 246.

SECTION 7.—THE COMMITTEE ON FOREIGN MISSIONS.

1. Origin of the committee. The Permanent Committee established.—2. The committee enlarged to twelve, and divided into three classes.—3. Duties of the committee.—4. Formation of Foreign Presbyteries encouraged. The Synod of New York and New Jersey empowered to form and receive such Presbyteries.—5. Report of 1860. The jubilee year.

1. *Origin of the Committee. Permanent Committee established.*

[In 1850, the subject of "erection of Presbyteries in foreign lands," was referred to a select committee, to report next year. Minutes, 1850, p. 320. This committee having failed to report, was discharged, and the subject recommitted to a new committee. Minutes, 1851, p. 10. Committee continued, 1852, p. 173; 1853, p. 342. In 1854, the committee reported, viz.:]

"The correspondence with ministers in connection with our Church on foreign missionary ground, laboring under the direction of the American Board of Commissioners for Foreign Missions, has been carried out according to the instructions of the General Assembly.

"More than twenty responses have been received, in answer to the committee's circular. These communications are characterized by a thoughtful discrimination, a spirit of sincere regard for our Church, and a desire to secure harmonious and successful action in the prosecution of the missionary work.

"From a careful review of this correspondence, and a consideration of the whole subject, your committee would recommend,

"1. That this Assembly regard it as inexpedient to take any measures, at present, for organizing Presbyteries or churches on foreign missionary ground.

"2. That an annual correspondence be recommended to be kept up between our foreign missionaries and the Presbyteries to which they respectively belong.

"3. That, inasmuch as it has hitherto been found to be impracticable to form distinctive Presbyterian organizations among the converted heathen, and inasmuch as the obstacles which have hitherto existed may possibly be removed by further conference with our foreign missionaries and with the Prudential Committee of the A. B. C. F. M., a Standing Committee of five ministers shall be appointed, who shall take charge of this whole subject, correspond further with our missionaries and the Prudential Committee above referred to, and report to the Assembly from year to year.

"The report was adopted; and Rev. Joel Parker, D.D., Rev. James W. McLane, D.D., Rev. David O. Allen, D.D., Rev. Edwin F. Hatfield, D.D., and Rev. Henry Darling, were appointed the Standing Committee provided for in this report."—*Minutes,* 1854, p. 511.

2. *The Committee Enlarged and Divided into Three Classes.*

"*Resolved,* That Rev. Albert Barnes, and Messrs. John A. Brown, W. E. Dodge, Treadwell Ketchum, Jesse W. Benedict, David Hoadley, and Walter S. Griffith, be added to the Permanent Committee on Foreign Missions, and that they be requested to divide the committee into three classes, one of which shall be elected annually by the Assembly."—*Minutes,* 1856, p. 212.

3. *Duties of the Committee.*

"The committee to whom was referred the report of the Permanent Committee on Foreign Missions, together with a resolution and memorial on the same subject, recommend the following:

"1. That the report of the Permanent Committee be approved. And we are grateful to God for the efficiency and harmony with which we have been enabled to prosecute the great work of foreign missions through the medium of the American Board of Commissioners for Foreign Missions.

"2. That, in addition to the duties already devolved upon this committee, it be made their further duty to ascertain, as far as possible, to what extent the churches in connection with the General Assembly are engaged in the work of foreign missions, and report the same to the next General Assembly. And that these missionary operations in which our churches are engaged, be made the subject of an annual report to the Assembly by this committee.

"In which reports, they shall spread before the Assembly such information as is calculated to excite and deepen an interest in this subject, and foster and develop the spirit of missions; giving the number of foreign missionaries of our Church who are in the field, the number of candidates for this work, the amount of annual contributions, so far as practicable, and the degree of interest which is manifested in this cause throughout our churches; together with the measure of success that has attended missionary effort; and communicate any information which they can gain, that may stimulate and develop foreign missionary enterprise.

"3. That the Presbyteries, through their stated clerks, or a committee appointed for that purpose, furnish to the Permanent Committee on Foreign Missions all the information on this subject that may be sought or they be able to furnish. And further, that the Presbyteries and Synods give special attention to this subject, adopting such measures as may rouse the spirit of missions among the churches."—*Minutes*, 1858, pp. 595, 596.

4. *Report and Resolutions of the Assembly. Formation of Foreign Presbyteries encouraged. The Synod of New York and New Jersey empowered to form and receive such Presbyteries.*

"The unfinished business of the last session was then taken up, being the consideration of the report on Foreign Missions; which, having been amended, was adopted, and is as follows:

"Your committee having taken into consideration the report of the Permanent Committee on Foreign Missions, and the overtures, Synodical and Presbyterial, bearing upon this part of our ecclesiastical work, which have been referred to your committee, respectfully submit the following report, and recommend its adoption by the General Assembly:

"1. The Assembly owe it to the Permanent Committee, to record their thanks for the lucid and deeply interesting narrative which they have furnished, in the report now submitted, of the past and present connection of our Church with the great Christian work of Foreign Missions:

"2. It is highly desirable that said report be printed and widely circulated among the members of our churches; and also that our pastors present to their congregations, at the monthly concert of prayer for Foreign Missions, the facts contained therein, as eminently calculated to induce thankfulness for that part which, in the providence of God, we have been permitted to take in this work in the past, as well as to incite us to more earnest zeal and labor as to the share which we may be hereafter called to assume in carrying the Gospel to the ends of the earth.

"3. It is desirable, also, that said report be printed in the Appendix to the Minutes of the General Assembly, so that there may exist, in an official form, a permanent record of the interesting facts which have been thus brought under the notice of this body.

"The following overtures or memorials on the subject of Foreign Missions have been forwarded to this Assembly:

"1st. From the Synod of Minnesota, praying the Assembly to decide such measures as, in their wisdom, may seem fit, for the purpose of securing a closer ecclesiastical relation of our Foreign Missionaries with the General Assembly, and of securing also direct reports from these brethren to our Assemblies, Synods, and Presbyteries; as tending, in the estimation of the memorialists, to a larger development of the missionary spirit in our beloved Church.

"2d. From the Presbytery of Newark, expressing their unanimous conviction of the expediency of instructing the Permanent Committee on Foreign Missions to concert measures with the Prudential Committee of the A. B. C. F. M., for the formation of Presbyteries on its foreign field, whenever such a step may be deemed practicable.

"3d. From the Presbytery of Philadelphia Third, stating that one of their members, a missionary in the foreign field, having been recommended by his Presbytery to propose to his Presbyterian brethren in the same mission, that they should form themselves into a Presbytery, declined, with his brethren, to do so, upon the understanding that it was the business of the Prudential Committee of the Board to arrange the ecclesiastical organizations of missionaries and mission churches in foreign lands; thereupon praying the Assembly to consider this subject; and expressing the conviction, that our churches are deficient in missionary spirit; that our young men are not coming forward to offer themselves as missionaries; and that, though actuated by no sectarian feeling, they are convinced that a proper missionary spirit cannot be created, or kept alive, without our having, in some way, a closer relation to our missionaries, and without, in some way, bringing home to our churches the feeling that this is our own work.

"This overture further reminds the General Assembly, that, after contributing millions of money, we have not a solitary mission church, or but one, in the entire foreign field; and respectfully suggests, without venturing to dictate, that a portion of the foreign field be set apart, to be occupied exclusively by missionaries of our Church, that every difficulty in the way of a homogeneous ecclesiastical organization may be removed.

"4th. From the Presbytery of Greencastle, recommending to the General Assembly to secure to our churches the direct control of our ministers laboring in foreign lands, as to their ecclesiastical relations.

"The Assembly, having considered these overtures and memorials, further resolve:

"1. That the General Assembly of the Presbyterian Church in the United States have reason to rejoice in God that they have been permitted to share, with their brethren of other denominations, the high privilege of bringing into efficiency the noblest of all the missionary institutions of our country; and that, in both funds and men, our churches have supplied so considerable a proportion of the expenditure which has been incurred in founding and sustaining, in the Turkish Empire, in Hindostan, in Ceylon, and elsewhere, missions and labors which have reflected so bright an honor upon American Christianity.

"2. That we rejoice in the successes which the Great Head of the Church continues to vouchsafe to the operations of the American Board in the varied and difficult fields which, in the providence of God, it is called to occupy; and fervently desire that its future career may be 'as the shining light that shineth more and more unto the perfect day.'

"3. That we deeply sympathize with the Board in its present pecuniary embarrassments, and commend the cause of missions, as conducted by it, to enlarged self-denying liberalities on the part of our churches.

"4. That the time has now come when, in order to a more thorough development of that missionary spirit which should pervade every portion of the Christian Church, the prayers of the memorialists, now enumerated, demand not only consideration, but action. These prayers ask not, in any instance, for a cessation from the co-operative principle in conducting this work, but simply for a closer connection with it, by means of the formation of Presbyteries in foreign lands, wherever numbers and circumstances will allow of such a course. In the judgment of this body, this request consists, not only with the highest reason, but with the broadest charity; for the Assembly cannot forget the fact, that, after long years of connection with the foreign missionary department of evangelistic labor, we have at this time but one Presbyterian church of our connection in the foreign field.

"The Presbyterian Church have had too great a share in laying the foundations of the American Board, and in building up its noble superstructure, to be willing, except for the most imperative reasons, to sever the tie which binds them, the one to the other. If they can do so with fidelity to their brethren abroad and to their churches at home, the Assembly will joyfully perpetuate their co-operation with brethren with whom it has been so long, so honorably, and so successfully associated, in advancing throughout the world the interests of the Redeemer's kingdom. They will sacrifice everything for this but the salvation of souls, and the edification and general prosperity of that portion of the Church over which the Holy Ghost hath made them overseers. But the General Assembly record it as their deliberate judgment, that it is due to the interests of our Church, and to its vital connection with our foreign work,

"1. That it should be distinctly understood, here and abroad, that the Board, its Prudential Committee, and officers, interpose no obstacles in the way of the formation of foreign Presbyteries.

"2. That the appointments of missionaries should be so disposed, wherever it is wise and practicable, as to facilitate the formation of such Presbyteries.

"3. That there should be a free correspondence of our missionaries with the Permanent Committee of the General Assembly.

"4. That less than this the Assembly cannot declare; because less than this would not lead our churches to identify themselves with the operations and successes of the Board, and to manifest that interest and zeal in its welfare and prosperity which are requisite for the perpetuity among ourselves of the true missionary spirit.

"5. That, in recording this their judgment, the General Assembly feel encouraged by the fact, that the Prudential Committee of the American Board have frequently professed their desire and purpose not to interfere with the ecclesiastical bias of the missionaries, or with the attempt of any one or more of them to form Presbyteries and Presbyterian churches on their fields of labor. Accepting these professions in good faith, the Assembly desire such an understanding with the Board as shall lead to the realization of all which is sought for by the before-mentioned Synod and Presbyteries, and demanded by the convictions of our whole Church.

"6. That this General Assembly are further encouraged, by information which has reached them from reliable sources, that our missionary brethren, in some portions of the work, are directing their thoughts and aims towards the perpetuation, in foreign countries, of our excellent Presbyterian polity.

"7. That it is regarded by the General Assembly as both desirable and important, that our brethren who are laboring in the foreign field correspond with the Permanent Committee on the subject of their labors; and that said committee be requested to prepare, from year to year, such a report of our foreign work as shall be calculated to quicken the zeal of our people in prayers and labors for the conversion of the whole world to Christ; such report to be submitted to the General Assembly.

"8. The General Assembly hereby appoint Rev. Albert Barnes, Rev. Jonathan F. Stearns, D.D., Rev. Edwin F. Hatfield, D.D., Rev. John Jenkins, Mr. Matthew W. Baldwin, and Hon. William Strong, a special committee to attend the next meeting of the A. B. C. F. M., to be held in Philadelphia, on the first Tuesday of October next, for the purpose of conveying to the Board the Assembly's views as herein expressed, and of conferring with it, or with any committee which it may appoint, as to the best mode by which these results may be most wisely and prudently secured; as well as to confer in regard to the localities where our missionaries can be most conveniently and speedily concentrated.

"9. That this report be printed in circular form, and transmitted to each of our foreign missionaries, with the recommendation to such missionaries that they proceed to form themselves into Presbyteries whenever and wherever, in their judgment, it is practicable and expedient.

"10. That the candidates for the missionary work, going out from our body, be recommended to give their attention to those fields where Presbyteries are or may be formed.

"11. The General Assembly hereby empower the Synod of New York and New Jersey to form and receive foreign Presbyteries whenever constitutionally requested so to do by our foreign missionaries.

"The committee have also had under consideration the report of the General Assembly's Permanent Committee on Foreign Missions, respecting a certain memorial referred to them by the last General Assembly, signed by Rev. George Duffield, D.D., and others, on the desirableness of our instituting missionary operations in Mexico and in Central and Southern America; also a second memorial, forwarded to this General Assembly by the same parties, on the same subject; in respect to which—

"The committee respectfully submit the following report, and recommend its adoption by the General Assembly:

"1. That the Assembly regard the proposal of the memorialists as entitled to both consideration and respect.

"2. That, in the present attitude of our work abroad, it is inexpedient for this General Assembly to initiate any new and independent foreign missionary undertaking.

"Because it is due to our missionary brethren in fields already occupied, that all our available men be commissioned to those parts of the world, in which it is deemed important to facilitate the formation of Presbyteries, and thus to increase the efficiency of particular missions.

"3. That it is yet due to the memorialists, and to the important subject which they thus bring to the notice of the Assembly, that it be held over for advisement for another year; and, for this purpose, the report of the Permanent Committee is referred back, together with the present memorial, to said committee; who are hereby requested to reconsider their report, to make further inquiries respecting the field indicated, and to report to the next General Assembly."—*Minutes*, 1859, pp. 21–25.

5. *Report of Standing Committee*, 1860. *The Jubilee Year.*

"The command, 'Go ye into all the world, and preach the Gospel to every creature,' is not surpassed for distinctness and impressiveness by any saying of our Lord Jesus Christ. No one, that pretends to love the Master, can be indifferent to this direction. Nor does it pertain alone to individual believers. It embraces every church in its organic character. Every denomination of Christians must see to it that its name is identified with the cause of foreign missions. It would be fatal to the hope of any professed disciple of the Son of God, to have no sympathy with the suffering Redeemer in his desire to save a perishing world. It is disgraceful to any company of believers not to recognize, somewhere in their system, the obligation resting upon them to take part, at whatever cost and sacrifice, in the conquest of the world to the dominion of the Cross. It may not be necessary that there should be as many distinct organizations, for sending out and sustaining missionaries upon the foreign field, as there are separate denominations; but if, upon careful investigation, it be thought that in this way the strength and efficiency of any portion of the people of God can thus be more completely developed, then no considerations of a worldly policy should be allowed, for a moment, to hinder the formation of a new missionary society. We are not called upon to convert the heathen, but we are bound, as individuals, as churches, and as a distinct branch of the Church of Jesus Christ, to do all in our power to preach the Gospel to every creature. We are debtors, made so by the command of Jesus, 'both to the Greeks and to the barbarians, both to the wise and to the unwise;' so, as much as in us is, we must be ready to preach the Gospel, not only to them that are at Rome, but to the crowded population of China and India, to the scattered inhabitants of Polynesia, and to the roving hordes in our own wilderness.

"The practical question at present is, whether, as a denomination, we can continue to work with the American Board, or whether the time has come to initiate a system, under which we can more rapidly and fully develop the strength and spirit of our people.

"The General Assembly finds an answer to this question in the report of its Permanent Committee, just presented, and that of the Committee of Conference with the American Board; which reports are to be printed in the Appendix to the Minutes, after so much of the first report as relates to the Presbyterial character of the churches of the Ahmednuggur Mission be modified, as the Permanent Committee now desire, to correspond to the facts in the case; and, after the paragraph be stricken out, relating to the communication of a missionary to a Presbytery, and the memorial of the Presbytery to the Assembly.

"The attention of the churches is called to certain particulars in this elaborate and excellent report of the Permanent Committee:

"1. The urging upon Presbyteries of the importance of securing a more perfect system, in respect to contributions for missionary purposes, and especially the necessity of reporting such collections, not in a spirit of boasting, but in order that full and correct statistics of our benevolent operations may be secured.

"2. The correspondence from the Dacotah, the Madura, and the African missions is worthy of notice, from the excellence of these communications and the important information which they convey; but more especially as constituting the beginning of an interchange of letters between the General Assembly and its absent and distant members, who are preaching the Gospel among the heathen.

"3. That portion of the report which is in reply to the memorial for the establishment of missions in Mexico, and Central or Southern America, may be accepted as the proper reply to the resolution of the Presbytery of Detroit, and a memorial signed by George Duffield and H. Kendall, submitted to the Standing Committee; as it argues at length the impracticability of attempting to establish separate and independent missions at the present time.

"It is only necessary to say, in respect to the report of the Special Committee of Conference with the American Board, that everything sought by our committee, or desired by the General Assembly, was cordially assented to; and we rely upon the good faith of the Prudential Committee to carry out their own declaration, 'that both "reason" and "charity" demand the facilitation of such organizations' (that is, foreign Presbyteries), 'whenever circumstances and a due regard to the great objects of this board will allow;' and, in view of the offer of the Prudential Committee, it is resolved, that the General Assembly will gladly welcome the annual delegation sent to confer with them by the American Board.

"The Assembly wish to be understood, as expressing their undiminished confidence in the noble institution with which they have been so long associated in the work of evangelizing the world, and their desire still to co-operate with their brethren of another denomination in spreading the news of salvation to the ends of the earth. Especially on this '*Jubilee year*,' would the Assembly enjoin upon all its churches to lend most liberal aid, in furthering a result so desirable as that which is sought, viz., to bring the board to its next anniversary free from debt, and prepared to begin with increased ardor and energy its second half century, in the glorious work of bringing all mankind into subjection to Christ."—*Minutes*, 1860, pp. 256–258.

CHAPTER XI.

CORRESPONDENCE WITH OTHER CHURCHES.

1. To correspond with foreign churches, belongs to the Assembly.—2. The Assembly grants permission to correspond with local bodies.—3. Proposals to correspond with the New England churches.—4. Plan of correspondence with the General Association of Connecticut.—5. The right to vote asked by the Assembly and conceded.—6. Conference on complaint of the Presbytery of Philadelphia.—7. For either body to receive a candidate, licentiate, or minister from the other, without regular testimonials and dismission, is irregular.—8. Correspondence with the General Convention of Vermont. Regulations same as with the General Association of Connecticut.—9. With the General Association of New Hampshire.—10. With the General Association of Massachusetts.—11. With the General Conference of Maine.—12. With the Evangelical Consociation of Rhode Island. The correspondence discontinued by the Consociation.—13. The Assembly requests that the right to vote be given up.—14. Replies of the Associations. New Hampshire agrees; Vermont refers the matter to a committee; Massachusetts declines.—15. The rule as to receiving candidates, licentiates, and ministers urged upon the Associations of Massachusetts, New Hampshire, and Vermont.—16. Reply of the Association of Massachusetts. The right to vote given up. The rule referred to the district associations.—17. Minute on correspondence with the New England churches.—18. Correspondence with the German Reformed Synod of North America.—19. With the General Synod of the Evangelical Lutheran Church.—20. With the Cumberland Presbyterian Church.—21. With the Presbyterian and Congregational Convention of Wisconsin.—22. With the General Association of New York. Further proceedings. The correspondence continued. The Association requested to couch its communications in courteous language. The right to review proceedings, rebuke or reprove, disavowed and denied.—23. The terms of correspondence defined.—24. Correspondence with the Union of the Evangelical Churches of France.—25. With the Reformed Presbyterian Church in North America, and with the General Synod of the Associate Reformed Church. Terms of correspondence.—26. Compensation of delegates to corresponding bodies.

1. *To correspond with Foreign Churches belongs to the Assembly.*

"The committee appointed to examine the Records of the Synod of

Tennessee reported, and the Records were approved, with the exception of a proposal to establish a plan of intercourse between said Synod and the Cumberland Presbyterians; of which proposal the Assembly disapprove, on the ground that it belongs to the Assembly to correspond with foreign churches, on such terms as may be agreed upon by the Assembly and the corresponding body."—*Minutes,* 1827, p. 219.

2. *The Assembly grants Permission to correspond with Local Bodies.*

a. "*Resolved,* That while this Assembly would not interfere authoritatively with the lower judicatories in the exercise of their prerogative, they would recommend that no ministers should be invited to sit as correspondents who do not belong to some body in correspondence with this Assembly."—*Minutes,* 1843, p. 23.

b. "The report of the committee in reference to correspondence with the Methodist Episcopal Conferences, which had been put upon the docket, was taken up, and the following resolution was adopted, viz.:

"Whereas, the communication of the Oneida Annual Conference of the Methodist Episcopal Church solicits only a correspondence between themselves and the Synod of New York and New Jersey, and not with the Presbyterian Church generally; and whereas the Synod has referred the matter to the Assembly, without submitting any specific proposition or plan for such correspondence: therefore,

"*Resolved,* That the communication be referred back to the Synod, to adopt such measures as they may deem proper, in pursuance of the request for a correspondence of the local bodies."—*Minutes,* 1850, pp. 323, 324.

c. "Overture, 'Is it orderly for our Presbyteries and Synods to invite ministers of the Methodist Episcopal Church to sit as corresponding members?' which was answered by the Assembly unanimously in the *affirmative.*"—*Minutes,* 1849, p. 174.

3. *Proposals for Correspondence with the New England Churches.*

[In 1766, the General Synod adopted an overture "to endeavor to obtain some correspondence between this Synod and the Consociated Churches of Connecticut." A committee was appointed to meet the delegates from Connecticut. *Minutes,* 1766, p. 364. A convention of the delegates was held at Elizabethtown, November 5, 1766. Its minutes were laid before the Synod, "seriously considered, and amended." Delegates were appointed to attend at New Haven September 10, "there finally, on the part of this body, to complete the plan of union." *Minutes*, 1767, p. 374. Under this plan, the Convention met alternately in New Jersey and Connecticut, until 1776, when the war interrupted it. In 1790, the General Assembly invited a renewal of the intercourse; "Resolved, that the ministers of the Congregational churches of New England be invited to renew their annual Convention with the clergy of the Presbyterian Church." *Minutes*, 1790, p. 29. A committee was appointed under the above resolution, and on their report, the next year, another committee was appointed, to meet at New Haven "such ministers of the New England churches as may be there present." *Minutes*, 1791, p. 33.]

4. *Plan of Correspondence with the General Association of Connecticut.*

"The minutes of the Convention of the Committees of the General Assembly of the Presbyterian Church in the United States, and of the General Association of the State of Connecticut, were taken into consideration, an extract of which is as follows, viz.:

"Considering the importance of union and harmony in the Christian Church, and the duty incumbent on all its pastors and members to assist each other in promoting, as far as possible, the general interests of the Redeemer's kingdom; and considering, further, that Divine Providence appears to be now opening the door for pursuing these valuable objects with a happy prospect of success; this Convention are of opinion that it will be conducive to these important purposes that a standing committee of correspondence be appointed in each body, whose duty it shall be, by frequent letters, to communicate to each other whatever may be mutually useful to the churches under their care, and to the general interests of the Redeemer's kingdom. That each body should, from time to time, appoint a committee, consisting of three members, who shall have a right to sit in the other's general meeting, and make such communications as shall be directed by their respective constituents, and deliberate on such matters as shall come before the body, but shall have no right to vote. That effectual measures be mutually taken to prevent injuries to the respective churches from irregular and unauthorized preachers. To promote this end, the Convention judge it expedient that every preacher travelling from the limits of one of these churches into those of the other, shall be furnished with recent testimonials of his regular standing and good character as a preacher, signed by the moderator of the Presbytery or Association in which he received his license; or, if a minister, of his good standing and character, as such, from the moderator of the Presbytery or Association where he last resided; and that he shall, previously to his travelling as a preacher into distant parts, further receive a recommendation from one member at least of a standing committee, to be hereafter appointed by each body, certifying his good qualifications as a preacher. Also, that the names of this standing committee shall be mutually communicated. And also, that every preacher, travelling and recommended as above, and submitting to the stated rules of the respective churches, shall be received as an authorized preacher of the Gospel, and cheerfully taken under the patronage of the Presbytery or Association within whose bounds he shall find employment as a preacher. And that the proceedings of the respective bodies on this report be communicated to our brethren of the Congregational and Presbyterian Churches throughout the States.

"Upon mature deliberation, the Assembly unanimously and cordially approved of the said plan; and to carry the same into effect, appointed the Rev. Drs. John Rodgers, John Witherspoon, and Ashbel Green, to be a committee of correspondence, agreeably to the said plan. And it is moreover agreed, that this Assembly will send delegates to sit and consult with the General Association of Connecticut, and receive their delegates to sit in this Assembly, agreeably to another article of the plan, as soon as due information shall be received that it is adopted on the part of the General Association of Connecticut."

[A standing committee was appointed] "to certify the good qualifications of the preachers travelling to officiate in the bounds of the Association of the State of Connecticut.

"And it was moreover agreed, that any preacher travelling as aforesaid, shall have at least the name of one of the committee who shall belong to the Synod from whose bounds he came."—*Minutes*, 1792, pp. 52, 53.

["The convention was ratified by the General Association of Connecticut, and Dr. Jonathan Edwards and Rev. Matthias Burnet took their seats in the Assembly."]—*Minutes*, 1793, p. 64.

5. *The right to Vote asked and conceded.*

"The Assembly proposed to the Association, 'That the delegates from these bodies respectively shall have a right, not only to sit and deliberate, but also to vote, in all questions which may be determined by either of them.'" *Minutes*, 1794, p. 80. The proposition was acceded to by the Association.—*Minutes*, 1795, p. 96.

6. *Conference on Complaint of the Presbytery of Philadelphia.*

"Overture No. 10 was taken up, viz.: A reference from the Presbytery of Philadelphia, relative to the ordination of Mr. John Chambers by the Association of the Western District of New Haven county, Connecticut. The papers on this business were read; after which the subject was discussed at considerable length."—*Minutes*, 1826, p. 172.

"The Assembly resumed the consideration of the reference from the Presbytery of Philadelphia in relation to the ordination of Mr. Chambers. After further discussion of the subject at considerable length, the following resolution was adopted, viz.:

"*Resolved*, That a committee of this Assembly, consisting of three, be appointed to attend at the meeting of the General Association of Connecticut, to be convened at Stamford in June next, to meet a similar committee of that Association, if said Association shall be pleased to appoint one, for the purpose of conferring on the grievance of which the Presbytery of Philadelphia complain; and of inquiring whether any, and if any, what further articles, or alteration of the present terms of intercourse between the Presbyterian Church in the United States and the members of the Congregational Churches in Connecticut, may be expedient for the better promotion of the purity, peace, and Christian discipline of the churches connected with the two bodies; which further articles or alterations of the present terms of intercourse, if any shall be proposed by the joint committee, shall be submitted to the General Association of Connecticut, and to the General Assembly of 1827, for adoption or rejection."—*Minutes*, 1826, p. 175.

[The Commission met in New York, August 1, 1826.]

7. *For either Body to receive a Candidate, Licentiate, or Minister, from the other, without regular Testimonials and Dismission, an infraction of the Plan.*

"From the commission and instructions of the committee from the General Association of Connecticut, it appeared that they had no power to do anything in relation to the case of the ordination of Mr. Chambers; but that they were appointed only on that part of the communication which respects the terms of intercourse between the General Assembly and the General Association of Connecticut.

"After mature deliberation, it was unanimously—

"*Resolved*, That the two following rules be proposed to the General Assembly and the General Association of Connecticut, for the future regulation of their intercourse with each other, viz.:

"1. That it shall be deemed irregular and unfriendly for any Presbytery or Association within the bounds of the corresponding churches, to receive any candidate for licensure, licentiate, or ordained minister, into connection with either, without regular testimonials, and a regular dismission from the Presbytery or Association from which the said candidate, licentiate, or minister may come.

"2. That the delegates commissioned respectively by the corresponding churches to attend the highest body of each be hereafter empowered, agreeably to the original plan of correspondence between the two churches, to sit and deliberate only, but not to vote.

"The above report was accepted; and the two resolutions recommended by the joint committee were adopted by the Assembly."—*Minutes*, 1827, pp. 199, 200.

8. *With the General Convention of Vermont.*

a. "A communication to this General Assembly from the General Convention of the regular ministers of the Gospel in the State of Vermont, proposing the formation of a plan of ministerial intercourse between them and the General Assembly of the Presbyterian Church in the United States of America, was brought in and read."—*Minutes*, 1802, p. 238.

b. "The committee appointed on the communication from the Convention of the regular ministers of the Gospel of the State of Vermont, reported. The report being considered and amended, was adopted, and is as follows:

"Your committee are of opinion that, although this Assembly have not received any answer to the request of last Assembly, proposed to the Convention of Vermont, yet the Assembly have received satisfactory information on the subjects alluded to, both from their own delegates to the General Association of Connecticut of last year, and also from the representatives of that body in the present Assembly. The committee therefore submit the following plan of union and intercourse between the said Convention and the General Assembly, viz.:

"1. Each body shall send one or two delegates to meet and sit with the other at the stated sessions of each body respectively.

"2. The delegate or delegates from each respectively shall have the privilege of joining in the discussions and deliberations of the body as freely and fully as their own members.

"3. That the union and intercourse may be full and complete between the said bodies, the delegate or delegates from each respectively, shall not only sit and deliberate, but also act and vote; which articles comprise the great principles of the union between the General Assembly and the General Association of Connecticut."—*Minutes*, 1803, p. 279.

"Ratified by the Convention."—*Minutes*, 1804, p. 297.

Regulations same as with the Association of Connecticut.

c. "*Resolved*, That the delegate appointed to represent this Assembly at the next meeting of the Convention of Vermont be, and he hereby is authorized to propose and agree upon the same regulations which have been agreed to be observed by this Assembly and the General Association of Connecticut, in relation to the credentials requisite for such ministers as may come within the bounds of this Assembly or the Convention of Vermont, for the purpose of preaching the Gospel."—*Minutes*, 1809, p. 422. [See pp. 436, 437.]

[The proposal "was agreed to with great unanimity" by the Convention.]—*Minutes*, 1810, p. 436.

9. *With the General Association of New Hampshire.*

"A proposal from the General Association of New Hampshire was made by the Rev. William F. Rowland and the Rev. John H. Church, commissioners appointed for that purpose, for a union between them and this Assembly similar to that subsisting between the General Association of Connecticut and this Assembly. The certificate of their appointment, and the papers accompanying it, were read.

"*Resolved*, That said union be formed.

"And it accordingly was formed."—*Minutes*, 1810, p. 435.

10. *With the General Association of Massachusetts.*

"A proposal from the General Association of Massachusetts proper, was made by the Rev. Joseph Lyman, D.D., and the Rev. Samuel Worcester, delegates appointed for that purpose, for the establishment of a union between them and this Assembly, similar to that subsisting between the Association of Massachusetts proper and the Associations of Connecticut and New Hampshire. The certificate of their appointment, and the articles of union with said Association were read.

"The articles of said union are as follows:

"1. The General Association of Connecticut and the General Association of Massachusetts proper, shall annually appoint each two delegates to the other.

"2. The delegates shall be admitted in each body to the same rights of sitting, debating, and voting with their own members respectively.

"3. It shall be understood that the articles of agreement and connection between the two bodies, may be at any time varied by their own consent.

"The same articles were adopted in their connection with the Association of New Hampshire.

"The delegates stated that the Shorter Catechism of the Westminster Assembly was adopted as the basis of their union, and by answering several questions proposed to them, fully satisfied the Assembly relative to the standard of their faith, and the object of their Association; whereupon,

"*Resolved, unanimously,* That said Union be formed."—*Minutes,* 1811, p. 462.

11. *With the General Conference of Maine.*

"The Rev. Benjamin Tappan, and William Ladd, Esq., appeared in the Assembly, and produced commissions as delegates from the General Conference of the State of Maine.

"The committee appointed to confer with the delegates from the General Conference of the State of Maine, made the following report, which was adopted, viz.:

"That after obtaining all the information which they deemed requisite, respecting the body proposing this connection, they have agreed to recommend to the General Assembly the adoption of the following articles of correspondence, which the above named delegates doubt not will be readily acceded to on the part of the General Conference.

"1. The General Assembly of the Presbyterian Church, and the General Conference of Maine, shall each appoint one or two delegates to attend these bodies respectively; and in case two are appointed, one may be a layman; for the purpose of communicating to each other whatever may be mutually useful to the churches under their care, and conducive to Christian harmony and co-operation, and to the general interest of the Redeemer's kingdom.

"2. These delegates shall have the privilege of proposing such measures as they may deem important or desirable, and of delivering their opinions on any questions under discussion, but shall have no vote in the decisions of the bodies respectively to which they shall be delegated.

"3. It shall be deemed irregular for any Presbytery, Conference, or Association within the bounds of the corresponding churches, to receive any candidate for licensure, licentiate, or ordained minister, into connection with either, without regular testimonials, and a regular dismission from the Presbytery, Conference, or Association from which the said candidate, licentiate, or minister may come.

"4. Each of the bodies forming these articles of correspondence shall appoint a committee for certifying the good standing of ministers travelling from the one to the other. The names of the persons composing these committees respectively, shall be mutually communicated by the two bodies; and it shall not be considered as a matter of offence if a licentiate or ordained minister, from either body, travelling without a certificate of regular standing, from one or more members of said committee, shall not be received or treated as such.

"5. It shall be understood that these articles of agreement and correspondence between the two bodies may be, at any time, modified by mutual consent, or terminated, when either body shall decide and announce that they are no longer considered as answering the great purposes intended to be promoted by them, and that their termination is desired."—*Minutes*, 1828, pp. 227, 228.

"The delegate from the General Conference of Maine, reported that said Conference has adopted the articles of union and correspondence proposed by the last General Assembly, with the exception of the third article, in place of which, they propose the following, viz.: While the General Conference of Maine has not, nor does it claim any ecclesiastical jurisdiction over the particular Conferences, Associations, Councils, or churches in its connection, it cheerfully unites with the General Assembly in the expression of the opinion, that it is irregular for any ordained minister, licentiate, candidate for licensure, or church member, to be received into ecclesiastical connection within the limits of one of the corresponding bodies, from the other, without due testimonials." [Accepted.]—*Minutes*, 1829, p. 255.

12. *With the Evangelical Consociation of Rhode Island.*

"The Rev. Isaac Lewis appeared in the General Assembly, and made application on behalf of the Evangelical Consociation of Rhode Island, for a correspondence with the General Assembly on the same terms with the other Congregational bodies of New England, in correspondence with this body. This subject was referred to Dr. Miller, Mr. Squier, and Mr. Armstrong.

"The committee reported that, after making careful inquiry of the delegate concerning the faith, order, and present state of the churches forming the body which he represents, they would respectfully recommend to the Assembly the adoption of the following resolutions, viz.:

"1. That the proposal of the Evangelical Consociation of Rhode Island be complied with; and that a plan of correspondence between that body and the General Assembly be, and the same hereby is adopted, on the same terms which regulate the correspondence between the General Assembly and the other Congregational bodies of New England.

"2. That there be an annual interchange of one delegate from each to the other respectively.

"3. That the Rev. Isaac Lewis, the bearer of this proposal from the Consociation of Rhode Island, be invited to take his seat in the General Assembly as the representative of that body.

"The report was adopted."—*Minutes*, 1831, pp. 319, 320.

[In 1856, the Consociation resolved to discontinue the correspondence. See Minutes, 1857, p. 426, Appendix.]

13. *Alteration asked for as to the Right to Vote.*

"The committee appointed to draught a memorial to the General Associations of Massachusetts and New Hampshire, and the General Convention of Vermont, in regard to some changes which the Assembly have deemed necessary to be made in the plan of correspondence and intercourse between the said ecclesiastical bodies and the Assembly, reported the following memorial in the form of an address to the aforesaid ecclesiastical bodies, which was adopted, and ordered to be signed by the moderator, viz.:

"The General Assembly of the Presbyterian Church, to the General Associations of Massachusetts and New Hampshire, and the General Convention of Vermont.

"Christian brethren, beloved in the Lord.

"It appears that, in the plan of intercourse between the Congregational churches of New England, and the General Assembly of the Presbyterian Church, an article was adopted, which is now believed to be inconsistent with a sound construction of the Constitution of the latter church. This article, it is due to truth and candor to remark, was proposed by the Presbyterian Church, without any overture from the Congregational churches, and in regard to which, they did nothing more than accede to the proposition submitted to them. The article to which we allude, relates to the powers granted to the delegates of the corresponding churches, to *vote* as well as to *deliberate* on the various subjects that may come before the representatives of these churches respectively. The right of voting in the General Assembly, cannot, it is believed, be constitutionally granted to any, but to the commissioners appointed by the Presbyteries, whose representatives compose that Assembly.

"We have therefore respectfully to request, that the plan of intercourse between you and us may be so modified, as that the delegates to each body may hereafter be empowered to sit and deliberate only, but not to vote. It is believed that the modification here contemplated, if it shall be consented to on your part, will not only place the Assembly on constitutional ground, but, by placing your Association on the same footing with other religious communities with which we hold a friendly correspondence, will destroy the appearance of an invidious distinction which now exists, and thus be calculated to promote extensively that mutual friendship and harmony which it is desirable to maintain and perpetuate, among all who love the truth as it is in Jesus.

"With Christian salutations.

"Signed in behalf of the General Assembly,

"FRANCIS HERRON, Moderator."

—*Minutes*, 1827, p. 213.

14. *Replies of the Associations.*

"From the report of the delegate to New Hampshire and Vermont, it appeared that the memorial of the last Assembly to these bodies was laid before each of them; and that the General Association of New Hampshire have adopted the proposition in the memorial, viz., that the delegates from each body to the other should hereafter sit and deliberate only, but not vote; and that the General Convention of Vermont had committed the subject to a committee, which are to report to the next Convention.

"From the Minutes of the General Association of Massachusetts, presented to the Assembly, it appears that that body have respectfully declined adopting the alteration proposed in the memorial of the Assembly."—*Minutes,* 1828, p. 229.

15. *Adoption of the Rule as to receiving Candidates urged upon the Associations.*

a. "The committee appointed to consider and report on the propriety of proposing to the General Associations of Massachusetts and New Hampshire, and the General Convention of Vermont, the adoption of the first of the two rules proposed by the last Assembly to the General Association of Connecticut, reported, that they view the adoption of said rule as necessary to the peaceful and harmonious correspondence of the bodies concerned; and would therefore recommend that the delegates appointed this year to the Associations and Conventions above named be instructed to present the rule referred to to their consideration.

"The above report was adopted.

"The rule referred to is as follows, viz.:

"That it shall be deemed irregular and unfriendly for any Presbytery or Association, within the bounds of the corresponding churches, to receive any candidate for licensure, licentiate, or ordained minister, into connection with either, without regular testimonials, and a regular dismission from the Presbytery or Association from which the said candidate, licentiate, or minister, may come."—*Minutes,* 1828, p. 233.

b. "The committee to whom was referred a motion on the subject of correspondence with the General Association of Massachusetts, made a report, which, being read and amended, was adopted, and is as follows, viz.:

"*Resolved*, That the delegates to the General Association of Massachusetts be instructed to inform that Association, that while this General Assembly do most cordially accept and approve the expression of their sentiments, with regard to candidates, licentiates, and ministers under censure for heresy or immorality, they do also most respectfully and affectionately represent to the Association, that they deem it highly important that it should be considered irregular that any candidate, licentiate, or minister, whose credentials are withheld on account of the violation of ecclesiastical order, should be received by either of the corresponding bodies."—*Minutes*, 1829, p. 274.

16. *Reply of the Association of Massachusetts.*

"The two following resolutions, adopted by the General Association of Massachusetts, and contained in the report of the delegates to that body, were approved by this Assembly, and ordered to be entered on the Minutes, viz.:

"*Resolved*, 1. That this Association, having learned that the existing rule of intercourse with the General Assembly, so far as it respects the right of voting in the legislative and judicial proceedings of that body, transcends the power vested in it, do waive their accustomed privilege of voting by their delegates in said body in such proceedings; desiring that as much of the same reciprocal intercourse, which has for a series of years so pleasantly existed between said bodies, may continue, as shall not conflict with the fundamental principles of their organization.

"2. That this Association regret that their proceedings, on the subject of receiving licentiates and candidates, &c., at the last meeting of the General Association, were not entirely satisfactory to the General Assembly. On the broad ground of heresy and immorality, they have no hesitancy in expressing their opinion, that it would be irregular for either body to receive licentiates, candidates, and ministers, without the usual certificates and recommendations; but as views of Christian ministers on the subject of ecclesiastical order may honestly differ, and as this Association has no control, either legislative or judicial, over the respective Associations of which it is composed, they can only refer the resolutions of the Assembly on this subject to the particular consideration of their district Associations, with the fullest confidence that on questions of 'ecclesiastical order,' as well as on every other subject, they will be disposed to meet the views and promote the interests of our highly respected and beloved brethren of the Presbyterian Church."—*Minutes*, 1830, p. 283.

17. *Minute on the Correspondence with the New England Churches.*

"*Resolved*, That this General Assembly see no cause either to terminate or modify the plan of correspondence with the Associations of our Congregational brethren in New England. That correspondence has been long established. It is believed to have been productive of mutual benefit. It is now divested of the voting power, which alone could be considered as infringing the Constitution of our Church, by introducing persons clothed with the character of plenary members of the Assembly. It stands at present substantially on the same footing with the visits of our brethren from the Congregational Union of England and Wales; and in the present age of enlarged counsel and of combined effort for the conversion of the world, ought by no means to be abolished. Besides, the Assembly are persuaded, that amidst the unceasing and growing intercourse between the Presbyterian and Congregational Churches, it is desirable to have that intercourse regulated by compact, and, of course, that it would be desirable to introduce terms of correspondence, even if they did not already exist."—*Minutes*, 1835, p. 487.

18. *With the German Reformed Church.*

"*Resolved*, That Dr. Ely, Rev. Timothy Alden, and the Rev. John M. Duncan, be a committee to confer with a committee from the General Synod of the Reformed German Church of North America, if such a committee should be appointed by that body, on the subject of a connection by correspondence between the two Churches, and to make a report to the next General Assembly."—*Minutes*, 1823, p. 87.

"The consideration of the report on a correspondence with the German Reformed Synod was resumed.

"After mature deliberation, it was

"*Resolved*, That the General Assembly will agree to an ecclesiastical correspondence with the German Reformed Synod of North America, on the following principles, viz.:

"First. The Churches are to remain separate and independent.

"Second. The German Reformed Synod, and the General Assembly of the Presbyterian Church, shall each appoint one minister and one elder, with an alternate of each, or two ministers, with their alternates, as either may wish, to sit in these judicatories respectively, with the privilege of deliberating on all subjects that may come before them.

"The Rev. Robert Cathcart, D.D., and the Rev. Alexander Boyd were appointed a committee to lay the above articles of correspondence before the German Reformed Synod at their next meeting, and when adopted by that body, the correspondence shall be considered as established."—*Minutes*, 1824, p. 102.

"Adopted by the Synod."—*Minutes*, 1825, p. 135.

19. *With the Evangelical Lutheran Church.*

"The Committee on Correspondence with Foreign Bodies made a report on the subject of correspondence with the Evangelical Lutheran Church, recommending that a delegate be appointed to attend their next meeting, and also to open a correspondence with them."

[Adopted, page 22.]—*Minutes*, 1843, pp. 20, 22.

"The Committee on Church Polity presented the following report, which was adopted, viz.:

"The Assembly have received with great pleasure the Rev. H. N. Pohlman, D.D., a delegate from the Evangelical Lutheran Church, and fully reciprocate the kind sentiments contained in the minutes of the last meeting of their Synod; and do, on the principles of action between the Assembly and other corresponding bodies, cordially adopt, and recommend for adoption by our inferior judicatories, the plan of correspondence proposed by the delegate, and unanimously adopted by the General Synod of the Evangelical Lutheran Church."—*Minutes*, 1846, pp. 16, 17.

20. *With the Cumberland Presbyterian Church.*

"The committee appointed by the last Assembly, on the subject of a correspondence with the Cumberland Presbyterian Church, presented a report, which was accepted, and the following article, agreed upon by the committee of the two bodies, was unanimously adopted:

"The General Assembly of each church shall appoint and receive delegates from the General Assembly of the other church, who shall be possessed of all the powers and privileges of other members of such Assemblies, except that of voting."—*Minutes*, 1849, p. 184.

21. *With the Presbyterian and Congregational Convention of Wisconsin.*

"On recommendation of the Committee of Correspondence with Foreign Bodies, it was—

"*Resolved,* That delegates be appointed to attend the Presbyterian and Congregational Convention of Wisconsin."—*Minutes,* 1843, p. 22.

22. *With the General Association of New York.*

a. "It was unanimously—

"*Resolved,* That a delegate be appointed to attend the next meeting of the General Association of New York."—*Minutes,* 1849, p. 171.

b. "The Committee on the Polity of the Church made a report on the subject of correspondence with the General Association of New York, as follows:

"That, from the position in which that body, and a large portion of the Presbyterian Church, are placed, in respect to each other, it is natural that a spirit of rivalry should exist between them; and that this should engender a spirit of proselytism, which appears to have been manifested, in a degree, in some of the past action of the Association, which, we hope, will not be persisted in on their part, and which, we trust, will never characterize the action of our Church. We are brethren of the same family, have the same Lord, the same faith, the same baptism, and the same great ends in view, and should live together in the strictest bonds of holy fellowship and union; striving together for the advancement of the kingdom of our Lord and Saviour Jesus Christ. Whether an individual church chooses to administer the discipline in the Presbyterian or Congregational way, is comparatively a matter of minor concern. Let each be persuaded in his own mind, and not interfere with the rights of his brother.

"We recommend that the correspondence be continued, and hope that it may be so conducted as to prove mutually satisfactory, and promotive of the interests of the kingdom of our dear Redeemer.

"The report was adopted."—*Minutes,* 1851, p. 22.

c. "The committee upon the communication from the delegate of the New York Association made their report, which, after amendment, was adopted, and is as follows:

"Whereas, The General Association of New York, at their meeting in Madrid, held August 23d, 1854, by resolution forwarded to this body, have addressed us in a discourteous and objectionable manner; therefore—

"*Resolved*, That the Assembly would respectfully request that the future communications of the Association to us be couched in courteous language."—*Minutes*, 1855, p. 35.

The Right to Review Proceedings, Reprove, or Rebuke, disavowed and denied.

d. "The Committee on the Correspondence between the General Assembly and the General Association of New York presented a report, which, having been read, was adopted, and is as follows:

"The committee, to whom was referred the question of the ecclesiastical relations of this Assembly with the General Association of New York, report:

"That they understand that our Congregational brethren of New York, by their resolution communicated to the General Assembly at St. Louis, and by the statements of their delegate on the floor of this Assembly, affirm, that one of the reasons for continuing their correspondence with this Assembly is, that they may reprove and rebuke them for not doing what is deemed a proper duty, or for doing what may by the Association be deemed improper.

"To such a position the committee can give no assent. The fraternal intercourse and interchange of delegates are for entirely different purposes. They have not been, and cannot be, maintained upon such grounds. We correspond for the purpose of co-operating in the great work in which we are mutually engaged. The *modus operandi* belongs exclusively to each. What may or may not be done by either body, in the prosecution of its legitimate business, and in carrying forward its own work, not affecting the rights and interests of the others, is not a subject of censure or rebuke; and the holding of such correspondence, with a view to the exercise of such censure, is a manifest breach of that comity which is indispensable to the proper intercourse of two ecclesiastical bodies of equal standing.

"Your committee therefore recommend the adoption of the following resolution:

"*Resolved*, That our delegate to that Association, while expressing the wishes of this Assembly to maintain Christian and fraternal fellowship, and the free interchange of a correspondence with our Congregational brethren, be instructed to state to our brethren that we can admit no right of theirs, by virtue of that correspondence, to review our proceedings, or to reprove or rebuke us for what we may or may not do.

"We do not claim or propose the exercise of any such right on the part of this Assembly."—*Minutes*, 1856, p. 212.

[Since 1855, no delegate has been appointed by the Assembly.]

23. *The Terms of Correspondence.*

"Whereas, Several of the Associations in correspondence with this body, have requested the views of this Assembly on the terms of correspondence, especially in regard to the right of reproof and rebuke, therefore—

"*Resolved*, That the General Assembly have never intended to refuse to corresponding bodies any rights or privileges which are compatible with true delicacy, courtesy, and Christian charity; in the light of which, this body respectfully requests all corresponding bodies to interpret all past acts of the Assembly."—*Minutes*, 1857, p. 408.

24. *With the Union of the Evangelical Churches of France.*

"The committee, to whom was referred the communication from the Union of the Evangelical Churches of France, presented a report, recommending the draft of a reply to their letter, and several resolutions, which were adopted, and are as follows:

"*Resolved*, 1. That this General Assembly do hereby cordially assent to the request of the brethren of the Union of the Evangelical Churches of France, to enter into correspondence with them."—*Minutes*, 1854, p. 510.

25. *With the "Reformed" and "Associate Reformed" Churches.*

a. "The Rev. Andrew W. Black, D.D., presented his credentials as a delegate from the General Synod of the Reformed Presbyterian Church in North America; his name was entered on the roll, and the Assembly proceeded to hear his statements, and the terms of correspondence proposed by the General Synod; which were referred to the Committee on the Polity of the Church.

"The same committee were directed to inquire into the expediency of entering into correspondence with the General Synod of the Associate Reformed Presbyterian Church."—*Minutes*, 1857, p. 386.

b. "The Committee on the Polity of the Church, to whom was referred the terms of correspondence with the General Synod of the Reformed Presbyterian Church in North America, made a report, which was adopted, and is as follows:

"The General Assembly of the Presbyterian Church in the United States of America, and the General Synod of the Reformed Presbyterian Church in North America, shall each appoint a minister with an alternate, to sit in the highest judicatories respectively, with the privilege of deliberating on all subjects coming before them, and of making suggestions on matters affecting the interests of both bodies mutually, or pertaining to the several interests of religion, but not of voting.

"The ministers, members, and judicatories of these churches, treating each other with Christian respect, shall always recognize the validity of each other's acts and ordinances consonant to the word of God; it being understood, that any ecclesiastical judicatory belonging to either body may examine persons, or review cases of discipline, on points at present peculiar or distinctive to themselves respectively.

"The same committee also recommended that a correspondence on the same terms be opened with the General Synod of the Associate Reformed Presbyterian Church in the United States, and that a delegate and alternate be appointed to attend their next meeting.

"Their report was adopted."—*Minutes*, 1857, p. 394.

26. *Expenses of Delegates to Corresponding Bodies.*

a. "*Resolved*, That the delegates to the General Association of Connecticut be allowed two dollars per day, during their attendance with the Association, and at the rate of two dollars for every forty miles in going and returning; which sums the treasurer is hereby ordered to pay out of the funds of the Assembly."—*Minutes*, 1796, p. 108.

[This was made general as correspondence was opened with other churches. Minutes, 1811, p. 470, &c.]

b. "The rule on the compensation of delegates to corresponding bodies (see Digest of 1820, p. 308, as above) was amended, by adding to it the words, 'not exceeding their necessary travelling expenses."—*Minutes*, 1849, p. 172.

CHAPTER XII.

THE PLAN OF UNION AND THE DIVISION OF THE CHURCH.

SECTION 1.—THE PLAN OF UNION.

1. Original proposition by the General Association of Connecticut.—2. Plan digested and adopted by the General Assembly.—3. Resolution declaring any change inexpedient and undesirable.—4. Resolutions to request the Association to consent to annul the Plan of Union.—5. The Plan of Union declared to be abrogated.

1. *Original Proposition by the Association of Connecticut.*

"A communication was read from the General Association of the State of Connecticut, appointing a committee to confer with a committee of the Presbyterian Church, to consider the measures proper to be adopted by the General Association and the General Assembly, for establishing an uniform system of Church government, between the inhabitants of the new settlements, who are attached to the Presbyterian form of government, and those who prefer the Congregational form.

"*Ordered*, That said communication lie on the table."

[It was as follows:]

"The Rev. John Smalley, Levi Hart, and Samuel Blatchford, are hereby appointed a committee of this General Association, to confer with a committee to be appointed by the General Assembly of the Presbyterian Church, if they see cause to appoint such committee, to consider the measures proper to be adopted both by this Association and the said Assembly, to prevent alienation, to promote harmony, and to establish, as far as possible, an uniform system of Church government, between those inhabitants of the new settlements who are attached to the Presbyterian form of Church government, and those who are attached to the Congregational form, and to make report to this Association. Any two of the said committee are hereby empowered to act.

"*Resolved*, That a copy of the foregoing proposals be transmitted to the said General Assembly, and that they be respectfully requested by the moderator of this General Association to concur in the measure now proposed.

"By order of the committee.

"NATHAN WILLIAMS, Chairman.

"A true copy.

"Attest: WM. LYMAN, Assistant Scribe."

—*Minutes*, 1801, p. 212.

2. *Plan adopted by the General Assembly.*

"The Rev. Drs. Edwards, McKnight, and Woodhull, the Rev. Mr. Blatchford, and Mr. Hutton, were appointed a committee to consider and digest a plan of government for the churches in the new settlements, agreeably to the proposals of the General Association of Connecticut, and report the same as soon as convenient."

"The report of the committee appointed to consider and digest a plan of government for the churches in the new settlements was taken up and considered, and, after mature deliberation on the same, approved, as follows:

"Regulations adopted by the General Assembly of the Presbyterian Church in America, and by the General Association of the State of Connecticut (provided said Association agree to them), with a view to prevent alienation, and to promote union and harmony in those new settlements which are composed of inhabitants from these bodies:

"1. It is strictly enjoined on all their missionaries to the new settlements, to endeavor, by all proper means, to promote mutual forbearance and a spirit of accommodation between those inhabitants of the new settlements who hold the Presbyterian, and those who hold the Congregational form of Church government.

"2. If in the new settlements any church of the Congregational order shall settle a minister of the Presbyterian order, that church may, if they choose, still conduct their discipline according to Congregational principles, settling their difficulties among themselves, or by a council mutually agreed upon for that purpose. But if any difficulty shall exist between the minister and the church, or any member of it, it shall be referred to the Presbytery to which the minister shall belong, provided both parties agree to it; if not, to a council, consisting of an equal number of Presbyterians and Congregationalists, agreed upon by both parties.

"3. If a Presbyterian church shall settle a minister of Congregational principles, that church may still conduct their discipline according to Presbyterian principles, excepting that if a difficulty arise between him and his church, or any member of it, the cause shall be tried by the Association to which the said minister shall belong, provided both parties agree to it; otherwise by a council, one-half Congregationalists and the other Presbyterians, mutually agreed upon by the parties.

"4. If any congregation consist partly of those who hold the Congregational form of discipline, and partly of those who hold the Presbyterian form, we recommend to both parties that this be no obstruction to their uniting in one church and settling a minister; and that in this case the church choose a standing committee from the communicants of said church, whose business it shall be to call to account every member of the church who shall conduct himself inconsistently with the laws of Christianity, and to give judgment on such conduct. That if the person condemned by their judgment be a Presbyterian, he shall have liberty to appeal to the Presbytery; if he be a Congregationalist, he shall have liberty to appeal to the body of the male communicants of the church. In the former case, the determination of the Presbytery shall be final, unless the church shall consent to a further appeal to the Synod, or to the General Assembly; and in the latter case, if the party condemned shall wish for a trial by a mutual council, the cause shall be referred to such a council. And provided the said standing committee of any church shall depute one of themselves to attend the Presbytery, he may have the same right to sit and act in the Presbytery as a ruling elder in the Presbyterian Church."—*Minutes,* 1801, pp. 221, 224, 225.

"Unanimously adopted by the Association."—*Minutes,* 1802, p. 237.

3. *Inexpedient and undesirable to interfere with the Plan.*

"*Resolved,* That it is deemed inexpedient and undesirable to abrogate or interfere with the Plan of Union between Presbyterians and Congregationalists in the new settlements, adopted in 1801."—*Minutes,* 1834, p. 440.

4. *Resolutions to request the Association to consent to annul the "Plan of Union."*

"*Resolved,* That this Assembly deem it no longer desirable that churches should be formed in our Presbyterian connection agreeably to the Plan adopted by the Assembly and the General Association of Connecticut, in 1801. Therefore,

"*Resolved*, That our brethren of the General Association of Connecticut be, and they hereby are, respectfully requested to consent that said Plan shall be, from and after the next meeting of that Association, declared to be annulled. And

"*Resolved*, That the annulling of said Plan shall not in anywise interfere with the existence and lawful operations of churches which have been already formed on this Plan."—*Minutes*, 1835, p. 486.

5. *The Plan of Union declared to be Abrogated.*

[See Sec. 2, 1, below.]

Section 2.—The Exscinding Acts of 1837.

1. The "Plan of Union" declared to be abrogated, on the ground of its unconstitutionality.—2. Protest against the abrogation of the Plan.—3. Answer to the protest.—4. Resolutions to cite to the bar of the Assembly such inferior judicatures as are charged by common fame with irregularities.—5. Protest against the foregoing resolutions.—6. Answer to the protest.—7. Proposal to inquire into the expediency of a voluntary division of the Presbyterian Church.—8. Committee of ten appointed.—9. Report of the committee of the majority.—10. Report of the committee of the minority.—11. The Synod of the Western Reserve declared to be no longer a part of the Presbyterian Church in the United States.—12. The Synods of Utica, Geneva, and Genesee declared out of the ecclesiastical connection with the Presbyterian Church.—13. Protest of the commissioners of the Synod of the Western Reserve.—14. Answer to the protest.—15. Protest of the commissioners of the Synods of Utica, Geneva, and Genesee.—16. Answer to the protest.—17. Dissolution of the Third Presbytery of Philadelphia.—18. Protest against the dissolution.—19. Answer to the protest.

1. *Plan of Union declared to be Abrogated.*

"The Assembly proceeded to the order of the day, viz., that part of the report of the Committee on Overture No. 1, which relates to the 'Plan of Union,' adopted in 1801.

"The report was read and adopted, in part, as follows, viz.:

"In regard to the relation existing between the Presbyterian and Congregational Churches, the committee recommend the adoption of the following resolutions:

"1. That between these two branches of the American Church, there ought, in the judgment of this Assembly, to be maintained sentiments of mutual respect and esteem, and for that purpose no reasonable efforts should be omitted to preserve a perfectly good understanding between these branches of the Church of Christ.

"2. That it is expedient to continue the plan of friendly intercourse, between this Church and the Congregational Churches of New England, as it now exists."—*Minutes*, 1837, p. 419.

"3. But as the 'Plan of Union' adopted for the new settlements, in 1801, was originally an unconstitutional act on the part of that Assembly—these important standing rules having never been submitted to the Presbyteries—and as they were totally destitute of authority as proceeding from the General Association of Connecticut, which is invested with no power to legislate in such cases, and especially to enact laws to regulate churches not within her limits; and as much confusion and irregularity have arisen from this unnatural and unconstitutional system of union, therefore it is resolved, that the Act of the Assembly of 1801, entitled 'A Plan of Union,' be, and the same is hereby abrogated." [Yeas, 143; nays, 110.]—*Ibid.* p. 421.

2. *Protest against the Abrogation.*

"The undersigned, members of the General Assembly, respectfully present the following protest against the resolution of said Assembly, adopted on the 23d ult., *abrogating* the Act of the General Assembly of 1801, entitled 'A Plan of Union,' &c., and for the following reasons, viz.:

"1. Because the said act is declared, in the resolution complained of, to have been *unconstitutional.* The utmost that can be said on this subject is, that it is an act neither specifically provided for, nor prohibited, in the Constitution. It cannot, therefore, be affirmed to be *contrary* to the Constitution.

"The Constitution provides, that before any constitutional rules proposed by the General Assembly to be established, shall be obligatory on all the churches, the approval of them by a majority of Presbyteries must be first obtained. (Form of Government, chap. xii, sec. 6.) The act of the Assembly adopting the Plan of Union, it is admitted, was not previously transmitted to the Presbyteries for their approval. It does not therefore follow, however, that that act was unconstitutional; because the provisions of the Plan of Union were, neither in fact, nor ever regarded by any of the Presbyteries as 'constitutional *rules*,' 'to be obligatory on *all* the churches.' They were the mere terms of an agreement, or treaty, between the General Assembly of the Presbyterian Church and the General Association of Connecticut, and through that Association with all the churches which have been formed according to the terms of that treaty.

"In the act of the Assembly adopting *that Plan of Union*, the General Assembly being constitutionally 'the bond of *union*, peace, correspondence, and mutual confidence, among all our churches' (Form of Government, chap. xii, sec. 4), merely exercised its legitimate functions, agreeably to the Constitution (Form of Government, chap. i, sec. 2), in declaring 'the terms of admission into the *communion*' of the Presbyterian Church, proper to be required on the frontier settlements, and in this light the entire Presbyterian Church has so regarded this Plan of Union from its adoption up to the present time, when the abrogation of it is publicly declared by the advocates of the measure to be *necessary* for the acquisition and perpetuation of power to accomplish the ends avowed and sought by the minority of the last General Assembly, and prosecuted by means of a convention, called at their instance, and holding its sessions cotemporaneously with those of the Assembly. For the following facts are undeniable, viz.: 1. That the Plan of Union now declared to be unconstitutional was formed TWENTY YEARS *before* the adoption of the present Constitution of the Presbyterian Church. 2. That this Plan, at the time of the adoption of the Constitution, was in full and efficient operation, and of acknowledged authority as common law in the Church. 3. That it had been recognized and respected in numerous precedents, in the doings of the General Assembly, from year to year; and 4. That for SIXTEEN YEARS *since* the adoption of this Constitution, it has been regarded of equal authority with any act whatever to which the General Assembly is constitutionally competent.

"Had the Plan of Union, and the act of the General Assembly adopting it, been regarded as unconstitutional and null, as being either an assumption of power not granted, or a trespass on the rights of Presbyteries, some remonstrance or objection to the imposition of constitutional rules for the government of all the churches, not legitimately enacted, would have been heard from some quarter before the lapse of one-third of a century. Had the Plan of Union been thought illegal, or had it been designed or desired by the Presbyteries in 1821, when the Constitution was revised, amended, and adopted by them a second time, to frustrate or resist the operation of this Plan, unquestionably either the revised and amended Constitution would have embodied in it some provision against it, or some attempt at least would have been made to that effect. The truth is that the Plan of Union adopted by the General Assembly was felt to be morally binding, as a solemn agreement or treaty duly ratified by the power constitutionally competent to do so, and by no means the enactment of constitutional rules, to be 'obligatory on all the churches' for their government.

"It is to no purpose, in our opinion, to allege the unconstitutionality of the Plan of Union, by pleading, that for a church to be regarded as a Presbyterian church, it must, according to our Constitution, be organized with ruling elders, while that Plan provides for the organization of churches, in certain cases, without such officers; because the Plan of Union designedly contemplates a process which the Assembly was constitutionally competent to prescribe, and which the entire Church had approved, by which churches on the frontier settlements may be organized, partially, at first, on the Presbyterian ground, and be gradually brought fully on to it; and because, if the provisions of the Constitution, prescribing the full form of organization proper for a Presbyterian church, must in every case be minutely and completely observed, and any deviation from it should vitiate the organization, then must those numerous churches among us in which there are no deacons be, for the same reason, pronounced unconstitutional.

"The attempt, too, to prove the unconstitutionality of the act of the Assembly adopting the Plan of Union, by attributing to the provisions of that Plan the character of constitutional rules obligatory on all the churches, and by objecting that the Presbyteries had not been previously consulted, strikes as directly, and is as conclusive, against the plans adopted for the organization and government of the Theological Seminaries at Princeton and Alleghany, of the Boards of Education and of Missions, and for the union and perpetuated existence of the Presbyteries belonging to the General Synod of the Associate Reformed Church, who were admitted into communion with the Presbyterian Church by the terms of a Plan of Union agreed upon between that Synod and the General Assembly; for the provisions of these plans have never been transmitted to the Presbyteries for their approval. If, therefore, the Plan of Union with the General Association of Connecticut is to be abrogated because of alleged unconstitutionality on these grounds, so must be the rules and regulations and the whole organization and government of the theological seminaries of the General Assembly, and also the act of the Assembly by which the Presbyteries of the Associate Reformed Synod were united with the Presbyterian Church of these United States, and by which the General Assembly became possessed of the valuable theological library known as the Mason library, now in Princeton, and formerly belonging to the Associate Reformed Synod.

"2. We protest against the resolution referred to, because the Plan of Union adopted by the General Assembly of 1801, was designed to suppress and prevent schismatical contentions, and for the promotion of charity, or, in the language of the Plan itself, 'with a view to prevent alienation and promote union and harmony,' which, through a long series of years, it has been efficient in doing, and has proved both itself efficacious to do and the wisdom of the Assembly in its projection and adoption; both which ends the General Assembly is constitutionally competent to design, and for which it is invested with ample authority by the Constitution (Form of Government, chap. xii, sec. 5), and held responsible by the great Head of the Church.

"3. We protest against the resolution referred to, because it declares the said Plan of Union to have been 'totally destitute of authority as proceeding from the General Association of Connecticut, which is invested with no power to legislate in such cases.' Even on the assumption that the said Association was invested with no such power—which, it seems to us, both indecorous and irrelevant for this General Assembly to assert as a reason for the resolution adopted—we cannot doubt that that Association had full power to agree to the stipulations of a treaty or contract proposed by the General Assembly, and urged on the acceptance of the General Association; and especially when it is considered, that, by acceding to the said stipulations, the said Association relinquished whatever right it had to the direction and regulation of the members of its own churches in the new settlements, and allowed and influenced them to increase, both the numbers and the pecuniary and spiritual strength of the Presbyterian Church. And even if the Plan referred to had not authority in so far as it emanated from the General Association of Connecticut, which we by no means admit, it was unquestionably binding on the General Assembly, by virtue of its own engagement, to fulfil its own obligations; and after numerous churches had been formed under their own care, the obligations of the Plan appear to us to have been common to the General Assembly, the General Association of Connecticut, and the churches, Presbyteries, and Synods formed in pursuance and in the faith of it, and that no one of these bodies could lawfully abrogate it without the consent of all the others. Our opinion therefore is, that the resolution of this General Assembly, abrogating the said Plan of Union, so far as it was intended to affect churches already formed under its provisions, is a breach of faith, and wholly void and of no effect; that all such churches have a right to continue their organization on the conditions of the said Plan; and that it is the duty of the Presbyteries, the Synods, and all future General Assemblies, to protect them in that right, until they shall voluntarily, under the kind and conciliatory influence of the aforesaid bodies, adopt the Presbyterian organization in full, as many of them have already done, and others, we are happy to learn, will probably soon do, if allowed to exercise their choice, unrestrained by the attempted exercise of assumed authority.

"4. We protest against the said resolution, because it denominates the Plan of Union unnatural, as well as unconstitutional, and attributes to it much confusion and irregularity; whereas, it appears to us to have been a most natural, wise, and benevolent plan for promoting the unity, increase, and purity of the Church in our new settlements, and that its operation for thirty-six years, with but such occasional irregularities as may occur under any system of government, has, on the whole, been productive of benign and happy effects; in view of which, this General Assembly and the whole Church ought to cherish sincere and devout gratitude to God.

"5. We protest against the said resolution, because the mode in which it was brought before the Assembly appears to us to have been exceedingly exceptionable, it having been in substance proposed in the memorial of a convention, of whose alleged cause and objects, and of most of whose declarations, because unaccompanied with satisfactory proof, we wholly disapprove, and which memorial, as coming from such a body, we think this Assembly ought not to have received and entertained, especially when it was found to contain representations of the state of the Church, in our opinion not justified by fact, and of very injurious tendency. Another objection to the mode in which the said resolution was brought before the Assembly is, that a majority of the committee to whom the memorial was referred, and who reported the resolution against which we protest, were members of the convention presenting the memorial.

"6. We protest, because, against the earnest remonstrances of many who are best acquainted with the happy effects of the Plan of Union, the debate on the subject was arrested by an impatient call for the previous question, more than eighty of the members voting for it having been members of the convention in whose name the said memorial was presented. The Assembly was thus forced to a decision without any proper evidence of the existence of the alleged irregularities, and before the subject of errors in doctrine had been discussed in the Assembly, notwithstanding the memorialists had declared that they 'complain and testify' against said Plan of Union 'chiefly because of their sincere belief, that the doctrinal purity of our ancient Confession of Faith is endangered, and not because of any preference for a particular system of mere Church government and discipline.'

"For these reasons, the undersigned enter this their solemn protest.

"PHILADELPHIA, June 1st, 1837.

"John P. Cleaveland, William Jessup, Baxter Dickinson, Absalom Peters, Henry Brown, Horace Bushnell, Harmon Kingsbury, Timothy Stillman, David Porter, E. W. Gilbert, Darius O. Griswold, John B. Richardson, James B. Shaw, Washington Thatcher, Thomas Brown, Thomas Lounsbury, Nahum Gould, Abner Hollister, Ephraim Cutler, William Fuller, Gardner Hayden, Robert Stuart, Silas West, Marcus Smith, John L. Grant, John Gridley, Nathaniel C. Clark, Varnum Noyes, Dudley Williams, George Spaulding, John Seward, Edwin Holt, Alanson Saunders, Jonathan Cone, J. M. Rowland, J. W. McCullough, Dewey Whitney, H. S. Walbridge, Horace Hunt, Samuel Reed, Rufus Nutting, Zina Whittlesey, James R. Gibson, Bennet Roberts, Joseph H. Breck, Enoch Kingsbury, James Boyd, Eldad Barber, David Schenck, Ira Pettibone, Lewis H. Loss, Jonathan Hovey, J. B. Preston, Ambrose White, Wilfred Hall, John S. Martin, George Painter, Benjamin Woodbury, Burr Bradley, Ira M. Wead, P. W. Warriner, T. D. Southworth, Adam Miller, Jacob Faris, Alexander Campbell, N. S. S. Beman, H. H. Hayes, Henry Brewster, N. E. Johnson, Solomon Stevens, Daniel Sayre, William C. Wisner, Isaac J. Rice, Felix Tracy, Bliss Burnap, E. Cheever, E. Seymour, Obadiah Woodruff, Frederick W. Graves, James I. Ostrom, Philip C. Hay, Jacob Gideon, David B. Ayres,

S. W. May, Ammi Doubleday, Robert Aikman, William Roy, Thomas McAuley, John Leonard, Calvin Cutler, Merit Harmon, F. A. McCorkle, James W. Phillips, George E. Delavan, James A. Carnahan, Obadiah N. Bush, John McSween, George Duffield, S. Benjamin, John Crawford, Fayette Shipherd, Thomas Williams, R. Campbell."—*Minutes*, 1837, pp. 454–458.

3. *Answer to this Protest.*

"The committee to whom that subject was referred, beg leave to present the following answer to the protest against the resolution abrogating 'the Plan of Union,' and request that both be placed on your minutes:

"The reasons of protest are numbered from one to six. No. 1 is the principal, and therefore we prefer leaving it to the last, and commencing with No. 2. 'We protest,' say the minority, 'against the resolution referred to, because the Plan of Union adopted by the General Assembly of 1801, was designed *to suppress and prevent schismatical contentions, and for the promotion of charity*, or, in the language of the Plan itself, 'with a view to prevent alienation and promote union and harmony.'

"To this a sufficient answer is found in the broad and undeniable fact, that 'the Plan of Union' has been a principal means of dividing the Church and this General Assembly into two parties, and been the main source of those schisms which for many years have distracted our Zion. Whilst it is admitted, that in some instances it may have beneficially affected certain localities, it has laid the deep foundation of lasting confusion, and opened wide the flood-gates of error and fanaticism. For proof of this, we have only to refer to the recorded votes of the last and the present General Assemblies, from which it abundantly appears, that the representatives of churches formed on this Plan have always opposed the Boards of Education and Missions, and the efforts toward reform, and the suppression of errors and of schismatical contentions.

"No. 3. 'Because it declares the said Plan of Union to have been totally destitute of authority, as proceeding from the General Association of Connecticut, which is invested with no power to legislate in such cases.'

"In reply to this, let it be remarked, 1st, that the protesters seeming to admit that the General Association of Connecticut had no power and authority to bind their churches, yet insist that the General Assembly could make a treaty or covenant that should be binding on the other side; and the brethren, in arguing the case, did insist on the 'Plan' being of the nature of a covenant (although no such term is contained in it), and yet one of the parties to this covenant had no authority to make a contract and to make it obligatory on their churches. That is, a contract, treaty, or covenant can exist and be and continue forever, binding in right and in law upon one party, whilst the other party, having no power or authority to bind themselves and those for whom they plead its benefits, never could be bound. That is, a treaty or covenant may exist without a mutual obligation!

"2dly. The protesters, without distinctly affirming it again, seem willing that the reader of their protest should believe that the General Association of Connecticut had power to bind their churches—that their acts participate of the nature of ecclesiastical authority. 'By acceding to said stipulations' (say they), 'the said Association relinquished whatever right it had to the direction and regulation of the members of its own churches in the new settlements.' Now these remonstrants know perfectly well, that the General Association of Connecticut never had, never claimed, and never exercised any right at all 'to the direction and regulation of the members of its own churches,' even in Connecticut itself, much less 'in the new settlements.' The 'right' of counsel and advice is the utmost stretch of their power and authority. And this General Assembly might give counsel and advice to the churches of Connecticut, and, should it be founded in truth, it is just as binding upon those churches as the counsels of their own General Association, *i. e.*, it comes *divested* entirely of all ecclesiastical *authority*.

"3dly. The resolution of abrogation is alleged to be 'a breach of faith, and wholly void and of no effect.' This is begging the question: it goes on the *assumption*, that faith was plighted of right, and the treaty, so called, lawfully constituted; which we have supposed to be the very point in question.

"No. 4. 'Because it denominates the Plan of Union *unnatural* as well as unconstitutional, and attributes to it much confusion and irregularity.' A sufficient answer to this is found in the preceding; to which may be added a single remark as to the irregularity, viz., that upon inquiry of brethren who came in upon this 'Plan,' it appeared from their own showing, to the abundant conviction of this General Assembly, that there were some members on this floor, deliberating and voting on the very resolutions in question, who had never adopted the Confession of Faith of this Church.

"No. 5. The fifth reason of protest is, that the resolution was concocted and brought before the Assembly by members of this body who had previously consulted, in the form of a convention, and memorialized this body on the subject: and that a majority of the committee to whom the memorial was referred were members of the convention.

"As to the former, let it suffice to say, that it is the right of every freeman and the duty of every Christian, before entering upon any great and important measure, to 'ponder the path of his feet,' because 'in the multitude of counsellors there is safety.' How the name 'convention,' any more than the name 'caucus,' should utterly vitiate their counsel, it may be difficult to discern.

"As to the latter, it may be remarked, that in all deliberative bodies, the principle is settled, that large committees ought to be selected in proportion to the respective party views that may be entertained on the subject committed. The wisdom of the rule is obvious to common sense, and the moderator of this Assembly simply carried out the rule in this case.

"No. 6. The sixth reason of protest is, 'because the debate on the subject was arrested by an impatient call for the previous question. The Assembly was thus forced to a decision without any proper evidence of the existence of the alleged irregularities, and before the subject of errors in doctrine had been decided on in the Assembly.'

"Here remark, *first*, the call for the previous question was not *impatient*,—it was asked for and seconded by a majority of the house, not in the spirit of violence and unjust oppression of the minority; and, *secondly*, there was no unreasonable curtailment of debate. The resolution was discussed two whole days,—a period of time perhaps more extended than was ever before allotted or allowed by any General Assembly to any single naked resolution. And, *thirdly*, the brethren of the minority occupied the floor more than one-half of the time. And on another resolution, where the discussion was arrested by the previous question, it was just at the close of two long speeches by the minority, and after they had consumed more than five hours in debate; whereas, the majority had not occupied the floor two hours and a half. So utterly groundless is the insinuation that a cruel and unjust use has been made of the previous question.

"'The Assembly was thus forced,' say the protesters—the Assembly was forced! 'Forced' by whom? Undoubtedly, by itself—'forced' to do just as it wished to do—'forced' to decide by a strong vote on a subject which had been discussed two whole days! Strange coercion this!!

"But, *fourthly*, the resolution in question was passed before the doctrinal errors were condemned. This is true. But it is also true, that 'the Assembly was thus forced,' by the opposition of the minority, to pass by the doctrinal discussion, because they could not have it in the order recommended by their committee. Certain alleged errors were offered by the minority, which they refused to have put in their proper place, but insisted on having first of all a decision upon them as amendments; which attempt, had it been successful, would have precluded their discussion, except upon a vote of reconsideration, which requires two-thirds: and thus the majority would have been completely, as to these alleged errors, in the power of the minority. Hence they were laid on the table, to be taken up at a future time. We now proceed to

"No. 1. The principal reason of protest is in these words, viz.: "Because the said act is declared, in the resolution complained of, to have been *unconstitutional*.'

"In opposition to the resolution declaring the Plan of Union unconstitutional, it would appear most reasonable that the protesters should affirm its constitutionality, *i. e.*, that the Constitution covers and provides for it. This ground, however, the protesters have not ventured to take. On the contrary, they explicitly admit, that the Constitution makes no provision for said act—'it is,' say they, 'neither specifically provided for, nor prohibited in the Constitution.'

"A remark or two will show that in this they have abandoned the ground. For, 1. The Constitution of the Presbyterian Church, like that of our National Union, is a constitution of specific powers, granted by the Presbyteries, the fountains of power, to the Synods and the General Assembly. 2. No powers, not specifically granted, can lawfully be inferred and assumed by the General Assembly, but only such as are indispensably necessary to carry into effect those which are specifically granted. 3. Therefore the burden of proof lies upon those who affirm that the Assembly had power to enact this 'Plan of Union.' They admit that there is no specific grant of such power; they are bound then to prove that its exercise was indispensably necessary, in order to carry out some other power specifically granted. Now we search in vain for any such proof in the protest. There is, we believe, but a single effort of the kind. This effort is made in view of two distinct and distant clauses in our book. (Form of Government, chap. xii, sec. 4.) The General Assembly 'shall constitute the bond of union, peace, correspondence, and mutual confidence among all our churches.' But surely here is no power granted to constitute a bond of union with churches of another denomination. It has exclusive reference to 'all our churches,' and yet the protesters refer to this as authority for forming a union with a denomination not holding the same form of government.

"An equally unsuccessful attempt is made upon chap. i, sec. 2, where the book affirms, that 'any Christian Church, or union or association of churches, is entitled to declare the terms of admission into its *communion.*' And the protesters assert here, that the General Assembly exercised this power in forming 'the Plan of Union,' and so declared 'the terms of admission into the *communion* of the Presbyterian Church, proper to be required in the frontier settlements.'

"On this statement two remarks seem requisite: *first*, the settling of the terms of communion, we had thought, was the highest act of power—an act beyond the reach of the General Assembly itself—an act which the Constitution itself provides, shall be done only by a majority of the Presbyteries. When, we ask, did the Presbyterian Church 'declare the terms of admission into its *communion?*' Most assuredly, when the Constitution was adopted. And yet the protesters in this case aver, that the 'Plan of Union' is a declaration of the terms of admission into our communion! Could they affirm more directly its unconstitutionality?

"The other remark is, that the Plan of Union itself does not prescribe the terms of admission into the communion of the Presbyterian Church. It prescribes the manner in which Congregationalists may remain out of this Church, and yet exercise a controlling and governing influence over its ecclesiastical judicatories.

"In the entire absence of all proof, that the power exercised in forming the Plan of Union, was indispensably necessary to carry out a power specifically granted, and in the face of their own admission, that such power is not specifically given to the General Assembly, we conclude, that the act in question was without any authority, and must be null and void.

"The next thing worthy of notice, is the criticism on the phrases 'constitutional rules,' and 'obligatory on all the churches.' This Plan of Union, it is argued, is not of the nature of constitutional rules, obligatory on all the churches, and therefore it was not necessary that it should have been sent down, and have received the sanction of a majority of the Presbyteries. In presenting this argument, the protesters admit, that if the Plan did embrace constitutional rules, the Assembly had no power to enact it. The book (Form of Government, chap. xii, sec. 6) declares: 'Before any overtures or regulations proposed by the Assembly to be established as constitutional rules, shall be obligatory on the churches, it shall be necessary to transmit them to all the Presbyteries, and to receive the returns of at least a majority of them in writing, approving thereof.'

"This was not done with the Plan; and the only question before us is, whether it is an alteration of the Constitution? This Assembly affirms that it is a radical and thorough change of the entire system. On which remark—

"1. Our book describes four church courts, viz., the Church Session, the Presbytery, the Synod, and the General Assembly. And (chap. ix) it defines 'the Church Session to consist of the pastor or pastors and ruling elders of a particular congregation,' and intrusts to these, as permanent officers, the government of that church. But the Plan of Union provides for no such thing. It expressly dispenses with the Church Session, and leaves the government in the hands of the people, or of a temporary committee.

"Again, chap. x, sec. 2: 'A Presbytery consists of all the ministers and one ruling elder from each congregation within a certain district.' But the Plan of Union abrogates this provision. It does not merely pass it by, but absolutely repeals and nullifies it. According to the Plan, a Presbytery may have committee-men less or more in it, and may have not a single elder. The book farther states, that 'Every congregation (i. e. of Presbyterians as before described) which has a stated pastor, has a right to be represented by one elder; and every collegiate church (i. e. a church with two or more ministers) by two or more elders, in proportion to the number of pastors.' Here it is perfectly obvious, that the principle of equal representation in Presbytery is aimed at. The same is true of a Synod (chapter xi): 'The ratio of the representation of elders in the Synod is the same as in the Presbytery.' That is, every congregation, governed by its own Session, shall be represented in Presbytery and Synod. But the Plan provides for Congregational committee-men, sitting and acting and voting in Presbytery, although it also provides that the congregation he represents shall not be under the government of the Presbytery, and no appeal can be taken from it to the Presbytery, even by a minister, unless the church agree to it. Thus the power of government is in the hands of men over whom that government does not extend. It is surely not necessary to proceed farther, to show that the Plan is an abrogation of the fundamental principles of the Presbyterian system. And yet the protesters say it does not contain constitutional rules. No, verily, but it is a mass of unconstitutional usurpations, resulting from an overstretch of power. By the criticism of the protest, it is denied that the Plan contains constitutional rules; whereas, in the first sentence of the instrument itself, it is called 'A plan of government for the churches in the new settlements.' And the second sentence runs thus: 'Regulations adopted by the General Assembly,' &c. Now, if *regulations* are not rules, language has lost its meaning; and if *regulations* containing 'a plan of government for the churches,' are not intended to be binding, and do not touch the Constitution, we are utterly at a loss to see how rules and regulations could be expressed. The article in question has been called 'a Plan of Union,' 'a contract,' 'a covenant,' none of which phrases is found in the document itself. It declares itself to be 'regulations,' containing 'a plan of government for the churches.' Now the General Assembly never had the power to establish 'regulations' and a new 'plan of government;' the Plan is therefore null and void.

"But, we are told, these governmental regulations were not binding on *all the churches*. Were they not, indeed? Have they not given rise to heterogeneous bodies, who have come up here and bound us almost to our undoing? Have they not bound with green withes and new cords this body and its Boards of Education and Missions? Have they not well-nigh shorn us of the locks of our strength, and forbidden us to go forth into the field of missionary conflict against the foes of our God and King? Surely, these protesters will not say the regulations are not binding upon all the churches.

"But, again, we are told in the protest, they are of long standing and have acquired the force of common law. Does long use constitute law? Then it would follow that concubinage and polygamy exist of moral right.

"Again, we are told, that this 'plan of government' was in existence twenty years prior to the last adoption of our Constitution; and the inference is, that therefore it is binding, and was viewed as a contract to be kept in good faith. The fair inferences, however, from the fact, ought to be, that this 'plan of government' was not submitted to our Presbyteries by the General Assembly, and is therefore not binding; and that this neglect was owing to the circumstance that it was then little known, and its evils were not all developed.

"Again, we are told in the protest, in reference to this new 'plan of government,' that its omission of elders, being expressly provided for and designed, does not 'vitiate the organization; for then must numerous churches among us, in which there are no deacons, be for the same reason pronounced unconstitutional.' And we are free to confess that, if the Constitution made the deacon a ruling officer in the Church, he must be found in our ecclesiastical courts, and his absence would nullify their constitutional existence. This, however, is not the case. The deacon's office in the New Testament, and in our book, is limited to 'serving tables.' The argument, therefore, is lame, and shows its eastern birth.

"Again, the protest affirms that the argument against this 'plan of government for the churches,' because it was not submitted to the Presbyteries, strikes equally against the Theological Seminaries, the Boards of Education and of Missions, and also against the admission of the Presbyteries of the Associate Reformed Synod into this Church.

"Let us touch these in their order; and first, the Theological Seminaries. Here, again, if our protesters can show that these Seminaries are, in the language of our book, 'constitutional rules, obligatory on the churches,' or even, in the language of their favorite Plan, 'regulations,' and 'a plan of government for the churches in the new settlements,' we will give up the argument, and Princeton and the Western seminaries and all. But if, as every one knows, the constitutions and regulations of these seminaries have nothing to do with the government of the churches, any more than the private regulations of a private clergyman for his private class of students, then is this argument null and void from the beginning. As to the power in the Assembly to organize a seminary, it may be found in the book (Form of Government, chap. xii, sec. 5), under the general power 'of superintending the concerns of the whole Church,' none of which concerns is of more vital importance than that of providing an efficient ministry. Also to them belongs the power of 'promoting charity, truth, and holiness, through all the churches under their care.' Now, the training of a pious and orthodox ministry is the most effectual mode of accomplishing this work, and clearly places Theological Seminaries within the Assembly's power.

"The same remarks are relevant and true, in reference to the Board of Education.

"As to the Board of Missions, 'the superintending of the concerns of the whole Church' cannot be carried out without missions; and the Form of Government, chap. xviii, expressly provides for them, and grants to the Assembly power over this very business. It reads thus: 'The General Assembly may, of their own knowledge, send missions to any part to plant churches or to supply vacancies: and, for this purpose, may direct any Presbytery to ordain evangelists or ministers, without relation to any particular churches.' How utterly unreasonable, then, for the protesters to deny the Assembly's power to institute a Board of Missions!

"As to the Mason Library and the Associate Reformed Churches, it may be necessary only to remark, that the two Presbyteries of New York and of Philadelphia—the only parts which came into this Presbyterian Church—were, from their beginning, *Presbyterian,* according to the strictest order; holding the same identical Westminster Confession of Faith and Presbyterian Form of Church Government. It is therefore difficult to perceive how the admission, by the General Assembly, of strict and rigid Presbyterians into their connection could be either extra or unconstitutional. The act of their admission did not create 'regulations,' and 'a plan of government for the churches,' as did 'the Plan' in question. It was not 'an overture or regulation for establishing constitutional rules, obligatory on the churches,' and therefore its transmission to all the Presbyteries was not necessary.

"Finally, the unconstitutionality of the 'plan of government for the churches in the new settlements,' abrogated by this resolution, is further demonstrated by reference to Form of Government, chap. xii, sec. 1, which says, 'The General Assembly is the highest judicatory of the Presbyterian Church. It shall represent, in one body, all the particular churches of this denomination;' and, subsequently, it defines the ratio of representation. Now, it has been proved, on the open floor of this General Assembly, by the protesters themselves, that the Synod of the Western Reserve, which was formed on this 'plan of government,' and which contains one hundred and thirty-nine particular churches, has only from twenty-four to thirty Presbyterian churches in it; and yet that Synod claims a right to twenty representatives here! Whom do these twenty represent? Certainly not 'particular churches of this denomination,' as our book says. No, but Congregational churches, which, by the terms of our book, and the whole representative spirit of our system, have no right to be represented here, and to judge and vote here, under a Constitution which they deny to be binding upon themselves. With no greater impropriety would unnaturalized foreigners claim the right of franchise in our country, and of eligibility to office in our legislatures, our supreme judicial tribunals, and the executive departments of our States and the nation. Besides, it has been shown by themselves here, that this 'plan of government' has been here violated, by those claiming privileges under it, sending men to the Assembly who had never adopted our Constitution.

"We therefore conclude that the reasonings of the protesters is fallacious; the 'plan of government' adopted in 1801 is, and ever has been, unconstitutional; and therefore this General Assembly ought to declare, as it has done in the resolution protested against, that it is, from the beginning, null and void."—*Minutes*, 1837, pp. 458–464.

4. *Resolutions to cite to the Bar of the Assembly such Inferior Judicatories as are charged by Common Fame with Irregularities.*

"1. *Resolved*, That the proper steps be now taken to cite to the bar of the next Assembly such inferior judicatories as are charged by common fame with irregularities.

"2. That a special committee be now appointed to ascertain what inferior judicatories are thus charged by common fame, prepare charges and specifications against them, and to digest a suitable plan of procedure in the matter; and that said committee be requested to report as soon as practicable.

"3. That as citations on the foregoing Plan is the commencement of a process involving the right of membership in the Assembly, therefore—

"*Resolved,* That, agreeably to a principle laid down, chap. v, sec. 9, of the Form of Government, the members of said judicatories be excluded from a seat in the next Assembly until their case shall be decided.

"Adopted by yeas 128, nays 122."—*Minutes*, 1837, p. 425.

"5. Mr. Hay for himself, and others, gave notice of a protest against the foregoing resolutions. The protest and answer were ordered to be entered on the minutes, viz.:

5. *Protest.*

"The undersigned, members of the General Assembly, beg leave respectfully to enter their solemn protest to the act of the Assembly, adopting the three resolutions relative to the citation of inferior judicatories; and likewise to the resolution of the Assembly, declaring the Synod of the Western Reserve not a part of the Presbyterian Church.* In support of our protest, we subjoin the following reasons:

"1. We object to the mode of investigation adopted, in the first-named resolutions, by the Assembly. They resolve, in the first place, 'to cite to the bar of the next Assembly such inferior judicatories as are charged, by common fame, with irregularities.' The first step, in our estimation, should have been to appoint a committee to inquire into the nature of the various rumors which are said to be afloat, and to report to the Assembly whether there was any cause for citation.

"2. The committee was empowered, by the second resolution, merely to ascertain what judicatories were charged by common fame; whereas, they ought to have been instructed, in this stage of the investigation, to ascertain whether there was or was not any foundation for existing rumors. It seems to be made imperative by the resolution, that all judicatories shall be reported by that committee for citation against which any unfavorable rumors are in circulation.

"3. The majority of the committee recommending these measures were members of the convention which originated all this business, and brought it into the Assembly. They acted upon it first in the convention, then in the Assembly; after that in the committee, and then are to pass a final vote in the Assembly. They petition themselves, consider their own petition, and then grant to themselves what they themselves ask.

* Pp. 483, 11.

"4. The investigation ought to have been expressly limited to Synods, because the Book of Discipline makes provision for the Assembly, in certain cases, to cite Synods, but no other judicatories. (See Gen. Rev. and Con., VI.)

"5. The resolution to deprive the judicatories to be cited, of a seat in the next Assembly is, in every respect, unconstitutional and void, '*ab initio*.' This Assembly has no power, by their vote, to deprive commissioners, duly elected, from a seat in the next Assembly, because that Assembly has the exclusive right of judging of the qualifications of its own members, and because to do so would be to inflict a penalty before trial or investigation. Besides, the Assembly has power to cite Synods only; and Presbyteries, and not Synods, are represented on this floor. To deprive every Presbytery in a whole Synod of a seat in the General Assembly, because a Synod, in its collective capacity, may have been irregular, is unprecedented in ecclesiastical proceedings.

"6. The provision in the Book of Discipline referred to in the third resolution, to justify the exclusion of members from seats in the next Assembly, has no application to this case. It applies only to a minister of the Gospel when on trial before his own Presbytery, and cannot justify the unconstitutional bearing of this resolution. Besides, the Book of Discipline expressly provides for those cases in which an inferior judicatory is to be excluded from a seat in the superior judicatory; and these cases are trials of appeals and complaints in which they are interested."—*Minutes*, 1837, pp. 473, 474.

6. *Answer to the Protest.*

"The signers to the protest object to the mode of investigation adopted in the first-named resolution, and contend that the first step should have been to appoint a committee to inquire into the nature of the rumors which are said to be afloat, and to report to the Assembly whether there was any cause for citation. The resolutions as to citation refer to supposed cases, and the committee were to cite, and designate, and report to the Assembly for its approval and further action. In this aspect of the case, the objections urged lose their force. No wrong was done to any Presbytery, nor any irregular process authorized, nor, indeed, any final step to be taken without action in the General Assembly. Upon the report of the committee to cite, the house would decide upon the foundation for existing irregularities, and a wholesome control as to the details of the whole subject would be exercised by the Assembly before the final disposition of the several cases; and the signers of the protest themselves affirm, in a subsequent part of the paper, and with the design of sustaining another position, that the citation contemplated by these resolutions was according to the book. Your committee deem it, therefore, unnecessary to dwell upon this part of the subject, it being evident, from the nature of the resolutions and the admission of the signers to the protest, that the steps contemplated by these resolutions were according to the book, and within the constitutional power of this Assembly.

"It is difficult to conceive how this regular constitutional action could be impaired or destroyed by the suggestion, whether true or untrue, that the committee recommending these measures were members of the convention; that they acted upon it first in the convention, then in the Assembly; after that in the committee, and then were to pass a final vote in the Assembly. It is even gravely charged as a ground of objection, that 'they petition themselves, consider their own petition, and then grant to themselves what they themselves ask.' It is a sufficient answer to this objection, that the majority of the duly-constituted members of this Assembly adopted and sanctioned the incipient as well as final steps in the case; and the acts of the Assembly are valid until it be shown that the provisions of the Constitution have been invaded, or that the majority consisted of persons who were not duly qualified commissioners. The fact of a majority or any number of members of the Assembly having been members of the convention cannot invalidate the acts of the Assembly. The right of petition is guaranteed by every well-regulated government, whether civil, political, or ecclesiastical, and it is just as competent for any number of the individuals composing the Assembly to meet publicly for consultation, as it would be for any number to meet privately for the same object. In neither case could the action of those members in the Assembly be supposed to be purified or contaminated by such consultations.

"The investigation contemplated by these resolutions was designed to apply to inferior judicatories, which includes Synods, and may not necessarily mean Presbyteries. The specification of such inferior judicatory was to be reported by the committee, and the fourth objection, as urged by the signers of the protest, could only be appropriate when a Presbytery should be cited. Any supposed restriction of the right of the General Assembly to cite any other inferior judicatories but Synods (which is regarded by the signers of the protest as being derived from the sixth part of the section of General Review and Control) is explained by the comprehensive character of the fifth part, which assigns to the superior judicatory power to 'examine, deliberate, and judge in the whole matter as completely as if it had been recorded, and thus brought up by the review of the records.' The General Assembly, by its very Constitution, is regarded as having a general control of the whole Church, and, in its conservative character, shall superintend all of its concerns. It is believed that the initiatory steps contemplated by the resolutions authorizing a committee to designate inferior judicatories who may have been guilty of irregularities, to cite them, and report as soon as practicable to this Assembly, do not infringe the spirit or letter of the inherent powers of the General Assembly. And the great principles of analogy would obviously dictate that the members of the inferior judicatories upon whom these preparatory measures are supposed to operate, should not be permitted to sit in the next General Assembly until their cases should be decided. If there be any sound principle contained in the clause, and the uniform practice which excludes an interested judicatory from voting, that principle and that practice should be applied to the members of such inferior judicatories as may be affected by these resolutions. This view of the subject is exceedingly strengthened by the fact that express power is vested in our judicatories to exclude at will their own members when on trial before them."—*Minutes*, 1837, pp. 476, 477.

7. *Proposal to inquire into the Expediency of a Voluntary Division of the Presbyterian Church.*

"Mr. Breckenridge gave notice that he would to-morrow morning offer a resolution to appoint a committee, to consist of equal numbers from the majority and minority on the vote to cite inferior judicatories, to inquire into the expediency of a voluntary division of the Presbyterian Church."—*Minutes*, 1837, p. 426.

"Agreeably to notice given last evening, Mr. Breckenridge moved that a committee of ten members, of whom an equal number shall be from the majority and minority of the vote on the resolutions to cite inferior judicatories, be appointed on the state of the Church.

"Dr. Junkin and Mr. Ewing, on the part of the majority, and Messrs. A. Campbell and Jessup, on the part of the minority, were appointed to nominate each five members of the committee on the foregoing resolutions."—*Ibid.* p. 427.

8. *Committee of Ten appointed.*

"Dr. Junkin and Mr. Campbell, from the committees to nominate the Committee of Ten on the State of the Church, respectively reported the following nominations, viz.: Mr. Breckenridge, Dr. Alexander, Dr. Cuyler, Dr. Witherspoon, and Mr. Ewing, on the part of the majority; and Dr. McAuley, Dr. Beman, Dr. Peters, Mr. Dickinson, and Mr. Jessup, on the part of the minority. The report was adopted; and the committee was directed to meet in this house, at the rising of the Assembly this morning, and afterwards on their own adjournments.

"On motion, the Assembly engaged in prayer, on behalf of this committee, and of the subject referred to them."—*Minutes*, 1837, p. 427.

"The Committee on the State of the Church reported, by their chairman, Dr. Alexander, that they had not been able to agree, and asked to be discharged.

"Both portions of the committee then made separate reports, accompanied by various papers, which reports and papers were ordered to be entered on the Minutes of the Assembly, and are as follows, viz.:

9. *Report of the Committee of the Majority.*

"The committee of the majority, from the united Committee on the State of the Church, beg leave to report:

"That having been unable to agree with the minority's committee on any plan for the immediate and voluntary separation of the New and Old School parties in the Presbyterian Church, they lay before the General Assembly the papers which passed between the committees, and which contain all the important proceedings of both bodies.

"These papers are marked 1 to 5 of the majority, and 1 to 4 of the minority. A careful examination of them will show that the two committees were agreed in the following matters, namely:

"1. The propriety of a voluntary separation of the parties in our Church, and their separate organization.

"2. As to the corporate funds, the names to be held by each denomination, the records of the Church, and its boards and institutions.

"It will further appear, that the committees were entirely unable to agree on the following points, namely:

"1. As to the propriety of entering at once, by the Assembly, upon the division, or the sending down of the question to the Presbyteries.

"2. As to the power of the Assembly to take effectual initiative steps, as proposed by the majority, or the necessity of obtaining a change in the Constitution of the Church.

"3. As to the breaking up of the succession of this General Assembly, so that neither of the new Assemblies proposed, to be considered *this* proper body continued; or that the body which should retain the name and institutions of the General Assembly of the Presbyterian Church in the United States of America, should be held in fact and law to be the true successors of *this* body. While the committee of the majority were perfectly disposed to do all that the utmost liberality could demand, and to use in all cases such expressions as should be wholly unexceptionable, yet it appeared to us indispensable to take our final stand on these grounds.

"For, *first*, we are convinced that if anything tending towards a voluntary separation is done, it is absolutely necessary to do it effectually, and at once.

"*Secondly*. As neither party professes any desire to alter any constitutional rule whatever, it seems to us not only needless, but absurd, to send down an overture to the Presbyteries on this subject. We believe, moreover, that full power exists in the Assembly, either by consent of parties, or in the way of discipline, to settle this and all such cases; and that its speedy settlement is greatly to be desired.

"*Thirdly*. In regard to the succession of the General Assembly, this committee could not, in present circumstances, consent to anything that should even imply the final dissolution of the Presbyterian Church, as now organized in this country; which idea, it will be observed, is at the basis of the plan of the minority, insomuch that even the body retaining the name and institutions should not be considered the successor of *this* body.

"*Finally*. It will be observed from our fifth paper, as compared with the fourth paper of the minority's committee, that the final shape which their proposal assumed was such that it was impossible for the majority of the house to carry out its views and wishes, let the vote be as it might; for if the house should vote for the plan of the committee of the majority, the other committee would not consider itself or its friends bound thereby; and *voluntary* division would therefore be impossible, in that case. But if the house should vote for the minority's plan, then—the foregoing insuperable objections to that plan being supposed to be surmounted—still the whole case would be put off, perhaps indefinitely.

"A. Alexander,
"C. C. Cuyler,
"J. Witherspoon,
"N. Ewing,
"R. J. Breckenridge."
—*Ibid.* pp. 430, 431.

10. *Report of the Committee of the Minority.*

"The subscribers, appointed members of the Committee of Ten on the State of the Church, respectfully ask leave to report, as follows:

"It being understood that one object of the appointment of said committee was to consider the expediency of a voluntary division of the

Presbyterian Church, and to devise a plan for the same, they, in connection with the other members of the committee, have had the subject under deliberation.

"The subscribers had believed that no such imperious necessity for a division of the Church existed, as some of their brethren supposed, and that the consequences of division would be greatly to be deprecated. Such necessity, however, being urged by many of our brethren, we have been induced to yield to their wishes, and to admit the expediency of a division, provided the same could be accomplished in an amicable, equitable, and proper manner. We have accordingly submitted the following propositions to our brethren on the other part of the same committee, who at the same time submitted to us their proposition, which is annexed to this report.

"[Here read the proposition marked Minority No. 1, and Majority No. 1.]

"Being informed by the other members of the committee that they had concluded not to discuss in committee the propositions which should be submitted, and that all propositions on both sides were to be in writing, and to be answered in writing, the following papers passed between the two parts of the committee :—

"Here read No. 2, Minority paper.
2, Majority "
3, Majority "
3, Minority "
4, Majority "
4, Minority "
5, Majority "

"From these papers it will be seen, that the only question of any importance upon which the committee differed, was that proposed to be submitted to the decision of the Assembly, as preliminary to any action upon the details of either plan. Therefore, believing that the members of this Assembly have neither a constitutional nor moral right to adopt a plan for a division of the Church, in relation to which they are entirely uninstructed by the Presbyteries; believing that the course proposed by their brethren of the committee to be entirely inefficacious, and calculated to introduce confusion and discord into the whole Church, and instead of mitigating, to enhance the evils which it proposes to remove; and regarding the plan proposed by themselves, with the modifications thereof, as before stated, as presenting in general the only safe, certain, and constitutional mode of division, the subscribers do respectfully present the same to the Assembly for their adoption or rejection.

"THOMAS MCAULEY,
"N. S. S. BEMAN,
"ABSALOM PETERS,
"B. DICKINSON,
"WILLIAM JESSUP."

No. 1, of the Majority.

"The portion of the committee which represents the majority, submit for consideration:

"1. That the peace and prosperity of the Presbyterian Church in the United States require a separation of the portions called respectively the Old and New School parties, and represented by the majority and minority in the present Assembly.

"2. That the portion of the Church represented by the majority in the present General Assembly, ought to retain the name and the corporate property of the General Assembly of the Presbyterian Church in the United States of America.

"3. That the two parties ought to form separate denominations, under separate organizations; that to effect this with the least delay, the Commissioners in the present General Assembly shall elect which body they will adhere to, and this election shall decide the position of their Presbyteries respectively, for the present; that every Presbytery may reverse the decision of its present commissioners, and unite with the opposite body by the permission of that body properly expressed; that minorities of Presbyteries, if large enough, or if not, then in connection with neighboring minorities, may form new Presbyteries, or attach themselves to existing Presbyteries, in union with either body, as shall be agreed on; that Synods ought to take order and make election on the general principles already stated; and minorities of Synods should follow out the rule suggested for minorities of Presbyteries, as far as they are applicable."

No. 1, of the Minority.

"Whereas, the experience of many years has proved that this body is too large to answer the purposes contemplated by the Constitution, and there appear to be insuperable obstacles in the way of reducing the representation:

"And whereas, in the extension of the Church over so great a territory, embracing such a variety of people, difference of view in relation to important points of church policy and action, as well as theological opinion, are found to exist:

"Now, it is believed, a division of this body into two separate bodies, which shall act independently of each other, will be of vital importance to the best interests of the Redeemer's kingdom. Therefore,

"*Resolved*, That the following rules be sent down to the Presbyteries for their adoption or rejection as constitutional rules, to wit:

"1. The General Assembly of the Presbyterian Church in the United States of America shall be, and it hereby is divided into two bodies; the one thereof to be called the General Assembly of the Presbyterian Church in the United States of America, and the other, the General Assembly of the American Presbyterian Church.

"2. That the Confession of Faith and Form of Government of the Presbyterian Church of the United States of America, as it now exists, shall continue to be the Confession of Faith and Form of Government of both bodies, until it shall be constitutionally changed and altered by either, in the manner prescribed therein.

"3. That in sending up their commissioners to the next General Assembly, each Presbytery, after having, in making out their commissions, followed the form now prescribed, shall add thereto as follows: 'That in case a majority of the Presbyteries shall have voted to adopt the plan for organizing two General Assemblies, we direct our said commissioners to attend the meeting of the General Assembly of the "Presbyterian Church of the United States of America," or the "American Presbyterian Church," as the case may be.' And after the opening of the next General Assembly, and before proceeding to other business than the usual preliminary organization, the said Assembly shall ascertan what is the vote of the Presbyteries, and in case a majority of said Presbyteries shall have adopted these rules, then the two General Assemblies shall be constituted and organized in the manner now pointed out in the Form of Government, by the election of their respective moderators, stated clerks, and other officers.

"4. The several Presbyteries shall be deemed and taken to belong to that Assembly with which they shall direct their commissioners to meet, as stated in the preceding rule. And each General Assembly shall, at their first meeting as aforesaid, organize the Presbyteries belonging to each into Synods. And in case any Presbytery shall fail to decide as aforesaid at that time, they may attach themselves within one year thereafter to the Assembly they shall prefer.

"5. Churches and members of churches, as well as Presbyteries, shall be at full liberty to decide to which of said Assemblies they will be attached, and in case the majority of male members in any church shall decide to belong to a Presbytery connected with the Assembly to which their Presbytery is not attached, they shall certify the same to the stated clerk of the Presbytery which they wish to leave and the one with which they wish to unite, and they shall, *ipso facto*, be attached to such Presbytery.

"6. It shall be the duty of Presbyteries, at their first meeting after the adoption of these rules, or within one year thereafter, to grant certificates of dismission to such ministers, licentiates, and students, as may wish to unite with a Presbytery attached to the other General Assembly.

"7. It shall be the duty of Church Sessions to grant letters of dismission to such of their members, being in regular standing, as may apply for the same within one year after the organization of said Assemblies under these rules, for the purpose of uniting with any church attached to a Presbytery under the care of the other General Assembly; and if such Session refuse so to dismiss, it shall be lawful for such members to unite with such other church in the same manner as if a certificate were given.

"8. The Boards of Education and Missions shall continue their organizations as heretofore, until the next meeting of the Assembly; and in case the rules for the division of the Assembly be adopted, those boards shall be, and hereby are, transferred to the General Assembly of the Presbyterian Church in the United States of America, if that Assembly at its first meeting shall adopt the boards as their organizations; and the seats of any ministers or elders in those boards, not belonging to that General Assembly, shall be deemed to be vacant.

"9. The records of the Assembly shall remain in the hands of the present stated clerk, for the mutual use and benefit of both General Assemblies, until, by such an arrangement as they may adopt, they shall appoint some other person to take charge of the same. And either Assembly, at their own expense, may cause such extracts and copies to be made thereof, as they may desire and direct.

"10. The Princeton Seminary funds to be transferred to the Board of Trustees of the Seminary, if it can be so done legally and without forfeiting the trusts upon which the grants were made; and if it cannot be done legally, and according to the intention of the donors, then to remain with the present Board of Trustees until legislative authority be given for such transfer. The supervision of said seminary, in the same manner in which it is now exercised by the General Assembly, to be transferred to and vested in the General Assembly of the Presbyterian Church in the United States to be constituted. The other funds of the Church to be divided equally between the two Assemblies.

"Pass a resolution suspending the operation of the controverted votes until after the next Assembly."

No. 2, of the Majority.

"The Committee of the Majority having considered the paper submitted by that of the minority, observe:

"1. That they suppose the propriety and necessity of a division of the Church may be considered as agreed on by both committees; but we think it not expedient to attempt giving reasons in a preamble; the preamble is therefore not agreed to.

"2. So much of No. 1, of the plan of the Committee of the Minority, as relates to the proposed names of the new General Assemblies, is agreed to.

"3. Nos. 1 to 8, inclusive, except as above, are not agreed to, but our proposition, No. 3, in our first paper, is insisted on. But we agree to the proposal in regard to single churches, individual ministers, licentiates, students, and private members.

"4. In lieu of No. 9, we propose that the present stated clerk be directed to make out a complete copy of all our records, at the joint expense of both the new bodies, and after causing the copy to be examined and certified, deliver it to the written order of the moderator and stated clerk of the General Assembly of the American Presbyterian Church.

"5. We agree, in substance, to the proposal in No. 10, and offer the following as the form in which the proposition shall stand: that the corporate funds and property of the Church, so far as they appertain to the Theological Seminary at Princeton, or relate to the professor's support, or the education of beneficiaries there, shall remain the property of the body retaining the name of the General Assembly of the Presbyterian Church in the United States of America; that all other funds shall be equally divided between the new bodies, so far as it can be done in conformity with the intentions of the donors; and that all liabilities of the present Assembly shall be discharged in equal portions by them; that all questions relating to the future adjustment of this whole subject upon the principles now agreed on, shall be settled by committees appointed by the new Assemblies at their first meeting respectively; and if these committees cannot agree, then each committee shall select one arbitrator, and these two, a third, which arbitrators shall have full power to settle finally the whole case in all its parts; and that no person shall be appointed an arbitrator, who is a member of either Church; it being distinctly understood that whatever difficulties may arise in the construction of trusts, and all other questions of power, as well as right, legal and equitable, shall be finally decided by the committees or arbitrators, so as in all cases to prevent an appeal by either party to the legal tribunals of the country."

No. 2, of the Minority.

"The Committee of the Minority, &c., make the following objections to the proposition of the majority.

"1. To any recognition of the terms 'Old and New Schools,' or 'Majority and Minority,' of the present Assembly; in any action upon the subject of division, the minority expect the division in every respect to be equal; no other would be satisfactory.

"2. Insisting upon an equal division, we are willing that that portion of the Church which shall choose to retain the present Boards, shall have the present name of the Assembly. The corporate property which is susceptible of division to be divided, as the only fair and just course.

"3. We object to the power of the commissioners to make any division at this time, and as individuals we cannot assume the responsibility.

No. 3 of the Majority.

"The Committee of the Majority, &c., in relation to paper No. 2, observe:

"1. That the terms 'Old and New School, Majority and Minority,' are meant as descriptive, and some description being necessary, we see neither impropriety nor unsuitableness in them.

"2. Our previous paper, No. 2, having, as we suppose, substantially acceded to the proposal of the minority in relation to the funds in their first paper, we deem any further statement on that subject unnecessary.

"3. That we see no difficulty in the way of settling the matter at present, subject to the revision of the Presbyteries, as provided in our first paper, under the third head; and as no 'constitutional rules' are proposed in the way of altering any principles of our system, we see no constitutional obstacle to the execution of the proposal already made. We therefore adhere to that plan as our final proposal. But if the commissioners of any Presbytery should refuse to elect, or be equally divided, then the Presbytery which they represent shall make such election at its first meeting after the adjournment of the present General Assembly.

No. 3 of the Minority.

"1. We accede to the proposition to have no preamble.

"2. We accede to the proposition No. 4, modifying our proposition No. 9, in relation to the records and copies of the records. The copy to be made within one year after the division.

"3. We assent to the modification of No. 10, by No. 5 of the propositions submitted, with a trifling alteration in the phraseology, striking out the words, 'shall remain the property of the body retaining the name of the General Assembly of the Presbyterian Church in the United States of America,' and inserting the words, 'shall be transferred and belong to the General Assembly of the Presbyterian Church of the United States of America, hereby constituted.'

"4. We cannot assent to any division by the present commissioners of the Assembly, as it would in no wise be obligatory on any of the judicatories of the Church, or any members of the churches. The only effect would be a disorderly dissolution of the present Assembly, and be of no binding force or effect upon any member who did not assent to it.

"5. We propose a resolution to be appended to the Rules, and which we believe, if adopted by the committee, would pass with great unanimity, urging in strong terms the adoption of the Rules by the Presbyteries; and the members of the minority side of the committee pledge themselves to use their influence to procure the adoption of the same by the Presbyteries."

No. 4 of the Majority.

"The committee of the majority, &c., in reply to paper No. 3 of the minority's committee, simply refer to their own preceding papers, as containing their final propositions."

No. 4 of the Minority.

"The committee of the minority, in reply to Paper No. 3 of the majority, observe:

"That they will unite in a report to the Assembly, stating that the committee have agreed that it is expedient that a division of the Church be effected, and in general upon the principles upon which it is to be carried out; but they differ as to the manner of effecting it. On the one hand, it is asked that a division be made by the present Assembly at their present meeting; and, on the other hand, that the plan of division, with the subsequent arrangement and organization, shall be submitted to the Presbyteries for their adoption or rejection. They will unite in asking the General Assembly to decide the above points previous to reporting the details, and, in case the Assembly decide in favor of immediate division, then the Paper No. 1 of the majority, with the modifications agreed on, be taken as the basis of the report in detail.

"If the Assembly decide to send to the Presbyteries, then No. 1 of the minority's papers, with the modifications agreed on, shall be the basis of the report in detail.

"The committee of the minority cannot agree to any other propositions than those already submitted, until the above be settled by the Assembly.

"If the above proposition be not agreed to, or be modified, and then agreed to, they desire that each *side* may make a report to the Assembly to-morrow morning."

No. 5 of the Majority.

"The committee of the majority, &c., in answer to No. 4, &c., reply, that, understanding from the verbal explanations of the committee of the minority, that the said committee would not consider either side bound by the vote of the Assembly, if it were against their views and wishes respectively on the point proposed to be submitted to its decision in said paper, to carry out in good faith a scheme which, in that case, could not be approved by them; and under such circumstances a *voluntary* separation being manifestly impossible, this committee consider No. 4 of the minority as virtually a waiver of the whole subject. If nothing further remains to be proposed, they submit that the papers be laid before the Assembly, and that the united committee be dissolved."

"The Committee on the State of the Church was discharged.

"The whole subject was laid on the table for the present. Yeas, 138; Nays, 107."—*Minutes*, 1837, pp. 430–437.

11. *The Synod of the Western Reserve declared to be no longer a Part of the Presbyterian Church in the United States of America.*

"*Resolved*, That, by the operation of the abrogation of the Plan of Union of 1801, the Synod of the Western Reserve is, and is hereby declared to be no longer a part of the Presbyterian Church in the United States of America. Yeas, 132; Nays, 105."—*Minutes*, 1837, p. 440.

12. *Synods of Utica, Geneva, and Genesee exscinded.*

"*Be it resolved*, by the General Assembly of the Presbyterian Church in the United States of America—

"1. That in consequence of the abrogation by this Assembly of the Plan of Union of 1801, between it and the General Association of Connecticut, as utterly unconstitutional, and therefore null and void from the beginning, the Synods of Utica, Geneva, and Genesee, which were formed and attached to this body under and in execution of said 'Plan of Union,' be, and are hereby declared to be out of the ecclesiastical connection of the Presbyterian Church of the United States of America, and that they are not in form or in fact an integral portion of said Church.

"2. That the solicitude of this Assembly on the whole subject, and its urgency for the immediate decision of it, are greatly increased by reason of the gross disorders which are ascertained to have prevailed in those Synods (as well as that of the Western Reserve, against which a declarative resolution, similar to the first of these, has been passed during our present sessions), it being made clear to us that even the Plan of Union itself was never consistently carried into effect by those professing to act under it.

"3. That the General Assembly has no intention by these resolutions, or by that passed in the case of the Synod of the Western Reserve, to affect in any way the ministerial standing of any members of either of said Synods; nor to disturb the pastoral relation in any church; nor to interfere with the duties or relations of private Christians in their respective congregations; but only to declare and determine, according to the truth and necessity of the case, and by virtue of the full authority existing in it for that purpose, the relation of all said Synods and all their constituent parts to this body, and to the Presbyterian Church in the United States.

"4. That inasmuch as there are reported to be several churches and ministers, if not one or two Presbyteries, now in connection with one or more of said Synods, which are strictly Presbyterian in doctrine and order, be it therefore further resolved, that all such churches and ministers as wish to unite with us, are hereby directed to apply for admission into those Presbyteries belonging to our connection which are most convenient to their respective locations; and that any such Presbytery as aforesaid, being strictly Presbyterian in doctrine and order, and now in connection with either of said Synods, as may desire to unite with us, are hereby directed to make application, with a full statement of their cases, to the next General Assembly, which will take proper order thereon."

"Yeas on resolution 1, 115; Nays, 88; on resolutions 2, 3, 4, Yeas, 113; Nays, 60."—*Minutes*, 1837, pp. 444, 445.

13. *Protest of the Commissioners from the Synod of Western Reserve.*

"We, the subscribers, commissioners to this General Assembly from the Presbyteries of Grand River, Trumbull, Portage, Cleveland, Lorain, Medina, Huron, and Maumee, feel it our duty to enter our solemn protest and remonstrance against what we regard the unconstitutional and unjust act of the Assembly, by which we are interrupted in the discharge of the duties assigned us by our respective Presbyteries, and excluded from the floor of this house, and from the Presbyterian Church of these United States of America; and by which the General Assembly of the said Church is actually dismembered; and for the following reasons, viz.:

"1. We were regularly appointed by our Presbyteries, commissioned in due form, and admitted to our seats in this Assembly, and exercised our undisputed rights as members for two weeks.

"2. The Presbyteries represented by us all have a regular Presbyterian existence, according to the Constitution of the Presbyterian Church, as interpreted and administered by all the courts of the Church; and some of these Presbyteries existed prior to the adoption of the Constitution in 1821, and participated in that act.

"3. If there was anything wrong in the original organization of our

Presbyteries (which we do not admit or believe), this wrong was chargeable, not upon us, but upon the Synod of Pittsburg, from whose act our original Presbyteries received their existence, and which act has been sanctioned by twenty-two General Assemblies, up to the present time.

"4. But if, after an administration of the Constitution for thirty-six years, on the assumption that the Plan of Union with the Association of Connecticut was constitutional, a different conclusion is now arrived at, we can see no reason why this new discovery, which legally concerns the 'accommodation churches' only, should be made a reason why Presbyteries, ministers, and elders, regularly introduced into the Presbyterian Church, according to its known and common forms, should be driven, without a constitutional trial, from the rights and privileges secured to them by our Constitution.

"5. If it be assumed that the existence of churches on the 'accommodation plan' rightfully annihilates the existence of all Presbyteries and Synods where such churches have been formed, we see not why this principle should be confined in its severe application to the Synod of the Western Reserve, when it is known that the same system has prevailed in the Synods of Albany, New Jersey, and South Carolina and Georgia, and extensively in other Synods under the care of the General Assembly. And, if the toleration of the 'accommodation plan' proves so fatal to the existence of inferior courts, we see not why the originating and the fostering of this plan for thirty-six years should not render nugatory all the acts of the Assembly itself, and even destroy its charter.

"A principle which leads to results so disastrous and suicidal to the Presbyterian Church, we cannot regard as constitutional.

"6. Once admit that regularly appointed commissioners may be excluded *instanter*, without a charge of discourtesy to the House, and without trial, and the way is open to drive from the General Assembly, under some pretext or other, any member, or any number of members, who, for the time being, may be obnoxious to the majority. This principle annihilates at once and forever the rights of Presbyteries on this floor, and renders the Constitution itself a dead letter.

"We complain not so much that we were denied a patient hearing; that it was professed we were not on trial, on the ground that we were already out of the House by the passage of a previous resolution; and that still testimony was elicited from us catechetically, which, we think, was abused to our condemnation; that the whole case on which hung the destiny of the Synod was hurried through, and finally closed by the 'previous question,' which shut up the mouths of ourselves and our friends; that, finally, we were furnished with no communication dismissing us from the House in a courteous manner. All this we have felt to be unkind and unjust treatment; but we have passed it over, to select our reasons for protest from the great principles of Presbyterianism, which, in our case, have been violated. We, therefore, wish to leave this our solemn protest on the records of a court of which we still regard ourselves as rightful members. Having done this, we commit our case to the calm decision of the Church at large, of posterity, of God.

"Rufus Nutting, Alanson Saunders, Henry Brown, Eldad Barber, John Seward, William Fuller, Joseph H. Breck, James Boyd, Harmon Kingsbury, Isaac J. Rice, Varnum Noyes, Benjamin Woodbury, Dudley Williams."—*Minutes*, 1837, pp. 449, 450.

14. *Answer to the Protest.*

"The General Assembly might not only decline to reply to the protest signed by the commissioners from the Presbyteries composing the Synod of the Western Reserve, but even refuse to admit it to record. For if the Plan of Union was unconstitutional, and therefore void, from the beginning, and the existence of these Presbyteries was founded on that Plan of Union, then they never had a constitutional existence, and their commissioners never had a constitutional right to a seat in the General Assembly. The Assembly, therefore, do not exclude those who they admit once had a right to seats here, but they simply declare that, from the unconstitutional organization of these Presbyteries, their commissioners never had, and of course now have not a right to seats in this Assembly. They, therefore, had no 'right to vote,' and consequently had no 'right to join in a protest' against any decision of this House, or to have their protest admitted to record. They did vote, however, in the decision against which they protest; but if they did that in one case which the Constitution did not authorize, that certainly gives them no right to do another thing which depended on their right to do the first act.

"But the Assembly desire to treat those brethren with all courtesy, and therefore allow their protest a place in the records.

"To their reasons for protesting, the following answers are given:

"It seems, however, to be proper in the first place to state the great principle on which the Assembly decided.

"We believe that our powers, as a judicatory, are limited and prescribed by the Constitution of the Presbyterian Church. Whatever any Assembly may do which it is not authorized by the Constitution to do, is not binding on any inferior judicatory, nor on any subsequent Assembly.

"The Constitution provides that all our judicatories shall be composed of bishops or ministers and ruling elders of the Presbyterian Church, and the General Assembly have no right to introduce into any of the judicatories any other persons claiming to hold any other offices, either in the Presbyterian Church or any other Church. And should they attempt to do this, no one is bound by it. But the General Assembly of 1801 did permit members of standing committees in churches not Presbyterian 'to sit and act' in our Presbyteries, and under this provision they have sat in the higher judicatories of the Church.

"On a thorough investigation, it is now fully ascertained that they had no authority from the Constitution to admit officers from any other denomination of Christians to sit and act in our judicatories; and therefore no Presbytery or Synod thus constituted is recognized by the Constitution of our Church, and no subsequent General Assembly is bound to recognize them.

"The Presbyteries of the Synod of the Western Reserve are thus constituted, for committee-men are permitted 'to sit and act' in all these Presbyteries; therefore this General Assembly cannot recognize the constitutional existence of these Presbyteries.

"The fact that they have been recognized by former Assemblies cannot bind this Assembly, when it is fully convinced of the unconstitutionality of the organization.

"In reply to the first reason in the protest, viz., that they were regularly appointed by their Presbyteries, &c., we say they were not regularly appointed, for it is admitted that these committee-men are allowed to vote for commissioners to the Assembly, and these illegal votes, of which there may have been a majority, render the appointment illegal. They held their seats in this Assembly for some time, it is true, but this gives them no right to continue to hold them after it is ascertained that they had no constitutional right to seats.

"As to the second reason, that their Presbyteries have a regular Presbyterian existence, it is denied by this Assembly, and on this ground they are denied seats. The existence of Presbyteries thus constituted is recognized neither in the former nor the amended Constitution of the Church.

"3. If the Synod of Pittsburg constituted Presbyteries in part of materials not allowed by the Constitution, this Assembly is not bound to recognize them.

"4. It is well known to those acquainted with the history of this General Assembly, that the Plan of Union, as an unconstitutional compact, has long been a subject of complaint, and as long ago as the year 1831, the Assembly resolved that the appointment of members of standing committees to be members of the General Assembly, was of questionable constitutionality, and therefore ought not in future to be made; and since that time none have been received in the Assembly known to be such. But their right to seats here is just as constitutional as in the Presbytery.

"The protestants still assume that their Presbyteries are regularly constituted, while we consider it a fundamental departure from our system to organize a Presbytery with one or two Presbyterian churches and ten or twelve of another denomination of Christians. And had none but Presbyterian churches been allowed to belong to the Presbyteries, some of these Presbyteries never would have existed. The representatives of these churches, on the accommodation plan, form a constituent part of these Presbyteries as really as the pastors or elders, and this Assembly can recognize no Presbytery thus constituted as belonging to the Presbyterian Church.

"5. The Assembly has extended the operation of this principle to other Synods which they find similarly constituted. But even if they did not, this injures not the Synod of the Western Reserve.

"6. 'Once admit that regularly appointed commissioners may be excluded,' &c. This is assuming what we deny. Many of those who voted for these commissioners, and, for aught we know, a majority, were neither bishops nor ruling elders in the Presbyterian Church, and therefore had no right to vote for those commissioners.

"The Constitution says expressly, it (the General Assembly) shall represent in one body all the particular churches of this denomination; but these commissioners were voted for by the delegates of churches of another denomination; therefore they represent churches of another denomination. According to their own showing, there is one Presbytery with only one Presbyterian church, another with two, and in the whole Synod, containing one hundred and thirty-nine churches, there are only twenty-five, or, at most, thirty Presbyterian churches, and one hundred and nine Congregational churches, or churches of a mixed character. It cannot, therefore, be a Presbyterian body where more than three-fourths of the churches are not Presbyterian. It is perfectly manifest that in a body thus constituted it would often occur that the commissioners elected would be chosen by those who had no right to vote, and so they would be the representatives not of the Presbyterian, but of the Congregational denomination.

"We would observe, in reference to the conclusion of the protest, that the members of the Synod of the Western Reserve, and their friends, occupied a larger space in the discussion than the majority of the Assembly; and the 'previous question' was not called for until it was manifest that the minds of members were made up. As the Assembly has already made provision for the organization into Presbyteries and annexation to this body of all the ministers and churches who are thoroughly Presbyterian, it is not necessary to reply to the closing remarks of the protest."—*Ibid.*, pp. 450, 452.

15. *Protest of the Commissioners from the Synods of Utica, Geneva, and Genesee.*

"Whereas, the General Assembly of the Presbyterian Church in the United States of America, now in session, has declared the Synods of Utica, Geneva, and Genesee, no longer constituent parts of the Presbyterian Church; and whereas, the commissioners from the Presbyteries constituting those Synods have been deprived of the right of deliberating and voting in this House, therefore—

"The undersigned, commissioners from the Synods of Utica, Geneva, and Genesee, claim their right to enter their protest and remonstrance against these acts, for the reasons following, viz.:

"1. Because we deem such acts utterly unconstitutional and unprecedented. In our Form of Government (chap. xii, secs. 4 and 5), the powers of the General Assembly are specifically defined, but no authority to exercise such summary process and excision is there granted. In our Book of Discipline (chapters iv and v), the mode of procedure in the trial and punishment of ministers of the Gospel is expressly and specifically prescribed, yet no one point of these laws of discipline has been conformed to in the excision and virtual excommunication of four or five hundred ministers, in good and regular standing in the Presbyterian Church; no citations have been issued or served; no charges have been specified or preferred, and no opportunity has been afforded for justification or defence.

"2. Because, when the regular and constitutional method of trial was proposed to this house, the majority rejected this plan, and proceeded, without trial in any form, and, in our judgment, in the face of all the regulations and provisions of our Constitution and rules of discipline, to declare the aforesaid Synods to be 'out of the ecclesiastical connection of the Presbyterian Church in the United States, and not in form or fact an integral portion of said Church.'

"3. Because the act of exclusion is professedly based on the previous act of the Assembly, purporting to abrogate the 'Plan of Union' formed by the Assembly of 1801, with the Connecticut Association, and acted upon for thirty-six years; whereas, in our estimation, that ancient compact could not, in good faith, be abrogated without previous conference with said Association; and even if it could be so abrogated, that abrogation would not destroy or invalidate the institutions established, and the rights vested under its operation. Besides, the majority of the churches within the bounds of said Synods are strictly Presbyterian in their structure, and, with few exceptions, even the small number of churches originally Congregational were not organized under the stipulations of the said 'Plan of Union,' but came in under a different arrangement, and possessed rights on this subject, separate from and independent of the 'Plan of Union' of 1801, secured to them by the Assembly of 1808, by which the Synod of Albany was authorized to take the 'Middle Association' under its care; in virtue of which arrangement commissioners from said Association were admitted to the floor of the General Assembly up to the period when the Association was dissolved and erected into two Presbyteries, regularly organized out of its materials.

"4. Because all our Synods and Presbyteries have been regularly and constitutionally formed and recognized, and, *as such*, have no necessary dependence whatever upon the 'Plan of Union,' or any other plan of accommodation, and, consequently, could not be affected either by the existence or abrogation of such plan.

"5. Because no proof was exhibited on the floor of the Assembly, that a single minister in these Synods was irregularly inducted into the office of the ministry, and we know of none such; and in every Presbytery belonging to these Synods there are churches formed on strict Presbyterian principles, and in most of our Presbyteries such churches compose a large majority.

"6. Because, while the resolution for the exclusion of these Synods was under discussion, members were permitted to read and refer to letters and publications containing what we consider unfounded statements, and to utter vague and injurious reports, and when requested, refused to give names, places, and dates; and, although the right was insisted upon, not a single commissioner from any one of the three Synods could obtain the floor to address the Assembly on the resolution, being put down by the motion for the previous question.

"7. Because no notice whatever was given to the Synods in question of the intention to sever them from the Presbyterian Church, nor the least opportunity afforded them for vindicating themselves from the vague and informal charges uttered against them on the floor of the General Assembly.

"8. Because there has been no definite or authentic evidence whatever regularly before this Assembly, of the existence within the bounds of the said Synods of those errors in doctrine, or those gross irregularities in practice which they are alleged to be guilty of tolerating.

"9. Because, in our view, these acts of the Assembly are not only unconstitutional and unwarrantable, but tend to disturb the peace of our churches, to injure our ministerial character and standing, and to impair our usefulness, and thus to retard the progress of truth and righteousness in one of the most populous and important sections of our country.

"10. Because, finally, while in the accompanying resolutions it is declared that these acts are not intended to affect our ministerial character, or to interfere with the organization and peace of our Synods or Presbyteries, the last resolution in the category directs Presbyteries, ministers, and churches, to detach themselves from the bodies with which they are now connected, and apply for admission into the nearest Presbyteries of the Presbyterian Church. Thus attempting to exercise authority over bodies already declared not to be constituent portions of the Presbyterian Church in the United States, and to disturb their order and peace.

"For these reasons, we do hereby enter our solemn protest and remonstrance against the proceedings in question.

"John W. McCullough, George Spalding, S. Benjamin, Philip C. Hay, Thomas Lounsbury, Merit Harmon, Solomon Stevens, Ira Pettibone, John Gridley, J. B. Richardson, Marcus Smith, Horace Hunt, Henry Brewster, Samuel W. May, Fayette Shipherd, Washington Thatcher, J. B. Preston."—*Minutes*, 1837, pp. 464–466.

16. *Answer to this Protest.*

"In reply to the protest of the commissioners from the Presbyteries composing the Synods of Utica, Geneva, and Genesee, against the act of this Assembly declaring them no longer a constituent portion of the Presbyterian Church, the Assembly remark:

"1. That the above-named Synods became connected with the Presbyterian Church by the Plan of Union of 1801, which Plan the Assembly had no constitutional power to adopt, and was accordingly null and void from the beginning. So it has been declared by this Assembly. And as these Synods became connected with the General Assembly by an unconstitutional Plan of Union, they never have been a constitutional part of it. And this is all the act in reference to them declares.

"Nor is there, as the protestants declare, an excommunication of four or five hundred ministers. The act itself asserts the contrary. As there was no judicial process instituted against them, no citations were necessary. Without impeaching the character or standing of the brethren composing these Synods, this Assembly, by a legislative act, merely declares them, in consequence of the abrogation of the Plan of Union of 1801, no longer a constituent part of the General Assembly of the Presbyterian Church in the United States.

"2. When resolutions were before the house for the citation of judicatures to the bar of the next Assembly, charged by common fame with sanctioning errors in doctrine and irregularities in practice, the protestants unanimously opposed them. And now they complain that they were not thus cited.

"3. The compact of the Assembly of 1808 with the Synod of Albany, in reference to the 'Middle Association,' is as unconstitutional as the Plan of Union of 1801; and the fact stated by the protestants, that two large Presbyteries were made out of that Middle Association, and that commissioners from said Association were admitted to the floor of the Assembly as members, only proves the constitutionality of the act against which they complain. So that their third specification of grievance contains its own answer.

"4. The contrary of their fourth specification of grievance is believed and proved to be the fact. The great majority of the churches of these Synods were formerly Congregational; and the great majority of those of them now Presbyterian retain much of their Congregational peculiarities and prejudices. They almost unanimously prefer the institutions of the Church they have abandoned, to those of the Church of their adoption. They are in form Presbyterian, but in prejudice, and in fact, Congregational.

"5. As no charge was brought against any minister or ministers, that they were irregularly inducted into the office of the ministry, no proof was needed to sustain it. The charge is, not that they were irregularly inducted into the Christian ministry, but that they were unconstitutionally connected with the Presbyterian Church.

"6. The papers complained of were official papers, published over the signatures of stated clerks of Presbyteries, and committees of Synods and Associations. The resolutions complained of were thirty-six hours under debate, and more than one-half of the time was occupied by those opposed to their adoption. A brother, in the midst of an argument, yielded the floor, that the protestants might make what statements they thought proper; but none were made. The previous question was once withdrawn, for the same purpose; and they were yet silent. And yet they complain because no time was given—that they were put down by the previous question!!

"7. This is founded on the supposition that they were constitutional parts of the Presbyterian Church, and that the act by which they were declared to be no longer a constitutional part of it, is not a legislative, but a judicial act. Both of which suppositions are incorrect.

"8. The evidence of great errors in doctrine and gross irregularities in practice prevailing to an alarming extent within the bounds of said Synods, and if not countenanced, certainly unsuppressed by them, is before the Church and the world.

"9. This is a mere expression of opinion by the protestants, to which, in this free country, every man has an undoubted right.

"10. In the resolution complained of, this Assembly merely tenders its advice to the ministers and churches sincerely Presbyterian, and points them to the constitutional door, by which they may speedily return to the Church of their preference and affection."—*Minutes*, 1837, pp. 466, 467.

17. *Dissolution of the Third Presbytery of Philadelphia.*

"*Be it resolved*, by the General Assembly of the Presbyterian Church in the United States of America:

"1. That the Third Presbytery of Philadelphia be, and is hereby dissolved.

"2. That the territory embraced in this Presbytery is reannexed to those to which it respectively appertained before its creation. Its stated clerk is directed to deposit all the records and other papers in the hands of the stated clerk of the Synod of Philadelphia, on or before the first day of the sessions of that Synod, at its first meeting after this Assembly adjourns.

"3. The candidates and foreign missionaries of the Third Presbytery of Philadelphia are hereby attached to the Presbytery of Philadelphia.

"4. The ministers, churches, and licentiates in the Presbytery hereby dissolved, are directed to apply, without delay, to the Presbyteries to which they most naturally belong, for admission into them. And upon application being so made by any duly organized Presbyterian Church, it shall be received.

"5. These resolutions shall be in force from and after the final adjournment of the present sessions of the General Assembly." [Yeas, 75; nays, 60.]—*Minutes*, 1837, p. 472.

18. *Protest against the foregoing Action.*

"The undersigned, members of the General Assembly, present the following protest against the resolutions of the General Assembly, by which the Third Presbytery of Philadelphia has been dissolved, and for the following reasons:

"1. Because the said resolutions are contrary to the acts of several successive General Assemblies, by which said Presbytery was, as we believe, constitutionally created, and has been sustained. This Presbytery was formed by the General Assembly of 1832,—justly said to have been one of the ablest Assemblies that ever sat in this city; and that too after long, full, and able discussion as to the constitutionality of creating it, the Assembly having deemed it the only effectual and constitutional way of suppressing the protracted and painful disputes among the brethren in the Presbytery of Philadelphia.

"Nor was this done until the Synod had refused to take steps for the division of the Presbytery of Philadelphia, as directed by the Assembly of 1831, and the case had been brought up before the Assembly by complaint and petition, and by the reference of the Synod. Subsequently this Presbytery having been dissolved by the Synod of Philadelphia, was restored by the Assembly in 1834. In 1836, the Assembly assigned geographical limits to this Presbytery, in the belief and with the general understanding, that it was to terminate the dispute in relation to its alleged unconstitutional existence, on the ground of elective affinity. Here it was hoped this Presbytery would have been permitted to pursue their labors without further molestation. We therefore regard it as not only doing injury to the Presbytery, but as being contrary to the repeatedly expressed decisions of the collected wisdom of the whole Church, and utterly subversive of all stability in our government, when the case had been fairly before them and fully discussed, again to disturb the organization of this Presbytery and agitate the churches of this city.

"2. We protest against the dissolution of this Presbytery, on the ground of its having been originally a mere elective affinity body, for this principle has been recognized and acted upon by the Presbyterian Church in this country for nearly a century, as a means of terminating painful disputes among brethren of the same Presbytery. It is a thing of frequent occurrence, to allow a minister unpleasantly situated, either from local circumstances or otherwise, to withdraw and connect himself with another Presbytery.

"3. Because the objections urged against the existence of this Presbytery, on the ground of its alleged defective geographical limits, are wholly without foundation, inasmuch as the geographical boundaries are completely and *throughout its whole extent* accurately defined, so that its future operations are restricted within limits much more distinctly defined than either of the two other Presbyteries in this city.

"4. We protest against the resolution, because of its unconstitutionality, inasmuch as the Presbytery has been dissolved without being accused, cited, tried, or condemned, and that too without any opportunity of defence, and in a manner as sudden and unexpected, as it has been in our apprehension contrary to justice and right; and inasmuch as it may have the effect to exclude from the Presbyterian Church some of its ministers in good standing, without the benefit of those forms of justice which our Book of Discipline provides shall be respected in all processes affecting the reputation of ministers, and guarantees to all.

"5. Because the resolution was passed after four Synods had been cut off, thus taking fifty-one commissioners from the floor of the Assembly, and thus dismembering the body, which we feel to be the more grievous, because, had the thing been attempted before such dismemberment, it could not have been carried.

"6. We protest, finally, because of the contentions which we fear it will excite again in this city, and which we had hoped had happily ceased. The Presbytery was at peace and peacefully pursuing its course. Its plans of usefulness have thus been broken up. Its way is embarrassed. The churches under its care are thrown into perplexity and confusion, and in our apprehension serious injury will be inflicted on the interests of religion in this city.

"John P. Cleaveland, William Jessup, Robert Stuart, Frederick W. Graves, James I. Ostrom, E. W. Gilbert, E. Seymour, Ambrose White, George Painter, John L. Grant, N. C. Clark, E. Cheever, Bliss Burnap, George Duffield, T. D. Southworth, Thomas Brown, Burr Bradley, N. S. S. Beman, Alexander Campbell, John Mines, Absalom Peters, Jacob Faris, Samuel Reed, Wilfred Hall, Adam Miller."—*Minutes*, 1837, pp. 486–488.

19. *Answer to the Protest.*

"*Resolved*, That the protest respecting the dissolution of the Third Presbytery of Philadelphia, is sufficiently answered by stating that the reasonings which it contains are foreign from the grounds on which the question was decided; that the evidence before this Assembly, establishing the evil effects of the existence of this Presbytery, is ample; that the principle on which it was formed, and on which it has existed up to this time, viz., that of elective affinity, is now on all hands admitted to be unconstitutional; and lastly, that being originally formed by the Assembly, none can question the right of that body to dissolve it, whenever its continued existence is found to be injurious to truth and charity."—*Minutes*, 1837, p. 488.

SECTION 3.—PERTAINING TO THE DIVISION.

1. Pastoral letter to the churches under the care of the General Assembly, 1837.—2. Circular letter to the Churches of Christ.—3. Assembly of 1838. Organization of the Assembly.—4. Demand for the records, books, papers, &c. of the General Assembly. The demand refused.—5. Trustees elected.—6. Committee of Twelve appointed with power to advise and direct.—7. The Assembly willing to agree to any reasonable measure for the amicable adjustment of difficulties.—8. Pastoral letter to the churches under the care of the General Assembly, 1838.—9. Report of the Committee of Twelve. Articles of agreement proposed. Result of the trial at law. Charge of the court.—10. A declaration of the General Assembly, setting forth its present position and its causes.—11. Withdrawal of the suits at law.—12. The roll of the Assembly rectified.—13. Proposal to unite in communion; refused.—14. Committee of Correspondence appointed. The result.—15. Detail of efforts for a harmonious understanding.

1. *Pastoral Letter to the Churches under the Care of the General Assembly*, 1837.

[Adopted by the majority of the Assembly of 1837, after the passage of the Exscinding Acts.—*Minutes*, 1837, p. 479.

"DEAR BRETHREN: As the doings of the present General Assembly have been of unusual character, and such as may produce important consequences, we think it proper to lay an abstract of our decisions and the reasons of them before the churches under our care. Discerning men have perceived for a number of years, that the affairs of our beloved Church were hastening to a crisis; and when the members of the present Assembly came together, the state of parties was such as to make it manifest, that a division of the Church was the most desirable object that could be effected. What are called the Old School and New School parties are already separated in fact; in almost every part of our country where those parties exist, they have less ministerial or Christian communion with one another than either of those parties have with Christians of other denominations; and they are so equally balanced in point of power, that for years past it has been uncertain, until the General Assembly was fully organized, which of those parties would predominate in that body.

"From these circumstances, as well as from other things not necessary to mention, it is known to our brethren, that the floor of our highest judicatory, as well as of our Synods and Presbyteries, has, for years, presented scenes of contention and strife such as many of us never expected to witness in the Presbyterian Church, and such as are highly disgraceful to our Christian character. This spirit of contention deprives the Church of all power for maintaining the purity of her standards, and securing that wholesome instruction, either in our pulpits or presses, which would conduce to the edification of the body of Christ; and until the parties are separated and formed into different denominations, there is no ground of hope that these contentions can be terminated.

"So fully was this Assembly convinced, that a separation of the parties was the only cure for the evils under which we labor, that a committee was appointed by common consent, composed of equal numbers from the different sides of the house, to adjust if possible the terms of an amicable division of the Church into two separate and independent denominations. This joint committee agreed upon the principles of the division, but could not agree upon the form. It was admitted on all hands, that the Old School party should retain the name and the funds of the Church, and especially all the funds and property connected with the Theological Seminaries at Princeton and Pittsburg. But on the mode of separation the committee could not agree. The New School party would consent to no other plan than that of referring it to the Presbyteries, in order to have the division made by the next General Assembly. To this plan the other party thought there were insuperable objections. It was believed that, our Presbyteries being so widely dispersed, the returns from them would be uncertain; that many things might occur to defeat the arrangement; and that, as the probable result, the parties would come to the next Assembly, with more determination to contend for the power and government of the whole Church than on any former occasion.

"On reviewing the causes from which our troubles have arisen, another plan presented itself to the view of the majority, which appeared better calculated to effect, in a peaceable manner, that division of the Church which all seemed to consider as a matter of indispensable necessity. The contentions which distract the Church evidently arose from the Plan of Union formed in 1801, between the General Assembly and the Association of Connecticut. This Plan was indeed projected and brought into operation by some of the wisest and best men the Presbyterian Church has ever known, and it evidently originated from the purest and most benevolent motives. It has, however, been disastrous in its effects. We mean no disrespect to the Congregationalists of New England, as such; indeed there is no denomination of Christians beyond the pale of our own Church whom we esteem and love more sincerely; and yet we believe that the attempt, by this Plan of Union, to bring Congregationalists and Presbyterians into the same denomination, has been the principal cause of those dissensions which now distract and rend the Church to pieces.

"We allude to these circumstances, merely for the purpose of explaining the only remedy which appears applicable to our present troubles. The Plan of Union adopted in 1801, was evidently unconstitutional in its nature, and of a tendency to subvert the institutions and distinctive character of the Presbyterian Church; and such being the fact, it was certainly the duty of the present Assembly to abrogate said Plan, and to declare it void from the beginning. From this act of abrogation, and from the declaration that it was void from the beginning, it would necessarily follow, that the churches, Presbyteries, and Synods formed under said Plan, were of course not to be considered as parts of the Presbyterian Church. From this view of the subject it appears, that the *separation*, so necessary for the well-being of the Presbyterian Church, exists already, and that we have nothing to do but to act on the facts of the case to secure our tranquillity.

"In the first place, we have said that the act of Union of 1801 was unconstitutional. It will be admitted that the most fundamental and sound parts of the constitution of any community, are those parts which form the legislative and judicial councils of the community, and designate the qualifications of the members of said councils. These are parts of the government, in all societies, deemed too sacred to be touched by any authority, excepting that which can make and unmake the constitution at its pleasure. Should any authority in the United States assume to introduce into the State legislatures or Congress, men not constitutionally qualified, and who were subjects of another political power, the alarm would be given at once that a most violent outrage had been inflicted on our governments and our rights. And although we would say it with respect, yet we *must say*, that this was the very thing which the act of 1801 effected in the Constitution of the Presbyterian Church. By *that act*, committee-men belonging to the Congregational Church, and under its government, were introduced into our Presbyteries, and by the subsequent execution of the act, into our Synods and our General Assembly. Men who were under the authority of a body without our Church, exercised the highest power of the Church. This was a most palpable infraction of our Constitution.

"In the next place, all the churches formed and constituted under the operation of this *act*, were at least as much trained in doctrine and church order on the Congregational as on the Presbyterian plan, and had just as much preparation for becoming members of a Congregational as of a Presbyterian church; and therefore any subsequent acts of any of our judicatories, forming such churches into Presbyteries or Synods, and connecting them with us as constituent parts of our body, were unconstitutional. This has been the source of all our present evils: the raising up of Presbyteries and Synods out of men who had at least as much of the Congregational as Presbyterian character, has scattered the elements of discord through all our regions, and torn our afflicted Church to pieces. These indeed were consequences not perceived from the beginning; it required the light of experience to teach us, that the amalgamation of such bodies as the Congregational and Presbyterian would produce a ferment sufficient to agitate the whole American nation.

"Having traced thus far the unconstitutional and pernicious tendency of this *act*, it only remains to say, that when this act is abrogated by the proper authority, as a matter of course everything which arose under its influence and training is abrogated with it. This we presume is the ground on which all the jurisprudence of our country stands, and upon which all our political courts and legislatures act. It has indeed been said, that when an unconstitutional law forms a contract, the abrogation of the law cannot set the contract aside, as this would suppose that a person might take the advantage of his own wrong to relieve himself from a just obligation. But to this it may be answered, that an unconstitutional law can give rise to no binding contract. The unconstitutionality supposes that the organ of government is granting what it has no right to grant, and therefore no obligation can be imposed. But in the present case, the *act in question* goes to the subversion of the Presbyterian Church, and therefore any contract which could arise under it, calculated to destroy that Church, would be of such an immoral tendency as could impose no obligation. It is one of the first principles of morals, that an unlawful contract is not to be fulfilled.

"It then appears plain to us, that, by the abrogation of the act of 1801, the Synods of the Western Reserve, Utica, Genesee, and Geneva, are independent bodies, standing on their own ground, and free to choose their future connections, and that thus far a separation exists between us and them, which may greatly conduce to the peace and comfort of both parties; and as both the majority and minority agree in expressing the opinion, that a division of the Church in conformity with the sympathies of the present parties, was both desirable and expedient, we were much surprised to find, that the minority would not agree with us in carrying out the existing separation, so as to form the Church into two distinct bodies, either of which would be sufficiently large to form a General Assembly, and which might act peaceably in promoting the common interests of our Redeemer's kingdom. In our present connection, there is no hope of peace. The controversy threatens to become more fierce, more extensive, and more destructive of all the vital principles of religion, the longer we continue together. Indeed, the great motives for all the measures of separation to which we have resorted on the present occasion, are the peace, prosperity, and holiness of our beloved Church; and these objects, we believe, can never be obtained until this separation is effected.

"Our brethren of the minority seemed to consider it as an insult, when we urged the fact, that the abrogation of an unconstitutional law left us as distinct and separate bodies: we intended no insult; the ground we took and the language we used implied none; we only said that they were separate from us, and we from them: if this implied disgrace on them, it implied the same on ourselves; we wished both parties to consider themselves as on equal ground; and as to the unconstitutional law from which all our misapprehensions had arisen, we were willing that the greater blame should lie on us. In fact, our wish was and is to part as brethren, and as in certain important points of doctrine and church order we cannot agree, let each party take the word of God as their rule of faith and practice, and pursue their course as those who must give account to the great Shepherd and Bishop of their souls.

"We have now, dear brethren, briefly explained the reasons for the course we have taken on the present occasion, and we believe it would have been a blessing to our Church, if the measures now adopted had been resorted to at an earlier period. The progress of controversy has greatly destroyed brotherly confidence. Indeed, the union between the parties, for several years, has only existed in name; in fact they have been two separate bodies, and we believe the sooner they are brought to consider themselves as forming distinct denominations, the sooner will they return to the spirit and principles of the Gospel of Christ.

"We must observe, in conclusion, that on whatever side the principal fault of our present disturbances may lie, the whole Church has abundant cause of deep humiliation and repentance before Almighty God. Our calamities have not arisen from the dust; our Heavenly Father has stretched forth his hand over us, and let us acknowledge 'the rod and him that hath appointed it.' Let us return to him that he may return to us; if he has wounded, it is he alone that can heal; if he hath broken down, he can build us up.

"By order of the General Assembly.

"DAVID ELLIOTT, *Moderator.*
"JOHN McDOWELL, *Stated Clerk.*

"PHILADELPHIA, June 8th, 1837."

—*Minutes*, pp. 499, 502.

2. *Circular Letter to the Churches of Christ.*

"Mr. Breckinridge, from the committee to prepare a letter to be addressed to all the Churches of Christ Jesus throughout the earth, made a report, which was read, accepted, and adopted" [by the majority of the Assembly of 1837, after the passage of the Exscinding Acts, as follows:]—*Minutes*, 1837, p. 494.

"The General Assembly of the Presbyterian Church in the United States of America, to all the Churches of Jesus Christ, wish grace, mercy, and peace from God, the Father, and the Lord Jesus Christ, through the Eternal Spirit:

"VERY DEAR BRETHREN: Assembled by the good providence of God, as the supreme judicatory of the Presbyterian Church in the United States of America, constituting by our ecclesiastical organization, not only 'the bond of union, peace, correspondence, and mutual confidence among all our churches,' but also the only organ 'of correspondence with foreign Churches,' we cannot consent to separate, after the unusually long, interesting, and important session which we are about to close, without pouring out the fulness of our hearts in reference to the weighty matters concerning which we have been called to act since we came together, into the ears and bosoms of all other Christian Churches, and especially those with which we are in friendly correspondence.

"You cannot be ignorant, dear brethren, that for a number of years past, the friends of truth and of regular Presbyterian order in our beloved Zion have been filled with painful apprehension at the manifest departure from our ecclesiastical standards which appeared to be gaining ground in a number of our judicatories. Firmly believing that the great purpose for which the Church was founded was, that she might maintain in their purity the doctrines and discipline of Christ, and hold them forth to a dark world; we have thought ourselves called upon to make inquiry respecting the errors and disorders alleged to exist, and, as far as possible, to banish them from that portion of the professing family of Christ with which we are connected. You have witnessed for a number of successive years our struggles for the attainment of this object. You have witnessed the mortifying disappointments which, from time to time, have attended our efforts to obtain, by constitutional means, a redress of the grievances of which we complained. You have seen what we regard as error becoming more extensive in its prevalence, and more bold and overbearing in its claims. You have seen certain voluntary societies, under the cover of professed zeal for the doctrines and order of our Church, in fact if not in intention, gradually subverting both. You have heard the motives of the friends of truth reproached; their name cast out as evil; their zeal for maintaining the purity of the Gospel represented as a mere struggle for power; and all their attempts to detect and censure heresy held up to public view as the efforts of restless and ambitious men to gain the pre-eminence for themselves. Amidst these ineffectual attempts to banish error and to restore order, vital piety has languished; mutual confidence has disappeared; the reviving and converting influences of the Holy Spirit have been withheld; and our time and strength have been painfully occupied with strife and debate, instead of being wholly given to the spread of the Gospel and the conversion of the world.

"We shall not stop to inquire by whose agency or by what steps this state of things has been produced. The adjustment of the proper award in regard to this question might be deemed an invidious task, and fail of commanding universal assent. But on the deplorable character of the situation in which we were placed, there can be but one opinion. Over our conflicts every friend of religion has mourned; every intelligent member of the Presbyterian Church has felt grieved and humbled; and we were becoming a reproach among all surrounding denominations. To every enlightened beholder it has been long manifest that parties so heterogeneous and discordant could no longer act together in the same body, either with comfort to themselves, or with honor and edification to the cause of our common Christianity.

"Such has been our melancholy history, especially for the last six years, and such were the discouraging and distressing circumstances in which this Assembly convened. On coming together, it was found to contain such a decided majority of the friends of truth and order as to place within our reach the most thorough measures of reform. And it is worthy of special notice, that this majority was created and brought together in full view of the measures adopted by the orthodox Assembly of 1835, and of all the conflicts and painful disclosures which characterized the Assembly of 1836. It was after the attention of the whole Church had been strongly called to these measures and disclosures, that our Presbyteries sent a delegation, the major part of whom declared in favor of the doctrines and order of our body. We felt ourselves, therefore, distinctly and solemnly called upon by the voice of the Church to go forward and rescue her struggling and bleeding interests from that humiliating and degrading perversion to which they had been so long exposed. This painful duty we have endeavored to perform in the fear of God, and although we do not claim that our manner of discharging it has been wholly free from the manifestation of human infirmity, we do hope and believe that our measures have been accompanied with much sincere and humble seeking for divine direction; and that they are such as the enlightened and impartial friends of our ecclesiastical Constitution will ultimately approve.

"As the great truths of the Gospel lie at the foundation of all Christian hope, as well as of the purity and prosperity of the Church, we feel ourselves bound to direct early and peculiarly solemn attention to those doctrinal errors which, there was but too much evidence, had gained an alarming prevalence in some of our judicatories. The advocates of these errors, on their first appearance, were cautious and reserved, alleging that they differed in words only from the doctrines as stated in our public standards. Very soon, however, they began to contend that their opinions were really new, and were a substantial and important improvement on the old creed of the Church; and, at length, that revivals of religion could not be hoped for, and that the souls of men must be destroyed, if the old doctrines continued to be preached. The errors thus promulged were, by no means, of that doubtful or unimportant character which seems to be assigned to them even by some of the professed friends of orthodoxy. You will see, by our published acts, that some of them affect the very foundation of the system of Gospel truth, and that they all bear relations to the Gospel plan of very serious and ominous import. Surely, doctrines which go to the formal or virtual denial of our covenant relation to Adam; the native and total depravity of man; the entire inability of the sinner to recover himself from rebellion and corruption; the nature and source of regeneration; and our justification solely on account of the imputed righteousness of the Redeemer, cannot, upon any just principle, be regarded as 'minor errors.' They form, in fact, 'another Gospel;' and it is impossible for those who faithfully adhere to our public standards to walk with those who adopt such opinions, with either comfort or confidence.

"It cannot be denied, indeed, that those who adopted and preached these opinions, at the same time declared their readiness to subscribe our Confession of Faith, and actually professed their assent to it, in the usual form, without apparent scruple. This, in fact, was one of the most revolting and alarming characteristics of their position. They declared that in doing this, they only adopted the Confession 'for substance,' and by no means intended to receive the whole system which it contained. Upon this principle, we had good evidence that a number of Presbyteries, in the ordination and reception of ministers and other church officers, avowedly and habitually acted; and hence it has not been uncommon for the members of such Presbyteries publicly and formally to repudiate some of the important doctrines of the formulary which they had thus subscribed; and even, in a few extraordinary cases, to hold up the system of truth which it contains as 'an abomination;' as a system which it were to be 'wished had never had an existence.' No wonder that men feeling and acting thus should have been found, in some instances, substituting entirely different Confessions of Faith in place of that which is contained in our Constitution. Who can doubt that such a method of subscribing to articles of faith is immoral in principle; that it is adapted to defeat the great purpose of adopting confessions; and that, if persisted in, it could not fail to open the door of our Church wider and wider to the introduction of the most radical and pestiferous heresies, which would speedily destroy her character as an evangelical body?

"Was it possible for us to doubt or hesitate as to our duty when such errors were evidently gaining ground among us, and when it was in our power judicially to condemn them—errors which, ever since the days of the apostles, have been pronounced by the true Church to be dangerous corruptions of Gospel truth? We are conscious that in pronouncing the errors in question to be unscriptural, radical, and highly dangerous, we are actuated by no feelings of narrow party zeal, but by a firm and growing persuasion that such errors cannot fail, in their ultimate effect, to subvert the foundation of Christian hope, and destroy the souls of men. As watchmen on the walls of Zion, we should be unfaithful to the trust reposed in us were we not to cry aloud and proclaim a solemn warning against opinions so corrupt and delusive.

"In the course of our attempt at reform, we have thought it our duty to annul the Plan of Union between Presbyterian and Congregational Churches in the new settlements formed in 1801, and evidently intended as a temporary system to meet a temporary exigency. By that Plan, Congregational Churches were brought into complete union with the Presbyterian Church, and their delegates, without having adopted our public standards, were introduced into our judicatories, and vested with the power of giving authoritative, and, in some cases, decisive votes on the most important questions of doctrine and discipline; and thus, in reality, of governing our Church. And it has happened, in fact, in a number of instances, that some of the most important decisions, in their bearing on the truth and order of our body, have been decided by the votes of those who had not subscribed to our ecclesiastical Constitution, and stood aloof themselves from its authority. Thus Congregationalists were found, in effect, to control the Presbyterian Church, and to prohibit her carrying into execution our appropriate system, while we had no more authority over them than they chose to recognize.

"It is impossible to contemplate this Plan of Union now without perceiving that it is most unnatural in its character; that it has not a shadow of foundation in the Constitution of the Presbyterian Church, and that it is adapted to be deeply injurious in its influence on us. It is but just, indeed, to say, that it was first proposed and commenced on our part, and that it was dictated by that spirit of unsuspecting simplicity and fraternal confidence which foresaw no evil. Its mischiefs gradually disclosed themselves, and it was not until they had taken wide and deep root, that they began to attract the attention and awaken the fears of the friends of truth and of Presbyterial order. It was more and more perceived, not only that this system, as before remarked, was most unequal, as it, in fact, conceded the right of governing us to those over whom we could exercise no controlling power, but that its effect must be, slowly, but inevitably, to subvert the order and discipline of the Presbyterian Church. Surely no impartial judge can blame us for wishing this mischievous system rescinded, or for annulling it when we had the power. It is due to ourselves, however, to say, that this measure was not either hastily conceived nor abruptly executed. The union in question has been for many years regarded by the great body of the Presbyterian Church as perhaps the most fertile source of the difficulties existing among us, especially when viewed, not merely as a violation of our Constitution and an invasion of our order, but as grievously abused by those who have taken advantage of it, in a manner not intended by its original framers, to disseminate their pernicious errors. Viewing the subject in this light, the General Assembly of 1835 respectfully requested the General Association of Connecticut to consent that the Plan of Union in question should be annulled. Having now waited two additional years in vain for any favorable action in the case on the part of our brethren of Connecticut, and having witnessed with the deepest sorrow the ever-growing evils of this relation, we have felt at this time solemnly called upon to abrogate the whole Plan, and to put an end, as far as in us lay, to the destructive effects which have so long resulted from its operation.

"If it were obviously equitable and important that the Plan of Union alluded to should be annulled, it was, in our view, no less equitable and important that the ecclesiastical bodies to which that Plan had given existence, and which were animated and governed by its spirit, should be declared to be no longer connected with our Church. It has been indeed painful to the Assembly to declare bodies, in which were brethren whose piety we cannot question, and whose activity in extending the visible Church we must regard with approbation, to be no longer connected with our body. But we were shut up to this painful duty. Being irregularly brought into our Church, and retaining all the feelings and habits growing out of the circumstances of their original introduction, we could not hope that they would walk together in peace with us, so long as the points of difference between us were so many and so serious. Although the creation of more churches on the Plan of Union was made to cease by the previous act of abrogation, still, as all must grant that the act which brought them in was wholly unconstitutional, and as, if this were the case, the act itself was, of course, void from the beginning, and all the acts and bodies growing out of it equally void, we have deemed it necessary to declare the brethren connected with those judicatories no longer connected with the Presbyterian Church. Fully aware of the painfulness of this decision to both parties, in order to avoid it, we made overtures to the brethren who were opposed to us in sentiment and in policy, which had for their object an amicable separation; offering them, in order to bring about such a separation, what we deemed equitable and even indulgent terms. These terms will be learned from the correspondence of the joint committee appointed to negotiate on the subject, which has been already made public. Our brethren saw fit to decline our proposal, and chose rather to abide the enforcing of the Constitution. They cannot complain of our course, when the only alternative was the ruin of the Church, or the restoration of our form of government to its legitimate and uniform reign.

"We are aware that some have called in question the constitutionality of our proceedings. On this subject, the more maturely we reflect, the more firmly are we persuaded that we have taken the most eligible and even the only practicable course. To have attempted to separate from us the brethren with whom we could no longer walk in peace, by personal process in each case, would obviously have been impossible, and even if possible, tedious, agitating, and troublesome in the highest degree. The General Assembly is vested by the Constitution of our Church with plenary power 'to decide in all controversies respecting doctrine and discipline; to reprove, warn, or bear testimony against error in doctrine or immorality in practice, in any church, Presbytery or Synod; to superintend the concerns of the whole Church; to suppress schismatical contentions and disputations; and, in general, to recommend and attempt reformation of manners, and the promotion of charity, truth, and holiness, through all the churches under their care.' It is manifest that no other body but the General Assembly is competent to sit in judgment on a Synod; and it is equally manifest that no other body can be vested with power to abolish a system which the General Assembly itself had formed, without consulting any of the Presbyteries. We have, therefore, not hesitated to apply the constitutional remedy in its fullest extent. And now, reposing on the high ground of our truly primitive and apostolical system of order, we appeal with unshaken confidence to the sympathy of all evangelical Churches, to the approval of the American people, and, above all, to the sanction of Him 'who sits as King upon the holy hill of Zion.'

"In the adoption of these measures, we are earnestly desirous that our views and feelings in regard to our Congregational brethren of New England should be correctly understood. We have no controversy with them, nor do we desire to have any, with respect to the Congregational form of Church government as it exists among themselves, nor with any other form of Church polity. Toward the excellent brethren, beloved in the Lord, in those and all other Churches, who are now testifying against the errors which are troubling *them*, as they are troubling *us*, we entertain the most cordial esteem and fraternal affection. They are engaged in the same hallowed cause with ourselves, and we cordially bid them God speed. Let there be no strife between us. There *ought* to be none, and there *will* be none, so long as there is no effort made by any party to intrude on the domestic concerns of any other. We cannot wisely attempt, with our different views and feelings, to inhabit the *same house;* but, as *neighbors*, we may be on the most amicable and even affectionate terms. We wish for no more than to be allowed the fair and unimpeded action of our own ecclesiastical principles. We desire to stand on our own responsibility, and not to be made involuntary sharers in the responsibility of other bodies and systems of action, with which we cannot entirely harmonize. We desire to perform our Master's work upon the principles which we conscientiously prefer, because we believe those principles to be found in the word of God; and we cannot consent to an alliance with any individuals or bodies of men in their system of action, without reserving to ourselves the right of review, of control, and, if necessary, of correction.

"It is our earnest hope, with respect to the brethren thus severed from us, that both parties will be essentially benefited by the separation. We trust that both will henceforth proceed in the conscientious discharge of duty, without being crippled or embarrassed by each other; and that hereafter there will be no other strife between us, than who shall love the Redeemer most, and who shall serve him with the warmest zeal.

"We have already adverted to the unhappy influence which has been exerted for a number of years past, by certain voluntary societies, which, though not responsible to any Church, and of course, therefore, not to us, were pursuing a train of measures adapted covertly, but effectually, to weaken her energies and govern her proceedings. We believe that if there be any department of Christian effort to which the Church of Christ is bound, in her appropriate character, to direct her attention and her unwearied labors, they are those which relate to the training of her sons for the holy ministry, and sending the Gospel to those who have it not, and planting churches in the dark and destitute portions of the earth. To be willing to commit either of these branches of her peculiar work to foreign and irresponsible hands, we are more and more persuaded is unfaithfulness to the best interests of Zion, and adapted fatally to injure the cause of Gospel truth and of Presbyterial order. Surely, if the Church is under obligations, not only to maintain in her own bosom, but also to impart as far as possible to the whole world, all such religious knowledge, worship, and ordinances as God hath revealed in his word, she is bound to see to it, that no persons shall be either educated or sent forth as ministers, who are not well instructed in her doctrine and order, and, as far as can be ascertained, firmly attached to both. This is equally a dictate of duty to our Master in heaven and to our own beloved institutions. To suffer boards constituted by ourselves, pledged to adhere to our own standards, and responsible to our own judicatories, to languish while we sustain and strengthen societies over which we have no control, and which are gradually undermining at once our purity, and, of course, our real strength, while professing to add to our numbers, would be manifestly as unwise as it would be criminal, in those who profess to love the Presbyterian Church, and to consider her as conformed, in her doctrine and order, to the apostolic model.

"One of the most formidable evils of the present crisis is the wide-spread and ever restless spirit of *radicalism*, manifest both in the Church and in the State. Its leading principle everywhere seems to be to level all order to the dust. Mighty only in the power to destroy, it has driven its deep agitations through the bosom of our beloved Church. Amidst the multiplied and revolting forms in which it has appeared, it is always animated by one principle. It is ever the same levelling revolutionary spirit, and tends to the same ruinous results. It has, in succession, driven to extreme fanaticism the great cause of revivals of religion, of temperance, and of the rights of man. It has aimed to transmute our pure faith into destructive heresy, our scriptural order into confusion and misrule. It has crowded many of our churches with ignorant zealots and unholy members, driven our pastors from their flocks, and with strange fire consumed the heritage of the Lord, filling our churches with confusion, and our judicatories with conflict; making our venerated name and beloved institutions, so far as its fearful influence extends, a hissing and a by-word before the American people, and even threatening the dissolution of our national Union, as well as the dismemberment of the Presbyterian Church.

"While we have endeavored to take, as our Master enabled us, decisive measures for securing, under the Divine blessing, the future purity and peace of our body, we would openly admit, dear brethren, that mere orthodoxy and regular scriptural government ought not to be considered by any Church as the *only*, or even as the *chief*, objects of her regard. Let it never be forgotten that truth, whether in respect to doctrine or discipline, is in order to godliness, and that the real prosperity and glory of any Church consists in the presence and power of the Holy Spirit, enlightening, reviving, and sanctifying her members, and adding to their numbers daily of such as shall be saved. We would, therefore, now that the adorable Head of the Church has enabled us in some measure to remove from our body the most prominent sources of division and strife, humble ourselves before God, and call upon all our brethren, of every name, with us to seek and pray without ceasing for those reviving and converting influences of the Holy Spirit, which alone can render any Church what it ought to be, a real blessing to the world and a nursery for heaven. And while we earnestly desire and implore this blessing, let us remember the great importance of distinguishing between genuine revivals of religion, and those which are spurious and fanatical. The former are the product of Gospel truth, impressed on the heart and conscience by the Holy Spirit of God. The latter are mere excitements of natural feeling, produced either by error or by some other form of human machinery. In proportion as the former prevail, the Church is prosperous and happy. The latter, however arrogant in claim or plausible in appearance, are only fitted to send a blight on the garden of the Lord, and to deceive and destroy the souls of men. We fear that not a little of that which has assumed the precious name of revivals, in various parts of our bounds, is of this latter description. This lamentable fact, however, creates no prejudice in our minds against genuine revivals of religion. It rather excites us to desire and long for them with more ardor; to pray for them with more importunity; to promote them with more care by an edifying example; and to guard against all counterfeits with more enlightened vigilance.

"Brethren, farewell. May the God of Israel bless you all—every one. We love, with tenderness which we cannot utter, our own portion of the Church of Jesus Christ our Lord. But we love also every other portion of the inheritance of that dear Saviour, and rejoicing in the confident hope that heaven will ring with praises of the redeemed from amongst every Christian denomination, our ardent and constant desire is to draw the bonds of union between us and all the rest as close as possible here below. Hence the present epistle to our brethren. Hence our earnest desire to explain clearly to them our posture, our action, and the solemn crisis which, having first overtaken several of our sister Churches, has at length fallen upon us, and will unquestionably overtake in succession all denominations of Christians.

"And now may God, of his infinite mercy, set the seal of his visible approbation upon what his providence and grace have enabled us to do. And may you, brethren, be preserved from the evils which we have endured, or be enabled to meet them with more promptitude and fidelity than we have done.

"And may the grace of our Lord Jesus Christ abide richly on all who love his holy name.

"By order of the General Assembly.

"DAVID ELLIOTT, *Moderator*.
"JOHN MCDOWELL, *Stated Clerk*.

"PHILADELPHIA, June 8th, 1837."

—*Minutes*, 1837, pp. 502–508.

3. *Assembly of* 1838. *Organization of the Assembly.*

"The General Assembly of the Presbyterian Church in the United States of America met, agreeably to appointment, in the 7th Presbyterian Church in the city of Philadelphia, on the third Thursday of May, 1838, at 11 o'clock A.M., and was opened with a sermon by the Rev. David Elliott, D.D., moderator of the last Assembly, from Isa. 60 : 1 : 'Arise, shine; for thy light is come, and the glory of the Lord is risen upon thee.'

"After public worship, the moderator of the last Assembly announced from the desk, that immediately after the benediction the moderator would take the chair on the floor of the church, and the Assembly would then be constituted.

"After the benediction, the moderator of the last Assembly took the chair, and opened the meeting with prayer.

"The Rev. William Patton, D.D., from the Third Presbytery of New York, then rose, and asked leave to offer the following preamble and resolutions:

"Whereas, the General Assembly of 1837 adopted certain resolutions intended to deprive certain Presbyteries of the right to be represented in the General Assembly. And whereas, the more fully to accomplish their purpose, the said Assembly of 1837 did require and receive from their clerks a pledge or promise that they would, in making out the roll of commissioners to constitute the General Assembly of 1838, omit to insert therein the names of commissioners from said Presbyteries. And whereas, the said clerks, having been requested by commissioners from the said Presbyteries to receive their commissions and enter their names on the roll of the General Assembly of 1838, now about to be organized, have refused to receive and enter the same; therefore—

"1. *Resolved*, That such attempts on the part of the General Assembly of 1837 and their clerks, to direct and control the organization of the General Assembly of 1838, are unconstitutional, and in derogation of its just rights as the general representative judicatory of the whole Presbyterian Church in the United States of America.

"2. *Resolved*, That the General Assembly cannot be legally constituted except by admitting to seats and to equality of powers, in the first instance, all commissioners who present the usual evidences of their appointment. And that it is the duty of the clerks, and they are hereby directed, to form the roll of the General Assembly of 1838, by including therein the names of all commissioners from Presbyteries belonging to the said Presbyterian Church, not omitting the commissioners from the several Presbyteries within the bounds of the Synods of Utica, Geneva, Genesee, and the Western Reserve; and in all things to form the said roll according to the known practice and established usage of previous General Assemblies."

"The moderator declared him to be out of order, and refused to allow them to be read. Dr. Patton then stated that he was very desirous to have them put and passed upon without remark or debate. The moderator again declared them out of order, as the next business was the report of the clerks upon the roll. Dr. Patton then appealed from the decision of the chair. The appeal was seconded, and the moderator declared the appeal to be out of order, and refused to put it, and directed the clerk to make his report upon the roll. Dr. Patton then declared to the moderator that the paper he wished read had relation to forming the roll. The moderator then stated that he was out of order, as the clerk was on the floor; whereupon the moderator was reminded by Dr. Patton that he had the floor before the clerk. The moderator directed the clerk to proceed with the report on the roll, and Dr. Patton thereupon took his seat.

"The Report of the clerks of the last Assembly upon the roll was then read by the Rev. John M. Krebs, one of the clerks of the last Assembly, and was as follows:

I. SYNOD OF ALBANY.

PRESBYTERIES.	MINISTERS.	ELDERS.
Londonderry,	John H. Church, D.D.	
Newburyport,	D. T. Smith.	
Champlain,	Phineas Bailey,	John Boynton.
Troy,	N. S. S. Beman, D.D.	
	Samuel Speer,	Nicholas M. Masters.
Albany,	Eliphalet Nott, D.D.	Isaac N. Beach.
	E. D. McMasters.	
Columbia,	J. B. Waterbury,	Lawrence Vandyke.
	Augustus L. Chapin,	Frederick Tyler.
St. Lawrence,		

II. SYNOD OF NEW YORK.

PRESBYTERIES.	MINISTERS.	ELDERS.
Hudson, ...	William Blain, ...	William L. Mapes.
	Samuel Pelton, ...	Norman Judson.
North River, . .	Eliphalet Price, ...	Aaron Raymond.
Bedford, ...	. . . .	John Owen.
New York, 1*st*, . .	William W. Phillips, D.D. .	Hugh Auchincloss.
	Elias W. Crane, ...	A. G. Blauvelt.
New York, 2*d*, . .	Ebenezer K. Maxwell, . .	Henry Rankin.
New York, 3*d*, . .	William Patton, D.D. . . .	Daniel Pierson.
	Erskine Mason, D.D. . . .	R. M. Hartley.
Long Island, . .	Ralph Smith.	
Long Island, 2*d*, .	James McDougall, ...	John Everett.

III. SYNOD OF NEW JERSEY.

PRESBYTERIES.	MINISTERS.	ELDERS.
Newark, ...	Samuel Fisher, D.D. . . .	O. Woodruff.
	William R. Weeks, D.D. . .	Israel Crane.
Elizabethtown, . .	James M. Hunting, ...	James Bower.
	Lewis Bond, ...	Robert Anderson.
New Brunswick, .	Eli F. Cooley, ...	D. W. Vail.
	John McLean, ...	William Wilson.
Newton, ...	John Gray, ...	Peter Thomson.
	J. Campbell, D.D.	William Long.
Susquehanna, . .	E. H. Snowden, ...	H. C. Anhauser.
Montrose, ...	. . . .	Isaac P. Foster.

IV. SYNOD OF PHILADELPHIA.

PRESBYTERIES.	MINISTERS.	ELDERS.
Philadelphia, . .	Ashbel Green, D.D.	Alexander Symington.
	William Latta, ...	A. W. Mitchell.
Philadelphia, 2*d*, .	William J. Gibson, ...	Robert Wallace.
Newcastle, . . .	William Finney.	
	Lindley C. Rutter, ...	John Robinson.
Wilmington, . .	E. W. Gilbert, ...	Willard Hall.
Lewes, ...	. . . .	S. K. Wilson.
Baltimore, . . .	Robert J. Breckinridge, . .	George Morris.
Carlisle, ...	John Moody, ...	John Clendenin.
	N. G. White, ...	Alexander McCoy.
Huntingdon, . . .	Joshua Moore, ...	William Smyth.
Northumberland, .	S. S. Sheddan, ...	Richard Matchin.

V. SYNOD OF PITTSBURG.

PRESBYTERIES.	MINISTERS.	ELDERS.
Blairsville, . . .	Samuel Swan, ...	Smith Agnew.
Redstone, ...	C. B. Bristol, ...	Dr. H. Campbell.
Washington, . . .	John Stockton, ...	James Lee.
Ohio, ...	David Elliot, D.D.	Hon. H. Denny.
	Thomas D. Baird, ...	W. H. Lowrie.
Alleghany, . . .	S. Caldwell, ...	Benjamin Junkin.
Steubenville, . . .	C. C. Beattie, ...	H. H. Leavitt.
Beaver, ...	A. O. Patterson, ...	John Clarke.
Erie, ...	Pierce Chamberlain, . . .	George Kellogg.

VI. SYNOD OF MICHIGAN.

PRESBYTERIES.	MINISTERS.	ELDERS.
Detroit,	John P. Cleaveland.	
Monroe,	Erastus N. Nichols,	Samuel G. Conklin.
St. Joseph,	Silas Woodbury,	A. G. Hammond.

VII. SYNOD OF OHIO.

PRESBYTERIES.	MINISTERS.	ELDERS.
Athens,	Luther G. Bingham,	Marcus Bosworth.
Columbus,	James Hoge, D.D.	John Entrekin.
Lancaster,	James Culbertson, D.D.	John C. Stockton.
Wooster,	Joseph S. Wylie,	John Elliot.
Richland,	Henry Hervey.	
Marion,	Henry Van Deman,	S. G. Strong.

VIII. SYNOD OF CINCINNATI.

PRESBYTERIES.	MINISTERS.	ELDERS.
Chilicothe,	Samuel Crothers,	Richard Long.
Miami,	John L. Bellville.	
Cincinnati,	Lyman Beecher, D.D.	Dr. George L. Weed,
	Baxter Dickinson,	John Q. A. Bassett.
Oxford,	Robert Irwin,	John Molyneaux.
Sidney,	Samuel Cleland,	John Ewing.

IX. SYNOD OF INDIANA.

PRESBYTERIES.	MINISTERS.	ELDERS.
Vincennes,	Matthew G. Wallace,	John Lagow.
Madison,	William G. Matthews,	Victor King.
Crawfordsville,	Samuel G. Lowry,	John S. Jennings.
Indianapolis,	William Sickels,	William M. Tate.
Logansport,	Alexander T. Rankin.	

X. SYNOD OF ILLINOIS.

PRESBYTERIES.	MINISTERS.	ELDERS.
Illinois,	Edward Beecher,	A. H. Burritt.
Kaskaskia,	Benjamin F. Spillman,	W. A. G. Posey.
Sangamon,	Cyrus L. Watson,	Joseph Young.
Ottawa,	John Blatchford.	
Schuyler,	Samuel Wilson.	
Peoria,	Flavel Bascom,	Charles Barrows.
Alton,	AlbertHa l.	

XI. SYNOD OF MISSOURI.

PRESBYTERIES.	MINISTERS.	ELDERS.
St. Louis,		James M. Covington.
St. Charles,		Alexander J. Dallas.

XII. SYNOD OF KENTUCKY.

PRESBYTERIES.	MINISTERS.	ELDERS.
Louisville,	James Hawthorn,	John Bemiss, M.D.
Muhlenburg,	John Lyle.	
Transylvania.		
West Lexington,	Robert Davidson,	Samuel M. Wallace.
Ebenezer,	R. C. Grundy,	Thomas H. Poage.

XIII. SYNOD OF VIRGINIA.

PRESBYTERIES.	MINISTERS.	ELDERS.
Lexington, . . .	John D. Ewing, ...	James McNutt.
	James C. Wilson, ...	William A. Bell.
Winchester, . . .	S. B. Wilson, D.D., ...	James H. Fitzgerald.
Dist. of Columbia,	William Hill, D.D.	Robert Jamieson.
West Hanover, . .	George A. Baxter, D.D. . .	Samuel McCorkle.
	Andrew Hart, ...	P. C. Venable, M.D.
East Hanover, . .	William S. Plumer, ...	William Maxwell.

XIV. SYNOD OF NORTH CAROLINA.

PRESBYTERIES.	MINISTERS.	ELDERS.
Roanoke, ...	William McPheeters, D.D. .	Thomas H. Willie.
Orange, ...	N. H. Harding, ...	Richard J. Smith.
Fayetteville, . . .	William N. Peacock, . . .	Alexander Martin.
Concord, ...	Samuel Williamson, . . .	W. L. Davidson.
	John Williamson, ...	William King.
Morgantown, . .	Albertus L. Watts.	

XV. SYNOD OF TENNESSEE.

PRESBYTERIES.	MINISTERS.	ELDERS.
Abingdon, . . .	Daniel H. Hoge.	
Union, ...	J. E. Montgomery, ...	Walter M. McGill.
	Levi R. Morrison, ...	Andrew Early.
French Broad, . .	Gideon S. White, ...	William Dick.
Holston, ...	Daniel Rogan, ...	John Patton.

XVI. SYNOD OF WEST TENNESSEE.

PRESBYTERIES.	MINISTERS.	ELDERS.
West Tennessee, .	Thomas F. Scott.	
Nashville, . . .	Robert A. Lapsley, ...	James C. Robinson.
Shiloh, ...	William Eagleton.	
North Alabama, .	James O. Stedman, ...	Thomas Childress.
Western District, .	Samuel Hodge, ...	John Ingram, M.D.

XVII. SYNOD OF SOUTH CAROLINA AND GEORGIA.

PRESBYTERIES.	MINISTERS.	ELDERS.
South Carolina, .	Hugh Dickson, ...	Alex. Chambers.
Bethel, ...	J. L. R. Davies, ...	John M. Doley.
Harmony, . . .	J. Witherspoon, D.D. . . .	Lawrence Prince.
Charleston Union, .	Elipha White.	
	Thomas Magruder.	
Georgia, ...	Horace S. Pratt, ...	Ebenezer S. Reese.
Hopewell, . . .	Samuel S. Davis, ...	William Shear.
Flint River, . . .	John S. Wilson, ...	David C. Campbell.

XVIII. SYNOD OF ALABAMA.

PRESBYTERIES.	MINISTERS.	ELDERS.
South Alabama, .	Robert Nall.	
Tuscaloosa, . . .	Joseph B. Adams, ...	James Knox.
Tombeckbee, . . .	Samuel Hind, ...	Eli Neely.

XIX. SYNOD OF MISSISSIPPI.

PRESBYTERIES.	MINISTERS.	ELDERS.
Mississippi, . . .	Samuel B. Jones, ...	John Chamberlain.
Clinton, ...	A. C. Dickerson, ...	Wm. M. Murdock.
Arkansas.		
Louisiana, . . .	John L. Montgomery, . . .	James Cooper.

"The reading of the report being finished, the moderator announced that if there were commissioners from any Presbyteries of the Presbyterian Church who had not been enrolled, then was the proper time to make application to have their names put upon the roll.

"Thereupon the Rev. Erskine Mason, D.D., from the Third Presbytery of New York, rose, and offered the following resolution:

"*Resolved*, That the roll be now completed by adding the names of all commissioners now present from the several Presbyteries within the bounds of the Synods of Utica, Geneva, Genesee, and the Western Reserve,

"And stated that the commissioners from the Presbyteries therein named had offered their commissions to the clerks, who had refused to receive them. The moderator asked Dr. Mason if they were from Presbyteries connected with the Assembly of 1837, at the close of its session. Dr. Mason replied that they were from Presbyteries within the bounds of the Synods of Utica, Geneva, Genesee, and the Western Reserve. The moderator then stated that they could not be received. Dr. Mason then formally tendered the commissions of commissioners from

THE PRESBYTERIES OF	MINISTERS.	ELDERS.
Lorain, ...	Daniel W. Lathrop, . . .	Henry Brown.
Geneva, ...	Wm. L. Strong, ...	Zenas Wheeler.
	Miles P. Squier, ...	Wm. B. Cook.
Genesse, ...	Erastus J. Gillett, ...	Augustus P. Hascall.
	Wm. Bridgman.	
Oneida, ...	Horace P. Bogue.	
	Joseph Myers.	
Angelica, ...	Asa J. Allen, ...	Thomson Bell.
Maumee, ...	J. H. Francis, ...	Levi Beebe.
Watertown, . . .	Isaac Brayton, ...	Jason Clark.
Portage, ...	George E. Pierce.	
	Sherman B. Canfield.	
Cayuga, ...	. . . .	Salem Town.
		Joseph Esty.
Ontario, ...	Silas C. Brown, ...	Hiram Ashley.
Rochester, . . .	Tryon Edwards, ...	George A. Avery.
	A. G. Hall.	
Delaware, . . .	Daniel Waterbury, ...	D. Penfield.

Otsego, ...	Joseph W. Paddock, . . .	David H. Little.
Trumbull, . . .	Selden Haynes, ...	M. Messer.
Onondaga, . . .	Hutchins Taylor.	
Chemung, . . .	John Frost.	
Huron, ...	E. P. Salmon.	
Buffalo, ...	Asa T. Hopkins, ...	Jabez Goodell.
	George R. Rudd, ...	Horace Allen.
Grand River, . .	Ferris Fitch.	
Niagara, ...	Herman Halsey.	
Cortland, . . .	Joseph R. Johnson.	
Chenango, . . .	John B. Hoyt, ...	Frederick Hotchkiss.
Cleveland, . . .	Samuel C. Aikin, ...	Stephen Whitaker.
Bath, ...	E. Everett, ...	Daniel S. Benton.
Tioga, ...	J. A. Nash, ...	Elias Hawley.

"And demanded that they be put upon the roll. The resolution was seconded. The moderator declared it out of order. Dr. Mason then said, that with the greatest respect for the chair, he must appeal from that decision. The appeal was seconded. The moderator declared the appeal out of order, and refused to put it.

"The Rev. Miles P. Squier, from the Presbytery of Geneva, then rose and addressed the chair, stating that he had a commission from the Presbytery of Geneva, which he had presented to the clerks, who refused to receive it, and he demanded his right to his seat, and required his name to be enrolled. The moderator asked him if the Presbytery of Geneva was within the Synod of Geneva. Mr. Squier replied that it was within the bounds of the Synod of Geneva. The moderator then said, 'We do not know you,' and refused the demand, declaring it out of order.

"These repeated refusals of the moderator and clerks of the General Assembly of 1837 to perform the duties of their respective offices in the organization of the General Assembly of 1838, till its own officers should be appointed, thus impeding the constitutional progress of business, the Rev. John P. Cleaveland, of the Presbytery of Detroit, rose, and stated in substance as follows: That as the commissioners to the General Assembly for 1838, from a large number of Presbyteries, had been refused their seats, and as we had been advised by counsel learned in the law, that a constitutional organization of the Assembly must be secured at this time and in this place, he trusted it would not be considered as an act of discourtesy, but merely as a matter of necessity, if we now proceed to organize the General Assembly for 1838, in the fewest words, the shortest time, and with the least interruption practicable. He therefore moved that Dr. Beman, from the Presbytery of Troy, be moderator, to preside till a new moderator be chosen. The motion was seconded by the Rev. Baxter Dickinson, from the Presbytery of Cincinnati, and no other person being nominated, the Rev. Dr. Beman was unanimously appointed such moderator.

"It was then moved and seconded that the Rev. Erskine Mason, D.D., from the 3d Presbytery of New York, and the Rev. E. W. Gilbert, from the Presbytery of Wilmington, be clerks *pro tempore*, and no other person being put in nomination, they were unanimously appointed.

"The following is the roll of the General Assembly as completed by the clerks.

I. SYNOD OF ALBANY.

PRESBYTERIES.	MINISTERS.	ELDERS.
Londonderry,	John H. Church, D.D.	
	E. P. Bradford.	
Newburyport,	D. T. Smith.	
Champlain,	Phineas Bailey.	
Troy,	N. S. S. Beman, D.D.	
	Samuel Speer,	Nicholas M. Masters.
Albany,	Eliphalet Nott, D.D.	Isaac N. Beach.
	E. D. McMasters.	
Columbia,	J. B. Waterbury,	Lawrence Vandyke.
	Augustus L. Chapin,	Frederick Tyler.

II. SYNOD OF UTICA.

St. Lawrence.		
Watertown,	Isaac Brayton,	Jason Clark.
Oswego.		
Oneida,	Horace P. Bogue.	
	Joseph Myers.	
Otsego,	Joseph W. Paddock,	D. H. Little.

III. SYNOD OF GENEVA.

Geneva,	Miles P. Squier,	Wm. D. Cook.
	Wm. L. Strong,	Zenas Wheeler.
Chenango,	John B. Hoyt,	Frederick Hotchkiss.
Onondaga,	Hutchins Taylor.	
Cayuga,		Joseph Esty.
		Salem Town.
Tioga,	J. A. Nash,	Elias Hawley.
Cortland,	J. R. Johnson.	
Bath,	E. Everett,	Daniel S. Benton.
Delaware,	D. Waterbury,	D. Penfield.
Chemung,	John Frost.	

IV. SYNOD OF GENESEE.

PRESBYTERIES.	MINISTERS.	ELDERS.
Genesee, ...	Wm. Bridgeman, ...	Augustus P. Hascall.
	E. J. Gillett.	
Ontario, ...	Silas C. Brown, ...	Hiram Ashley.
Rochester, . . .	Tryon Edwards, ...	George A. Avery.
	A. G. Hall.	
Niagara, ...	Herman Halsey.	
Buffalo, ...	A. T. Hopkins, ...	Jabez Goodell.
	George R. Rudd, ...	Horace Allen.
Angelica, ...	Asa S. Allen, ...	Thomson Bell.

V. SYNOD OF NEW YORK.

PRESBYTERIES.	MINISTERS.	ELDERS.
Hudson, ...	William Blain, ...	William L. Mapes.
	Samuel Pelton, ...	Norman Judson.
North River, . .	Eliphalet Price, ...	Aaron Raymond.
Bedford, ...	. . . .	John Owen.
New York, 1*st*, . .	Wm. W. Phillips, D.D. . .	Hugh Auchincloss.
	Elias W. Crane, ...	A. G. Blauvelt.
New York, 2*d*, . .	Ebenezer K. Maxwell, . .	Henry Rankin.
New York, 3*d*, . .	William Patton, D.D. . . .	Daniel Pierson.
	Erskine Mason, D.D. . . .	R. M. Hartley.
Long Island, . .	Ralph Smith.	
Long Island, 2*d*, .	James McDougall, ...	John Everett.

VI. SYNOD OF NEW JERSEY.

PRESBYTERIES.	MINISTERS.	ELDERS.
Newark, ...	Samuel Fisher, D.D. . . .	O. Woodruff.
	Wm. R. Weeks, D.D. . . .	Israel Crane.
Elizabethtown, . .	James M. Hunting, ...	James Bower.
	Lewis Bond, ...	Robert Anderson.
New Brunswick, .	Eli F. Cooley, ...	D. W. Vail.
	John McLean, ...	Wm. Wilson.
Newton, ...	John Gray, ...	Peter Thomson.
	J. Campbell, D.D.	Wm. Long.
Susquehanna, . .	E. H. Snowden, ...	H. C. Anhauser.
Montrose, ...	. . . .	Isaac P. Foster.

VII. SYNOD OF PHILADELPHIA.

PRESBYTERIES.	MINISTERS.	ELDERS.
Philadelphia, . .	Ashbel Green, D.D. . . .	Alex. Symington.
	William Latta, ...	A. W. Mitchell, M.D.
Philadelphia, 2*d*, .	William J. Gibson, ...	Robert Wallace.
New Castle, . . .	William Finney.	
	Lindley C. Rutter, ...	John Robinson.
Wilmington, . . .	E. W. Gilbert, ...	Willard Hall.
Lewes, ...	. . . .	S. K. Wilson.
Baltimore, . . .	Robert S. Breckinridge, . .	George Morris.
Carlisle, ...	John Moody, ...	John Clendenin.
	N. G. White, ...	Alex. McCoy.
Huntingdon, . . .	Joshua Moore, ...	Wm. Smyth.
Northumberland, .	S. S. Sheddan, ...	Richard Matchin.

VIII. SYNOD OF PITTSBURG.

PRESBYTERIES.	MINISTERS.	ELDERS.
Blairsville,	Samuel Swan,	Smith Agnew.
Redstone,	C. B. Bristol,	Dr. H. Campbell.
Washington,	John Stockton,	James Lee.
Ohio,	David Elliot, D.D.	Hon. H. Denny.
	Thomas D. Baird,	W. H. Lowrie.
Alleghany,	S. Caldwell,	Benj. Junkin.
Steubenville,	C. C. Beattie,	H. H. Leavitt.
Beaver,	A. O. Patterson,	John Clarke.
Erie,	Pierce Chamberlain,	George Kellogg.

IX. WESTERN RESERVE.

Grand River,	Ferris Fitch.	
Portage,	George E. Pierce.	
	Sherman B. Canfield.	
Huron,	E. P. Salmon.	
Maumee,	J. H. Francis,	Levi Beebe.
Trumbull,	S. Haynes,	Moses Messer.
Lorain,	Daniel W. Lathrop,	Henry Brown.
Cleveland,	S. C. Aikin,	Stephen Whitaker.

X. SYNOD OF MICHIGAN.

Detroit,	John P. Cleveland.	
Monroe,	Erastus N. Nichols,	Henry Disbrow.
St. Joseph's,	Silas Woodbury,	A. G. Hammond.

XI. SYNOD OF OHIO.

Athens,	Luther G. Bingham,	Marcus Bosworth.
Columbus,	James Hoge, D.D.	John Entrekin.
Lancaster,	James Culbertson, D.D.	John C. Stockton.
Wooster,	Joseph S. Wiley,	John Elliott.
Richland,	Henry Hervey.	
Marion,	Henry Vandeman,	S. G. Strong.

XII. SYNOD OF CINCINNATI.

Cincinnati,	Lyman Beecher, D.D.	Dr. George L. Weed.
	Baxter Dickinson,	John Q. A. Bassett.
Chilicothe,	Samuel Crothers,	Richard Long.
Miami,	John L. Bellville.	
Oxford,	Robert Irwin,	John Molyneaux.
Sidney,	Samuel Cleland,	John Ewing.

XIII. SYNOD OF INDIANA.

Salem,	William W. Martin,	Henry L. Fabrigue.
Vincennes,	Matthew G. Wallace,	John Lagow.
Madison,	William C. Matthews,	Victor King.

PRESBYTERIES.	MINISTERS.	ELDERS.
Crawfordsville,	Samuel G. Lowry,	John S. Jennings.
Indianapolis,	William Sickels,	Dr. Wm. M. Tate.
Logansport,	Alex. T. Rankin.	

XIV. SYNOD OF ILLINOIS.

Illinois,	Edward Beecher,	A. H. Burritt.
Kaskaskia,	Benjamin F. Spillman,	W. A. G. Posey.
Sangamon,	Cyrus L. Watson,	Joseph Young.
Ottawa,	John Blatchford.	
Schuyler,	Samuel Wilson.	
Palestine.		
Peoria,	Flavel Bascom,	Charles Barrows.
Alton,	Albert Hall.	

XV. SYNOD OF MISSOURI.

Missouri.		
St. Louis,		James M. Covington.
St. Charles,		Alex. J. Dallas.

XVI. SYNOD OF KENTUCKY.

Louisville,	James Hawthorn,	John Bemis, M.D.
Muhlenburg,	John Lysle.	
Transylvania.		
West Lexington,	Robert Davidson,	Samuel M. Wallace.
Ebenezer,	R. C. Grundy,	Thomas H. Poage.

XVII. SYNOD OF VIRGINIA.

Lexington,	John D. Ewing,	James McNutt.
	James C. Wilson,	Wm. A. Bell.
Winchester,	S. B. Wilson, D.D.	James H. Fitzgerald.
Dist. of Columbia,	William Hill, D.D.	Robert Jamieson.
West Hanover,	George A. Baxter, D.D.	Samuel McCorkle.
	Andrew Hart,	P. C. Venable, M.D.
East Hanover,	Wm. S. Plumer,	Wm. Maxwell.

XVIII. SYNOD OF NORTH CAROLINA.

Roanoke,	Wm. McPheeters, D.D.	Thomas H. Willie.
Orange,	N. H. Harding,	Richard J. Smith.
Fayetteville,	Wm. N. Peacock,	Alex. Martin.
Concord,	Samuel Williamson,	W. L. Davidson.
	John Williamson,	Wm. King.
Morgantown,	Albertus L. Watts.	

XIX. SYNOD OF TENNESSEE.

PRESBYTERIES.	MINISTERS.	ELDERS.
Abingdon, . . .	Daniel H. Hoge.	
Union, ...	J. E. Montgomery, ...	Walter M. McGill.
	Levi R. Morrison, ...	Andrew Early.
French Broad, . .	Gideon S. White, ...	William Dick.
Holston, ...	Daniel Rogan, ...	John Patton.

XX. SYNOD OF WEST TENNESSEE.

West Tennessee, .	Thomas F. Scott.	
Nashville, . . .	Robert A. Lapsley, ...	James C. Robinson.
Shiloh, ...	Wm. Eagleton.	
North Alabama, .	James O. Stedman, ...	Thomas Childress.
Western District, .	Samuel Hodge, ...	John Ingram, M.D.

XXI. SYNOD OF SOUTH CAROLINA AND GEORGIA.

South Carolina, .	Hugh Dickson, ...	Alex. Chambers.
Bethel, ...	J. Le Roy Davies, ...	John M. Doby.
Harmony, . . .	J. Witherspoon, D.D. . . .	Lawrence Prince.
Charleston Union, .	Elipha White, ...	S. Glover.
	Thomas Magruder, ...	Robert L. Stewart.
Georgia, ...	Horace S. Pratt, ...	Ebenezer S. Reese.
Hopewell, . . .	Samuel S. Davis, ...	William Shear.
Flint River, . . .	John S. Wilson, ...	David C. Campbell.

XXII. SYNOD OF ALABAMA.

South Alabama, .	Robert Nall.	
Tuscaloosa, . . .	Joseph B. Adams, ...	James Knox.
Tombeckbee, . . .	Samuel Hurd, ...	Eli Neely.

XXIII. SYNOD OF MISSISSIPPI.

Mississippi, . . .	Samuel B. Jones, ...	John Chamberlain.
Clinton, ...	A. C. Dickerson, ...	Wm. M. Murdock.
Arkansas.		
Louisiana, . . .	John L. Montgomery, . . .	James Cooper.

CORRESPONDING BODIES.

Evangelical Consociation of Rhode Island,	Rev. Orin Fowler.
General Association of Connecticut, . .	Rev. Nathaniel W. Taylor, D.D.
General Convention of Vermont, . . .	Rev. Harvey Curtis.
General Association of New Hampshire, .	Rev. Henry Wood.

"The Rev. Samuel Fisher, D.D., of the Presbytery of Newark, was nominated as Moderator of the General Assembly, and no other person being put in nomination, he was chosen by a very large majority. The Rev. Dr. Beman thereupon announced to Dr. Fisher that he was duly elected the Moderator of the General Assembly; and on leaving the chair, informed him that he was to be governed in his office by the rules of the General Assembly hereafter to be adopted.

"The Rev. Erskine Mason, D.D., was then chosen Stated Clerk, and the Rev. E. W. Gilbert Permanent Clerk of the General Assembly.

"The following notice had been previously delivered to the Rev. Dr. Beman:

"Resolution of the trustees of the Seventh Presbyterian Church, adopted May 7th, 1838.

"*Resolved,* That the General Assembly of the Presbyterian Church, which is to convene in Philadelphia on the 17th inst., and which shall be organized under the direction of the moderator and clerks officiating during the meeting of the last Assembly, shall have the use of the Seventh Presbyterian Church during their sessions, to the exclusion of every other assembly or convention which may be organized during the same period of time.

(Signed) "JAMES SCHOTT,
"*President of the Board of Trustees.*

"It was moved and seconded that the General Assembly now adjourn to meet forthwith in the lecture room of the First Presbyterian Church in this city. The motion to adjourn was carried unanimously.

"The moderator then audibly announced that the General Assembly was so adjourned, and gave notice that any commissioners who had not presented their commissions should do so at the First Presbyterian Church.

"The Assembly being again met at the lecture room of the First Presbyterian Church, Dr. Patton again offered his preamble and resolutions, as follows, which were unanimously adopted:

"Whereas the General Assembly of 1837 adopted certain resolutions intended to deprive certain Presbyteries of the right to be represented in the General Assembly; and whereas, the more fully to accomplish their purpose, the said Assembly of 1837 did require and receive from their clerks a pledge or promise, that they would, in making out the roll of commissioners to constitute the General Assembly of 1838, omit to insert therein the names of commissioners from said Presbyteries; and whereas the said clerks, having been requested by commissioners from the said Presbyteries to receive their commissions and enter their names on the roll of the General Assembly of 1838, now about to be organized, have refused to receive and enter the same. Therefore,

"1. *Resolved*, That such attempts on the part of the General Assembly of 1837 and their clerks, to direct and control the organization of the General Assembly of 1838, are unconstitutional, and in derogation of its just rights as the general representative judicatory of the whole Presbyterian Church in the United States of America.

"2. *Resolved*, That the General Assembly cannot be legally constituted except by admitting to seats and to equality of powers, in the first instance, all commissioners, who present the usual evidences of their appointment; and that it is the duty of the clerks, and they are hereby directed, to form the roll of the General Assembly of 1838, by including therein the names of all commissioners from Presbyteries belonging to the said Presbyterian Church, not omitting the commissioners from the several Presbyteries within the bounds of the Synods of Utica, Geneva, Genesee, and the Western Reserve; and in all things to form the said roll according to the known practice and established usage of previous General Assemblies.

"Commissions were called for, and committed to the hands of the stated and permanent clerks.

"Adjourned to meet in this place at 4 o'clock, P.M.

"Concluded with prayer."—*Minutes*, 1838, pp. 635–646.

4. *Demand for the Records, Books, Papers, &c., of the General Assembly.*

a. "The following resolution was offered and adopted:

"*Resolved*, That the Rev. Erskine Mason, D.D., clerk of this Assembly, be directed to demand of the Rev. John McDowell, D.D., and Rev. John M. Krebs, clerks of the last General Assembly, all the commissions of the commissioners to the Assembly of 1838, which have been put into their hands; also the Records of the General Assembly of the Presbyterian Church in the United States of America, and all the books and papers belonging to the Assembly that may be in their possession."—*Minutes*, 1838, p. 647.

The Demand Refused.

b. "The stated clerk presented the following report, which was accepted, and ordered to be entered on the Minutes:

"The stated clerk reports that he transmitted to the Rev. John McDowell, D.D., stated clerk, and the Rev. John M. Krebs, the permanent clerk of the last Assembly, a certified copy of the resolution of May 17th, demanding of the said clerks the commissions of commissioners to the Assembly of 1838, and all the records, papers, and documents belonging to the General Assembly, and which may now be in the possession of the said clerks; that the Rev. John McDowell, D.D., formally declined, in the presence of the Rev. Samuel H. Cox, D.D., to deliver any record or document whatsoever belonging to the General Assembly, and now in his possession; and that the Rev. John M. Krebs, in answer to the demand of your clerk, returned a written communication, of which the following is an extract:

"In reply to your favor, I would respectfully inform you that I am the permanent clerk of the General Assembly of the Presbyterian Church in the United States of America; that the Minutes of the Assembly for May 17th are now before me; and that there is no record on the Minutes either of such a resolution as you have communicated, or of your appointment as stated clerk in the place of Dr. John McDowell; and consequently I have no authority to comply with your demand.

(Signed) "JOHN M. KREBS."

—*Minutes*, 1838, p. 653.

5. *Trustees Elected.*

"At 10 o'clock the Assembly proceeded to the order of the day, viz., the election of six trustees of the General Assembly. Messrs. Bogue, Brown, and Chapin were appointed to receive the ballots and report the result. The Assembly ascertained that no vacancies in the Board of Trustees have occurred by death or otherwise. They then proceeded to try whether they could elect any of that third of the number of trustees which they are permitted by law to change, by voting for a person to fill the place of the Rev. Ashbel Green, D.D., the first on the list. On counting the votes, it was ascertained that all the votes given were for James Todd, who was accordingly declared by the moderator to be a trustee duly chosen in the place of Ashbel Green. In the same manner the Assembly proceeded to vote, and unanimously elected John R. Neff in the place of George C. Potts, Frederick A. Raybold in the place of William Latta, George W. McClelland in the place of Thomas Bradford, William Darling in the place of Solomon Allen, and Thomas

Fleming in the place of Cornelius C. Cuyler; thus changing as many of the trustees as they are permitted by law to change. Whereupon James Todd, John R. Neff, Frederick A. Raybold, George W. McClelland, William Darling, and Thomas Fleming, were declared to be duly elected trustees of the General Assembly of the Presbyterian Church in the United States of America."—*Minutes*, 1838, pp. 654, 655.

6. *Committee of Twelve appointed, with Powers.*

a. "Overture No. 13 was reported and adopted, and is as follows:

"In view of the peculiar attitude of the Presbyterian Church—

"*Resolved*, That a *committee of twelve* be appointed, with power to advise and direct in respect to any legal questions and pecuniary interests that may require attention during the ensuing year.

"The following persons were appointed that committee, viz., Hon. William Darling, Rev. John L. Grant, Rev. Nathan S. S. Beman, D.D., Ambrose White, Esq., Thomas Fleming, Esq., George W. McClelland, Esq., Rev. Albert Barnes, Rev. Thomas Brainerd, Rev. Absalom Peters, D.D., Rev. William Patton, D.D., Rev. Erskine Mason, D.D., and Rev. E. W. Gilbert.

"*Ordered*, That the committee meet immediately after the dissolution of this Assembly, and afterwards on their own adjournment."—*Minutes*, 1838, p. 657.

b. "Overture 15 was presented and adopted, and is as follows, viz.:

"*Resolved*, That the 'Committee of Twelve,' appointed on the 24th instant, be, and they are hereby authorized to adopt all such measures as they in their judgment may deem proper to preserve and maintain inviolate the rights and privileges of the General Assembly and of the churches under their jurisdiction."—*Minutes*, 1838, p. 660.

7. *The Assembly willing to agree to any reasonable Measures for the amicable Adjustment of Difficulties.*

"Overture No. 8 was presented, and, after discussion, unanimously adopted, viz.:

"*Resolved*, That this body are willing to agree to any reasonable measures, tending to an amicable adjustment of the difficulties existing in the Presbyterian Church, and will receive and respectfully consider any proposition which may be made for that purpose."—*Minutes*, 1838, p. 654.

8. *Pastoral Letter to the Churches under the care of the General Assembly.*

"BELOVED IN THE LORD: It is well known as a matter of history, that the Presbyterian Church in our nation commenced in the union of pious natives and foreigners of Congregational and Presbyterian origin. These differences, in her early and feeble state, occasioned no interruption of her peace and efficiency. But as her numbers increased, they produced contentions, which resulted in the violent expulsion of one Synod by another, and a separation of seventeen years.

"The terms of reunion were, a subscription to the Confession of Faith, 'as containing the system of doctrine taught in the Holy Scriptures,' notwithstanding any such 'scruples with respect to any article or articles of said Confession as the Presbytery or Synod shall judge not essential or necessary in doctrine, worship, or discipline;' and 'the Synod do solemnly agree that none of us will traduce or use any opprobrious terms of those who differ from us in those extra essential and not necessary points of doctrine, but treat them with the same friendship, kindness, and brotherly love as if they had not differed from us in such sentiments.'

"By this Plan of Union the peace of the Church was restored and her prosperity augmented, though, from some circumstances, the administration of her policy was continued without envy in the hands of the immigrant Presbyterian portion of the Church.

"When the tide of population began to roll westward, and the territories of our Church were fast filling up with pious emigrants from the East, a proposal was made by the General Assembly of our Church to the Association of Connecticut, to permit the union in the same church of Presbyterians and Congregationalists, in the new settlements, for the greater facility of supporting and extending the institutions of religion. This union, so congenial with the spirit of the Gospel, exerted for a long time an auspicious influence in the extension of Presbyterian churches from the Hudson to the Mississippi.

"But at length, in the mysterious providence of God, it came to pass that the very causes of our prosperity became the occasions of disaster. For, in the rapid multiplication of new States and Presbyterian churches, it soon became apparent that native American Presbyterians must unavoidably become a majority of the Church; and though the slight variations of doctrine and policy created no alarm while the helm of power was supposed to be safe, the prospect of its passing to other hands created a strong sensation.

"About this time, a Plan of Union was formed with the Associate Reformed Church, and a considerable accession was made to our Church from that body; and soon after, the system of ecclesiastical organization commenced for the administration of the charities of the Church, with increasing unfriendliness to voluntary associations, till the one was established and the others were disclaimed and opposed.

"During the progress of these movements, the slight shades of doctrinal difference always known and permitted to exist in the Church, before and since the Adopting Act, and recognized in every form as consistent with the Confession of Faith and the unity of the Spirit in the bonds of peace, became the occasions of alarm, and whisperings, and accusations, and at length of ecclesiastical trials for heresy, while doctrines and measures unknown to the Confession were selected as tests of orthodoxy.

"As the result of these efforts to change the terms of subscription and union, the General Assembly of 1837, 'convinced that a separation of the parties was the only cure,' and 'that a separation by personal process was impossible, or, if possible, tedious, agitating, and troublesome in the highest degree,' proceeded without charges, citation, witnesses, or a judicial trial, to separate four Synods and one Presbytery from the Presbyterian Church. In these circumstances, apprised by counsel of the unconstitutionality of the disfranchising act, and advised of a constitutional mode of organization, we did, in a meeting for consultation and prayer, on the 15th day of May, 1838, send the following proposal to a large number of commissioners to the Assembly, met in another place, viz.:

"*Resolved*, That while we regard with deep sorrow the existing difficulties in our beloved Church, we would fondly hope that there are no insurmountable obstacles in the way of averting the calamities of a violent dismemberment, and of securing such an organization as may avoid collisions, and secure the blessings of a perpetuated harmonious action.

"*Resolved*, That we are ready to co-operate in any efforts for pacification which are constitutional, and which shall recognize the regular standing, and secure the rights of the entire Church, including those portions which the acts of the last General Assembly were intended to exclude.

"*Resolved*, That a committee of three be now appointed, respectfully to communicate the foregoing resolutions to those commissioners now in session in this city, who are at present inclined to sustain the acts of the last General Assembly, and inquire whether they will open a friendly conference for the purpose of ascertaining if some constitutional terms of pacification may not be agreed upon.

"While this proposal was under consideration, it was resolved by the meeting,

"That, should a portion of the commissioners to the next General Assembly attempt to organize the Assembly without admitting to their seats commissioners from all the Presbyteries recognized in the organization of the General Assembly of 1837, it will then be the duty of the commissioners present to organize the General Assembly of 1838, in all respects according to the Constitution, and to transact all other necessary business consequent upon such organization.

"To our communication, we received the following answer:

"The committee on the communication from 'the meeting of commissioners,' now in session in the lecture-room of the First Church, presented the following preamble and resolutions, which were adopted, viz.:

"Whereas, the resolutions of 'the meeting,' whilst they profess a readiness 'to co-operate in any efforts for pacification which are constitutional,' manifestly proceed upon the erroneous supposition that the acts of the last General Assembly, declaring the four Synods of the Western Reserve, Utica, Geneva, Genesee, out of the ecclesiastical connection of our Church, were unconstitutional and invalid, and the convention cannot for a moment consent to consider them in this light; therefore—

"*Resolved unanimously*, That the convention regard the said overture of 'the meeting,' however intended, as founded upon a basis which is wholly inadmissible, and as calculated only to disturb that peace of our Church which a calm and firm adherence to those constitutional, just, and necessary acts of the last General Assembly can alone, by the blessing of Divine Providence, establish and secure.

"*Resolved*, That, in the judgment of the convention, the resolution of the last General Assembly which provides, in substance, that all churches and ministers within the said four Synods which are strictly Presbyterian in doctrine and order, and wish to unite with us, may apply for admission into those Presbyteries belonging to our connection which are most convenient to their respective locations; and that any such Presbyteries as aforesaid, being strictly Presbyterian in doctrine and order, and now in connection with either of the said Synods, as may desire to unite with us, are directed to make application, with a full statement of their case, to the next 'General Assembly, which will take order therein,' furnishes a fair and easy mode of proceeding, by which all such ministers, churches, and Presbyteries, within the said Synods, as are really desirous to be recognized as in regular standing with us, and as proper parts of our 'entire Church,' may obtain their object without trouble and without delay.

"By this answer, all prospect of conciliation or an amicable division being foreclosed, we did, after mature consideration and fervent prayer, proceed, at a proper time and place, to organize, in a constitutional manner, the General Assembly of 1838; which being accomplished on our part without violence or tumult, the Assembly adjourned to the First Presbyterian Church.

"During the session of the Assembly on Wednesday, May 24th, the following resolution was passed, viz.:

"*Resolved*, That this body is willing to agree to any reasonable measures tending to an amicable adjustment of the difficulties existing in the Presbyterian Church, and will receive and respectfully consider any propositions which may be made for that purpose.

"Beside these overtures for peace, influential members of the Assembly held personal conference with members of the other body, till it was ascertained that there was no hope of an amicable settlement of differences.

"In the retrospect of this mournful history, we are compelled to regard the excision of the four Synods and the Third Presbytery of Philadelphia, with the setting up a new test of doctrine and measures, as an exercise of power by the Assembly unknown to the Constitution, and dangerous to the purity and liberty of the Church, perpetuating to an accidental majority unlimited and irresponsible power, and affording to minorities only such protection as may be found in passive obedience and non-resistance.

"We could not fail to perceive, in a General Assembly concentrating in itself legislative, judicial, and executive power, and dispensing the discipline, the honors, and the copious revenues of the Church, the elements of an ecclesiastical organization, which, with less pretension in the beginning, had once, for more than ten centuries, subverted the liberties and rolled back the civilization of the world.

"To have acquiesced in such concentration of irresponsible ecclesiastical power and patronage, would have been to abandon the Constitution of the Church, which we had solemnly engaged to defend; to expose large amounts of property to diversion from its intended use; to subject the churches to a wide-spread, vexatious litigation; to abandon to aggression and division a large and efficient body of concordant churches with their pastors; to surrender the rights of conscience, and free inquiry, and charitable enterprise, to an organization never recognized by Heaven as their keeper, or clothed by our Constitution with their power; and, finally, to throw apparently the example of an extended and powerful Church—the patron, hitherto, of constitutional liberty—on the side of those elements of strife and violence which already so powerfully agitate the nation.

"We love and honor the Confession of Faith of the Presbyterian Church, as containing more well-defined fundamental truth, with less defect, than appertains to any other human formula of doctrine, and as calculated to hold, in intelligent concord, a greater number of sanctified minds than any which could now be formed; and we disclaim all design, past, present, or future, to change it. But it is not the Bible, nor a substitute for the Bible, nor a stereotyped page, to be merely committed to memory by unreflecting, confiding minds, without energy of thought, and a prayerful, faithful searching of the Scriptures. It is itself an illustrious monument of the independent investigation of the most gifted minds, and breathes and inspires the spirit which formed it.

"We impute to our brethren no intention of producing the results which we anticipate from their measures, but good intentions do not change the nature or avert the mischiefs of erroneous principles and injurious actions. It is a matter of history, that some of the greatest calamities of the Church have flowed from principles and innovations introduced by good men, and with the best intentions.

"And now, beloved brethren, we beseech you to unite with us in thanksgiving to God for the harmony, and kind feeling, and decision which have pervaded our deliberations and action, and for those wide-spread and exuberant effusions of the Spirit the past year which, amid unusual sorrows and fears of deserved judgments, have caused the tide of spiritual prosperity to flow deep and broad, the expression of sovereign mercy and the pledge of future love.

"It is our desire and expectation that ye will persevere in well doing, and not be seized with any sudden amazement, through manifold temptations and trials of your faith and patience, and that you will not be moved away from the Gospel which ye have heard, and the 'form of sound words' and salutary discipline, so influential in our past prosperity.

"We exhort that fervent charity be maintained among you, and a spirit of prayer for the continued presence and power of the Holy Spirit, and devotedness to those labors which God especially employs for the promotion of revivals of religion, the great end of all means, and the comprehension of all spiritual good.

"But while these things are faithfully done, we pray you that other duties of imperious obligation and urgent necessity be not neglected; particularly that your charity for home and foreign missions, and the education of a holy ministry, and for all our long-cherished voluntary associations, be not suffered to decline, but rather to flow on with augmented power, and faith, and prayer.

"That especial care be taken to send and sustain a full representation of the Church, as a mean of a mutual communication of knowledge, the culture of confidence, and the production of wise counsels.

"And now, brethren, we commend you to Him who 'is able to keep you from falling, and to present you faultless before the presence of His glory with exceeding joy,' praying 'that ye might be filled with the knowledge of His will in all wisdom and spiritual understanding, that ye might walk worthy of the Lord unto all pleasing, being fruitful in every good work, and increasing in the knowledge of God; strengthened with all might according to His glorious power, unto all patience and long-suffering with joyfulness.'

"Now our Lord Jesus Christ himself, and God, even our Father, which have loved us, and given us everlasting consolation and good hope through grace, comfort your hearts, and stablish you in every good word and work."

"SAM'L FISHER, *Moderator.*
"ERSKINE MASON, *Stated Clerk.*

"PHILADELPHIA, May 25th, 1838."

—*Minutes*, 1838, pp. 663–667.

9. *Report of the Committee of Twelve to the General Assembly of the Presbyterian Church.*

a. "In the General Assembly, May 20, 1839, Judge Darling, from the Committee of Twelve, made the following report in part:

"The committee appointed on the 21st May, 1838, 'to advise and direct in respect to any legal questions and pecuniary interests that might require attention during the ensuing year,' and who were authorized to adopt all such measures as they in their judgment might deem proper, to preserve and maintain inviolate the rights and privileges of the General Assembly and of the churches under its jurisdiction, entered upon the discharge of their duties immediately after the adjournment of the last General Assembly, deeply impressed with the importance of the interests intrusted to them, with their responsibilities to the Presbyterian Church, and with a determination to exert their influence to bring the controversy in the Presbyterian Church to a speedy termination, on just and equitable terms, which would restore peace and harmony to our beloved Zion. They resolved not to resort to the civil courts for redress, until every reasonable hope of an amicable adjustment should be abandoned, and unless it became necessary so to do to protect and preserve the rights and privileges of the Church which they represented. The trustees elected by the General Assembly of 1838, having been denied the right to take their seats at a regular meeting of the Board of Trustees, as then constituted, and our opponents manifesting a determination to persist in their acts of injustice and oppression, the committee, with the notice and under the direction of their counsel, Josiah Randall and William Meredith, Esqs., of Philadelphia, and George Wood, Esq., of New York, caused a writ of *quo warranto* to be issued, in the name of the Commonwealth of Pennsylvania, at the relation of the Hon. James Todd *et al.* *vs.* the Rev. Ashbel Green, D.D., *et al.*, to show cause by what authority they continue to usurp and hold the office of trustees, &c. The committee adopted this mode of proceeding at the suggestion of their legal advisers, believing that, in this form of action, they would be enabled to obtain a more speedy trial and decision on the merits of the controversy between the Reformed and Constitutional General Assemblies, and on the various points of law involved in the same, and with less expense and excitement than in any other form of action which could be devised. While this cause was pending, and previous to the trial before Judge Rogers, at *Nisi Prius*, the committee were informed by one of their counsel, that John K. Kane, Esq., one of the trustees of the General Assembly, and who was of counsel for the respondents, had stated to him that those he represented were disposed to adjust, amicably and equitably, all matters in controversy in this cause, and had requested him to ascertain what terms the committee would propose, as a basis for an amicable division of the Presbyterian Church, and the final adjustment of all the matters in dispute between the Reformed and Constitutional General Assemblies. Upon inquiry, the committee ascertained that neither Mr. Kane, nor any other person, was authorized to enter into a negotiation with the committee on the subject of a compromise; that Mr. Kane was probably acting on his own responsibility, influenced by a most laudable desire to promote union and peace among the professed friends of the Redeemer. The committee duly appreciated the motives which prompted the efforts of Mr. Kane, and keeping in view the resolution of the General Assembly of 1838, viz., 'That this body is willing to agree to any reasonable measures, tending to an amicable adjustment of the difficulties in the Presbyterian Church, and will receive, and respectfully consider, any propositions made for that purpose,' they waived all exceptions which might have been taken to enter into any negotiation with, or to making any propositions to, one irresponsible individual, and promptly requested their counsel to furnish Mr. Kane with a copy of the following articles of agreement:

b. "Articles of Agreement Proposed.

"In order to secure an amicable and equitable adjustment of the difficulties existing in the Presbyterian Church in the United States of America, it is hereby agreed by the respective parties, that the following shall be articles on which a division shall be made and continued:

"Art. I. The successors of the body which held its sessions in Ranstead Court shall hereafter be known by the name and style of 'The General Assembly of the Presbyterian Church in the United States of America.' The successors of the body which held its sessions in the First Presbyterian Church shall hereafter be known by the name and style of 'The General Assembly of the American Presbyterian Church.'

"Art. II. Joint application shall be made by the parties to this agreement to the Legislature of Pennsylvania, for a charter to incorporate trustees of each of the respective bodies, securing to each the immunities and privileges now secured by the existing charter to the trustees of the General Assembly of the Presbyterian Church in the United States of America, subject, nevertheless, to the limitations and articles herein agreed on; and when so obtained, the existing charter shall be surrendered to the State.

"Art. III. Churches, ministers, and members of churches as well as Presbyteries, shall be at full liberty to decide to which of the said Assemblies they will be attached; and in case the majority of legal voters of any congregation shall prefer to be connected with any Presbytery connected with the Assembly to which their Presbytery is not attached, they shall certify the same to the stated clerk of the Presbytery which they wish to leave, and their connection with said Presbytery shall thenceforth cease.

"Art. IV. The Theological Seminary of Princeton, the Western Theological Seminary, the Board of Foreign Missions, the Board of Domestic Missions, the Board of Education, with the funds appertaining to each, shall be the property and subject to the exclusive control of the body which, according to this agreement, shall be chartered under the title of 'The General Assembly of the Presbyterian Church in the United States of America.'

"This agreement shall not be considered a secession on the part of either body from the Presbyterian Church in the United States of America, but a voluntary and amicable division of this Church into two denominations, each retaining all the ecclesiastical and pecuniary rights of the whole body, with the limitations and qualifications in the above articles specified.

"The only reply which the committee received to these propositions was, that they could not be accepted, but that the Old School party would agree that the members of the Constitutional General Assembly, and all who adhered to this General Assembly, should be at liberty to leave the Presbyterian Church without *molestation* from them, and that they should not be called *seceders*. This reply, in the opinion of the committee, cut off all hope of an amicable and just settlement, and closed the door of reconciliation. They, therefore, formally resolved that it was inexpedient to make any further attempt to effect a compromise, and that the necessary preparations be made for the trial of the cause now pending.

c. "The result of the trial of this cause before Judge Rogers, at *Nisi Prius*, and of the subsequent motion to set aside the verdict of the jury in this cause, is known to all the members of the General Assembly. But the committee forbear entering into the history of this trial, or of the causes which probably influenced the court in bank to award a new trial; believing that this will be done in due time by another committee.

"The committee cannot close this report without bearing their testimony to the zeal and distinguished ability which the counsel for the relators displayed, in the preparation, trial, and argument of this cause; and although we have not obtained all which the justice of our cause warranted us to hope for and expect, yet much has been gained. The true history of the proceedings of the Assemblies of 1837 and 1838, at Ranstead's Court, has been extensively circulated. The nature of the difficulties in the Presbyterian Church is now better understood. The public mind has been, in a great measure, disabused of the misrepresentations industriously circulated by certain presses, respecting the motives, views, and intentions of the friends and adherents of the Constitutional Presbyterian Church; while the manifest injustice which has been inflicted upon us will lead to the development of Christian character, which will be of incalculable value to the Church. It is true, we have been disappointed, but not defeated; cast down, but not destroyed. Our cause, the committee believe, is not lost; but we trust the judgment on a just and righteous verdict of a jury of our country, is suspended only for a season.

"The committee view with pain and regret the scene of protracted litigation which lies in prospect before them, but they believe that the path of duty is the only path of safety, and that they are bound to maintain and defend the great principles of civil and religious rights involved in this case, and to preserve and protect inviolate the rights and privileges of the Church under the care of this General Assembly. The committee, therefore, recommend a firm adherence to the standards and Constitution of the Presbyterian Church; to cultivate union, that all may act in harmonious concert, guided by the immutable principles of truth and justice; leaving our cause, with explicit trust and confidence, with the great Head of the Church, believing that He will send us deliverance, and cause truth and righteousness to prevail."

Presbyterian Church Case. Charge of the Court.

d. "*Rogers, J.*—Gentlemen of the Jury,—Before the year 1758, the Presbyterian churches in this country were under the care of two separate Synods and their Presbyteries,—the Synod of New York and the Synod of Philadelphia.

"In the year 1758 these Synods were united, and were called 'The Synod of New York and Philadelphia.' This continued until the year 1788, when the General Assembly was formed. The Synod was then divided into four Synods, the Synod of New York and New Jersey, Philadelphia, Virginia, and the Carolinas; of these four Synods the General Assembly was constituted.

"In 1803, the Synod of Albany was erected. This Synod has been from time to time subdivided, and the Synods of Genesee, Geneva, and Utica, have been formed.

"The Synod of Pittsburg has been also erected, out of which the Synod of the Western Reserve has been formed.

"These constitute the four exscinded Synods, viz., the Synods of Genesee, Geneva, Utica, and the Western Reserve.

"The General Assembly was constituted by every Presbytery, at their last stated meeting preceding the meeting of the General Assembly, deputing to the General Assembly commissioners, in certain specific proportions.

"The Westminster Confession of Faith is part of the Constitution of the Church. The Constitution could not be altered, unless two-thirds of the Presbyteries under the care of the General Assembly prepare alterations or amendments, and such alterations or amendments were agreed to by the General Assembly.

"The form of government was amended in 1821. The General Assembly now consists of an 'equal delegation of bishops and elders from each Presbytery, in certain proportions.'

"The judicatories of the Church consist of the Session, of the Presbyteries, of Synods, and the General Assembly.

"The church Session consists of the pastor, or pastors, and ruling elders of a particular congregation. A Presbytery, of all the ministers and one ruling elder from each congregation within a certain district. A Synod is a convention of bishops and elders, including at least three Presbyteries; and the General Assembly, of an 'equal delegation of bishops and elders from each Presbytery,' in the following proportions, viz.: Each Presbytery consisting of not more than twenty-four ministers, sends one minister and one elder; and each Presbytery consisting of more than twenty-four ministers, sends two ministers and two elders; and in the like proportion for every twenty-four ministers in any Presbytery. The delegates so appointed are styled Commissioners to the General Assembly.

"The General Assembly is the highest judicatory of the Presbyterian Church. It represents, in one body, all the particular churches of this denomination of Christians.

"In relation to this body, the most important undoubtedly are the various Presbyteries; for, as was before said, the General Assembly consists of an equal delegation of bishops and elders from each of the Presbyteries. If the Presbyteries are destroyed, the General Assembly falls, as a matter of course, as there would no longer be any constituent bodies in existence from which delegates could be sent to the General Assembly.

"The Presbyteries are essential features in the form of government in another particular, for before any overtures or regulations proposed by the General Assembly to be established as constitutional rules, can be obligatory on the churches, it is necessary to transmit them to all the Presbyteries, and to receive the returns of at least a majority of them in writing, approving thereof.

"A Synod, as has been before observed, is a convention of bishops and elders within a district, including at least three Presbyteries. The Synods have a supervisory power over Presbyteries, but unlike Presbyteries, as such they are not essential to the existence of the General Assembly. If every Synod in the United States were exscinded and destroyed, still the General Assembly would remain as the highest tribunal in the Church. In this particular there is a vital difference between Presbyteries and Synods. The only connection between the General Assembly and the Synods is, that the former has a supervisory power over the latter.

"Having thus given you an account of such parts of the form of church government as may in some aspects of the cause, be material, I shall now call your attention to the matter in issue.

"This proceeding is what is called a '*quo warranto*.' It is issued by the commonwealth, at the suggestion of James Todd and others, against Ashbel Green and others, to show by what authority they claim to exercise the office of Trustees of the General Assembly of the Presbyterian Church in the United States of America. I must here remark, that it is not only an appropriate, but the best method of trying the issue in this case.

"It is admitted that, until the 24th of May, 1838, the respondents were the rightful trustees; but it is contended by the relators, that on that day, the 24th of May, 1838, in pursuance of the act of incorporation, the General Assembly of the Presbyterian Church changed one-third of the trustees, by the election of the relators in the place and stead of the respondents.

"The 28th March, 1799, the Legislature of Pennsylvania declared Ashbel Green and seventeen others (naming them), a body politic and corporate, by the name and style of Trustees of the General Assembly of the Presbyterian Church in the United States of America.

"The sixth section provides that the corporation shall not, at any time, consist of more than eighteen persons; whereof, the General Assembly may, at their discretion, as often as they shall hold their sessions in the State of Pennsylvania, change one-third in such a manner as to the General Assembly may seem proper.

"It was the intention of the legislature, by the act of incorporation, to provide for the election of competent persons, who as an incorporated body, might, with more ease and in a better manner, manage the temporal affairs of the Church. It is only in this aspect that we have cognizance of the case.

"In this country, for the mutual advantage of Church and State, we have wisely separated the ecclesiastical from the civil power. The court has as little inclination as authority to interfere with the Church and its government, farther than may be necessary for its protection and security. It is only as it bears upon the corporation, which is the creature of the civil power, that we have any right to determine the validity, or to construe the acts and resolutions of the General Assembly.

"Although neither the members of the General Assembly, as such, nor the General Assembly itself, are individually or aggregately members of the corporation, yet the Assembly has power, from time to time, as they may deem proper, to change the trustees, and to give special instructions for their government. They stand in the relation of electors, and have been properly denominated, in the argument, *quasi* corporate. The trustees only are the corporation by express words of the act of the Assembly.

"Unhappily, differences have arisen in the Church (the nature of which it is not necessary for us to inquire into), which have caused a division of its members into two parties, called and known as the Old and New School. These appellations we may adopt for the sake of designating the respective parties, the existence of which will have an important bearing on some of the questions involved in this important cause. It gives a key to conduct, which it would be otherwise difficult to explain.

"The division continued to increase in strength and virulence until the Session of 1837, when certain decisive measures, which will be hereafter stated, were taken by the General Assembly, which at this time was under the control of members who sympathize (as the phrase is) with the principles of the Old School.

"At an early period the Presbyterian Church, at their own suggestion, formed unions with cognate churches, that is, with churches whose faith, principles, and practice assimilated with their own, and between whom there was no essential difference in doctrine.

"On this principle a Plan of Union and correspondence was adopted by the Assembly in 1792, with the General Association of Connecticut, with Vermont in 1803, with that of New Hampshire in 1810, with Massachusetts in 1811, with the Northern Associate Presbytery of Albany in 1802, and with the Reformed Dutch Church and the Associate Reformed Church in 1798.

"These conventions, as is stated, originated in the measures adopted by the General Assembly in 1790 and 1791. The delegates from each of the associated churches not only sat and deliberated with each other, but also acted and voted by virtue of the express terms of the Union.

"In further pursuance of the settled policy of the Church to extend its sphere of usefulness, in the year 1801, a Plan of Union between the Presbyterians and Congregationalists was formed.

"The Plan, which was devised by the fathers of the Church to prevent alienation and to promote harmony, was observed by the General Assembly, without question by them, until the year 1835, a period of thirty-four years.

"At that time it was resolved by the General Assembly, that they deemed it no longer desirable that churches should be formed in their Presbyterian connection, agreeably to the Plan adopted by the Assembly and General Association of Connecticut, in 1801. They, therefore, resolved that their brethren of the General Association of Connecticut be, and they hereby are, respectfully requested to *consent* that the said Plan shall be, from and after the next meeting of that Association, declared to be annulled. And also resolved that the annulling of said Plan shall not in anywise interfere with the existence and lawful association of churches which *have been already formed* on this Plan.

"To this resolution no reasonable objection can be made, and if the matter had been permitted to rest here, we should not have been troubled with this controversy. It had not then occurred to the Assembly that the Plan of Union was unconstitutional. The resolutions are predicated on the belief that the agreement or compact was constitutional. They request that the Association of Connecticut would *consent* to rescind it. It does not seem to have been thought, that this could be done without their consent. And moreover, the resolution expressly saves the right of existing churches which had been formed on that Plan.

"I must be permitted to regret, for the sake of peace and harmony, that this business was not permitted to rest on the basis of resolutions which breathe the spirit of peace and good feeling. But unfortunately the General Assembly, in 1837, which was then under another influence, took a different view of the question.

"'As the "Plan of Union" adopted for the new settlements, in 1801, was originally an unconstitutional act on the part of that Assembly,—these important standing rules having never been submitted to the Presbyteries,—and as they were totally destitute of authority as proceeding from the General Association of Connecticut, which is invested with no power to legislate in such cases, and especially to enact laws to regulate churches not within their limits; and as much confusion and irregularity have arisen from this unnatural unconstitutional system of union, therefore it is

"'*Resolved*, That the Act of the Assembly of 1801, entitled a "Plan of Union," be, and the same is hereby abrogated.' See Digest, pp. 297–299.

"The resolution declares the Plan of Union to be unconstitutional: 1st, because those important standing rules, as they call them, were not submitted to the Presbyteries; and secondly, because the General Association of Connecticut was invested with no power to legislate in such cases, and especially to enact laws to regulate churches not within their limits.

"The court is not satisfied with the force of these reasons, and do not think the agreement or Plan of Union, comes within the words or spirit of that clause in the Constitution which provides, that before any overture or regulations shall be proposed by the General Assembly, to be established as constitutional rules, shall be obligatory on the churches, it shall be necessary to transmit them to all the Presbyteries, and to receive the returns of at least a majority of them approving thereof. Nor is it in the opinion of the court, in conflict with the Constitution before its amendment in 1821, which provides that no alteration shall be made in the Constitution, unless two-thirds of the Presbyteries under the care of the General Assembly propose alterations or amendments, and such alterations or amendments are agreed to by the Assembly.

"It was a regulation made by competent parties, and not intended by either as a constitutional rule; nor was it obligatory on any of the Presbyterian churches within their connection. Those who were competent to make it, were competent to dissolve it without the assent of the Presbyteries, as such, which could not be done were it a constitutional rule, within the meaning of the Constitution. Whether one party may dissolve it without the consent of the other, it might be unnecessary to decide. My opinion is that they can. The Plan of Union is intended to prevent alienation, and to promote union and harmony in the new settlements.

"It is not the union of a Presbyterian church with a Congregational church or churches, but it purports to be, and is a Plan of Union between individual members of the Presbyterian and Congregational Churches, in that portion of the country which was then denominated the new settlements. It is advisory and recommendatory in its character—has nothing obligatory about it. A Congregational church as such, is not by force of the agreement incorporated with the Presbyterian Church. It has no necessary connection with it; for it is only when the congregation consists partly of those who hold the Congregational form of discipline, and partly of those who hold the Presbyterian form, and there is an appeal to the Presbytery (as there may be in certain cases), that the Standing Committee of the Congregational Church, consisting partly of Presbyterians and partly of Congregationalists, may or shall attend the Presbytery, and may have the same right to sit and act in the Presbytery as a ruling elder. And whatever may have been occasionally the instances to the contrary, this I conceive to be the obvious construction of the regulation. That part of the agreement was intended as a safeguard, or protection of the rights of all the parties to be affected by it, without any design to confer upon the Standing Committee all the rights of a ruling elder.

"I view it as a matter of discipline and not of doctrine, the effect of which is to exempt those members of the different communions who adopted it, from the censures of the church to which they belong, and particularly the clerical portion of them.

"The court is also of the opinion, that after an acquiescence of nearly forty years, and particularly after the adoption by the Presbyteries of the amended Constitution of 1821, the Plan of Union is not now open to objection. The Plan has been recognized by the Presbyteries, at various times and different manners, under the old and amended Constitution. It has been acted on by them and the General Assembly in repeated instances, and is equally as obligatory as if it had received the express sanction of the Presbyteries, in all the forms known to the Constitution.

"That acquiescence gives right, is a principle which we must admit. The constitutionality of the purchase and admission of Louisiana as a member of the Union, was doubted by some of the wisest heads and purest hearts in the country, but he would be a very bold man, indeed, who would now deny that State, and Mississippi, Arkansas, and Missouri to be members of the Confederation. In the memorable struggle for the admission of Missouri into the Union, this objection was never taken.

"Nor am I satisfied with the second reason, that the General Association of Connecticut was invested with no power to legislate in such cases, and especially to enact laws to regulate churches not within their limits. Although the General Assembly had the right to annul the Plan of Union without the assent of the General Association of Connecticut, yet I must be permitted to say, that after having acted on the Plan, and reaped all the advantages of it, it is rather discourteous, to say the least of it, to attempt to abrogate it without the consent of the other party. Although the Association may be an advisory body, yet it does not appear that any difficulty has been started by them, or by the churches under their control. All parties acquiesced in it for thirty-six years, and it would be too late for either now to object to its validity. Nor is there anything in the idea that they have no power to regulate churches not within their limits. This is a matter of consent, and there is nothing to prevent the churches in one State, from submitting themselves to the ecclesiastical government of churches located in another State. The Presbyterian Church has furnished us with repeated examples of this kind.

"So far from believing the Plan of Union to be unconstitutional, I concur fully with one of the counsel, that confined within its legitimate limits, it is an agreement or regulation, which the General Assembly not only had power to make, but that it is one which is well calculated to promote the best interests of religion.

"If as is stated, the Standing Committee of Congregational Churches have claimed and exercised the same rights as ruling elders in Presbyteries, and in the General Assembly itself, it is an abuse which may be corrected by the proper tribunals, but surely that is no argument, or one of but little weight, to show that the Plan of Union is unconstitutional and void.

"Although in the opinion of the court, the Assembly have the right to repeal the Plan of Union without the consent of the General Association of Connecticut, yet it was unjust to repeal it, without saving the rights of existing ministers and churches.

"But whether the Plan of Union be constitutional or not, is only material so far as it is made the basis of some subsequent resolutions, to which your attention will now be directed.

"At the same session, and after failure of an attempt at compromise, the character of which has been the subject of much comment, the General Assembly resolved, 'that by the abrogation of the Plan of Union of 1801, the Synod of the Western Reserve is, and is hereby declared to be no longer a part of the Presbyterian Church.'

"'*Resolved*, That in consequence of the abrogation by this General Assembly of the Plan of Union of 1801, between it and the General Association of Connecticut, as utterly unconstitutional, and therefore null and void from the beginning, the Synods of Utica, Geneva, and Genesee, which were formed and attached to this body, under and in execution of said 'Plan of Union,' be, and are hereby declared to be out of the connection of the Presbyterian Church in the United States of America, and that they are not, in form or in fact, an integral portion of said church.'

"These resolutions refer only in name to the four Synods, and if we were called on for the construction alone, it might be well doubted whether they were intended, or could be made to include the Presbyteries within their limits, the constituents or electoral bodies of the General Assembly itself. I should be inclined, for the purpose of protecting their rights from a resolution so penal in its character, to say that they were not included, neither in the spirit nor the words of the resolution. But this construction we are prevented from giving by their declarative resolution. It is there in effect said, that it is the purpose of the General Assembly to destroy the relations of all such Synods, and all their constituent parts, to the General Assembly, and to the Presbyterian Church in the United States. In the fourth resolution it is declared, that any Presbytery within the four Synods, being strictly Presbyterian in doctrine and order, who may desire to be united with them, are hereby directed to make application, with a full statement of their case, to the next General Assembly, which will take proper order thereon.

"There is no mistaking the character of these resolutions. It is an immediate dissolution of all connection between the four Synods and all their constituent parts, and the General Assembly. They are destructive of the rights of electors of the General Assembly. The connection might be renewed, it is true, by each of the Presbyteries making application to the next General Assembly, but they are at liberty to accept or refuse them, provided they, the General Assembly, deem them strictly Presbyterian in doctrine and order. As they had the right to admit them, they had the right also to refuse them, unless in their opinion, they were strictly Presbyterian in doctrine and order.

"By these resolutions, the commissioners, who had acted with the General

Assembly up to that time, were deprived of their seats. At the same time, four Synods, with twenty-eight Presbyteries, were cut off from all connection with the Presbyterian Church. The General Assembly resolved, that because the Plan of 1801 was unconstitutional, those Synods and their constituent parts are no longer integral parts of the Presbyterian Church.

"You will observe, that I have already said the Plan of Union is constitutional. That reason therefore fails. They have resolved that it is not only unconstitutional, but that it is null and void from the beginning. Instead of a *prospective*, they have given their resolutions a *retrospective* effect, the injustice of which is most manifest.

"But admitting that the Plan of Union is unconstitutional, null and void, from the beginning, I cannot perceive what justification that furnishes for the exscinding resolutions. The infusion of Congregationalists with the Presbyteries, or the General Assembly itself, does not invalidate the acts of the General Assembly. They had a right, notwithstanding the charter which recognizes elders and ministers as composing the Presbyterian Church, to perform the functions committed to them by the Constitution. And among them to establish and divide Synods, to create Presbyteries, as in their judgment the exigencies of the Church might demand.

Accordingly, we find that the four Synods, and all the Presbyteries attached to them, have been formed since the year 1801. The Assembly creates the Synods, and the Synods the Presbyteries. Sometimes the Assembly creates the Presbyteries—a course pursued with some of the Presbyteries which have been exscinded. They have been established since, but this is no evidence that the four exscinded Synods were formed and attached to the General Assembly under, and in execution of, the Plan of Union. The compact, as has been before observed, was intended for a different purpose, and imposed on the Presbyterian Church no obligation to admit churches formed on the Plan as members. It was a voluntary act, and not the necessary result of the agreement; nor does it appear that the Presbyteries were formed and incorporated with the Church on any other terms or conditions than other Presbyteries, who were in regular course taken into the Presbyterian connection.

"But, gentlemen, when resolutions of so unusual a character, so condemnatory, and so destructive of the rights of electors, the constituents of the Assembly itself, are passed, we have a right to require that the substantial forms of justice be observed. But so far from this, the General Assembly, in the plenitude of its power, has undertaken to exclude from all their rights and privileges twenty-eight Presbyteries, who are its constituents, without notice, and without even the form of trial. By the resolutions, the commissioners, who had acted as members of the General Assembly for two weeks, were at once deprived of their seats. Four Synods, 28 Presbyteries, 509 ministers, 599 churches, and 60,000 communicants, were at once disfranchised and deprived of their privileges in this Church.

"This proceeding is not only contrary to the eternal principles of justice, the principles of the common law, but it is at variance with the Constitution of the Church.

"This proceeding is not in the nature of a *legislative*, but it is a *judicial* proceeding to all intents and purposes. It is idle to deny that the Presbyteries within the infected districts, as they are called, were treated as enemies and offenders against the rules, regulations, and doctrines of the Church. If there is anything that a man values, it is his religious rights.

"And of this opinion were the General Assembly themselves, for, only a few days before, they came to the following resolutions:

"'*Resolved*, 1. That the proper steps be now taken to cite to the bar of the next Assembly, such inferior judicatories as are charged by common fame with irregularities.

"'2. That a special committee be now appointed to ascertain what inferior judicatories are thus charged by common fame, prepare charges and specifications against them, and to digest a suitable plan of procedure in the matter, and that said committee be requested to report as soon as practicable.'

"Nothing further appears to have been done in this matter in the General Assembly, for, after failure of the attempt at compromise, they appear to have discovered a much more expeditious, if not a more agreeable, method of effecting their object.

"I have said that exscinding the Presbyteries without notice and without trial, was not only contrary to the common law, but it was contrary to the Constitution of the Church. And it is only necessary to open the Book of Discipline to see how very careful the fathers of the Church have been to secure to the accused a full, fair, and impartial trial.

"Notice is given to the parties concerned at least ten days before the meeting of the judicatory. The accused are informed of the names of all the witnesses to be adduced against them. When the charges are exhibited, the time, places, and circumstances are stated, if by possibility they can be ascertained, citations are issued, signed by the moderator or clerk by order, and in the name of the judicatory.

"Judicatories are enjoined to ascertain, before proceeding to trial, that their citations have been duly served. And, to secure a fair and impartial trial, the witnesses are to be examined in the presence of the accused, who is permitted to ask any question tending to his own exculpation. The judgment, when rendered, is regularly entered on the records of the judicatory.

"If these proceedings, before judgment, are requisite in the case of the meanest member of the Church (the omission of which, by any of the inferior judicatories, would call down on the offenders the severest censure of the General Assembly), it is inconceivable that similar precautions are not necessary to protect the rights of Presbyteries, which consist of many individuals, from the injustice, violence, and party spirit of the General Assembly itself. Constitutions are intended to protect the weak, the minority, from the injustice of the majority.

"The majority, for the most part, are able to protect themselves. It is the minority that need protection; and for this purpose it is necessary to encircle them with at least all the *forms* of justice.

"This, as has been before observed, is a judicial act; and if a regular trial had been had and judgment rendered, the sentence would have been conclusive. We should not have attempted to examine the justice of the proceeding, but inasmuch as there have been no citations and no trial, I instruct you that the resolution of the General Assembly exscinding the four Synods of Utica, Geneva, Genesee, and the Western Reserve, are *unconstitutional*, *null*, and *void*.

"The judgments of all courts, whether ecclesiastical or civil, whether of inferior or superior judicatories, are absolutely void when rendered without citations and without trial, and without the opportunity of a hearing.

"But admitting this to be in the nature of a legislative proceeding, still it is void; for I deny the right of any legislature to deprive an elector of his right to vote, either with or without trial.

"This is a power which can only be exercised by a judicial tribunal who act under the sanction of an oath, who examine witnesses on oath, and who conform to all the rules of evidence established by the sages of the law.

"If the legislature of Pennsylvania should dare, by resolution or otherwise, to deprive one of you, gentlemen, of your rights as an elector, it would be the duty of the court to declare such an act null and void. I am unable to distinguish the difference between the two cases.

"Whether the General Assembly is the proper tribunal, in the first instance, for the trial of offence, or whether the Presbyteries are amenable to their judicatories in this or any other mode, it is unnecessary to decide, as the court are clearly of the opinion, that if they have the right, it must be exercised with the same rules and regulations which are applicable to the inferior judicatories.

"Personal process in such case may be tedious, agitating, and troublesome in the highest degree, but it is obviously not impossible. Nor does it strike me as impossible to devise a plan under the Constitution to correct heresy and schism without resort to personal process in such case. But if it were so, this is an excuse, but it is no justification of the exscinding resolutions.

"Offenders, according to the rules of the Church, may be brought before a judicatory by common fame. But I perceive no power given to convict on common fame.

"You will remark, gentlemen, that the Presbyteries, by the Constitution of the Church, are the electors of the General Assembly. Their right of representation has been taken away without trial, without the examination (as far as we know) of a single witness.

"Whether these Presbyteries have Congregational churches in their connection, is not now material. It is possible that, had a trial been had, that point, which is deemed so important, may have been disproved. At any rate, it would seem a singular reason for dissolving a whole Presbytery, that one church was contaminated with false and heretical doctrines, or doctrines not strictly Presbyterian; that a whole Presbytery should be ejected, because a single church was governed without the benefit of ruling elders. It would be a reason, perhaps a good one, for cutting off that church from the Presbyterian connection, but none for casting out the whole Presbytery. And this, gentlemen, would be particularly severe on the members and congregations, when the fact was known, at the time the Presbytery was created, such connection did exist.

"If, however, after having condemned this (as it is called) unnatural connection, the Presbyteries should obstinately continue to adhere to it, then they would justly expose themselves to the severest censures of the Church. But whether there is any mode known to the Constitution by which a Presbytery can be deprived of the right of representation on the floor of the General Assembly, is a point which is not necessary to the case, and which I shall not undertake to decide.

"I have been requested by the respondents' counsel to instruct you that the introduction of lay delegates from Congregational establishments into the judicatories of the Presbyterian Church was a violation of the fundamental principle of Presbyterianism, and a contradiction of the act of the Legislature of Pennsylvania, incorporating the trustees of the Church. But any act permitting such introduction would therefore have been void, although submitted to the Presbyteries. As an abstract question on this point, I give an affirmative answer, although, gentlemen, I am unable to see the bearing it has on the matter at issue in this case.

"You have already seen that the court is of the opinion, that the exscinding resolutions are unconstitutional, null, and void; yet this did not of itself dissolve the General Assembly. The Assembly was dissolved at the termination of its session. You will perceive in the course of the remarks which I shall have to make to you, that the acts of this Assembly will have an important influence on the proceedings of the Assembly of 1838.

"The General Assembly of the Presbyterian Church is entitled to decide upon the right claimed by any one to a seat in that body, but unlike legislative bodies, their decision is the subject of revision. Ecclesiastical judicatories are subject to the control of the law.

"I also instruct you that a *mandamus* would not reach the case, for before the remedy could be applied, the General Assembly would be dissolved, and it would be impossible to foresee whether the next Assembly would persist in their illegal and unconstitutional course of conduct. You will recollect that the commissioners are elected a short time before the meeting of the General Assembly, and that that body, which sits but a few weeks for the transaction of business, is dissolved, and a new General Assembly is called at the termination of the sessions.

"Having thus disposed of the proceedings of the General Assembly of 1837, we will now proceed to the acts of 1838. It will perhaps conduce to a proper understanding of the somewhat extraordinary proceedings which then took place, to advert to the practice of the General Assembly in times of less excitement and interest than existed on that occasion.

"After the business of the Assembly is finished, the General Assembly is dissolved, and another General Assembly is directed to be chosen in the same manner, to meet at a time and place designated by the Assembly.

"The moderator, or, in case of his absence, another member appointed for the purpose, opens the next meeting with a sermon; he is directed to hold the chair till a new moderator be chosen. As this is for the purpose of organization, it is not necessary that he be a member, nor is it necessary that the clerks should be members who are requested to attend for the same purpose.

"By the practice of the Assembly, in pursuance of a regulation for that purpose, the stated and permanent clerks are a standing committee on commissions. To them are submitted the commissions of members; they decide on them in the first place, and if unexceptionable in form or substance, they are enrolled as members of the house; if exceptionable, they report them as such in a separate list. The moderator, after divine service, opens the session with prayer. He takes his seat as moderator, and proceeds to organize the house. The first business in order is the report of the clerks, who are the Committee on Commissions, who make a report, stating on the roll those who are members, and designating, either in the roll or in a separate list, those whose commissions have been examined and found defective, either in form or in substance.

"The next business in order is to appoint a Committee on Elections from the list of members who have been enrolled.

"To that committee are referred the commissions of such persons as may claim seats whose commissions have been examined and rejected.

"It is usual to appoint the Committee on Elections on the morning of the first day of the session, and they, unless in cases of difficulty, report to the house in the afternoon, and the house decides upon the propriety of the report. It would seem also to be the practice, that when a commissioner has omitted to hand in his commission to the clerks before the meeting of the Assembly, he may do so in the Assembly, and the Committee of Commissions may add his name to the roll of members.

"After the house is organized, they proceed to the choice of a moderator and stated and permanent clerks to preside over their deliberations, and to keep their records during their session.

"You will observe that I am speaking of the rules of practice in the sessions of 1837 and 1838.

"As the Church increased in numbers, and, I may add, without giving offence, after the spirit of contention increased also in the same or greater ratio, the simplicity of the ancient practice gradually changed. The changes have been stated with great clearness by one of our venerable fathers, but as we have to do with existing rather than ancient rules, it is not necessary for me to notice them.

"The jury will recollect that the court has decided that the exscinding resolutions of the General Assembly of 1837 were unconstitutional, null, and void.

"It results from this opinion, that the commissioners from the Presbyteries within the bounds of these Synods had the same right to seats in the General Assembly as the members from other Presbyteries within the jurisdiction of the Assembly, liable to be dealt with by them in the same manner as commissioners from other Presbyteries.

"It was under these circumstances they presented themselves with commissions, in proper form, to Mr. Krebs and Dr. McDowell, the clerks of the former Assembly. They not only rejected their commissions, but refused to put their names on the roll at all.

"I shall not now stop to inquire whether these gentlemen were or were not pledged to the course they thought proper to pursue, nor into the question, whether they were the judges of the constitutionality of an act of a former Assembly, as I am clearly of the opinion, and so I instruct you, that they grossly erred in refusing to place their names on the list of rejected applicants. They were the Committee on Commissions to whom such questions are in the first place referred. It was their duty to decide on the propriety of the application, and to refer the decision to the further action of the house, by adding their names to the roll of members whose commissions had been examined and rejected.

"They cannot consider commissions, in other respects regular, as alien and outlawed, merely because they proceeded from Presbyteries that had been unconstitutionally put out of the pale of the Church without citation and without trial.

"It is, therefore, the opinion of the court, that in this there was a palpable violation of the rights of the proscribed commissioners. And this, gentlemen, was the second error committed, and which led to the scene of disorder which ensued, so little creditable to a Christian assembly.

"After the moderator, Dr. Elliott, had taken the chair, Dr. Patton addressed the chair, and stated that he had certain resolutions to offer. The moderator decided that he was out of order; that the first business was the report of the clerks, who, you will recollect, were the Committee on Commissions.

"Dr. Patton stated that his motion or resolution had reference to the formation of the roll; that it was his intention to make his motion, and have the question taken without debate. The moderator said the clerks were proceeding with their report. Dr. Patton reminded the moderator that he had the floor before the clerks. The moderator still decided that he was out of order; whereupon Dr. Patton respectfully appealed from the decision of the chair. The moderator decided that the appeal was out of order, and stated as a reason for the decision, that there was no house to which the appeal could be taken.

"The Court is of the opinion that the decision of the moderator was correct, for the reason given by him. It is a rule of the Assembly, that no persons shall be permitted to vote, unless they are enrolled, and until the report of the Committee on Commissions, it cannot be judicially known who are members of the house, and as such, privileged to take part in the organization. If, however, there was a majority for it, arising from the absence of the moderator, or the refusal of the clerks to report the roll, there would be no difficulty in organizing the Assembly. The decision of the moderator was correct, if the reason assigned was the true reason.

"After this disposition of Dr. Patton's motion, the clerks made a report, omitting, improperly, as has been before stated, the names of the commissioners from the exscinded Presbyteries; and the moderator announced to those who had not presented their commissions, that now was the time to present them, and have themselves enrolled. Some of the witnesses say that the moderator announced that, if there were any names *omitted*, this was the time to present their commissions. The one side say that this was a distinct intimation from the moderator himself, that now was the time to present the commissions of the commissioners from the exscinded Presbyteries. The other say it included those only who had *not* presented their commissions to the clerks; that the only course to be pursued, as to those who had presented their commissions, and had their claim to be enrolled refused, was to have their case referred to the Committee on Elections, on whose report only would it come properly before the Assembly.

"However the fact may be,—and this of course you will decide,—at this time Dr. Mason, a member whose seat was uncontested, and who had been reported by the clerks to the house as a member, moved that the names of the commissioners from the exscinded Synods should be added to the roll. He had the commissions in his hand, and at the time of the motion, stated that they were the commissions of commissioners, which had been rejected by the clerks. The moderator inquired from what Presbyteries those commissioners came. Dr. Mason replied, they came from the Synods of Utica, Geneva, Genesee, and the Western Reserve. The moderator declared Dr. Mason *out of order*, or said that he was out of order at that time. The witnesses differ as to the precise expression; but, whatever may have been the reason assigned, they all concur that the moderator declared Dr. Mason out of order. Dr. Mason said that, with great respect to the chair, he must appeal from the decision. The appeal was seconded. The moderator refused to put the appeal, declaring the *appeal* to be out of order.

"In this stage of the cause, it is unnecessary to decide whether the original motion was or was not out of order. I shall put this part of the case on the refusal of the moderator to put the question on the appeal. The question is not, whether an appeal may not be out of order, but it is, whether this appeal was out of order. If the moderator had put the question on the appeal, it is possible that the house would have decided that the original motion was out of order. They might have thought that the matter was properly referable to the Committee of Elections—that it was a privileged question; or the Assembly might by possibility have taken a different view of the question. And whatever they might have thought and decided would have been conclusive.

"But, by refusing to put the question, the moderator took all power to himself over this question. No reason was given by the moderator. It rested simply upon *his will*. In the opinion of the court, it was a dereliction of duty, a usurpation of authority, which called for the censure of the house. He could not then allege, as he had done on a former occasion, that there was no house to which the appeal could be taken. At that time, you will recollect, that the clerks had made their report, and it was then ascertained what members had a right to vote.

"Had the question on the appeal been allowed, it could then have been ascertained whether a motion had been made for the appointment of the Committee on Elections. As it is, it is doubtful whether the motion was made before or after the motion made by Dr. Mason.

"And here let me remark, that I look upon the refusal of the clerks to put the names of the commissioners on the roll, and this refusal of the moderator to put the question on the appeal to the house, as most unfortunate.

"If the excitement did not *then* commence, yet it, with the uproar and confusion which ensued, from this time greatly increased. After the refusal of the moderator to allow an appeal, the Rev. Miles Squier arose and said, that *he* had presented his commission to the clerks, which they had refused to receive. The moderator asked from what Presbytery *he* came. He said from the Presbytery of Geneva. The moderator asked if it was within the bounds of the Synod of Geneva. He said it was. The moderator then replied, *We do not know you*. The precise meaning and import of these words has been the subject of comment. It will be for you to give them such weight as you think them entitled to, in another part of this cause.

"And here, let me remark, that the witness had not a right, whatever injustice he may have suffered, either to speak or vote on any question before the house. He had not been reported as a member by the clerks; and the rules of the General Assembly required, that before a member speak or vote he must be enrolled.

"To this time the witnesses substantially agree in their statement. There was but little noise, and but little confusion. Every person saw, and every person heard, all the transactions in the Assembly.

"And here, gentlemen, it will be your solemn duty respectfully, but firmly, to decide upon the conduct of the moderator.

"Was he performing his duty, as the presiding officer of the house, in its organization? or was he carrying out the unconstitutional and void proceeding of the General Assembly of 1837, which cut off from the body of the Presbyterian Church four Synods, twenty-eight Presbyteries, five hundred and nine ministers, and near sixty thousand communicants, without citation, and without trial?

"I put the question to you, because it is the opinion of the court that the General Assembly has a right to depose its moderator, upon sufficient cause.

"This power is necessary for the protection of the house, otherwise the moderator, instead of being the *servant* would be the *master* of the house. There is nothing in the Constitution of the Church that restricts or impairs the right.

"It applies to all moderators, whether moderators for the session, or moderators for organization. The right is, perhaps, less questionable in the latter than in the former case. He is a ministerial as well as a judicial officer.

"Nor do I think that they are restrained in their choice to a moderator of a former year, who may be present. That rule applies only to ordinary cases, when the moderator of the last year is not in attendance, or is unable, from some physical reason, to discharge the duties of the office. It does not apply to the peculiar and extraordinary circumstances of this case.

"The deposition of a moderator, and the election of another in his place, it appears, is not without precedent in the history of the Church.

"There is one thing certain, that the deposition of a moderator, and the election of another, if in other respects regular, will not of itself vitiate the organization.

"After Mr. Squier had taken his seat, upon the emphatic declaration of the moderator, *we do not know you*, Mr. Cleveland arose.

"Mr. Cleveland held in his hand a paper, from which he read, at the same time accompanying it with remarks not on the paper. It is not distinctly in evidence what he did say, but in substance it was perhaps this:

"That as the commissioners to the General Assembly of 1838, from a large number of Presbyteries, had been refused their seats, and as we have been advised by counsel, learned in the law, that a constitutional organization of the Assembly must be secured at this time and in this place, he trusted it would not be considered as an act of discourtesy, but merely a matter of necessity, if we now proceed to organize the General Assembly of 1838, in the fewest words, the shortest time, and with the least interruption practicable.

"Mr. Cleveland then moved that Dr. Beman, of the Presbytery of Troy, be moderator, or, as some of the witnesses say, that he take the chair. The motion being seconded, the question was put by Mr. Cleveland, and was carried, as the witnesses for the relators say, by a large majority, and by this they mean that a large majority of voices voted in the affirmative. The question was reversed, and, as the same witnesses say, there were some voices coming from the southwest corner of the church, who voted in the negative. This is denied by the respondents.

"Dr. Beman, who was sitting in a pew, the locality of which has been described to you, stepped into the aisle and called the house to order. A motion was then made that Dr. Mason and Mr. Gilbert be appointed clerks. There being no others put in nomination, the question was put by the moderator, Dr. Beman, in the affirmative and negative, and there was a majority of voices in their favor.

"Dr. Beman then stated that the next business in order was the election of a moderator. A member nominated Dr. Fisher, and no other person being in nomination, the question was put affirmatively and negatively, and Dr. Fisher was elected by a large majority of voices. There were no negative votes on this nomination; several of the witnesses say he was unanimously elected.

"Dr. Beman then announced the election of Dr. Fisher as moderator, and said he should govern himself by the rules which might be hereafter adopted.

"Dr. Fisher stepped into the aisle, moved towards the north end of the church, and called for business; and Dr. Mason and Mr. Gilbert were chosen clerks, no others being put in nomination.

"Dr. Beman stated that some difficulties had been made by the trustees about the occupation of the church in which they were then sitting. To avoid difficulty, a motion was made to adjourn to meet forthwith at the lecture-room of the First Presbyterian Church. The question was taken on the motion, and was decided in the affirmative, there being no votes in the negative. The result of the vote was announced by Dr. Fisher, who then stated if there were any commissioners who had not presented their commissions, they might then and there attend for that purpose. The members of the house then repaired to the lecture-room of the First Presbyterian Church, proceeded with their business, and on the 24th of May, 1838, elected the relators trustees, in the place and stead of the respondents.

"This is the relators' case, and here I will direct your attention to some of the points which have been raised by the respondents' counsel.

"The respondents contend that Mr. Cleveland had no right to put the question. They object, also, to the time and manner of putting the question. Under one or other of these points I will endeavor to include the question which has been raised, and which has been argued with such force and with such a variety of illustrations.

"Had Mr. Cleveland a right to put this question? It must be conceded, that unless he was authorized to take the sense of the house, the members were not bound to vote against it. In ordinary cases, it is usual for a member who moves a question, to put it in writing, and deliver it to the speaker, who, when it has been seconded, proposes it to the house, and the house are then said to be in possession of the question. But this, the relators say, is not an *ordinary* question, but one of a peculiar nature. They allege, that the moderator had shown gross partiality and injustice in the chair; that he was engaged in a plan or scheme to carry out the unconstitutional and void Act of 1837, which deprived certain commissioners of their seats; that this authorized the house to displace him, and to elect another to discharge the duties which he failed or was unwilling to perform. If this were so, of which you are the judges, Mr. Cleveland had a right to take the sense of the house on the propriety of the moderator's conduct. It would be worse than useless to require him to put the question on his own deposition, for this the house were authorized to believe he would refuse to perform, as he had failed in the performance of his duty before. The law compels no person to do a vain or nugatory thing. The law maxim is, '*Lex neminem cogit ad vana, seu impossibile.*' Nor, gentlemen, was it necessary that it should be taken by clerks, if they, as well as the moderator, were engaged in the same plan, to deprive members of their seats, to which they were justly and constitutionally entitled. It is the opinion of the court, that a member, although not an officer, is entitled to put a question to the house in such circumstances.

"The motion which Mr. Cleveland made, after explaining his object, was either that Dr. Beman be moderator, or that Dr. Beman be called to the chair. It is of no consequence in which form the motion was made. They are substantially the same. The motion amounted to this: that Dr. Elliott, who occupied the chair, should be deposed, and that Dr. Beman should be elected chairman and moderator in his stead. It was a pertinent question, easily understood, and not calculated to mislead the dullest member of the Assembly. It was in proper form, and in proper time; for, gentlemen, it was not necessary to precede it by a motion that the house should now proceed to the choice of a moderator. All these requisites are substantially comprised in the motion which was made. There was nothing in the question, or in the manner of putting, which was disorderly, or which might have led to disorder. Mr. Cleveland put the question to the house, which, under certain circumstances, of which I have already said you are the judges, he had a right to do. In the course of his remarks, he turned himself partly round from the moderator; but this, so far as any point of law is involved, is of no sort of consequence. It is also contended by the respondents, that the claim of members to seats, according to the standing order of the house, was referable to the Committee on Elections, and further that the house cannot enter into business until the organization is complete. The latter point the court answers in the negative. There is no doubt the house may elect a moderator, although the seats of some of the members are contested. In general, they would prefer to await the report of the Committee on Elections; but this would be a matter of discretion. The right to seats would be as well, if not better decided, after the house was organized by the election of a moderator, as when it was in its inchoate or incipient state. Such an objection would not vitiate the organization, whatever cause there might be on the part of those who had been deprived of seats, to complain of the precipitation of the Assembly in proceeding to business, particularly if done with a view of preventing them from partaking in the business.

"In deciding on the first point, and others which have been raised by the respondents, it is necessary to advert to the nature of the questions themselves.

"Dr. Mason moved that the names of certain members who had been unconstitutionally and unjustly deprived of seats in the Assembly, should be added to the roll. The motion of Mr. Cleveland, and the subsequent resolutions or motions, were the consequences of the decision of the moderator, that Dr. Mason's motion was out of order, and the refusal of the moderator to allow an appeal to the house. The right of members was unjustly invaded, and from this moment it became a question of privilege, which overrides all other questions whatever. A question of privilege is always in order, to which privileged questions, such as the appointment of a committee of elections, must give way. The cry, therefore, of 'order' from the moderator, or from any member whatever, under such circumstances, would be disorderly. Two inconsistent rights cannot exist at the same time, and it is obvious that if a member, or the moderator, may put a stop to a proceeding which involves in it the conduct of the moderator himself in the discharge of his high functions, and a question of privilege, by the cry of order, it would be an easy and effectual mode of destroying the rights of members in any deliberative assembly. It is usual, when it is intended to prevent a member from proceeding with a motion, to rise to order, and a requisition is then made by the moderator that the member take his seat. It is the opinion of the court that Dr. Mason had the right to make his motion before the appointment of the committee on elections. Indeed, I know of no other mode of getting this question before the committee on elections, except by bringing it before the house, who might either decide it for themselves, or, if they thought proper, refer it to that committee, in whose report it would again come before the house. In this point, I wish you distinctly to understand, that it is the opinion of the court, and that I so instruct you, that if you believe that the conduct of the moderator and clerks was the result of a preconcerted plan with a portion of the members, to carry out the unconstitutional and void Act of 1837, which deprived the members from certain Presbyteries of seats in the Assembly, then, in this particular, the requisitions of the law have been substantially complied with.

"The fact that Mr. Cleveland put the question instead of the moderator, the cries of order when this was in progress, the omission of some of the formulæ usually observed when there is no contest and no excitement, such as standing in the aisle, instead of taking the chair occupied by the moderator, not using the usual insignia of office, putting the question in an unusual place, and the short time consumed in the organization of the house, and three or more members standing at the same time, will not vitiate the organization, if you should be of the opinion that this became necessary from the illegal and improper conduct of the adverse party.

"It is a singular point, gentlemen, that this part of the respondents' case rests upon standing rules which were not then in existence. You will recollect, that each Assembly adopted its own rules; indeed, both the relators and respondents have appealed to these rules. I will remark, that the roll of members reported by Mr. Krebs and Dr. McDowell, was the roll of the house. As such, it was virtually in the possession of the clerks afterwards chosen, provided they were regularly and duly elected. It is the opinion of the court, that the existence of a house competent to perform all the functions of a General Assembly, does not depend on the observance or non-observance of the standing order of the house. You, however, must take this opinion with the qualification that you believe that the house had been substantially organized for the transaction of business; that you should believe that the deviation from the accustomed course was the necessary result of a preconcerted plan unconstitutionally to exclude the members from the exscinded Presbyteries from their seats in the Assembly. And here, gentlemen, let me request your particular attention to the point in issue. The relators say that they are trustees regularly appointed by the General Assembly of the Presbyterian Church. In other words, they affirm that the house which assembled in the lecture-room of the First Presbyterian Church was the General Assembly of the Presbyterian Church. This is an affirmative proposition, which the relators are bound to support.

"The question is not which is the General Assembly, but whether they are the General Assembly, and as such had a right to elect the relators trustees. This allegation the relators must sustain to your satisfaction, otherwise your verdict must be in favor of the respondents.

"The respondents strenuously deny that the portion of brethren who assembled in the First Presbyterian Church, are the General Assembly. On this point, both parties, the relators and respondents, have put themselves upon the country, and you, gentlemen, are that country.

"Let me now briefly call your attention to the relators' case. The moderator, Dr. Elliott, proceeded to organize the house. The clerks, Mr. Krebs and Dr. McDowell, reported to the house the roll of members, omitting those who were not entitled to seats. Dr. Patton offered a resolution on the formation of the roll. This motion was declared by the moderator to be out of order. Dr. Mason then moved that the names of the members from the Presbyteries within the exscinded Synods should be added to the roll. This motion was declared by the moderator to be out of order. An appeal from the decision was demanded, which was also declared to be out of order. On motion of Mr. Cleveland, the former moderator was deposed for sufficient cause, and Dr. Beman was elected moderator, and Mr. Gilbert and Dr. Mason were elected clerks. After organization, Dr. Fisher was elected moderator, and Mr. Gilbert and Dr. Mason elected clerks for the Assembly. The Assembly being thus organized by the appointment of officers, adjourned to meet forthwith at the lecture-room of the First Presbyterian Church, and accordingly met in pursuance of the adjournment, and on the 24th of May, 1838, in due form, elected the relators trustees. This, gentlemen, is a summary of the plaintiffs' case; and if the facts are as stated, your verdict should be rendered in favor of the relators.

"The respondents deny that the portion of brethren who assembled in the First Presbyterian Church are the General Assembly.

"Their objection, in addition to the points which have been already stated, is that there was not a full and free expression of the opinion of the house.

"They allege that the various motions for the appointment of moderator and clerks, and for the adjournment, were not carried by a majority of the house.

"It is hardly necessary to observe that spectators had no right to vote, nor had members not enrolled by the clerks, although entitled to seats, a right to vote. But notwithstanding this, it is the opinion of the court, that if after deducting those who voted and were not entitled to vote, there was a clear majority in favor of several motions, irregularity, or, if you please, something worse, would not vitiate the organization. The presumption is, that none but qualified persons voted; but there is a proof that some voted who were not enrolled, yet this itself will not destroy the relators' right of action. You, gentlemen, will, in the first place, inquire whether there was a majority of affirmative voices of members entitled to vote.

"If there was not, there is an end of the question, and your verdict must be in favor of the respondents.

"But if there was a majority, you will further inquire whether the questions on the several motions were reversed.

"If they were not reversed, your verdict must be in favor of the respondents, for in that case it is very clear the members had no opportunity of showing their dissent to several motions or propositions which were submitted to them.

"These, gentlemen, are questions of fact for your decision. I will content myself with referring to the evidence and arguments of the counsel, and at the same time observing to you that it is your duty to reconcile the testimony of the case, and with one other observation, that affirmative testimony is more to be relied on than negative testimony.

"And here, gentlemen, I wish you distinctly to understand that it is the majority of those who were entitled to vote, and who actually voted, that is to be counted on the various questions which were submitted to the house. I wish you also to understand that it is the majority of members that had been enrolled that must determine this question. When there is a quorum of members present, the moderator can only notice those who actually vote, and not those who do not choose to exercise their privilege of voting. 'Whenever,' says Lord Mansfield, 'electors are present and don't vote at all, they virtually acquiesce in the decision of those that do.'

"And with this principle agrees one of the rules of the General Assembly itself, which must be familiar to every member.

"Members (30th rule) ought not, without weighty reasons, to decline voting, as this practice might leave the decision of very interesting questions to a small portion of the judicatory. Silent members, unless excused from voting, must be considered as acquiescing with the majority.

"This is not only the doctrine of the common law, of the written law as you have seen, but it is the doctrine of common sense, for without the benefit of this rule, it would be almost impossible, certainly very inconvenient, to transact business in a large deliberative assembly.

"Of this rule, gentlemen, we have had very lately a most memorable instance. The fundamental principles of your government have been altered; a new Constitution has been established by a plurality of votes; forty thousand electors, who deposited their votes for one, or other, of the candidates for governor, did not cast them at all on that most interesting and important of all questions. But notwithstanding this the amended Constitution has been proclaimed by your executive, and recognized by your legislature, and by the people, as the supreme law of the land. This, gentlemen, has been stigmatized as a technical rule of law, a fiction and intendment in law. It is sufficient for us, gentlemen, that it is a rule of law. We must not be wiser than the law; for if we attempt this, we endanger everything we hold dear,—our life, our liberty, our property.

"Nor, gentlemen, can we know anything of any fancied equity as contradistinguished from the law. The law is the equity of the case, and it must be so considered under the most awful responsibility, by this court, and this jury. In my opinion, a court and jury can never be better employed than when they are vindicating the safe and salutary principles of common law.

"But the respondents further object that the design of the New School brethren was not to organize a General Assembly according to the forms prescribed by the Constitution, but that they intended, and it was so understood by them, to effect an *ex parte* organization, with a view to a peaceable separation of the Church. If this was the intention, and was so understood at the time, the house which assembled in the First Presbyterian Church, cannot be recognized as the General Assembly, competent to appoint trustees under the charter. Having chosen voluntarily to leave the Church, they can no longer be permitted to participate in its advantages and privileges. If a member, or a number of individuals choose to abandon their Church, they must at the same time be content to relinquish all its benefits.

"But this is a question of fact, which you must decide. In this part of the case, the burden of proof is thrown upon the respondents. They must satisfy you that such was the intention of the New School party in organizing the house and adjourning to the First Presbyterian Church. But, granting that the motion of Mr. Cleveland was in order; that Drs. Beman and Fisher, and the clerks, had a majority of votes; that the intention was to organize the General Assembly, and that they did not intend an ex parte organization; the respondents say that such was the precipitation and haste of these proceedings, their extraordinary and novel character, the noise, tumult, and confusion, that they and the other members of the house had no opportunity of hearing and voting, if they had wished to do so, and that therefore this is an attempt at organization, which is null and void.

"It is very certain, that if individual members of a deliberative assembly, by trick or artifice, by surprise, noise, tumult, or confusion, carry such a question as this, it ought not, it cannot be regarded. The members must have an opportunity to debate, to vote, if they desire it; and for this reason it is, the negative question must be put, and that the several questions must be reversed.

"It will be for you to say whether the members had this opportunity. To this part of the case I request your particular attention.

"If you believe that the several motions were made and reversed, that they were carried by a majority of affirmative voices, whatever may be your opinion of the relative strength of two parties in the Assembly, your verdict must be for the relators. I hold it to be a most clear proposition, that silent members acquiesce in the decision of the majority. It is of no sort of consequence for what reason they were silent; whether from a previous determination or otherwise. The effect is the same, provided they had an opportunity of hearing and voting on the question. It is not necessary that all should hear or vote.

"If persons who are members of an assembly, by surprise, by noise, or violence, carry such a question, such a vote cannot be considered as the deliberate sense of the Assembly; but when the members are aware of the nature of the proceedings, and choose to treat them with contempt, or to interrupt the business themselves by stamping, noise, talking, cries of order, shame! shame! or requesting silence with a view to interruption, or attending to other business when they ought to be attending to this, they cannot be permitted afterwards to allege that they had no opportunity to vote. They cannot take advantage of their own wrong, or their own folly. In such a case, their silence, or, if you choose, noise, shall be viewed as an acquiescence in the vote of the majority. But when members are prevented from hearing and understanding the question by the noise and confusion, or by the indecent haste with which the business is conducted, the organization is not such as can give it any legal validity. It is of no consequence whether the members are prevented from voting understandingly on the question by the persons engaged in conducting the business, or by the spectators. But when it comes from the members of the other party, they shall not be permitted to object, when they themselves are the causes of the difficulty.

"If the facts be so, they (the members of the Old School) did not hear, because they would not hear. They caused the disorder, and let them reap the bitter fruits of their injustice. The court and you, gentlemen of the jury, have nothing to do with consequences, with fancied majorities and minorities, but with majorities legally ascertained. We are placed at this bar under an awful responsibility to do justice, without regard to the numerical strength of the contending parties.

"If you, gentlemen, believe that the questions were not reversed, that they were not carried, that the members of the Assembly had not an opportunity of hearing and voting upon them, your verdict should be in favor of the respondents. But if, on the other hand, you believe they intended to organize the Assembly; that the questions were severally put; that the noise, tumult, and confusion which prevailed in the Assembly were the result of a preconcerted plan or combination, or conspiracy between the clerks, the moderator, and the members of the Old School party, to sustain the unconstitutional and void resolutions of 1837, which deprived members of seats to which they were justly entitled, your verdict should be in favor of the relators.

"And here I do not wish to be understood as having expressed, or even intimated, an opinion as to the facts of the case. The facts are for you, the law is for the court.

"And now, gentlemen, I intreat you, *as you shall answer to God at the great day*, that you discard from your minds all partiality, if any you have, fear, favor, and affection; that you decide this interesting cause according to the evidence; and that you remember that the law is part of your evidence.

"[After the delivery of the charge, the jury retired, and in about an hour returned a verdict for the plaintiffs.]"—*Minutes*, 1839, pp. 40–56.

[The decision of the *court in banc* granting a new trial, with other decisions needful to an understanding of the legal *status* of the Assembly, not printed in the Minutes, will be found in the Appendix at the close of the Digest.]

10. "*A Declaration of the General Assembly, setting forth the Present Position of our beloved Zion, and the Causes which have brought us into our Peculiar Condition.* 1839.

"It is manifest to the Christian world, that a great and grievous schism has taken place in the Presbyterian Church in the United States of America, insomuch that brethren who used to walk together in the fellowship of the Gospel, now meet in separate ecclesiastical bodies, and have no organic relation to each other.

"We, therefore, the commissioners of that portion of our once united Church, which was separated from their brethren by the acts of the Assembly of 1837, wishing to free ourselves and our churches from the imputation of the sin of causing division and offences in the Church of the living God, do hereby set forth and declare to our brethren throughout the Christian world, the present attitude of that portion of the Church which we represent, and the causes which have produced the existing difficulties.

"Rightly to understand the present posture of our affairs, and properly to appreciate the causes which have resulted in the rending of the American Presbyterian Church, it will be necessary to take a retrospective view of the introduction of Presbyterianism in our land, and of its history from the period of its introduction to the present time.

"It will be found, upon a reference to the history of bygone days, that on the 6th day of April, 1691, the Presbyterian and Congregational denominations of Christians in Great Britain met at Stepney, and there, by the blessing of Almighty God, after talking over their differences and their agreements, consummated a union of the two denominations, by adopting what was then called the 'Heads of Agreement,' embracing a few cardinal principles which were to govern them in their fraternal intercourse.

"This Presbyterian and Congregational Union sent over one of their number, by the name of McKemie, as a missionary to the new settlements in America, who, in connection with Messrs. McNish, Andrews, Hampton, Taylor, Wilson, and Davis, in 1704, formed the first Presbytery which ever existed in America, by the name of the Presbytery of Philadelphia. This mother Presbytery was formed upon the liberal Christian principles which governed the London Association, by which Mr. McKemie was sent to this country, and was composed partly of Presbyterian and partly of Congregational ministers and churches. Mr. Andrews, the first pastor of the Metropolitan or First Church in Philadelphia, was a decided Congregational Presbyterian; and the church over which he was placed was under the care of the Presbytery *sixty-four* years, before they elected any ruling elders. This state of things continued until 1716, when the Synod of Philadelphia was formed out of the Presbyteries of Philadelphia, New Castle, Snow Hill, and Long Island, the last three having grown up after the formation of the first, in 1704.

"In 1730, fourteen years after the formation of the Synod of Philadelphia, the Rev. Mr. Andrews, in a letter to Mr. Prince, says that, in the then existing state of things, 'We all call ourselves Presbyterians, none pretending to be called Congregationalists, and our ministers are all Presbyterians, though most of them are from New England.'

"During all this period, the Church of Scotland, instead of imbibing the liberal principles of the age, which had resulted in the fraternal union of 1691, in London, and in the establishing of a modified Presbyterianism in America, still adhered to her arbitrary principles, as will appear from the fact that during the reign of Queen Anne, in 1712, only four years before the formation of the Synod of Philadelphia, they solemnly bore their testimony against religious toleration.

"In 1724, those ministers from Scotland who came over to this country, and who, in the language of the Rev. Dr. Miller, 'were desirous to carry into effect the system to which they had been accustomed in all its extent and strictness,' began to insist that the entire system of the Scottish Church be received in this country. This demand led to the Adopting Act of 1729, which was a return to the liberal principles of 1691, upon which the Presbyterian Church in America was based, and is as follows: 'Although the Synod do not claim or pretend to any authority of imposing our faith on other men's consciences, but do profess our just dissatisfaction with, and abhorrence of, such impositions, and do not only disclaim all legislative power and authority in the Church, being willing to receive one another as Christ has received us to the glory of God, and admit to fellowship in Church ordinances all such as we have grounds to believe that Christ will at last admit to the kingdom of heaven, yet we are undoubtedly obliged to take care that the faith once delivered to the saints be kept pure and uncorrupt among us, and so handed down to our posterity; and do therefore agree, that all the ministers of this Synod, or that shall hereafter be admitted to this Synod, shall declare their agreement in, and approbation of the Confession of Faith, with the Larger and Shorter Catechisms of the Assembly of Divines at Westminster, as being in all essential and necessary articles, good forms and sound words and systems of Christian doctrine; and do also adopt the said Confession of Faith and Catechisms as the confession of our faith. And we do also agree that the Presbyteries within our bounds shall always take care not to admit any candidate for the ministry into the exercise of the sacred functions, but what declares his agreement in opinion with all the essential and necessary articles of said Confession, either by subscribing the said Confession of Faith and Catechisms, or by a verbal declaration of his assent thereto, as such minister or candidate shall think best. And in case any minister of this Synod, or any candidate for the ministry, shall have any scruples with regard to any article or articles of said Confession of Faith or Catechisms, he shall, at the time of his making such declaration, declare his sentiments to the Presbytery or Synod, who shall, notwithstanding, admit him to the exercise of the ministry within our bounds, and to ministerial communion, if either the Presbytery or Synod shall judge his scruples or mistakes to be only about articles not essential and necessary in doctrine, worship, or government. But if the Synod or Presbytery shall judge such minister or candidate erroneous in essential and necessary articles of faith, the Synod or Presbytery shall declare him incapable of communion with them. And the Synod do solemnly agree, that none of us will traduce or use any opprobrious terms towards those who differ from us in those extra essential and not necessary points of doctrine, but treat them with the same friendship, kindness, and brotherly love as if nothing had happened.'

"In 1730, we find the Presbytery of New Castle, in the face of these conciliatory measures of the Synod, adopting the Confession of Faith and Catechisms, as being in all things agreeable to the word of God;

and, in 1732, the new Presbytery of Donegal followed their example, and promised 'forever thereafter to adhere thereto.'

"In 1736, that party who were in favor of the strong measures of the Scottish Church, had gained so much ascendency that they brought a majority of the Synod to follow the example of the two Presbyteries of New Castle and Donegal, and adopt the Confession, Catechisms, and Directory of the Westminster divines, without alteration or exception; thus establishing the power of the civil magistrate to control Synods and persecute the Church.

"This rash departure from the tolerant and fraternal principles of 1691 in England, and of 1704 and 1729 in America, led to the painful schism of 1741, which resulted in the organization of the Synod of New York in 1745.

"In 1758, the Synods of New York and Philadelphia came together in one body, and took the name of the Synod of New York and Philadelphia; and in the sixth article of their union, they agreed to adopt the Confession of Faith, Catechisms, and Directory as they had been adopted in 1728.

"In 1766, eight years after the union of the Synods under the name of the Synod of New York and Philadelphia, that body proposed an Annual Convention of delegates of the pastors of the Congregational, Consociated, and Presbyterian Churches in North America, which recommendation was complied with, and the convention was held annually for ten years, when it was interrupted by the American Revolution. In 1788, the General Assembly was organized, and, in 1790, the Assembly, to use their own language, 'being peculiarly desirous to renew and strengthen every bond of union between brethren so nearly agreed in doctrine and forms of worship as the Presbyterian and Congregational Churches evidently are, and remembering with much satisfaction the mutual pleasure and advantage produced and received by their former intercourse, do resolve that the Congregational Churches in New England be invited to renew their annual convention with the clergy of the Presbyterian Church.' This resolution resulted in the plan of correspondence with the Congregational bodies of New England, which exists to this day. This plan provides that 'every preacher travelling from one body to the other, and properly recommended, shall be received as an authorized preacher of the Gospel, and cheerfully taken under the patronage of the Presbytery or Association within whose limits he shall find employment as a preacher.'

"In 1801, the enlightened piety of the two denominations produced another Plan of Union, designed to promote the interests of religion in our new settlements, which strictly enjoined on all their missionaries to endeavor by all proper means to promote mutual forbearance and accommodation between those inhabitants who hold the Presbyterian and those who hold the Congregational form of government, and provided a plan for establishing a uniform system of government among them, when associated in the same church.

"These Plans of Union between the two denominations were a virtual recognition of the benign principles established in 1691, in England, and afterwards adopted in America, and made the basis of Presbyterianism in the original Presbytery and Synod of Philadelphia.

"These fundamental principles continued to be recognized and acted upon by the Assembly of the Presbyterian Church and the subordinate judicatories, with few exceptions, until 1837, when a majority of the commissioners abrogated the Plan of Union of 1801, and cut off from the Presbyterian Church, 4 Synods, 28 Presbyteries, 509 ministers, 599 churches, and 60,000 communicants, more than one-fifth of the whole denomination, alleging that as they were brought into the Church under the Plan of Union of 1801, they necessarily fell with it.

"As an alleged consequence of this act, they next proceeded to expel from the house all the commissioners who were present from the Presbyteries composing the exscinded Synods, and dissolved the Third Presbytery of Philadelphia.

"In 1838, the commissioners from the exscinded Synods came up to the General Assembly, and offered their commissions to the clerks, who refused to receive them or enrol the names of the said commissioners. After the moderator, Rev. David Elliot, D.D., had taken his chair, and the names of the enrolled members had been reported, Rev. Erskine Mason, D.D., one of the enrolled members, presented the commissions of the commissioners from the exscinded Presbyteries, and moved that their names should then be enrolled. The moderator decided that the motion was out of order. Dr. Mason then appealed to the house, and the moderator refused to put the appeal. By this refusal, the rights of Dr. Mason and the rights of the house were invaded, and a question of privilege, which takes the precedence of all other questions, and is always in order, was raised. Hereupon Rev. John P. Cleveland, another enrolled member, moved that Rev. N. S. S. Beman, D.D., should be appointed moderator in the room of Rev. David Elliot, D.D., who had invaded the rights of the Assembly, and put the question to the house, which was carried, as has since been proved in a civil court, by a majority of those who voted from the enrolled members. Rev. E. Mason, D.D., and Rev. E. W. Gilbert were then elected clerks, and Dr. Fisher was chosen moderator; and having been notified that they must leave the place where they were assembled, they forthwith adjourned to the First Presbyterian Church, and invited all the commissioners to meet with them.

"After this organization of what we consider the constitutional Assembly, the commissioners who adhered to the acts of 1837 organized themselves into an Assembly, and have subsequently taken measures to divide the Presbyterian Church, by organizing into separate Synods, Presbyteries, and churches, such minorities in different parts of the country as adhered to them, and when they had the majority, casting out such minorities as adhered to this Assembly.

"After the proceedings of that portion of our brethren who had cast out and cut off the four Synods, and formed themselves into an Assembly, were published and known, the constitutional Assembly did, by its committee, issue a quo warranto out of the Supreme Court of Pennsylvania, to test the legality of the Exscinding Acts of 1837, and of the subsequent proceedings founded upon them, and if possible, to restore the unity of the Church and secure religious liberty. This cause was tried in March last, at Philadelphia, before the Hon. Molton C. Rogers, one of the justices of said Supreme Court, when it was ruled by the said judge, and decided by the verdict of an enlightened jury, that the Plan of Union of 1801, 'was not only a regulation which the General Assembly had power to make, but that it was one which was well calculated to promote the best interests of religion;' and that the acts of the Assembly of 1837, exscinding the four Synods, were 'not only contrary to the eternal principles of justice, the principles of common law, but at variance with the Constitution of the Church;' and that the Assembly, of which we are the successors, was the constitutional Assembly of the Presbyterian Church.

"The counsel for that Assembly, which was formed after the constitutional one which we represent, not satisfied with this decision, moved the court in banc for a new trial, and the said court in banc, the Hon. Molton C. Rogers dissenting, and the Hon. Judge Sergeant being absent, did award a new trial, upon the ground that the Exscinding Acts of 1837 were legislative and not judicial, expressly declaring that if they had been judicial, they 'would have been contrary to the cardinal principles of natural justice, and consequently void.' The court in banc did, moreover, decide and declare that the Assembly of 1837 'did, at first, resolve to proceed judicially, but that the measure was abandoned, probably because it came to be perceived that the Synods had committed no offence.' Now the Supreme Court of Pennsylvania, the very tribunal which granted a new trial, have made a solemn decision, that the Assembly of 1837, determined at all events to get rid of 60,000 of their brethren, 'first resolved to proceed judicially against them, but perceiving that they had committed no offence, changed their purpose, and by a legislative act, cut them off from the Church, disfranchised them of their privileges, and deprived them of their share of the property and funds, which had been contributed in part by themselves.'

"While we would submit to the decision of the court in banc, and recognize it as the law of Pennsylvania, till it shall be reversed, still we may lawfully appeal to the Christian public, as to the morality of those ecclesiastical proceedings of the Assemblies of 1837 and 1838, which are the basis of such opinion.

"What must be thought of Christian ministers and elders, convened as a General Assembly of the Presbyterian Church, who were so intent upon depriving 60,000 of their brethren of their religious privileges and church property, that they did, as the Supreme Court has decided was the case, first resolve to proceed judicially against them, and when they perceived that this would not answer their purpose, because they had been guilty of no offence, resolved to expel them by a legislative act.

"From whence did the Assembly derive this legislative power? By the Adopting Act of 1729, which was made the basis of the union of the Synods of New York and Philadelphia in 1758, all legislative powers are expressly disclaimed, and in book 1, chapter i, section 7, of the Form of Government, as amended and ratified by the Assembly of 1821, we are told that the Assembly 'were unanimously of the opinion, that all church power, whether exercised by the body in general, or in the way of representation by delegated authority, is only ministerial and declarative.' The General Assembly acts by delegated authority, and yet after a unanimous decision in their constitutional Form of Government in 1821, that their power is only ministerial and declarative, in 1837, they, by what the court say can only be sustained as a legislative act, disfranchise 60,000 of the members of the Presbyterian Church. If they had no legislative powers, then, according to the decision of the court in banc, as well as of Judge Rogers at Nisi Prius, the act of excision in 1837 'was contrary to the cardinal principles of natural justice, and consequently void.'

"But if we should, for one moment, grant what the whole Presbyterian Church in 1758 and 1821 especially disclaimed, that the Assembly possessed legislative power, could they either legally or righteously legislate 60,000 of their brethren out of the Church? We ask, in the language of Judge Rogers, what would be thought of a State that should legislate one of its members out of his elective franchise? It is a well-known principle of law, as that learned judge well remarks, that no man can be deprived of his elective franchise by a legislative act, this being a power which can only be exercised by a judicial tribunal.

"But it is said, that as the four Synods came in under the Plan of Union, they must fall with that Plan. If by the Synods coming in under this Plan, we are to understand that they were organized in any different manner from all other Synods, the allegation is not true; and if it be meant that they were formed during its existence, the same is true of every Presbytery and Synod formed since 1801. How, then, would we ask, are the Synods or Presbyteries affected by the Plan of Union? No minister was ever received into any Presbytery according to any provision in that Plan, for it contains no such provision. But it is alleged by the exscinding brethren of 1837, that the Plan of Union of 1801 was unconstitutional and void from the beginning; but this, both Judge Rogers and the court in banc declare to be incorrect, so that we have the anomaly of an ecclesiastical court justifying their acts on the ground that the Union of 1801 was unconstitutional, and a civil court sustaining this same decision, upon the ground that the Union was constitutional.

"But there is another important fact which ought to be noticed, and that is, that in 1821, twenty years after the Plan of Union had been adopted, a new and amended Constitution was framed and solemnly adopted by the Presbyteries which have been exscinded, as well as their brethren of other Presbyteries, and that the whole Church, after living and acting together for sixteen years under this new Constitution, is rent asunder by this act of excision, and 60,000 of its members attempted to be cut off from all participation in the privileges of that Church.

"In view of these facts, we, the General Assembly, convened in the First Presbyterian Church at Philadelphia, on the 16th day of May,

1839, appealing to Almighty God for the purity of our motives and the rectitude of our measures, and professing a deep regret for this grievous breach in the professed body of Christ, and solemnly protesting that the sin of this schism does not lie at our door, throw ourselves upon the candor and wisdom of the Christian world, for the rectitude of our proceedings in the painful circumstances in which we have been placed.

(Signed) "BAXTER DICKINSON, *Moderator.*
"ERSKINE MASON, *Stated Clerk.*"
—*Minutes*, 1839, pp. 56–60.

11. *Withdrawal of the Suit at Law.*

a. "In relation to the case at law of the Commonwealth *v.* Green and others, the committee came deliberately and unanimously to the result, on the 15th of November, 1841, to instruct their counsel to withdraw the suit, and thus 'for the present,' and they hope forever, to end the legal controversy."—*Letter of the Committee ad interim,* 1842, p. 19.

b. "*Resolved,* That this Assembly would commend the zeal and fidelity manifested by the committee *ad interim,* in the novel circumstances in which, by the Providence of God, they have been placed; and their proceedings are hereby approved.

"This Assembly further declares, that the withdrawing the suit against Ashbel Green and others, in the nature of a *quo warranto,* and the ceasing, for the present, of this Assembly to prosecute its claims for property belonging to it, in law and in equity, shall not be considered as any waiving or relinquishment of any of its legal and equitable rights in and to any property which did, now does, or hereafter may, belong to the trustees of the Presbyterian Church in the United States of America."—*Minutes,* 1843, p. 21.

12. *The Roll of the Assembly rectified.*

"The Assembly, on the motion of Dr. Cox, took up the report of the Committee on the Polity of the Church; which, after being amended, was adopted, and is as follows:

"Whereas, it appears, by abundant evidence, to this Assembly, that another body, claiming to be the General Assembly of the Presbyterian Church in the United States of America, at present exists, organized expressly on a 'new basis,' wholly unknown to the Constitution of our

Church, and now holding their sessions in Ranstead Court, in this city; and,

"Whereas, it is also ascertained that a considerable number of the Presbyteries formerly in connection with us have, within the space of two years, withdrawn in fact from us, and are now in connection with the other body, to which we refer above; and,

"Whereas, in times so extraordinary and so distressing to those who love the unity of the Church, and stand alone on the old basis of the Constitution of the same, rejecting every idea of any new basis; the conduct of our withdrawing brethren having made the exigency in which we are under the necessity of acting without a precedent and without a parallel; therefore,

"*Resolved*, 1. That, having waited a sufficient time, sincerely desiring the return of our withdrawing brethren to the old basis, which we have never deserted, it is now the duty of this Assembly to declare their disunion, by their own act, from us; and to rectify the roll of the Presbyteries that are the constituents of this Assembly accordingly.

"2. That the following sixteen Synods be recognized as constitutionally remaining with us on the old and the true basis of the Presbyterian Church, viz.: Albany, Utica, Geneva, Genesee, New York, Newark, Pennsylvania, Western Reserve, Michigan, Ohio, Cincinnati, Indiana, Illinois, Missouri, Virginia, and Tennessee."—*Minutes*, 1840, p. 16.

13. *Proposal to Unite in the Communion.*

a. "Rev. A. W. Campbell moved that the Committee on Devotional Exercises be authorized to confer with a similar committee of the General Assembly, meeting in the Tenth Presbyterian Church of this city, in reference to a united celebration of the Lord's Supper.

"The motion was carried unanimously."—*Minutes*, 1846, p. 11.

The Result.

b. "The Committee on Devotional Exercises presented a report as to the result of a conference with a similar committee of the other Assembly, in reference to a united celebration of the Lord's Supper, which was adopted, and is as follows:

"The Committee on Devotional Exercises, to whom was referred the resolution authorizing them to confer with a similar committee of the Assembly meeting in the Tenth Presbyterian Church, in reference to a united celebration of the Lord's Supper, report:

"That they presented to the committee of the Annual Assembly a certified copy of the resolution passed by this body, accompanied by the following letter, addressed to the chairman of said committee:

"DEAR BROTHER: It devolves upon us, as chairman and secretary of the Committee on Devotional Exercises of the Triennial General Assembly of the Presbyterian Church, convened in the First Presbyterian Church in this city, to present for your consideration the above resolution.

"Should the foregoing proposal meet the approval of yourself and of your Assembly, it would afford us great pleasure, as a committee, to confer with you at such time and place as you may designate.

"Wishing you, and the Assembly with whom you are associated, grace, mercy, and peace from our Lord Jesus Christ, we are yours, affectionately,

"ALFRED E. CAMPBELL, *Chairman*,
"CHARLES H. READ, *Secretary*.

"To our proposal we have received the following answer, through the Rev. Daniel Baker, one of the Committee on Devotional Exercises:

"Extract from the Minutes of the General Assembly, in session at Philadelphia, May 28th, 1846.

"The committee to whom were referred the papers relating to the joint celebration of the Lord's Supper by the two Assembles, with instructions to bring in a minute expressive of the views of the Assembly, presented a report, which was adopted, and is as follows, viz.:

"The Committee on Devotional Exercises, having reported to the General Assembly a communication from a similar committee of the General Assembly in session at the First Presbyterian Church, representing that the said Assembly has authorized its committee to confer with the committee of this Assembly in relation to a joint celebration of the Lord's Supper by the two bodies; it was ordered, that the committee respectfully acknowledge and reciprocate the courtesy of the communication, and say in reply, that, while this Assembly recognize the above-mentioned body as a branch of the Church of our common Lord, and for this reason would, as individuals, under appropriate circumstances, unite with our brethren in the celebration of divine ordinances, yet, as this Assembly has never, in its corporate and official capacity, united with any other ecclesiastical body in celebrating the Lord's Supper, it judges it inexpedient to institute a new usage at this time.

"On motion, the Committee on Devotional Exercises were directed to communicate a copy of the above minute to the committee of the other Assembly.

"Attest, WILLIS LORD,
"*Stated Clerk of the General Assembly.*

"We can only regret that the proposal, made in the most fraternal manner, and passed by a unanimous vote, did not meet with a cordial response in the other Assembly. We have long seen that while the two Assemblies were holding correspondence with many of the same ecclesiastical bodies, and in their respective Synods and Presbyteries maintaining the usual courtesies of correspondence, and freely exchanging pulpits with each other, nothing has been done, in our official capacity, to show the world that we recognized each other as brethren. And as the world had seen the jarring and contention that existed in former years between the two Assemblies, it seemed to be demanded from both to manifest, by some public act, like that of the united celebration of the Lord's Supper, that, though we were separated, we were one in Christ, and would love and treat each other as brethren; and, though we are the injured party, our motives and our ministerial character having been impeached, and some of us belonging to Presbyteries and churches which were exscinded by the acts of 1837, still it was our earnest wish to extend to them the hand of Christian charity—to forgive and forget, as we pray to be forgiven of our God.

"It is, therefore, to us a source of deep regret, that our brethren of the other Assembly did not manifest a disposition to unite with us, and by their influence and example, aid us in doing away the reproach and the odium which have been heaped upon the Presbyterian Church. But though we may not, as an Assembly, under existing circumstances, unite with our brethren of the other Assembly in a joint celebration of the Lord's Supper, still, it is our sincere prayer that we may meet with them in the General Assembly and Church of the First Born in Heaven, and sit down with them at the Marriage Supper of the Lamb."—*Minutes*, 1846, pp. 21, 22.

14. *Committee of Correspondence Appointed.*

a. "The Committee on Bills and Overtures reported an overture in these words:

"*Resolved*, That a proposal be made to the General Assembly of the Presbyterian Church, now holding its sessions in the city of Pittsburg, to institute fraternal correspondence by the interchange of delegates."—*Minutes*, 1849, p. 174.

"The unfinished business of yesterday, viz., the indefinite postponement of the notice to send delegates to the Assembly at Pittsburg, was resumed.

"The motion to postpone was lost.

"The Rev. G. R. H. Shumway then moved to refer the whole subject to a special committee of five, to report to the next General Assembly, which was carried, and Rev. Thomas Brainerd, D.D., Rev. James G. Hamner, D.D., Rev. Henry G. Ludlow, and Messrs. Ambrose White and Frederick A. Raybold were appointed."—*Minutes*, 1849, p. 175.

The Result.

b. "A letter was received from the Rev. Thomas Brainerd, D.D., chairman of the committee appointed by the last Assembly, to correspond with a committee of the other General Assembly of the Presbyterian Church, if such should be appointed, stating that 'as no corresponding committee was appointed by our brethren of the Assembly which met in Pittsburg last year, no opportunity has been had to carry out the fraternal and Christian spirit of our Assembly.

"The committee were thereupon discharged."—*Minutes*, 1850, p. 306.

15. *Detail of our Efforts for a Harmonious Understanding.*

"A communication was received, and read, from the Presbytery of Rochester, in reference to a reunion of the two branches of the Presbyterian Church." [It was referred to a committee (Minutes, 1850, p. 310), who report, viz.:]

"Rev. E. Mason, D.D., from the committee to whom was referred the subject of correspondence with the other General Assembly, made a report, which, after being amended, was unanimously adopted, and is as follows:

"The committee, to whom was referred the subject of the letter from the Presbytery of Rochester, report,

"That this Assembly has always deplored, and continues to deplore, the unhappy division in the Presbyterian Church, as well as the causes which produced it. For this sundering of the body of Christ they do not feel themselves at all responsible, as, in everything they have done, they have stood upon the defensive, to protect their dearest rights, secured to them under the Constitution of the Church.

"They have always, moreover, been ready to meet their brethren in any plan consistent with principle, to heal the breach, and restore the Church to its former integrity; and have even taken the first step towards such a result.

"Feeling that a separation between brethren of a common faith, common sympathies, and a common creed, could not be without sin, they did, immediately after the separation in 1838 (see Minutes, p. 634), publish to the world their willingness to 'agree to any reasonable measures tending to an amicable adjustment of the difficulties existing in the Presbyterian Church.'

"In 1839, to avert all unpleasant controversy, and prevent all unhappy litigation, they proposed a plan of amicable settlement, designed only to secure our constitutional privileges as Presbyterians, while it relinquished to our brethren of the other body all the chartered rights, institutions, and funds of the Presbyterian Church. (See Minutes of 1839, p. 21.)

"The idea of an amicable settlement, and even of reunion, was cherished for some time by this body; and it was not until 1840, three years after the separation, that they relinquished it; and coming reluctantly to the conclusion that union was impracticable, they corrected their roll, and dropped from it the names of these brethren, in deference to their feelings. (See Minutes of 1840, p. 16.)

"Again, in 1846, they expressed the desire for union with their brethren; and, pained by the unseemly exhibition of two such bodies at apparent strife with each other, they proposed to their brethren of the other Assembly, a mutual recognition of each other, by communing together at the Table of our Master.

"These propositions and overtures were all made in good faith, and with an earnest desire and hope that they might be met in the spirit which prompted them.

"The result is a matter of history, and is now before the world. We do not pretend to question the motives of our brethren in rejecting them; we yield to them what we claim for ourselves, honesty of purpose, and sincere convictions of duty. We stated only the facts, and do so, to show that we cannot, as a body, at the present time, take any farther action in this matter.

"While we are constrained to come to this conclusion, we should be untrue to ourselves before God and the world, did we not frankly avow our readiness to meet in a spirit of fraternal kindness and Christian love any overture which may be made to us by the other body."—*Minutes*, 1850, pp. 322, 323.

CHAPTER XIII.

MISCELLANEOUS.

SECTION 1.—SECESSION OF THE SOUTHERN CHURCHES.

1. The protest against the action of the Assembly at Cleveland, and the answer.—2. Withdrawal of the Synods of Missouri, Virginia, Kentucky, Tennessee, West Tennessee, and Mississippi. Claims of the United Synod.—3. Report of the Trustees of the Church Erection Fund on these claims.—4. Adjustment of the roll. The Synods of Mississippi, Kentucky, Tennessee, and West Tennessee stricken from the roll.—5. The Synod of Virginia stricken from the roll, and the bounds of the Synod of Pennsylvania enlarged.

1. *Protest against the Action of the Assembly at Cleveland.*

[In 1857, the General Assembly, in sessions at Cleveland, adopted a paper on slavery (see *ante*, pp. 291–295), to which the following protest was offered, and ordered to be put upon the Minutes, viz. :]

"We, the undersigned Southern ministers and ruling elders, protest against the present decision of the General Assembly.

"We protest, because, while past General Assemblies have asserted that the system of slavery is wrong, they have heretofore affirmed, that the slaveholder was so controlled by State laws, obligations of guardianship and humanity, that he was, as thus situated, without censure or odium as the master. This averment in the testimony of past Assemblies has so far satisfied the South, as to make it unnecessary to do more than protest against the mere anti-slavery part of such testimony.

"We protest then, now, that the present act of the Assembly is such an assertion of the sin of slavery, as degrades the whole Southern

Church,—an assertion without authority from the word of God, or the organic law of the Presbyterian body.

"We protest, that such action is, under present conditions, the virtual exscinding of the South, whatever be the motives of those who vote the deed.

"We protest, that such indirect excision is unrighteous, oppressive, uncalled for,—the exercise of usurped power,—destructive of the unity of our branch of the Church,—hurtful to the North and the South,—and adding to the peril of the union of these United States.

"Fred. A. Ross,	Robt. P. Rhea,
"Jas. G. Hamner,	F. R. Gray,
"Isaac W. K. Handy,	M. S. Shuck,
"Gideon S. White,	W. E. Caldwell,
"George W. Hutchins,	E. A. Carson,
"George Painter,	R. M. Morrison,
"Henry Mathews,	Robert McLain,
"John F. Chester,	A. J. Modie,
"J. V. Barks,	Peachy R. Grattan,
"J. B. Logan,	Thomas H. Cleland,
"C. M. Atkinson,	Archer C. Dickerson."

—*Minutes*, 1857, p. 406.

[To this protest the Assembly record the following answer:]

"In reply to the protest against the action taken by the Assembly on the subject of slavery, the Assembly make the following remarks:

"1. The present action of the Assembly on this subject is in perfect harmony with the testimonies of former Assemblies, and consists chiefly in a reaffirmation of those testimonies. The General Assembly has never 'affirmed that the slaveholder was so controlled by State laws, obligations of guardianship and humanity, that he was, as thus situated, without censure or odium as the master.' It has only conceded, that certain exceptional cases may exist, such as are defined in the resolutions of the Assembly of 1850, and approved by this Assembly.

"2. We see nothing in the present action which is unconstitutional, or which 'degrades,' or even reflects upon, any portion of the Southern Church, which still abides by the old doctrine of the Presbyterian Church in relation to this subject.

"3. With respect to the complaint, 'that such action is, under present conditions, the virtual exscinding of the South,' the Assembly observe, that no such excision is intended, and we cannot perceive that it is in anywise involved even by remote implication. We have simply re-affirmed the established views of the Presbyterian Church on the subject of slavery, and distinctly condemned the new and counter doctrines which have been declared and defended by some within our bounds.

"4. With regard to the allegation, that our action in this case is 'unrighteous, oppressive, uncalled for,' usurpatory, and destructive of great interests, we need only say, that it rests on the groundless assumption, that this action is an 'indirect excision' of the South. If our Southern brethren shall break the unity of the Church, because we stand by our former position, as in duty bound, the responsibility for the consequences will not rest on the Assembly."—*Minutes*, 1857, pp. 408, 409.

2. *Withdrawal of the Synods. Claims of the United Synod.*

[In the Assembly of 1858, the Synods of Missouri, Virginia, Kentucky, Tennessee, West Tennessee, and Mississippi were not represented,—"The United Synod" having been formed in the meantime by portions of each of these Synods; no notice, however, of withdrawal was given by any of the Presbyteries and Synods.]

"Communications were received from the Presbytery of Harmony. They were read and referred to a committee, consisting of Rev. S. H. Gridley, D.D., Hon. Robert Denniston, and Samuel M. Blatchford."—*Minutes*, 1858, p. 575.

"A communication was received, and read, from Rev. A. H. H. Boyd, D.D., in behalf of the 'United Synod of the Presbyterian Church.' It was referred to the special committee already appointed upon the communication from the Presbytery of Harmony, which, by order of the Assembly, was increased by the addition of Rev. George W. Gale, D.D., Rev. Elias J. Richards, Rev. James Eels, and Hon. John Porter."—*Minutes*, 1858, p. 579.

"The Assembly proceeded to the consideration of the report of the special Committee on the Communications of the Presbytery of Harmony, and of the commissioner from the 'United Synod of the Presbyterian Church.'

"The report was adopted, and is as follows:

"The committee to whom were referred the communications from the Presbytery of Harmony, and from the 'United Synod of the Presbyterian Church,' beg leave to recommend the following resolutions as the action of the Assembly in relation to these communications:

"*Resolved*, 1. That this Assembly recognize and reciprocate the friendly greetings and fraternal spirit evinced in these communications, as well as in the Christian bearing and courtesy of the Rev. A. H. H. Boyd, D.D., the accredited representative of the United Synod.

"*Resolved*, 2. That this Assembly regret the unnatural separation which these bodies have felt themselves constrained to create, by the action which they have taken, both because of our family affinities and sympathies, and because it weakens our ability, and diminishes our opportunities, for mutual aid and encouragement, in the great work for which the Church exists. We had hoped that, by perpetuating our relations, by kind interchange of views, and mutual prayers, and by that light which time and patient inquiry secure, we should ultimately be of one mind touching the subject of slavery, as we now are in relation to other moral questions.

"*Resolved*, 3. That the consideration and adjustment of the claims to the funds of the Assembly preferred by the Presbytery of Harmony and the United Synod be postponed to the next General Assembly, for the following reasons: 1. That suitable time may be given for a full examination of questions bearing on the equitable character, and of the legal consequences, of granting the claims preferred. 2. That the Assembly may be able to ascertain what and how many churches under the care of the Presbyteries and Synods which have withdrawn and may withdraw from our connection, may desire to retain their relations to the Assembly, and whose claims to a share in the distribution of the Church Erection Fund will consequently remain undisputed. 3. That the final adjustment of these claims, made as the result of due deliberation, mutual conference of the parties, and prayer to Him who giveth wisdom to his servants, may be satisfactory, if possible, to all concerned.

"*Resolved*, 4. That the whole subject of these claims be referred to the board of trustees of the Church Erection Fund, to consider and report thereon to the next General Assembly."—*Ibid.* pp. 588, 589.

3. *Report of the Trustees.*

"The trustees of the Church Erection Fund have presented two special reports, on subjects referred to them by the last General Assembly, the adoption of both which is recommended by this committee.

"The first of these special reports relates to three papers: one from the Presbytery of Harmony, discussing the action of the General Assembly of 1857, on slavery, and assigning the reasons for the withdrawal of that body from our ecclesiastical connection; a second paper from the same Presbytery, asking for a payment, to it and to the Synod of Kentucky, of what it calls its 'proportional share' of the Church Erection Fund; and a third paper, signed by A. H. H. Boyd, in behalf of a body styled 'The United Synod of the Presbyterian Church,' and represented as consisting of the Synods of Virginia, Tennessee, West Tennessee, and Mississippi, which it is stated have withdrawn from our connection; asking for the payment to that body of the sums allotted to those Synods in the first apportionment of the Church Erection Fund.

"The trustees of the Church Erection Fund justly remark, in their special report, that the first paper calls for no action on our part; and, the charter by which they are incorporated explicitly defines 'feeble congregations in connection with' the 'General Assembly,' as the only bodies to which their grants can be made, and these trustees as the only persons by whom the fund, or any portion of it, can be held."—*Minutes*, 1859, p. 26.

4. *Adjustment of the Roll.*

"On the adjustment of the roll, the committee recommend that the Synod of Mississippi, having notified the Assembly of their withdrawal from our connection, be stricken from the roll.

"The committee further state, that they have information that the Synod of Kentucky has been dissolved; and that the Synods of East and West Tennessee have abjured the jurisdiction of the Assembly, and formally connected themselves with another ecclesiastical body; and we would therefore recommend that these Synods be stricken from the roll.

"The committee further state, that though the Synod of Virginia has formally withdrawn, and the Synod of Missouri assumed an independent position in reference to this Assembly, still there is evidence to believe that there are many brethren, and even Presbyteries, in the bounds of these Synods who sympathize with us. We therefore advise that the names of these Synods be retained until these brethren have determined upon the relation they desire to occupy. Adopted."—*Minutes*, 1859, p. 44.

5. *Synod of Virginia stricken from the Roll. Bounds of the Synod of Pennsylvania enlarged.*

"The Committee on Church Polity beg leave to report on the adjustment of the roll:

"Whereas, the Presbyteries of Winchester, Piedmont, and Hanover, constituent portions of the Synod of Virginia, have followed up their previous vote of withdrawal from the Assembly by a positive connection with another ecclesiastical body; therefore, the committee recommend that the bounds of the Synod of Pennsylvania be so extended as to embrace the State of Maryland and the District of Columbia; that the Presbytery of the District of Columbia be transferred to the said Synod; and that the Synod of Virginia be stricken from the roll. Adopted."—*Minutes,* 1860, p. 240.

SECTION 2.—BIBLE-CLASSES AND SUNDAY-SCHOOLS.

1. The forming of Bible-classes recommended. Plan of instruction not to supersede the Catechism.—2. Sabbath-schools and the instruction of the young. American Sunday-School Union indorsed.—3. Catechetical instruction urged on pastors, parents, and teachers.

1. *The forming of Bible-classes recommended.*

"The committee to which was referred the overture from the Synod of New York and New Jersey, on forming classes of young people, for studying and reciting the Bible, reported; and their report, being read and amended, was adopted, viz.:

"*Resolved,* 1. That it be recommended, and it is hereby recommended earnestly, to the Ministers and Sessions which are in connection with the General Assembly, to pay especial attention to this subject, and provide, without delay, for the stated instruction of the children and youth in the sacred Scriptures within their respective congregations.

"2. That although the particular manner of instruction and recitation in the congregations ought to be left to the discretion of their Ministers and Sessions respectively; yet as some degree of uniformity is desirable in a business of so much magnitude, it is recommended as the most effectual means of promoting the knowledge of the Holy Scriptures, that in all our churches, classes be formed of the youth, to recite the

Scriptures in regular order; that the recitations, if convenient, be as often as once a week, and from two to five chapters appointed for each recitation; that the youth be examined on,

"1. The history of the world, but more especially of the Church of God, and of the heathen nations who were God's agents in accomplishing his purposes towards his Church.

"2. Persons noted for their piety or ungodliness, and the effects of their example in promoting or injuring the best interests of mankind.

"3. Doctrines and precepts, or 'what man is to believe concerning God, and what duty God requires of man.'

"4. Positive ordinances, or the directions which God has given as to the way in which he is to be worshipped acceptably.

"5. The particular features of character of which the Spirit of God has given notice, both in wicked and good persons; in the last particularly regarding those who were types of Christ, and in what the typical resemblance consisted.

"6. The gradual increase from time to time of information concerning the doctrines contained in the Scriptures; noting the admirable adaptation of every new revelation of doctrine to the increased maturity of the Church. The nature of God's law, its immutability as constituting an everlasting rule of right and wrong, the full and perfect illustration of its precepts given by Christ.

"7. The change which God has made from time to time in the positive ordinances, together with the reasons of that change. The difference between the moral law, and those laws which are positive.

"8. The illustrations of the divine perfections in the history, biography, doctrines and precepts, together with the positive ordinances of the Scriptures.

"9. The practical lessons to regulate our conduct in the various relations of life.

"On all these particulars the meaning of the words used in Scripture must be ascertained, that thus we may understand what we read.

"*Resolved*, 3. That the Presbyteries under the care of the Assembly be directed to take order on this subject; and they are hereby informed that this is not to come into the place of learning the Catechism of our Church, but to be added to it as an important branch of religious education."—*Minutes*, 1816, pp. 627, 628.

2. *On Sabbath-Schools and Instruction of the Young.*

a. "In all parts of the Church, Sunday-schools are established, and there is but one sentiment respecting them. The Assembly consider them as among the most useful and blessed institutions of the present day. They have a most extensive reforming influence. They apply a powerful corrective to the most inaccessible portions of the community. They begin moral education at the right time, in the best manner, and under the most promising circumstances. They act indirectly, but most powerfully, upon teachers and parents, and frequently become the means of bringing them to the church, and to the knowledge and love of the truth. Sunday-schools are highly useful *everywhere;* but they are peculiarly adapted to new and destitute regions of the Church. The plan is simple, and easily accomplished. It requires comparatively little knowledge and experience to conduct them with ability. Very much good has been accomplished by the instrumentality of young ladies and gentlemen. The pleasing scene is often witnessed in some of our new settlements, of large meetings of children on the Lord's day, in schoolhouses, or beneath the shade of the original forest. The voice of praise and prayer is heard, and the word of the living God is proclaimed, amid the most beautiful works of his hand."—*Minutes,* 1824, p. 129.

b. "*Resolved,* That the General Assembly do cordially approve of the design and operations of the American Sunday-School Union; and they do earnestly recommend to all ministers and churches under their care to employ their vigorous and continued exertions in the establishment and support of Sabbath-schools."—*Minutes,* 1826, p. 181.

c. "After the recess the Assembly met. The committee to whom was recommitted the report of the committee on the religious education of the rising generation, made the following report, which was adopted, viz.:

"*Resolved,* 1. That the Assembly regard the religious education of youth as a subject of vital importance, identified with the most precious interests and hopes of the Christian Church.

"2. That the present indications of Divine Providence are such as imperiously to demand of the Christian community unusual effort to train up the rising generation in the nurture and admonition of the Lord.

"3. That the Board of Missions be and hereby are instructed to enjoin it on their missionaries sedulously to attend to the religious education of the *young;* and particularly that they use all practicable effort to establish *Sabbath-schools,* and to extend and perpetuate the blessings of Sabbath-school instruction.

"4. That the system of Sabbath-school instruction, now in prevalent and cheering operation, be and hereby is most earnestly recommended to the attention of the pastors and sessions of all our churches.

"5. That the Presbyteries be and hereby are enjoined to make the progress of the Sabbath-school cause within their bounds the subject of special inquiry, and annually to transmit the results of such inquiry to the General Assembly.

"6. That inasmuch as the advantages of the Sabbath-school may, in some cases, be the occasion of remissness in the important duty of *family* instruction, it be and hereby is earnestly recommended to heads of families not to relax in their personal religious efforts at *home,* and in the domestic circle; but that they abound more and more in the use of all appropriate means, to promote sound knowledge and experimental piety, in every member of their households.

"7. That as there is reason to apprehend that the *Catechisms of this Church* have not, in some parts of our Zion, received that measure of attention to which their excellence entitles them, it be and hereby is recommended to pastors, sessions, heads of families, superintendents of Sabbath-schools, and all charged with the education of youth in our connection, to give these admirable summaries of Christian truth and duty a prominent place in their instructions to the youth and children under their care.

"8. That it be and hereby is recommended to the pastors and sessions of our churches to make themselves acquainted with the system of *Infant School* instruction, now in happy progress in many places, and if practicable, to establish such schools in their congregations."—*Minutes,* 1830, pp. 303, 304.

d. "*Resolved,* That the General Assembly regard with an increased and lively interest the efforts of the American Sunday-school Union, especially in their endeavors to open, in the destitute portions of the land, Sabbath-schools for the instruction and training of the young; that we acknowledge them in many instances to have formed the nucleus of a Christian congregation; and we desire renewedly to commend this noble cause to the sympathy, prayers, and benefactions of the Church." —*Minutes,* 1853, p. 314.

3. *Catechetical Instruction.*

a. "The Synod, considering the education of youth, and their being early instructed in just principles of religion, as one of the most useful means of promoting the influence of the Gospel in our churches,

"*Resolved*, That it be enjoined on every Presbytery, in appointing supplies to their vacant congregations, to take order that every vacant congregation within their limits be carefully catechized at least once in the year, in the same manner as is required by the order of our Church in congregations supplied with regular pastors, and that the ministers appointed to this duty be required at the next meeting of the Presbytery to render an account of their fidelity in this respect, and that the Presbyteries be required to render an account of their attention to this order at the next meeting of Synod."—*Minutes*, 1785, p. 513.

b. "*Resolved*, That as there is reason to apprehend that the Catechisms of this Church have not in some parts of our Zion received that measure of attention to which their excellence entitles them, it be, and hereby is recommended to pastors, sessions, heads of families, superintendents of Sabbath-schools, and all charged with the education of youth, in our connection, to give these admirable summaries of Christian truth and duty a prominent place in their instructions to the youth and children under their care."—*Minutes*, 1830, p. 304.

c. "*Resolved*, That the use of the Catechism in the religious instruction of the young, and of the children under the care of the Church, be affectionately and earnestly recommended to the Sessions in connection with the General Assembly, as the most effectual means under God of preserving the purity, peace, and unity of our Church."—*Minutes*, 1832, p. 372.

d. "The following resolutions, on the subject of *Catechetical Instruction*, were offered by the Rev. W. H. Smith, and unanimously adopted, viz.:

"1. *Resolved*, That this General Assembly considers the practice of *Catechetical Instruction* as well adapted to the prosperity and purity of our Zion.

"2. *Resolved*, That this Assembly view also with deep regret the neglect, on the part of many of our churches, of this good old practice of our fathers—a practice which has been attended with such blessed results to the cause of pure and undefiled religion.

"3. *Resolved*, That the institution of Sabbath-schools does not exonerate ministers and parents from the duty of teaching the Shorter Catechism to the children of the Church.

"4. *Resolved,* That this Assembly earnestly and affectionately recommend to all the ministers and ruling elders in its connection, to teach diligently the young of their respective congregations, the Assembly's Shorter Catechism."—*Minutes,* 1849, p. 181.

SECTION 3.—ON THE SUPPORT OF THE MINISTRY.

1. Support of the Ministry. Early action. Glebe and parsonage recommended.—2. Adequate provision urged. Presbyteries to inquire into the fulfilment of contracts.—3. Congregational libraries for the use of ministers.—4. Liberality in the support of the ministry urged.

1. *Early Action. Glebe and Parsonage recommended.*

a. "That in every congregation a committee be appointed, who shall twice in every year collect the minister's stipend, and lay his receipts before the Presbytery preceding the Synod; and at the same time, that ministers give an account of their diligence in visiting and catechizing their people.

"The Synod recommends that a glebe, with a convenient house and necessary improvements, be provided for every minister."—*Minutes,* 1766, p. 359.

b. "As it appears the interest of religion is in danger of suffering greatly at present, from the many discouragements under which the ministers of the Gospel labor from the want of a sufficient support and liberal maintenance from the congregations they serve, the Synod appoint a committee to take this matter into consideration, and report thereon to the next Synod.

"*Ordered,* That Drs. Witherspoon, Ewing, and Spencer, be a committee for this purpose."—*Minutes,* 1782, p. 495.

"Said committee brought in their report, which was read and considered. Whereupon,

"*Ordered,* That Drs. Witherspoon and Spencer, with Mr. S. Smith, be a committee to prepare a draught of a pastoral letter to the congregations under the inspection of Synod, as also to prepare some resolves to be passed by Synod, and accompany said letter; the whole to be brought in to-morrow morning."—*Minutes,* 1783, p. 499.

[The letter was brought in, amended, and ordered to be published.]

2. *Adequate Provision to be urged.*

[The Assembly enjoins it upon all the Presbyteries] "that they will endeavor, as far as the state of society in different parts of our Church will permit, to withdraw the ministers of the Gospel from every worldly avocation for the maintenance of themselves and families, that they may devote themselves entirely to the work of the ministry; and that, for this end, they labor to convince the people of the advantage that will accrue to themselves from making such adequate provision for the support of their teachers and pastors, that they may be employed wholly in their sacred calling; and, in those places where it may be found prudent and practicable, that they devise means to have the contracts between congregations and pastors examined in the Presbyteries at stated periods, inquiries instituted with regard to the reciprocal fulfilment of duties and engagements, and endeavors used to promote punctuality and fidelity in both parties, before distress on one side, or complaint on the other, grow to a height unfavorable to the interests of religion."—*Minutes*, 1799, p. 181.

3. *Congregational Libraries.*

"That inasmuch as the clergy, in many situations in the country, have it not in their power to furnish themselves with libraries so various and extensive as to enable them to discharge their office in the manner most useful to the people, most dignified for the pulpit, and most honorable for religion, it be recommended to the Presbyteries to take measures to promote the establishment of congregational libraries, under such regulations that the Presbyteries shall have the principal direction in the choice of the books with which those libraries shall be furnished. The ministers of the respective churches shall have the immediate care and the constant use of them, and that means be used to make annual augmentations to them."—*Minutes*, 1799, p. 182.

4. *Liberality in the Support of the Ministry urged.*

"The following preamble and resolution, proposed by Elder Walter S. Griffith, were unanimously adopted:

"Whereas, it is highly important to our churches that they be served by competent ministers, who shall be free from worldly cares and avocations; whereas, the law of Christ expressly declares, 'that they which preach the Gospel should live of the Gospel,' and that he 'that is taught in the word' should 'communicate unto him that teacheth in all good things,' thus making it the solemn duty, as it is clearly the interest, of Christian churches to provide for their ministers a competent and liberal support; whereas, the cost of the necessities of life has advanced so greatly as to render the salaries heretofore paid to many of our ministers entirely inadequate, causing to them and to their families great anxiety and distress; and whereas, this subject demands at this time, and should not fail to attract, the special attention of every Christian; therefore,

"*Resolved,* That the General Assembly earnestly exhort all the churches under their care to consider this question in the spirit of Christian fidelity and liberality, and to make ample provision for those who minister to them in word and doctrine; stipulating so to increase their compensation, when necessary, as to make their salaries fully adequate to their comfortable support, in view of the enhanced expenses of living, and paying the amount agreed upon with honorable and Christian promptitude."—*Minutes,* 1854, pp. 499, 500.

SECTION 4.—ON FASTING AND PRAYER.

1. Prayer for the General Assembly.—2. Special seasons for prayer recommended. —3. Revivals consequent on special prayer.—4. The monthly concert. Time of observing it.—5. Appointment of a day of fasting and prayer for the conversion of the world,—first Monday in January. Standing custom.—6. Prayer for magistrates.

1. *Prayer for the General Assembly.*

"An overture from the Synod of North Carolina was received and read, and is as follows:

"Whereas, the General Assembly is the highest and most important judicatory of the Presbyterian Church; and whereas, to obtain the Divine blessing on that judicatory must appear, to every Christian of our denomination, to be a matter of the utmost moment; therefore,

"*Resolved,* That this Synod do respectfully suggest to the General Assembly the propriety of recommending to all the churches under their care to observe the afternoon or evening previous to the meeting of that body, as a season of special prayer to Almighty God for his blessing; that he would, of his infinite mercy, condescend to superintend and direct all their measures, deliberations and decisions, so that all may redound to the promotion of his own glory, and the general prosperity of that particular Church to which we belong.

"After some discussion, the above overture was adopted."—*Minutes*, 1821, p. 10.

2. *Special Seasons for Prayer recommended.*

"The General Assembly, taking into serious consideration the general aspect of religion, the great decay of vital piety, and the prevalence of infidelity and immorality, and being deeply affected thereby (especially considering the many blessings which, as a nation and a people, we enjoy), agreed to urge, in the most earnest manner, upon all their members, the utmost diligence, perseverance, and zeal, in the discharge of the duties of their offices and stations; and that they prosecute those measures, agreeably to the word of God, which they may judge most conducive to counteract the existing evils, and most effectually serve the interests of evangelical principles, and of true and undefiled religion; and would recommend that some particular times be set apart as special seasons of prayer with respect to those objects, as may be found most convenient in their respective circumstances."—*Minutes*, 1796, p. 116.

3. *Revivals in connection with Special Prayer.*

"The Assembly consider it as worthy of particular attention, that most of the accounts of revivals communicated to them stated that the institution of praying societies, or seasons of special prayer to God for the outpouring of the Spirit, generally preceded the remarkable displays of Divine grace with which our land has been recently favored. In most cases, preparatory to the signal effusions of the Holy Ghost, the pious have been stirred up to cry fervently and importunately that God would appear and vindicate his own cause. The Assembly see in this a confirmation of the word of God, and an ample encouragement of the prayers and hopes of the pious for future and more extensive manifestations of Divine power; and they trust that the churches under their care, while they see cause of abundant thankfulness for this dispensation, will also perceive that it presents new motives to zeal and fervor in applications to that throne of grace from which every good and perfect gift cometh."—*Minutes*, 1803, p. 275.

4. *The Monthly Concert.*

a. "Whereas, the King and Head of the Church has during the last year poured out his Spirit in a remarkable and glorious manner on many of the churches within our bounds, and has manifestly succeeded the efforts of Christians in past years, in their endeavors to diffuse the light of revealed truth among the heathen; and has hereby encouraged and urged the pious to united and importunate wrestling at the throne of grace; and whereas many Christians in Asia, Africa, and Europe, have agreed to set apart the first Monday evening of every month, that they may meet together, and say with one heart, to the prayer-hearing God, 'Thy kingdom come; come, Lord Jesus, and fill the world with thy glory.' Therefore,

"*Resolved,* That this General Assembly do approve of concerts of prayer for the advancement of the Redeemer's kingdom, and do recommend it to the friends of Zion in their connection, as far as may be convenient, to spend the first Monday in every month in special prayer to God, for the coming and glorious reign of Christ on earth."—*Minutes,* 1815, p. 601, 602.

b. "In reference to the time of observing the *Monthly Concert,* on motion of Dr. Cox, the Assembly agreed to recommend, that it be continued permanently *on the first Monday evening of every month,* without change; since it is now to be considered as a concert of Protestant Christendom throughout the world, urging the petition *Thy kingdom come,* in the same spirit, and, as nearly as may be, according to the different meridians of their habitation, at the same time."—*Minutes,* 1839, p. 26.

5. *Appointment of a Day of Prayer for the Conversion of the World.*

a. "The committee to whom was referred Overture No. 11, viz., 'on the appointment of a day of prayer for the conversion of the world,' made the following report, which was unanimously adopted, viz.:

"It being understood, that Christians and churches, both in this country and in Europe, have at different times desired the public designation of a day to be observed by all Christians throughout the world, as a day of fasting and prayer for the outpouring of the Holy Spirit on the whole family of man, and this Assembly being deeply impressed with the importance and high privilege of such an observance, and feeling urged and encouraged to more importunate supplications in view of the recent revivals of religion in this land, as well as the signs of the present time in relation to the prospects of the Church in other nations, therefore,

"*Resolved,* That it be recommended to the ministers and churches under the supervision of the General Assembly of the Presbyterian Church in the United States of America, and the churches in correspondence with the same, to observe the first Monday in January, 1833, as a day of *fasting* and *prayer,* for the divine blessing on the ministry of the Gospel throughout the world, for the revival of religion in the whole of Christendom, and for the entire success of those benevolent enterprises which have for their object the world's conversion to God.

"*Resolved,* That other denominations of Christians in the United States, and the Christian churches in all other countries, be, and they hereby are affectionately, and with Christian salutations, invited to concur in the observance of the day above specified.

"*Resolved,* That these resolutions be published with the signature of the Moderator and Clerk of the General Assembly, for the information of such Synods, Assemblies, Associations, Conferences, Conventions, and other ecclesiastical bodies as may choose to recommend the above observance to the churches under their care. And may grace, mercy, and peace be multiplied to all throughout the world who love our Lord Jesus Christ."—*Minutes,* 1832, p. 365.

b. "At the meeting of the General Assembly of the last year, an additional measure was adopted, in compliance with overtures from various quarters, calling for the public designation of a day to be observed by all Christians throughout the world, as a day of fasting and prayer for the outpouring of the Holy Spirit on the whole family of man. For this purpose, the first Monday of January last was accordingly designated; and it is understood that the day was observed, both in the Old World and the New, with much solemnity, and in many instances with a sacred pleasure and humble hope in God, the recollection of which is still delightful and animating. This General Assembly, therefore, do earnestly recommend to all the churches and people under their pastoral superintendence, to continue the observance of the same day of the coming year, and for the same purpose as that to which the specified day of the present year was set apart. Let the whole of the first Monday of January, 1834, be observed as a season of special prayer—of united, fervent, believing prayer, for the conversion of the world to

God. And if it be thus observed, prayer will of course be accompanied with deep humiliation—with a sincere prostration of soul before the holy and all-seeing God, in view of personal guilt, and of the sin of the Christian world in so long neglecting to obey, as they ought to have done, one of the last commands of their redeeming God, before he ascended to his throne in the heavens, to disciple all nations, and to preach the Gospel to every creature—to send the messages of salvation to the perishing millions of the unevangelized world. And the Assembly would earnestly recommend that this observance be connected with *fasting*, and abstinence from secular labor. The great *spiritual* object is a union of hearts, and of unfeigned, ardent, and repeated aspirations, supplications, and intercessions at the throne of eternal mercy, through the prevalent intercession of the great Mediator and Advocate of his people there, that the Holy Spirit may come down in a copious effusion of his special, new-creating, soul-saving influence, for the conversion of the world to God—for the consolation, encouragement, and abundant success of the missionaries who are now in the field of labor; for raising up, qualifying, sending forth, and blessing the labors of additional missionaries—a host of apostolic, devoted, self-sacrificing men, into all heathen lands, and all destitute portions of lands already partially Gospelized; for enlightening, directing, and animating all missionary associations, and for a special benediction on all theological seminaries, colleges, academies, common and Sabbath-schools; for the translators of the Holy Scriptures, and for all Bible and tract societies and distributors; for inclining the minds of the whole Christian community to devote a liberal portion of the worldly substance which God has given them, for the promotion of his cause, and the building up of his kingdom on the ruins of Satan's empire; and generally for a rich divine blessing on all the benevolent and Christian associations, plans, and exertions which characterize and are the glory of the day in which we have our lot in life."—*Minutes*, 1833, p. 398.

[It has become a standing custom of the Assembly to designate the first Monday in January as a day of fasting and prayer for the conversion of the world, and also to recommend the observance of the last Thursday in February as a day of prayer for colleges, theological seminaries, and other institutions of learning. See Minutes, *passim*.]

6. *Prayer for Magistrates.*

"It is the duty of the people to pray for magistrates; to honor their persons, to pay them tribute and other dues, to obey their lawful commands, and to be subject to their authority for conscience' sake. Infidelity, or differences in religion doth not make void the magistrate's just and legal authority, nor free the people from their due obedience to him." [Confession of Faith, chap. xxiii, sec. 4.]—*Minutes*, 1830, p. 300.

Section 5.—On Psalmody.

1. Narrative of early action. A new collection to be prepared, and a committee appointed. The Book approved.—2. Movement for a new Book of Psalmody; referred to the committee *ad interim*.—3. The Church Psalmist recommended. —4. The Church Psalmist purchased for the Assembly; a supplement added.—5. Book of Tunes prepared and published.

1. *The Assembly's Narrative of what has hitherto been done. A new Collection to be prepared, and a Committee appointed.*

"The committee to which the resolution on the subject of Psalmody was committed, the consideration of which was deferred by the last Assembly, to be taken up by this Assembly, reported, and their report being read and amended, was adopted, and is as follows, viz.:

"That the subject of the resolution, in their opinion, is of such magnitude as to demand the serious attention of this Assembly.

"Psalmody has in all ages been considered a most important part of the worship of God. The Church, therefore, has ever been careful to preserve its purity for the edification of her members; whilst they who have departed from the faith once delivered to the saints, have availed themselves of it to accomplish their divisive plans with the best success. Mindful of their duty in this matter, the General Assembly have, from time to time, authorized the use of Rouse's version of the Book of Psalms, Watts's Imitation of the Psalms of David with his three books of Hymns, Barlow's alterations of, and addition to Watts's Imitation, and Dwight's revision of Watts, with his additional versifications and collection of hymns, in the churches under their care.

"Whilst the committee grant that each of these systems of psalmody has its excellencies, they respectfully recommend that one uniform system of psalmody be prepared, under the direction of the Assembly, for the use of the churches under their care. They believe that the time has come when such a measure may be adopted without offending any of our churches, and with the prospect of complete success.

"If they are correct in this belief, of which the Assembly must judge, it appears to them that uniformity in this matter will furnish a strong bond of peace and harmony between the different sections of our Church.

"The committee further recommend that this uniform system of psalmody consist of two parts, viz.:

"1. A compilation of metrical versions of the Book of Psalms, adhering to the order and connection of the same as far as practicable.

"In this compilation the preference ought to be given to the authorized versions now in use, so far as the poetry and conformity to the text allow. The committee, in recommending this compilation, disavow any design of committing the Assembly on the difference of opinion which exists about the Book of Psalms. They also wish it to be distinctly understood that they do not disapprove of Watts. But they think that a compilation, such as is recommended, if judiciously executed, will satisfy the friends of Dr. Watts's Imitation, and the advocates of the exclusive authority of the Book of Psalms.

"2. A copious collection of hymns and spiritual songs from various authors, giving the preference to those now authorized, so far as good taste, sound sense, and enlightened piety admit.

"Such a system of psalmody, the committee think, besides producing harmony among ourselves in this part of public worship, will tend to enlarge that growing disposition among Christians of different denominations, to union of exertions for promoting the kingdom of Christ.

"They therefore submit the following resolutions, viz.:

"1. That a committee be appointed to digest and prepare a uniform system of psalmody, as recommended in this report; the whole, when prepared agreeably to the views of the committee, to be submitted to the General Assembly for their adoption.

"2. That the committee appointed to carry this resolution into effect be authorized to procure, at the expense of the Assembly, such versions of the Book of Psalms, and such collections of hymns and sacred songs, as they may deem necessary.

"The Assembly appointed Drs. Romeyn, Alexander, Nott, Blatchford, and Spring, a committee to prepare and digest a system of psalmody, as recommended in the foregoing report."—*Minutes*, 1820, p. 740.

[The book was finally laid before the Assembly in 1830, and approved.]

"The report of the Committee on Psalmody, which was laid on the table, was taken up, when it was—

"*Resolved*, That the Book of Psalms and Hymns, with the alterations and additions submitted by the committee, be approved by the Assembly, and its use in the worship of God be authorized in all the churches under its care."—*Minutes*, 1830, p. 306.

2. *Movement for a new Book of Psalmody.*

a. "On motion of Dr. Cox, the whole subject of psalmody, with the procuring and furnishing an edition of psalms and hymns for our general use in a way involving no pecuniary responsibility to the Assembly, was referred to the Consulting Committee for their deliberation and action, as they may deem proper and practicable."—*Minutes*, 1840, p. 24.

3. *The Church Psalmist recommended.*

a. "Whereas, the General Assembly of 1840, for the purpose of bringing about a greater degree of uniformity in the psalmody used in our churches, appointed a committee on this subject, and after much consultation and reports in part, committed 'the whole subject, with the procuring and furnishing an edition of psalms and hymns for our general use, in a way involving no pecuniary responsibility to the Assembly,' to the Consulting Committee, or committee *ad interim;*

"And whereas, that committee, agreeably to the powers intrusted to them, have, after much time and labor devoted to the subject, procured and furnished such a Book of Psalms and Hymns as they deem suited to general use in our Church;

"And whereas, so far as we are enabled to judge, the said book, entitled the 'Church Psalmist,' fully merits the recommendation the committee have given it;

"Therefore, that this General Assembly recommend the collection of psalms and hymns entitled the 'Church Psalmist,' to the churches under our care, leaving them at the same time free to continue the books now in use if they deem it most for edification.

"Ordered, that the stated clerk pay to Dr. Beman $400, the amount of his claim, out of the first funds which may come into his hands after discharging the debt due to the counsel engaged in the late lawsuit."—*Minutes*, 1843, p. 20–21.

b. "The unfinished business of the morning, viz., the consideration of the report on Psalmody, was resumed, and after long discussion, the report was amended and adopted, and is as follows, viz.:

"Whereas, the subject of Psalmody is one of great importance, and it is highly desirable that there should be uniformity in respect to the book used for this purpose;

"And, whereas, the Assembly of 1840, after repeated discussions, 'referred the whole subject of Psalmody, with the procuring and furnishing an edition of psalms and hymns for general use,' to the Consulting Committee;

"And, whereas, this committee, agreeably to the powers intrusted to them, after a patient and thorough examination of different books submitted to them, unanimously adopted and recommended to the churches the book entitled 'The Church Psalmist,' as in their judgment possessing greater excellencies than any other known to them.

"And, whereas, the Assembly of 1843 adopted the report of the committee, thereby adopting 'The Church Psalmist' as the authorized psalmody of the Presbyterian Church in these United States, and giving their approbation to the arrangement entered into with the editor and publisher, in accordance with which ten per cent. of the proceeds of all sales of fifty copies and over was received into the treasury of the Assembly, therefore be it

"*Resolved*, 1. That it is earnestly recommended to the churches in connection with this Assembly, for the purpose of carrying out the matured action of our highest ecclesiastical judicatories, and thus securing uniformity, an increasing revenue, and the possession of a work of high intrinsic merit, whenever they deem it best to make a change in their psalmody, to adopt the book of the Assembly.

"*Resolved*, 2. That by the permission of the editor, the second part of the 51st Psalm in L. M. of Dr. Watts's version be substituted for the third part of the 51st Psalm in C. M. of the Church Psalmist."—*Minutes*, 1846, p. 19.

4. *The Church Psalmist purchased. The Supplement added.*

"In 1855, *Minutes*, p. 32, and again in 1856, *Minutes*, p. 215, the Publication Committee were authorized and directed to 'negotiate with the compilers and publishers of the Church Psalmist, and to purchase that book if this can be done on reasonable terms.' In 1857, the committee report to the Assembly that they have purchased the Psalmist, upon which the Assembly

"*Resolved,* That we recognize with gratitude to God the completion of the labors of the Publication Committee, by which the Assembly is furnished with a book of psalmody which they can call their own; the profits of which will materially aid the funds of the Church in the Publication cause; and the Assembly hereby recommend to the pastors and the churches that they use all reasonable diligence in promoting uniformity by the introduction of this book.

"*Resolved,* That the preparation of an appendix to the Church Psalmist of such hymns as may be necessary to make the work complete be committed to N. S. S. Beman, D.D., Rev. Albert Barnes, and S. W. Fisher, D.D., and that this Committee report to the next General Assembly."—*Minutes,* 1857, pp. 410, 411.

[The committee were directed to report to the Publication Committee (Minutes, 1858, p. 585), by whom the supplement was published, and the book thus completed.]—*Minutes,* 1859, p. 38.

5. *The Book of Tunes.*

a. "*Resolved,* That a committee of three be appointed by the Publication Committee to prepare a Book of Tunes adapted to the Church Psalmist, and that this committee be instructed to consult and correspond with pastors and leaders of choirs in the churches, as to the particular tunes most in use and most popular in the congregations, and that this committee report to the next General Assembly."—*Minutes,* 1857, p. 410.

b. "The committee appointed to prepare a Book of Tunes adapted to the Church Psalmist, presented the following report:

"The Committee on the preparation of a Book of Tunes respectfully report to the General Assembly that the work intrusted to them is in progress, and will shortly be completed. It was not until near the close of the last year that they received notice of their appointment by the Publication Committee. Shortly after, they addressed a circular letter to the ministers in connection with the Assembly, requesting them to confer with the leader of music in their respective congregations and forward such information and suggestions on the whole subject as occurred to them. Numerous responses have been received, some of them of great value, and the most of them giving assurance of hearty cooperation in the work. From every part of the Church, almost without exception, the call has been made for congregational singing. 'Give us the good old tunes that our fathers sung, the tunes that our children love, the tunes that all can use in the worship of God.' Such is the demand; and the committee will endeavor to comply with it, fully persuaded as they themselves are that it is both Scriptural and reasonable. The work will be carefully prepared under the supervision of a competent professor of sacred music.

"If the Assembly desire, as some have suggested, a hymn book with tunes incorporated after the manner of the 'Temple Melodies,' it will be necessary for them to give the committee specific instructions to that effect.

"The report was adopted."—*Minutes*, 1858, p. 585.

"The book was published and laid before the Assembly in 1860."—*Minutes*, pp. 246, 295.

SECTION 6.—AMENDMENTS TO FORM OF GOVERNMENT, BOOK OF DISCIPLINE, AND DIRECTORY FOR WORSHIP, ADOPTED OR PROPOSED.

1. Amended in 1821, and adopted substantially as at present.—2. Proposal to amend chap. x, Form of Government, refused.—3. Amendment of chap. xiii, sec. 2, Form of Government, refused.—4. Proposals to amend Form of Government, chap. xii, sec. 4; Book of Discipline, chap. vii, sec. 1, art. iv, secs. 2, 3, 4, On Appeals, Complaints, and References; Form of Government, chap. xii, sec. 7, and chap. xiv, sec. 6.—5. Answers of the Presbyteries. Form of Government, chap. xii, sec. 7, altered. Five of the six proposed amendments agreed to, but the sixth being rejected, the Assembly refuse to make the alterations proposed.—6. Proposal to alter the ratio of representation in the Assembly; also to make it Synodical and not Presbyterial.—7. Proposal of an overture in reference to calling special meetings of Synod. Not adopted.—8. Reports of the Presbyteries. The ratio of representation altered. Form of Government, chap. xii, sec. 2.—9. Proposal to limit the appellate jurisdiction of the Assembly to charges against a minister, and to processes originating in a Synod.—10. Proposal to make the Synods, in all cases, the courts of final jurisdiction, to hold the Assembly triennially, and to authorize the calling of the Assembly *pro re nata*.—11. Answers of the Presbyteries, affirming the proposed amendments. Alterations of the Constitution made in accordance. Form of Government, chap. xii, secs. 2, 7, 8.—12. Proposal to return to Annual Assemblies, Form of Government, chap. xii, sec. 7, and to restore appellate jurisdiction to the Assembly.—13. The pro-

posal more clearly defined. Revision of the Standards committed to a committee.—14. The Overtures 1 and 2, respecting Annual Assemblies, chap. xi, sec. 7, and chap. xii, sec. 7, Form of Government, adopted. Overture 3, 4, and 5, pertaining to appeals in the case of ministers, Book of Discipline, chap. 7, par. 2, sec. iii, par. 2, and sec. iv, par. 4, not adopted.—15. Report on changes of the Constitution. Proposal to restore it as in 1840, or before the division. Overtures sent down, Book of Discipline, chap. xii, sec. 4, chap. vii, sec. 2, chap. vii, sec. 3, sub sec. 2, chap. vii, sec. 4, sub sec. 1; Form of Government, chap. xii, a new section after sec. 7, and xii, sec. 2.—16. These overtures rejected. The Book restored as before the division.

1. *The Form of Government, Book of Discipline, and Directory for Worship, amended,* 1821.

"In 1820, a paper containing proposed amendments to the Form of Government was sent down to the Presbyteries with the following result.

"The committee appointed to ascertain the decisions of the several Presbyteries, on the subject of the revised Form of Government and forms of process, and the amendments to the Directory, sent down by the last Assembly, reported, and their report being read, was adopted, and is as follows, viz.:

"That there are connected with this Assembly sixty-two Presbyteries; that, therefore, the affirmative vote of thirty-two Presbyteries is necessary to make any one article binding; that forty-five Presbyteries have reported to the Assembly their decisions on each chapter, section, and article; that from these reports it appears that the most of the articles have been adopted unanimously, and that every chapter, section, and article has been adopted by a majority of the whole number of Presbyteries; that the smallest number of votes given for any one article is thirty-seven; that, therefore, *the whole of the proposed amendments* sent down by the last Assembly to the Presbyteries is ratified, and becomes a part of the Constitution."—*Minutes*, 1821, p. 9.

[This brings the Constitution substantially to its present form. Other amendments, since proposed or adopted, are given below as a matter of history, and in some cases as defining the true meaning of the Constitution.]

2. *Proposal to amend Chap. X, Form of Government, refused.*

"The following overture from the Presbytery of Baltimore was received and read, viz., That after the 12th article of the 10th chapter of the revised Form of Government, the following be added: '13. Every Presbytery shall judge of the qualifications of its own members.'

"*Resolved*, That it is inexpedient to grant the request contained in this overture, or to make any new alterations at present in the Book of Discipline."—*Minutes*, 1821, p. 10.

3. *Proposal to amend Chap. XIII, Sec. 2, Form of Government, refused.*

"The Committee on Overture No. 9, relating to an amendment in the Form of Government, chap. xiii, sec. 2 (on the election of elders), reported, and their report was adopted, and is as follows: see chap. ii, sec. 2, p. 50."—*Minutes*, 1826, p. 187.

4. *Proposal to amend Form of Government, Chap. XII, Sect.* 4; *Book of Discipline, Chap. VII, Sect.* 1, 2, 3, 4, *On Appeals, Complaints, and References; Form of Government, Chap. XII, Sect.* 7, *and Chap. XIV, Sect.* 6.

"The committee to whom was recommitted the report on the propriety of making certain alterations in the existing rules which govern the proceedings of the General Assembly, and, if necessary, alterations in the Constitution of our Church, recommended,

"1st. That the *Form of Government*, chap. xii, sect. 4, be so altered as to read thus: 'The General Assembly shall act upon all cases relating to complaints and appeals, which may be regularly brought before them from inferior judicatories.'

"2dly. That the *Book of Discipline*, chap. vii, sect 1, art. 4, be made to read thus: 'No judicial decision, however, of a judicatory shall be revised, unless it be regularly brought up by appeal, or complaint, or order of the General Assembly.'

"3dly. That the *Book of Discipline*, chap. vii, sect. 1, receive two new articles, to be numbered vii and viii, the *first* of which shall read thus: 'Should it appear to the General Assembly, in reviewing the records of a Synod, that a Synod has, in the case of a complaint or appeal, acted *unconstitutionally*, or done something manifestly unjust or oppressive, the General Assembly may pass a censure on its proceedings; but no judicial decision of a Synod shall be reversed by the General Assembly until due notice has been given to the original parties to appear before the next General Assembly, and to the inferior courts to send up all the documents, papers, and testimony relative to the case, duly authenticated:' and the *second* of which shall read thus, viz.: 'When a case shall be brought up, in the manner prescribed in the foregoing article, the Assembly shall be governed in their proceedings by the rules which regulate appeals before a lower judicature.'

"4thly. That to the *Book of Discipline*, chap. vii, sect. 2, shall be added a new article, to be numbered x, in these words, viz.: 'References made by Presbyteries or Synods to the General Assembly shall not be for the trial of any cause, but only for advice.'

"5thly. That the *Book of Discipline*, chap. vii, sect. 3, receive an additional article, to be numbered xviii, in the following words, viz.: 'All appeals from any Session or Presbytery shall terminate in the Synod to which those inferior courts belong.'

"6thly. That to the *Book of Discipline*, chap. vii, sect. 4, shall be added an article, to be numbered viii, in these words, viz.: 'Complaints, like appeals, shall terminate in the Synods within whose jurisdiction they shall have originated.'

"In support of the foregoing propositions for alteration and amendment, the committee remark, that the time which is now consumed by the Assembly in the consideration of complaints and appeals is such as greatly to interfere with a due attention to other important and more general concerns of the Church; and this demand of time for complaints and appeals will, if the existing system remains unaltered, speedily become so great, that the very limited period during which the Assembly can sit will scarcely suffice for attending to this single object. The foresight of this had, it is believed, a principal influence in the appointment of your committee; and after considering a variety of suggestions, insurmountable objections occurred to the adoption of any one, except that which has now been submitted. But to this, every objection, when closely and candidly examined, seemed to your committee to vanish.

"The right of complaint and appeal is indeed one of great importance, and the security of it fully is known to be regarded as among the most attractive features of the whole system of Presbyterian Church government. But this right, it is believed, may be provided for in all its extent, although the change in the Form of Government now contemplated should be made. It will be recollected, that before the formation of the General Assembly all appeals were terminated in a Synod—the Synod of New York and Philadelphia—not then more numerous than several of our local Synods now are; and with the final decisions of that Synod the churches were satisfied; quite as much so as they have ever been with the decisions of the General Assembly. Indeed, it is believed by your committee, that from the greater advantages possessed by Synods for obtaining an accurate knowledge of the true state and circumstances of the controversies which arise within their bounds, and from having more time for a careful investigation and a full hearing of everything relating to complaints and appeals that are brought before them, they are more likely than the Assembly to make an equitable and satisfactory award. Nor should it be forgotten, that if an inequitable and unsatisfactory award is ever made by the Assembly, the evil consequences are extensive and numerous; the authority and respect of subordinate judicatures are diminished; litigious individuals are encouraged to persist in an evil course; erroneous principles are established by the supreme tribunal of our Church, and eventually attachment to, and respect for, the General Assembly are enfeebled, and the bond of union among our churches is weakened, and its dissolution threatened.

"Experience has taught us that a considerable part of the complaints and appeals on which the General Assembly has ultimately decided, had their origin from church Sessions. In all such cases, if the proposed amendments to the Constitution should be adopted, two appeals will still remain,—one to the Presbytery and the other to the Synod. If local feelings may be supposed in some cases to influence a Presbytery, they seldom if ever extend to a whole Synod; and as the placing of the last appeal here will bring controversies to a more speedy issue than if carried further, the most formidable objection ever made to the discipline of our Church—that it occasions delay in settling disputes and ending discord—will, in no inconsiderable degree, be removed.

"If, after all, a decision, manifestly unconstitutional or unjust, should be made by a Synod in the case of a complaint or an appeal, this will of course appear on the records, will probably be accompanied by a protest or dissent, will thus attract the notice of the committee of the Assembly appointed to review the book, will by that committee be reported to the house, and thus a full opportunity will be given to correct the error.

"The committee moreover recommend,

"7thly. That in the *Form of Government*, chap. xii, sect. 7, the words '*publicly read*,' should be exchanged for the word 'examined.' In favor of this amendment, the committee stated, that probably much time, which is now occupied by the whole Assembly in having the commissions publicly read, might be saved, and stricter order be observed, by the adoption of rules of the following import: that immediately after the opening of the General Assembly and the constituting of the house, a Committee of Commissions be appointed, with instructions; and that the house adjourn till the usual hour in the afternoon. That the Committee of Commissions be instructed to examine the commissions, and report to the Assembly, immediately after its opening in the afternoon, on those commissions which are unobjectionable, and on those, if such there be, which are materially incorrect, or that are otherwise objectionable. That those whose commissions are unobjectionable, immediately take their seats as members, and proceed to business; and that the first act be the appointment of a Committee of Elections, to which shall be referred all the informal, or otherwise objectionable commissions, with instructions to report thereon as soon as practicable.

"The committee finally recommend,

"8thly. That the *Form of Government*, chap. xiv, sect. 6, be so altered as to read *three years* instead of *two years*.

"It is believed by the committee, that since the formation of the Constitution of the Presbyterian Church, in the year 1788, a change has taken place in the state of this Church and society in our country at large, which may render proper a change in the period during which candidates for the Gospel ministry should be required to study, previously to their licensure to preach the Gospel. Candidates for the Gospel ministry now are in general younger than such candidates were thirty years ago; there are more facilities for education; and the diffusion of knowledge and increase of mental improvement, seem to demand a correspondent increase of ministerial furniture, in those who preach the Gospel. For these reasons the committee submit that in their apprehension the article of the Constitution which directs that the period of two years of previous study shall be indispensable to license, may advantageously be increased to the period of three years, except in extraordinary cases.

"Having considered and approved of the foregoing eight propositions, the Assembly resolved that they be transmitted to the Presbyteries, and said Presbyteries hereby are instructed to report in writing, to the next General Assembly, *their adoption or rejection of the alterations and additions*, thus proposed to be made in the Constitution of the Presbyterian Church."—*Minutes*, 1826, pp. 188–190.

5. *Answers of the Presbyteries. Chap. XII, Sect. 7, of Form of Government altered. Five of the Six Amendments proposed agreed to; but the alteration is not made by the Assembly.*

"The committee to whom was referred the report of the Committee on the Returns of the Presbyteries, in relation to the proposed alterations and amendments of the Constitution, that they might report what ought to be done in consequence of the state of these returns, made the following report, viz.: That there are connected with the Assembly, eighty-eight Presbyteries; forty-five, therefore, are necessary to make any alteration in the Constitution of the Church.

"In regard to the proposed erasure of the 4th section of the 24th chapter of the Confession of Faith, sixty-eight Presbyteries have reported: fifty of them against the erasure, and eighteen in favor of it. The section, therefore, is not to be erased. [See chap. vii, p. 241, *e*, for the overture alluded to.]

"In relation to No. 7 of the proposed amendments to the Form of Government, it appears that *fifty-three* Presbyteries have voted in favor of the alteration and thirteen against it; wherefore,

"*Resolved*, That the proposed amendment, viz.: That in the Form of Government, chap. xii, sect. 7, the words '*publicly read*,' should be exchanged for the word '*examined*,' be, and the same is hereby adopted as a part of the Constitution of this Church.

"In relation to No. 8, *thirty* Presbyteries have voted in favor of it, and *thirty-seven* against it. This amendment, therefore, cannot be adopted, a majority of the Presbyteries not having approved of it.

"In relation to the first six of the proposed amendments to the Form of Government,* the committee made the following report, which was adopted, viz.:

"That, on examining the proposed amendments to the Constitution, sent down to the Presbyteries by the last General Assembly, as they stand on the printed Minutes, page 37, it appears that the whole of them, from Nos. 1 to 6, inclusive, were framed with such reference to each other, and to their common object, as that they ought to have been either adopted or rejected altogether; and further, that the Presbyteries, by rejecting the *sixth*, have in effect defeated the very end which they must have intended to secure by the adoption of the rest; and have otherwise involved the whole subject in difficulties, which, from the

* Of these, No. 1 is an amendment to the Form of Government, and Nos. 2, 3, 4, 5, 6, are amendments to the Book of Discipline. Digest, p. 587.

peculiar nature of the case, it is but fair and reasonable to suppose they could not have distinctly designed or foreseen. In this state of things your committee beg leave to submit the following resolution, as in their judgment proper to be adopted by the General Assembly, viz.:

"Whereas, the Presbyteries having failed to report their decisions upon the subject of the proposed amendments, Nos. 1, 2, 3, 4, 5, 6, as recorded in page 37 of the printed Minutes of the Assembly of last year, in the full and distinct manner contemplated in the overture submitted by that Assembly, the General Assembly do not deem it desirable to renew the said overture at the present time: Therefore, *Resolved*, That the consideration of the said proposed amendment be and the same is hereby indefinitely postponed."—*Minutes*, 1827, pp. 217, 218.

6. *Proposal to reduce the ratio of Representation; also, to make Representation Synodical, and not Presbyterial.*

"The report of the committee on Overture No. 3, viz., on reducing the ratio of representation to the General Assembly, was taken up, and after mature deliberation and amendment was adopted, and is as follows, viz.:

"That your committee, having attended to the business confided to them, and read the various documents put into their hands from several ecclesiastical bodies and ministers of our Church on the subject, and considered at large the different methods of change and ratios of representation proposed, have come with great unanimity to the following result, viz.:

"1. That a change materially reducing the present representation, by increasing its ratio, is expected and required by all, and proper to be attempted at the present Assembly.

"2. That in view of the growing number of our members and ministers, amounting already to more than twenty Synods and a hundred Presbyteries, it has become a question whether the *form* of representation, as well as the *ratio*, ought not to be changed, and the *Synodical* form substituted for the *Presbyterial;* that is to say, that hereafter the election of commissioners to the General Assembly should be by Synods and not by Presbyteries.

"3. That both questions be overtured by the present Assembly to the Presbyteries, for their consideration and votes on each distinctly, so as to secure, if possible, a constitutional result at the next Assembly, fixing the proper changes; and hence the committee recommend to the Assembly, for their adoption, the following form of overture to the Presbyteries, viz.: That every Presbytery be required to decide on the following questions:

"1. Shall the form of representation be changed from Presbyterial to Synodical?

"2. If so changed, shall the ratio of Synodical representation, omitting fractions, be *one minister* and *one elder* for every *twenty-five* ministers belonging to the Synod, with the privilege of nomination in the Presbyteries in such ratio and mode as each Synod may adopt?

"3. If not changed in form, shall the second section of the twelfth chapter of the Form of Government be so altered as to read as follows, viz.:

"The General Assembly shall consist of an equal delegation of bishops and elders from each Presbytery in the following proportion, viz.: each Presbytery consisting of not more than twenty-four ministers shall send one minister and one elder, and each Presbytery consisting of more than twenty-four ministers shall send two ministers and two elders, and in the like proportion for every twenty-four ministers in every Presbytery; and these delegates so appointed shall be styled Commissioners to the General Assembly."—*Minutes*, 1832, p. 370.

[For action on these proposals, see 8, on next page.]

7. *Proposal of an Overture in reference to calling Special Meetings of Synod.*

"*Resolved*, That the following rule be sent down to the Presbyteries for their consideration and decision; and they are hereby required to send up their decision respectively in writing to the next General Assembly, whether the same shall become a constitutional rule or not, viz.:

"When any emergency shall require a meeting of the Synod sooner than the time to which it stands adjourned, the Moderator, or, in case of his absence, death, or inability to act, the Stated Clerk shall, with the concurrence or at the request of three ministers and three elders, the ministers and elders being of at least two different Presbyteries, call a special meeting. For this purpose, he shall send a circular letter, specifying the particular business of the intended meeting, to every minister belonging to the Synod, and to the Session (if practicable) of every vacant congregation; and between the time of issuing the letters of convocation and the time of meeting shall elapse at least twenty days; and nothing shall be transacted at such special meetings besides the particular business for which the judicatory has been convened. It shall also be the duty of the Moderator to cause notice to be given in the public prints of the time and place of such intended meeting of the Synod."—*Minutes*, 1832, p. 372.

8. *Reports of the Presbyteries on these Alterations. The Ratio of Representation altered.*

"The committee appointed to receive the returns from the Presbyteries, on the proposed alterations in the Constitution, and to state the results, made the following report, which was adopted, viz.:

"There are *one hundred and eleven* Presbyteries, of which *fifty-six* are requisite to authorize any alteration of the Constitution; *forty-six* appear to have voted for, and *seventeen* against, the proposed article relative to the calling of special meetings of Synod, which proposed amendment is of course not adopted.*

"That *twenty* Presbyteries have voted in favor of a Synodical representation, in the General Assembly; and that *sixty-seven* Presbyteries have voted in favor of the proposed increase in the ratio of Presbyterial representation. *Three* Presbyteries have voted against any change, and *one* for such an alteration as the Assembly has never proposed.

"The committee therefore recommend that the Assembly, in conformity with the authority thus constitutionally intrusted to them, should adopt the following minute, viz.:

"*Resolved*, that the 2d section of the 12th chapter of the Form of Government be, and the same is hereby so amended as to read thus: "The General Assembly shall consist of an equal delegation of bishops and elders from each Presbytery, in the following proportion, viz.: each Presbytery consisting of not more than twenty-four ministers shall send one minister and one elder; and each Presbytery consisting of more than twenty-four ministers shall send two ministers and two elders, and in like proportion for every twenty-four ministers in every Presbytery; and these delegates so appointed shall be styled Commissioners to the General Assembly."—*Minutes*, 1833, pp. 400, 401.

[In 1826, the ratio had been increased from *nine* and *eighteen*, as fixed in 1821, to *twelve* and *twenty-four*.—*Minutes*, p. 168. See chap. v, sec. 4, p. 158.]

* This overture was again sent down, but a majority failed to report, and it was dropped.—*Minutes*, 1834, p. 429.

9. *Proposal to limit the appellate Jurisdiction of the Assembly.*

a. "The Assembly took up the report of the Committee to examine the reports of the Presbyteries respecting certain changes of the Constitution overtured by the last two General Assemblies."—[See *Minutes*, 1835, p. 475; 1836, pp. 247, 274.] And it was

"*Resolved*, That the following overture be sent down to all the Presbyteries, for their adoption or rejection, viz.:

"*Resolved*, That so much of the Constitution of the Church as empowers the General Assembly to issue appeals, complaints, and references, brought before them from the lower judicatories, except in cases of charges against a minister of the Gospel for error or heresy, and of process commencing in the Synods, be, and the same is hereby so amended, that hereafter the Synods, except in the cases above mentioned, be the judicatories of the last resort."—*Minutes*, 1837, p. 497.

b. "The committee to whom was referred the reports of the Presbyteries in relation to an overture sent down by the last Assembly (p. 497, Minutes), proposing a change of the Constitution, so as to make Synods, in the cases proposed, the judicatories of last resort, reported that the following twenty Presbyteries, viz., Newark, Marion, Peoria, Third New York, Athens, Columbia, Oneida, Cayuga, Delaware, Crawfordsville, Wilmington, Onondaga, Portage, Newburyport, Detroit, Monroe, Cincinnati, St. Louis, Otsego, and Sangamon have reported in favor of the proposed change; and that two Presbyteries, viz., St. Charles and Clinton, have reported against the proposed change.

"As only a minority of the Presbyteries had sent up their answer to this Assembly, it was ordered that the same overture be again sent down to all the Presbyteries, and that they be earnestly requested to send their answers to the next Assembly."—*Minutes*, 1838, p. 656.

c. "The answers of Presbyteries to the overture sent down by the last Assembly (Minutes, p. 656), in reference to stopping appeals, in ordinary cases, at the Synods, were called for, and referred to the Committee on the State of the Church."—*Minutes*, 1839, p. 12.

10. *Proposals to stop Appeals at the Synod; to hold the Assembly Triennially; and to authorize pro re nata Meetings of the Assembly.*

"The Committee on the State of the Church having had before them sundry petitions and memorials requesting a modification of our present ecclesiastical organization, recommend that the following overtures be sent down to the Presbyteries for their action:

"1. Shall the Constitution be so amended as to limit the power of the General Assembly, and make the Synods in all cases the courts of ultimate appeal and final authoritative jurisdiction, and the General Assembly an advisory council for all the churches?

"2. Shall the Constitution be so amended as to require the General Assembly to hold its sessions triennially, as a bond of union between the churches, retaining its present functions, with the exceptions specified in the first overture?

"3. Shall the last moderator and the stated and permanent clerks be empowered to call a *pro re nata* meeting of the General Assembly, in case of any emergency which, in their opinion, solemnly demands such meeting: providing that four full months shall intervene between the call and the time of holding such meeting?

"The committee further recommend that, should the Presbyteries agree to the amendments above proposed, the next General Assembly make the arrangement of Synods, and fix the ratio of representation best adapted to the organization of the Church, as thus modified. The plan which best commends itself to the minds of the committee is substantially that proposed, in the year 1832, by the Rev. Dr. Alexander, and published in the Princeton Biblical Repertory, vol. iv, of the New Series, pp. 28–47."—*Minutes*, 1839, p. 27.

11. *Answers of the Presbyteries, affirming the proposed Amendments. Alterations in the Constitution made in accordance.*

"The Committee [on Polity] report:

"1. That the overtures sent down to the Presbyteries by the Assembly of 1839 have been affirmed in the responses, all three of them: there being 59 affirmatives for the first overture; 57 for the second; and for the third, 44.

"The whole number of our Presbyteries last year was 85; of which, consequently, the lowest majority is 43; and this number the committee have therefore assumed as their criterion of the majority, according to the words of the Constitution. See Form of Government, chap. xii, sec. 6.

"2. That the paragraph *appended* to the overtures having been also affirmed by 49 votes, the committee have digested their results accordingly, and recommend that the Assembly now rule and ordain the following changes in the polity of the Presbyterian Church in these United States, viz.:

"(1.) That the ratio of Presbyterial representation be reduced to its minimum, altering our Form of Government, chap. xii, sec. 2, so that said section shall be hereafter alone and in all, and read as follows, viz.: The General Assembly shall consist of an equal delegation of bishops and ruling elders from the Presbyteries, in the simple proportion of one minister and one elder from each Presbytery; and these commissioners so appointed shall be styled, '*Commissioners to the General Assembly.*'" [See chap. v, sec. 4, p. 159.]

"(2.) That Section 7 of the same chapter (xii) be so altered in its first sentence as to read as follows, viz.: 'The General Assembly shall meet triennially, or once in three years, and ordinarily on the third Thursday of the month of May in every third year.

"(3.) That Section 8 of the same be so practically modified, and every other part and provision of the Constitution with it conformably, that the present changes, as hereinabove specified, shall be maintained inviolate, and shall go into full force and operation as the Constitution of the Presbyterian Church in the United States of America."—*Minutes*, 1840, pp. 16, 17.

12. *Proposal to return to Annual Assemblies, and to restore Appellate Power to the Assembly, so far as it respects Ministers.*

a. "Ordered, on motion of the Rev. S. Haynes, that the following overture be sent down to the several Presbyteries for their action, and that they report to the meeting of this Assembly in 1847: 'Shall the Form of Government, chap. xii, sec. 7, be so altered as to require the General Assembly to hold its sessions *annually* instead of *triennially*, retaining its present functions."—*Minutes*, 1846, p. 30.

"The Committee on Church Polity presented a report recommending that the following overture be sent down to the Presbyteries for their action: 'Shall appellate power be restored to the Assembly, so far as respects ministers?' And the report was adopted."—*Minutes*, 1846, p. 35.

13. *The Proposals more clearly defined. Revision of the Standards committed to a Committee.*

"The following resolution was adopted:

"Whereas, there is a doubt about the propriety of the *forms of over-*

tures submitted to the Presbyteries by this Assembly, at its sessions in Philadelphia; therefore,

"*Resolved,* That the Presbyteries be requested to forward their reply to them in the following form:

"1. Shall Section 7th of Chapter xi, Form of Government, be altered so as to read 'annually,' instead of 'triennially?'

"2. Shall the first sentence of Section 7th of Chapter xii, Form of Government, be altered so as to read, 'The General Assembly shall meet at least once in every year,' or shall it read, 'The General Assembly shall meet at least once in every third year?'

"3. Shall paragraph 2d of Chapter vii, Book of Discipline, be altered so as, after the word 'Synod,' to insert the words, 'except in cases affecting the character of ministers of the Gospel?'

"4. Shall paragraph 2d of Section 3 of Chapter vii, Book of Discipline, be altered so as to prefix to it the words, 'All appeals, except in cases affecting the character of ministers of the Gospel, shall terminate with the Synod?' and

"5. Shall paragraph 4th, of Section 4 of Chapter vii, Book of Discipline, be altered so as to annex to it the words, 'And all complaints shall terminate with the Synods, except in cases affecting the character of ministers of the Gospel?'

"On motion of Rev. I. Ingraham, it was

"*Resolved, unanimously,* That in the judgment of this Assembly, *the Constitution, as contained in the book which is now authenticated to the churches,* is authoritative and binding, until it shall be regularly amended by proper overtures submitted to the Presbyteries.

"The remainder of the report on the revision of the standards was recommitted, with instructions to report to the next Assembly."—*Minutes,* 1847, pp. 148, 149.

14. *The Overtures* 1 *and* 2 *respecting Annual Assemblies adopted. Overtures* 3, 4, *and* 5 *on Appeals negatived.*

"The Committee on the Polity of the Church reported on the subject of the overtures sent down by the last Assembly:

"That it appears from the roll that there are one hundred and four Presbyteries connected with the Assembly; of which fifty-three are a majority; that eighty-one Presbyteries have sent in their answers to the overtures, and twenty-three have not.

"That to the first and second overtures, which respect the return to Annual Assemblies, sixty-three Presbyteries have answered in the affirmative, and twenty-six have answered in the negative.

"These overtures are affirmed, and the Constitution is changed accordingly, viz.:

"1. Section 7 of Chapter xi,* Form of Government, is altered, so as to read 'annually' instead of 'triennially.'

"2. The first sentence of Section 7 of Chapter xii, Form of Government, is so altered as to read: 'The General Assembly shall meet at least once in every year,' instead of 'The General Assembly shall meet at least triennially, or once in every third year.'

"To the overtures Nos. 3, 4, and 5, pertaining to appeals in the case of ministers, forty Presbyteries have answered in the *affirmative*, and forty-seven Presbyteries have answered in the *negative*.

"The changes proposed by these overtures are, therefore, not adopted."—*Minutes*, 1849, p. 175.

15. *Report on Changes of the Constitution. Proposal to Restore it, as in* 1840. *Overtures sent down.*

In 1849, the following paper was adopted in reference to the changes made in the Constitution:

"Whereas, this General Assembly has ascertained, as is fully set forth in the report of the Committee on the Revision of the Standards (which is hereby directed to be published in the Appendix to the Minutes), that the alterations made in the Constitutional Rules, by a Committee of the Assembly of 1840, were made in a manner so irregular and unconstitutional as to occasion great doubt and perplexity as to their authenticity;

"And whereas, one of the three overtures on which these alterations were based, relating to the frequency of the meetings of the General Assembly, has now been constitutionally reversed:

"And whereas, serious doubt has been expressed as to the passage of the third overture of the Assembly of 1839; and the occasion for its passage has now been taken away by the restoration of annual assemblies:

"And whereas, a change in the basis of representation in General Assembly, as established in a constitutional manner by the Assembly of

* This refers to the Book as altered in 1840. Section 7 is Section 6 of the present Book.

1833, has never been submitted to the Presbyteries and constitutionally adopted:

"Therefore, in order to ascertain the wishes of the Presbyteries more clearly and fully, as to the expediency of restoring the Constitution to its condition previous to 1840, and, if this be thought inexpedient, in order to incorporate the principles then introduced in a perfectly regular and constitutional manner:

"*Resolved*, That the Book be restored to the form in which it was published previous to the year 1840, and that the following overtures be submitted to the Presbyteries:

"I. LIMITATION OF APPEAL.

"1. Shall Form of Government, chapter xii, section 4, be altered so as to omit the words 'appeals and,' before the word 'references?'

"2. Shall Book of Discipline, chapter vii, section 2, be altered so as to insert the words 'the General Assembly and the Synod in judicial cases,' instead of the words 'the highest?'

"3. Shall Book of Discipline, chapter vii, section 3, subsec. 2, be altered so as to read, 'any judicatory not higher than a Synod,' instead of 'a higher judicatory?'

"4. Shall Book of Discipline, chapter vii, section 4, subsec. 1, be altered so as to read, 'any judicatory inferior to a Synod,' instead of 'an inferior judicatory?'

"II. PRO RE NATA ASSEMBLIES.

"5. In Form of Government, chapter xii, shall a new section be introduced after section 7, as follows: 'VIII. The last moderator and the stated and permanent clerks are empowered to call a *pro re nata* meeting of the General Assembly, in case of any emergency, which, in their opinion, demands such a meeting, by circular letter, addressed to each of the Presbyteries, at least four months before the time of holding such meeting?'—and the subsequent section be numbered ix instead of viii?

"III. REPRESENTATION IN ASSEMBLY.

"6. Shall Form of Government, chapter xii, section 2, be altered so as to read: 'The General Assembly shall consist of an equal delegation of bishops and elders, one from each Presbytery; and these delegates so appointed, shall be styled *Commissioners to the General Assembly.*

"*Resolved further*, That till an expression of the will of the Presbyteries in regard to these overtures be obtained, it be understood that all appeals and complaints shall terminate with the Synods, and that the basis of representation in the Assembly shall be the same as at present." —*Minutes*, 1849, pp. 183, 184.

[See Appendix to Minutes, pp. 195–212.]

16. *These Overtures rejected and the Constitution restored as before the Division.*

"The Committee on the Polity of the Church made a report in reference to the 'Answers of Presbyteries to the overtures sent down by the last Assembly,' which was adopted, and is as follows:

"It appears from the roll, that there are one hundred and two Presbyteries connected with the Assembly; that eighty-seven Presbyteries have sent up their answers to the first three overtures, on the subject of the 'Limitation of Appeals,' and fifteen have not; and that of these, thirty Presbyteries have answered in the affirmative, and fifty-seven Presbyteries have answered in the negative.

"That to the fourth overture, on the subject of 'Complaints,' the answers vary only by the addition of the Presbytery of Pataskala to the number of those answering in the negative; thus making the number of Presbyteries replying in the affirmative to this overture, twenty-nine; and in the negative, fifty-eight.

"That to the fifth overture, on the subject of 'Pro re nata Meetings of the Assembly,' eighty-six Presbyteries have sent answers, the same as have replied to the other overtures, with the exception of the Presbytery of Newark; and that of these only three Presbyteries have answered in the affirmative, viz., Champlain, Erie, and Hanover; the remaining eighty-three having answered in the negative.

"That to the sixth overture, on the subject of the 'Ratio of Representation in the Assembly,' answers have been returned by eighty-four Presbyteries, the same as before, with the exception of the Presbyteries of Newark, Grand River, and Huron; and that of these, twenty-eight Presbyteries have answered in the affirmative, and fifty-six Presbyteries have answered the same overture in the negative. The Assembly therefore declares that a majority of the whole number of Presbyteries has decided against each and all of the proposed changes in the Constitution.

The Book therefore remains as in 1840; or, as it was before the division of the church."—*Minutes*, 1850, pp. 317, 318.

NOTE.—The amendments made or proposed have never affected the Confession of Faith proper, the Larger and Shorter Catechisms, or the Directory for Worship. These remain, word for word and letter for letter, as they were adopted at the formation of the Assembly in 1788.

SECTION 7.—RULES FOR JUDICATORIES.*

[See page 172 for Amendments.]

1. The moderator shall take the chair precisely at the hour to which the judicatory stands adjourned; shall immediately call the members to order; and, on the appearance of a quorum, shall open the session with prayer.

2. If a quorum be assembled at the hour appointed, and the moderator be absent, the last moderator present shall be requested to take his place without delay.

3. If a quorum be not assembled at the hour appointed, any two members shall be competent to adjourn, from time to time, that an opportunity may be given for a quorum to assemble.

4. After calling the roll, and marking the absentees, the minutes of the last sitting shall be read, and, if requisite, corrected.

5. It shall be the duty of the moderator at all times to preserve order, and to endeavor to conduct all business before the judicatory to a speedy and proper result.

6. It shall be the duty of the clerk, as soon as possible after the commencement of the sessions of every judicatory, to form a complete roll of the members present, and put the same into the hands of the moderator. And it shall also be the duty of the clerk, whenever any additional members take their seats, to add their names, in their proper places, to the said roll.

* The following rules not having been submitted to the Presbyteries, make no part of the Constitution of the Presbyterian Church. Yet the General Assembly of 1821, considering uniformity in proceedings in all the subordinate judicatories as greatly conducive to order and dispatch of business, and having revised and approved these rules, recommend them to the Synods, Presbyteries, and Sessions as a system of regulations which, if they think proper, may be advantageously adopted by them.

7. It shall be the duty of the clerk immediately to file all papers in the order in which they have been read, with proper indorsements, and to keep them in perfect order.

8. It shall be the duty of the moderator carefully to keep notes of the several articles of business which may be assigned to particular days, and to call them up at the time appointed.

9. The moderator may speak to points of order in preference to other members, rising from his seat for that purpose; and shall decide questions of order, subject to an appeal to the judicatory by any two members.

10. Business left unfinished at the last sitting is, ordinarily, to be taken up first.

11. A motion made must be seconded, and afterwards repeated by the moderator, or read aloud before it is debated; and every motion shall be reduced to writing, if the moderator or any member require it.

12. Any member who shall have made a motion, shall have liberty to withdraw it, with the consent of his second, before any debate has taken place thereon, but not afterwards, without the leave of the judicatory.

13. On questions of order, adjournment, postponement, or commitment, no member shall speak more than once. On all other questions, each member may speak twice, but not oftener, without express leave of the judicatory.

14. When a question is under debate, no motion shall be received unless to amend it, to commit it, to postpone it for the previous question, or to adjourn.

15. An amendment may be moved on any motion, and shall be decided before the original motion.

16. If a motion under debate contains several parts, any two members may have it divided, and a question taken on each part.

17. The previous question shall be put in this form: *Shall the main question be now put?* It shall only be admitted when demanded by a majority of the members present; and its effect shall be to put an end to all debate, and bring the body to a direct vote; first, on a motion to commit the subject under consideration (if such motion shall have been made); secondly (if the motion to commit does not prevail), on pending amendments; and, lastly, upon the main question.

18. The call for the previous question shall not be debatable.

19. A question shall not be again called up or reconsidered at the same sessions of the judicatory at which it has been decided, unless by

the consent of two-thirds of the members who were present at the decision; and unless the motion to reconsider be made and seconded by persons who voted with the majority.

20. A subject which has been indefinitely postponed, either by the operation of the previous question or by a direct motion for indefinite postponement, shall not be again called up during the same sessions of the judicatory, unless by the consent of three-fourths of the members who were present at the decision.

21. Every member, when speaking, shall address himself to the moderator, and shall treat his fellow-members, and especially the moderator, with decorum and respect. Nor shall members address one another, nor any person present, but through the moderator.

22. Without express permission, no member of a judicatory, while business is going on, shall engage in private conversation.

23. No speaker shall be interrupted unless he be out of order, or for the purpose of correcting mistakes or misrepresentations.

24. It is indispensable that members of ecclesiastical judicatories maintain great gravity and dignity while judicially convened; that they attend closely in their speeches to the subject under consideration, and avoid prolix and desultory harangues; and, when they deviate from the subject, it is the privilege of any member and the duty of the moderator to call them to order.

25. No member in the course of debate shall be allowed to indulge in personal reflections.

26. If more than one member rise to speak at the same time, the member who is most distant from the moderator's chair shall speak first.

27. When more than three members of the judicatory shall be standing at the same time, the moderator shall require all to take their seats, the person only excepted who may be speaking.

28. If any member act in any respect in a disorderly manner, it shall be the privilege of any member and the duty of the moderator to call him to order.

29. If any member consider himself as aggrieved by a decision of the moderator, it shall be his privilege to appeal to the judicatory; and the question on such appeal shall be taken without debate.

30. Members ought not, without weighty reasons, to decline voting, as this practice might leave the decision of very interesting questions to a small proportion of the judicatory. Silent members, unless excused from voting, must be considered as acquiescing with the majority.

31. It is the duty of the moderator to appoint all committees, except in those cases in which the judicatory shall decide otherwise.

32. The person first named on any committee shall be considered as the chairman thereof, whose duty it shall be to convene the committee; and, in case of his absence or inability to act, the second named member shall take his place and perform his duties.

33. When various motions are made, with respect to the filling of blanks with particular numbers or times, the question shall always be first taken on the highest number and the longest time.

34. When the moderator has commenced taking the vote, no further debate or remark shall be admitted, unless there has evidently been a mistake; in which case, the mistake shall be rectified, and the moderator shall recommence taking the vote.

35. When a vote is taken by ballot in any judicatory, the moderator shall vote with the other members; but he shall not vote in any other case unless the judicatory be equally divided; when, if he do not choose to vote, the question shall be lost.

36. The yeas and nays on any question shall not be recorded, unless it be required by one-third of the members present.

37. All judicatories have a right to sit in private on business which, in their judgment, ought not to be matter of public speculation.

38. Besides the right to sit judicially in private, whenever they think it right to do so, all judicatories have a right to hold what are commonly called "interlocutory meetings," or a sort of committees of the whole judicatory, in which members may freely converse together without the formalities which are usually necessary in judicial proceedings.

39. Whenever a judicatory is about to sit in a judicial capacity, it shall be the duty of the moderator solemnly to announce from the chair that the body is about to pass to the consideration of the business assigned for trial; and to enjoin on the members to recollect and regard their high character, as judges of a court of Jesus Christ, and the solemn duty in which they are about to act.

40. In all process before a judicatory, where there is an accuser or prosecutor, it is expedient that there be a committee of the judicatory appointed (provided the number of members be sufficient to admit of it without inconvenience), who shall be called the *Judicial Committee;* and whose duty it shall be to digest and arrange all the papers, and to prescribe, under the direction of the judicatory, the whole order of the proceedings. The members of this committee shall be entitled, not-

withstanding their performance of this duty, to sit and vote in the cause as members of the judicatory.

41. But in cases of process on the ground of *general rumor*, where there is, of course, no particular accuser, there may be a committee appointed (if convenient) who shall be called the *Committee of Prosecution*, and who shall conduct the whole cause on the part of the prosecution. The members of this committee shall not be permitted to sit in judgment in the case.

42. No member shall retire from any judicatory without the leave of the moderator, nor withdraw from it to return home without the consent of the judicatory.

43. The moderator of every judicatory above the church Session, in finally closing its sessions, in addition to prayer may cause to be sung an appropriate psalm or hymn, and shall pronounce the apostolic benediction.

APPENDIX.

LEGAL DECISIONS.

New Trial Accorded.

After the verdict of the jury in favor of the plaintiffs (given in connection with the charge of Judge Rogers, upon page 530) a motion for a new trial was made on the behalf of the defendants (the "Old School" body), before the Supreme Court of Pennsylvania in banc, and on May 8th, 1839, Chief Justice Gibson delivered the opinion of the Court, awarding a new trial. Although this decision is not upon the Minutes of the General Assembly, it is needful to a fair and full presentation of the legal history of the case. It was as follows:

Opinion of the Court.

"GIBSON, C. J.—To extricate the question from the multifarious mass of irrelevant matter in which it is enclosed, we must, in the first place, ascertain the specific character of the General Assembly, and the relation it bears to the corporation which is the immediate subject of our cognizance. This Assembly has been called a *quasi* corporation; of which it has not a feature. A *quasi* corporation has capacity to sue and to be sued as an artificial person; which the Assembly has not. It is also established by law; which the Assembly is not. Neither is the Assembly a particular order or rank in the corporation, though the latter was created for its convenience; such, for instance, as the shareholders of a bank or joint-stock company, who are an integrant part of the body. It is a segregated association, which, though it is the reproductive organ of corporated successions, is not itself a member of the body; and in that respect it is anomalous. Having no corporate quality in itself, it is not a subject of our corrective jurisdiction, or of our scrutiny, further than to ascertain how far its organic structure may bear on the question of its personal identity or individuality. By the charter of the corporation, of which it is the handmaid and nurse, it has a limited capacity to create vacancies in it, and an unlimited power over the form and manner of choice in filling them. It would be sufficient for the civil tribunals, therefore, that the Assembled Commissioners had constituted an actual body; and that it had made its appointment in its own way, without regard to its fairness in respect to its members; with this limitation, however, that it had the assent of the constitutional majority, of which the official act of authentication would be, at least, *prima facie* evidence. It would be immaterial to the legality of the choice that the majority had expelled the minority, provided a majority of the whole body concurred in the choice. This may be safely predicated of an undivided Assembly, and it would be an unerring test in the case of a division, could a quorum not be constituted of less than such a majority; but unfortunately, a quorum of the General Assembly may be constituted of a very small minority, so that two, or even more, distinct parts may have all the external organs of legitimate existence. Hence, where, as in this instance, the members have formed themselves into separate bodies, numerically sufficient for corporate capacity and organic action, it becomes necessary to ascertain how far either of them was formed in obedience to the conventional law of the Association, which, for that purpose only, is to be treated as a rule of civil obligation.

"The division which, for purposes of designation, it is convenient to call the Old School party, was certainly organized in obedience to the established order; and, to legitimate the separate organization of its rival, in contravention, as it certainly was, of everything like precedent, would require the presentation of a very urgent emergency. At the stated time and place for the opening of the session, the parties assembled, without any ostensible division; and, when the organization of the whole had proceeded to a certain point, by the instrumentality of the Moderator of the preceding session, who, for that purpose, was the constitutional organ, a provisional Moderator was suddenly chosen, by a minority of those who could be entitled to vote, including the exscinded Commissioners. The question on the motion to elect, was put, not by the Chair, but by the mover himself; after which, the seceding party elected a permanent Moderator, and immediately withdrew, leaving the other party to finish its process of organization, by the choice of its Moderator for the session.

"In justification of this apparent irregularity, it is urged that the constitutional Moderator had refused an appeal to the Commissioners in attendance, from his decision, which had excluded from the roll the names of certain Commissioners who had been unconstitutionally severed, as it is alleged, from the Presbyterian connection by a vote of the preceding session. It is conceded by the argument, that if the Synods with the dependent Presbyteries by which those Commissioners were sent, had been constitutionally dissolved, the motion was one which the Moderator was not bound to put, or the Commissioners to notice; and that whatever implication of assent to the decision which ensued, might otherwise be deduced from the silence of those who refused to speak out, about which it will be necessary to say something in the sequel, there was no room for any such implication in the particular instance. It would follow also, that there was no pretence for the deposal of the Moderator, if indeed such a thing could be legitimated by any circumstances, for refusing an appeal from his exclusion of those who had not color of title, and consequently, that what else might be reform, would be revolution. And this leads to an inquiry into the constitutionality of the act of excision.

"The sentence of excision, as it has been called, was nothing else than an ordinance of dissolution. It bore that the Synods in question, having been formed and attached to the body of the Presbyterian Church under, and in execution of, the Plan of Union, 'be, and are hereby declared to be, out of the ecclesiastical connection of the Presbyterian Church in the United States of America; and that they are not, in form or in fact, an integral portion of said Church.' Now, it will not be said that if the dissolved Synods had no other basis than the Plan of Union, they did not necessarily fall along with it, and it is not pretended that the Assembly was incompetent to repeal the union prospectively, but it is contended that the repeal could not impair rights of membership which had grown up under it. On the other hand, it is contended that the Plan of Union was unconstitutional and void from the beginning, because it was not submitted to the Presbyteries for their sanction; and that no right of membership could spring from it. But viewed, not as a constitutional regulation which implies permanency of duration, but as a temporary expedient, it acquired the force of a law without the ratification of those bodies. It was evidently not intended to be permanent, and it consequently was constitutionally enacted and constitutionally repealed by an ordinary act of legislation; and those Synods which had their root in it, could not be expected to survive it. There never was a design to attempt an amalgamation of ecclesiastical principles which are as immiscible as water and oil; much less to effect a commixture of them only at particular geographical points. Such an attempt would have compromised a principle at the very root of Presbyterial government, which requires that the officers of the Church be set apart by special ordination for the work. Now, the character of the Plan is palpable, not only in its title and provisions, but in the minute of its introduction into the Assembly. We find in the proceedings of 1801, page 256, that a committee was raised 'to consider and digest a Plan of Government for the Churches in the *new settlements*, agreeably to the proposal of the General Association of Connecticut;' and that the plan adopted in conformity to its report, is called 'A Plan of Union for the new settlements.' The avowed object of it was to prevent alienation,—in other words, the affiliation of Presbyterians in other churches, by suffering those who were yet too few and too poor for the maintenance of a minister, temporarily to call to their assistance the members of a sect who differed from them in principles, not of faith, but of ecclesiastical government. To that end, Presbyterian ministers were suffered to preach to Congregational churches, while Presbyterian churches were suffered to settle Congregational ministers; and mixed congregations were allowed to settle a Presbyterian or a Congregational minister at their election, but under a Plan of Government and discipline adapted to the circumstances. Surely this was not intended to outlast the inability of the respective sects to provide separately for themselves, or to perpetuate the innovations on Presbyterial government which it was calculated to produce. It was obviously a missionary arrangement from the first; and they who built up Presbyteries and Synods on the basis of it, had no reason to expect that their structures would survive it, or that Congregationalists might, by force of it, gain a foothold in the Presbyterian Church, despite of Presbyterial discipline. They embraced it with all its defeasible properties plainly put before them; and the power which constituted it might fairly repeal it, and dissolve the bodies that had grown out of it, whenever the good of the Church should seem to require it.

"Could the Synods, however, be dissolved by a legislative act? I know not how they could have been legitimately dissolved by any other. The Assembly is a homogeneous body, uniting in itself, without separation of parts, the legislative, executive, and judicial functions of the government; and its acts are referable to the one or the other of them, according to the capacity in which it sat when they were performed. Now, had the exscinded Synods been cut off by a judicial sentence without hearing or notice, the act would have been contrary to the cardinal principles of natural justice, and consequently void. But though it was at first resolved to proceed judicially, the measure was abandoned; probably because it came to be perceived that the Synods had committed no offence.

"A glance at the Plan of Union is enough to convince us that the disorder had come in with the sanction of the Assembly itself. The first article directed *missionaries* (the word is significant), to the new settlements to promote a good understanding betwixt the kindred sects. The second and third permitted a Presbyterian congregation to settle a Congregational minister, or a Presbyterian minister to be settled by a Congregational church; but these provided for no recognition of the people in charge as a part of the Presbyterian body—at least they gave them no representation in its government. But the fourth allowed a mixed congregation to settle a minister of either denomination; and it committed the government of it to a standing committee, but with a right to appeal to the body of male communicants if the appellant were a Congregationalist, or to the Presbytery if he were a Presbyterian. Now, it is evident the Assembly designed that every such congregation should belong to a Presbytery as an integrant part of it, for if its minister were a Congregationalist, in no way connected with the Presbyterian Church, it would be impossible to refer the appellate jurisdiction to any Presbytery in particular. This alone would show that it was designed to place such a congregation in ecclesiastical connection with the Presbytery of the district; but this is not all. It was expressly provided in conclusion, that if the 'said standing committee of any church shall depute one of themselves to attend the Presbytery, he may have the same right to sit and act in the Presbytery as a ruling elder of the Presbyterian Church.' For what purpose if the congregation were not in Presbyterial fellowship?

"It is said that this *jus representationis* was predicated of the appeal precedently mentioned; and that the exercise of it was to be restrained to the trial of it. The words, however, were predicated without restriction; and an implied limitation of their meaning would impute to the Assembly the injustice of allowing a party to sit in his own cause, by introducing into the composition of the appellate court a part of the subordinate one. That such an implication would be inconsistent with the temper displayed by the Assembly on other occasions, is proved by the order which it took as early as 1791, in the case of an appeal from the sentence of the Synod of Philadelphia, whose members it prevented from voting on the question (Assembly's Digest, p. 332), as well as by its general provision, that 'members of a judicatory may not vote in the superior judicatory on a question of approving or disapproving their records.' (*Id.* page 333.)

"The principle has since become a rule of the Constitution, as appears by the Book of Discipline, chap. vii, sec. 3, paragraph 12. As the representatives of those anomalous congregations therefore could not sit in judgment on their own controversies, it is pretty clear that it was intended they should be represented generally, else they would not be represented at all in the councils of the Church, by those who might not be Presbyterians; and that to effect it, the principle of Presbyterial ordination was to be relaxed, as regards both the ministry and eldership; and it is equally clear that had the Synods been cited to answer for the consequent relaxation as an offence, they might have triumphantly appeared at the bar of the Assembly with the Plan of Union in their hand. That body, however, resorted to the only constitutional remedy in its power; it fell back, so to speak, on its legislative jurisdiction, in the exercise of which the Synods were completely represented and heard by their commissioners.

"Now the apparent injustice of the measure arises from the contemplation of it as a judicial sentence pronounced against parties who were neither cited nor heard; which it evidently was not. Even as a legislative act, it may have been a hard one, though certainly constitutional, and strictly just. It was impossible to eradicate the disorder by anything less than a dissolution of those bodies with whose existence its roots were so intertwined as to be inseparable from it, leaving their elements to form new and less heterogeneous combinations. Though deprived of Presbyterial organization, the Presbyterian parts were not excluded from the Church, provision being made for them, by allowing them to attach themselves to the nearest Presbytery.

"It is said there is not sufficient evidence to establish the fact that the exscinded Synods had actually been constituted on the Plan of Union, in order to have given the Assembly even legislative jurisdiction. The testimony of the Rev. Mr. Squier, however, shows that in some of the three which were within the State ot New York, congregations were sometimes constituted without elders; and the Synod of the Western Reserve, when charged with delinquency on that head, instead of denying the fact, promptly pointed to the Plan of Union for its justification. But what matters it whether the fact were actually what the Assembly supposed it to be? If that body proceeded in good faith, the validity of its enactment cannot depend on the justness of its conclusion. We have, as already remarked, no authority to rejudge its judgments on their merits; and this principle was asserted with conclusive force by the presiding judge who tried the cause. Upon an objection made to an inquiry into the composition of the Presbytery of Medina, it was ruled that 'with the reasons for the proceedings of 1837 (the act of excision), we have nothing to do. We are to determine only what was done: the reasons of those who did it are immaterial. If the acts complained of were within the jurisdiction of the Assembly, their decision must be final, though they decided wrong.' This was predicated of a judicial jurisdiction, but the principle is necessarily as applicable to jurisdiction for purposes of legislation. I cite the passage, however, to show that after a successful resistance to the introduction of evidence of the fact, it lies not with the relators to allege the want of it.

"If, then, the Synods in question were constitutionally dissolved, the Presbyteries of which they had been composed were, at least for purposes of representation, dissolved along with them; for no Presbytery can be in connection with the General Assembly, unless it be at the same time subordinate to a Synod also in connection with it, because an appeal from its judgment can reach the tribunal of the last resort only through that channel. It is immaterial that the Presbyteries are the electors: a Synod is a part of the machinery which is indispensable to the existence of every branch of the Church. It appears, therefore, that the commissioners from the exscinded Synods were not entitled to seats in the Assembly, and that their names were properly excluded from the roll.

"The inquiry might be rested here: for if there were no color of right in them, there was no color of right in the adversary proceedings which were founded on their exclusion. But even if their title were clear, the refusal of an appeal from the decision of the Moderator, would be no ground for the degradation of the officer at the call of a minority; nor could it impose on the majority an obligation to vote on a question put unofficially, and out of the usual course. To all questions put by the established organ, it is the duty of every member to respond, or be counted with the greater number, because he is supposed to have assented beforehand to the result of the process pre-established to ascertain the general will; but the rule of implied assent is certainly inapplicable to a measure which, when justifiable even by extreme necessity, is essentially revolutionary, and based on no pre-established process of ascertainment whatever.

"To apply it to an extreme case of inorganic action, as was done here, might work the degradation of any presiding officer in our legislative halls, by the motion and actual vote of a single member, sustained by the constructive votes of all the rest; and though such an enterprise may never be attempted, it shows the danger of resorting to a conventional rule, when the body is to be resolved into its original elements, and its rules and conventions to be superseded, by the very motion. For this reason, the choice of a Moderator, to supplant the officer in the chair, even if he were removable at the pleasure of the commissioners, would seem to have been unconstitutional.

"But he was not removable by them, because he had not derived his office from them; nor was he answerable to them for the use of his power. He was not *their* Moderator. He was the mechanical instrument of their organization; and till that was accomplished, they were subject to his rule—not he to theirs. They were chosen by the authority of his mandate, and with the power of self-organization, only in the event of his absence at the opening of the session. Corporeally present, but refusing to perform his function, he might be deemed constructively absent, for constitutional purposes, insomuch that the commissioners might proceed to the choice of a substitute without him; but not if he had entered on the performance of his task; and the reason is that the decision of such questions as were prematurely passed here, is proper for the decision of the body when prepared for organic action, which it cannot be before it is fully constituted and under the presidency of its own Moderator, the Moderator of the preceding session being *functus officio*. There can be no occasion for its action sooner; for though the commissioners are necessarily called upon to vote for their Moderator, their action is not organic, but individual. Dr. Mason's motion and appeal, though the clerks had reported the roll, were premature; for though it is declared in the twelfth chapter of the Form of Government, that no commissioner shall deliberate or vote before his name shall have been enrolled, it follows not that the capacity, consummated by enrolment, was expected to be exercised during any part of the process of organization, but the choice of a Moderator; and moreover, the provision may have been intended for the case of a commissioner appearing for the first time, when the House was constituted.

"Many instances may doubtless be found among the minutes, of motions entertained previously, for our public bodies, whether legislative or judicial, secular or ecclesiastical, are too prone to forget the golden precept—'Let all things be done decently and in order.' But these are merely instances of irregularity which have passed, *sub silentio*, and which cannot change a rule of positive enactment. It seems, then, that an appeal from the decision of the Moderator did not lie; and that he incurred no penalty by the disallowance of it. The title of the exscinded commissioners could be determined only by the action of the House, which could not be had before its organization was complete; and in the meantime he was bound, as the executive instrument of the preceding Assembly, to put its ordinance into execution: for to the actual Assembly, and not to the Moderator of the preceding one, it belonged to repeal it.

"It would be decisive, however, that the motion, as it was proposed, purported not to be in fact a question of degradation for the disallowance of an appeal, but one of new and independent organization. It was, ostensibly as well as actually, a measure of transcendental power, whose purpose was to treat the ordinance of the preceding Assembly as a nullity, and its Moderator as a nonentity. It had been prepared for the event avowedly before the meeting. The witnesses concur that it was propounded as a measure of original organization transcending the customary order; and not as a recourse to the *ultima ratio* for a specific violation of it. The ground of the motion as it was opened by the mover, was not the disallowance of an appeal, which alone could afford a pretext of forfeiture, but the fact of exclusion. To affect silent members with an implication of assent, however, the ground of the motion and nature of the question must be so explicitly put before them as to prevent misconception or mistake; and the remarks that heralded the question in this instance, pointed at, not a removal of the presiding incumbent, but a separate organization to be accomplished with the least practicable interruption of the business in hand; and if they indicated anything else they were deceptive. The measure was proposed not as that of the body, but as the measure of a party; and the cause assigned for not having proposed it elsewhere, was that individuals of the party had been instructed by counsel that the purpose of it could not be legally accomplished in any other place. No witness speaks of a motion to degrade; and the rapidity of the process by which the choice of a substitute, not a successor, was affected, left no space for reflection or debate. Now before the passive commissioners could be affected by acquiescence implied from their silence, it ought to have appeared that they were apprised of what was going on; but it appears that even an attentive ear-witness was unable to understand what was done. The whole scene was one of unprecedented haste, insomuch that it is still a matter of doubt how the questions were put. Now, though these facts were fairly put to the jury, it is impossible not to see that the verdict is, in this respect, manifestly against the current of the evidence.

"Other corroborative views have been suggested; but it is difficult to compress a decision of the leading points in this case into the old-fashioned limits of a judicial opinion. The preceding observations, however, are deemed enough to show the grounds on which we hold that the Assembly which met in the First Presbyterian Church was not the legitimate successor of the Asembly of 1837; and that the defendants are not guilty of the usurpation with which they are charged.

"Rule for a new trial made absolute.

"ROGERS, J.—After the patient and impartial investigation, by me, of this cause, at *Nisi Prius*, and in bank, I have nothing at this time to add, except that my opinion remains unchanged on all the points ruled at the trial. This explanation is deemed requisite, in justice to myself, and because it has become necessary (in a case, in some respects without precedent, and presenting some extraordinary features) to prevent misapprehension and misrepresentation."

York Church Case.

[The first case that was tried, after the delivering of the foregoing Opinion, was that of the Presbyterian Church, at York, Pa. A minority of that church, adhering to that body which had been pronounced by this Opinion of the Court to be "the General Assembly of the Presbyterian Church in the United States of America," seceded from the congregation, and, worshipping in another place, claimed to be "The English Presbyterian Congregation in the Borough of York,"—its chartered name,—and as such elected trustees, and sued for the church property.

The case came on for trial in the court below, and was decided in favor of the Congregation (the majority). The minority appealed to the Supreme Court, and the Opinion of that court was delivered by Chief

Justice Gibson. It materially modifies his former Opinion, and is as follows (see 1 Watts & Sergeant's Reports, p. 35):

"This ejectment is brought in the name of the corporation by a minority of the congregation, who, having withdrawn from its stated worship in the church building, insist that the majority have forfeited their corporate rights by dissolving the connection of the congregation with the Presbytery of Carlisle, and the primitive General Assembly; and to understand the grounds on which they have placed the controversy, it is necessary to state the case with its circumstances.

"The congregation was formed in 1762; for it was proved at the trial that ministerial supplies were furnished in that year by the Presbytery of Donegal, and subsequently by the Presbytery of Carlisle, under whose care it remained until the late convulsion of the Presbyterian body induced it, while disclaiming all intention to become an independent church, to decline for the present the jurisdiction of the conflicting judicatories. Its pulpit seems not to have been regularly filled till the installation of the Rev. Dr. Cathcart, in 1793. Such were its origin and ecclesiastical relations. The property in contest was conveyed by John Penn, Sr., and John Penn, Jr., late proprietaries of the province of Pennsylvania, to George Irwin, William Scott, and Archibald McLean, 'in trust for, and as a site for a house of *religious worship*, and a burial place for the use of the said religious society of English Presbyterians and their successors, in and near the said town of York, in the county of York; and in confidence that they, the said George Irwin, William Scott, and Archibald McLean, and the survivor of them, their and his heirs and assigns, shall and will permit and suffer the said lot or piece of ground and premises and the buildings thereon hereafter to be erected, to be from time to time, and at all times hereafter, at the disposal and under the care, regulation, and management of the said religious society and their successors in and near the town of York aforesaid; and to and for no other use, intent, or purpose whatsoever.' The church seems to have been built shortly afterwards, but it was not finished before the installation of Dr. Cathcart. The congregation obtained a patent of incorporation, in 1813, by the style of 'The Trustees of the English *Presbyterian* Congregation in the borough of York;' but the legal title of the original trustees has not been conveyed to it, and the corporation is now, what the congregation were before, the party beneficially entitled. It will be perceived, therefore, that the minority attempt to use the corporate name in order to oust the majority for an alleged forfeiture of the corporate rights, incurred, as it is supposed, by an application of the property to uses differing from those which the founders prescribed.

"By the common law he who gives the first possessions to a corporation is the founder of it, and entitled to the rights which the foundership gives. Viner's Abr. Tit. Corporations H. 1. These consist in visitation, and correction of any misapplication of his bounty to purposes foreign to its original destination. What then was the purpose prescribed by the Messrs. Penn? It was no more than to carry out the generous policy of their ancestor, the founder of the province, who, though rigidly attached to the principles of the Society of Friends, was bigoted to no particular sect, but munificent to all; and who left each to apply his gifts to such pious uses as it might think fit. That his descendants followed his example in this instance, is shown by the terms of the trust, which prescribed no form of doctrine or discipline, the beneficiary being described as the English Presbyterian Congregation, evidently to individuate it; and that subjection to a particular Assembly, was not a condition of the grant, is proved by the fact that there was at that time no such Assembly in America. The conveyance was executed in 1785; and the General Assembly of the American Presbyterian Church was constituted by the Synod of New York and Philadelphia, in 1788. It may be said that this congregation was connected with the elements of which the General Assembly was formed, and that it is bound to conform to those subsequent changes to which its representatives in the Synod assented. But were the founders, or the subject of their bounty bound by terms to which the founders did not originally assent? The original terms could not be altered even with their own consent; for that they are as incompetent as any one else to add to, or take away from them, was ruled in Philips *v.* Bury, Skin. 513, in which it was agreed that the founder having given statutes to a college, cannot alter them unless he has reserved a right to do so. As tests of sectarian denomination and character, therefore, the divisions that have since taken place about the Constitution of the General Assembly must be laid out of the case. The founders foresaw them not; and had they foreseen them, they would have left them to be dealt with by the congregation at its pleasure. The members of the congregation who erected the building may be thought to have had a separate interest of their own in the purpose to which it was to be dedicated; but even they cannot be said to have erected it with a view to a particular union, for though it was not finished till after the Assembly was constituted, it was begun, and the pecuniary responsibilities incident to the plan were contracted previously. But by the common law, even subsequent contributors have no other right of direction than that which the founder has prescribed; for they come in and give their money on a basis already established, and they can neither add to it nor take anything from it. If then the Messrs. Penn necessarily gave the ground in contest, subject to the direction of a majority bearing the name of Presbyterians, subsequent contributors with particular views, could not change the destination of it. But though no standard of discipline or faith be prescribed in the conveyance or charter of incorporation, I entirely concur in what Lord Eldon said in The Attorney General *v.* Pearson, 3 Meriv. Rep. 353, that 'when a house is created for religious worship, and it cannot be discovered what was the nature of the worship intended by it, it must be implied from the usage of the congregation; and that it is the duty of the court to administer the trust in such a manner as best to establish the usage, considering it as a matter of implied contract with the congregation.' I understand by this, that contemporaneous usage is evidence of an implied contract betwixt the founder and the congregation, and consequently of the purpose intended by him; but when, as here, neither the usage nor the purpose could possibly have existed at the time material to the question, subsequent usage cannot add to that which he intended. I agree with him also, 'that when the members of a congregation become dissentient among themselves, it is not in the power of individuals to say, we have changed our opinions, and you who assemble in this place for the purpose of hearing the *doctrines* and joining in the *worship* prescribed by the founder, shall no longer enjoy the benefit he intended for you unless you conform to the alterations which have taken place in our opinions.' With all this and much more, I promptly agree when predicated of a congregation adhering as nearly as it can to the principles of its original faith, and not, as in that case, swerving from the tenets of trinitarianism and embracing the hostile tenets of unitarianism. I concede also that subjection to a particular judicatory may be made a fundamental condition of a grant, as it expressly was in Duncan *v.* The Ninth Presbyterian Congregation, in which the trust was declared to be for 'such congregation of persons as shall belong to the present reformed Synod to which the Rev. Robert Annan's church in Spruce Street belongs,'—a case which was ultimately settled by the parties, but in which I differed from some of my brethren who thought the congregation had not lost its property in the trust by putting off its distinctive character and merging itself in the mass of the Presbyterian Church. That was a strong case; but it is altogether unlike the present, in which no such condition was expressed or implied. Even without an express condition, it might be a breach of the compact of association for the majority of a congregation to go over to a sect of a different denomination, though it were different only in name. For instance, the majority of a congregation of Seceders could not carry the church property into the Presbyterian connection, though these two sects have the same standards and plan of government. But this principle is inapplicable to a change of connection as regards different parts of the same denomination or sect.

"Now, since the foundation of this congregation, an event has happened which the founders did not contemplate, and which would not have been provided for, had it been foreseen. This was no less than a dismemberment of the Presbyterian body, not indeed by disorganization of it, or an entire reduction of it to its primitive elements, but by an excision, constitutional though it was, of whole Synods with their Presbyteries and congregations. There was not merely a secession of particles, leaving the original mass entire, but the original mass was split into two fragments of nearly equal magnitude; and though it was held by this court, in The Commonwealth *v.* Green, 5 Whart. Rep. 531, that the party which happened to be in office by means of its numerical superiority at the time of the division, was that which was entitled to represent it, and perform the functions of the original body, it was not because the minority were thought to be anything else than Presbyterians, but because a popular body is known only by its government or head. That they differed from the majority in doctrine or discipline, was not pretended, though it was alleged that they did not maintain the scriptural warrant of ruling elders. But the difference in this respect had been tolerated if not sanctioned by the Assembly itself, which, with full knowledge of it, had allowed the heterodox Synods to grow up as part of the Church; and it could not, therefore, have been viewed as radical or essential. We were called on, however, to pass, not on a question of heresy, for we would have been incompetent to decide it, but on the regularity of the meeting at which the trustees were chosen. I mention this to show that we did not determine that the excision was expurgation and not division. Indeed, the measure would seem to have been as decisively revolutionary, as would be an exclusion of particular States from the federal Union for the adoption of an anti-republican form of government. The excluded Synods, gathering to themselves the disaffected in other quarters of the Church, formed themselves into a distinct body, governed by a supreme judicatory, so like its fellow as to pass for its twin brother, and even to lay claim to the succession. That the Old School party succeeded to the privileges and property of the Assembly, was not because it was more Presbyterian than the other, but because it was stronger; for had it been the weaker, it would have been the party excluded, and the New School party, exercising the government as it then had done, would have succeeded in its stead, and thus the doctrine pressed upon us, would have made title to church property the sport of accident. In that event, an attempt to deprive the Old School congregations of their churches, for an act of the majority, in withdrawing from the jurisdiction of the Assembly, would have loaded the New School party with such a weight of popular odium as would have sunk it. Here then was the original mass divided into two parts of nearly equal magnitude and similar structure; and what was a congregation in the predicament of the one before us to do? It surely was not bound to follow the party which was successful in the conflict, merely because superiority of numbers had given it the victory.

"Before the American Revolution, the Church of England in America, as it was called, was annexed to the diocese of the Bishop of London; and it will scarce be pretended that, after its separation from it as a natural, but not inevitable consequence of our political independence, a single American parishioner might have recovered the church with its parsonage and glebe, when there was any, from his dissentient brethren, by insisting on a continuance of the ancient connection. Public opinion would not have borne it. Yet every Episcopal congregation in America had been founded on the basis of that connection, and our independence in other matters had raised no unanswerable objection to its permanence, especially, after the Bishop of London had procured an act of Parliament to dispense with engagements by the American Episcopal clergy that would have interfered with their political allegiance. It is true that the separation was effected with the assent of the mother Church; but it was the parishioner here, and not the Church abroad, whose consent was necessary to a dissolution of his ecclesiastical relation, in order to impair his civil rights. Besides, the consent of the mother Church was only formal, and given to the separation as to a measure which she could not prevent. She indeed conferred the Episcopate, and thus secured a continuance of the apostolic succession to the American Episcopal Church; but that might have been had from the nonjuring bishops in Scotland, as it was by Dr. Seabury, or from the Danish Episcopal Church, which indeed offered it on terms of signing the thirty-nine articles of the Church of England, with the exception of their political parts. Had the offer been accepted, there would have been an adverse withdrawal of ecclesiastical allegiance—in principle the very case before us—and it will not be pretended that the majority of an Episcopal congregation here would not have been at liberty, in that event, to form a connection with an independent Episcopal Church government, without forfeiting the interest of each in the Church property.

"The revolution led to no severance of the Presbyterian Church in America from the Church of Scotland, for there had been neither connection nor correspondence between them, and no illustration of the principle proposed, can be had from that quarter; but might not one of these very congregations which were severed from the primitive General Assembly here, have formed a new connection when driven from the old one, without forfeiting its interest in the Church property? or could a strictly orthodox minority strip them of it by organizing themselves as a congregation, on strictly Presbyterian principles, and regaining the former connection? To cut off the dissenters in the first instance, and to confiscate their property for what was declared to be a heresy for the first time, would be an act of power, not of justice. It will not be denied that they were Presbyterian in doctrine and discipline, or that if they were not, they had been received as such into the bosom of the Church; and what is the difference betwixt such a congregation and the one before us? It is, that the one was turned out of the connection, and that the other withdrew from it voluntarily; but the minority of the one has as much right as the minority of the other to seize the Church property for a violation of conditions supposed to be implied by the act of association. It will not do to say the Assembly sanctioned the separation in the one case and not in the other; for the Assembly had no power over the civil rights of the parties, and could not impair them. Nor did it mean to impair them. On the contrary, it allowed what it considered to be the sound parts of those congregations to attach themselves to the nearest orthodox Presbytery. This was done, most assuredly, not to enable them to despoil their congregational brethren; but had they attempted to do so, it is hazarding little to say they would have been disappointed.

"In a case like the present, it may be demanded, to what is the minority of a dissentient congregation to appeal? It might be replied, that for the contingency of revolution, it made no provision in its articles of association, and the law makes none; but that to the justice and forbearance of the majority of association, whose very object is to deal justly, love mercy, and walk humbly, it is to be supposed that the minority cannot appeal in vain. Nor has such an appeal in any instance been unsuccessful. The schism which a few years since shook the Methodist Church to its centre, is heard of no more; and perhaps this happy termination of it has been effected in a great measure by the good sense of the parties in following the advice of this court in The Methodist Church *v.* Remington, 1 Watts, 227, 'to part in peace, having settled their claims to the property on the basis of mutual and liberal concession.' And the same thing has been done with like effect by the original Presbyterian congregation in Carlisle.

"In conclusion, we are of opinion that no particular Presbyterian connection was prescribed by the founders, or established by the charter; and that if such connection had been prescribed, there has been no adhesion to a connection essentially different, and that the breaking up of the original Presbyterian confederation, has released this congregation from the duty of adhering to any particular part of it in exclusion of another. Instead of examining each specific error, it has been thought better to examine the principles on which the title depends; and though the jury were inaccurately instructed that an action could not be maintained by the corporation on its equitable title, yet as other principles in the cause are decisive against its right to recover, the record is free from any error which could do the party an injury."

Case of Lane Seminary.

Near the close of the year 1845, two suits at law were brought against Lane Seminary by David R. Kemper, one of the donors of the land on which the Seminary is built. The first was instituted in the Supreme Court of Ohio, in the form technically denominated "*quo warranto*," calling upon the faculty to show why they hold their offices contrary to the charter, which requires that they be "*members of the Presbyterian Church, under the General Assembly of that Church in the United States of America.*" This suit was decided at the December term of the court in banc, December, 1847, in favor of the faculty, on the ground that the action was barred by the Statute of Limitation, which provides that such action must be commenced within three years of the alleged forfeiture of office. 16 Ohio Reports, 358.

The other was a suit in chancery, brought in the Court at Cincinnati, in the form of a petition, by Mr. Kemper as a donor, that the court would require the trustees to conform to their charter, which, he alleged, had been violated by the neglect of manual labor, and by putting men into the offices of instruction, who are not "members of the Presbyterian Church under the General Assembly."

On this suit, the defendants demurred to the right of the plaintiff to institute the suit, and the court sustained the demurrer.

From this decision, the plaintiff then appealed to the Supreme Court.

On his appeal the plaintiff, having obtained leave to amend his plea, substituted for "D. R. Kemper, a donor," "D. R. Kemper, a Presbyterian, in behalf of himself and other Presbyterians." The defendants still demurred, and their demurrer was sustained by the higher court. 17 Ohio Reports, 293.

A third suit was then instituted in the Court of Common Pleas, in the name of the State of Ohio, on the relation of D. R. Kemper. This suit was abated by the death of the relator, in 1849. In 1850, the suit was renewed, on the relation of Samuel B. Findlay,—the means of carrying it on being furnished by subscription among those interested in changing the ownership of the Seminary.

This suit was decided in favor of the trustees of the Seminary, at the November term of the court, 1854. The following is the language of the court:

"The court finds and decrees that the trustees of said institution, the officers and members of the executive committee of said institution, the professors and teachers in said institution or seminary are, and always have been, while in such connections with said institution or seminary, members of the Presbyterian Church, in good standing, under the care of the General Assembly of the Presbyterian Church in the United States of America; and in their religious character and professions have always conformed to the requirements of the laws incorporating said institution or seminary, and of the deed of James Kemper and others to the trustees of said seminary, &c.

"The court further finds and decrees, that the trustees and officers of the Lane Seminary have not, in any respect or at any time, disregarded or broken the trusts confided to, or imposed upon them by the various donors and contributors to the funds, real and personal, of the said institution, and by the said deed from James Kemper and others. On the contrary, the court finds and decrees that they have, in all respects and always, fully and faithfully kept and performed each and all of the trusts of every kind confided and imposed upon them by the various donors and contributors to the funds, real and personal, and all trusts of every kind imposed by deed, statute law, or otherwise."

From this decision no appeal was taken. Hence no report of this decision appears in the Reports of the State of Ohio.

The time for taking an appeal having expired, this decision is final, and fixes the standing of the General Assembly in the State of Ohio.

ADDENDUM.

Synod of Minnesota Erected 1858.

The committee also reported, that a memorial from the Presbytery of Blue Earth has been placed in their hands, praying that a new Synod may be created, to consist of the Presbyteries of Blue Earth, Minnesota, and Dacotah, which last Presbytery is not now in connection with any higher ecclesiastical body. There has also been placed in the hands of the committee a certified copy of a resolution by the Presbytery of Minnesota, concurring with said memorial from the Presbytery of Blue Earth. They have further received verbal information, from the commissioner of the Presbytery of Minnesota, that it is believed that the members of the Presbytery of Dacotah are favorable towards the arrangement, though no definite communication has been received from the Presbytery itself.

The said Presbytery of Dacotah not being now under the jurisdiction of the Assembly, it is not competent for this body *absolutely* to create the proposed Synod according to the prayer of the memorialist. But inasmuch as it is urged upon the committee that a strong necessity exists for the immediate construction of such a Synod, they recommend to the Assembly the following action:

Resolved, 1. That the Presbyteries of Blue Earth and Minnesota be directed to meet at St. Paul, Minnesota, in the First Presbyterian Church, on the second Wednesday of September, 1858, at 7 o'clock P.M., with the view of uniting, if the way be prepared, with the Presbytery of Dacotah, in the organization of a Synod.

Resolved, 2. That the stated clerk of the Assembly address a letter to the Presbytery of Dacotah, inviting them to meet with the Presbyteries of Blue Earth and Minnesota, at the above time and place, and, if the way be prepared, to become incorporated with them in a Synod under the care of this General Assembly.

Resolved, 3. That, in the event of compliance with this invitation by the Presbytery of Dacotah, the Presbyteries of Blue Earth, Minnesota, and Dacotah, shall then and there become a Synod under the name of the *Synod of Minnesota;* and that the Rev. Thomas S. Williams, or in case of his absence, the oldest minister present, shall preach a sermon, and preside until a new moderator be chosen.

The report was adopted.—*Minutes*, 1858, pp. 591, 592.

ERRATA.

Page 50, line 7. For "sec. 20," read "sec. 2."
" 210, lines 12, 17, 22. For "Form of Government," read "Book of Discipline."
" 216, line 21. For "over to," read "over."
" 295, line 7. For "CHICAGO," read "PITTSBURG."

INDEX.

Organization and Government of the Apostolic Church. By REV. ALBERT BARNES. A standard and valuable work on the claims of Episcopacy. 18mo., cloth, . 40

Paleario. *The Benefit of Christ's Death.* By AONIO PALEARIO. 18mo., cloth, - - - - - - - - - 38
Red edged, - - - - - - - - - - 45

This interesting and remarkable book was written by a learned Italian in the 16th century. The writer was burned by the Inquisition at Rome, and the book, after gaining a circulation of 40,000 copies, proscribed and lost. It is now again produced, with a sketch of the writer, and has been received with the greatest interest and satisfaction.

"Buy it and read it."—*Presbyter.*

"A most remarkable book."—*Philadelphia Evening Bulletin.*

"Its publication well shows that even in the darkest days and lands of Romanism, God never left himself without a witness."—*Christian Instructor.*

Money; *or, The Ainsworths.* A Prize Book, illustrating the proper use of money, - - - - - - - - 60
Gilt, - - - - - - - - - - - 75

This little volume took the prize offered by the Presbyterian Publication Committee for a book for the Sunday-school Library. It is a book for boys.

Says the *New York Observer:* "It is a premium book, $100 having been offered for the best; and this book is worth more money than that."

Says the *Episcopal Recorder:* "There is a great deal of good advice given in this book, in a form which is not hard to take."

Says the *Christian Observer:* "A book that will give pleasure and profit."

Martyrs of the Mutiny; *or, The Trials and Triumphs of Christians in the Sepoy Rebellion in India.* With an Introduction by the Rev. JOHN JENKINS, D.D. 16mo., cloth, 50

In this book are given deeply interesting narrations of the sufferings of Christians in the late *Sepoy Rebellion* in India. From them we see that amid the horrors of that fearful struggle, Hindoos as well as Americans and Europeans had grace to confess the name of Christ, even at the cost of life itself. Four illustrations.

"It affords us pleasure to commend this handsome volume to the old and the young, and to every family."—*Christian Observer.*

"A remarkable memorial, that will be read with melancholy interest by thousands."—*N. Y. Observer.*

"It deserves a wide circulation in the libraries of Sabbath-schools and in Christian families. We can give it our hearty commendation."—*Presbyterian Banner.*

"A volume of more than ordinary interest."—*Central Christian Herald.*

"It is, in truth, a book for the times."—*Presbyterian Witness.*

The Bible Read with Profit. By REV. THOMAS WATSON, a Nonconformist Divine of the 17th Century. An excellent companion to the Bible. 32mo., cloth, - - - - 12

Confession of Faith and Form of Government. 18mo., half-morocco, - - - - - - - - - 38

The Prayer-Meeting. By REV. J. FEW SMITH, D.D.
Cloth, - - - - - - - - - - - 15
Paper, - - - - - - - - - - - 10

It enforces the value of the Prayer-Meeting to the individual and the Church, and gives such instructions and suggestions as will add to its pleasure and profitableness. Especially adapted for general distribution.

www.ingramcontent.com/pod-product-compliance
Lightning Source LLC
LaVergne TN
LVHW021055110826
845150LV00001B/76

* 9 7 8 1 4 2 5 5 6 7 1 6 3 *